Principles of Modern Operating Systems

SECOND EDITION

José M. Garrido
Richard Schlesinger
Kenneth Hoganson

Kennesaw State University

JONES & BARTLETT
LEARNING

World Headquarters
Jones & Bartlett Learning
5 Wall Street
Burlington, MA 01803
978-443-5000
info@jblearning.com
www.jblearning.com

Jones & Bartlett Learning books and products are available through most bookstores and online booksellers. To contact Jones & Bartlett Learning directly, call 800-832-0034, fax 978-443-8000, or visit our website, www.jblearning.com.

Substantial discounts on bulk quantities of Jones & Bartlett Learning publications are available to corporations, professional associations, and other qualified organizations. For details and specific discount information, contact the special sales department at Jones & Bartlett Learning via the above contact information or send an email to specialsales@jblearning.com.

Copyright © 2013 by Jones & Bartlett Learning, LLC, an Ascend Learning Company

All rights reserved. No part of the material protected by this copyright may be reproduced or utilized in any form, electronic or mechanical, including photocopying, recording, or by any information storage and retrieval system, without written permission from the copyright owner.

Production Credits
Publisher: Cathleen Sether
Senior Acquisitions Editor: Timothy Anderson
Managing Editor: Amy Bloom
Director of Production: Amy Rose
Associate Marketing Manager: Lindsay White
Online Products Manager: Dawn Mahon Priest
V.P., Manufacturing and Inventory Control: Therese Connell
Composition: Northeast Compositors, Inc.
Cover and Title Page Design: Scott Moden
Cover and Title Page Image: © Rob McKay/ShutterStock, Inc.
Printing and Binding: Malloy, Inc.
Cover Printing: Malloy, Inc.

Library of Congress Cataloging-in-Publication Data
Principles of modern operating systems. — 2nd ed. / José Garrido ... [et al.].
    p. cm.
  Rev. ed. of: Principles of modern operating systems / José M. Garrido, Richard Schlesinger. c2008.
  Includes bibliographical references and index.
  ISBN 978-1-4496-2634-1 (casebound)
  1. Operating systems (Computers) I. Garrido, José M. II. Garrido, José M. Principles of modern operating systems.
  QA76.76.O63G3844 2012
  005.4'3—dc22
                              2011008938

6048

Printed in the United States of America
15 14 13 12 11   10 9 8 7 6 5 4 3 2 1

Contents

Preface ... xv

1 Basic Concepts of Operating Systems ... 1
- 1.1 Introduction ... 1
  - 1.1.1 Software Components ... 1
- 1.2 Operating Systems ... 2
  - 1.2.1 Operating System Interfaces ... 3
  - 1.2.2 Multi-Level Views of an Operating System ... 4
- 1.3 Categories of Operating Systems ... 7
- 1.4 Small and Specialized Operating Systems ... 8
- 1.5 Brief History of Operating Systems ... 9
- 1.6 Contemporary Operating Systems ... 10
  - 1.6.1 Unix ... 10
  - 1.6.2 Microsoft Windows ... 11
  - 1.6.3 Mac OS ... 11
- 1.7 64-bit Operating Systems ... 11
  - 1.7.1 Microsoft 64-bit Windows 7 ... 12
  - 1.7.2 Mac OS X ... 12
- 1.8 Summary ... 12
- Exercises and Questions ... 13

2 Processes and Threads ... 15
- 2.1 Introduction ... 15
- 2.2 Processes ... 15
  - 2.2.1 Process States ... 16
  - 2.2.2 Process Descriptor ... 18
- 2.3 Threads ... 19
  - 2.3.1 Multithreading ... 20
  - 2.3.2 User-Level Threads ... 21
  - 2.3.3 Kernel-Level Threads ... 22
  - 2.3.4 Java Threads ... 22

	2.4	POSIX Threads		28
		2.4.1 Creating POSIX Threads		29
		2.4.2 Basic Synchronization of Pthreads		30
		2.4.3 Scheduling and Priorities of POSIX Threads		30
	2.5	Multiprogramming		31
		2.5.1 CPU and I/O Requests		31
		2.5.2 Interrupting Processes		32
		2.5.3 Context Switch		33
	2.6	Summary		34
		Exercises and Questions		35

3 System Performance and Models — 37

	3.1	Introduction		37
	3.2	General Concepts of Modeling		37
	3.3	Simple Models of Computer Systems		38
	3.4	Performance of Computer Systems		39
		3.4.1 Performance Metrics		40
		3.4.2 Workload and System Parameters		41
	3.5	Simulation Models		43
		3.5.1 Types of Simulation Models		43
		3.5.2 Discrete-Event Models		44
		3.5.3 Stochastic Models		45
	3.6	A Model of the Simple Batch System		45
		3.6.1 Description of the Model		46
		3.6.2 Implementations of the Model		48
		3.6.3 Simulation Output of the Console Implementation		49
		3.6.4 Output of the GUI Implementation		56
	3.7	System Capacity and Bottleneck		58
	3.8	Summary		59
		Exercises and Questions		60

4 Systems with Multiprogramming — 61

	4.1	Introduction		61
	4.2	Systems with Multiple Stations		61
		4.2.1 CPU and I/O Bursts		63
		4.2.2 Overlapping of CPU and I/O Processing		63
		4.2.3 Context Switches		64
	4.3	Studying Systems with Multiprogramming		64
		4.3.1 Model of a System with Multiprogramming		64
		4.3.2 Model of a System Without Multiprogramming		68
		4.3.3 Comparison of the Two Models		70

		4.3.4	Models with GUI and Graphical Animation	71
	4.4	Summary		74
		Exercises and Questions		75

5 Processor Scheduling — 77

	5.1	Introduction		77
	5.2	General Types of Scheduling		78
	5.3	Processor Scheduling Concepts		78
		5.3.1	The CPU Scheduler	79
		5.3.2	Scheduling Multiple Classes of Processes	80
	5.4	CPU Scheduling Policies		80
		5.4.1	First-Come-First-Served	82
		5.4.2	Shortest Process Next	92
		5.4.3	Round Robin Scheduling	98
		5.4.4	Shortest Remaining Time	108
		5.4.5	Brief Comparison of the Four Scheduling Policies	114
		5.4.6	Dynamic Priority Scheduling	115
		5.4.7	Other Scheduling Policies	116
	5.5	Multiprocessor Systems		118
	5.6	Summary		123
		Exercises and Questions		124

6 Synchronization Principles — 129

	6.1	Introduction		129
	6.2	Basic Synchronization Principles		129
		6.2.1	No Synchronization	130
		6.2.2	Mutual Exclusion	130
		6.2.3	Critical Sections	130
	6.3	Approaches for Implementing Synchronization		132
	6.4	Semaphores		132
	6.5	Synchronization with Semaphores		134
		6.5.1	Critical Section Problem	134
		6.5.2	Event Ordering	135
	6.6	Synchronization Case Studies		136
		6.6.1	The Bounded-Buffer Problem	136
		6.6.2	Synchronization with Semaphores in Java	138
		6.6.3	Simulation Models of the Bounded-Buffer Problem	141
		6.6.4	The Readers-Writers Problem	146
		6.6.5	Simulation Models of the Readers-Writers Problem	148
	6.7	POSIX Threads		152
		6.7.1	Creating POSIX Threads	152

		6.7.2	Basic Synchronization of Pthreads	153
		6.7.3	Mutual Exclusion	154
		6.7.4	Semaphores	155
	6.8	Monitors		156
		6.8.1	Synchronization with Monitors	156
		6.8.2	The Producer-Consumer Problem with a Monitor	157
		6.8.3	Monitor Synchronization with Java	158
		6.8.4	Simulation Models Using Monitors	160
	6.9	Interprocess Communication		162
		6.9.1	Asynchronous Communication	162
		6.9.2	Simulation Model for Asynchronous Communication	163
		6.9.3	Synchronous Communication	166
		6.9.4	Simulation Model for Synchronous Communication	167
	6.10	Atomic Transactions		170
	6.11	Summary		172
		Exercises and Questions		173

7 Deadlocks 175

	7.1	Introduction		175
	7.2	Basic Principles of Deadlock		175
		7.2.1	Resource Allocation Graph	177
		7.2.2	Conditions for the Existence of Deadlock	178
	7.3	The Dining Philosophers		181
		7.3.1	Modeling Deadlock	182
		7.3.2	Informal Solution to Deadlock	185
	7.4	Methods for Handling Deadlock		188
	7.5	Deadlock Prevention		189
		7.5.1	Disallowing Hold and Wait	189
		7.5.2	Disallowing Circular Wait	194
		7.5.3	Model with Graphical Animation	198
	7.6	Deadlock Avoidance		201
		7.6.1	Banker's Algorithm	201
		7.6.2	Applying the Banker's Algorithm	201
	7.7	Deadlock Detection and Recovery		203
		7.7.1	Deadlock Detection	203
		7.7.2	Recovery	204
	7.8	Summary		205
		Exercises and Questions		205

8 File Management 207

| | 8.1 | Introduction | 207 |

8.2	Files		207
	8.2.1	File Attributes	208
	8.2.2	Folders	209
	8.2.3	Pathnames	209
8.3	Access Methods		211
	8.3.1	Open	211
	8.3.2	Close	212
	8.3.3	Read	213
	8.3.4	Write	214
	8.3.5	Sequential Access	215
	8.3.6	Streams, Pipes, and I/O Redirection	215
	8.3.7	Other I/O System Calls	217
8.4	Directory Functions		217
8.5	File Space Allocation		217
	8.5.1	Cluster Allocation	218
	8.5.2	Calculating Read/Write Addresses	219
	8.5.3	Free Space Management	220
	8.5.4	Disk Fragmentation	221
	8.5.5	Reliability of Disk Space Management	222
8.6	Real-World Systems		222
	8.6.1	Microsoft FAT System	223
	8.6.2	Microsoft NTFS System	225
	8.6.3	Linux Ext2 and Ext3 Systems	226
	8.6.4	Mac OS X HFS+ Systems	227
	8.6.5	Other File Systems	228
8.7	Virtual File System		228
8.8	Removable Media		229
8.9	Seeing the Future Now		231
8.10	Summary		231
	Exercises and Questions		232

9   The I/O System   233

9.1	Introduction		233
9.2	I/O Hardware		233
	9.2.1	Direct Memory Access	235
	9.2.2	Hard Disk Drives	237
	9.2.3	Solid State Disks	238
9.3	Device I/O Structure		238
	9.3.1	Intelligent Buses	241
	9.3.2	Handling Multiple Devices Simultaneously	243
9.4	I/O Performance Optimization		244

		9.4.1	Reducing the Number of I/O Requests	245
		9.4.2	Buffering and Caching	245
		9.4.3	I/O Scheduling	248
	9.5	Hard Disk I/O Scheduling		248
		9.5.1	First-Come First-Served Algorithm	249
		9.5.2	Shortest Seek Time First Algorithm	249
		9.5.3	Elevator (SCAN) Algorithm	250
		9.5.4	Circular Scan Algorithm	251
		9.5.5	Optimizing Rotational Latency	251
		9.5.6	Interaction of Disk Scheduling and Other System Functions	252
	9.6	System Configuration		252
	9.7	Hard Disk Scheduling Simulation Model		254
	9.8	Summary		257
		Exercises and Questions		257

10 Memory Management   259

	10.1	Introduction		259
	10.2	Process Address Space		260
		10.2.1	Binding	261
		10.2.2	Static and Dynamic Loading	262
		10.2.3	Static and Dynamic Linking	262
	10.3	Contiguous Memory Allocation		262
		10.3.1	Fixed Partitions	263
		10.3.2	Dynamic Partitions	264
		10.3.3	Swapping	267
	10.4	Noncontiguous Memory Allocation		268
		10.4.1	Paging	268
		10.4.2	Segmentation	271
	10.5	Virtual Memory		272
		10.5.1	Basic Concepts	273
		10.5.2	Process Locality	273
		10.5.3	Using Segments	275
		10.5.4	Memory Protection	275
		10.5.5	Shared Memory	276
		10.5.6	Address Translation	277
		10.5.7	Page Size Considerations	278
	10.6	Paging with Virtual Memory		278
		10.6.1	Paging Policies	279
		10.6.2	Frame Allocation	281
		10.6.3	Page Faults and Performance Issues	281

10.7	Paging Algorithms		282
	10.7.1	Static Paging Algorithms	282
	10.7.2	Dynamic Paging Algorithms	299
10.8	Thrashing		304
	10.8.1	Combining Paging with Segmentation	305
10.9	Summary		306
	Exercises and Questions		307

11 Security and Protection 309

11.1	Introduction		309
11.2	Problems of Security		310
11.3	Security and Protection Components		311
	11.3.1	Physical Security	311
	11.3.2	User Authentication	311
	11.3.3	Protection	312
	11.3.4	Secure Communications	319
	11.3.5	Digital Certificates	320
	11.3.6	People	323
11.4	System Vulnerabilities		323
	11.4.1	Social Engineering	323
	11.4.2	Trojan Horse Programs	323
	11.4.3	Spyware	324
	11.4.4	Trap Doors	324
	11.4.5	Database Access Vulnerabilities	324
	11.4.6	Buffer and Stack Overflow	324
11.5	Invasive and Malicious Software		325
11.6	Defending the System and the User		326
11.7	Intrusion Detection Management		327
11.8	Security and Privacy		328
11.9	Secure Systems Versus Systems Security		328
11.10	Summary		329
	Exercises and Questions		330

12 Networking and Distributed Systems 333

12.1	Introduction		333
12.2	Ethernet		335
12.3	Internetworking and TCP/IP		337
	12.3.1	Connection Oriented Versus Connectionless	339
	12.3.2	Streaming Data	340
12.4	World Wide Web		340
12.5	DNS and DHCP		341

		12.5.1	DNS Caching	342
		12.5.2	DHCP	343
	12.6	Parallel Computing	344
		12.6.1	Simple Model of Parallel Speedup	346
		12.6.2	Limitations of Parallel Speedup	347
		12.6.3	Multiple Levels of Parallelism	349
	12.7	Cluster and Grid Computing	350
	12.8	Distributed Application Technologies	356
		12.8.1	Distributed Software Architectures	357
		12.8.2	Software Interface: ODBC	358
		Exercises and Questions	359

13 Virtual Machines — 361

	13.1	Introduction	361
	13.2	Overall Virtual Machine Structure	362
	13.3	Hardware Interface	363
		13.3.1 Instruction Execution	363
		13.3.2 Software Trap Handling	365
		13.3.3 Device Input/Output	367
		13.3.4 Memory Management	367
	13.4	Hardware Enhancements	368
		13.4.1 Additional Execution Modes	368
		13.4.2 Memory Mapping Enhancements	370
	13.5	Mapping Devices to Host OS Structures	370
	13.6	Unmapped Devices	371
	13.7	Virtual Machine Integration	372
	13.8	Summary	373
		Exercises and Questions	374

Appendix A Introduction to Using Linux — 375

	A.1	Introduction	375
	A.2	Command-Line Interface	376
	A.3	Files and Directories	377
		A.3.1 Specifying Paths	377
		A.3.2 Wildcards	378
	A.4	Basic Commands	378
		A.4.1 The `passwd` Command	378
		A.4.2 The `man` Command	379
		A.4.3 The `ls` Command	379
		A.4.4 The `cp` Command	381
		A.4.5 The `mv` Command	382

Contents   xi

		A.4.6	The `rm` Command	382
		A.4.7	The `cd` Command	383
		A.4.8	The `mkdir` Command	383
		A.4.9	The `rmdir` Command	384
		A.4.10	I/O Redirection and Pipe Operators	384
	A.5	Shell Variables		385
		A.5.1	The `pwd` Command	386
		A.5.2	The `more` Command	388
		A.5.3	The `exit` Command	388
	A.6	Text Editing		388
	A.7	File Access Permissions		389
	A.8	The `cat` Command		389
	A.9	Commands for Process Control		390
	A.10	Foreground and Background Processes		391
	A.11	Script Files		392
		A.11.1	Comments in Scripts	392
		A.11.2	Positional Parameters	392
		A.11.3	Command Substitution	393
		A.11.4	The `test` Command	393
		A.11.5	The `if` and the `test` Commands	394
		A.11.6	The `set` Command	395
		A.11.7	Mutibranch with the `if` Command	396
		A.11.8	Repetition with the `for` Command	397
		A.11.9	Repetition with the `while` Command	398
	A.12	Searching Data in Files		398
	A.13	Evaluating Expressions		401
	A.14	Connecting to a Remote Linux Server		402
		A.14.1	The Putty Program	402
		A.14.2	SSH Client	403
		A.14.3	X-Window and Graphical Desktops	406
		A.14.4	Using the K Desktop Environment	407

Appendix B Java and POSIX Threads 409

	B.1	Introduction		409
	B.2	Threads		409
	B.3	Object-Oriented Concepts and Threads in Java		410
		B.3.1	Inheritance	410
		B.3.2	Abstract Classes	412
		B.3.3	Polymorphism	412
		B.3.4	Classes and Interfaces	413
		B.3.5	Exceptions	414

		B.3.6	Java Threads	415
	B.4	POSIX Threads		423
		B.4.1	Creating POSIX Threads	423
		B.4.2	Basic Synchronization of Pthreads	424
		B.4.3	Mutual Exclusion	425
		B.4.4	Semaphores	426
		B.4.5	Condition Variables	427
		B.4.6	Scheduling and Priorities of POSIX Threads	429

Appendix C The Java Modeling Framework — 431

C.1	Introduction		431
C.2	Basic Structure of a Model		432
	C.2.1	Simulation Model	432
	C.2.2	Input Parameters	432
	C.2.3	Class Input	433
	C.2.4	Class UI	434
	C.2.5	Processes	434
	C.2.6	The `RequestProcessor`	434
	C.2.7	Request	434
	C.2.8	Schedular	435
	C.2.9	The `IncomingRequestGenerator` Class	438
	C.2.10	`ResourceManager`	439
	C.2.11	The `Output` Class	439
	C.2.12	Simulation Display	439
	C.2.13	The `Plotter` Class	439
	C.2.14	The `QPlotter` Subclass	441
	C.2.15	Animation	441
	C.2.16	The `QGraphic` Abstract Class	441
	C.2.17	The `SchedularGraphic` Concrete Subclass	442
	C.2.18	Random Number Generator Classes	442
	C.2.19	The `Statistic` Class	445
C.3	Java Coding Recommendations		447
C.4	The Simulation Package on CD-ROM		447
	C.4.1	Files on the CD-ROM	447
	C.4.2	Compiling with Java and the PsimJ Library	447
	C.4.3	Example Program	448

Appendix D Psim3 — 471

D.1	The Psim3 Library		471
	D.1.1	The Time Dimension	471
	D.1.2	Defining Active Objects	472

		D.1.3	Running a Simulation	472
		D.1.4	Features in Class `process`	473
		D.1.5	Scheduling a Process	476
		D.1.6	Suspending a Process	476
		D.1.7	Interrupting a Process	476
		D.1.8	Terminating a Process	477
	D.2	The Queue Library		478
		D.2.1	General Description	478
		D.2.2	Features of Class `squeue`	478
		D.2.3	Features of Class `pqueue`	480
	D.3	The Resource Library		483
		D.3.1	General Description	483
		D.3.2	Relevant Features of the `res` Class	484
		D.3.3	Features in Class `bin`	485
	D.4	The `waitq` Class		486
	D.5	The `condq` Class		487
	D.6	Random Numbers		489
		D.6.1	Class `randint`	489
		D.6.2	Class `erand`	491
		D.6.3	Class `normal`	491
		D.6.4	Class `poisson`	492
		D.6.5	Class `urand`	493
	D.7	The Simulation Package on CD-ROM		494
		D.7.1	Files on the CD-ROM	494
		D.7.2	Brief Instructions for Compiling and Linking	495

Appendix E Overview of Probability Theory — 497

E.1	Introduction		497
E.2	Basic Concepts		497
E.3	Probability of an Event		498
E.4	Random Numbers		499
E.5	Probability Distribution Functions		501
	E.5.1	The Geometric Distribution	503
	E.5.2	The Binomial Distribution	504
	E.5.3	The Exponential Distribution	504
	E.5.4	The Poisson Distribution	505
	E.5.5	The Uniform Distribution	506
	E.5.6	The Normal Distribution	506
E.6	Statistics		507
E.7	Analyzing Sample Data		508
E.8	State-Dependent Models		509

Contents

	E.8.1	State Dependence	509
	E.8.2	Stochastic Matrices	509

Appendix F Using the C++ Models — 511
F.1	Using Linux	511
F.2	Using Unix (Sun Solaris)	513
F.3	Using Microsoft Windows	513

Appendix G The Computer System: An Overview — 515
G.1	Computer System Components	515
G.2	The Central Processing Unit (CPU)	516
G.3	Computer Instructions	519
G.4	Fetch/Decode/Execute/Interrupt Cycle	520
G.5	Simple Computer Instructions	521
G.6	Computer Architecture Layers	524
G.7	Operating Systems	526
	G.7.1 Manage the Resources of the Computer System	526
	G.7.2 Provide a User Interface	527
	G.7.3 Provide a Programming Interface	528
	G.7.4 Process Execution Mode	528
	G.7.5 Provide a Networking Interface	529
G.8	Language Translation	529
	G.8.1 Assembly Language	531
	G.8.2 High-Level Languages	531
	G.8.3 Byte Code and the Virtual Machine	533
G.9	CPU Internal Structure	535
	G.9.1 Adding the System Bus Interface	536
	G.9.2 Supporting the Instruction Fetch	539
	G.9.3 Detailed Program Execution	539
G.10	CPU Performance Enhancement: Pipeline	542
G.11	System Performance Enhancement: Cache	544
	G.11.1 The Need for Cache	544
	G.11.2 Cache Performance	548
	G.11.3 Fully Associative Cache	550
Exercises and Questions		551

Bibliography — 555

Index — 557

Preface

Principles of Modern Operating Systems, Second Edition presents a practical introduction to the fundamental principles of operating systems. These principles are illustrated by using relatively simple simulation models to study the general behavior and performance of various aspects of operating systems. These models are object-oriented discrete event simulation models implemented in Java and C++ and are used throughout the book.

Using a non-traditional approach, the book introduces the basic principles and concepts of operating systems and provides the hands-on component for an undergraduate course. The hands-on component consists of a set of simulation models that are used by students to carry out and analyze simulation runs on Linux and Windows systems. The results of these runs provide students the opportunity to carry out experiments related to the various concepts discussed. Conventional textbooks on operating systems describe the theoretical aspects with much detail and do not emphasize the study of performance to analyze these systems.

This text can be used as an alternative to conventional (and more traditional) textbooks for undergraduate courses in computer science, information systems, software engineering, electrical engineering, systems engineering, and information technology. It attempts to simplify most of the complexity in dealing with the concepts, techniques, and methods discussed. For the systems professional, the book provides an overview of the theory of operating systems supplemented by a practical introduction to systems performance using simulation models.

After teaching operating systems with this approach for several years, the authors have taken the following assumptions in writing this book:

- The use of simulation models is useful as a hands-on component and does not replace basic conceptual material. Multiple simulation models are provided for the students who are not required to develop models but to run them in studying OS behavior and performance.

- The authors' experience teaching multiple sections of the OS course at Kennesaw State University for the last ten years has shown that using simulation models to study operating systems is a good way to give students an appreciation of the components and behavior of an operating system. It also gives them basic techniques in computing the various performance metrics. Students are not required to construct simulation models for performance study, but are required to use these in studying the various aspects of operating systems.

- Most students at KSU like the Java implementation and the fact that Java is one of the most widely-used programming languages today. Other students prefer to experiment with the simulation models provided in C++.

For every important topic discussed, one or more complete case studies are presented and explained with the corresponding simulation model implemented in Java and C++. The intention is for students to use and analyze simulation runs that correspond to some aspects of operating systems. This book does not include principles on simulation or explanation in developing simulation models.

For interested readers, the simulation principles are discussed in detail in more advanced books on operating systems.

All the simulation models discussed and the simulation software packages can be found on the included CD-ROM. A set of PowerPoint presentations for all the material discussed is also available for instructor download.

The case studies presented as simulation models, the simulation software, answers to end-of-chapter exercises, and the corresponding PowerPoint presentations for every chapter, are available at go.jblearning.com/garrido. The simulation models are provided for academic purposes only and have been validated mainly to fulfill this purpose. The simulation models presented have not formally been validated, but we have compared results of some of the models with the theoretical calculations. We assume this is acceptable because these models are intended only for educational purposes.

Important features of the book/software and the specific benefits a reader can expect to derive from these features include the following:

- Java is used as one of the implementation languages for the simulation models. This is one of the most widely-used programming languages today and offers several advantages compared to other programming languages. The simulation models implementation emphasizes programming-in-the-large. The simulation models are also presented in C++ with POSIX threads. The two constitute a good match to study synchronization, concurrency, and all other important topics related to operating systems.

- The practical aspects of performance measures of operating systems are presented using object-oriented simulation models.

- The simulation models and techniques can be applied to other types of systems (communication systems, transportation systems, etc.).

- The object-oriented approach to modeling and simulation uses threads with Java and C++ (with POSIX threads).

- A relatively simple approach is applied for modeling and simulation of complex systems, for example systems dealing with concurrency and timing constraints.

Appendix A includes an introduction to Linux, which we use in our courses on operating systems. In fact, the first set of assignments must be run and solved on a Linux server. Appendix B introduces Java and POSIX threads.

Appendix C includes a brief documentation of the PsimJ package and the Java modeling framework. Appendix D includes the documentation of Psim3, the C++ version of PsimJ. Appendix E is an overview of probability theory. Appendix F presents a summary set of instructions on using the simulation models. The most recent versions of the PsimJ and Psim3 simulation software packages are available on the Psim website: http://science.kennesaw.edu/~jgarrido/psim.html.

Appendix G provides basic information on computer organization and architecture. This can be used for review or as an introduction to this material.

Updates to the 2nd Edition

Chapter 1, Basic Concepts of Operating Systems, has been redesigned so that the architecture sections have been removed and placed in a new appendix. A few section titles have been changed for better clarity. A new section, Small and Specialized Operating Systems, has been added and follows the trend of industry for small devices. Another section on 64-bit Operating Systems has also been added.

Chapter 2, Processes and Threads, has also been revised. Some section titles have been changed. Several output values of the simulation run of the simple batch system have been changed and the output listing of this simulation run has been completely replaced with a newer version of the simulation run. An updated version of the simulation software is used.

Chapter 3, System Performance and Models, has been revised and expanded to improve and enhance the explanation of the various subtopics. Some material on Java and POSIX threads has been added. A few new exercises have been added to the last section of this chapter.

Chapter 5 has a revised title, Processor Scheduling, and has been extensively revised and expanded. A few numbers in the results of the scheduling simulation runs have been updated or corrected. Clarifications have been provided in various sections to improve the understanding of scheduling using several policies. A new section on multiprocessors has been added.

The chapter on Synchronization Principles (Chapter 6) has also been revised to improve explanation of the topics. A new section on thread synchronization has been added.

Chapter 7, Deadlocks, has also been revised to improve explanation of the topics. Figures 7.3 and 7.4 have been updated.

Chapters 8 and 9 on File Management and The I/O System, respectively, have been updated to reflect hardware changes since the first edition was published. References to floppy disks have been removed and material has been added about solid state disks.

The chapter on Memory Management (Chapter 10) has also been revised. A few paragraphs have been added to improve explanation of the topics. The original Figure 10.4 has been removed.

Chapter 12 on Networking and Distributed Systems has been completely rewritten and now includes material about grid systems.

A new chapter on Virtual Machines (Chapter 13) has been added.

A new Appendix G has been added to provide basic material on computer organization and architecture.

Acknowledgments

Gbodi Odaibo, a graduate student of the Master of Science in Applied Computer Science (MSACS) program at KSU, developed the simulation model of the Bankers algorithm for deadlock avoidance that appears in Chapter 7. The CD-ROM also contains several animations of synchronization problems that have been included by permission of Stephan Fischli, Berner Fachhochschule Software/Schule Schweiz.

We would like to acknowledge and thank the following professionals who provided insightful reviews of the manuscript at various stages of development:

- Patrick Otoo Bobbie, Southern Polytechnic State University
- John Connely, California Polytechnic State University
- Richard V. Ezop, DePaul University
- Ramana M. Gosukonda, Fort Valley State University
- Matthew Jaffe, Embry-Riddle Aeronautical University
- Jianhua Lin, Eastern Connecticut State University
- Dmitris Margaritis, Iowa State University
- Donald Miller, Arizona State University
- Ronald Schroeder, Southern Polytechnic State University
- Ralph Zegarelli, University of Hartford

We would like to express our deep thanks to our wives Gisela Garrido, Merle Schlesinger, and Mary Hoganson, as well as our children: Max and Tino Garrido, Ryan Schlesinger, and Lyssa, Elyse, and Kyle Hoganson.

Chapter 1

Basic Concepts of Operating Systems

1.1 Introduction

The operating system is an essential part of a computer system; it is an intermediary component between the application programs and the hardware. The ultimate purpose of an operating system is twofold: (1) to provide various services to users' programs and (2) to control the functioning of the computer system hardware in an efficient and effective manner.

This chapter presents the basic concepts and the *abstract* views of operating systems. This preliminary material is important in understanding more clearly the complexities of the structure of operating systems and how the various services are provided. General and brief references to Unix and Windows are included throughout the chapter. Appendix A presents a detailed explanation of the Linux commands.

1.1.1 Software Components

A *program* is a sequence of instructions that enables a computer to execute a specific task. Before a program executes, it has to be translated from its original text form (source program) into a machine language program. The program then needs to be linked and loaded into memory.

The *software components* are the collection of programs that execute in the computer. These programs perform computations and control, manage, and carry out other important tasks. There are two general types of software components:

- System software
- Application software

System software is the set of programs that control the activities and functions of the various hardware components, programming tools and abstractions, and other utilities to monitor the state of the computer system. This software forms an environment for the programmers to develop and execute their programs (collectively known as application software). There are actually two types of users: application programmers and end users.

The most important part of system software is the operating system (OS) that directly controls and manages the hardware resources of the computer. The OS also provides a set of services to the user programs. The most common examples of operating systems are Linux, Unix, Windows, MacOS, and OS/2.

Application software are the user programs and consists of those programs that solve specific problems for the users and execute under the control of the operating system. Application programs are developed by individuals and organizations for solving specific problems.

1.2 Operating Systems

An operating system (OS) is a large and complex set of system programs that control the various operations of a computer system and provide a collection of services to other (user) programs. The purpose of an operating system involves two key goals:

- Availability of a convenient, easy-to-use, and powerful set of services that are provided to the users and the application programs in the computer system

- Management of the computer resources in the most efficient manner

Application and system programmers directly or indirectly communicate with the operating system in order to request some of these services.

The services provided by an operating system are implemented as a large set of system functions that include scheduling of programs, memory management, device management, file management, network management, and other more advanced services related to protection and security. The operating system is also considered a huge resource manager and performs a variety of services as efficiently as possible to ensure the desired performance of the system.

Figure 1.1 shows an external view of a computer system. It illustrates the programmers and end users communicating with the operating system and other system software.

The most important active resource in the computer system is the CPU. Other important resources are memory and I/O devices. Allocation and deallocation of all resources in the system are handled by various resource managers of the operating system.

General-purpose operating systems support two general modes of operation: (1) user mode and (2) kernel mode, which is sometimes called the supervisor, protected, or privilege mode. A user process will normally execute in user mode. Some instructions, such as low-level I/O functions and memory access to special areas where the OS maintains

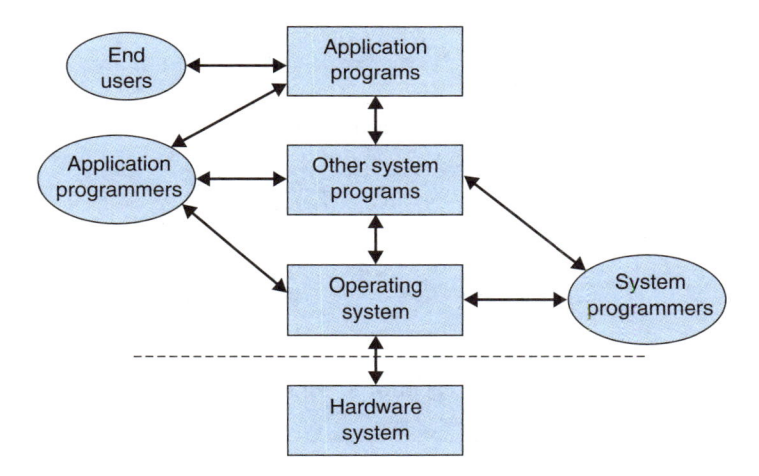

Figure 1.1 An external view of a computer system.

its data structures, can execute only in kernel mode. As such, the OS in kernel mode has direct control of the computer system.

1.2.1 Operating System Interfaces

Users and application programmers can communicate with an operating system through its interfaces. There are three general levels of interfaces provided by an operating system:

- Graphical user interface (GUI)
- Command line interpreter (also called the shell)
- System-call interface

Figure 1.2 illustrates the basic structure of an operating system and shows the three levels of interfaces, which are found immediately above the kernel. The highest level is the graphical user interface (GUI), which allows I/O interaction with a user through intuitive icons, menus, and other graphical objects. With these objects, the user interacts with the operating system in a relatively easy and convenient manner— for example, using the click of a mouse to select an option or command. The most common GUI examples are the Windows desktop and the X-Window in Unix.

The user at this level is completely separated from any intrinsic detail about the underlying system. This level of operating system interface is not considered an essential part of the operating system; it is rather an add-on system software component.

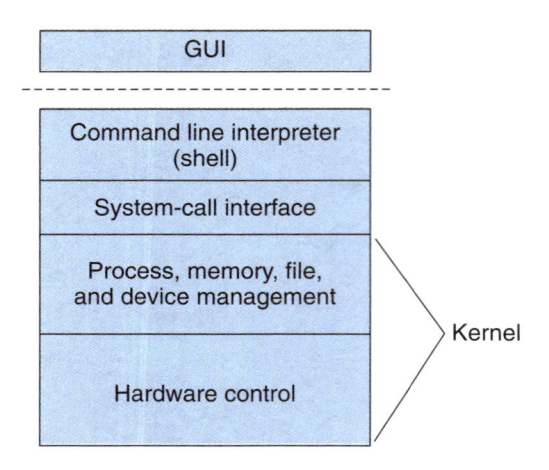

Figure 1.2 Basic structure of an operating system.

The second level of interface, the command line interpreter, or shell, is a text-oriented interface. Advanced users and application programmers will normally directly communicate with the operating system at this level. In general, the GUI and the shell are at the same level in the structure of an operating system.

The third level, the system-call interface, is used by the application programs to request the various services provided by the operating system by invoking or calling system functions.

1.2.2 Multi-Level Views of an Operating System

The overall structure of an operating system can be more easily studied by dividing it into the various software components and using a top-down (layered) approach. This division includes the separation of the different interface levels, as previously discussed, and the additional components of the operating system. The higher the level of the layer, the simpler the interaction with the system. The top layer provides the easiest interface to the human operators and to users interacting with the system. Any layer uses the services or functions provided by the next lower layer.

As mentioned previously, the main goal of an operating system is to provide services to the various user and system programs. The operating system is structured into several components, each one providing its own group of services. For a more clear understanding of the complexities of how the various services are provided, two abstract views of the OS are presented: (1) the external view and (2) the internal view.

1.2.2.1 External View of an Operating System

The external view of an operating system is the set of interfaces discussed previously. These are sometimes referred to as the *abstract views*. Users of a computer system directly or indirectly communicate with the operating system in order to request and receive some type of service provided by the operating system. Users and application programs view the computer system at the higher level(s) of the operating system interface. The low-level OS structures (internal view) and the hardware details are hidden behind the OS interface.

Figure 1.3 illustrates the abstract views of a computer system. Only the upper-level abstract views are important to users of the OS. The low-level OS view and the hardware view are relevant only to system specialists.

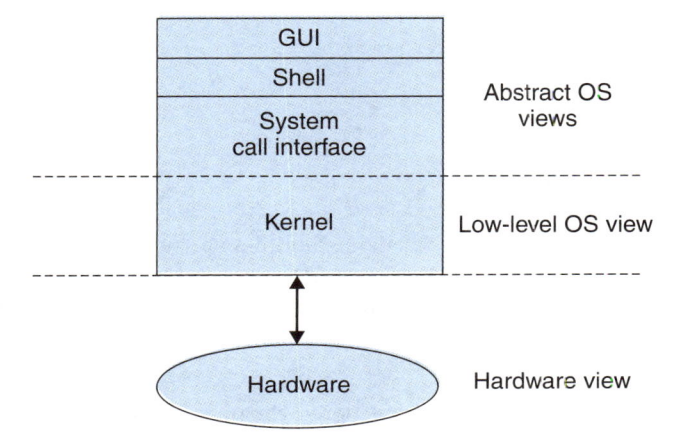

Figure 1.3 Abstract views of a computer system.

One of the main principles applied in the design of the external view concept is simplicity. The system interfaces hide the details of how the underlying (lower-level) machinery operates. The operational model of the computer system presented to the user should be relatively easy to use and is an abstract model of the operations of the system.

The abstraction provided by the OS interfaces gives users and application programs the appearance of a simpler machine. The various programs also convey the illusion that each one executes on its own machine; this abstraction is sometimes called the *abstract machine view*.

1.2.2.2 Internal View of an Operating System

The system services interface (or the system call interface) separates the *kernel* from the application layer. Located above the hardware, the kernel is the core and the most critical part of the operating system and needs to be always resident in memory. A detailed knowledge about the different components of the operating system, including these lower-level components, corresponds to an internal view of the system.

In studying the internal view of the operating system, it becomes important to identify the various components of the OS that establish policies for the various services they support and the mechanisms used to implement these policies.

It was previously noted that the various services provided by the operating systems include process management, memory management, device management, file management, network management, and other more advanced services related to protection and security. The most important functional components of the operating system are as follows:

- Process manager
- Memory manager
- Resource manager
- File manager
- Device manager

These components are actually modules of the operating system and are strongly related. In addition to these basic functions, most operating systems have some type of network management, security management, and other more advanced functions.

Process Manager

The *process manager* can be considered the most important component of the operating system. It carries out several services such as creating, suspending (blocking), executing, terminating, and destroying processes.

With multiprogramming, several active processes are stored and kept in memory at the same time. If there is only one CPU in the system, then only one process can be in execution at a given time; the other processes are waiting for CPU service. The decision regarding which process to execute next is taken by the scheduler. The dispatcher allocates the CPU to a process and deallocates the CPU from another process. This switching of the CPU from one process to another process is called *context switching* and is considered overhead time.

Memory Manager

The *memory manager* controls the allocation and deallocation of memory. It imposes certain policies and mechanisms for memory management. This component also includes policies and mechanisms for memory protection. Relevant memory management schemes are paging, segmentation, and virtual memory.

Resource Manager

The *resource manager* facilitates the allocation and deallocation of resources to the requesting processes. Functions of this component include the maintenance of resource tables with information such as the number of resources of each type that are available and the number of resources of each type that have been allocated to specific processes. The access mode for the various resources is another type of function.

File Manager

The *file manager* allows users and processes to create and delete files and directories. In most modern operating systems, files are associated with mass storage devices such as magnetic tapes and disks. Data can be read and/or written to a file using functions such as open file, read data from file, write data to file, and close file. The Unix operating system also uses files to represent I/O devices (including the main input device and a main output device such as the console keyboard and video screen).

Device Manager

For the various devices in the computer system, the *device manager* provides an appropriate level of abstraction to handle system devices. For every device type, a device driver program is included in the OS. The device manager operates in combination with the resource manager and file manager. Usually, user processes are not provided direct access to system resources. Instead, processes request services to the file manager and/or the resource manager.

1.3 Categories of Operating Systems

A common way to classify operating systems is based on how user programs are processed. These systems can be classified into one of the following categories:

- *Batch systems*, in which a set of jobs is submitted in sequence for processing. These systems have a relatively long average turnaround period (interval from job arrival time to completion time) for jobs.

- *Interactive systems*, which support interactive computing for users connected to the computer system via communication lines. The most common type of operating systems that support interactive computing is *time-sharing*. Figure 1.4 illustrates the general structure of a time-sharing system. A time-sharing system is an example of a multiuser system, which means that multiple users are accessing the system at the same time.

- *Real-time systems*, which support application programs with very tight timing constraints.

- *Hybrid systems*, which support batch and interactive computing.

The most general classification of operating systems is regarding the application environment and includes the following categories:

- *General purpose*, which are used mainly to develop programs and execute these on most types of platforms.

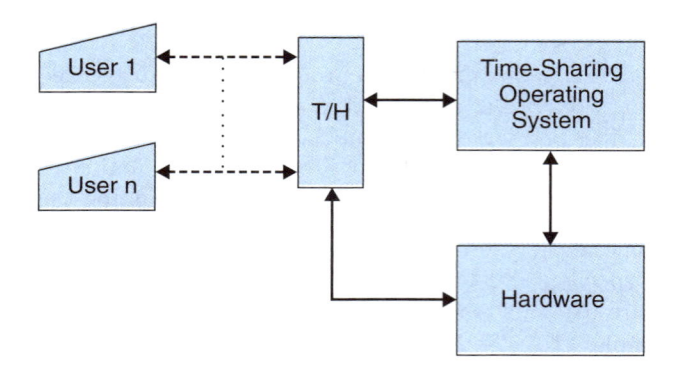

Figure 1.4 General structure of a time-sharing system.

- *Application-dependent*, which are designed for a special purpose. An example of this type is a real-time operating system that controls a power plant for the generation of electricity.

Systems can also be classified as being single user or multiuser. In single-user systems, the single user has access to all resources of the system all the time. In multiuser systems, several users request access to the resources of the system simultaneously.

The term *job* refers to a unit of work submitted by a user to the operating system. A typical job consists of the following parts:

- A sequence of commands to the operating system
- A program either in a source language or in binary form
- A set of input data used by the program when it executes

The sequence of commands in a job includes commands for compiling the source program provided (with an appropriate compiler), linking the program with appropriate libraries, loading the linked program, and executing the program with the input data provided. The term *job* was used in the early batch operating systems. The term *process* basically refers to an execution instance of a program.

1.4 Small and Specialized Operating Systems

A mobile operating system, also known as a mobile OS, a mobile platform, or a handheld operating system, is the operating system that controls a mobile device. Compared to the standard general-purpose operating systems, mobile operating systems are currently somewhat simpler, and focus on wireless versions of broadband and local connectivity, mobile multimedia formats, and different input methods.

Mobile operating systems that can be found on smartphones include Nokia's Symbian OS, Apple's IOS, RIM's BlackBerry OS, Windows Phone, Linux, Palm WebOS, Google's Android, and Nokia's Maemo. Android, WebOS, and Maemo are in turn built on top of Linux, and the iPhone OS is derived from the BSD and NeXTSTEP operating systems, which are all related to Unix.

An embedded operating system is an operating system for embedded computer systems. These operating systems are designed to be very compact and efficient, with similar functions that non-embedded computer operating systems provide, but which are more specialized depending on the applications they run. Most embedded operating systems are real-time operating systems.

Examples of systems that use embedded operating systems include: Automated Teller Machines, cash registers, CCTV systems, a TV box set, a GPS, jukeboxes, and missiles.

1.5 Brief History of Operating Systems

The development of operating systems can be summarized as follows:

1. Early computer systems had no operating systems and the programs had to directly control all necessary hardware components.

2. The first types of operating systems were the simple batch operating systems in which users had to submit their jobs on punched cards or tape. The computer operator grouped all the jobs in batches and stacked these on the main input device, which was a fast card reader or tape reader.

   One of the most important concepts for these systems was automatic job sequencing. An important performance metric for these systems was the CPU idle time, which affected the CPU utilization. The most important performance metric from the user point of view was the turnaround time, which is the interval from the submission of a job until the output was generated.

3. The next types of operating systems developed were batch systems with multiprogramming. These systems were capable of handling several programs active in memory at any time and required more advanced memory management. When a program stopped to wait for I/O in these systems, the OS was able to switch very rapidly from the currently executing program to the next. The short interval was called *context switch time*. Multiprogramming normally improves the processor and device utilization.

4. Time-sharing operating systems were the next important generation of systems developed. The most significant advantage of these systems was the capability to provide interactive computing to the users connected to the system. The basic technique employed on these systems was that the processor's time was uniformly shared by the user programs. The operating system provided CPU service during a small and fixed interval to a program and then switched to the next program.

5. Variations of multiprogramming operating systems were developed with more advanced techniques. These included improved hardware support for interrupt mechanisms and allowed implementation of better scheduling techniques based on priorities. Real-time operating systems were developed.

6. Advances in hardware and memory management techniques allowed development of operating systems with newer and more powerful features, such as paging and virtual memory, multi-level cache, and others.

Most of the development of modern operating systems has focused on networking, distribution, reliability, protection, and security. Several widely used operating systems are available today:

- Microsoft Windows, a family of systems that includes 98, Me, CE, 2000, XP, Vista, Windows 7, and others
- Linux (Linus Torvalds, FSF GNU)
- OSF-1 (OSF, DEC)
- Solaris (Sun Microsystems)
- IRIX (Silicon Graphics)
- OS2 (IBM)
- OS/390 (IBM)
- VMS (Dec/Compaq/HP)
- MacOS X (Apple)

1.6 Contemporary Operating Systems

The three most widely used operating systems are Linux, Unix, and Windows. These actually represent two different families of operating systems that have evolved over the years: Unix/Linux and Microsoft Windows.

1.6.1 Unix

Unix was originally introduced in 1974 by Dennis Ritchie and Ken Thompson while working at AT&T Bell Labs. The operating system was developed on a small computer and had two design goals: small size of the software system and portability. By 1980, many of the users were universities and research labs. Two versions became the best known systems: System V Unix (AT&T) and BSD Unix (University of California at Berkeley).

Unix became the dominant time-sharing OS used in small and large computers. It is one of the first operating systems written almost entirely in C, a high-level programming language.

The Unix family includes Linux, which was primarily designed and first implemented by Linus Torvals and other collaborators in 1991. Torvals released the source code on the Internet and invited designers and programmers to contribute their modifications and enhancements. Today Linux is freely available and has been implemented in many small and large computers. This operating system has also become important in commercial software systems.

1.6.2 Microsoft Windows

Windows operating systems are considered the most widely used family of operating systems released by Microsoft. These systems were developed for personal computers that use the Intel microprocessors. This group of operating systems consists of Windows 95, 98, ME, and CE, which can be considered the smaller members of the family. The larger and more powerful members of the Windows family of operating systems are Windows NT, 2000, XP, Vista, and Windows 7.

The larger Windows operating systems include a comprehensive security model, more functionality facility for network support, improved and more powerful virtual memory management, and full implementation of the Win32 API functions.

1.6.3 Mac OS

Mac OS X is an operating system that is really a very good development platform. Mac OS X is based on BSD (Berkeley System Distribution) UNIX and provides support for many POSIX, Linux, and System V APIs. Apple integrated the widely used FreeBSD 5 UNIX distribution with the Mach 3.0 microkernel.

This OS supports multiple development technologies including UNIX, Java, the proprietary Cocoa and Carbon runtime environments, and several open source, web, scripting, database, and development technologies. MacOS X provides several runtime environments integrated under a single desktop environment. The system provides an object-oriented application framework, procedural APIs, a highly-optimized and tightly integrated implementation of Java Standard Edition (JSE), BSD UNIX APIs and libraries, and X11.

1.7 64-bit Operating Systems

These are operating systems for 64-bit processors and systems with 64-bit computer architecture. They appeared more than three decades ago for the large mainframes of the '70s. Less than 10 years ago, microprocessors with 64-bit architecture were introduced.

1.7.1 Microsoft 64-bit Windows 7

With Windows 7 operating system, more computers are able to use the 64-bit edition. One of the important benefits of running a 64-bit OS is that it can address more memory. A 32-bit version of Windows can address only up to 4GB of RAM, and effectively use only around 3GB, since that extra gigabyte is reserved. A 64-bit OS can theoretically address around 17 billion gigabytes of RAM. In practice, the more expensive and advanced versions of 64-bit Windows 7 can handle up to 192GB, while the lower-end editions are more limited.

Of course, 64-bit operating systems still pose some challenges. The 64-bit flavors of Windows 7 and Vista need specific hardware drivers written for them—their 32-bit counterparts won't work. And although manufacturers have been developing 64-bit drivers for their newer peripherals, users with older printers, scanners, and other hardware face a tougher time trying to find 64-bit drivers. Microsoft's Windows 7 Compatibility page lets you browse or search for different hardware and software to determine whether it will run under 64-bit Windows.

1.7.2 Mac OS X

Mac OS X is considered not only the world's most advanced operating system but also extremely secure, compatible, and easy to use. Mac OS X Snow Leopard incorporates new technologies that offer immediate improvements while also smartly setting it up for the future.

64-bit systems provide all users the tools to apply the power of 64-bit to speed up everything from everyday applications to the most demanding scientific computations. Although Mac OS X is already 64-bit capable in many ways, Snow Leopard takes the next big step by rewriting nearly all system applications in 64-bit code and by enabling the Mac to address massive amounts of memory. Mac OS X is faster, more secure, and completely ready to support future applications.

1.8 Summary

The two basic components of a computer system are the hardware and the software components. An operating system is a large and complex software component of a computer system that controls the major operations of user programs and manages all the hardware resources. The main type of system studied in this book is the general-purpose operating system. This chapter has presented the fundamental concepts of operating systems. Discussions on the general structure, user interfaces, and functions of an operating system have also been presented. Two examples of well-known operating systems are Linux and Microsoft Windows.

This chapter also described various views of the operating system, the high-level external view, also called the abstract machine view, and the low-level or internal view. The abstract machine view is seen by the programs that request some type of service from the operating system. The internal details of the OS are hidden below the interfaces. The internal view includes the components that represent the modules of the OS for carrying out various functions: the process manager, memory manager, resource manager, file manager, and device manager. The process manager is considered the most important component of the OS.

Key Terms		
abstract view	file manager	OS interface
access time	hardware component	process
application software	input	process manager
batch system	interactive system	processing
command	job	real-time system
computer system	kernel	software components
context switching	Linux	system software
CPU	Mac OS	Unix
external view	memory manager	Windows

Exercises and Questions

1. Explain the main facilities provided by an operating system. Give examples.

2. What type of computing do you normally use with your personal computer: batch or interactive? Explain and give examples.

3. Explain when you would prefer time-sharing processing instead of batch processing.

4. Describe the general type of work that you regularly do with Windows. Explain the type or level of operating system interface that you normally use. Describe any other possible interface level that you could use with Windows.

5. Get a Unix/Linux account and log in to the system; start experimenting with a small set of commands. Get acquainted with the system's prompt, which is normally a dollar sign. Investigate the use and purpose of the following commands: `who`, `cd`, `pwd`, `ls`, `finger`, `mkdir`, `cp`, `more`, `cat`, and `pico`.

6. From the user point of view, list and explain the main differences between Windows and Linux.

7. From your point of view, what are the main limitations or disadvantages of Windows?

8. From your point of view, what are the main limitations or disadvantages of Linux?

9. Search the Internet and, from the user point of view, list and explain the main differences between Unix and Linux.

10. Explain the main advantages and disadvantages of using internal and external views for the operations of a computer system, such as the one presented in this chapter. Give good arguments.

11. Log in to Linux. At the command prompt, type **man ps** to read the online manual documentation for the **ps** command. After reading this documentation, type **ps**. How many programs are active? How are they identified? Are these all the programs in the OS? Investigate with the options in the **ps** command.

12. Search the Internet and write a brief report on the differences between Windows 7 Home Edition and the Professional Edition.

13. Search the Internet to find data on the commercial support and commercial applications developed for Linux.

Chapter 2

Processes and Threads

2.1 Introduction

Processes and threads are two important types of dynamic entities in a computer system. A process is basically a program in memory either in execution or waiting for CPU, I/O, or other service. Thus, a process is the fundamental computational unit that requests various types of services in the computer system. A process can contain one or more threads of execution. These two types of entities are handled by the process management module of the operating system. System resources are required by the processes and threads in order to execute. This chapter discusses how operating systems represent processes and threads, the various operating system interfaces, and the general principles involved in multiprogramming, which is the technique of supporting several processes in memory at the same time. Appendix B contains more detailed information on Java and POSIX threads.

2.2 Processes

A *process* is a program in execution, ready to execute, or one that has executed partially and is waiting for other services in the computer system. In simpler terms, a process is an instantiation of a program, or an execution instance of a program. A process is a dynamic entity in the system because it exhibits behavior (state changes), and is capable of carrying out some (computational) activity, whereas a program is a static entity. This is similar to the difference that exists between a class (a static entity) and an object (a dynamic entity) in object-oriented programming.

Two basic types of processes are system processes and user processes. System processes execute operating system services, user processes execute application programs.

The operating system (OS) manages the system hardware and provides various computing services for the processes. The OS hides from the user processes all details of the operation of the underlying hardware and how the various services are implemented. To accomplish this, several abstract models and views of the system are provided.

A typical and simplified scenario of how the OS manages the various processes can be described as follows: processes request CPU and I/O services at various times and usually wait for these services. The OS maintains a waiting line or queue of processes for every one of these services. At some time instance, the process will be in a queue waiting for CPU service. At some other instance, the process will be in a different queue waiting for I/O service. When the process completes all service requests, it terminates and exits the system.

Process management is one of the major functions of the operating system; it involves creating processes and controlling their execution. In most operating systems, several processes are stored in memory at the same time and the OS manages the sharing of one or more processors (CPUs) and other resources among the various processes. This technique implemented in the operating system is called *multiprogramming*.

One of the requirements of multiprogramming is that the OS must allocate the CPUs and other system devices to the various processes in such a way that the CPUs and other devices are maintained busy for the longest total time interval possible, thus minimizing the idle time of these devices. If there is only one CPU in the computer system, then only one process can be in execution at any given time. Some other processes are ready and waiting for CPU service while other processes are waiting or receiving I/O service.

The CPU and the I/O devices are considered *active resources* of the system because these resources provide some service to the various processes during some finite interval of time. Processes also request access to *passive resources*, such as memory.

The operating system can be represented by an *abstract machine view*, in which the processes have the illusion that each one executes on its own machine. Using this abstraction, a process is defined as a computational unit with its own environment, and components that include a process identifier, address space, program code, data, and resources required. For every program that needs execution in the system, a process is created and is allocated resources (including some amount of memory). The address space of a process is the set of memory addresses that it can reference.

2.2.1 Process States

The process manager controls execution of the various processes in the system. Processes change from one state to another during their lifetime in the system. From a high level of abstraction, processes exhibit their behavior by changing from one state to the next. The state changes are really controlled by the OS. For example, when the process manager blocks a process because it needs a resource that is not yet available, the process changes from the *running* state to the *waiting for resource* state. When a process is waiting for service from the CPU, it is placed in the ready queue and is in the *ready state*. In a similar manner, when a process is waiting for I/O service, it is placed in one of several I/O queues and it changes to a *wait state*.

The OS interrupts a process when it requests a resource that is not available. If a process is interrupted while executing, the OS selects and starts the next process in the ready queue. During its lifetime, a process will be in one of the various states mentioned previously:

- Created
- Waiting for CPU (i.e., the process is ready)
- Executing (i.e., receiving service from the CPU)
- Waiting for I/O service (the process is blocked)
- Receiving I/O service
- Waiting for one or more passive resources
- Interrupted by the OS
- Terminated

A state diagram represents the various states of a process and the possible transitions in the behavior of a process. Figure 2.1 shows the state diagram of a typical

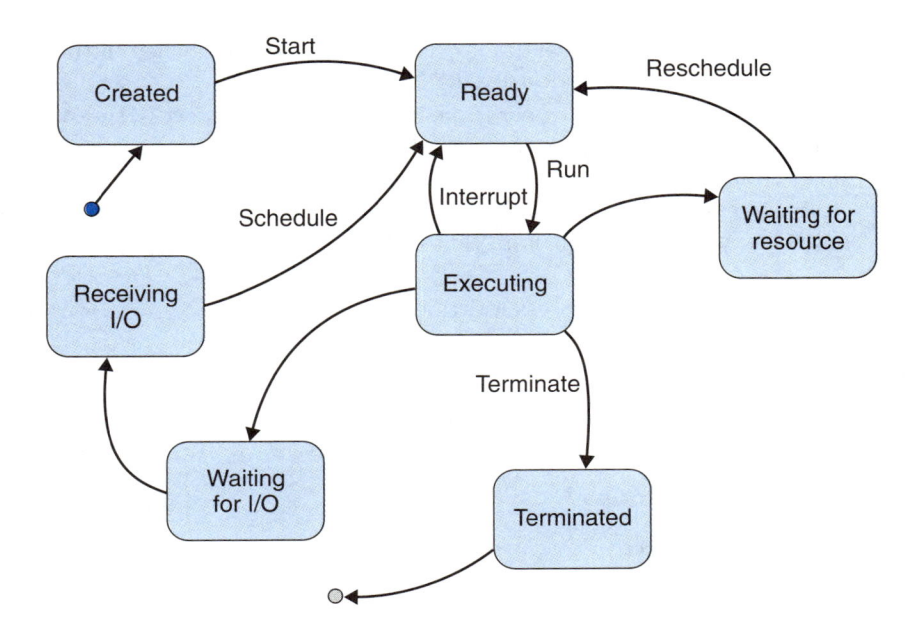

Figure 2.1 State diagram of a typical process.

process. Each state is indicated by a rounded rectangle and the arrows connecting the states represent transitions from one state to the next. The small blue circle denotes that the state it points to is the initial state. In a similar manner, the state before the small gray circle is the last state in the behavior of a process. Normally, a process spends a finite time in any of its states.

When a job arrives, and if there are sufficient resources (such as memory) available, a corresponding process is created. In a time-sharing system, when a user logs in, a new process is created. After being created, the process becomes ready and waits for CPU service. It eventually receives this service, then waits for I/O service, and at some later time receives I/O service. The process then goes back to the ready state to wait for more CPU service. The state in which a process is waiting for I/O service is normally called the *blocked state*. After satisfying all service requests, the process terminates.

Another possible wait state is defined when the process is swapped out to disk if there is not sufficient memory. This means that the operating system can move a process from memory to disk and have the process wait in a *suspended state*; at some other time the process is moved back to memory.

2.2.2 Process Descriptor

For every new process in the system, a data structure called the *process descriptor*, also known as a *process control block* (PCB), is created. It is on this data structure that the OS stores all data about a process. The various queues that the OS manipulates thus contain process descriptors or pointers to the process descriptors, not actual processes. A process descriptor represents a process in the system and when the process terminates, its descriptor is normally destroyed.

For a user process, its owner is the user, for a system process, the owner is the system administrator or the system service that created the process. If a process creates another process, this second process is referred to as a *child process*.

A process descriptor includes several data items or fields that will be defined in the next subsection. The most important of these data fields are as follows:

- Process name or process identifier

- Process owner

- Process state

- List of threads

- List of resources

- List of child processes

- Address space

- Process privileges or permissions

- Current content of the various hardware registers in one of the CPUs before the context switch

The address space is normally a set of parameters that indicate the memory locations allocated to the process. In addition to the fields listed, every descriptor contains a pointer to the actual process located at some location in memory. In Unix, every process has a unique process identifier called the PID, which is an integer value assigned to every new process. Figure 2.2 shows a simplified structure of a process descriptor.

Process ID
State
User
Resources
Permissions
CPU registers
Parent pointer
Child list
Stack and code pointers

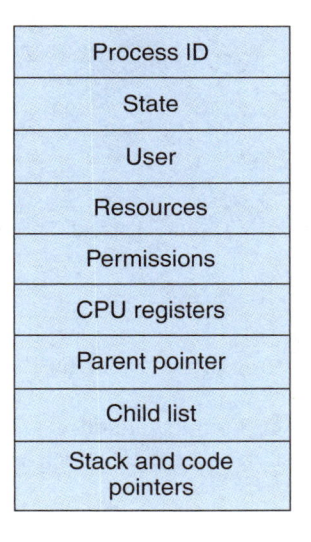

Figure 2.2 Simplified structure of a process descriptor.

2.3 Threads

In addition to processes, modern operating systems support computational units called *threads*. A process can have multiple threads or sequences of executions. A thread is often called a *lightweight process* and is a (dynamic) component of a process. Several threads are usually created within a single process. These threads share part of the program code and the resources that have been allocated to the process.

Most modern operating systems support *multithreading*—a feature that allows multiple threads to execute within a single process. Multithreading enables a programmer to define several tasks in a single process; each task is assigned to a thread.

2.3.1 Multithreading

The operating system manages processes and threads in a multiprogramming environment. From a computational point of view, the execution of threads is handled much more efficiently than the execution of processes. According to this view, threads are the active elements of computation within a process. All threads that belong to a process share the code and resources of the process, as illustrated in Figure 2.3.

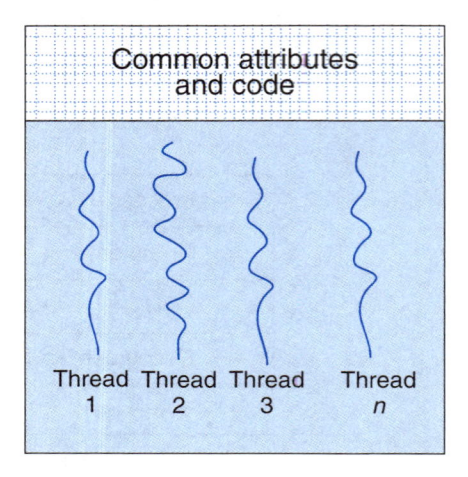

Figure 2.3 Several threads sharing the code and resources in a process.

The thread identifier uniquely identifies the thread. The process that owns the thread represents the environment in which the thread executes. Threads have their own attributes, such as

- Execution state
- Context (the program counter within the process)
- Execution stack
- Local memory block (for local variables)
- Reference to the parent process to access the shared resources allocated to the process

A thread descriptor—a data structure used by the OS to store all the relevant data of a thread—contains the following fields:

- Thread identifier
- Execution state of the thread
- Process owner of the thread

- List of related threads
- Execution stack
- Thread priority
- Thread-specific resources

Some of the fields of a thread descriptor also appear as part of the corresponding process descriptor.

When a process is created, the only thread initially created is called the *base thread* of the process; other threads of the process may then be created by the process or by the base thread.

A thread will exist in different states and will transition from one of its states to another state while executing. A subset of the states of a process, the relevant states of a thread are: *ready*, *running*, and *blocked* (waiting for an I/O operation to complete). A process may terminate when all the threads in the process terminate.

For every process, there is a single process descriptor and an address space assigned to the process. In addition to this, there are several stacks for each thread and a separate thread descriptor for each thread.

One of the advantages of threads from the system point of view is that there is much less overhead managing threads than managing processes. Thus, all the operations related to thread management—creating a new thread, terminating a thread, switching between threads (context switching), and communication between threads—take considerably less time. The reason for this is clear: Because threads share the code and resources of the process, there is no need to change the code and resources from one thread to another thread in the same process.

In a typical small user application, one thread displays one window with a graphic on the screen, another thread handles the user interaction with a GUI, and another carries out a computational task, and so on.

There are two general types of threads: user-level threads and kernel-level threads.

2.3.2 User-Level Threads

With the user-level threads (ULT), the thread management is carried out at the level of the application without kernel intervention. The application carries out threads management using a thread library, such as the POSIX Pthreads Library. Using this standard library, the application invokes the appropriate functions for the various thread management tasks such as creating, suspending, and terminating threads.

As mentioned previously, an application starts executing as a process with the base thread. The process can then create new threads and pass control to one of them to execute. Thread switching and other thread management tasks are carried out by the process using other functions of the thread library. All the necessary data structures are within the address space of a process. The scheduling of threads is normally independent of the scheduling of processes, which is carried out at the kernel level.

The Java programming language supports threads at the language level. For example, every Java application is implemented as a process and the Java Virtual Machine (JVM) supports multiple Java threads in a single application.

The C++ and C programming languages do not directly support threads. The Pthreads library is used in programming with threads.

2.3.3 Kernel-Level Threads

With kernel-level threads (KLT), the thread management tasks are carried out by the kernel. A process that needs these thread-handling services has to use the system call interface of the kernel thread facility. The kernel maintains all the information for the process and its threads in the descriptors previously described.

One of the advantages of kernel-level threads is that the process will not be blocked if one of its threads becomes blocked. Another advantage is the possibility of scheduling multiple threads on multiple CPUs.

Linux, Unix (several implementations), Windows, and OS/2 are examples of operating systems that provide kernel-level threads. Sun Solaris (Sun Microsystems) provides a facility with combined user-level and kernel-level threads.

2.3.4 Java Threads

A program can have multiple execution paths (sequential flows of control) called *threads*. Java provides various ways to create and manipulate threads as objects. A thread is called a lightweight process because it executes concurrently with other threads within a single program.

As mentioned in Chapter 1, the *active* objects in the conceptual model are implemented as threads in Java. These objects execute concurrently to compete for exclusive access to resources and/or to interact among themselves in some synchronized fashion.

2.3.4.1 Using Threads

There are five general steps for using threads in Java:

1. Define one or more classes with thread behavior. These are the user-defined thread classes that:

    - inherit class `Thread`, or
    - implement the `Runnable` interface.

2. Redefine the special thread method `run` for each thread class.

3. Create one or more thread objects from each of these classes.

4. Start the thread objects with the special thread method, `start`.

5. Manipulate the thread objects with the thread methods available from the `Thread` class (or from the `Runnable` interface).

The simplest way to define a class with thread behavior is to use the `Thread` class (from the Java library) as the base class. In addition to the inherited attributes and methods, the subclass will normally include its own methods with additional behavior. Method `run` has to be overridden (redefined). This method defines and controls the behavior of a user-defined thread class, and it is implicitly invoked by method `start`. For a given program, several classes with thread behavior would normally be defined.

In addition to the object threads created from the user-defined thread classes, the Java Virtual Machine (JVM) creates and starts several system threads implicitly. One of these is the main thread that starts when the main method begins execution. Another system thread is the garbage collector thread. If the application includes graphics, the JVM starts one or more graphics threads.

2.3.4.2 Inheriting the Thread Class

A user-defined class will normally extend the Java `Thread` library class. The following code defines class `Mythread`:

```
public class Mythread extends Thread
{
  private String thread_name;
   // constructor
   Mythread ( String tname ) {
      thread_name = new String ( tname );
   }
   // override method run()
   public void run () {
     setName ( thread_name );
     System.out.println ( " New thread: " + thread_name );
   }
   //
   // define additional features
} // end of class Mythread
```

Class `Mythread` inherits the `Thread` class and overrides method `run`. It defines a constructor to initialize the name of the object. From method `main` of the program, for example, a thread of class `Mythread` can be created and started. Using this method for defining threads, every instance of class `Mythread` is a thread object. The following code creates a thread object and starts it, in addition to this object; it also implicitly creates the main thread:

```
public static void main (String [] args) {
   Mythread mythr_obj = new Mythread ("my new thread");
   mythr_obj.start(); // start execution of the thread object
     ...
   System.out.println("Main thread");
}
```

Method `start` is one of the methods of class `Thread`. After the thread object is created, it needs to start execution. Invoking the `start` method begins execution of the thread object. As mentioned previously, this method implicitly invokes method `run`, which defines the actual behavior of the thread object.

The first activity carried out by the previous thread object and defined in method `run` is to set the name of the thread object. Method `setName` of class `Thread` is invoked to set the name of the thread object. This is one of several methods defined in the `Thread` class.

One of the most common applications of threads is GUI implementations, and one of the major concerns in user-interface implementations is to keep the user interface alive and responding to user-generated events. To accomplish this, a thread is defined for the basic GUI, and different threads are defined for the major tasks of the application.

2.3.4.3 Other Basic Thread Methods

There are several methods defined in the `Thread` class. The previous section explained the use of three of them: `run`, `start`, and `setName`. Since more than one thread may execute a method, it can be very convenient or useful to have a reference to the thread that is currently executing a portion of code.

The static method `currentThread` returns a reference to the currently executing thread at the particular point in time. A thread reference needs to have been declared before invoking `currentThread` to get the value of the reference to the current thread. The following portion of code declares a thread reference, then gets the reference to the current thread by invoking the static method `currentThread`:

```
Thread mythread;    // a thread reference declaration

...
// get reference to the currently running thread
mythread = Thread.currentThread();
```

After a reference to the current thread is known, several nonstatic `Thread` methods can be invoked. One of these is the method to get the name of the current thread. The method `getName` returns a string with the name of the thread. Assume that the method to set the name of the thread has been previously called. The following statements simply get the name of the thread and assign it to a string object:

```
String mythread_name;   // a string object ref declaration
...
mythread_name = mythread.getName(); // get name of current thread
```

A thread begins execution when its `start` method is invoked; at this point in time, the thread becomes alive. It will remain alive until its `run` method returns, or when it is terminated. To check if a thread is alive, the boolean method `isAlive` can be used. The following code checks if a thread is alive, then prints a message on the screen:

```
// mythread is a reference to a thread object
...
if ( mythread.isAlive() ) {
   System.out.println("Thread: " + mythread.getName() +

       " is alive");
   ...
}
else {
   system.out.println ("Thread is not alive");
   ...
}
```

2.3.4.4 A Thread Suspending Itself

A thread can be suspended for a given period, then reactivated. Method `sleep` can be used by a thread to suspend itself; the method is a static method that requires an argument of type `long`. The following line of code calls method `sleep` with an argument of value 10000 to suspend a thread for 10 seconds:

```
Thread.sleep ( 10000 );
```

While the thread is suspended, it can be interrupted by another thread; Java requires placing this call within a `try` block so it can check for an exception. The code is as follows:

```
try {
    Thread.sleep ( 10000 );
}
catch (InterruptedException e)  {
    // ignore exception
}
```

2.3.4.5 Implementing the Runnable Interface

As mentioned before, in Java a class can only inherit a single base class—that is, multiple inheritance is not supported. However, a class can implement multiple interfaces. Therefore, when it becomes impractical for a class to inherit the `Thread` class, it can implement the `Runnable` interface.

Similar to the manner used previously to define a class for thread objects, implementing the `Runnable` interface requires the class to completely define method `run`. There is a minor difference in defining a thread class by implementing the `Runnable` interface, compared to the technique used before. An instance of the class is passed as an argument to the `Thread` constructor.

There are six general steps used to declare and define a thread object:

1. Define a thread class by implementing the `Runnable` interface.

2. Declare and create an object of the class implementing the `Runnable` interface.

3. Declare and create a thread object by invoking the thread constructor using the instance of the class in the previous step, as an argument.

4. Start the thread object by invoking its start method.

5. Manipulate the thread object by invoking the various thread methods.

6. Indicate to the garbage collector to destroy the thread object.

The following Java code defines a class that implements the `Runnable` interface and includes a definition of the `run` method:

```java
public class Otherthread implements Runnable {
  // declaration of attributes
  ...
  // definition of private and public methods
  ...
  // definition of the run() method
  public void run () {
     System.out.println ("Thread: " + getName () );
     ...
  }
}        // end of class
```

This class can now be instantiated, and `Thread` objects can be created and manipulated. This is accomplished by the following code of method `main`:

```java
public static void main ( String [] args ) {
   private Otherthread classobj;
   ...
   // create object of this class
   classobj = new Otherthread ();
   // now create thread object
   Thread mythread = new Thread ( classobj );
   mythread.start ();   // start execution of thread

   ...
}      // end main()
```

2.3.4.6 Interrupting a Thread Object

There are several ways for one thread to stop another thread. The most straightforward way is to have one thread interrupt a second thread. The first thread can do this by invoking the `interrupt` method of the second thread. In the following example, the main thread interrupts the thread that it has created and started previously. The main method described previously now includes a call to the interrupt method of the second thread:

```
...
// time after starting thread object mythread, interrupt it
mythread.interrupt ();
...
```

The interrupted thread will have a special interrupt flag set to indicate that it has been interrupted. If the thread being interrupted is sleeping, an exception is thrown (as shown above). The block of instructions to execute when this event occurs (interrupt) is placed in a `catch` block.

```
try {
    Thread.sleep ( 10000 );
}
catch ( InterruptedException e ) {
    // just a message to screen
    System.out.println ("Thread interrupted ....");
}
```

When a thread is interrupted, its interrupted flag is set. This is reflected in its interrupted status, which will indicate whether the thread was interrupted. The call to method `sleep` above clears the interrupted flag when it throws the exception. Usually, when a thread is executing a method and it is interrupted, it should be able to raise an exception of type `InterruptedException`.

To check the interrupted status of a thread, the `isInterrupted` method is called. This method returns `true` if the thread has been interrupted and `false` if the thread has not been interrupted. This method does not change the interrupted status of the thread. For example, the following code checks for the interrupted flag and executes appropriate instructions in a thread:

```
...
if ( isInterrupted () ) {
    ...        // appropriate instructions
    System.out.println ( "Thread was interrupted, ..." );
}
else {
    ...        // other instructions
    System.out.println ( "Thread was not interrupted, ..." );
}
...
```

To check and clear the interrupted flag in a thread, the `interrupted` method is invoked; it is a static method of class `Thread`. The following code invokes this method and displays the interrupted status of the thread:

```
System.out.println ( "Status for thread: " +
    Thread.interrupted () );
```

2.3.4.7 Thread Priorities in Java

Scheduling is the selection of which thread to execute next. Threads are normally scheduled with their default priorities. The application threads (including the main thread) have a default priority of 5. The system threads, such as the thread of the garbage collector and AWT windows thread, have a higher priority (in the range of 6 to 10).

To change the priority of threads, Java provides several constants and methods used for priority assignments. Any priority changes must be done with care, and JVM may not actually use the new priorities in the expected manner.

To get the current priority of a thread, the `getPriority` method is invoked. To set the priority of a thread to a different value, the `setPriority` method is invoked. The priority is an integer value. A thread can be rescheduled to execute any time after a pause by relinquishing the processor to another thread. The `yield` static method indicates the scheduler to execute the next pending thread. The code that follows gets the priority of a thread. If it is 5 or less, it is set to the maximum priority possible; otherwise the current thread yields the processor to another scheduled thread.

```
int my_prior;
...
my_prior = mythread.getPriority();
if ( my_prior <= 5 )
    mythread.setPriority ( Thread.MAX_PRIORITY);
else
    Thread.yield();     // yield execution of this thread
...
```

2.4 POSIX Threads

POSIX threads, also known as *Pthreads*, are not really object-oriented; they were developed to be used with the C programming language. For C++, we can define a wrapper class as the defining basic thread class, then instantiate or inherit the class from a subclass. The Psim3 simulation package, which is used to implement the simulation models discussed in this book, was developed with Pthreads.

Pthreads follow the IEEE Portable Operating System Interface (POSIX) standards. Part of this standard covers threads and includes the application programming interface (API) that supports threads.

Every thread has the following parameters associated with it:

- A thread ID, which uniquely identifies the thread. The thread ID is returned when the thread is created.
- An attribute object, which is used to configure the thread. Normally the default values are used for the attribute object.
- A *start function*, which is called when the thread is created.
- An argument of the start function call. If more than one argument is required in the function call, then the argument should point to a data structure.

2.4.1 Creating POSIX Threads

The prototype of the function to create a thread within a process is as follows:

```
int pthread_create (pthread_t *thread_id,
                    pthread_attr_t *attr,
                    void *(*start_function)(void *),
                    void *arg);
```

A process, or application, may create several threads by invoking the `pthread_create` function.

The following portion of code is an example of creating a thread that calls the `func1` function when it is created:

```
Pthread_t tid;
int error_code;
//
// create a new thread
//
error_code = pthread_create (&tid, NULL, func1, arg1);

. . .
void * func1 (void *arg) {
  //
  // code for func1
  //
}
```

In the Psim3 simulation package, member function `pstart()` of class `process` includes the Pthread function `pthread_create` to create a thread. Thus, a new thread is created when the `pstart()` function is called on a process object—an instance of a user-defined class that inherits class `process`.

2.4.2 Basic Synchronization of Pthreads

2.4.2.1 Waiting for Termination

When a thread has to wait for another thread to complete, the first thread has to invoke `pthread_join(..)`. A call to this function suspends the first thread until the second thread exits or returns. The first thread invokes `pthread_join(..)` and needs the thread ID of the second thread as one of the arguments in the function call. The following line of code invokes the function using the thread ID, `Tid2`, of the second thread.

```
error_code = pthread_join(Tid2, NULL);
```

Threads that can be *joined* are also called *nondetached threads*; threads that cannot be joined are called *detached threads*. By default, threads that are created are joinable. Threads that are to be detached can be created by first changing the attribute in the attribute object of the thread. The following line of code changes this:

```
pthread_attr_setdetachstate(&attr, PTHREAD_CREATE_DETACHED);
```

An existing thread can be detached by invoking the following function:

```
int pthread_detach( pthread_t tid);
```

2.4.2.2 Termination of a Thread

A thread normally terminates when it returns from its *start function*, which is the code body of the thread. Another way a thread terminates is by calling the `pthread_exit()` function. The prototype of this function is

```
int pthread_exit( void *thes);
```

Parameter `thes` is the thread's exit status. A detached thread should not exit with this parameter different than NULL.

A thread may be terminated by another thread. If a first thread needs to terminate a second thread with a thread ID, `tid2`, then the following line of code in the first thread will terminate the second thread:

```
pthread_cancel(tid2);   // cancel thread tid2
```

2.4.3 Scheduling and Priorities of POSIX Threads

The default scheduling approach used in POSIX threads is the *process scheduling scope*, a process in which each thread competes for system resources with all other similar threads within the process. These threads are unbound, which means that a thread does not directly bind to a kernel entity.

A thread can temporarily change its scheduling by releasing or yielding the CPU to another thread. The function call `sched_yield()` in a thread will allow another thread to run.

POSIX defined three real-time scheduling policies for threads: (1) FIFO (with priorities), (2) round robin, and (3) another policy that may be specified by a particular implementation. When a thread is created, it has a given scheduling policy and a priority. These two can be changed dynamically after the thread starts execution.

The scheduling policies contain at least 32 priority values. To get the minimum and maximum priority values, POSIX provides two functions that are specified by the following function prototypes:

```
int sched_get_priority_min (int sched_policy);

int sched_get_priority_max (int sched_policy);
```

The integer parameter `sched_policy` has three possible values: (1) SCHED_FIFO, (2) SCHED_RR, and (3) SCHED_OTHER.

The scheduling parameter of a thread is a data structure having several components, with scheduling priority being one of them. The scheduling policy and scheduling parameter can be changed with the function call in the following code:

```
struct sched_param s_param;   // scheduling parameter
. . .
s_param.sched_priority = priority_val;
err_val = pthread_setschedparam (th_id, sched_policy, &s_param);
```

2.5 Multiprogramming

An operating system can support several processes in memory through a facility known as *multiprogramming*. The system performs CPU processing (CPU service) to one process and I/O processing (I/O service) to another process, while the other processes are waiting for service in the various queues (waiting lines). The number of processes in memory is called the *degree of multiprogramming*.

The operating system maintains several queues for processes that wait for services or for resources. The processes that are waiting for CPU service are in the ready state and are placed in the ready queue. The processes that are waiting for an I/O device are placed in the I/O queue corresponding to that device.

2.5.1 CPU and I/O Requests

Processes demand CPU and I/O processing. These are provided in short time intervals known as CPU and I/O bursts. During the execution of a process, it usually runs for the length of its current CPU burst, then it requests I/O service. For the next cycle, the process runs for the duration of its next CPU burst, then requests I/O service, and so on until the process completes all its service demands.

A simple way to describe the behavior of a process is by stating that the process alternates its CPU and I/O requests, and it cycles through the CPU and I/O devices. The total service demand of a process will usually consist of several CPU and I/O requests. The servicing of a CPU request is called a *CPU burst*, and the servicing of an I/O request is called an *I/O burst*.

The total processing or service of process P_i typically consists of several CPU and I/O bursts. The duration of CPU burst j of process P_i is τ_{ij}. If m is the total number of CPU bursts of process P_i, then the total CPU service of process P_i is

$$\tau_i = \tau_{i1} + \tau_{i2} + \ldots \tau_{im}.$$

The duration of I/O burst k of process P_i is δ_{ik}. If n is the total number of I/O bursts of process P_i, then the total I/O service of process P_i is

$$\delta_i = \delta_{i1} + \delta_{i2} + \ldots \delta_{in}.$$

The actual behavior of process P_i is represented by a sequence of wait, CPU burst, and I/O burst time intervals, as represented by the following expression:

$$\langle\ w_{\tau_1}, \tau_1, w_{\delta_1}, \delta_1, w_{\tau_2}, \tau_2, w_{\delta_2}, \delta_2, \ldots, w_{\tau_{m-1}}, \tau_{m-1}, w_{\delta_n}, \delta_n, w_{\tau_m}, \tau_m\ \rangle.$$

Usually, before a CPU burst τ_{ij} of process P_i, the process has to wait for a time interval w_{τ_j} and before an I/O burst δ_{ik} of process P_i, the process has to wait for a time interval w_{δ_k}.

Because of the overlapping of operations of the I/O devices and the CPU, one of the various processes receives CPU service and another process receives I/O service. This way, the I/O devices and the CPU spend most of their time busy, which means that their utilization is relatively high.

2.5.2 Interrupting Processes

When a process is executing, it is in the running state. At any time instant, the OS may interrupt the process and switch to the next process that is waiting for CPU service. There are three basic reasons for interrupting this process:

- The running process needs an I/O operation, such as reading data from a file. In this case, the process invokes a system function of the OS and suspends itself. When the I/O operation is complete, the process is reactivated and placed again in the ready queue to wait for CPU service. In the meantime, the OS has switched to the next process and starts to execute it.

- The running process is interrupted by a timer under OS control. The process returns to its ready state in the ready queue to wait for CPU service. The OS removes the next process from the ready queue and switches to this process.

- A high priority process arrives or is made to transition to the ready state, and the OS interrupts the running process if it has a lower priority. The interrupted process is normally returned to the ready queue to wait for CPU service.

Figure 2.4 illustrates the basic queues in the CPU and I/O devices (servers) that a process joins while waiting for service in the computer system. There is one CPU and its ready queue, and n I/O devices, each one with an I/O queue.

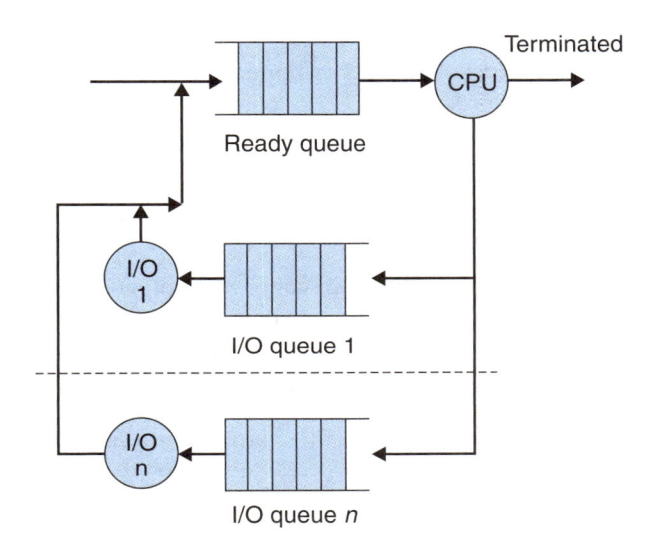

Figure 2.4 Basic queues for processes in a computer system.

The selection of the next process to select from the ready queue is carried out by the *scheduler*. The allocation of the CPU to this new process is carried out by the *dispatcher*, another component of the OS.

Assume that there is one CPU and several I/O devices. Only one process is receiving CPU service—that is, only one process is actually executing. Another process is receiving I/O service from a specific I/O device. Other processes in memory are waiting either for CPU or for I/O service. Processes in memory could also be waiting for an event (such as the unlocking of a list) to occur.

As mentioned earlier, computer systems have the capabilities to overlap CPU and I/O service—that is, they provide these various services simultaneously to different processes. For example, the CPU is servicing process $P1$ while the I/O device 1 is servicing process $P2$, while the I/O device 2 is providing service to process $P3$. These three activities are occurring at the same time; processes $P1$, $P2$, and $P3$ are all receiving different services at the same time. The computer system controls this overlapping of CPU and I/O devices via its interrupt mechanisms.

2.5.3 Context Switch

When the OS interrupts an executing process, it carries out a *context switch*—the changing of the CPU from one process to another. This involves deallocating the CPU from the current process and allocating the CPU to the next process selected by the scheduler. This is a simplistic explanation of a context switch. The context of the current process includes the complete information of the process and it is stored in its PCB. For the other process, its complete context is loaded from its PCB.

Context switching is carried out with hardware support. The time it takes for this changeover is called the context switch time. This time interval should be very short because it is considered overhead or nonproductive time during which the CPU is not servicing any (user) processes.

2.6 Summary

Processes and threads are the main concepts explained in this chapter. The process is the fundamental unit of computation. It is a dynamic entity, unlike a program, which is a static entity. The process descriptor is the main data structure that the OS uses to manipulate processes. This descriptor contains essential data about a process. A thread is a sequential flow of execution; it is also called a lightweight process and is a dynamic component of a process. The threads within a process share part of the code and resources of the process. A process goes through several possible states during its lifetime in the system. The operating system handles a process in such a way that it changes state until the process terminates. The state changes are shown in the process state diagram. Appendix B contains more detailed information on Java and POSIX threads.

There are several queues created and managed by the operating system. Processes wait for service or for resources in queues. The various examples of queues include the ready queue, I/O queue, and input queue. Multiprogramming is a facility of the OS for supporting several processes in memory; this increases the CPU and device utilizations. Context switching is needed to change the CPU allocation from one process to another.

\	Key Terms	\
abstract machine	lightweight process	queue
active resource	multiprogramming	ready state
base thread	overhead time	server
blocked state	passive resource	service request
context switch	PID	state diagram
CPU burst	process	suspended
CPU utilization	process control block (PCB)	thread
device utilization	process descriptor	transition
I/O burst	process management	user thread (ULT)
kernel thread (KLT)	process state	

Exercises and Questions

1. Investigate how Java handles threads. A Java application can have several threads. Is this consistent with the basic notion of threads in the OS?

2. Discuss the importance of the process descriptor (PCB). What data does it contain? Is there any other relevant data about a process that would need to be included in the PCB?

3. Consult a Linux manual and find out the actual content of a process descriptor in Linux.

4. Repeat the previous exercise for Sun Solaris OS.

5. Repeat the previous exercise for Microsoft Windows XP.

6. Explain the notion of a context switch. What would happen if the context switch time were too long? Discuss your arguments.

7. Explain why the context switch time is considered overhead. Give examples.

8. Explain the differences among processes, programs, and threads. List the basic possible states for a process. Discuss any additional state. Is it possible to have intermediate states?

9. Is multiprogramming more useful in a multiuser system or a single-user system? Discuss your arguments.

10. A system has several processes that request I/O services in long time intervals compared with very short CPU service. For example, the processes request services that about 95 percent of the total service request time are I/O requests and only 5 percent are CPU requests. What potential problems can this system exhibit? Explain.

11. A system has several processes that request CPU services in long time intervals compared with the I/O service. For example, the processes request services that about 95 percent of the total service request time are CPU requests and only 5 percent are I/O requests. What potential problems can this system exhibit? Explain.

12. Write a simple program in Java that creates and starts three or more threads. These should display a message then terminate.

13. Repeat the previous exercise using C++ instead of Java.

Chapter 3
System Performance and Models

3.1 Introduction

This chapter introduces basic concepts and principles of modeling in the study of the dynamic behavior of simple systems and in calculating their performance. This study is carried out by using object-oriented simulation models.

A model is a simplified or abstract representation of a real system and has a specific purpose and goal. Abstraction is the ability to hide nonessential properties and behavior of the system so the model is used to describe, study, and/or design the system. The main reason for using a model is that it can help predict the behavior of the real system.

Models of computer systems typically consist of several service stations, each one including a queue and a server. The queue is used to hold processes that are waiting for service. The types of service are normally CPU processing and I/O processing. This modeling approach can also be used in studying computer networks.

A few diagrams included in this chapter use Unified Modeling Language (UML), a standard notation that describes conceptual models of systems.

3.2 General Concepts of Modeling

A model includes only those aspects of the real system that were considered to be important according to the initial requirements of the model. The limitations of the model must be clearly understood and documented. The behavior of the model depends on the environment inputs. The model should allow the user to carry out the following:

- Observe its behavior and measure its output when given some input.
- Predict the behavior of the system by analyzing the behavior of its model, under the same circumstances.

There are many types of models that would be of interest in studying computer systems:

- *Physical models*: Models constructed to resemble the physical attributes of an actual object by scaling down the physical properties of a real system. Examples of physical models are: train, airplane, or ship models. Physical models have certain attributes:

    - They are dedicated or specialized in the type of system that they represent. For example, the model of a building is not used to represent a house.
    - They have some rigid physical properties that are difficult and expensive to change and therefore may require rebuilding the model.
    - They are static because the dynamic behavior of the system cannot be represented.

- *Graphical models*: Models that use graphical representations to display the behavior of a system. They are used as high-level descriptions of the system in diagrammatic form.

- *Mathematical models*: Models that are represented by a set of mathematical expressions and logical relations to express the relationships among entities or objects of the system. Performance analysis is carried out by using mathematical models, and expressions and relations represent the structure and behavior of the real system. There are two subtypes of mathematical models: analytical and empirical. With the first, mathematical relations and expressions are used to describe the model. With the second, numerical techniques are used. The simulation models in this book are mathematical models.

3.3 Simple Models of Computer Systems

The previous chapter explained how early operating systems, which were mainly batch systems, used jobs—work requests consisting of a sequence of commands to the OS. For example, such a sequence of commands might be to compile a source program and run a program using the data included in the job for running the program. A process, however, is a modern term and is considered an execution instance of a program; the process is the fundamental unit of computation.

Models of computer systems consist of a network of stations, each one including a server and a queue. These models are often called *queuing models*. A server is a system component that provides a particular service (e.g., CPU or I/O processing) to the processes; a server is thus considered an active resource. Figure 3.1 shows the main components of a simple model of a batch system that consists of a single station that provides computing service to jobs arriving into the system. These jobs arrive from some environment (population) and join the *input queue* to wait for memory allocation.

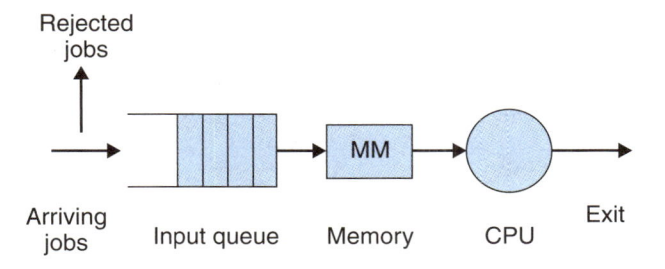

Figure 3.1 A simple model of a batch system.

This model represents a simple batch system with no multiprogramming, which means that there is only one program instance in memory at any given time and there is only a single queue, the *input queue*, which holds the jobs that arrive and wait for memory allocation. In this and similar systems, the single server is the *processor* (CPU). From a functional perspective, the dynamic behavior of this system can be described as follows:

1. When memory is available, the memory manager removes the program instance at the head of the input queue and allocates memory to it.

2. After memory allocation, the processor starts to service this program instance.

3. At the end of the service period, the program instance terminates, memory is deallocated, and the program exits the system.

All the state changes that occur in the system are analyzed when studying the dynamic behavior of the system. In the model of the simple batch operating system described previously, the system changes state when a process arrives, completes, starts service, and so on. These instantaneous occurrences are called *events*—actions that normally trigger (or cause) state changes in the system and changes in its behavior.

One way to define a system state is by the number of processes in the queue at a specific point in time, including when the queue is empty and when it is full. When a job arrives into the system, a process is created and the number of processes in the system is increased by one. The new process has to wait in the queue. When a process completes service, it terminates and leaves the system, and the number of processes is decremented by one.

A process is rejected when it finds that the queue is full. A rejected process will not be accepted by the system and is lost forever.

3.4 Performance of Computer Systems

The study of the performance of a computer system involves determining the various performance metrics when the system is subject to some workload. This workload

40 Chapter 3 System Performance and Models

is characterized by several workload parameters, and the performance of a system is usually calculated for different sets of these parameters. System parameters are more system-dependent and also affect the performance of the system.

Three approaches are often considered in studying the performance of systems:

- Measurements
- Simulation models
- Analytical (mathematical) models

The last two approaches require the development of *performance models*—simulation or mathematical analytical models that determine some specified performance metrics.

A complete performance study includes the definition of the following components:

- Set of relevant objectives and goals
- Performance metrics
- System parameters
- System factors
- System workload perameters

3.4.1 Performance Metrics

A *performance metric* (or performance measure) of a computer system is a measurement or quantity that helps characterize, together with other performance metrics, the effectiveness of the system—that is, how well it is carrying out its functions, considering some particular aspect. This quantity is usually related to the efficiency and/or usage of the components of the system. A set of several different performance metrics is necessary, one for every aspect considered, of the system being modeled.

The results of running a performance model yield the values of the performance metrics. The most common performance metrics for computer systems are as follows:

- *Average wait time*, the average period that jobs wait in the system since their arrival time.
- *Average throughput*, the average number of jobs completed in some specified time interval.
- *CPU utilization*, the portion of time the CPU is used relative to the total observation time interval (usually a percentage).
- *Resource utilization*, the proportion of the interval the resource is used relative to the total observation time interval.
- *Average response time*, the average time interval that the system takes to respond to a particular command or request of a user process. This metric is mainly useful in interactive systems.

- *Average turnaround time*, the average time interval that elapses from the time a job is submitted until the time the system writes the output results. This metric is also referred to as the *sojourn time* and is used mainly in batch systems.

- *Availability*, the fraction of time (percentage) that an external observer finds the system capable of carrying out some work. The time interval during which the system is not available is called the *downtime*.

- *Reliability*, the mean time between failures or the probability of failures.

- *Capacity*, the maximum achievable throughput under ideal workload conditions.

- *Fairness*, a measure of the variability of throughput across the various types of jobs or processes.

- *Speedup*, a factor of gains in speed usually achieved by adding more processors to a system.

The performance study of a system, such as the simple batch system given some workload, usually attempts to achieve the following performance criteria:

- Reduce waiting periods for the processes.

- Improve the processor (CPU) utilization.

- Maximize throughput.

In most computer systems, the processor *utilization* is considered one of the important performance metrics of a system. When the processor has no work to carry out, it is in the idle state and the time duration is the idle time of the CPU. When the processor has to carry out some overhead task, the time spent can be considered nonproductive work because the processor is not actually carrying out the execution of user processes.

If the system workload increases, the processor utilization will also increase. The speed of the processor also affects the processor utilization. The faster the processor, the lower the utilization—that is, it provides service at a higher rate and it spends more time waiting for processes to arrive. In this case, the processor will spend part of its time in an idle state.

3.4.2 Workload and System Parameters

The workload consists of a set of service requests demanded by the processes in a system. Predicting the values of the performance metrics depends not only on the workload parameters but also on the software and hardware parameters.

The workload submitted to a system consists of jobs arriving into the batch system. The workload characterization is a set of workload parameters that affect the performance of the system. A typical set of workload parameters for a model of a computer system consists of:

- Average memory demand, M, of the jobs

- Average arrival rate, λ, of the jobs

- Average service rate, μ, of the jobs

In most simulation models discussed in this book, instead of the average arrival rate, the average interarrival period is used and denoted by $1/\lambda$, which is the inverse. Instead of the average service rate, the average service period is used and denoted by $1/\mu$, which is the inverse.

Since it is important to model the variability between job arrivals and the variability of the job service requirements, the average of these two quantities is given. The actual period between job arrivals is random, with the average of all those random periods being the parameter used. In a similar manner, the service period requested by a job is random, and the average of all these random periods is the workload parameter used.

Most of the models discussed follow the assumption that the time interval between job arrivals and the service period are exponentially distributed random values and are calculated by a random number generator that uses an exponential probability distribution. The random number generator uses a given mean value. A similar random number generator is used for other random numbers needed in the simulation models. The other two common probability distributions are the normal and the uniform distributions. For the queuing model of the simple batch system, three parameters are defined:

- Average memory demand, M

- Average interarrival period, $1/\lambda$

- Average service demand, D

The average service demand is the time it takes the CPU to service a job, $D = 1/\mu$.

For the model of the simple batch system considered in the previous section, the following system parameters are identified:

- Input queue size

- Total memory of the computer

- Speed of the processor

From the previous discussion, the average arrival rate, λ, represents the arrival pattern of processes from the environment. This workload parameter is given by the average arrival rate (λ)—for example, 25 processes per minute. This parameter is alternatively given by the average interarrival period.

For this model, the interarrival period follows an exponential probability distribution that is used to generate randomly the individual interarrival period for each process. Every interarrival interval is a random number generated by a random number generator using the calculations of an exponential probability distribution provided by the simulation package.

The average service demand for the processes is another important parameter in the workload characterization. Each individual process has a different service demand that follows an exponential distribution. In the simulation model of this system, an exponential distribution is used to generate randomly the individual service demand for each process.

The queue is always assumed to be of a finite size. When the model reaches the capacity of the queue, subsequently arriving processes are rejected. This parameter also affects the computation of some of the performance metrics, such as the average waiting time and the throughput. The simulation model of the simple batch system shows this dependency in a very clear form.

The memory demand of the process and memory capacity of the computer system affect the rejection of the process. Processes that demand more memory than the total system memory are rejected. On the other hand, if the computer system has too much memory, it will reflect low memory utilization.

The speed of processing (CPU speed) is another relevant system parameter that affects performance. This is considered a hardware workload parameter.

3.5 Simulation Models

There are two general goals for a simulation model:

- To analyze some relevant aspects of the system using the sequence of events or trace from the simulation runs

- To estimate various performance metrics of the system

Simulation models include sufficient level of detail needed to represent the complexity of a system. These models can be much more accurate than analytical models because any desired level of detail can be potentially achieved in the solution.

3.5.1 Types of Simulation Models

Simulation models are often divided into two categories: *deterministic models* and *stochastic models*. Deterministic models exhibit a completely deterministic behavior. A stochastic model includes some uncertainty implemented with random variables, whose values are represented by a probabilistic distribution. Most simulation models are stochastic because the real systems being modeled usually exhibit inherent uncertainty properties. Informally, these models use random inputs and produce random outputs.

The values of most workload parameters change randomly and are represented by a probability distribution. For example, in a model of a computer system, the inter-arrival intervals of jobs usually follow an exponential distribution. Other probability distributions that are used in the models discussed in this book are normal, uniform, and Poisson. In the simulation models considered, most workload parameters are implemented as random variables.

One of the advantages of using a simulation model is the observation of the dynamic behavior of a system—that is, the state changes in the model as time advances. The state of the model is defined by the values of its attributes represented by state variables. For example, the number of waiting jobs to be processed by the simple computer batch system changes its value with time. Whenever this attribute (number of jobs waiting) changes value, the system changes its state.

Simulation models are also divided into two other general categories: *continuous models* and *discrete-event models*. In continuous models, the changes of state occur continuously with time, and the state variables in the model are represented as continuous functions of time. For example, a model that represents the temperature in a boiler as part of a power plant can be considered a continuous model because the state variable that represents this temperature is implemented as a continuous function of time. These types of models are usually deterministic and are modeled as a set of partial differential equations.

3.5.2 Discrete-Event Models

In *discrete-event models*, changes of state occur at discrete points in time—that is, at specific instants. Most practical discrete-event models are also stochastic models. The simple batch system is a discrete-event model. An arrival event occurs at a specific instant and there is a change in the number of jobs waiting to receive processing from the CPU (the server).

Figure 3.1 shows this simple arrangement of an input queue and CPU in the model of a computer system. Jobs arrive at discrete points in time, requesting memory and CPU service. The jobs must join the input queue to wait for memory. At some later time, each job receives some amount of CPU time. After this, the job terminates and exits the system.

A simulation run is an experiment carried out on the simulation model, during some time interval of observation. Every run, the result of experimenting with a simulation model, provides two groups of output:

- *Trace* or *sequence events* that occur during the simulation time interval
- *Performance metrics* that summarize the statistics of the simulation run

The trace allows users to verify that the model is actually interacting in compliance with the model's requirements and design. The performance metrics are the outputs that are analyzed for estimates used for capacity planning or for improving the current real operating system. These outputs are used to validate the model and then to derive useful predictions of the system.

The main simulation approach applied to all the simulation models presented in this book is the process interaction approach to discrete-event simulation. This approach is the most powerful one since it is adequate for large and complex systems and lends itself very well to modeling computer systems and studying various aspects of their behavior. The other advantage of this approach is that it is inherently object-oriented.

3.5.3 Stochastic Models

Simulation models have variables that change values in a nondeterministic manner (i.e., with uncertainty). A stochastic model includes random variables to implement the uncertainty attributes. Thus, systems are usually simulated with stochastic models. Typical random events of a stochastic model can be described as follows:

- The arrival events are random—that is, it is not known exactly when a job arrival event will occur.

- The service time intervals are also random—that is, it is not known exactly how much time it will take the CPU to service a particular process.

For example, there are two random variables in the model of a simple batch system:

- The interarrival time interval for each job

- The CPU service time interval for each process

The important issue is that the variability between job arrivals and the variability of job service requirements are very important. The actual values for these attributes depend on some probabilistic distribution. For this model, the interarrival period follows an exponential probability distribution that is used to generate randomly the individual interarrival period for each process.

The service demand of a process follows an exponential distribution. In the simulation model of this system, an exponential distribution is used to generate randomly the individual service demand for each process.

3.6 A Model of the Simple Batch System

The simulation model of the simple batch system is an example of a single-server queuing system (see again Figure 3.1). This model represents a batch system that services one process at a time, which means it is not a multiprogramming system. There is only one process in memory at any time and it uses as much memory as it needs, assuming that it does not take more than the maximum memory available in the system. This model represents a single-class system—that is, there is only one type of process.

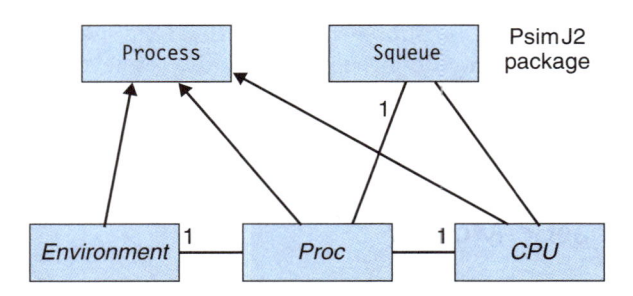

Figure 3.2 The UML class diagram for a batch system.

3.6.1 Description of the Model

Running the simulation model of the simple batch system will show all the types of events and state changes in the queuing system described previously. For every process created, its interarrival time interval, service time interval, and memory demands are generated as random numbers.

A typical model includes a set of active objects and a set of passive objects. Active resources of the system, such as the CPU and I/O devices, are normally modeled as active objects, and passive system resources, such as memory, are modeled as passive objects. In a simulation model, the active objects have a life of their own; once they are started, they execute as a separate thread. The passive objects are acted upon by the active objects; the operations of the passive objects are invoked by the active objects.

The *PsimJ2* and *Psim3* simulation packages are used to implement simulation models with Java and C++, respectively. More details on how these models use the packages are found in the appendices.

The Unified Modeling Language (UML) is a standard graphical notation used to describe models. UML consists of several types of diagrams, of which only the class, collaboration, and state diagrams are mentioned here.

The structure of a simulation model consists of several classes, some of which are predefined in the PsimJ2 and Psim3 simulation packages. The model representation for the simple batch system is defined by the various UML diagrams. The UML class diagram for the simple batch system is shown in Figure 3.2. The figure shows the top classes, `Process` and `Squeue`, which are defined in the PsimJ2 package (and also defined in the Psim3 package). The classes defined in the simulation model (*Proc*, *Environment*, and *CPU*) inherit (or extend) the PsimJ2 library class `Process` to acquire the definition for the behavior of active objects. The library class `Squeue` is normally instantiated when a simple (FIFO) queue object is needed, which is an example of a passive object. The model of a simple batch system has one queue, the input queue for jobs arriving into the system.

The following classes define active objects and are the main components of the Java implementation for the simulation model of the simple batch system:

- Class *Proc*, which defines the processes to be serviced (executed) by the processor (CPU). Several instances of this class are created and actually executed; each one is an object of class Proc.

3.6 A Model of the Simple Batch System

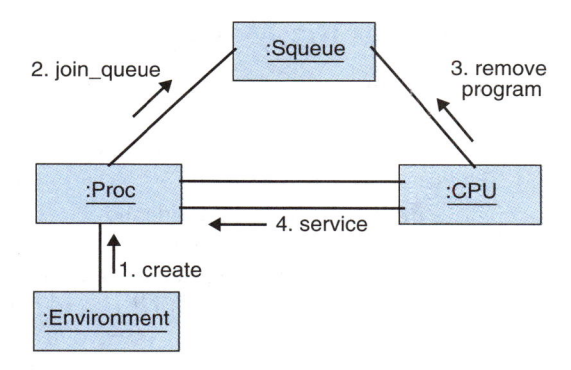

Figure 3.3 The UML collaboration diagram for the batch operating system.

- Class *Environment*, which defines an object that creates instances of class Proc according to the interarrival time interval. An object of this class represents the environment.

- Class *CPU*, which defines the object that represents the processor that provides services (executes) to the objects of class Proc, according to their service demands.

Figure 3.3 shows the UML collaboration diagram with the interactions among the processes mentioned above. Objects of class *Proc* arrive and join the input queue, an instance of class `Squeue`. The single instance of class *CPU* removes an object from the queue and provides execution service to it. When this service is completed, the *CPU* object removes the next object from the queue, and so on.

For a more complex system, a state diagram is necessary. Figure 3.4 shows the UML state diagram of a typical process.

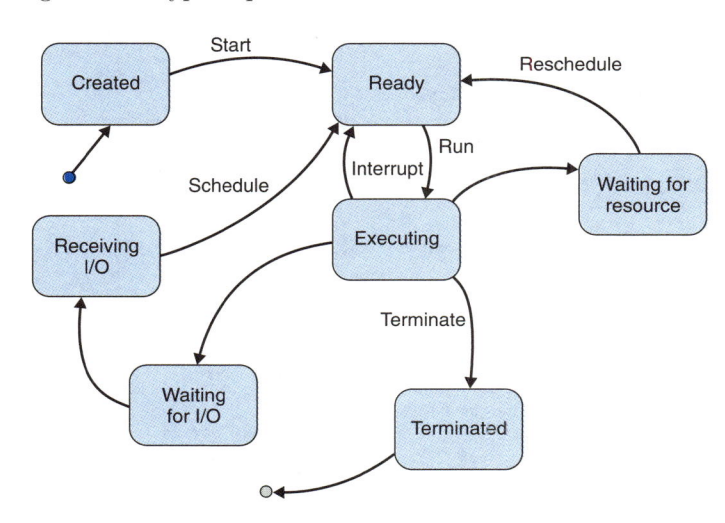

Figure 3.4 UML state diagram of a typical process.

3.6.2 Implementations of the Model

The simulation described in the previous section has been implemented in Java and C++. There are several good tools for developing Java programs. The software tools that have been used for developing the simulation models in Java are jGRASP (Auburn University) and Eclipse.

There are two Java implementations for this model, the console implementation and the GUI implementation. The implementation of the simulation model for the simple batch system includes four classes that define active objects, written in Java and using PsimJ2: (1) *Simplebatch*, (2) *Environment*, (3) *CPU*, and (4) *Proc*. The Java files for this model are `Simplebatch.java`, `Environment.java`, `CPU.java`, and `Proc.java`. These files are stored in the archive file `batch.jar` in the Java folder. Listing 3.1 shows a partial listing of class *CPU* of the console implementation.

Listing 3.1 Partial listing of the Java source code for the simple batch system.

```java
...
public void Main_body()
{
   double simperiod;
   fmt = new DecimalFormat("0.###");
   simperiod = SimpleBatch.get_simp();
   while ( get_clock() <= simperiod )
   {
      System.out.println("Test input queue");
      if(SimpleBatch.in_queue.empty() ) // queue empty?
      {
         goIdle();      // yes, no processes to service
         leaveIdle();
      }
      else {            // no,
         executeJob();  // provide CPU service to process
      }
   }
}
/** The input queue is not empty
 ** get the process at the head of the queue
 ** provide the requested CPU service to the process
 */
private void executeJob()
{
   double t_service;              // service period
   startTime = get_clock();
   curr_proc = (Proc) SimpleBatch.in_queue.out();
```

```
        curr_proc.setStart();
        t_service = curr_proc.getService(); // req service time
        System.out.println("CPU to service "+curr_proc.get_name()
            + " for: "+ fmt.format(t_service));
        delay(t_service);                   // service period
        completeproc();
    }
...
```

The listing shows only part of the code of class *CPU*. The main method of the class is `Main_body`, which is the method of every class that defines the structure and behavior of active objects. In this method, the behavior described is the following: The CPU object repeatedly examines the input queue for waiting processes. If the queue is empty, the CPU object goes to an idle state; otherwise the CPU object removes the process from the head of the queue and executes it. This is implemented by invoking method `executeJob`. This method is also shown in the listing; the CPU object gets the execution time from the process object and invokes the library method `delay` that waits for the period in the argument.

The C++ implementation uses the Psim3 package and is stored in the `batch.cpp` file. This implementation has been tested on Windows, Linux, and Solaris. The software tool for developing the C++ models are also jGRASP and Eclipse.

3.6.3 Simulation Output of the Console Implementation

For the console implementation of the simple batch system, the output of the simulation run includes the workload: the average interarrival time interval and the average service time interval. The system parameters included are the total system memory and the input queue size.

Listing 3.2 shows the first part of a simulation run. The output listing shows the first part of the trace, which is the sequence of different events that occurred during the simulation run. The first relevant event is the arrival of `Process1` at simulation time `4.309`. This process requires a CPU service time of 5.307 and 11 units of memory. `Process2` arrives at time `6.981` with a CPU service requirement of `1.038` and a memory requirement of 10 units. `Process3` arrives at simulation time `9.46` while `Process1` is being serviced, so it has to wait in the queue. `Process1` completes and terminates at time `9.616` and `Process2` starts immediately. This process completes and terminates at time `10.659`.

`Process8` is rejected because its memory requirement is 14 memory units, more than the total system memory, which is 12. The trace continues to list the rest of the events that occur during the simulation run until the total simulation run expires.

Listing 3.2 First part of the output of a simulation run for the simple batch system.

```
PsimJ2 simulation model: Simple Batch System
Simulation date: 8/24/2010 time: 15:17


Average inter-arrival: 3.2 avg service: 4.5
Total system memory: 12 queue size: 10


Process1 requiring service period 5.307 and memory: 11 arrives at: 4.309
CPU is reactivated at 4.309
Process1 starts at 4.309 with service period 5.307
CPU to service Process1 service period: 5.307
Process2 requiring service period 1.038 and memory: 10 arrives at: 6.981
Process3 requiring service period 7.399 and memory: 8 arrives at: 9.46
Process2 starts at 9.616 with service period 1.038
CPU to service Process2 service period: 1.038
Process1 completed, wait period 0 sojourn 5.307
Process1 terminates at time 9.616
Process3 starts at 10.654 with service period 7.399
CPU to service Process3 service period: 7.399
Process2 completed, wait period 2.635 sojourn 3.674
Process2 terminates at time 10.654
Process4 requiring service period 2.096 and memory: 10 arrives at: 10.929
Process5 requiring service period 0.219 and memory: 11 arrives at: 11.938
Process6 requiring service period 8.317 and memory: 9 arrives at: 15.857
Process7 requiring service period 2.918 and memory: 10 arrives at: 16.458
Process4 starts at 18.053 with service period 2.096
CPU to service Process4 service period: 2.096
Process3 completed, wait period 1.194 sojourn 8.593
Process3 terminates at time 18.053
Process8 requiring service period 2.6 and memory: 14 arrives at: 18.872
Process8 rejected.
Process5 starts at 20.15 with service period 0.219
CPU to service Process5 service period: 0.219
Process4 completed, wait period 7.124 sojourn 9.22
Process4 terminates at time 20.15
Process6 starts at 20.368 with service period 8.317
CPU to service Process6 service period: 8.317
Process5 completed, wait period 8.212 sojourn 8.43
Process5 terminates at time 20.368
Process7 starts at 28.685 with service period 2.918
CPU to service Process7 service period: 2.918
Process6 completed, wait period 4.511 sojourn 12.828
Process6 terminates at time 28.685
```

```
Process9 requiring service period 24.677 and memory: 12 arrives at: 30.48
Process10 requiring service period 1.349 and memory: 9 arrives at: 30.619
Process9 starts at 31.603 with service period 24.677
CPU to service Process9 service period: 24.677
Process7 completed, wait period 12.227 sojourn 15.145
Process7 terminates at time 31.603
Process11 requiring service period 7.286 and memory: 14 arrives at: 33.104
Process11 rejected.
Process12 requiring service period 12.778 and memory: 14 arrives at: 33.757
Process12 rejected.
Process13 requiring service period 11.197 and memory: 10 arrives at: 39.589
Process14 requiring service period 5.786 and memory: 10 arrives at: 40.395
Process15 requiring service period 5.627 and memory: 12 arrives at: 44.68
Process16 requiring service period 1.464 and memory: 12 arrives at: 44.869
Process17 requiring service period 5.002 and memory: 11 arrives at: 48.272
Process18 requiring service period 4.69 and memory: 8 arrives at: 51.914
Process19 requiring service period 1.264 and memory: 14 arrives at: 55.746
Process19 rejected.
Process20 requiring service period 10.351 and memory: 14 arrives at: 55.791
Process20 rejected.
Process10 starts at 56.28 with service period 1.349
CPU to service Process10 service period: 1.349
Process9 completed, wait period 1.123 sojourn 25.8
Process9 terminates at time 56.28
Process21 requiring service period 2.482 and memory: 10 arrives at: 56.769
Process13 starts at 57.629 with service period 11.197
CPU to service Process13 service period: 11.197
Process10 completed, wait period 25.661 sojourn 27.01
Process10 terminates at time 57.629
Process22 requiring service period 4.675 and memory: 13 arrives at: 63.006
Process22 rejected.
Process23 requiring service period 1.516 and memory: 12 arrives at: 66.203
Process14 starts at 68.826 with service period 5.786
CPU to service Process14 service period: 5.786
Process13 completed, wait period 18.04 sojourn 29.237
Process13 terminates at time 68.826
Process24 requiring service period 9.443 and memory: 11 arrives at: 72.481
Process15 starts at 74.612 with service period 5.627
CPU to service Process15 service period: 5.627
Process14 completed, wait period 28.431 sojourn 34.217
Process14 terminates at time 74.612
Process25 requiring service period 12.062 and memory: 8 arrives at: 75.283
Process16 starts at 80.239 with service period 1.464
CPU to service Process16 service period: 1.464
```

```
Process15 completed, wait period 29.932 sojourn 35.559
Process15 terminates at time 80.239
Closing Environment
Process26 requiring service period 1.219 and memory: 10 arrives at: 81.373
Process17 starts at 81.703 with service period 5.002
CPU to service Process17 service period: 5.002
Process16 completed, wait period 35.37 sojourn 36.834
Process16 terminates at time 81.703
Process18 starts at 86.705 with service period 4.69
CPU to service Process18 service period: 4.69
Process17 completed, wait period 33.431 sojourn 38.433
Process17 terminates at time 86.705
Process21 starts at 91.395 with service period 2.482
CPU to service Process21 service period: 2.482
Process18 completed, wait period 34.79 sojourn 39.481
Process18 terminates at time 91.395
Process23 starts at 93.877 with service period 1.516
CPU to service Process23 service period: 1.516
Process21 completed, wait period 34.626 sojourn 37.108
Process21 terminates at time 93.877
Process24 starts at 95.393 with service period 9.443
CPU to service Process24 service period: 9.443
Process23 completed, wait period 27.674 sojourn 29.19
Process23 terminates at time 95.393
Process25 starts at 104.836 with service period 12.062
CPU to service Process25 service period: 12.062
Process24 completed, wait period 22.912 sojourn 32.355
Process24 terminates at time 104.836
Process26 starts at 116.898 with service period 1.219
CPU to service Process26 service period: 1.219
Process25 completed, wait period 29.553 sojourn 41.615
Process25 terminates at time 116.898
CPU goes idle at 118.117
Process26 completed, wait period 35.525 sojourn 36.744
Process26 terminates at time 118.117
-----------------------------------------------------------
End Simulation: Simple Batch System date: 8/24/2010 time: 15:17

Results of simulation:
-----------------------------------------------------------
Service factor: 0.225
Processor utilization: 0.379
Total arrived:   26
Total rejected:   6
Throughput:  20
```

3.6 A Model of the Simple Batch System

```
Proportion Rejected: 0.231
Average wait period: 19.649
Average memory used: 3.882
-------------------------------------------------------------
```

Listing 3.3 includes the output lines (in the trace) to the end of the simulation run. The last events are shown in the trace. The simulation run ends after the termination of `Process26` at time `118.117`. The values of the performance metrics are shown after the trace.

Listing 3.3 Second part of the output of a simulation run for the simple batch system.

```
PsimJ2 simulation model: Simple Batch System
Simulation date: 8/24/2010 time: 15:17



Average inter-arrival: 3.2 avg service: 4.5
Total system memory: 12 queue size: 10

CPU created at: 0.0
CPU goes idle at 0
Process1 requiring service period 5.307 and memory: 11 arrives at: 4.309
CPU is reactivated at 4.309
Process1 starts at 4.309 with service period 5.307
CPU to service Process1 service period: 5.307
Process2 requiring service period 1.038 and memory: 10 arrives at: 6.981
Process3 requiring service period 7.399 and memory: 8 arrives at: 9.46
Process2 starts at 9.616 with service period 1.038
CPU to service Process2 service period: 1.038
Process1 completed, wait period 0 sojourn 5.307
Process1 terminates at time 9.616
Process3 starts at 10.654 with service period 7.399
CPU to service Process3 service period: 7.399
Process2 completed, wait period 2.635 sojourn 3.674
Process2 terminates at time 10.654
Process4 requiring service period 2.096 and memory: 10 arrives at: 10.929
Process5 requiring service period 0.219 and memory: 11 arrives at: 11.938
Process6 requiring service period 8.317 and memory: 9 arrives at: 15.857
Process7 requiring service period 2.918 and memory: 10 arrives at: 16.458
Process4 starts at 18.053 with service period 2.096
CPU to service Process4 service period: 2.096
Process3 completed, wait period 1.194 sojourn 8.593
```

Chapter 3 System Performance and Models

```
Process3 terminates at time 18.053
Process8 requiring service period 2.6 and memory: 14 arrives at: 18.872
Process8 rejected.
Process5 starts at 20.15 with service period 0.219
CPU to service Process5 service period: 0.219
Process4 completed, wait period 7.124 sojourn 9.22
Process4 terminates at time 20.15
Process6 starts at 20.368 with service period 8.317
CPU to service Process6 service period: 8.317
Process5 completed, wait period 8.212 sojourn 8.43
Process5 terminates at time 20.368
Process7 starts at 28.685 with service period 2.918
CPU to service Process7 service period: 2.918
Process6 completed, wait period 4.511 sojourn 12.828
Process6 terminates at time 28.685
Process9 requiring service period 24.677 and memory: 12 arrives at: 30.48
Process10 requiring service period 1.349 and memory: 9 arrives at: 30.619
Process9 starts at 31.603 with service period 24.677
CPU to service Process9 service period: 24.677
Process7 completed, wait period 12.227 sojourn 15.145
Process7 terminates at time 31.603
Process11 requiring service period 7.286 and memory: 14 arrives at: 33.104
Process11 rejected.
Process12 requiring service period 12.778 and memory: 14 arrives at: 33.757
Process12 rejected.
Process13 requiring service period 11.197 and memory: 10 arrives at: 39.589
Process14 requiring service period 5.786 and memory: 10 arrives at: 40.395
Process15 requiring service period 5.627 and memory: 12 arrives at: 44.68
Process16 requiring service period 1.464 and memory: 12 arrives at: 44.869
Process17 requiring service period 5.002 and memory: 11 arrives at: 48.272
Process18 requiring service period 4.69 and memory: 8 arrives at: 51.914
Process19 requiring service period 1.264 and memory: 14 arrives at: 55.746
Process19 rejected.
Process20 requiring service period 10.351 and memory: 14 arrives at: 55.791
Process20 rejected.
Process10 starts at 56.28 with service period 1.349
CPU to service Process10 service period: 1.349
Process9 completed, wait period 1.123 sojourn 25.8
Process9 terminates at time 56.28
Process21 requiring service period 2.482 and memory: 10 arrives at: 56.769
Process13 starts at 57.629 with service period 11.197
CPU to service Process13 service period: 11.197
Process10 completed, wait period 25.661 sojourn 27.01
Process10 terminates at time 57.629
Process22 requiring service period 4.675 and memory: 13 arrives at: 63.006
```

3.6 A Model of the Simple Batch System

```
Process22 rejected.
Process23 requiring service period 1.516 and memory: 12 arrives at: 66.203
Process14 starts at 68.826 with service period 5.786
CPU to service Process14 service period: 5.786
Process13 completed, wait period 18.04 sojourn 29.237
Process13 terminates at time 68.826
Process24 requiring service period 9.443 and memory: 11 arrives at: 72.481
Process15 starts at 74.612 with service period 5.627
CPU to service Process15 service period: 5.627
Process14 completed, wait period 28.431 sojourn 34.217
Process14 terminates at time 74.612
Process25 requiring service period 12.062 and memory: 8 arrives at: 75.283
Process16 starts at 80.239 with service period 1.464
CPU to service Process16 service period: 1.464
Process15 completed, wait period 29.932 sojourn 35.559
Process15 terminates at time 80.239
Closing Environment
Process26 requiring service period 1.219 and memory: 10 arrives at: 81.373
Process17 starts at 81.703 with service period 5.002
CPU to service Process17 service period: 5.002
Process16 completed, wait period 35.37 sojourn 36.834
Process16 terminates at time 81.703
Process18 starts at 86.705 with service period 4.69
CPU to service Process18 service period: 4.69
Process17 completed, wait period 33.431 sojourn 38.433

Process17 terminates at time 86.705
Process21 starts at 91.395 with service period 2.482
CPU to service Process21 service period: 2.482
Process18 completed, wait period 34.79 sojourn 39.481
Process18 terminates at time 91.395
Process23 starts at 93.877 with service period 1.516
CPU to service Process23 service period: 1.516
Process21 completed, wait period 34.626 sojourn 37.108
Process21 terminates at time 93.877
Process24 starts at 95.393 with service period 9.443
CPU to service Process24 service period: 9.443
Process23 completed, wait period 27.674 sojourn 29.19
Process23 terminates at time 95.393
Process25 starts at 104.836 with service period 12.062
CPU to service Process25 service period: 12.062
Process24 completed, wait period 22.912 sojourn 32.355
Process24 terminates at time 104.836
Process26 starts at 116.898 with service period 1.219
CPU to service Process26 service period: 1.219
```

```
Process25 completed, wait period 29.553 sojourn 41.615
Process25 terminates at time 116.898
CPU goes idle at 118.117
Process26 completed, wait period 35.525 sojourn 36.744
Process26 terminates at time 118.117
-----------------------------------------------------------
End Simulation: Simple Batch System date: 8/24/2010 time: 15:17

Results of simulation:
-----------------------------------------------------------
Service factor: 0.225
Processor utilization: 0.379
Total arrived:   26
Total rejected:   6
Throughput:  20
Proportion Rejected:  0.231
Average wait period: 19.649
Average memory used: 3.882
-----------------------------------------------------------
```

The performance metrics appear at the end of the output listing, which shows the value of the following performance metrics:

- Processor utilization
- Throughput
- Proportion of rejected processes
- Number of rejected processes
- Average wait time for the processes
- Average memory used

The simulation run includes a derived performance quantity known as the *service factor*—the percentage of time spent by a process when actually receiving service from the processor. An additional performance metric that is not included in the output of the simulation run is the *sojourn time*, also called the *turnaround time*—the total time that the process spends inside the computer system. It is computed as the interval from the time the process arrives until it exits the system.

3.6.4 Output of the GUI Implementation

The second implementation of the simple batch model uses a graphical user interface (GUI). The Swing and AWT Java packages are used with the Java program that

3.6 A Model of the Simple Batch System

implements the simulation model. The main advantage gained from using graphics is the enhanced feature of the Java program that facilitates the input and output of data during the program execution. This is similar to a Windows environment. The console implementation is more adapted to a command level interface with the operating system—for example, using a command window on Windows, or the text command mode on Unix. Figure 3.5 shows the GUI window during the execution of the Java program.

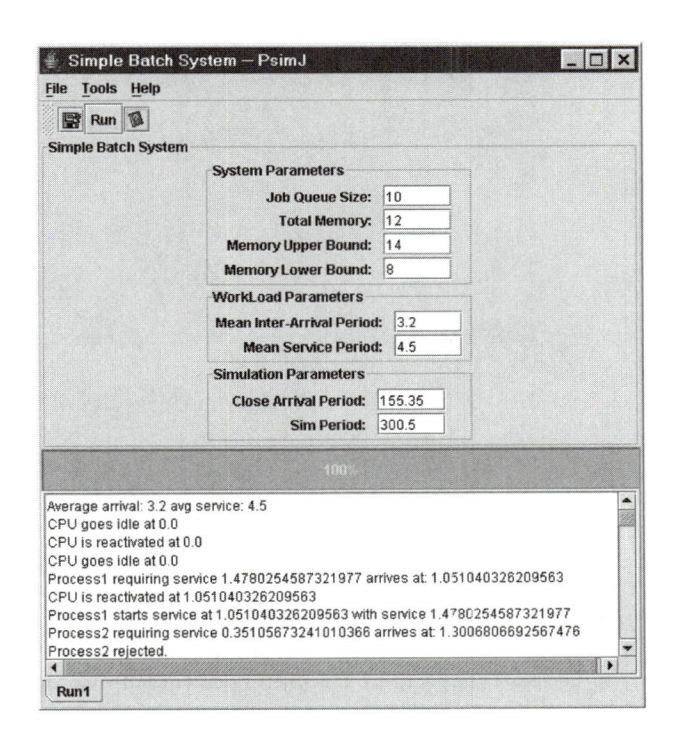

Figure 3.5 The GUI for I/O in the simple simulation model.

The simulation model described has two implementations, one in Java and the other in C++. The one listed in this section is one of the four classes of the Java implementation. The four classes are each stored on a separate file: `SimpleBatch.java`, `Proc.java`, `CPU.java`, and `Environment.java`. The archive file `batchg.jar` contains the four source Java files, the compiled classes, and output samples. Figure 3.6 shows the GUI window for the summary results of the simulation run.

The third implementation is the C++ implementation, which consists of only one file called `batch.cpp` with the four classes *CPU*, *job*, *environment*, and *batch*. These files, the simulation packages (PsimJ2 and Psim3), and further instructions are available on the website for this book.

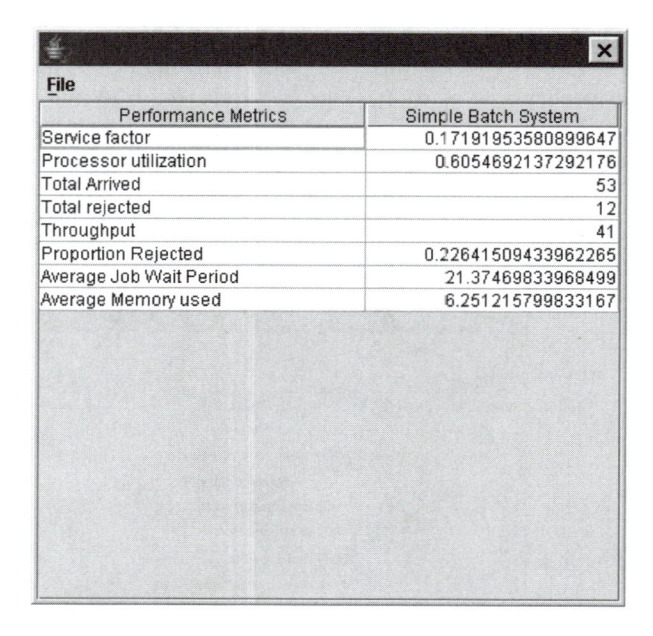

Performance Metrics	Simple Batch System
Service factor	0.17191953580899647
Processor utilization	0.6054692137292176
Total Arrived	53
Total rejected	12
Throughput	41
Proportion Rejected	0.22641509433962265
Average Job Wait Period	21.37469833968499
Average Memory used	6.251215799833167

Figure 3.6 The GUI for the summary results of a simulation run.

3.7 System Capacity and Bottleneck

The capacity of a computer system is determined by its maximum performance. Functionality is the ability of the system to perform correctly. In today's complex environment, the use and demand of computers and computer networks are increasing at an extremely rapid rate, so the capacity planning and performance modeling are very important for the design and operation of these systems.

The computer system is simply modeled as a network of service stations. Each station includes a queue and a server. The computer system reaches capacity when one or more of its servers or resources reaches a utilization of 100 percent. The *bottleneck* of the system will be localized in the server or resource with a utilization of 100 percent, while the other servers and resources each have utilization significantly below this level. In a single-server system, this situation is much more simplified.

The bottleneck in the model of the simple batch computer system described here can be localized at the processor, the queue, or the memory. The queue may become full (may reach capacity) very often as the processor utilization increases. The memory capacity may also be used at capacity (100 percent). Thus, in any of the three cases, the processor, the queue, or the memory will need to be replaced or increased in capacity.

3.8 Summary

A computer system has one or more servers, arriving jobs (or processes), and queues for every server to hold waiting processes. The manner in which jobs arrive, how they leave the queue to receive service, how service is provided, and how they leave the system is of interest in studying these systems. In computer systems, the CPU is a server and the arriving entities are the processes; the queue is used to hold processes that wait for processing in the CPU.

Simulation rather than analytical techniques is preferred because determining the performance metrics for larger models with analytical techniques can become a very complex and tedious task. This chapter also discussed the different performance metrics that are estimated, and the performance parameters that need to be considered in studying operating systems.

An introduction to performance calculation of operating systems has been included as an important component of the study of operating systems. The three common techniques for performance evaluation are measurements, analytical models, and simulation models. The performance evaluation of operating systems is carried out with simulation models. Starting with the goals of the operating system study and given the workload, performance modeling estimates the appropriate performance metrics as output. The most important performance metrics are throughput, average response time, and CPU utilization. The process model is a simple abstraction used to understand in a more clear and easy manner, the internal dynamic handling of the processes in the computer system.

This chapter also discussed a simple simulation model used for studying the dynamic behavior of a simple batch system and calculation of some basic performance metrics.

Key Terms

arrival rate	memory demand	sojourn time
bottleneck	model type	stochastic model
capacity	performance metric	system parameter
console implementation	queue size	throughput
continuous model	queuing model	trace
deterministic model	random variable	turnaround time
discrete-event model	response time	UML
dynamic behavior	service factor	utilization
events	service rate	wait time
GUI implementation	simulation model	workload parameter
input queue	single-server	

Exercises and Questions

1. How does a simulation of the simple process model help you understand the dynamic behavior of the simple batch operating system? Explain.

2. Comparing two models with different processor speeds—one with a slow service rate and the other with a very fast rate—can be simulated by changing the workload and providing two different values for the average service time demands of the processes. Change the simulation model of the simple process model to replace the processor with a faster one. How much faster is the new processor? Change the program and run several simulations. Explain the change in the performance metrics.

3. Add more memory to the simulation model (i.e., increase the memory capacity of the model). Run the simulation several times. Give your conclusions.

4. Change the queue size in the simulation model. Run the simulation several times. Give your conclusions.

5. Identify the performance metrics that conflict with each other in the simulation model studied. State your reasons for this. Which ones are more important? How will you solve the conflict?

6. Change the arrival and service rates of the processes in the simulation model. Run the simulation several times. Answer the same questions as in the previous exercises.

7. Add the computation of the standard deviation for the waiting periods of the processes to the simulation model. Run the simulation a few times. What additional information can you get from this value?

Chapter 4
Systems with Multiprogramming

4.1 Introduction

This chapter discusses the general behavior and basic performance metrics of systems with multiprogramming. Some of the concepts discussed were initially introduced in Chapter 2 and are repeated here with additional explanation. To study multiprogramming, simulation models with multiple servers (CPU and I/O) are presented. These models represent batch operating systems with two servers—the CPU and an I/O device—in addition to memory allocation. The models help to better explain the concept of multiprogramming in an operating system. The computer systems that are modeled provide services to processes requesting CPU and I/O processing. Graphical animation is included in one of the simulation models to allow visualization of the sequence of events that occur, such as arrival of a process and service completion of a process, during a simulation run. This chapter also compares the behavior of models representing systems with and without multiprogramming.

4.2 Systems with Multiple Stations

Recall from Chapter 2 that a computer system can support several processes in memory. The operating system with multiprogramming manages the system to support multiple processes in memory. While one process receives service from the CPU, another process receives service from an I/O device, and the other processes are waiting in the queues; all of this occurs at the same time.

On a typical system, a process is created in response to a new job arriving, a new user who carries out a login, and/or a currently executing process that creates a new process. A process is created if there is sufficient memory available, and the process waits if other resources it needs are not available.

The number of processes that the system supports is called the *degree of multiprogramming*. Such a system can be represented by a simple model of a queuing network. The general structure of queuing networks consists of several *stations*, each one with a server and a queue and interconnected in such a manner that processes follow the flow from one station to the next.

Figure 4.1 shows a model of a computer system with multiple stations. The first station is the *memory manager* (MM), which allocates memory to the waiting jobs in the input queue. The second station includes the ready queue and the CPU, which provides CPU service to the processes waiting in the ready queue. The other stations in the model each include an I/O queue and an I/O device that provide service to the processes waiting in the corresponding I/O queue.

The model described here simplifies the understanding of the overall process behavior. A new process has certain memory, CPU, and I/O requirements. If the memory request of the process is equal to or less than the total system memory and if the input queue is not full, the process joins the input queue. Otherwise, the process is rejected and it abandons the system (forever). When there is sufficient memory available, the OS allocates memory to the process waiting at the head of the input queue, or else the process continues waiting.

Once the process is in the memory of the system, it joins the *ready queue* to wait for CPU processing. When the CPU is available, the process at the head of the ready queue is removed from the queue and CPU service is provided to the process. After the

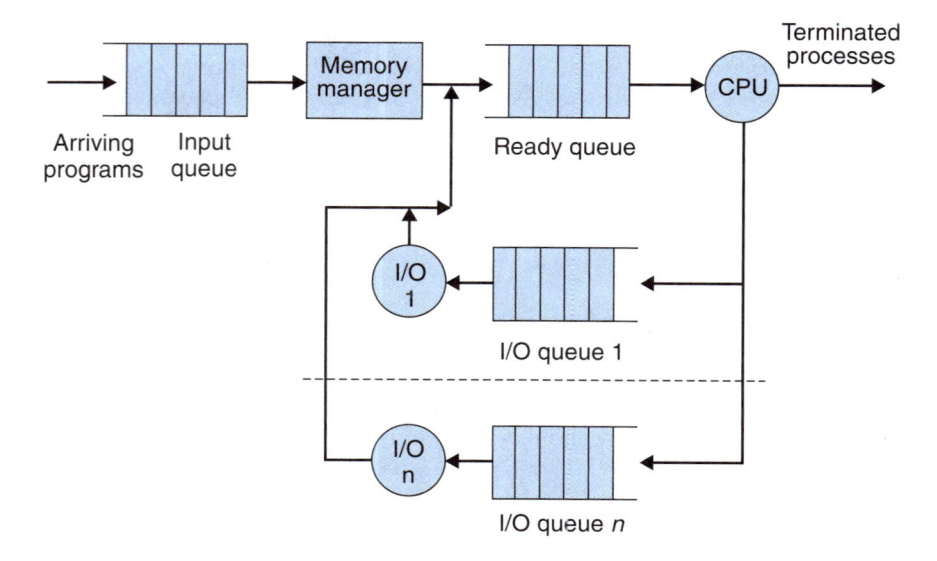

Figure 4.1 A model of a computer system with multiple stations.

process receives the requested CPU processing, it joins the I/O queue to wait for I/O processing.

When the corresponding I/O device is available, it removes the process from the head of the I/O queue and provides I/O service to the process. The process then returns to the ready queue for more CPU processing, if it needs more CPU service.

In this manner, a process can cycle through the CPU and I/O servers several times depending on its total CPU and I/O requirements (demands). Eventually, all the CPU and I/O requirements are met and the process terminates and exits the system.

4.2.1 CPU and I/O Bursts

The total service requirement, also known as service demand, of a process consists of several short CPU and I/O service requests. Each CPU request is called a *CPU burst* and each I/O request is called an *I/O burst*. A process usually exhibits a series of alternating CPU and I/O bursts.

A typical process, P, requires a total of C_T time units of CPU service and D_T time units of I/O service. These will be divided into j CPU bursts and k I/O bursts. Each CPU burst will have a different duration. The total CPU service required by process P is
$$C_T = c_1 + c_2 + \ldots c_j.$$

Each I/O burst will also have a different duration, and the total I/O service required by process P is
$$D_T = d_1 + d_2 + \ldots d_k.$$

Process P usually waits a finite time interval in the corresponding queue before every CPU and I/O burst. The process waits for time interval w_{c1} in the ready queue before it can be provided CPU service for the time interval of the CPU burst c_1, and waits for w_{cj} in the ready queue before it receives CPU service for burst c_j, and so on. In a similar manner, w_{dk} denotes the time interval in the I/O queue that the process waits to receive service for I/O burst d_k.

The sequence of activities of process P—waiting in the ready queue, receiving CPU service, waiting in the I/O queue, and receiving I/O service—is denoted by
$$\langle w_{c1}, c_1, w_{d1}, d_1, w_{c2}, c_2, w_{d2}, d_2, \ldots w_{cj}, c_j, w_{dk}, d_k \rangle.$$

4.2.2 Overlapping of CPU and I/O Processing

The computer system can *overlap* I/O device operation with processor operation; it accomplishes this with hardware support. The ability to carry out this overlapping involves using the interrupt mechanism of the computer system. While the system is providing CPU service to process P_a, it is providing I/O service to process P_b simultaneously, under control of the operating system. This results in a more efficient utilization of the system facilities.

The most significant advantage of overlapped CPU and I/O services is that they make *multiprogramming* possible. Multiprogramming is the ability of the operating system to coordinate the presence of several processes in memory with CPU and I/O services that are provided in bursts. Multiprogramming has significant implications on system performance—from throughput and CPU and I/O device utilizations to average process wait times and turnaround times.

4.2.3 Context Switches

As explained in Chapter 2, *context switches* are an inherent characteristic of multiprogramming, representing the changeover from the current process being executed to the next process to execute. The complete context of the current process is saved in its descriptor or process control block (PCB) and the context of the next process is loaded from its PCB.

The context switch time is a very short and finite interval of time. Because there is no process receiving service from the CPU during this interval, it is considered overhead work that the CPU must carry out. This is very different from a CPU idle time, which is a time interval during which the CPU does nothing.

4.3 Studying Systems with Multiprogramming

This section introduces several models representing batch systems. The first model represents a batch system with multiprogramming and the second represents a system with no multiprogramming. These two models are implemented in Java as console applications. The third model includes a GUI for user input and output. The fourth model includes a GUI for input and output and shows a graphical animation of the sequence of events. The fifth model is implemented in C++ and represents a similar batch system.

4.3.1 Model of a System with Multiprogramming

The model of a batch system studied here includes one CPU server and one I/O server. Three queues are used: the first queue is used for processes that have arrived and are waiting for memory allocation; one of the other two queues is used for the CPU server, and the other is used for the I/O server. Each server provides service independently of the other servers.

This model represents a system with a larger memory (512 K memory units) than the model of the simple batch system discussed in Chapter 2 and supports several processes in memory.

The simulation model includes the following major components:

- *The processes*, each one representing a computational unit to be serviced in the computer system, under control of the operating system. The processes are implemented as active objects of class *Job*.

- *The environment*, which generates the arriving processes. This is an active object of class *Arrivals*. This object creates instances of class *Job* according to the interarrival period.

- *The CPU*, which represents the processor that provides CPU service (execution) to the processes according to their service demands. The CPU is an active object of class *Processor*.

- *The disk device*, which represents an I/O device providing I/O service to the processes according to their demands. The disk device is an active object of class *Disk*.

- *The main memory*, which represents a major resource of the system and is modeled as a passive object of class *Res*.

- *The queues*, which are modeled as passive objects of class *Squeue*.

This list includes the active objects in the model and the passive objects that are represented by the memory resource and the queues.

Random variables are used in the model to represent several parameters, and each of these variables is derived from a specific probability distribution. The interarrival periods are generated from an exponential distribution. The CPU and I/O service periods, also known as service demands, are each generated from an exponential distribution. The memory demands for the processes are generated from a uniform distribution.

The simulation model is implemented in Java using the PsimJ2 simulation class library. The model implementation is stored in files `BatchmIO.java`, `Arrivals.java`, `Job.java`, `Disk.java`, and `Processor.java`. These files are stored in the archive file `batchmio.jar`. The model was developed using the jGRASP integrated development environment.

Listing 4.1 shows the first part of the output of a simulation run of the model that represents a batch system with multiprogramming and I/O. This part of the output includes the values of the workload parameters, the system parameters, and the first portion of the trace. This output shows the value of three system parameters: (1) the degree of multiprogramming with a value of 20, (2) the total system memory with a value of 512, and (3) the size of the queues with a value of 125.

Listing 4.1 First part of a simulation run of the system with multiprogramming.

```
Psim/Java project: System with Multiprogramming - CPU and I/O
Simulation date: 2/18/2006 17:34
Avg. (mean) inter-arrival per.: 2.3
 mean CPU service per.: 18.5; mean I/O service per.: 18.75
Min memory req.: 10 Max memory req: 65
Total system memory: 512
Degree of multiprogramming: 20; Queue size: 125
```

Chapter 4 Systems with Multiprogramming

```
Job1 requiring service 5.456 arrives at time 0.721
Processor starting CPU burst of Job1 at 0.721
Processor completed CPU burst of Job1 at 2.752
I/O dev starting I/O burst of Job1 at 2.752
I/O dev completed burst Job1 at 4.811
Processor starting CPU burst of Job1 at 4.811
Processor completed CPU burst of Job1 at 6.092
I/O dev starting I/O burst of Job1 at 6.092
Job2 requiring service 13.976 arrives at time 6.804
Processor starting CPU burst of Job2 at 6.804
I/O dev completed burst Job1 at 7.391
Processor completed CPU burst of Job2 at 12.008
Processor starting CPU burst of Job1 at 12.008
I/O dev starting I/O burst of Job2 at 12.008
Job3 requiring service 0.906 arrives at time 13.017
Job4 requiring service 8.145 arrives at time 13.624
Processor completed CPU burst of Job1 at 14.151
Processor starting CPU burst of Job3 at 14.151
Processor completed CPU burst of Job3 at 14.488
Processor starting CPU burst of Job4 at 14.488
Job5 requiring service 20.763 arrives at time 17.031
```

The CPU and I/O requests of each job that arrives have several alternating CPU and I/O bursts. `Job1` arrives at time `0.721` and starts executing immediately because there are no other jobs in the system. `Job1` completes at time `2.752` and starts immediately its I/O burst. This I/O burst completes at time `4.811`. At this time, `Job1` starts immediately its next CPU burst because no other job has arrived yet (and the CPU is idle). At time `6.092` its CPU burst completes and starts its next I/O burst.

While `Job1` is receiving service for its I/O burst, `Job2` arrives at time `6.804` and starts immediately because the CPU is idle at that time. `Job1` completes its current I/O burst at time `7.391` and begins to wait in the ready queue because `Job2` is still receiving CPU service for its first CPU burst. At time `12.008`, `Job2` completes its CPU burst and `Job1` starts its next CPU burst. At this time, `Job2` starts its I/O burst. Shortly, `Job3`, `Job4`, and `Job5` arrive at times `13.017`, `13.624`, and `17.031`. The system will continue this cycle, maintaining the CPU and the I/O device as busy as possible servicing the various jobs.

Listing 4.2 Second part of a simulation run of the system with multiprogramming.

```
Processor completed CPU burst of Job41 at 793.846
Processor starting CPU burst of Job60 at 793.846
I/O dev completed burst Job49 at 796.039
I/O dev starting I/O burst of Job54 at 796.039
```

4.3 Studying Systems with Multiprogramming

```
I/O dev completed burst Job54 at 797.197
Terminating process Job54
I/O dev starting I/O burst of Job53 at 797.197
I/O dev completed burst Job53 at 797.612
Terminating process Job53
I/O dev starting I/O burst of Job51 at 797.612
Processor completed CPU burst of Job60 at 800.445
Processor starting CPU burst of Job42 at 800.445
Adjusting Simulation at: 800.6 for: 9.790508682229529
I/O dev completed burst Job51 at 804.064
Terminating process I/O dev
Processor completed CPU burst of Job42 at 810.391
Terminating process Processor
Simulation closing at: 811.1911086822296
-----------------------------------------------------
Memory usage: 0.9150302684027927
 avg num items used: 476.90258114299934
% of time spent resource usage: 0.9823714862255094
Avg waiting time: 6.656902785992291
Avg. num waiting processes: 7.359561328105059
% of time spent waiting: 0.925497386494413
End Simulation of System with Multiprogramming -
  CPU and I/O servers, clock: 811.1911086822296
Results of simulation:
Service factor: 0.048
Total number of jobs that arrived:   231
Total number of rejected jobs:  56
Throughput:   44
Maximum number of jobs in memory: 20
Proportion rejected/arrived jobs:  0.242
Proportion of rejected/completed jobs: 1.273
Average job wait period: 177.092
Processor utilization: 0.969
I/O dev utilization: 0.935
```

Listing 4.2 shows the last part of the simulation run of the model. This output shows the last part of the trace and the summary statistics with the resultant value of several performance metrics. Note in the listing that Job54 terminates after it completes its last I/O burst at time 797.197. In a similar manner, Job53 terminates at time 797.612. Some jobs did not have time to complete during the simulation period.

The relevant performance metric to observe is the CPU utilization with value 0.969, which is relatively high (compared to the model with no multiprogramming in the following subsection). The utilization of the I/O device with value 0.935 is also relatively high.

68   Chapter 4   Systems with Multiprogramming

The C++ implementation of this model is implemented using the Psim3 simulation package and the Pthreads POSIX package. The model is stored in file `batchmio.cpp`. The simulation runs of this model give similar outputs to the Java implementation.

4.3.2 Model of a System Without Multiprogramming

Using the same configuration of the system modeled in the previous section, consider the model of a system without multiprogramming. The system configuration is the same, which includes the total system memory, a CPU server, and an I/O server.

To compare the behavior of both models, the workload is also the same: the mean interarrival rate, the mean memory demands, and the mean CPU and I/O service demands. The only system parameter that is different is the degree of multiprogramming (because the model considered here supports only a single process in memory at any time) set to 1.

Listing 4.3 shows the partial output of the first part of a simulation run using the model of the batch system without multiprogramming. This listing shows the value of the workload and system parameters. The output also shows the first part of the trace, the sequence of events represented in the simulation run.

Listing 4.3 First part of a simulation run of the system without multiprogramming.

```
Psim/Java project: System with no Multiprogramming -
  CPU and I/O servers
Simulation date: 2/20/2006 15:29
Avg. (mean) inter-arrival per.: 2.3
mean CPU service per.: 18.5 mean I/O service per.: 18.75
Min memory req.: 10 Max memory req: 65
Total system memory: 512
Degree of multiprogramming: 1
Queue size: 125

Job1 requiring service 5.088 arrives at time 0.721
Processor starting CPU burst of Job1 at 0.721
Processor completed CPU burst of Job1 at 2.65
I/O dev starting I/O burst of Job1 at 2.65
I/O dev completed burst Job1 at 4.605
Processor starting CPU burst of Job1 at 4.605
Processor completed CPU burst of Job1 at 5.952
I/O dev starting I/O burst of Job1 at 5.952
Job2 requiring service 34.386 arrives at time 6.804
I/O dev completed burst Job1 at 7.317
Processor starting CPU burst of Job1 at 7.317
Processor completed CPU burst of Job1 at 9.09
I/O dev starting I/O burst of Job1 at 9.09
```

4.3 Studying Systems with Multiprogramming

```
I/O dev completed burst Job1 at 10.886
Processor starting CPU burst of Job1 at 10.886
Processor completed CPU burst of Job1 at 10.926
I/O dev starting I/O burst of Job1 at 10.926
I/O dev completed burst Job1 at 10.966
Terminating process Job1
Processor starting CPU burst of Job2 at 10.966
Job3 requiring service 6.27 arrives at time 13.017
Job4 requiring service 106.834 arrives at time 13.624
Job5 requiring service 12.81 arrives at time 17.031
Job6 requiring service 7.175 arrives at time 17.986
Job7 requiring service 3.254 arrives at time 18.48
Processor completed CPU burst of Job2 at 24.003
I/O dev starting I/O burst of Job2 at 24.003
```

The output illustrates the behavior of a system with no multiprogramming. Job1 arrives at time 0.721 and gets service for several CPU and I/O bursts. Job2 arrives at time 6.804 and has to wait in the input queue because Job1 has not yet completed all its CPU and I/O bursts. Only one job at a time is allowed to receive CPU and I/O service. Only when Job1 terminates at time 10.966 is Job2 allocated memory and able to start to execute. While Job2 receives service, Job3, Job4, Job5, Job6, and Job7 arrive and wait in the input queue.

Listing 4.4 shows the last part of the simulation run of the model. This part includes the last part of the trace and the summary statistics with the resultant value of several performance metrics. The output shows the usage of the memory as a passive resource.

Listing 4.4 Second part of a simulation run of the system without multiprogramming.

```
I/O dev completed burst Job18 at 756.122
Processor starting CPU burst of Job18 at 756.122
Processor completed CPU burst of Job18 at 776.718
I/O dev starting I/O burst of Job18 at 776.718
I/O dev completed burst Job18 at 797.593
Processor starting CPU burst of Job18 at 797.593
Processor completed CPU burst of Job18 at 799.447
I/O dev starting I/O burst of Job18 at 799.447
Adjusting Simulation at: 800.6 for: 0.726
I/O dev completed burst Job18 at 801.326
Terminating process I/O dev
Terminating process Processor
Simulation closing at: 802.126
-------------------------------------------------
Memory usage: 0.06801679476336829
 avg num items used: 40.62852469209889
```

```
% of time spent resource usage: 0.857


End Simulation of System with no Multiprogramming -
  CPU and I/O servers, clock: 802.126
Results of simulation:
-----------------------------------------------------
Service factor: 0.057
Total number of jobs that arrived:  231
Total number of rejected jobs:  94
Throughput:  17
Maximum number of jobs in memory: 1
Proportion rejected/arrived jobs:  0.407
Proportion of rejected/completed jobs: 5.529
Average job wait period: 373.162
Processor utilization: 0.497
I/O dev utilization: 0.503
```

The simulation model is implemented in Java using the PsimJ2 simulation class library. The classes of the model are stored in files `BatchIO.java`, `Arrivals.java`, `Job.java`, `Processor.java`, and `Disk.java`. The only difference between this model and the previous one (of a system with multiprogramming) is that the degree of multiprogramming is set to 1. The files of this model are stored in the archive file `batchnmio.jar`.

4.3.3 Comparison of the Two Models

Table 4.1 Comparison of Simulation Results for the Two Batch Operating Systems

Performance Metric	*Multiprogramming*	*No multiprogramming*
CPU utilization	0.985	0.203
I/O utilization	0.969	0.206
Processes arrived	231	231
Throughput	28	10
Rejected processes	60	96
Average wait	115.26	137.93

The relevant advantages of multiprogramming become clear when comparing the behavior of the two models discussed above. Table 4.1 presents the performance metrics from the outputs of a simulation run for each model. The average process wait time is shorter in the model with multiprogramming. The model with multiprogramming shows higher CPU and I/O server utilizations because these servers spend less time idle.

During the same simulation period and with the same total number of processes that arrived, the number of processes that are completed (throughput) is larger in the model with multiprogramming. In the model without multiprogramming, not all processes that arrived actually received service, and only a very small percentage of the processes were completed.

4.3.4 Models with GUI and Graphical Animation

Java is a good language for implementing graphical user interfaces (GUIs) and graphical animation of the simulation outputs. The standard Java packages are well-documented and used widely.

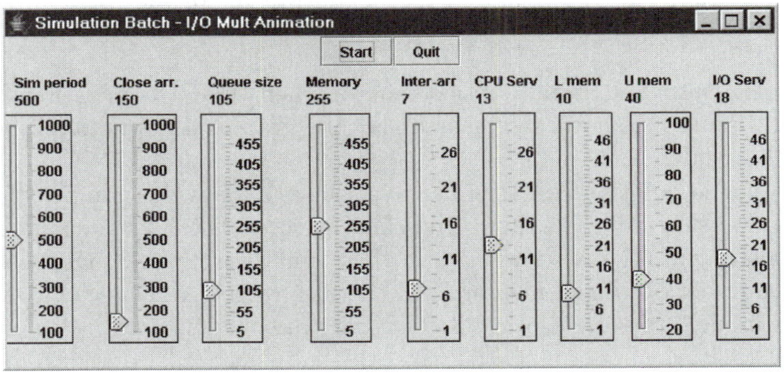

Figure 4.2 GUI of a simulation run of a batch system with multiprogramming.

The model described in this section is similar in functionality to the Java model discussed before; it represents a batch system with multiprogramming. The model has a GUI that presents default values and allows the user to change these values. The GUI displays and accepts input values for the simulation parameters (simulation period and the close arrival time), the workload parameters, and several system parameters. Figure 4.2 shows the GUI for a simulation run.

After the user enters all desired input parameters, the model presents two dialog boxes for the user to select a file on which the model will store the complete output of the simulation run (trace of the simulation run and performance metrics). Figure 4.3 shows the first dialog box.

When the simulation starts, the model shows another window with the animation of all relevant events that occur during the run. These include a job arriving to the input queue and the number of jobs currently in the input queue, a job being placed in the ready queue (after being allocated memory), a job starting execution (CPU service), a job being placed in the I/O queue, a job starting to get I/O processing, and a job

72   Chapter 4   Systems with Multiprogramming

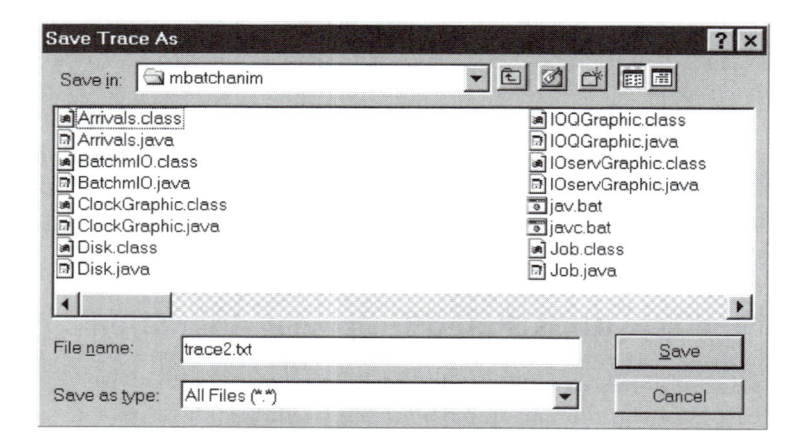

Figure 4.3   Dialog box for the output file of the trace of a simulation run.

terminating. The animation also shows when the CPU and/or the I/O device become idle. Figure 4.4 shows a screen shot of the graphical animation during a simulation run of the model.

The simulation run also displays a line chart of the number of jobs in memory as a function of simulation time. The chart is constructed as the simulation proceeds. This is one of several state variables in the simulation model. Figure 4.5 shows the chart of the number of jobs in memory. All the files with Java classes for the implementation of this model are stored in the archive file `mbatchanim.jar`.

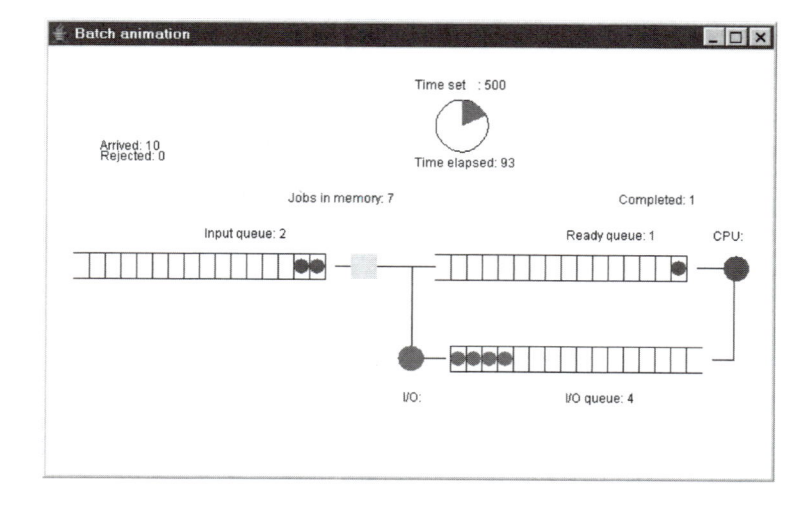

Figure 4.4   Screen shot of the graphical animation during a simulation run.

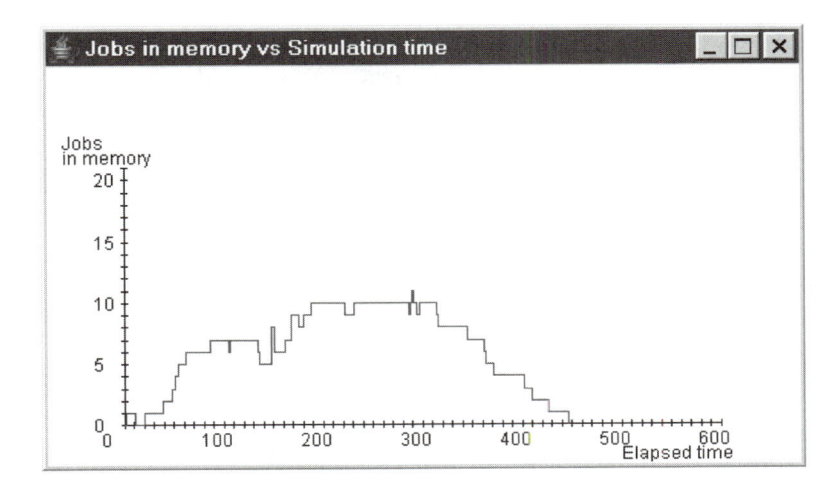

Figure 4.5 Chart of the number of jobs in memory in a simulation run.

A C++ version of the model with a GUI is stored in file `batchmiog.cpp`. This model uses OpenGL and GLUT graphical packages, in addition to Psim3 and Pthreads. Figure 4.6 shows the GUI for the model implemented in C++.

The output values of this model are presented in two different forms. At the end of a simulation run, another window appears with the summary statistics—that is, the values of the performance metrics. The model also writes two text files: `batchmiog.dat`,

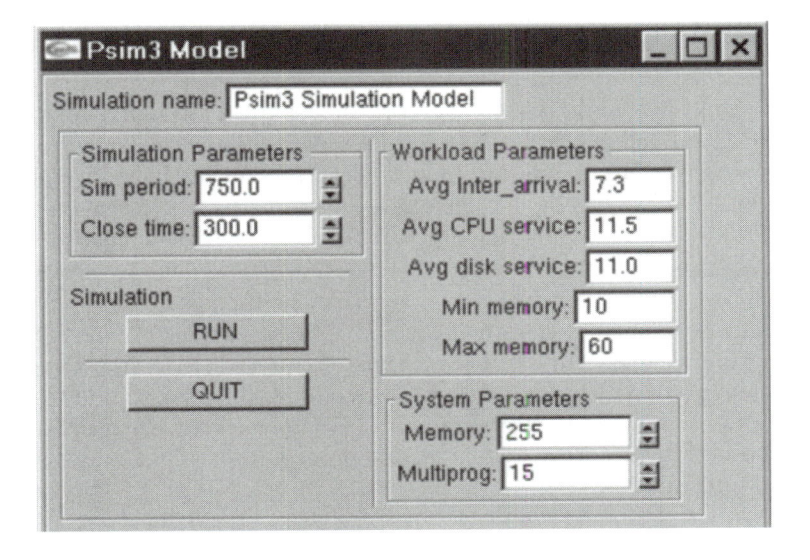

Figure 4.6 GUI of a simulation run of a batch system with multiprogramming using Psim3.

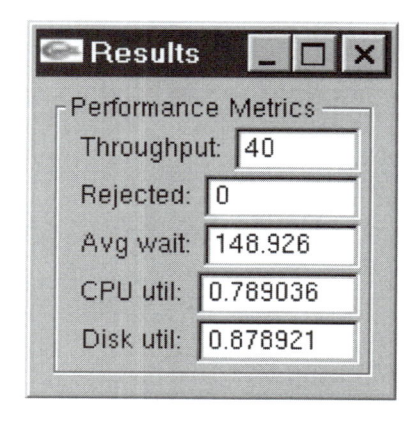

Figure 4.7 Window with the values of performance metrics of a simulation run.

which contains all the detailed output, and `resources.dat`, which contains details about the resources used and in this case is the system memory. Figure 4.7 shows the window with the performance metrics computed by the simulation model in a typical simulation run.

4.4 Summary

Two important concepts discussed in this chapter are multiprogramming and context switches. Batch operating systems with and without multiprogramming are modeled and studied. The simulation models of these systems have two servers: the CPU and the I/O device. The models also have three queues: the input queue, the ready queue, and the I/O queue. In normal operation, after having been allocated memory, a process cycles through the CPU and the I/O stations, demanding service in CPU and I/O bursts.

A brief comparison of the behavior of two systems with and without multiprogramming is included. The simulation runs of the models for these two systems show the advantages of multiprogramming. The comparison is based on the various performance metrics calculated. Multiprogramming is implemented using the overlapped CPU and I/O processing, context switching, and processes with demand service in relatively short time intervals (bursts).

	Key Terms	
active object	I/O device	probability distribution
context switch	I/O queue	queuing network
CPU burst	memory manager	ready queue
CPU idle time	model components	server
degree of multiprogramming	multiprogramming	service demand
I/O burst	overlapped processing	station

Exercises and Questions

1. Estimate the largest possible value of the context switch time that a system can support in order for multiprogramming to be useful. Discuss your arguments.

2. Discuss the advantages and disadvantages of short CPU burst times for processes.

3. Repeat the previous question for I/O burst times.

4. Discuss the advantages and disadvantages of having a large degree of multiprogramming.

5. Using the CPU and I/O bursts, write an expression that represents the total execution period of a process.

6. Using the CPU and I/O bursts, write an expression that represents the total I/O processing period of a process.

7. Using the CPU and I/O bursts, write an expression that represents the total period that a process spends in the system.

8. The various simulation models presented in this chapter are very similar. Is the number of queues the same as the number of servers? There are two severs in the systems and three queues. Explain.

9. What are the differences in the implementation between the models presented in this chapter?

10. The model that represents a system without multiprogramming includes an object of class *Arrivals* that creates objects of class *Job*. The object of class *Arrivals* generates random periods for the CPU burst and for the I/O burst of a process (object of class *Job*). Modify the model implementation so that this is done within the definition of class *Job*. Is there any other way to handle the random burst periods for CPU and for I/O? Discuss the possibilities and describe them in an example.

11. Explain why a context switch is considered an overhead task. How does the context-switch time affect performance? Recall that the data in the PCB of a process is called the context of the process.

12. The models for the batch system compute the accumulated processor service time in the global variable `sum_proc_time`. Is there any other similar variable that would be helpful in order to get more complete summary statistics from the model?

13. From the simulation runs, it can be observed that the number of completed processes in the model that represents a system with multiprogramming is different than the model that represents a system without multiprogramming. Change the Java implementation of the second model so that the number of completed processes is the same as those in the first model. After running the modified model, do you observe an average wait time for the processes that is lower than the first model? Explain.

14. The models studied use objects of class *Job* as active objects. Modify the implementation of one of the models and change objects of class *Job* to be passive objects. Are there any advantages gained?

Chapter 5
Processor Scheduling

5.1 Introduction

The main goal of scheduling is the sharing of one or more processors among the processes in the ready queue. The critical activities that the operating system scheduler must carry out are the ordering of the allocation and deallocation of the processor(s) to the various processes and threads, one at a time. The other activity is deciding when to deallocate a processor from a process. These activities must be carried out in a way that meets the performance objectives of the system. Since the processors are the most important resource in a computer system, the operating system must manage it in the most efficient and effective manner.

The previous chapter explained and described several aspects of multiprogramming, in which an operating system supports several processes in memory. To carry out multiprogramming, the operating system provides scheduling policies and mechanisms, which is the topic of this chapter.

A scheduling policy defines the order in which processes are selected from the ready queue for processing. The scheduling mechanism decides when and how to carry out the context switch to the selected process—i.e., the deallocation of a processor from the current process and the allocation of the processor to the selected process.

This chapter begins with a brief discussion of the general types of scheduling, and then it focuses on the two general types of processor scheduling policies: nonpreemptive and preemptive. Four scheduling policies are discussed: first come, first served (FCFS); shortest job first (SJF), also known as shortest process next (SPN); round robin (RR); and shortest remaining time (SRT). Simulation models are used to illustrate each of the scheduling policies. These models are compared with respect to the performance metrics. Priorities and multiclass systems are also discussed. For simplicity, assume that the computer system has only one processor (CPU).

5.2 General Types of Scheduling

Three general types of scheduling are often considered in studying operating systems:

- *Long-term scheduling*: The operating system decides to create a new process from the jobs waiting in the input queue. This decision controls the degree of multiprogramming. The operating system may decide to create a new process when a currently executing process terminates or when it needs to increase or limit the degree of multiprogramming. The selection of which job to select from the waiting list is based on several criteria.

- *Medium-term scheduling*: The operating system decides when and which process to swap out or swap in from or to memory. This also controls the degree of multiprogramming.

- *Short-term scheduling*: The operating system decides which process to execute next. In other words, the operating system decides when and to which process the CPU will be allocated next. This type of scheduling is often called CPU scheduling and is the one considered in this chapter.

Long-term and medium-term scheduling are described in the chapter on memory management.

5.3 Processor Scheduling Concepts

In a system with a multiprogramming operating system, there are usually several processes in the ready queue waiting to receive service from the CPU. The *degree of multiprogramming* represents the number of processes in memory.

As seen in the previous chapter, the total service demand of a process consists of a sequence of several alternating *CPU bursts* and *I/O bursts*. CPU scheduling focuses on selecting the next process from the ready queue and allocating the CPU to that process for the duration of its current CPU burst. Figure 5.1 shows a simple model of CPU scheduling.

Every process that requests CPU service carries out the following sequence of actions:

1. Join the ready queue and wait for CPU processing.

2. Execute (receive CPU service) for the duration of the current CPU burst or for the duration of the time slice (timeout).

3. Join the I/O queue to wait for I/O service or return to the ready queue to wait for more CPU service.

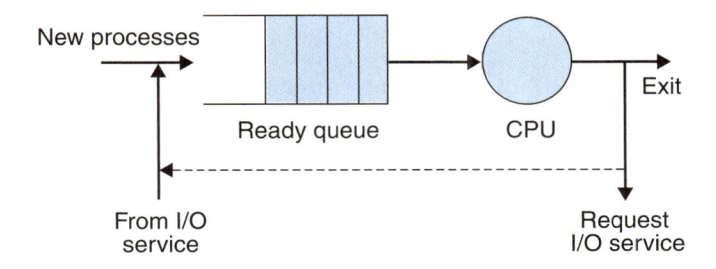

Figure 5.1 A simple CPU scheduling model.

4. Terminate and exit if service is completed—i.e., if there are no more CPU or I/O bursts. If more service is required, return to the ready queue to wait for more CPU service.

5.3.1 The CPU Scheduler

The CPU scheduler is the part of the operating system that selects the next process to which the CPU will be allocated, deallocates the CPU from the process currently executing, and allocates the CPU to the newly selected process. The basic mechanism used by the scheduler defines three basic functions:

- Insertion of processes that request CPU service into the *ready queue*. This queue is normally implemented as a linked list of process control blocks (PCBs) belonging to the processes waiting for CPU service. This queue is usually a data structure that represents a simple first-in-first-out (FIFO) list, a set of simple lists, or a priority list. Recall that all the information about a process is stored in its PCB, which is explained in Chapter 2. This function is carried out by the *enqueuer*, a component of the scheduler.

- The occurrence of a context switch, carried out by the context switcher that saves the context of the current process and deallocates the CPU from that process.

- The selection of the next process from the ready queue and loading its context. This can be carried out by the *dispatcher*, which then allocates the CPU to the newly selected process.

The context switch involves overhead work, and the context switch time must be very short; if it is not, it will degrade performance of the system. The context switch time is mainly dependent on the supporting hardware. A context switch can occur at any of the following times:

- The executing process has completed its current CPU burst. This is the normal case in simple batch systems.

- The executing process is interrupted by the operating system because its allocated time (time slice) has expired. This is a normal case in time-sharing systems.

- The executing process is interrupted by the operating system because a higher priority process has arrived requesting CPU service.

The basic scheduling functions listed above are carried out by several components of the scheduler: the enqueuer, the context switcher, and the dispatcher. These are system processes that compete with the user processes for CPU service.

5.3.2 Scheduling Multiple Classes of Processes

If the operating system treats all processes in the same manner, the system is referred to as a *single-class system*. Fairness is an important issue in defining the performance of a system. A single-class system is said to be *fair* because there is only one group of processes and normally the system treats all of these processes in the same manner.

Processes requesting service from the computer system may be classified into different classes or groups. It is often necessary that the processes in one group get preference compared to processes in another group. The operating system will give preference to a group of processes with respect to other groups of processes based on the *priority* of the group. Every group is assigned a *priority* depending on some criteria. The priority can be based on the relative importance or urgency of the processes. Systems that give preference to some processes in relation to other processes are less fair than single-class systems.

A system with different groups of processes is called a *multiclass system*. Each group or class of processes will usually be given a different set of workload parameters. For example, one group would have a high average arrival rate compared to other groups. The various groups may each have a different average CPU service demand and different average memory demand.

The ready queue may actually be organized as a set of queues, one for each priority. Figure 5.2 illustrates a scheduling model with multiple ready queues.

In multiclass systems, there is potential for *starvation* (indefinite waiting) of one or more of the lower-priority processes. This will normally happen if higher-priority processes continue to arrive, and the lower-priority processes may then have to wait indefinitely. The operating system can have the capability of using different scheduling policies, one for every group (or class) of processes.

5.4 CPU Scheduling Policies

There are two general categories of CPU scheduling policies:

- Nonpreemptive scheduling
- Preemptive scheduling

5.4 CPU Scheduling Policies

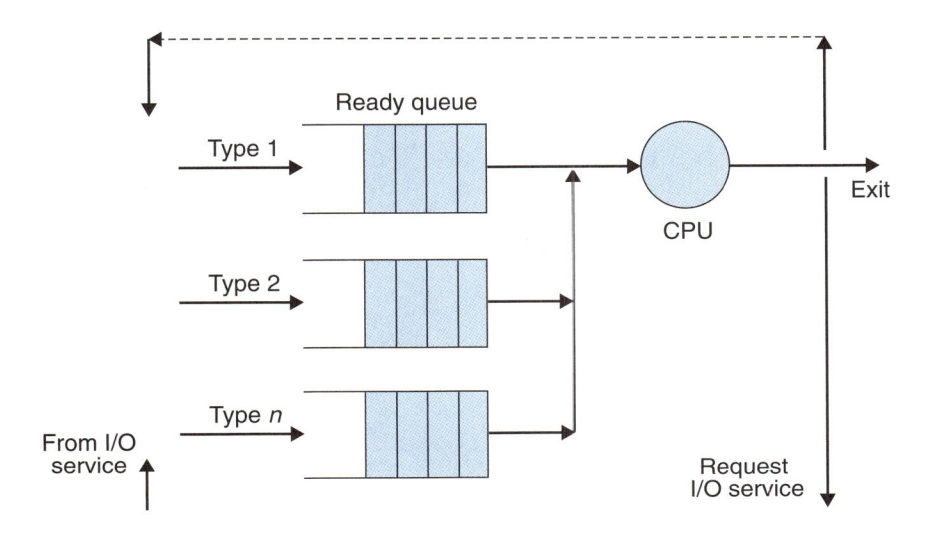

Figure 5.2 A CPU scheduling model with multiple ready queues.

In *nonpreemptive scheduling*, a process that is executing will continue until completion of its CPU burst. The process will then change to its wait state for I/O service, or terminate (change to the terminate state) and exit the system.

In *preemptive scheduling*, the process that is executing may be *interrupted* before completion of its current CPU burst and moved back to the ready queue. A process can be interrupted for one of the following reasons:

- The allocated service interval (time slice) expires.

- Another process with a higher priority has arrived into the ready queue.

Priorities can be used with either preemptive or nonpreemptive scheduling. Depending on the goals of an operating system, one or more of various scheduling policies can be used; each will result in a different system performance. The criteria are based on relevant performance measures and the various scheduling policies are evaluated based on the criteria. There are several relevant performance measures to consider:

- *CPU utilization*: The proportion of time that the CPU spends executing processes.

- *Throughput*: The total number of processes that are executed and completed during some observation period.

- *Process average waiting time*: The average of the waiting intervals of all processes that are completed.

- *Average turnaround time*: The average of the intervals from arrival until completion, for all processes.

- *Average response time*: The average of the intervals from the time a process sends a command or request to the operating system until a response is received, for all processes. This metric is used mainly in interactive systems.

- *Fairness*: A metric that indicates if all processes are treated in a similar manner. The normalized turnaround time is often used for this purpose.

The most relevant scheduling policies in general-purpose operating systems are as follows:

- *First-come-first-served* (*FCFS*): The order of process arrival to the ready queue determines the order of selection for CPU service. This policy is normally single-class and nonpreemptive.

- *Shortest job first* (*SJF*): The process with the shortest CPU burst is the one selected next from the ready queue. Also called shortest process next (SPN), it is typically considered a multiclass and a nonpreemptive scheduling policy.

- *Longest job first* (*LJF*): The process with the longest CPU burst is selected next from the ready queue. Also called longest job next (LJN), it is considered a multiclass policy and typically a nonpreemptive scheduling policy.

- *Priority scheduling*: A priority is assigned to each type of process. The process with the highest priority is the one selected next. These scheduling policies are multiclass and can be preemptive or nonpreemptive.

- *Round robin* (*RR*): Processes are basically selected in the same order of arrival to the ready queue but can only execute until the time slice expires. The interrupted process is placed at the back of the ready queue. This scheduling policy can be single-class or multiclass, and it is the most common preemptive scheduling policy used in time-sharing systems.

- *Shortest remaining time* (*SRT*), also known as *shortest remaining time first* (*SRTF*): A new process that arrives will cause the scheduler to interrupt the currently executing process if the CPU service period of the newly arrived process is less than the remaining service period of the process currently executing (receiving CPU service). There is then a context switch and the new process is started immediately.

5.4.1   First-Come-First-Served

First-come-first-served (*FCFS*) is the most basic and simplest scheduling policy; it is implemented with a *first-in-first-out* (*FIFO*) queue. The arrival order of the processes into the ready queue determines the selection of the next process to service. In other words, the process that has been waiting the longest period in the ready queue is selected next for execution.

5.4.1.1 Simple Analysis with FCFS

The following example illustrates the concepts and techniques for the basic analysis of this scheduling policy and how to calculate some of the performance metrics. Let five processes arrive to the ready queue in the order $P1$, $P2$, $P3$, $P4$, and $P5$ at time zero. Assume that the context switch interval is negligible (zero). Table 5.1 shows the CPU bursts for the processes; assume that the time units are in microseconds.

Table 5.1 CPU Service Demands for Five Processes

Process	CPU Burst
$P1$	135
$P2$	102
$P3$	56
$P4$	148
$P5$	125

The Gantt chart (or execution diagram) in Figure 5.3 shows the starting times, execution intervals, and completion times for the five processes. This chart is used to build simple deterministic models that represent the scheduling of processes.

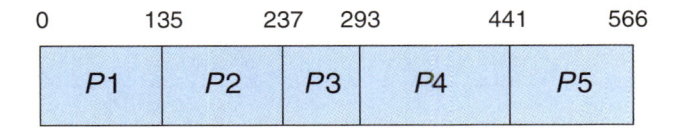

```
0        135      237  293       441       566
|   P1   |   P2   | P3 |   P4    |   P5    |
```

Figure 5.3 Gantt chart of FCFS scheduling for five processes.

For this problem, process $P1$ starts immediately, so its waiting time is zero. Process $P2$ waits until $P1$ completes, process $P3$ waits until $P2$ completes, process $P4$ waits until $P3$ completes, and process $P5$ waits until $P4$ completes.

Table 5.2 shows the starting times, completion times, and wait intervals for every process. From this data, the average turnaround time can be calculated using the completion times from the table. The average turnaround time for the five processes is 334.4 microseconds. In a similar manner, the average wait time can be calculated using the wait time for every process, and this value is 221.2 microseconds. The throughput is 5 because all five processes completed execution, and the CPU utilization is 100 percent because the CPU was never idle. The FCFS scheduling policy is not very good with respect to performance, but it is a fair policy.

Table 5.2 Data for Five Processes Using FCFS Scheduling

Process	Start	Completion	Wait	Turnaround	Normalized Turnaround Time (Ntat)
P1	0	135	0	135	1.0
P2	135	237	135	237	2.323
P3	237	293	237	293	5.232
P4	293	441	293	441	2.979
P5	441	566	441	566	4.528

The normalized turnaround time (Ntat) for each process is computed by dividing its turnaround time by its service time (CPU burst).

Since the FCFS scheduling policy is basically a single-class nonpreemptive policy, the scheduler handles all processes in the same manner. Even if there are several types of processes, there is no preference for the processes of one group over the processes of another. Arriving processes enter the queue at the tail, and the scheduler always takes the process from the head of the queue.

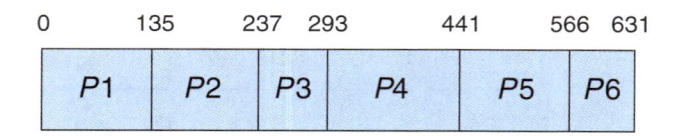

```
0        135      237  293       441      566  631
| P1     | P2     | P3 | P4      | P5     | P6 |
```

Figure 5.4 FCFS scheduling for six processes.

In addition to the five processes already mentioned, suppose that another process, P6, arrives at time 200 with a CPU burst of 65 microseconds. This process has to wait until process P5 completes. Therefore, P6 starts at time 566 and completes at time 631. Figure 5.4 shows the Gantt chart for the six processes. Table 5.3 includes the data for process P6.

The wait interval for process P6 is 366 (566 − 200) microseconds. The turnaround time for the process is 431 (631 − 200) microseconds, and its normalized turnaround time is 6.631. With process P6 included, the average wait time is now 245.33 microseconds, the average turnaround time is 350.5 microseconds, and the average normalized turnaround time is 3.782.

Consider now the first problem but with the following arrival times for the five processes. Process P1 arrives at time 0, process P2 arrives at time 145, process P3 arrives at time 200, process P4 arrives at time 300, and process P5 arrives a time 400.

5.4 CPU Scheduling Policies

Table 5.3 Data for Six Processes Using FCFS Scheduling

Process	Start	Completion	Wait	Turnaround	Ntat
P1	0	135	0	135	1.0
P2	135	237	135	237	2.323
P3	237	293	237	293	5.232
P4	293	441	293	441	2.979
P5	441	566	441	566	4.528
P6	566	631	366	431	6.631

Table 5.4 CPU Service Requests and Arrival Times

Process	CPU Burst	Arrival Time
P1	135	0
P2	102	145
P3	56	200
P4	148	300
P5	125	400

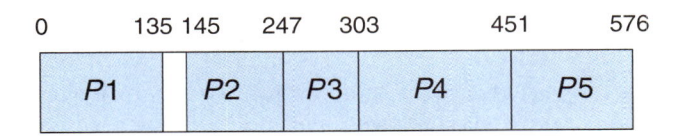

```
0       135 145   247   303         451         576
        |  P1  | P2 | P3 |   P4    |    P5    |
```

Figure 5.5 Gantt chart for the modified FCFS problem.

Table 5.4 shows the CPU bursts and the arrival times for the processes; assume that the time units are in microseconds.

The execution diagram (Gantt chart) for this new problem is slightly different than the one for the original problem. Figure 5.5 shows the chart with the new values of start and completion times for every process.

Note that process $P1$ starts immediately at time 0 and completes at time 135. Process $P2$ arrives at time 145, so the CPU is idle from time 135 until time 145. Upon arrival, process $P2$ starts immediately. Process $P3$ arrives before $P2$ completes, so it waits until $P2$ completes. Process $P4$ waits until $P3$ completes and process $P5$ waits until $P4$ completes. Table 5.5 shows the various measures for the modified problem. The turnaround time for each process is calculated as the completion time minus the arrival time.

Table 5.5 Measures for the Modified FCFS Scheduling Problem

Process	Start	Completion	Wait	Turnaround	Ntat
$P1$	0	135	0	135	1
$P2$	145	247	0	102	1
$P3$	247	303	47	103	1.839
$P4$	303	451	3	151	1.02
$P5$	451	576	51	176	1.408

For this problem, the average wait time is 20.2, the average turnaround time is 133.4, and the average normalized turnaround time is 1.253. The throughput is 5, and the CPU utilization is 98.26 percent because the CPU was idle during 10 microseconds.

Several assumptions are taken in solving the simple scheduling problems discussed (see Exercise 1 at the end of the chapter).

5.4.1.2 Simulation Model for FCFS Scheduling

A more complete model for scheduling processes can be constructed using simulation modeling. As in previous chapters, Java and C++ are used to implement the simulation models that represent the various scheduling policies.

In the simulation models presented in this chapter, there are five different types of processes, and every process type or group is given its own mean arrival rate, mean CPU service period, and mean memory request. The simulation runs will show a different throughput, process average wait period, and average turnaround time for each group (class) of processes.

To study FCFS scheduling, several simulation runs can be carried out with the simulation model described next, which is implemented in Java and PsimJ2. The model consists of five Java classes: (1) *BatmFCFS*, (2) *Arrivals*, (3) *Mmanager*, (4) *Job*, and (5) *Processor*. These classes are stored in files `BatmFCFS.java`, `Arrivals.java`,

`Mmanager.java`, `Job.java`, and `Processor.java`, and all these Java files are stored in the archive file `batmfcfs.jar`.

The simulation model represents the FCFS scheduler and the workload includes five types of processes. However, this model represents a *single-class system*, which means that the processes from the different groups or classes are treated in the same manner. In other words, there is no preference for the processes of one group over another group, so priorities are not used. The queues defined in the model are simple queues—that is, FIFO queues.

The simulation model of the FCFS scheduler consists of the following major components:

- The processes, which represent the units of work to be serviced by the CPU. The processes are implemented as active objects of class *Job*.

- The environment that generates the arriving processes. The environment is an active object of class *Arrivals*. There are several of these objects created; each one creates processes of a specific group.

- The CPU, which represents the processor that executes the processes according to their service demands. This is an active object of class *Processor*.

- The memory manager, which represents the module of the OS that allocates memory to the waiting jobs. This is an active object of class *Mmanager*.

The simulation model also includes the following passive objects:

- A random number generator called `arr_period` for the process interarrival periods. This generator is an object of class *Erand*, which uses an exponential distribution.

- A random number generator called `serv_period` that generates the values for the process CPU service demand periods. This generator is an object of class *Erand*, which uses an exponential distribution.

- A random number generator called `random_mem` that generates the values for the process memory demands. This generator is an object of class *Normal*, which uses a normal distribution.

- The input queue, called `in_queue`, which represents the queue for arriving jobs that request memory. This is implemented as a passive object of class *Squeue*, which defines simple queues (FIFO queues).

- The ready queue, called `ready_queue`, which represents the queue of processes waiting for the CPU. This is implemented as a passive object of class *Squeue*, which defines simple queues (FIFO queues).

- The system memory, which is a resource called *memory* that can be acquired, used, and then released by processes. This is implemented as a passive object of class *Res*, which defines resources that can be acquired only by processes in a mutually exclusive manner.

A partial output of the first part of a simulation run of the model for the FCFS scheduling is shown in Listing 5.1. This part of the output is called the trace. It can be observed that the servicing of the processes is strictly in the order of arrival.

Listing 5.1 Output listing of a simulation run of the FCFS scheduling model.

```
Psim/Java project: FCFS Scheduling Model
Simulation date: 7/31/2006 16:25
FCFS Scheduling Model
Starting Simulation
Job1 type 1 req service 7.551 mem req 49 arrives at 2.059
Job1 starting at: 2.059 serv: 7.551
Job2 type 2 req service 12.728 mem req 37 arrives at 2.064
Job3 type 3 req service 18.576 mem req 42 arrives at 2.064
Job4 type 4 req service 26.587 mem req 39 arrives at 2.064
Job5 type 0 req service 1.125 mem req 39 arrives at 2.25
Job6 type 2 req service 1.958 mem req 32 arrives at 2.381
Job7 type 3 req service 2.858 mem req 40 arrives at 2.381
Job8 type 4 req service 22.118 mem req 47 arrives at 2.381
Job9 type 0 req service 0.066 mem req 40 arrives at 2.383
Job10 type 1 req service 1.568 mem req 43 arrives at 2.487
Job11 type 0 req service 0.177 mem req 45 arrives at 2.738
Job12 type 2 req service 2.662 mem req 26 arrives at 2.813
Job13 type 3 req service 3.885 mem req 49 arrives at 2.813
Job14 type 4 req service 137.277 mem req 35 arrives at 2.813
Job15 type 2 req service 0.322 mem req 41 arrives at 2.865
Job16 type 3 req service 0.47 mem req 39 arrives at 2.865
Job17 type 4 req service 1.83 mem req 47 arrives at 2.865
Job18 type 2 req service 14.853 mem req 43 arrives at 5.274
Job19 type 3 req service 21.678 mem req 33 arrives at 5.274
Job20 type 4 req service 27.211 mem req 42 arrives at 5.274
Job21 type 2 req service 5.31 mem req 40 arrives at 6.135
Job22 type 3 req service 7.749 mem req 47 arrives at 6.135
. . .
Job710 terminating at: 20328.137
Processor completed service of Job839 at: 20384.907895438642
Job845 starting at: 20384.908 serv: 31.119
Job839 terminating at: 20384.908
Processor completed service of Job845 at: 20416.02698787303
Job848 starting at: 20416.027 serv: 29.524
Job845 terminating at: 20416.027
```

```
Processor completed service of Job848 at: 20445.551043038344
Job966 starting at: 20445.551 serv: 8.968
Job848 terminating at: 20445.551
Processor completed service of Job966 at: 20454.51949275445
Job982 starting at: 20454.519 serv: 46.185
Job966 terminating at: 20454.519
Processor completed service of Job982 at: 20500.704104714434
Job998 starting at: 20500.704 serv: 162.386
Job982 terminating at: 20500.704
Processor completed service of Job998 at: 20663.090355416527
Job1017 starting at: 20663.09 serv: 1.111
Job998 terminating at: 20663.09
Processor completed service of Job1017 at: 20664.201574514056
Job1017 terminating at: 20664.202
Simulation closing at: 25000.0
```

The second part of the output of a simulation run is the summary statistics. This includes the final results and the relevant performance metrics calculated by the simulation model. Listing 5.2 shows the second part of the output listing of a simulation run of the FCFS scheduling model. Two categories of performance metrics are shown. The first includes the global performance metrics:

- Total number of processes that arrived
- Total number of processes that completed (throughput)
- Maximum number of processes in memory (the degree of multiprogramming)
- Average turnaround time
- Average normalized turnaround time
- Average process wait time
- CPU utilization

The second category of performance measures includes the performance metric for every process type:

- Number of completed processes for the type (class) of process (throughput)
- Average wait time for the type of process
- Average turnaround time for the type of process
- Average normalized turnaround time for the type of process

When carrying out the simulation runs of the models, the results may show that some jobs are rejected. This may happen when either the input queue is full or the memory demand of a job is higher than the total system memory.

Listing 5.2 Second part of the listing of a simulation run of the FCFS scheduling model.

```
Memory
Memory usage: 0.3986062081549838
Avg num items used: 987.7309778322333
% of time spent resource usage: 0.8264856854981253
End Simulation of FCFS Scheduling Model, clock: 25000.0
Final Results: FCFS Scheduling Model
--------------------------------------------
Total number of jobs that arrived: 1026
Total number of rejected jobs: 443
Total number of completed jobs: 583
Maximum number of jobs in memory: 25
The proportion of rejected jobs: 0.432
Average total wait time: 831.457
Average turnaround time: 9939.16
Average normalized turnaround time: 16463.433
CPU utilization: 1
--------------------------------------
Number of completed jobs of type 0: 130
Average waiting time for type 0: 880.775
Average turnaround time for type 0: 10781.616
Average normalized turnaround time for type 0: 67952.545
Number of completed jobs of type 1: 101
Average waiting time for type 1: 841.918
Average turnaround time for type 1: 10367.935
Average normalized turnaround time for type 1: 3198.889
Number of completed jobs of type 2: 122
Average waiting time for type 2: 802.393
Average turnaround time for type 2: 9833.541
Average normalized turnaround time for type 2: 769.498
Number of completed jobs of type 3: 115
Average waiting time for type 3: 804.701
Average turnaround time for type 3: 9298.554
Average normalized turnaround time for type 3: 522.715
Number of completed jobs of type 4: 115
Average waiting time for type 4: 824.109
Average turnaround time for type 4: 9362.897
Average normalized turnaround time for type 4: 2498.017
```

The performance of FCFS scheduling does not compare well with the other scheduling policies. This will become clear for the average process waiting time after studying the other scheduling policies.

Figure 5.6 shows the GUI of the simulation model for the FCFS scheduler. All data input is carried out on this window. Figure 5.7 shows a summary of the output data calculated by the simulation model.

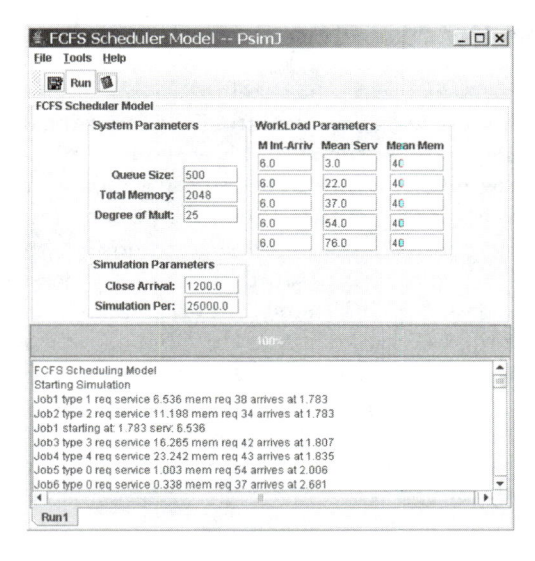

Figure 5.6 GUI for data input with the FCFS scheduler model.

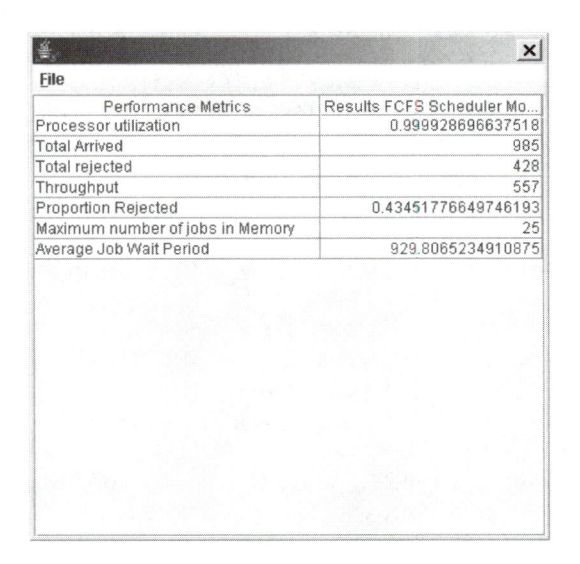

Figure 5.7 Output window with summary statistics for the FCFS scheduler model.

The C++ version of the simulation model is stored in file `batmfcfs.cpp`.

5.4.2 Shortest Process Next

Shortest process next (SPN), also known as *shortest job first (SJF)*, is a scheduling policy in which the scheduler selects from the ready queue the process with the shortest CPU service time interval (burst). This scheduling policy can be considered multiclass because the scheduler gives preference to the group of processes with the shortest CPU burst. It is also a nonpreemptive scheduling policy.

An internal priority is used for each group or class of processes. The operating system assigns a higher priority to the group of processes that has the shortest CPU service time interval (or CPU burst). In other words, the scheduler gives preference to the groups of processes with shorter CPU bursts over other groups of processes. This scheduling policy is not *fair* compared to FCFS scheduling.

Shortest process next scheduling is provably optimal because it results in the minimum wait time for processes. However, when processes with shorter service periods continue arriving into the ready queue, the processes with longer service demand periods may be left waiting indefinitely. This situation is known as *starvation*.

5.4.2.1 Simple Analysis with SPN

Consider the first scheduling problem that was described for FCFS scheduling, which also helps to illustrate SPN scheduling. Table 5.1 provides the original data with the durations of the CPU bursts for the five processes that arrive at time zero. The Gantt chart in Figure 5.8 shows the SPN scheduling of the five processes, including the starting times, the execution intervals, and the completion times.

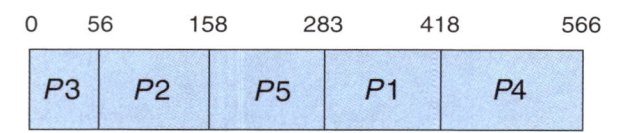

```
 0    56      158       283        418          566
 ┌─────┬───────┬─────────┬──────────┬────────────┐
 │ P3  │  P2   │   P5    │    P1    │     P4     │
 └─────┴───────┴─────────┴──────────┴────────────┘
```

Figure 5.8 Gantt chart with SPN scheduling of five processes.

The data with the starting and completion times and the wait periods for the five processes is shown in Table 5.6 for SPN scheduling. From this data, the average turnaround time can be calculated. This value for the five processes is 296.2 microseconds. In a similar manner, the average wait time can be calculated using the wait time for every process, and this value is 183.0 microseconds. These two average periods are very low compared to the corresponding values calculated for FCFS scheduling. Therefore, SPN scheduling is a great improvement with respect to these two performance metrics: average turnaround and average wait periods. The main difficulty of SPN scheduling is estimating the service time for each process.

Suppose that another process, *P6*, arrives at time 200 with a CPU burst of 65 microseconds. This process arrives while *P5* is executing and has to wait until process *P5* completes. It is placed in the ready queue before processes *P1* and *P4* because it has a smaller CPU burst. Therefore, *P6* starts at time 283 and completes at time 348.

The Gantt chart in Figure 5.9 shows the SPN scheduling of the six processes, including the starting times, the execution intervals, and the completion times.

5.4 CPU Scheduling Policies 93

Table 5.6 Measures for Five Processes Using SPN Scheduling

Process	Start	Completion	Wait	Turnaround	Ntat
P1	283	418	283	418	3.096
P2	56	158	56	158	1.549
P3	0	56	0	56	1.0
P4	418	566	418	566	3.824
P5	158	283	158	283	2.264

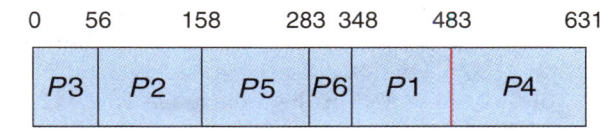

```
0      56        158     283 348      483         631
|  P3  |   P2    |   P5  | P6 |  P1   |    P4     |
```

Figure 5.9 Gantt chart with SPN scheduling of six processes.

The wait interval for process $P6$ is $(283 - 200)$, which is 83 microseconds. The turnaround time for the process is $(348 - 200)$ 148 microseconds and its normalized turnaround time is 2.276. The data with the starting, completion, wait, and turnaround times for the six processes is shown in Table 5.7 for SPN scheduling.

Table 5.7 Measures for Six Processes Using SPN Scheduling

Process	Start	Completion	Wait	Turnaround	Ntat
P1	348	483	348	483	3.577
P2	56	158	56	158	1.549
P3	0	56	0	56	1.0
P4	483	631	483	631	4.263
P5	158	283	158	283	2.264
P6	283	348	83	148	2.276

94   Chapter 5   Processor Scheduling

With process *P*6 included, the average wait time is now 188 microseconds. The average turnaround time is 293.166 microseconds, and the average normalized turnaround time is 2.488.

5.4.2.2   Simulation Model for SPN Scheduling

As in FCFS scheduling, a much more complete example for SPN scheduling can be illustrated using a simulation model. This model is very similar to the one shown for FCFS scheduling; it is implemented using Java and the PsimJ2 simulation package.

In this simulation model, each of the five types of processes is treated differently. The workload parameters are different for each group or class of processes. The model assigns an internal priority to every type or group of process. The highest priority is assigned to the group of processes with the shortest CPU service demand. The next highest priority is assigned to the group with the next shortest CPU demand, and so on.

The simulation model for the SPN scheduling consists of the same major components and the same passive objects as in the FCFS model. The model consists of five Java classes: *Batmsjf*, *Job*, *Mmanager*, *Processor*, and *Arrivals*. These classes are stored in files `Batmsjf.java`, `Job.java`, `Mmanager.java`, `Processor.java`, and `Arrivals.java`. All of these Java files are stored in the archive file `batmsjf.jar`.

Instead of a simple queue (FIFO queue), a *priority queue* is used to implement the ready queue, in which the processes are ordered by priority. The queue is declared and created as a passive object of type `Pqueue` in class *Batmsjf*. In class *Job*, the priority of an object is assigned the value of the type of the object.

A partial output of the first part of a simulation run of the model for SPN (SJF) scheduling is shown in Listing 5.3. The workload parameters are the same as the ones used with the model for a FCFS scheduling policy. It can be noticed from this output listing that the order of servicing of the processes depends on the average CPU burst duration.

Listing 5.3 Partial trace of a simulation run of the SPN scheduling model.

```
Psim/Java project: SJF Scheduler Model
Simulation date: 7/15/2006 17:21
Constructor of Multiprog SJF Scheduler
SJF Scheduling Model
Constructing Processor object
Starting Simulation
Job1 type 1 req service 6.375 mem req 49 arrives at 1.739
Job2 type 2 req service 10.721 mem req 36 arrives at 1.739
Job3 type 3 req service 15.648 mem req 41 arrives at 1.739
Job1 starting at: 1.739 serv: 6.375
Job4 type 0 req service 0.874 mem req 34 arrives at 1.766
Job5 type 4 req service 22.369 mem req 41 arrives at 1.766
Job4 starting at: 8.114 serv: 0.874
Job6 type 4 req service 36.078 mem req 39 arrives at 8.114
```

5.4 CPU Scheduling Policies

```
Job1 terminating at: 8.114
Job2 starting at: 8.987 serv: 10.721
Job4 terminating at: 8.987
Job7 type 0 req service 4.627 mem req 40 arrives at 12.048
Job8 type 1 req service 37.802 mem req 50 arrives at 12.048
Job9 type 2 req service 63.575 mem req 41 arrives at 12.048
Job10 type 3 req service 92.786 mem req 38 arrives at 12.048
Job11 type 1 req service 18.597 mem req 38 arrives at 17.12
Job12 type 2 req service 31.277 mem req 41 arrives at 17.12
Job13 type 3 req service 45.647 mem req 39 arrives at 17.12
Job14 type 4 req service 174.45 mem req 46 arrives at 18.79
Job15 type 0 req service 3.895 mem req 26 arrives at 18.79
Job7 starting at: 19.709 serv: 4.627
Job2 terminating at: 19.709
Job15 starting at: 24.335 serv: 3.895
Job16 type 4 req service 23.661 mem req 34 arrives at 24.335
Job7 terminating at: 24.335
Job17 type 0 req service 2.8 mem req 46 arrives at 24.728
Job18 type 4 req service 56.661 mem req 48 arrives at 24.728
Job19 type 0 req service 0.491 mem req 38 arrives at 26.971
Job20 type 4 req service 28.409 mem req 37 arrives at 26.971
Job17 starting at: 28.23 serv: 2.8
Job15 terminating at: 28.23
Job19 starting at: 31.031 serv: 0.491
Job21 type 4 req service 44.306 mem req 37 arrives at 31.031
Job17 terminating at: 31.031
Job8 starting at: 31.522 serv: 37.802
Job19 terminating at: 31.522
Job22 type 0 req service 4.939 mem req 48 arrives at 39.212
 . . .
Job489 terminating at: 21758.268
Job493 starting at: 21852.03 serv: 18.995
Job490 terminating at: 21852.03
Job494 starting at: 21871.025 serv: 7.412
Job493 terminating at: 21871.025
Job498 starting at: 21878.437 serv: 79.776
Job494 terminating at: 21878.437
Job506 starting at: 21958.213 serv: 92.593
Job498 terminating at: 21958.213
Job517 starting at: 22050.807 serv: 292.585
Job506 terminating at: 22050.807
Job530 starting at: 22343.392 serv: 349.133
Job517 terminating at: 22343.392
Job532 starting at: 22692.525 serv: 11.957
Job530 terminating at: 22692.525
Job538 starting at: 22704.482 serv: 252.682
```

```
Job532 terminating at: 22704.482
Job540 starting at: 22957.164 serv: 34.554
Job538 terminating at: 22957.164
Job545 starting at: 22991.717 serv: 120.903
Job540 terminating at: 22991.717
Job550 starting at: 23112.621 serv: 140.784
Job545 terminating at: 23112.621
Job577 starting at: 23253.404 serv: 11.244
Job550 terminating at: 23253.404
Job606 starting at: 23264.648 serv: 79.108
Job577 terminating at: 23264.648
Job691 starting at: 23343.756 serv: 33.155
Job606 terminating at: 23343.756
Job823 starting at: 23376.911 serv: 74.73
Job691 terminating at: 23376.911
Job841 starting at: 23451.641 serv: 35.938
Job823 terminating at: 23451.641
Job860 starting at: 23487.579 serv: 87.037
Job841 terminating at: 23487.579
Job860 terminating at: 23574.616
Simulation closing at: 25000.0
```

The second part of the output of a simulation run is the summary statistics. Listing 5.4 shows the second part of the output of a simulation run with SPN scheduling. As with the FCFS scheduling, the output of the simulation run with SPN scheduling consists of two groups of performance metrics. The first group includes the following:

- Total number of processes that arrived
- Total number of processes that completed (throughput)
- Maximum number of processes in memory (the degree of multiprogramming)
- Average turnaround time (sojourn time)
- Average normalized turnaround time
- Average total process wait time
- CPU utilization

The second category of performance measures includes the following for every process type:

- Number of completed processes for the class of processes (throughput)
- Average turnaround time for the class of processes
- Average normalized turnaround time for the class of processes
- Average waiting time for the class of processes

5.4 CPU Scheduling Policies

Listing 5.4 Second part of the listing of a simulation run of the SPN scheduling model.

```
Memory
Memory usage: 0.43152171902333075
 avg num items used: 937.2598745491734


Percent of time spent resource usage: 0.9429150917026855
End Simulation of SJF Scheduler Model, clock: 25000.0

Final Results: SJF Scheduling Model
---------------------------------------------
Total number of jobs that arrived: 983
Total number of rejected jobs: 414
Total number of completed jobs: 569
Maximum number of jobs in memory: 25
The proportion of rejected jobs: 0.421
Average total wait time: 984.938
Average turnaround time: 10252.478
Average normalized turnaround time: 7357.132
CPU utilization: 1
--------------------------------------
Number of completed jobs of type 0: 132
Average waiting time for type 0: 52.419

Average turnaround time for type 0: 9439.028
Average normalized turnaround time for type 0: 28109.141
Number of completed jobs of type 1: 107
Average waiting time for type 1: 64.552
Average turnaround time for type 1: 9365.255
Average normalized turnaround time for type 1: 1601.821
Number of completed jobs of type 2: 104
Average waiting time for type 2: 99.981
Average turnaround time for type 2: 9118.992
Average normalized turnaround time for type 2: 967.45
Number of completed jobs of type 3: 104
Average waiting time for type 3: 273.27
Average turnaround time for type 3: 9315.544
Average normalized turnaround time for type 3: 671.457
Number of completed jobs of type 4: 122
Average waiting time for type 4: 4162.173
Average turnaround time for type 4: 13675.693
Average normalized turnaround time for type 4: 1098.037
```

This simulation run has the same workload and system parameters as the model with FCFS scheduling. It also has the same total number of processes that arrived. There are significant improvements in performance compared with the model with FCFS. The value of the average process waiting period and the average turnaround (sojourn) period are much lower than in the model with FCFS scheduling. It is possible that if the arrival of processes were allowed to continue for a longer time, the results would show that some of the lower priority processes might starve.

Figure 5.10 shows the GUI of the simulation model for the SPN scheduler. All data input is carried out on this window. Figure 5.11 shows a summary of the output data calculated by the simulation model.

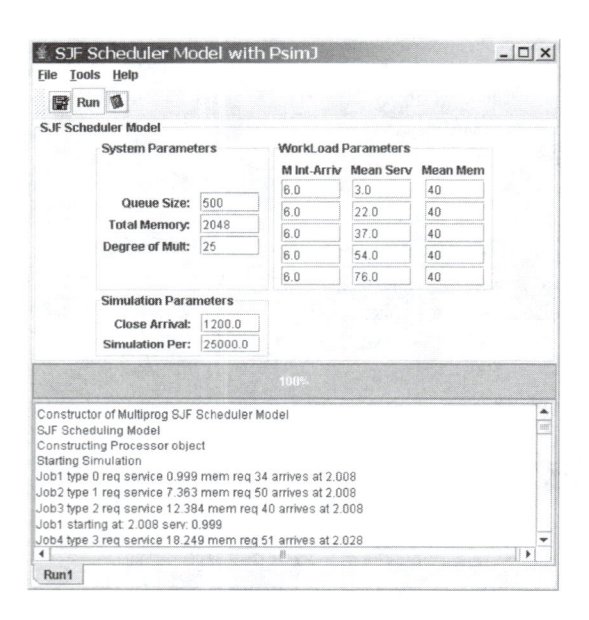

Figure 5.10 GUI for data input with the SPN scheduler model.

The C++ version of the simulation model is stored in file `batmsjf.cpp`.

5.4.3 Round Robin Scheduling

Round robin (RR) scheduling is used in time-sharing systems. It is the most common of the preemptive scheduling policies. Every process is allocated the CPU for a short fixed interval called the *time quantum*, or *time slice*. After this short interval expires, the process that is executing (receiving CPU service) is interrupted by the operating system.

The time slice is usually much shorter than the average CPU burst of the processes. When the time slice expires, the scheduler carries out a context switch to the next process selected from the ready queue. After a process executes for the duration of the time slice, it is interrupted and cycled back to the ready queue. In this manner, the ready queue is treated as a circular queue. The path back to the ready queue is shown in Figure 5.12. A process will continue to cycle through the CPU and ready queue until it completes its current CPU burst.

5.4 CPU Scheduling Policies

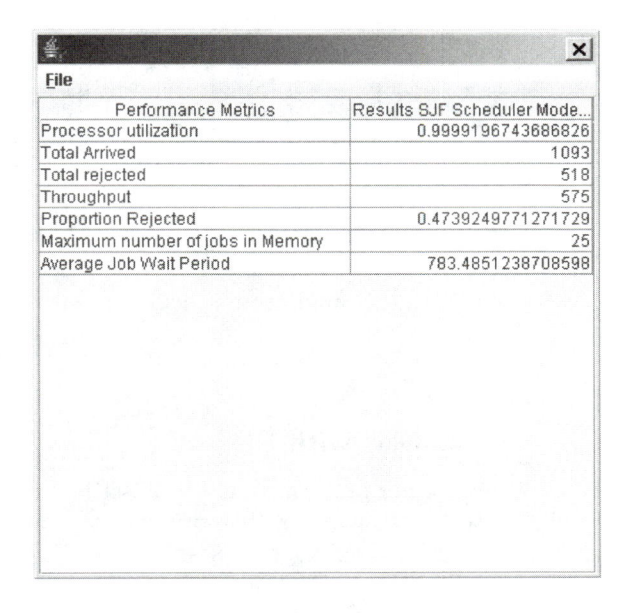

Performance Metrics	Results SJF Scheduler Mode...
Processor utilization	0.999919674368682
Total Arrived	1093
Total rejected	518
Throughput	575
Proportion Rejected	0.4739249771271729
Maximum number of jobs in Memory	25
Average Job Wait Period	783.4851238708598

Figure 5.11 Output window with summary statistics for the SPN scheduler model.

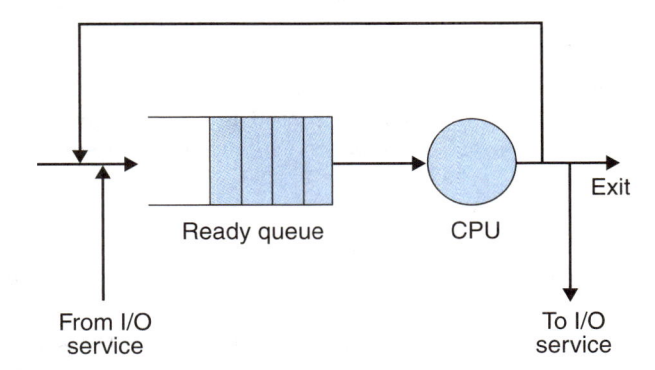

Figure 5.12 A model for RR scheduling.

The operating system using this scheduling scheme attempts to allocate the CPU in a uniform manner to all processes in the ready queue for a fixed short interval (the time slice). Thus all processes in the ready queue are given an equal chance to receive service from the CPU for a short fixed period. The main advantage that this policy provides to users is *interactive* computing.

The time quantum (or time slice) is considered a system parameter. Its value is usually less than the CPU burst for most processes, and it is much longer than the context switch time. If the time quantum is too long or too short, performance will be affected significantly.

100 Chapter 5 Processor Scheduling

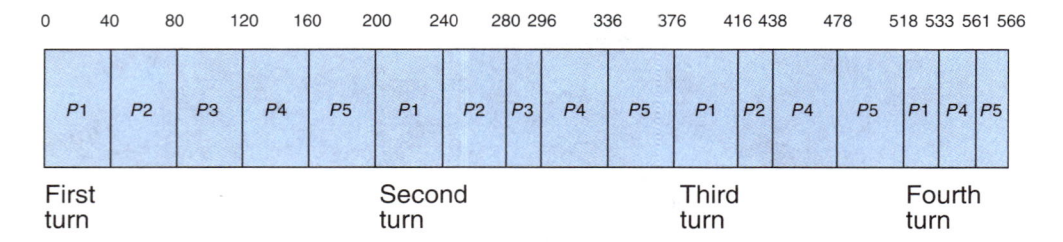

```
0    40   80   120  160  200  240  280 296  336  376  416 438  478  518 533 561 566
┌────┬────┬────┬────┬────┬────┬────┬──┬────┬────┬───┬────┬────┬───┬──┬──┐
│ P1 │ P2 │ P3 │ P4 │ P5 │ P1 │ P2 │P3│ P4 │ P5 │P1 │ P2 │ P4 │ P5│P1│P4│P5│
└────┴────┴────┴────┴────┴────┴────┴──┴────┴────┴───┴────┴────┴───┴──┴──┘
 First                    Second                Third              Fourth
 turn                     turn                  turn               turn
```

Figure 5.13 Round robin scheduling for five processes.

5.4.3.1 Simple Analysis with RR

Consider the same scheduling problem that was described for FCFS scheduling, which also helps to illustrate RR scheduling. The original data appears in Table 5.1, which includes the CPU bursts for the five processes.

The Gantt chart in Figure 5.13 shows the RR scheduling of the five processes including the starting times, the execution intervals, and the completion times. The time slice is 40 time units. Note that a process can execute several times, as needed, until its current CPU burst interval has been completed. After every turn, the process has to wait.

The Gantt chart shows that every process executes only up to the length of the time slice and then it is interrupted. For example, process $P1$ starts at time zero and executes until time 40. Then $P1$ is placed into the ready queue to wait for additional CPU service. Process $P2$ starts at time 40 and executes until time 80, and so on for the other processes.

Process $P1$ is selected again from the ready queue and started at time 200. It executes until time 240. $P1$ is selected four times to complete its current CPU burst. The last time that $P1$ is started, it executes for only 5 microseconds, the remaining CPU service time for this process.

In other words, $P1$ takes the following four turns to execute this process:

- The first turn, in which the process starts execution at time zero and the wait period is zero.

- The second turn, in which the process starts execution at time 200 and the wait period is 160 (200 − 40) microseconds.

- The third turn, in which the process starts execution at time 376 and the wait period is 136 (376 − 240) microseconds.

- The fourth turn, in which the process starts execution at time 518 and the wait period is 102 (518 − 416) microseconds. In this time interval, process $P1$ only executes for 5 microseconds.

5.4 CPU Scheduling Policies 101

Table 5.8 Measures for Five Processes Using RR Scheduling

Process	Start	Completion	Wait	Turnaround	Ntat
P1	0	533	398	533	3.948
P2	40	438	336	438	4.294
P3	80	296	240	296	5.285
P4	120	561	413	561	3.790
P5	160	566	441	566	4.528

The data with the times for the five processes is shown in Table 5.8. The time slice for this problem is 40 microseconds. The table shows only the first starting times for the processes as they go through the cycle. The fourth column in the table shows the total wait time for each process. With this data, the average turnaround time can be calculated using the completion times from the table. The average turnaround time for the five processes is 478.8 microseconds; the average normalized turnaround time is 4.369. In a similar manner, the average wait time is calculated using the wait time for every process, and this average value is 365.6 microseconds.

Round robin scheduling can be single or multiclass. In a multiclass system with round robin scheduling, the different groups (classes) of processes are each given a different priority, and the selection of a process from the ready queue is based on that priority. Each group of processes usually has different workload parameters, and can have a different time slice.

Suppose that process *P6* arrives at time 200 with a CPU burst of 65 microseconds. This process arrives when *P5* has just completed executing its first time slice. The scheduler places *P5* in the ready queue, behind processes *P1*, *P2*, *P3*, and *P4*. Process *P6* is placed in the ready queue behind *P5* and has to wait until process *P5* completes its second time slice. Therefore, *P6* starts at time 376 and completes at time 583.

The Gantt chart in Figure 5.14 shows the RR scheduling of the six processes, including the starting times, the execution intervals, and the completion times. The data

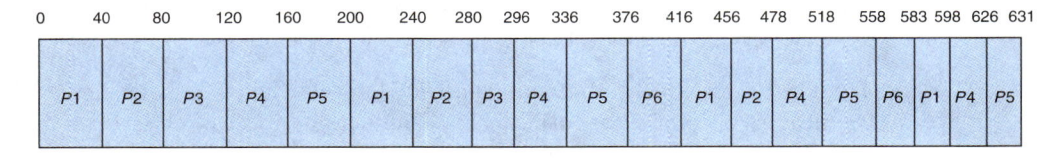

Figure 5.14 Gantt chart with RR scheduling of six processes.

Chapter 5 Processor Scheduling

Table 5.9 Measures for Six Processes Using RR Scheduling

Process	Start	Completion	Wait	Turnaround	Ntat
P1	0	598	463	598	4.43
P2	40	478	376	478	4.686
P3	80	296	240	296	5.285
P4	120	626	478	626	4.23
P5	160	631	506	631	5.048
P6	376	583	318	383	5.892

with the starting, completion, wait, turnaround times, and the normalized turnaround time for the six processes is shown in Table 5.9 for RR scheduling.

With process *P*6 included, the average wait time is now 396.83 microseconds. The average turnaround time is 502 microseconds, and the average normalized turnaround time is 4.976.

5.4.3.2 Simulation Model for RR Scheduling

As with the other scheduling policies, a much more complete example for RR scheduling is shown using a simulation model. This model is implemented in Java and uses the PsimJ2 simulation package. The model is stored in files `BatmRR.java`, `Job.java`, `Processor.java`, `Arrivals.java`, `Os_timer.java`, and `Mmanager.java`. These Java files are stored in the archive file `batmrr.jar`.

The simulation model of the RR scheduler is slightly different from the ones shown for the other scheduling policies. It consists of the following major components:

- The processes, which represent the units of work to be serviced by the processor (CPU). The processes are implemented as active objects of class *Job*.

- The environment, which is an active object of class *Arrivals*. There are several of these objects created; each one creates processes of a certain type.

- The CPU, which represents the processor that executes the processes depending on their service demand. This is an active object of class *Processor*.

- The OS timer, which interrupts the CPU object when the time slice expires for the process currently executing. This is an active object of class *Os_timer*.

- The memory manager, which allocates memory to the processes waiting in the input queue. This is an active object of class *Mmanager*.

The simulation model also includes the following passive objects:

- A random number generator called `arr_period` that generates random values for the process interarrival periods. This generator is an object of class *Erand*, which uses an exponential distribution.

- A random number generator called `serv_period` that generates random values for the process CPU service demand periods. This generator is an object of class *Erand*, which uses an exponential distribution.

- A random number generator called `random_mem` that generates random values for the process memory demands. This generator is an object of class *Normal*, which uses a normal distribution.

- The input queue, called `in_queue`, which represents the queue for arriving processes that request memory. This is implemented as a passive object of class *Squeue*, which defines simple queues (FIFO queues).

- The ready queue, called `ready_queue`, which represents the queue of processes waiting for the CPU. This is implemented as a passive object of class *Squeue*, which defines simple queues (FIFO queues).

- The system memory, which is a resource called `memory` that can be acquired, used, and then released by processes. This is implemented as a passive object of class *Res*, which defines resources that can only be acquired by processes in a mutually exclusive manner.

Although there are five different groups or types of processes in this model, all processes are treated in the same manner. Listing 5.5 shows a partial output for the first part (trace) of a simulation run of the RR scheduler model. This listing shows that the RR scheduler selects the processes from the ready queue in the same order that they arrived. In addition to this, the preemptive behavior of the model follows the previous discussion. The processes are interrupted when the time slice expires and there is a context switch to the next process.

Listing 5.5 Partial output of the trace in a simulation run of the RR scheduler simulation model.

```
Psim/Java project: RR Scheduling Model
Simulation date: 8/2/2006 14:53
RR Scheduling Model
Starting Simulation
Job1 type 0 req service 0.931 mem req 47 arrives at 1.863
Job2 type 1 req service 6.83 mem req 38 arrives at 1.863
Job3 type 2 req service 11.487 mem req 46 arrives at 1.863
```

Chapter 5 Processor Scheduling

```
Job1 starting at: 1.863 serv: 0.931
Job4 type 3 req service 16.764 mem req 35 arrives at 1.863
Job5 type 4 req service 23.594 mem req 38 arrives at 1.863
Service completed for Job1
Job1 terminating at: 2.794
Job2 starting at: 2.794 serv: 6.83
Timer interrupting processor at: 4.794040723208941
Job2 with remaining time 4.829877323399634 to ready queue
Job3 starting at: 4.794 serv: 11.487
Timer interrupting processor at: 6.794040723208941
Job3 with remaining time 9.486611862081203 to ready queue
Job4 starting at: 6.794 serv: 16.764
Timer interrupting processor at: 8.79404072320894
Job4 with remaining time 14.764244339253647 to ready queue
Job5 starting at: 8.794 serv: 23.594
Timer interrupting processor at: 10.79404072320894
Job5 with remaining time 21.594121662653283 to ready queue
Job2 starting at: 10.794 serv: 4.83
Job6 type 0 req service 5.29 mem req 39 arrives at 12.443
Job7 type 1 req service 38.794 mem req 33 arrives at 12.443
Job8 type 2 req service 65.244 mem req 31 arrives at 12.443
Job9 type 3 req service 95.22 mem req 41 arrives at 12.443
. . .
Job530 with remaining time 57.85142303314325 to ready queue
Job538 starting at: 24977.61 serv: 4.795
Timer interrupting processor at: 24979.610233500025
Job538 with remaining time 2.794593887448258 to ready queue
Job539 starting at: 24979.61 serv: 37.322
Timer interrupting processor at: 24981.610233500025
Job539 with remaining time 35.32183972762719 to ready queue
Job542 starting at: 24981.61 serv: 32.317
Timer interrupting processor at: 24983.610233500025
Job542 with remaining time 30.316948486476633 to ready queue
Job543 starting at: 24983.61 serv: 95.26
Timer interrupting processor at: 24985.610233500025
Job543 with remaining time 93.26032245452888 to ready queue
Job827 starting at: 24985.61 serv: 39.328
Timer interrupting processor at: 24987.610233500025
Job827 with remaining time 37.32780794974384 to ready queue
Job529 starting at: 24987.61 serv: 15.368
Timer interrupting processor at: 24989.610233500025
Job529 with remaining time 13.368116365654416 to ready queue
Job544 starting at: 24989.61 serv: 174.596
Timer interrupting processor at: 24991.610233500025
Job544 with remaining time 172.5961462849881 to ready queue
```

5.4 CPU Scheduling Policies

```
Job545 starting at: 24991.61 serv: 266.913
Timer interrupting processor at: 24993.610233500025
Job545 with remaining time 264.9130947714647 to ready queue
Job540 starting at: 24993.61 serv: 81.416
Timer interrupting processor at: 24995.610233500025
Job540 with remaining time 79.41592257962347 to ready queue
Job550 starting at: 24995.61 serv: 0.922
Service completed for Job550
Job550 terminating at: 24996.532
Job445 starting at: 24996.532 serv: 43.552
Timer interrupting processor at: 24998.53233612718
Job445 with remaining time 41.55165736753918 to ready queue
Job852 starting at: 24998.532 serv: 10.564
Simulation closing at: 25000.0
```

The second part of the output of a simulation run of the model for the RR scheduling is shown in Listing 5.6. It presents the summary statistics, which include the two categories of performance metrics also used in the models previously discussed. The output of the simulation run with RR scheduling consists of two groups of performance metrics. The first group includes the following metrics:

- Total number of processes that arrived
- Total number of processes that completed (throughput)
- Maximum number of processes in memory (the degree of multiprogramming)
- Average turnaround time (sojourn time)
- Average normalized turnaround time
- Average total process wait time
- CPU utilization

The second category of performance metrics includes the following for every process type:

- Number of completed processes for the class of processes (class throughput)
- Average turnaround time for the class of processes
- Average normalized turnaround time for the class of processes
- Average waiting time for the class of processes

Listing 5.6 A simulation run of the model with RR scheduling.

```
Memory
Memory usage: 0.4914841096974845
 avg num items used: 1006.7741153062841
% of time spent resource usage: 0.9997867856924684
End Simulation of RR Scheduling Model, clock: 25000.0
Final Results: RR Scheduler Model
---------------------------------------------
Total number of jobs that arrived: 855
Total number of rejected jobs: 292
Total number of completed jobs: 547
Maximum number of jobs in memory: 26
The proportion of rejected jobs: 0.342
Average total wait time: 11273.501
Average turnaround time: 10941.121
Average normalized turnaround time: 2301.65
CPU utilization: 1
--------------------------------------
Number of completed jobs of type 0: 115
Average waiting time for type 0: 10903.294
Average turnaround time for type 0: 10503.792
Average normalized turnaround time for type 0: 8316.379
Number of completed jobs of type 1: 111
Average waiting time for type 1: 10989.985
Average turnaround time for type 1: 10636.002
Average normalized turnaround time for type 1: 1182.269
Number of completed jobs of type 2: 109
Average waiting time for type 2: 11198.167
Average turnaround time for type 2: 10870.829
Average normalized turnaround time for type 2: 716.459
Number of completed jobs of type 3: 107
Average waiting time for type 3: 11466.044
Average turnaround time for type 3: 11164.967
Average normalized turnaround time for type 3: 506.112
Number of completed jobs of type 4: 105
Average waiting time for type 4: 11860.675
Average turnaround time for type 4: 11587.512
Average normalized turnaround time for type 4: 372.756
```

Figure 5.15 shows the GUI of the simulation model for the RR scheduler. All data input is carried out within this window. Figure 5.16 shows a summary of the output data calculated by the simulation model.

The C++ version of the simulation model is stored in file `batmrr.cpp`.

5.4 CPU Scheduling Policies 107

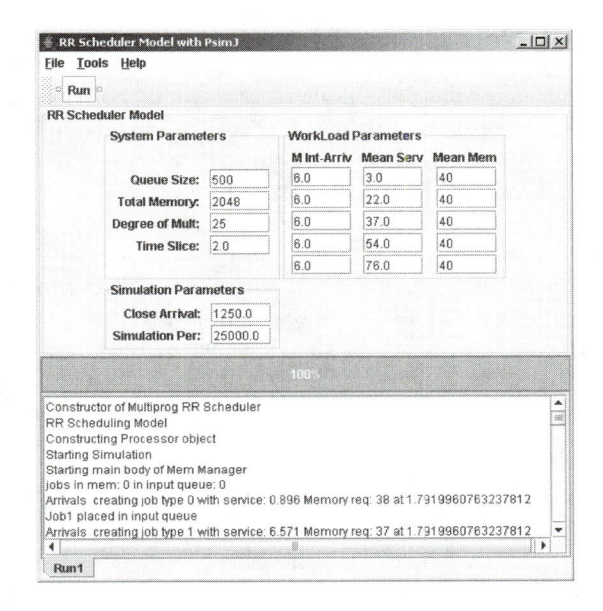

Figure 5.15 GUI for data input with the RR scheduler model.

Figure 5.16 Output window with summary statistics for the RR scheduler model.

5.4.4 Shortest Remaining Time

Shortest remaining time (*SRT*), also known as *shortest remaining time first* (*SRTF*), is a preemptive version of SPN scheduling. With this scheduling policy, a new process that arrives will cause the scheduler to interrupt the currently executing process if the CPU service time interval of the newly arrived process is less than the remaining service time interval of the process currently executing (receiving CPU service). A context switch occurs and the new process is started immediately.

When a process completes CPU service, the next process selected from the ready queue is the one with the shortest remaining service time. The scheduler selects from the ready queue the process with the shortest CPU service period (burst). As with SPN, this scheduling policy can be considered multiclass because the scheduler gives preference to the group of processes with the shortest remaining service time and the processes with the shortest CPU burst.

An internal priority is used for each group or class of processes. The operating system assigns the highest priority to the groups of processes that have the shortest CPU service period (or CPU burst). In other words, the scheduler gives preference to the groups of processes with shorter CPU bursts over other groups of processes. This scheduling policy is not *fair* compared to FCFS and RR scheduling.

When processes with shorter service time continue arriving into the ready queue, the processes with longer service demand times will always be interrupted and may be left waiting indefinitely. As mentioned before, this situation is known as *starvation*.

5.4.4.1 Simple Analysis with SRT

Consider the second scheduling problem that has been used to explain the other scheduling policies previously discussed. Suppose process *P*6 arrives at time 200 with a CPU burst of 65 microseconds. Table 5.10 provides the data with the arrival times and the durations of the CPU bursts for the six processes.

The Gantt chart in Figure 5.17 shows the SRT scheduling of the six processes, including the starting times, the execution intervals, the time *P*5 is interrupted, and the completion times.

At time zero, *P*3 starts executing because it has the shortest CPU burst among the first five processes. At time 56, *P*3 completes execution and *P*2 starts execution because it has the next shortest CPU burst. At time 158, *P*2 completes and *P*5 starts execution. At time 200, *P*6 arrives and the scheduler compares the CPU burst of process *P*6 with the remaining CPU service time of process *P*5, which is the currently executing process. At time 200, *P*5 has a remaining service time of 83 microseconds, which is greater than the CPU burst of *P*6. Therefore, *P*5 is interrupted and a context switch to *P*6 is carried out, enabling *P*6 to start immediately.

At time 265, *P*6 completes execution of its CPU burst, and the scheduler selects *P*5 to resume execution because its remaining time is shorter than *P*1 and *P*4. At time 348, process *P*5 completes and terminates. *P*1 starts executing its CPU burst and completes at time 483. At this time, *P*4 starts and completes execution of its CPU burst at time 631.

5.4 CPU Scheduling Policies

Table 5.10 CPU Service Demands for Six Processes

Process	Arrival Time	CPU Burst
P1	0	135
P2	0	102
P3	0	56
P4	0	148
P5	0	125
P6	200	65

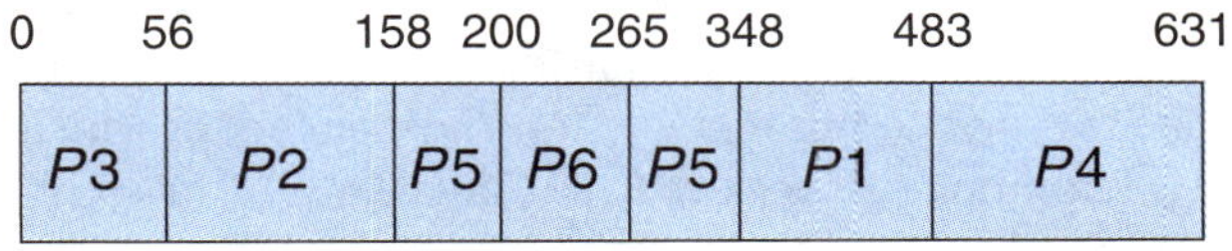

```
0     56        158 200 265 348      483         631
| P3  |   P2   |P5|P6|P5|   P1      |     P4      |
```

Figure 5.17 Gantt chart with SRT scheduling for six processes.

The data with the starting and completion times and the wait periods for the six processes for SRT scheduling is shown in Table 5.11. From this data, the average turnaround time calculated for the six processes is 290.16 microseconds. In a similar manner, the average wait period calculated using the wait period for every process is 185.0 microseconds, and the average normalized turnaround time is 2.362.

Table 5.11 Measures for Six Processes Using SRT Scheduling

Process	Start	Completion	Wait	Turnaround	Ntat
P1	348	483	348	483	3.577
P2	56	158	56	158	1.549
P3	0	56	0	56	1.0
P4	483	631	483	631	4.263
P5	158	348	223	348	2.784
P6	200	265	0	65	1.0

5.4.4.2 Simulation Model for SRT Scheduling

As with the other scheduling policies previously discussed, a much more complete example for SRT scheduling can be illustrated using a simulation model. This model is very similar to the one shown for SPN scheduling; it is implemented in Java and uses the PsimJ2 simulation package.

In this simulation model, there are five types of processes, and they are all treated differently. The workload parameters are different for each group or type of processes, and the model assigns an internal priority to each one. The highest priority is assigned to the group of processes with the shortest CPU service demand. The next highest priority is assigned to the group with the next shortest CPU demand, and so on.

The simulation model for the SPN scheduling consists of the same major components and the same passive objects as in the FCFS model. The model consists of five Java classes: (1) *Batmsrt*, (2) *Job*, (3) *Mmanager*, (4) *Processor*, and (5) *Arrivals*. These classes are stored in files `Batmsrt.java`, `Job.java`, `Mmanager.java`, `Processor.java`, and `Arrivals.java`. These Java files are stored in the archive file `batmsrt.jar`.

An arriving process interrupts the CPU if it has a shorter CPU burst than the remaining time of the current executing process. This is implemented in class *Job*. A *priority queue* is used to implement the ready queue, in which the processes are ordered by priority. The queue is declared and created as a passive object of type `Pqueue` in class *Bamsjf*. In class *Job*, the priority of an object is assigned the value of the type of the object.

A partial output of the first part of a simulation run of the model for SRT scheduling is shown in Listing 5.7. The workload parameters are the same as the ones used with the other models for scheduling. It can be noticed from this output listing that the order of servicing of the processes depends on the CPU burst duration. It can also be observed when an arriving process interrupts the CPU, which would be servicing a process with a remaining time longer than the arriving process.

Listing 5.7 Partial trace of a simulation run of the SRT scheduling model.

```
Psim/Java project: SRTF Scheduling Model
Simulation date: 8/3/2006 14:4
Constructor of Multiprog SRT
SRT Scheduling Model
Starting Simulation
CPU finds ready queue empty
Job1 placed in input queue
Job2 placed in input queue
Job3 placed in input queue
Job4 placed in input queue
Job5 placed in input queue
Job1 joining ready queue
Job1 starting at: 1.974 serv: 0.987
Job2 joining ready queue
```

5.4 CPU Scheduling Policies

```
Job3 joining ready queue
Job4 joining ready queue
Job5 joining ready queue
Service completed for Job1 at: 2.9616510317702285
Job1 terminating at: 2.962
Job2 starting at: 2.962 serv: 7.24
Job6 placed in input queue
Job7 placed in input queue
Job8 placed in input queue
Job9 placed in input queue
Job10 placed in input queue
Job6 interrupting CPU at: 3.5218165570369875
Job2 with remaining time 6.679425885727133 to ready queue
CPU interrupted by Job6 at 3.5218165570369875
Job6 starting at: 3.522 serv: 0.774
Job7 joining ready queue
Job8 joining ready queue
Job9 joining ready queue
Job10 joining ready queue
Service completed for Job6 at: 4.295507824965405
Job6 terminating at: 4.296
Job2 starting at: 4.296 serv: 6.679
Service completed for Job2 at: 10.974933710692538
Job2 terminating at: 10.975
Job7 starting at: 10.975 serv: 5.674
Service completed for Job7 at: 16.648669675500933
Job7 terminating at: 16.649
Job3 starting at: 16.649 serv: 12.176
Job11 placed in input queue
Job12 placed in input queue
Job13 placed in input queue
Job14 placed in input queue
Job15 placed in input queue
Job11 interrupting CPU at: 19.90451472676237
Job3 with remaining time 8.919831412682838 to ready queue
CPU interrupted by Job11 at 19.90451472676237
Job11 starting at: 19.905 serv: 8.191
   . . .
CPU interrupted by Job685 at 24242.079740421977
Job685 starting at: 24242.08 serv: 76.996
Service completed for Job685 at: 24319.0759465979
Job685 terminating at: 24319.076
Job235 starting at: 24319.076 serv: 552.345
Job700 interrupting CPU at: 24319.0759465979
Job235 with remaining time 552.3454379683917 to ready queue
```

Chapter 5   Processor Scheduling

```
CPU interrupted by Job700 at 24319.0759465979
Job700 starting at: 24319.076 serv: 434.488
Service completed for Job700 at: 24753.564265169753
Job700 terminating at: 24753.564
Job235 starting at: 24753.564 serv: 552.345
Service completed for Job235 at: 25305.909703138146
Job235 terminating at: 25305.91
Job260 starting at: 25305.91 serv: 132.132
Service completed for Job260 at: 25438.04202124097
Job260 terminating at: 25438.042
Job265 starting at: 25438.042 serv: 103.405
Service completed for Job265 at: 25541.44661282675
Job265 terminating at: 25541.447
Job270 starting at: 25541.447 serv: 53.566
Service completed for Job270 at: 25595.012230871554
Job270 terminating at: 25595.012
Job285 starting at: 25595.012 serv: 297.047
Service completed for Job285 at: 25892.058794638844
Job285 terminating at: 25892.059
Job290 starting at: 25892.059 serv: 82.055
Service completed for Job290 at: 25974.114089353126
Job290 terminating at: 25974.114
Job295 starting at: 25974.114 serv: 121.691
Simulation closing at: 26000.0
```

Listing 5.8 shows the summary statistics that include several general performance metrics and the ones corresponding to each type of process.

Listing 5.8 Summary statistics of a simulation run of the SRT scheduling model.

```
Memory
Memory usage: 0.49897439283501177
 avg num items used: 1022.9957493788598
% of time spent resource usage: 0.9989284482819979
End Simulation of SRTF Scheduling Model, clock: 26000.0
Final Results: SRTF Scheduling Model
----------------------------------------------
Total number of jobs that arrived: 960

Total number of rejected jobs: 233
Total number of completed jobs: 709
Maximum number of jobs in memory: 25
The proportion of rejected jobs: 0.243
Average total wait time: 1300.197
Average turnaround time: 7223.832
Average normalized turnaround time: 428.213
```

```
CPU utilization: 1
---------------------------------------
Number of completed jobs of type 0: 162
Average waiting time for type 0: 4.069
Average turnaround time for type 0: 18.272
Average normalized turnaround time for type 0: 19.564
Number of completed jobs of type 1: 150
Average waiting time for type 1: 260.53
Average turnaround time for type 1: 1498.062
Average normalized turnaround time for type 1: 169.162
Number of completed jobs of type 2: 139
Average waiting time for type 2: 1391.649
Average turnaround time for type 2: 6043.372
Average normalized turnaround time for type 2: 492.944
Number of completed jobs of type 3: 138
Average waiting time for type 3: 2889.494
Average turnaround time for type 3: 12363.49
Average normalized turnaround time for type 3: 702.388
Number of completed jobs of type 4: 120
Average waiting time for type 4: 2415.929
Average turnaround time for type 4: 19565.312
Average normalized turnaround time for type 4: 913.422
```

Figure 5.18 shows the GUI of the simulation model for the SRT scheduler. All data input is carried out within this window. Figure 5.19 shows a summary of the output data calculated by the simulation model.

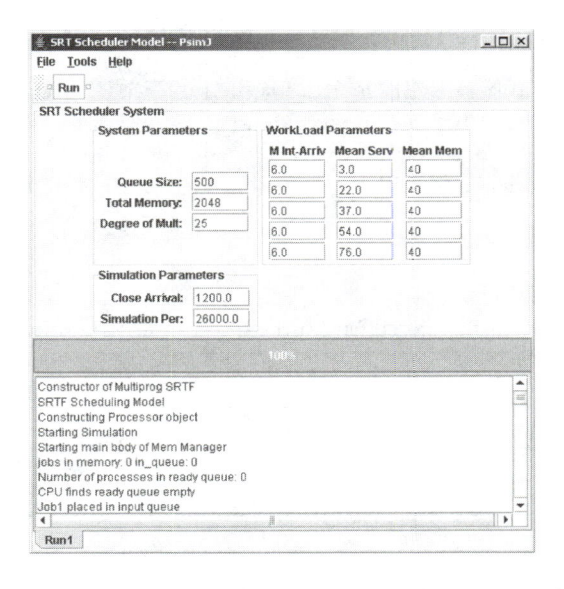

Figure 5.18 GUI for data input with the SRT scheduler model.

114   Chapter 5   Processor Scheduling

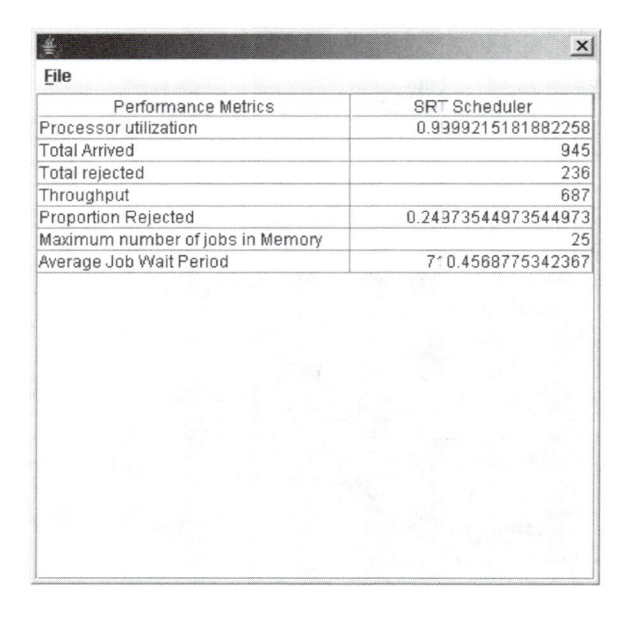

Figure 5.19 Output window with summary statistics for the SRT scheduler model.

5.4.5 Brief Comparison of the Four Scheduling Policies

Only two of the performance measures for these models are compared here: the average turnaround period and the average wait period. The data is taken from the second sample problem explained for the four scheduling policies discussed in this chapter. These results appear in Table 5.12 for the FCFS, SPN, RR, and SRT scheduling policies.

As mentioned before, the workload parameters for the four simulation models are the same. More detailed analysis will consider the results from running the various simulation models and will require different values of arrival rates, service periods, and

Table 5.12 Performance Measures of Sample Problem for Four Scheduling Policies

Performance measure	FCFS	SPN	RR	SRT
Average turnaround	350.5	293.166	502.0	290.16
Average wait	245.33	188.0	396.83	185.0

5.4.6 Dynamic Priority Scheduling

In Chapter 4, which discussed systems with multiprogramming, the typical behavior of processes was discussed. Most processes will exhibit a sequence of alternating CPU and I/O bursts. In simple terms, we can observe that programs requesting I/O service will typically start with CPU service for a short time, request another I/O operation, and release the CPU. Thus, if these processes are given higher priority, they can keep the I/O devices busy without using a significant amount of CPU time. This will tend to maximize I/O utilization while using a relatively small amount of CPU time. Thus the remaining CPU capacity will be available for processes that are requesting CPU bursts.

How do we know which processes to give higher priority? Any fixed decision about whether a process will carry out I/O will tend to be wrong a large part of the time. Thus *fixed priority scheduling* cannot maximize system performance. It makes sense only in specialized circumstances, where overall system performance is not a concern.

In *dynamic priority scheduling*, the CPU scheduler dynamically adjusts the priority of a process as it is executing. The typical approach is to adjust the priority based on the level of expectation that the process will carry out a system call (typically an I/O request). However, this requires the CPU scheduler to predict future process requests. Although we cannot precisely predict the future, we can use an approximation (also known as a heuristic) that is based on observed program behavior:

> *A process will tend to carry out in the near future what it has done in the recent past.*

Thus a process that has just carried out an I/O operation will tend to request another I/O operation. This leads to the following algorithm:

1. Allocate the CPU to the highest priority process.

2. When a process is selected for execution, assign it a time slice.

3. If the process requests an I/O operation before the time slice expires, raise its priority (i.e., assume it will carry out another I/O request soon).

4. If the time slice expires, lower its priority (i.e., assume it is now in a CPU burst) and allocate the CPU to the highest priority ready process.

Some operating systems that implement dynamic priority scheduling will use a fixed time slice value. Other operating systems will make the time slice a function of the priority (giving a shorter time slice to processes that are expected to perform I/O, thus allowing a relatively quick decision that the process is now computing). Figure 5.20 illustrates this approach.

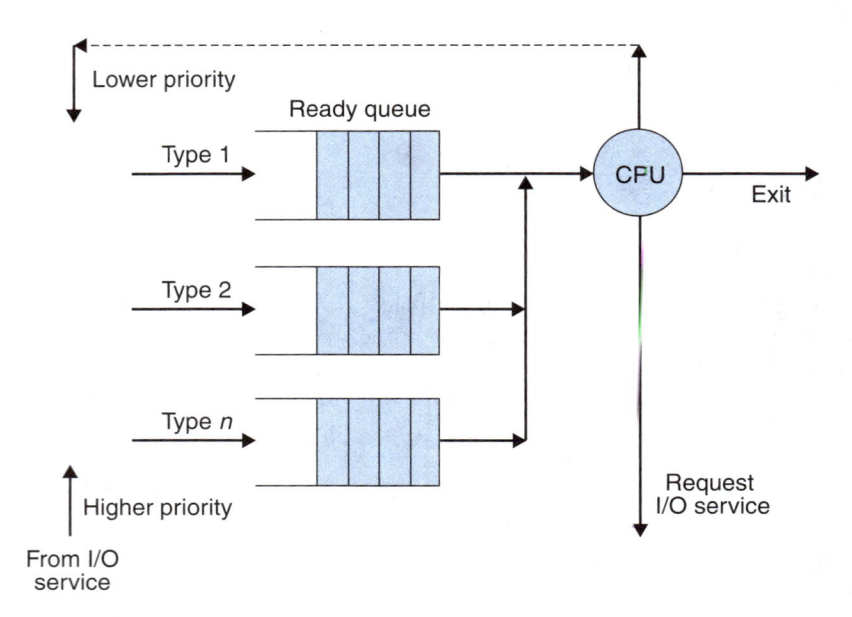

Figure 5.20 Dynamic priority in a simple CPU scheduling model.

5.4.7 Other Scheduling Policies

5.4.7.1 Longest Process Next

Longest process next (LPN) scheduling, also known as longest job first (LJF), is not a very common scheduling policy. Similar to SPN scheduling, it is a multiclass scheduling policy that can be preemptive or nonpreemptive. The only difference with SPN is that higher priorities are assigned to the group of processes with longer CPU bursts.

LPN scheduling does not exhibit the fairness shown by FCFS scheduling as processes are given different priorities. Processes with low average CPU service demand may starve or may have to wait too long compared to the processes in the other groups.

As an example, consider the same scheduling problem that was described for FCFS and SJF scheduling, which helps to illustrate LPN scheduling. The original data appears in Table 5.1, which shows the CPU bursts for the five processes. The Gantt chart in Figure 5.21 shows the LPN scheduling of the five processes, including the starting times, the execution intervals, and the completion times.

The data with the starting and completion times and the wait time for the five processes appear in Table 5.13. From this data, the average turnaround time can be calculated using the completion times from the table. The average turnaround time for the five processes is 384.2 microseconds. In a similar manner, an average wait time of 269.8 microseconds can be calculated using the wait period for every process. These results involve a longer average turnaround and wait times compared to SJF scheduling.

Table 5.13 Measures for Five Processes Using LPN Scheduling

Process	Starting Time	Completion Time	Wait Period
P1	148	289	148
P2	408	510	408
P3	510	566	510
P4	0	148	0
P5	283	408	283

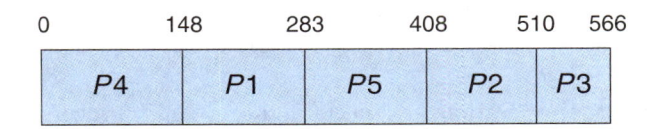

```
0        148      283      408     510  566
    P4   |   P1   |   P5   |  P2  | P3
```

Figure 5.21 LPN scheduling for five processes.

5.4.7.2 Real-Time Scheduling Policies

Real-time systems are ones that continuously interact with an external environment. In these systems, the behavior is defined by the specified *timing constraints*. Real-time systems are sometimes known as *reactive systems*.

One of the goals of real-time scheduling is to guarantee fast response of the high-priority real-time processes.

The second general goal of real-time scheduling is to guarantee that the processes can be scheduled in some manner in order to meet their individual deadlines. The performance of the system is based on this guarantee.

A real-time process has a deadline requirement. This process will normally have relatively high priority and must complete its service before the deadline expires. A real-time process can be periodic or sporadic.

A *periodic process* is started every p time units. This specific time interval is known as the period. The other two relevant timing properties of a periodic process are its computation time requirement, c, and its deadline, d. The process must complete execution before its deadline expires. A *sporadic process* is normally started by an external random event. After the occurrence of the specified event, the process must start and complete before its deadline expires.

Real-time scheduling normally includes priorities and preemption. There are two widely known real-time scheduling policies: rate monotonic and the earliest deadline first.

With *rate monotonic scheduling* (*RMS*), priorities of the processes are statically assigned in reverse order of period length. Higher priorities are assigned to processes with shorter periods, which implies that more frequently executing processes are given higher priority.

With *earliest deadline first* scheduling (*EDFS*), the priorities of the processes are assigned statically or dynamically. Processes with earlier deadlines are given higher priorities.

5.5 Multiprocessor Systems

A multiprocessor computer system has two or more processors. The main goal of these systems is to improve the overall performance of the system. There are two general categories of multiprocessor computer systems: tightly coupled and loosely coupled.

Tightly coupled computer systems have two or more processors that share the system main memory or a common block of memory, and are controlled by the operating system of the computer system. Loosely coupled computer systems are composed of several semi-autonomous units, each with a processor, memory, and communication facilities.

The actual operation and performance of multiprocessor systems depend on the granularity of the configuration. This relates to the synchronization needed among the various processes that execute concurrently or simultaneously. On one extreme (an ideal situation), there are several processes executing in the system; each process is allocated a processor and the execution is completely independent of the other processes. The other extreme is a very fine granularity of parallelism, in which a task needs parallel computing to perform its complex algorithm. Between these extreme levels of granularity, we can identify course, medium, and fine levels of parallelism.

Coarse granularity is used with concurrent processes that need some level of synchronization to share resources and/or to communicate. Medium granularity is used with threads that are executed concurrently and that need synchronization.

A multicore processor is a processing unit composed of two or more cores. Each core is capable of executing instructions. Computer systems may be designed using cores configured tightly or loosely. Multicore processors are used in many applications.

As with general multiprocessor systems, performance gained by the use of a multicore processor depends very much on the software algorithms and implementation. Many typical applications, however, do not realize significant speedup factors. The parallelization of software is a significant ongoing topic of research.

One of the goals of conventional processor scheduling is to keep execution units busy by assigning each processor a thread to run. Recent research on scheduling multicore systems focus on high utilization of on-chip memory, rather than of execution cores, to reduce the impact of expensive DRAM and remote cache accesses.

A simplified model of a multiprocessor system consists of a single ready queue and follows a FCFS scheduling policy. This model is an example of a model of a multiprocessor system with coarse granularity. More advanced configurations and techniques for example, parallel computing, are outside the scope of this book.

Figure 5.22 shows a model of a system with N processors and a single ready queue. A simulation model that implements a simple FCFS scheduling policy using this configuration of multiple processors is implemented in the OOSimL simulation language

5.5 Multiprocessor Systems

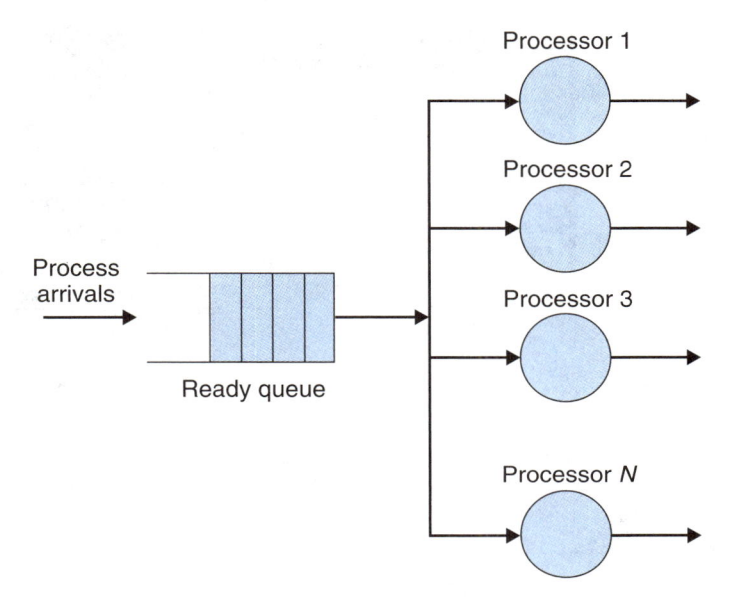

Figure 5.22 Multiple processors and a single queue.

and stored in the archive file `mulservsq.jar`. The Java code of the implementation is also included.

The model represents a system that has several servers to service arriving processes. An arriving process joins the ready queue. It examines the available server queue; if there is an available idle server, it signals the server to start service. If there are no servers available, the process waits in the queue. Figure 5.23 shows the initial GUI for data input of a simulation run. Figure 5.24 shows partial results of a simulation run. Listing 5.9 shows the output results of a simulation run with this model.

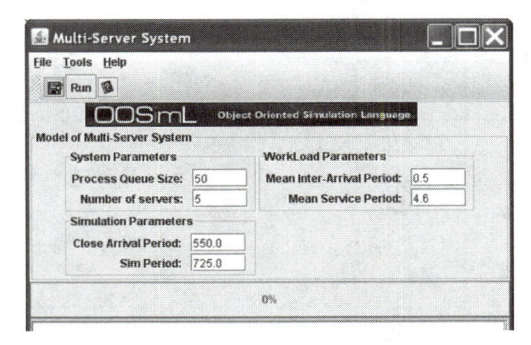

Figure 5.23 Input for a simulation run of the multiprocessor model.

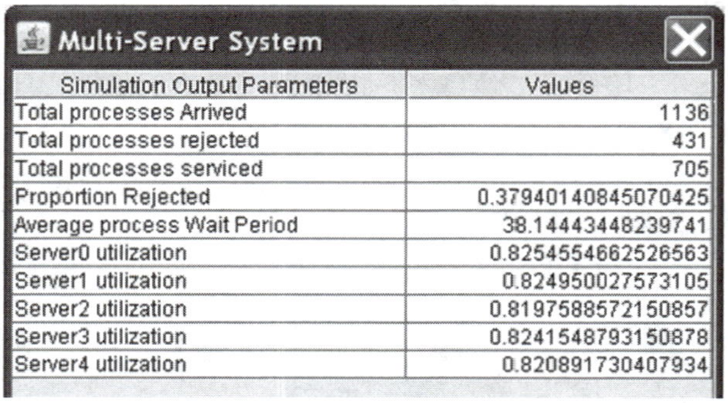

120 Chapter 5 Processor Scheduling

Simulation Output Parameters	Values
Total processes Arrived	1136
Total processes rejected	431
Total processes serviced	705
Proportion Rejected	0.37940140845070425
Average process Wait Period	38.14443448239741
Server0 utilization	0.8254554662526563
Server1 utilization	0.824950027573105
Server2 utilization	0.81975885721 50857
Server3 utilization	0.8241548793150878
Server4 utilization	0.820891730407934

Figure 5.24 Results of a simulation run of the multiprocessor model.

Listing 5.9 Summary statistics of a simulation run of the multiserver model.

```
OOSimL model: Multiple-server Model
Simulation date: date: 9/2/2010 time: 8:33
--------------------STATISTICS REPORT----------------------------
----------------------------------------------------------
Squeue: Available Server Queue
Capacity of queue: 5
Number of observations: 19
Max number of objects in queue: 5
Average number of objects in queue: 0
Average time in queue: 0.3335221740564266
Queue utilization: 0.008974407360988172
Queue usage: 0.0035882385622622447
----------------------------------------------------------
Squeue: Process Queue
Capacity of queue: 50
Number of observations: 1410
Max number of objects in queue: 50
Average number of objects in queue: 37
Average time in queue: 0.42454298517736966
Queue utilization: 0.8154323901426993
Queue usage: 0.7418434844162793
----------------------------------------------------------
Random generator: Process Service Intervals
Distribution: Negative exponential
Number of obs: 1136
Seed: 782
Mean: 4.6
----------------------------------------------------------
Random generator: Process Inter-Arrivals
Distribution: Negative exponential
Number of obs: 1136
```

```
Seed: 765
Mean: 0.5
----------------------------------------------------------------
End Simulation of Multiple-server Model
date: 9/2/2010 time: 8:33
Elapsed computer time: 1283430800325 millisec


Total number of processes that arrived: 1136
Total number of rejected processes: 431
Total number of processes serviced: 705
Average process wait time: 38.144
Server0 utilization: 0.825
Server1 utilization: 0.825
Server2 utilization: 0.82
Server3 utilization: 0.824
Server4 utilization: 0.821
```

Figure 5.25 shows a model of a system with N processors, each one with its own ready queue. A simulation model that implements a simple FCFS scheduling policy using this configuration of multiple processors is implemented in the OOSimL simulation language and stored in the archive file `mulservmq.jar`. The Java code of the implementation is also included.

The model is similar to the model previously discussed. It represents a system that has several servers to service arriving processes, each server with its own queue. An

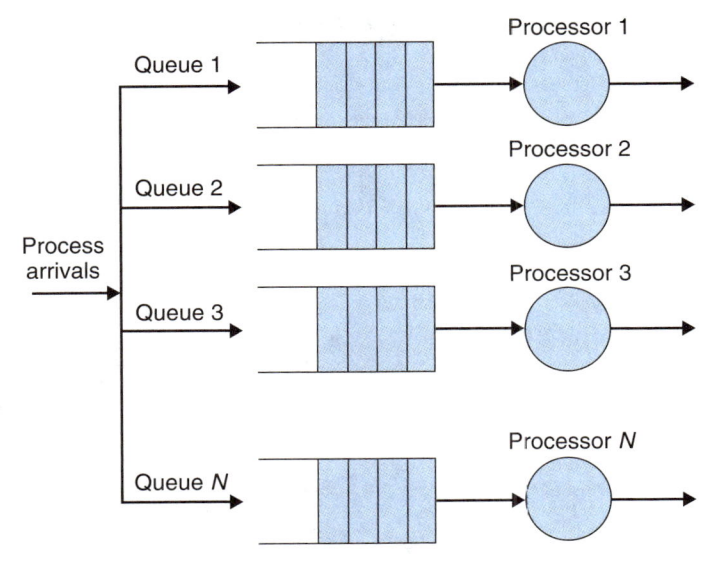

Figure 5.25 Multiple queues and multiple processors.

arriving process joins the shortest queue. It examines the process queue; if there is an empty queue, it joins the queue and signals the server to start service. Listing 5.10 shows the output results of a simulation run with this model.

Listing 5.10 Summary statistics of a simulation run of the multiserver model.

```
OOSimL model: Model of Multiserver Multi-queue System
Simulation date: date: 9/2/2010 time: 8:14
--------------------STATISTICS REPORT---------------------------
----------------------------------------------------------
Squeue: Process Queue4
Capacity of queue: 60
Number of observations: 126
Max number of objects in queue: 18
Average number of objects in queue: 7
Average time in queue: 7.175996396071741
Queue utilization: 0.7308698186805673
Queue usage: 0.39567646795006683
----------------------------------------------------------
Squeue: Process Queue3
Capacity of queue: 60
Number of observations: 128
Max number of objects in queue: 19
Average number of objects in queue: 7
Average time in queue: 7.1530027129990685
Queue utilization: 0.743724080509029
Queue usage: 0.38839549818828273
----------------------------------------------------------
Squeue: Process Queue2
Capacity of queue: 60
Number of observations: 128
Max number of objects in queue: 19
Average number of objects in queue: 7
Average time in queue: 7.450906424092661
Queue utilization: 0.7508960548857849
Queue usage: 0.3999960290828692
----------------------------------------------------------
Squeue: Process Queue1
Capacity of queue: 60
Number of observations: 128
Max number of objects in queue: 19
Average number of objects in queue: 7
Average time in queue: 7.527072335158235
Queue utilization: 0.7629015934502612
```

```
Queue usage: 0.414649247936787
-----------------------------------------------------------
Squeue: Process Queue0
Capacity of queue: 60
Number of observations: 130
Max number of objects in queue: 19
Average number of objects in queue: 7
Average time in queue: 7.3057257691724
Queue utilization: 0.7686982858151991
Queue usage: 0.4168749660391795
-----------------------------------------------------------
Random generator: Inter-arrival
Distribution: Negative exponential
Number of obs: 320
Seed: 431
Mean: 2.0
-----------------------------------------------------------
Random generator: Service Interval
Distribution: Uniform
Number of obs: 320
Seed: 0
Lower bound: 12.25
Upper bound: 16.5
-----------------------------------------------------------

End Simulation of Model of Multiserver Multi-queue System
date: 9/2/2010 time: 8:14
Elapsed computer time: 2016 millisec

Total number of processes serviced: 320
Process average wait period: 142.127
Average period process spends in the subsystem: 156.494
Server0 utilization: 0.998
Server1 utilization: 0.996
Server2 utilization: 0.993
Server3 utilization: 0.989
Server4 utilization: 0.987
```

5.6 Summary

Scheduling policies include two important issues: (1) the selection of the next process to allocate the CPU and (2) when to carry out the context switch to the newly selected process. This involves the allocation and deallocation of the CPU, as well as the time instant to carry out a context switch to another process. The scheduling policies discussed are FCFS, SPN, RR, and SRT. These policies include general concepts of priority scheduling. The scheduling policies can be nonpreemptive and preemptive. Appendix B includes more detailed information on Java and POSIX threads.

The performance of operating systems depends on the scheduling policy used and on the workload parameters. For every scheduling policy included here, the concepts are discussed, a simple analysis is carried out with two numerical problems, and a simulation model is presented. The resulting performance measures for the various policies are briefly compared using the data of the numerical problems discussed. The simulation models help illustrate the behavior of the scheduler under various workloads and show the performance metrics calculated.

Key Terms

CPU burst	nonpreemtive	shortest process
CPU idle time	scheduling	next (SPN)
deadline	normalized turnaround	shortest remaining
dynamic priority scheduling	periodic process	time (SRT)
earliest deadline first	preemptive scheduling	simulation trace
scheduling (EDFS)	priority	single class system
fairness	priority queue	sporadic process
first-come-first-served (FCFS)	process group	starvation
first-in-first-out (FIFO)	process interrupt	summary statistics
fixed priority scheduling	rate monotonic	throughput
Gantt chart	ready queue	time quantum
interactive computing	real-time scheduling	time slice
longest process next (LPN)	round robin (RR)	time-sharing
multiclass system	scheduling	turnaround period
multiprocessor system	scheduling policies	wait period

Exercises and Questions

1. Several assumptions are made to simplify the solution in using the simple deterministic modeling technique discussed in this chapter. This technique is used to calculate several performance metrics for the various scheduling schemes. List these assumptions and provide a brief explanation for each one.

2. Discuss the most important advantages of FCFS scheduling. What are its limitations?

3. Describe the difference in the results that you would get if the five processes from the example in this chapter belong to two different groups, each group with a different time slice.

4. Discuss an example in which LJF scheduling would be practical.

5. Discuss in some detail the changes in result for the example with RR scheduling using a much smaller time slice.

6. Discuss in some detail the changes in result for the example with RR scheduling using a much larger time slice.

7. Table 5.4 shows the CPU bursts and arrival times for five processes; assume that the times units are in microseconds. Use this data to construct a Gantt chart and calculate the various performance metrics for SPN scheduling.

8. Use the data in Table 5.4 to construct a Gantt chart and calculate the various performance metrics for RR scheduling.

9. Use the data in Table 5.4 to construct a Gantt chart and calculate the various performance metrics for SRT scheduling.

10. Calculate the relevant performance metrics for FCFS scheduling using the data from Table 5.4. Assume that process $P6$ arrives at time 200 with a CPU burst of 65 microseconds.

11. Calculate the relevant performance metrics for SPN scheduling using the data from Table 5.4. Assume that process $P6$ arrives at time 200 with a CPU burst of 65 microseconds.

12. Calculate the relevant performance metrics for RR scheduling using the data from Table 5.4. Assume that process $P6$ arrives at time 200 with a CPU burst of 65 microseconds.

13. Calculate the relevant performance metrics for SRT scheduling using the data from Table 5.4. Assume that process $P6$ arrives at time 200 with a CPU burst of 65 microseconds.

14. Run the simulation models corresponding to the various scheduling policies. Write a table to compare the relevant performance metrics. Include a brief conclusion.

15. Modify the simulation model of FCFS scheduling and change the value of the simulation period. What are your conclusions?

16. Modify the simulation model of SPN scheduling and change the value of the simulation period. Consider starvation. What are your conclusions?

17. Modify the simulation model of RR scheduling and change the value of the simulation period. What are your conclusions?

18. Modify the simulation model of SRT scheduling and change the value of the simulation period. Consider starvation. What are your conclusions?

19. Consider assigning a priority to every process in the example of the five processes with RR scheduling. Assume that process $P1$ has the lowest priority and process $P5$ has the highest priority. How will this change the results?

20. Consider assigning a priority to every process in the example of the five processes with RR scheduling. Assume that process $P1$ has the lowest priority and process $P5$ has the highest priority. The processes arrive at different times, with process $P1$ arriving first and process $P5$ last. When a high priority process arrives, any lower priority process executing is interrupted. How will this change the results?

21. Explain why interactive computing is made possible with RR scheduling.

22. Explain why context switching is necessary for implementing scheduling.

23. Modify the simulation model for the FCFS scheduling policy. Change the system memory and the workload parameters so that there are processes rejected at the input queue. Carry out several simulation runs. What can you observe? What can you conclude about the memory capacity of the system?

24. Design and implement some type of animation using Java's AWT and Swing packages to illustrate the dynamic behavior of the FCFS scheduling.

25. List the performance measures that are outputted and the ones that can also be shown, in the simulation model for FCFS scheduling. Which ones are more important?

26. Assume that the memory demand of processes is the most important workload parameter. Change any one of the simulation models so that priorities are given to the processes with larger memory demands. Carry out several simulation runs. Discuss your results.

27. Change the time slice of the model with an RR scheduling policy; increase the value of the time slice. Compare this with the model based on an FCFS scheduling policy. What are your conclusions after analyzing the trace and performance measures from the simulation runs?

28. Change the simulation model for the RR scheduling policy so that there is only one class of processes. Is it possible to use priorities? If there are only two classes—foreground and background processes—how would you assign priorities to the various processes? Discuss.

29. Include an additional level of preemption in the simulation model with RR scheduling. How does the system behave? Does it improve the values of the performance measures?

30. Observe the output of a simulation run (the trace and performance measures) in the simulation model with RR scheduling. What advantages does RR have, in addition to interactive computing? Discuss.

31. Does scheduling with an LJF policy have any practical value? Observe the outputs of the corresponding simulation runs.

32. In what way can the normalized turnaround times be a useful way to measure fairness? Give good arguments.

33. How can you apply the concept of *bottleneck* in the simulation models presented in this chapter? Write your arguments.

34. Design and implement a simulation model for earliest deadline first scheduling (EDFS). What are the main differences with the other models presented?

Chapter 6
Synchronization Principles

6.1 Introduction

The focus of synchronization is the coordination of the activities of the active processes in the computer system. Processes need to be synchronized when they compete for shared resources or when they need to cooperate in carrying out their activities. The operating system incorporates a collection of mechanisms and tools for the coordination of the activities of multiple processes. The study of synchronization mainly includes the principles, techniques, and tools provided by the operating system.

This chapter discusses the basic synchronization principles and problems. The possible solutions to such problems with synchronization tools such as semaphores and monitors are also discussed. Two classical synchronization problems are studied: the consumer-producer problem (also called the bounded-buffer problem) and the readers-writers problem. Interprocess communication (IPC) is also discussed as a set of mechanisms that facilitate the exchange of messages among processes.

This chapter also discusses several simulation models that help illustrate the various types of synchronization problems and their solutions. Two simulation models are presented for the producer-consumer synchronization problem, for the readers-writers problem, and for interprocess communication.

6.2 Basic Synchronization Principles

Synchronization is the coordination of the activities of two or more processes that usually need to carry out the following activities:

- Compete for resources in a mutually exclusive manner.

- Cooperate in sequencing or ordering specific events in their individual activities.

6.2.1 No Synchronization

When two or more processes execute and independently attempt to simultaneously share the same resources, their executions generally will not produce correct results. Since synchronization is absent, the results of these process executions depend on their relative speeds and on the order of use of the resources.

A simple example is a global variable shared by several processes. One process increases the value of the global variable, while another is taking its value to add to a local variable. This leads to unpredictable results and is sometimes called a *race condition*. To avoid this problem, synchronization is used so that processes will be made to compete in some appropriate manner and ensure correct results.

6.2.2 Mutual Exclusion

To solve the race condition problem when a group of processes are competing to use a resource, only one process must be allowed to access the shared resource at a time. In other words, two or more processes are prohibited from simultaneously or concurrently accessing a shared resource.

When one process is using a shared resource, any other process that needs access to that resource is excluded from using it at the same time. This condition is called *mutual exclusion*. At any given time, only one process is allowed to access a shared resource; all other processes must wait.

6.2.3 Critical Sections

A simple analogy to help understand the concept of a critical section is the example of a road intersection shown in Figure 6.1. Two vehicles, one moving on Road A and the other moving on Road B, are approaching the intersection. If the two vehicles reach the

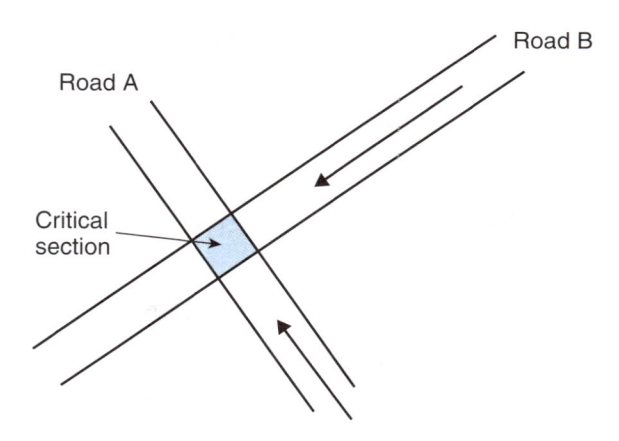

Figure 6.1 A simple analogy for a critical section: A road intersection.

intersection at the same time, there will be a collision. which is an undesirable event. The road intersection is critical for both roads because it is part of Road A and also part of Road B, but only one vehicle should enter the intersection at any given time. Therefore, mutual exclusion should be applied on the road intersection.

The part or segment of code in a process that accesses and uses a shared resource is called the *critical section*. Every process that needs to access a shared resource has its own critical section. Figure 6.2 shows two processes, $P1$ and $P2$, each with a critical section in which access to a global variable x is carried out.

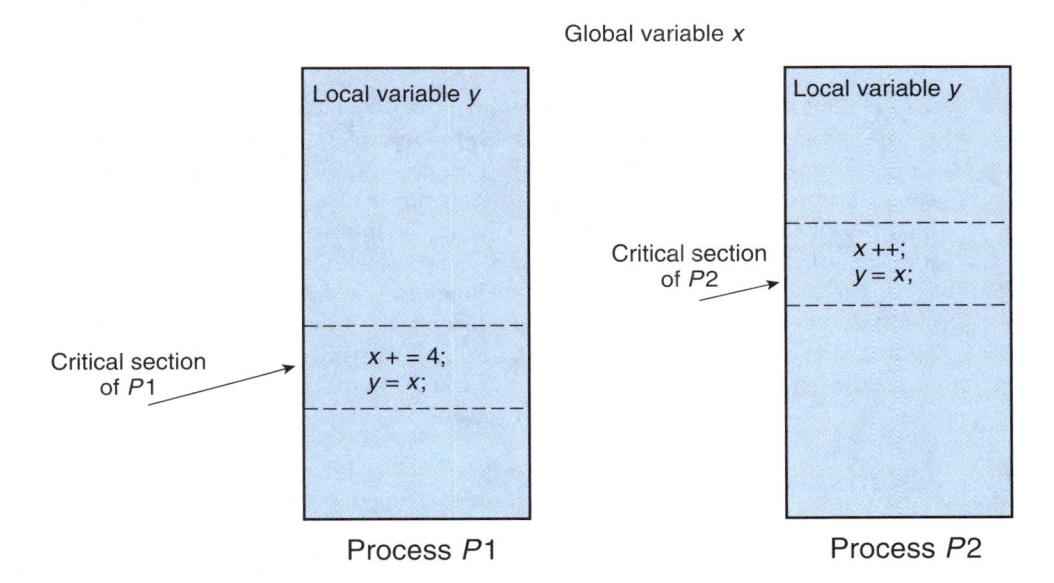

Figure 6.2 Critical sections in processes.

To achieve mutual exclusion, the approach used is to coordinate the group of processes that access shared resources such that only one process can execute its critical section at any instant, and the other processes are excluded. The following conditions must be met for mutual exclusion on the critical sections:

- Mutual exclusion: Only one process may be executing its critical section at any time.

- Absence of starvation: Processes wait a finite time interval to enter their critical sections.

- Absence of deadlock: Processes should not block each other indefinitely.

- Progress: A process will take a finite time interval to execute its critical section.

6.3 Approaches for Implementing Synchronization

There are several approaches for implementing solutions to the critical section problem. These can be grouped into three categories:

- Busy waiting
- Hardware support
- Operating system support

The most notable of the many algorithms that have been proposed for the solution to the critical section problem are Dekker's algorithm and Peterson's algorithm. Using the first approach, a process executes and continuously examines variables and loops, thus consuming CPU cycles. Using the second involves directly accessing the hardware facilities of the computer system. Disabling the interrupts is the simplest of these techniques. Other techniques include using special machine instructions such as *test and set lock* (TSL). In the third approach—the one discussed in detail in this and the following chapter—mechanisms and tools provided by the operating system are used with an appropriate programming language to implement the synchronization needed. The two important synchronization tools involved are semaphores and monitors.

6.4 Semaphores

The solution to the road intersection analogy shown in Figure 6.1 is the installation of a traffic light to coordinate the use of the shared area in the intersection.

A *semaphore* is the equivalent of a traffic light. It is an abstract data type that functions as a software synchronization tool that can be used to implement a solution to the critical section problem.

A semaphore is an object whose methods are invoked by the processes that need to share a resource. An object-oriented definition of a semaphore is given as a class specification. The following portion of code includes the definition of class *Semaphore*:

```
class Semaphore {
   private int sem;
   private Pqueue sem_q;           // semaphore queue
   public Semaphore ( int initval);
   public wait ();                 // P ()
   public signal ();               // V ()
} // end of class Semaphore
```

Class *Semaphore* has two attributes: an integer variable named **sem** and a reference, *sem_9*, to a queue object (of class *Pqueue*). A semaphore reference variable is declared, and the object created and initialized in a manner similar to that shown in the following portion of code:

```
Semaphore mutex;      // declaration
mutex = new Semaphore (1);   // create semaphore object
```

A semaphore object, after initialization, can be used only with two indivisible operations: `wait` (or P) and `signal` (or V). A process can invoke the operations `wait` and `signal` of the semaphore object:

```
mutex.wait();     // invoke the wait method
  . . .
mutex.signal(); // invoke the signal method
```

There are two general types of semaphores:

- The *binary semaphore*, whose integer attribute `sem` can take only two values, 0 or 1, and is used basically to allow mutual exclusion.

- The *counting semaphore*, whose integer attribute `sem` can take any nonnegative integer value.

To implement a solution to the critical section problem, the critical section in every process is enclosed between the `wait` and the `signal` operations. Every process follows this sequence of instructions:

1. Invoke the `wait` operation on a semaphore `mutex`, which tests the value of its integer attribute `sem`. If the value of `sem` is greater than 0, it is decremented and the process is allowed to proceed to enter its critical section. If the value of `sem` is zero, the `wait` operation suspends the process and places it in the semaphore queue.

2. Execute the critical section of the process.

3. Invoke the `signal` operation on the semaphore `mutex`, which increments the value of the attribute `sem` and reactivates the process waiting at the head of the semaphore queue.

4. Continue executing the normal sequence of instructions; the reactivated process will become the current process.

The following portion of pseudocode represents a high-level implementation of operations *wait* and *signal* of a semaphore:

```
public void wait() {
  if sem > 0 then
        sem--;
  else
        place process into waiting queue;
        sleep();
}

public void signal() {
  sem++;
  if queue is non-empty then
        remove a process from waiting queue;
        wakeup process;
}
```

6.5 Synchronization with Semaphores

Semaphores can be used to solve general synchronization problems. In direct competition of processes for a shared resource, the critical section problem defines the mutually exclusive access of a shared resource by a group of processes. Since processes also need to cooperate, another basic type of synchronization is event or execution ordering.

6.5.1 Critical Section Problem

The critical section problem is to impose a protocol to the processes that share a resource. With this protocol, the critical section in each process is identified, then two additional sections have to be implemented: an *entry section* before and an *exit section* after the critical section of the process. Figure 6.3 shows the three sections that appear in every process that shares a resource.

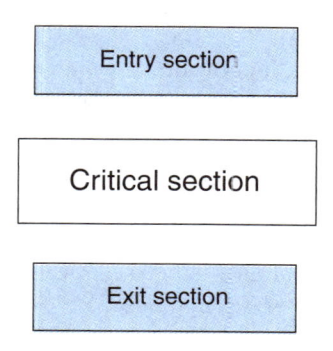

Figure 6.3 Entry and exit sections.

As mentioned before, the simple solution to the critical section problem involves the use of a semaphore by all the processes that share a resource. If `mutex` is a reference to

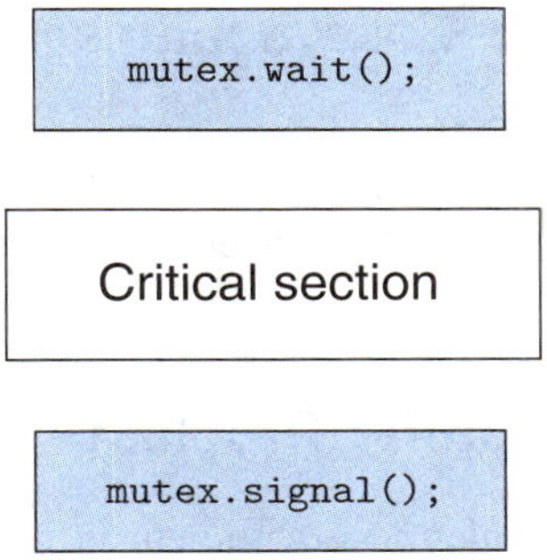

```
          mutex.wait();

         Critical section

         mutex.signal();
```

Figure 6.4 The entry and exit sections implemented with a binary semaphore.

a binary semaphore object that has been initialized to 1, the semaphore-based solution to the problem is simply to have every process invoke the `wait` in its entry section, before its critical section, and invoke the `signal` operation in its exit section, after its critical section. Figure 6.4 shows the entry and exit sections implemented with a binary semaphore.

```
mutex.wait();
  [ critical section ]
mutex.signal();
```

6.5.2 Event Ordering

Event ordering is a type of synchronization based on process cooperation, where the processes exchange synchronization signals in order to coordinate the order of executions. Assume that two processes $P1$ and $P2$ need to synchronize their executions in the following order: in $P1$, `write(x)` must be executed before `read(x)` executes in $P2$. This synchronization problem can also be solved with semaphores; the following is a solution that uses semaphore `exord`, initialized to zero:

```
// process P1}                     // process P2
. . .                              . . .
write(x);                          exord.wait()}
exord.signal();                    read(x);}
. . .                              . . .
```

Since the initial value of the integer attribute of the semaphore object is 0, invoking the `wait()` operation on semaphore `exord` suspends process $P2$. At the same time, process $P1$ can proceed to execute `write(x)`, then it invokes the `signal()` operation, which increments the value of the integer attribute of semaphore `exord`. After this, process $P2$ is reactivated and it invokes the `wait()` operation on semaphore `exord`, then executes `read(x)`.

6.6 Synchronization Case Studies

Two classical case studies will help clarify the synchronization mechanisms: the bounded-buffer problem and the readers-writers problem. A simulation model is presented for each case study.

6.6.1 The Bounded-Buffer Problem

The *bounded-buffer problem*, also known as the *producer-consumer problem*, involves two processes: (1) the producer process, which produces data items and inserts them in the buffer, one by one; and (2) the consumer process, which removes the data items from the buffer and consumes them, one by one.

The producer and consumer processes continuously need access to the shared buffer, and both processes operate at their own individual speeds. The problem is to synchronize the activities of both of them.

The shared buffer has N slots, each one capable of storing a data item. Figure 6.5 shows the producer and consumer processes, as well as the buffer with full and empty slots. The producer-consumer problem has the following restrictions:

- The producer cannot deposit a data item into the buffer when the buffer is full.

- The consumer cannot remove a data item from the buffer when the buffer is empty.

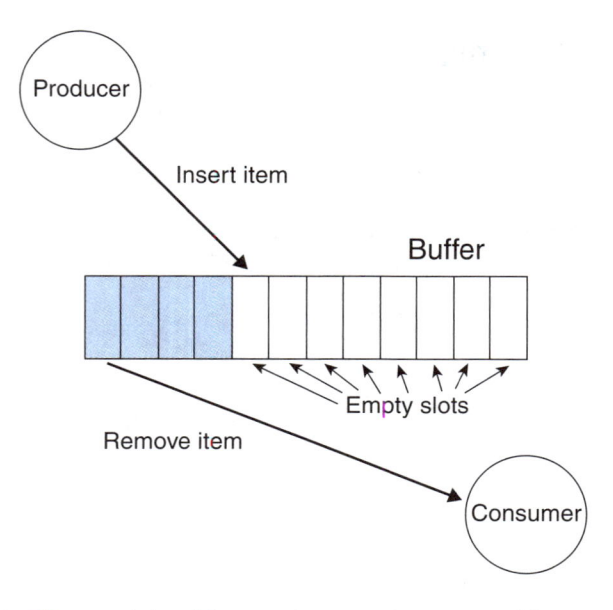

Figure 6.5 The producer-consumer problem.

6.6 Synchronization Case Studies

- The operations to insert (deposit) a data item into a slot in the buffer and to remove a data item from a slot in the buffer are mutually exclusive.

The general solution to the producer-consumer problem requires three semaphores:

- A counting semaphore, `full`, for counting the number of full slots.

- A counting semaphore, `empty`, for counting the number of empty slots.

- A binary semaphore, `mutex`, for mutual exclusion.

The following high-level implementation in pseudocode of the producer process is used:

```
while (true) {
  [ produce an item ]
  empty.wait();              // are there any empty slots?
    mutex.wait();            // acquire exclusive access
      [ deposit an item into an empty slot of the buffer ]
    mutex.signal();          // release mutual exclusion
  full.signal();             // increment full slots
} // end while loop
```

The following high-level implementation in pseudocode of the consumer process is used:

```
while (true) {
  full.wait();               // are there any full slots?
    mutex.wait();            // acquire exclusive access
      [ remove an item from a full slot of the buffer ]
    mutex.signal();          // release mutual exclusion
  empty.signal();            // increment empty slots
  [ Consume data item ]
} // end while loop
```

The statements in the pseudocode that define the producer process are enclosed in an endless loop, which implies that the producer process is a nonterminating process. The producer executes the following sequence of steps:

1. It produces a data item.

2. When the producer process invokes `wait` on semaphore `mutex`, it will be blocked (suspended) if there are no empty slots available.

3. It will be reactivated after the consumer removes an item from a full slot of the buffer.

4. It invokes `wait` on semaphore `mutex` to gain exclusive access to the buffer, which is its critical section. The producer will be suspended if the consumer has already gained access to the buffer by executing its own critical section.

5. It will be reactivated when the consumer releases mutual exclusion.

6. It executes the critical section, which involves inserting the data item into an empty slot of the buffer.

7. It releases mutual exclusive access to the buffer by invoking the `signal` of semaphore `mutex`.

8. It invokes *signal* of semaphore *full*; this increments the value of semaphore `full` and reactivates the consumer if it has been suspended to wait for a full slot.

As with the producer process, the statements in the pseudocode that define the consumer process are enclosed in an endless loop, which implies that the consumer process is a nonterminating process. The consumer follows a similar sequence of instructions using the three semaphores and executes the following sequence of steps:

1. It checks if there are any full slots by invoking `wait` on semaphore `full`.

2. If there is at least one full slot, it proceeds to the next statement; otherwise, it is blocked.

3. It attempts to gain exclusive access to the buffer by invoking `wait` on semaphore `mutex`.

4. It executes its critical section, which involves removing an item from a full slot.

5. It releases mutual exclusion by invoking `signal` on semaphore `mutex`.

6. It increments the number of empty slots by invoking `signal` on semaphore `empty`.

7. It consumes the data item.

6.6.2 Synchronization with Semaphores in Java

The previous section explained how the semaphores provided by the OS are used as synchronization tools.

The Java programming language has facilities for defining and creating *Java threads*. One way to define a thread class is by extending (inheriting) the Java `Thread` library class. The body of a thread is normally coded in method `run`.

After a thread object is created, method `start` of the thread needs to be invoked in order for the thread object to start executing its `run` method. A thread object can be assigned a priority, and this could influence the way the Java Virtual Machine (JVM) schedules the threads. Static variables are shared among the threads, and the access to shared variables and to other resources needs to be synchronized.

The Java language provides a mechanism for basic mutually exclusive access to shared resources. Each object is provided a lock, but the lock can be acquired by only one thread at a time. Appropriate methods of the shared object must have `synchronized` methods. When a thread invokes a `synchronized` method on a shared object, a lock is acquired on that object. All other threads must wait until the lock is released by the thread that holds it. A synchronized method is used to guarantee mutually exclusive access to a shared object by the various threads.

Java includes the *wait/notify mechanism* to help synchronize Java threads. Two methods are provided in the language: `wait` and `notify`. The `wait` method suspends a process invoking this method and puts the thread into a waiting state. The `notify` method reactivates a thread from waiting and puts it back in the ready queue.

A semaphore is an object that can be shared by several thread objects. It can be defined to have two *synchronized* methods, `swait` and `signal`. The semaphore object will also have an integer attribute, `sem`. A semaphore can be defined in Java as follows:

```
class Semaphore {
  private int sem;
  //
  public synchronized void wait() {
    while ( sem <= 0) {
      try {
        swait();
      } catch (Exception e) { System.exit(0);};
    }  // end while
    sem--;            // decrease value of sem
  }// end swait
  //
  public synchronized void signal() {
    sem++;
    notify();
  }  // end signal
  //
  // constructor
  public Semaphore ( int intval) {
    sem = intval;    // initialize attribute sem
}  // end class Semaphore
```

Assume that the producer and consumer processes are implemented as threads and the buffer is implemented as an array of size `N`. The producer is defined with the following class, which inherits the Java class *Thread*:

Chapter 6 Synchronization Principles

```
public class Producer extends Thread {
 private Semaphore mutex;
 private Semaphore full;
 private Semaphore empty;
 public Producer (Semaphore m, Semaphore f, Semaphore e) {
   mutex = m;
   full = f;
   empty = e;
 } // end constructor

 public void run() {
   while (true) {
     [ produce an item ]
     empty.wait();              // are there any empty slots?
     mutex.wait();              // acquire exclusive access
       [ deposit an item into an empty slot of the buffer ]
     mutex.signal();            // release mutual exclusion
     full.signal();             // increment full slots
   } // end while loop
 } // end run
} // end class Producer
```

In a similar manner, the consumer is defined by the following class, which inherits (extends) the Java class *Thread*:

```
public class Consumer extends Thread {
 private Semaphore mutex;
 private Semaphore full;
 private Semaphore empty;
 public Consumer (Semaphore m, Semaphore f, Semaphore e) {
   mutex = m;
   full = f;
   empty = e;
 } // end constructor
 //
 public run() {
   while (true) {
     full.wait();               // are there any full slots?
     mutex.wait();              // acquire exclusive access
       [ remove an item from a full slot of the buffer ]
     mutex.signal();            // release mutual exclusion
     empty.signal();            // increment empty slots
       [ Consume data item ]
   } // end while loop
  } // end while
 } // end run
} // end class Consumer
```

The main class defines method `main`, which creates and initializes the semaphore objects, creates the two thread objects (producer and consumer objects), and starts execution of the thread objects:

```
public class ProdconSync {
  static final int N = 100;    // number of slots in buffer
  public static void main (String args[]) {
    Semaphore mutex = new Semaphore (1);
    Semaphore full = new Semaphore (0);
    Semaphore empty = new Semaphore (N);
    Producer prod = new Producer (mutex, full, empty);
    Consumer cons = new Consumer (mutex, full, empty);
    prod.start();
    cons.start();
  } // end main
}   // end class ProdconSync
```

6.6.3 Simulation Models of the Bounded-Buffer Problem

The basic simulation model of the bounded-buffer problem (producer-consumer problem) includes five classes: (1) *Semaphore*, (2) *Buffer*, (3) *Producer*, (4) *Consumer*, and (5) *Consprod*. The model with graphics and animation includes additional classes for displaying the GUI and the animation. The models are implemented in Java with the PsimJ2 simulation package, and they are stored in the archive files: `consprod.jar` and `consprodanim.jar`.

Class *Semaphore* is implemented with the PsimJ2 resource class *Bin*. The `swait` operation on this semaphore class is implemented with the `take` method of class *Bin*, and the `signal` operation is implemented with the `give` method of class *Bin*.

In the model, semaphore `mutex` is an object of class *Semaphore* initialized to 1. The two counting semaphores are also objects of class *Semaphore*. One object is called `empty` and is initialized to `numSlots`. The other object is called `full` and is initialized to zero.

Class *Buffer* consists of an array of characters. The operations are `put` and `get`. The capacity of the buffer is a constant value, `numSlots`. The producer takes a finite time to produce an item before it deposits it into the buffer. This is a random period generated from an exponential distribution given a mean period for producing an item. In a similar manner, the consumer takes a random period to consume an item that it has taken from the buffer. Both processes execute their activities in an endless loop. Each process spends a random time executing its critical section.

Figure 6.6 shows the graphical user interface (GUI) for a simulation run of the consumer-producer simulation model. The following input parameters can be set:

- Simulation time interval
- Average time interval that the producer takes to produce a data item

142   Chapter 6   Synchronization Principles

Figure 6.6   Graphical user interface (GUI) for the consumer-producer model.

- Average time interval that the producer spends in its critical section
- Value of the coefficient of variance for the normal distribution random time for the random times that a process spends in its critical section
- Average time interval that the consumer takes to consume a data item
- Average time interval that the consumer spends in its critical section
- Buffer size

Figure 6.7 presents a screenshot of the graphical animation during a simulation run of the consumer-producer model. It shows the producer placing a data item into the

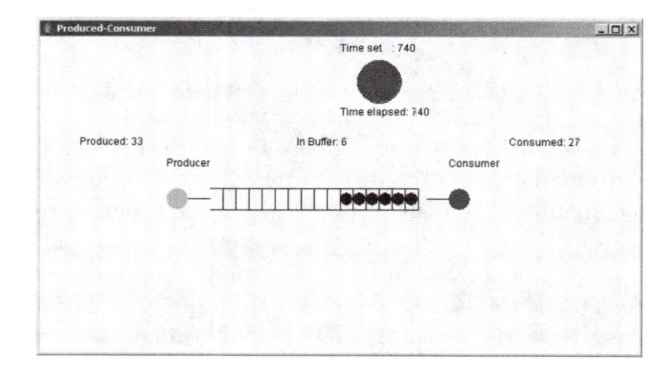

Figure 6.7   Graphical animation for the consumer-producer model.

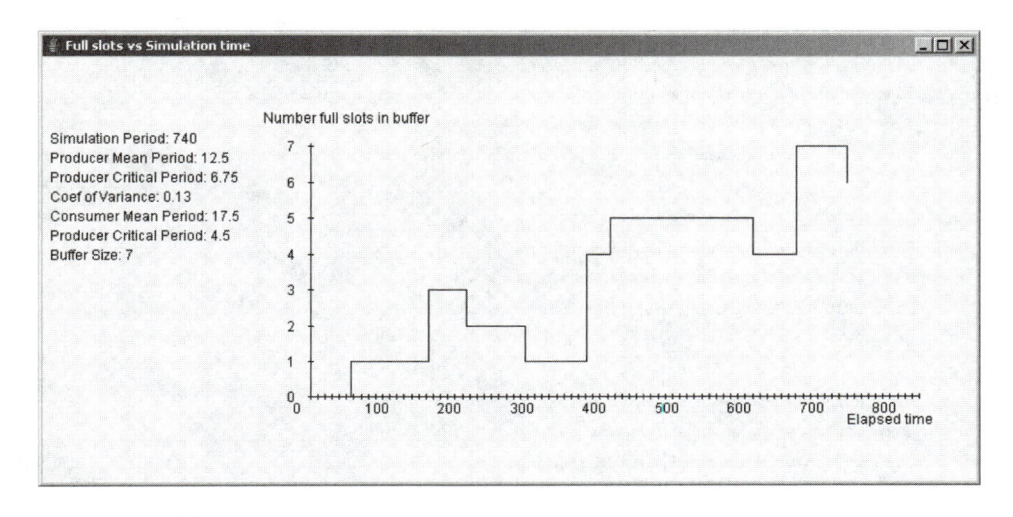

Figure 6.8 Plot output for the consumer-producer model.

buffer, the current data items in the buffer, and the times when the consumer removes data items from the buffer. The animation also shows when either process needs to wait.

Figure 6.8 shows a small chart with the plot of the variation of the number of data items in the buffer with time, until the value of time reaches the end of the simulation time interval.

This simulation model generates two output text files: the trace file and the summary file. Listing 6.1 includes the partial output listing of the trace of a simulation run for the producer-consumer simulation model. The trace shows the sequence of events that accomplish the synchronization of the two processes.

Listing 6.1 Trace output of the producer-consumer model.

```
Project: Producer-Consumer Model
Run at: Thu Sep 15 00:00:11 EDT 2006 by jgarrido on Windows XP, localhost
-----------------------------------------------------
Input Parameters
Simulation Period: 740
Producer Mean Period: 12.5
Prod Mean Buffer Access Period: 6.75
Coef of Variance: 0.13
Consumer Mean Period: 17.5
Cons Mean Buffer Access Period: 4.5
Buffer Size: 7
Time 0000.000 Producer producing item
```

```
Time 0000.000 Consumer requesting full slot
Time 0003.338 Producer requesting empty slot
Time 0003.338 Character put by Producer: k
Time 0010.285 Producer releases mutex
Time 0010.285 Producer adds 1 full slot
Time 0010.285 Producer producing item
Time 0010.285 Character removed by consumer: k
Time 0015.400 Consumer releases mutex
Time 0015.400 Consumer retrieved char
Time 0016.123 Producer requesting empty slot
Time 0016.123 Character put by Producer: e
Time 0020.073 Consumer requesting full slot
Time 0023.579 Producer releases mutex
Time 0023.579 Producer adds 1 full slot
Time 0023.579 Producer producing item
Time 0023.579 Character removed by consumer: e
Time 0024.455 Producer requesting empty slot
Time 0027.313 Consumer releases mutex
Time 0027.313 Consumer retrieved char
Time 0027.313 Character put by Producer: n
Time 0033.185 Producer releases mutex
Time 0033.185 Producer adds 1 full slot
Time 0033.185 Producer producing item
Time 0035.486 Consumer requesting full slot
Time 0035.486 Character removed by consumer: n
Time 0035.849 Producer requesting empty slot
Time 0039.759 Consumer releases mutex
Time 0039.759 Consumer retrieved char
Time 0039.759 Character put by Producer: n
Time 0040.985 Consumer requesting full slot
Time 0047.382 Producer releases mutex
Time 0047.382 Producer adds 1 full slot
Time 0047.382 Producer producing item
Time 0047.382 Character removed by consumer: n
Time 0051.459 Consumer releases mutex
Time 0051.459 Consumer retrieved cha
Time 0055.188 Consumer requesting full slot
Time 0061.391 Producer requesting empty slot
  . . .
Time 0665.097 Consumer releases mutex
Time 0665.097 Consumer retrieved char
Time 0666.943 Producer producing item
Time 0674.126 Cons time exceeds simulation per
Time 0684.487 Producer producing item
Time 0688.586 Producer producing item
```

```
Time 0694.831 Producer producing item
Time 0696.607 Producer producing item
Time 0716.297 Producer producing item
Time 0719.678 Producer producing item
Time 0738.700 Producer producing item
Simulation closing
```

The summary statistics of the simulation run for the producer-consumer model are shown in Listing 6.2.

Listing 6.2 Summary statistics of the producer-consumer model.

```
Project: Producer-Consumer Model
Run at: Thu Sep 15 00:00:11 EDT 2006 by jgarrido on Windows XP, localhost
Input Parameters
Simulation Period: 740
Producer Mean Period: 12.5
Prod Mean Buffer Access Period: 6.75
Coef of Variance: 0.13
Consumer Mean Period: 17.5
Cons Mean Buffer Access Period: 4.5
Buffer Size: 7
----------------------------------------------------
Results of simulation: Producer-Consumer Model
Total Items Produced: 23
Mean Prod Buffer Access Time: 0006.735
Total Prod Buffer Access Time: 0154.916
Mean Producer Wait Time: 0000.760
Total Producer Wait Time: 0017.480
Total Items Consumed: 23
Mean Cons Buffer Access Time: 0004.575
Total Cons Buffer Access Time: 0105.218
Mean Consumer Wait Time: 0007.896
Total Consumer Wait Time: 0181.597
```

This model calculates the total wait time for each process for the simulation period given. Since the "faster" process always has to wait for the "slower" process, changing the mean periods to produce and to consume an item will have an effect on the performance measures. Typically, one type of process will have to wait longer than the other type of process. This illustrates that the solution to such problems is not fair.

The C++ implementation of the model uses the Psim3 simulation package and includes the five classes mentioned previously. This model is stored in the archive file consprod.cpp.

6.6.4 The Readers-Writers Problem

The readers-writers problem is another classic synchronization problem, slightly more complex than the consumer-producer problem.

The readers-writers problem includes two types of processes: *readers* and *writers*. There are several processes of each type, and all of these processes share a data resource. The readers access the data resource to read only; the writers need access to the data resource to update the data. The problem must satisfy the following conditions:

- Any number of reader processes can access the shared data resource simultaneously.

- If a writer process has gained access to the shared data resource, the process has exclusive access to the shared data.

In this problem, there is a need to define two levels of mutual exclusion:

- Individual mutually exclusive access to the shared data resource

- Group exclusive access to the shared data resource

The first level is used in the producer-consumer problem and in most problems where mutually exclusive synchronization is applied. The second level of exclusive access to a shared resource allows the processes of a group to access a shared resource simultaneously and exclude other processes.

Two levels of mutual exclusion are used in the readers-writers problem. Since a group of readers can access the shared data object simultaneously, group mutual exclusion is applied. Any writer process is excluded from accessing the shared data object when there are one or more reader processes already accessing the shared data object.

Several variations of the problem have been proposed for solution. One variation gives readers implicit priority. When a reader process arrives, it starts to read immediately if there are one or more reader processes already reading. If new reader processes continue to arrive, any writer process must wait.

The first reader process that needs access to the shared data must compete with any writer process. In this variation of the problem, readers have implicit priority. Once a single reader has gained access to the shared data area, readers can retain access to the data area as long as there is at least one reader accessing the data area. In this situation, starvation is possible for writers.

A solution to the first variation (readers have priority) of this problem uses two binary semaphores, `wrt`, which is used by all the processes, and `mutex`, which is used only by the reader processes. Readers also share a variable called `readcount`. The following short listing declares and creates the semaphore objects, `wrt`:

```
Semaphore wrt;          // binary semaphore for all processes
wrt = new Semaphore(1);
```

Each writer needs exclusive access to update data in the shared data area. The `wrt` semaphore is used by any writer to gain exclusive access to the shared data area. As long as a writer is accessing data, no other writers and no readers may access the shared data area. The following pseudocode is used for the body of a writer:

```
. . .
wrt.wait ();  // get access to the shared object
   [ write to shared data object (exclusive access) ]
wrt.signal ();
. . .
```

Reader processes have a slightly more complex body of code. In order to allow multiple readers, when there are no readers accessing the shared data area, the first reader will attempt to gain exclusive access to the shared data area. When there is at least one reader accessing the shared data area, subsequent readers can proceed without waiting to access the shared data. To accomplish this, the first reader uses semaphore `wrt` to gain exclusive access to the shared data area. This implies that the first reader will compete with writers in attempting to access the shared data.

The last reader, after reading data, will release exclusive access to the shared data and give a chance to the waiting writers, if any. In order to identify the first reader that will attempt to read data from the shared data area and to identify the last reader that has accessed the shared data, a global variable shared by readers only is used. Called `readcount`, this variable maintains a count of the number of readers accessing the shared data.

Variable `readcount` is shared among reader processes. The access to this variable must be done in a mutually exclusive manner because individual readers are incrementing and decrementing this variable. The other binary semaphore, `mutex`, is used by readers to gain exclusive access to shared variable `readcount`. The following high-level pseudocode is used for the body of a reader:

```
Semaphore mutex;           // binary semaphore for readers only
int readcount = 0;         // shared variable for readers only
mutex = new Semaphore(1);  // create semaphore mutex
. . .
mutex.wait ();
  increment readcount;     // access shared variable
  if readcount equals 1 then
     wrt.wait ();          // attempt access to shared data area
mutex.signal ();
  [ read from the shared data area ]
mutex.wait();
  decrement readcount;     // access shared variable
  if readcount equals zero then
     wrt.signal ();        // release access to shared data area
mutex.signal();
. . .
```

Another variation of the problem gives priorities to writer processes. But in this other situation, starvation is possible for readers. The implementation to this second version of the solution to the problem needs two additional semaphores and a shared variable for the writers. The other way to implement this second variation of the problem is to use a priority queue in the semaphore definition. Explicitly giving a higher priority to the writer processes will guarantee that no new readers will be allowed access to the data area if there is at least one writer waiting.

6.6.5 Simulation Models of the Readers-Writers Problem

The simulation models of the readers-writers problem follow very closely the theoretical discussion. The Java implementation of the model includes nine classes: (1) *Buffer*, (2) *Condition*, (3) *Reader*, (4) *ReaderArrivals*, (5) *ReaderWriter*, (6) *SimDisplay*, (7) *SimInputs*, (8) *Writer*, and (9) *WriterArrivals*. These files are stored in the archive file `readwrite.jar`. The model with the GUI is stored in the archive file `rwrite2.jar`. The C++ version of this model is stored in file `reawriter.cpp`. The model implements the first strategy for solving the readers-writers problem.

In this model, two binary semaphore objects are used: `mutex` and `wrt` of class *Semaphore*. The first reader object is the only reader to use the `wrt` semaphore and invokes the `swait` operation, competing with the writer objects for exclusive access to the shared data area. The last reader releases mutually exclusive access to the shared data area by invoking the `signal` operation of semaphore `wrt`. This model uses the same Java implementation of class *Semaphore* that is used in the model of the producer-consumer problem.

Figure 6.9 shows the graphical user interface of the readers-writers model. The two files generated by the model are the trace and the summary statistics. Listing 6.3 shows a partial listing of the trace of a simulation run of this model.

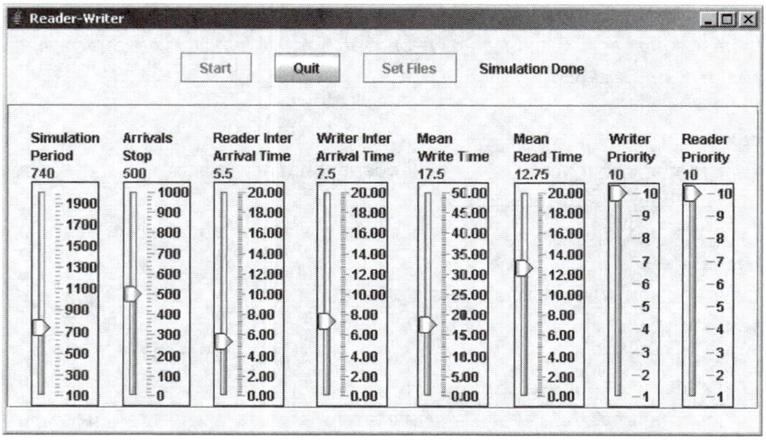

Figure 6.9 Graphical user interface of the readers-writers model.

Normally, different mean intervals to read from or to write to the shared data resource are assigned to the reader and writer processes. This model assumes that the relative speeds of the processes are different so a random period is generated for each process from an exponential distribution, given a mean read period for readers and a mean write period for writers.

Listing 6.3 Trace of a simulation run of the readers-writers model.

```
Project: Concurrent Readers/Writers Problem
Run at: Thu Mar 02 15:20:37 EST 2006
-----------------------------------------------------
Input Parameters
Simulation Period: 740
Arrivals Stop: 400
Reader Inter Arrival Time: 5.5
Writer Inter Arrival Time: 7.5
Mean Write Time: 17.5
Mean Read Time: 12.75
Writer Priority: 10
Reader Priority: 10
Project: Concurrent Readers/Writers Problem
Run at: Thu Mar 02 15:20:37 EST 2006
Start Simulation
Time 0004.359 Reader1 arrives
Time 0004.359 Reader1 is first reader
Time 0004.359 Reader1 starting to read data
Time 0004.801 Reader1 finished reading data
Time 0004.801 Reader1 last reader
Time 0008.174 Reader2 arrives
Time 0008.174 Reader2 is first reader
Time 0008.174 Reader2 starting to read data
Time 0008.895 Reader3 arrives
Time 0008.895  2 readers accessing data
Time 0008.895 Reader3 starting to read data
Time 0009.224 Reader4 arrives
Time 0009.224  3 readers accessing data
Time 0009.224 Reader4 starting to read data
Time 0011.481 Reader3 finished reading data
Time 0011.481 2 readers left accessing data
Time 0011.754 Reader2 finished reading data
Time 0011.754 1 readers left accessing data
Time 0011.825 Reader5 arrives
Time 0011.825  2 readers accessing data
```

```
Time 0011.825 Reader5 starting to read data
Time 0012.134 Writer1 arrives
Time 0017.100 Reader6 arrives
Time 0017.100  3 readers accessing data
Time 0017.100 Reader6 starting to read data
Time 0018.519 Reader6 finished reading data
Time 0018.519 2 readers left accessing data
Time 0020.509 Reader4 finished reading data
Time 0020.509 1 readers left accessing data
Time 0020.853 Reader7 arrives
Time 0020.853  2 readers accessing data
Time 0020.853 Reader7 starting to read data
Time 0023.236 Reader8 arrives
Time 0023.236  3 readers accessing data
Time 0023.236 Reader8 starting to read data
Time 0026.830 Reader9 arrives
Time 0026.830  4 readers accessing data
Time 0026.830 Reader9 starting to read data
Time 0027.614 Writer2 arrives
Time 0029.552 Writer3 arrives
Time 0030.300 Reader9 finished reading data
Time 0030.300 3 readers left accessing data
Time 0030.554 Writer4 arrives
Time 0031.054 Reader10 arrives
Time 0031.054  4 readers accessing data
Time 0031.054 Reader10 starting to read data
Time 0031.139 Reader8 finished reading data
  . . .
Time 0682.935 Reader54 finished reading data
Time 0682.935 4 readers left accessing data
Time 0687.830 Reader60 finished reading data
Time 0687.830 3 readers left accessing data
Time 0700.476 Reader68 finished reading data
Time 0700.476 2 readers left accessing data
Time 0701.504 Reader53 finished reading data
Time 0701.504 1 readers left accessing data
Time 0720.782 Reader81 finished reading data
Time 0720.782 Reader81 last reader
Time 0720.782 Writer28 starts to write data
Time 0740.200 Writer28 completed to write data
```

Listing 6.4 shows the listing with the summary statistics of a simulation run. The performance measures computed by this model are the throughput for each type of process, and their average wait time.

Listing 6.4 Summary statistics of a simulation run of the readers-writers model.

```
Project: Concurrent Readers/Writers Problem
Run at: Thu Mar 02 15:20:37 EST 2006
------------------------------------------------------
Input Parameters
Simulation Period: 740
Arrivals Stop: 400
Reader Inter Arrival Time: 5.5
Writer Inter Arrival Time: 7.5
Mean Write Time: 17.5
Mean Read Time: 12.75
Writer Priority: 10
Reader Priority: 10
Project: Concurrent Readers/Writers Problem
Run at: Thu Mar 02 15:20:37 EST 2006
------------------------------------------------------
Results of simulation: Concurrent Readers/Writers Problem
------------------------------------------------------
Results of simulation:
Number of Readers that Arrived:   87
Number of Readers that completed: 87
Average reader wait period: 0164.1250
Number of Writers that Arrived:   45
Number of Writers that completed: 28
Average writer wait period: 0234.5263
```

The model of the readers-writers problem gives the reader processes an implicit priority. If the reader processes are allowed to arrive continuously, a writer process may never have a chance to enter its critical section. The system modeled is not a *fair system*, and it has a potential for *starvation*. In this situation, a process may be left waiting indefinitely. This can more easily be observed by changing the workload of the simulation model so that a simulation run would exhibit starvation of several writer processes. Starvation is also possible in scheduling when the scheduling policy is not fair, although operating systems can solve this with a technique called *aging*.

The second strategy for the solution to the readers-writers problem involves giving writer processes a higher priority. Reader processes are allowed to read the shared data resource only when there are no writer processes writing or waiting to write. This approach can easily be implemented in a second simulation model of the readers-writers model using PsimJ2 and Java.

The general goals of the problem are similar to the bounded-buffer problem, which are to synchronize the activities of the processes and to maintain data consistency (and integrity).

6.7 POSIX Threads

POSIX threads, also known as *Pthreads*, are not really object-oriented; they were developed to be used with the C programming language. For C++, we define a wrapper class as defining the basic thread class, then instantiate or inherit the class from a subclass. The Psim3 simulation package, which is used to implement the simulation models discussed in this book, was developed with *Pthreads*.

Pthreads follow the IEEE Portable Operating System Interface (POSIX) standards. Part of this standard covers threads and includes the application programming interface (API) that supports threads.

Every thread has several parameters associated with it. These parameters are the following:

- A thread ID, which identifies uniquely the thread. The thread ID is returned when the thread is created.

- An attribute object, which is used to configure the thread. Normally the default values are used for the attribute object.

- A *start function*, which is called when the thread is created.

- An argument of the start function call. If more than one argument is required in the function call, then the argument should point to a data structure.

6.7.1 Creating POSIX Threads

The prototype of the function to create a thread within a process is as follows:

```
int pthread_create (pthread_t *thread_id,
                    pthread_attr_t *attr,
                    void *(*start_function)(void *),
                    void *arg);
```

A process, or application, may create several threads and for each one invokes the `pthread_create` function.

The following portion of code is an example of creating a thread that calls the `func1` function when it is created.

```
Pthread_t tid;
int error_code;
//
// create a new thread
//
error_code = pthread_create (&tid, NULL, func1, arg1);
```

```
...
void * func1 (void *arg) {
  //
  // code for func1
  //
}
```

In the Psim3 simulation package, member function `pstart()` of class `process` includes the Pthread function `pthread_create` to create a thread. Thus, a new thread is created when the `pstart()` function is called on a process object. A process object is an instance of a user-defined class that inherits class `process`.

6.7.2 Basic Synchronization of Pthreads

6.7.2.1 Wait for Termination

When a thread has to wait for another thread to complete, the first thread has to invoke the `pthread_join(..)`. A call to this function suspends the first thread until the second thread exits or returns. The first thread invokes the `pthread_join(..)` and needs the thread ID of the second thread as one of the arguments in the function call. The following line of code invokes the function using the thread ID, Tid2, of the second thread.

```
error_code = pthread_join(Tid2, NULL);
```

Threads that can be *joined* are also called *non-detached* threads. Threads that cannot be joined are called *detached* threads. By default, threads that are created are joinable. Threads that are to be detached can be created by first changing the attribute in the attribute object of the thread. The following line of code changes this.

```
pthread_attr_setdetachstate(&attr, PTHREAD_CREATE_DETACHED);
```

An existing thread can be detached by invoking the following function.

```
int pthread_detach( pthread_t tid);
```

6.7.2.2 Termination of a Thread

A thread normally terminates when it returns from its *start function*, which is the code body of the thread. Another way a thread terminates is by calling the `pthread_exit()` function. The prototype of this function is:

```
int pthread_exit( void *thes);
```

Parameter `thes` is the thread's exit status. A detached thread should not exit with this parameter different than NULL.

A thread may be terminated by another thread. If a first thread needs to terminate a second thread with a thread ID, `tid2`, then the following line of code in the first thread will terminate the second thread.

```
pthread_cancel(thid2);   // cancel thread thid2
```

6.7.3 Mutual Exclusion

Mutual exclusion is an important approach used for a set of processes, (and/or threads) to share resources in a mutually exclusive manner.

With POSIX, mutual exclusion is used with *mutex variables*, also called *mutexes*. These are normally declared as global static variables of type `pthread_mutex_t`. The usage of these variables is similar to binary semaphores used for mutual exclusion.

In order to initialize a *mutex* variable, its attribute object needs to be initialized. The following lines of code declare and initialize a *mutex* attribute object with its default values.

```
pthread_mutex_t mymtx;          // mutex variable declaration
pthread_mutexattr_t mymtx_attr; // attributes object of a mutex
...
err_val = pthread_mutexattr_init (&mymtx_attr); // initialize attr
```

The default attributes object will allow sharing the *mutex* variable by threads within the same process. If needed, the `process-shared` attribute will have to be set to share the *mutex* variable by all threads in multiple processes. The following line of code sets this attribute.

```
err_val = pthread_mutexattr_setpshared (&mymtx_attr,
            THREAD_PROCESS_SHARED);
```

Once the attributes object of a *mutex* variable is initialized, then the *mutex* variable can be used as a simple mutually exclusive lock in the critical sections of the threads that share a resource.

Recall that before the critical section of a process, the *entry section* executes, and after the critical section, the *exit section* executes.

Function `pthread_mutex_lock()` is used to implement the *entry section* and function `pthread_mutex_unlock()` is used to implement the *exit section*.

The critical section in the *start* function of a thread accesses a shared resource in a mutually exclusive manner. The *mutex* variable, `mymtx` has been declared and initialized. The attributes object, `mymtx_attr` of the *mutex* variable has also been initialized. The threads that accessed a shared resource have been created. The following lines of code implement the *entry section*, the *critical section*, and the *exit section* in a thread.

```
pthread_mutex_lock(mymtx);     // entry section with mutex 'mymtx'
   // critical section
pthread_mutex_unlock(mymtx);   // exit section
```

6.7.4 Semaphores

Semaphores are used to synchronize threads within a process and are similar to *mutex* variables. Semaphores are variables of type `sem_t` and have to be initialized to an appropriate value.

6.7.4.1 Initializing Semaphores

Function `sem_init()` is used to initialize the semaphore to an integer value. The following lines of code declare and initialize a semaphore to the value 4.

```
sem_t mysem;                 // semaphore variable
. . .
sem_init(&mysem, 0, 4);      // initialize semaphore to 4
```

In the call to function `sem_init()`, the first argument is a reference to the semaphore variable, the second argument with value zero indicates that the semaphore is shared among threads within a process, and the third argument is the value to which the semaphore variable is initialized. Thus, the semaphore `mysem` is defined as a counting semaphore.

6.7.4.2 Decrementing and Incrementing Semaphores

Decrementing the value of a semaphore is carried out by function `sem_wait()` and if the semaphore cannot be decremented because its current value is zero, the thread invoking this function is suspended. Incrementing a semaphore is carried out by function `sem_post()`. This function also reactivates any waiting threads that have been suspended. The following lines of code invoke both functions with semaphore `mysem`, which was intialized previously.

```
sem_wait(&mysem);    // decrement semaphore 'mysem'
. . .
sem_post(&mysem);    // increment semaphore 'mysem'
```

With these functions to increment and decrement semaphores, and the use of mutex variables, synchronization problems such as the *bounded buffer* problem and the *readers-writers* problem can be easily solved using threads.

To check if a semaphore can be decremented without the thread, which invokes the function, being suspended, function `sem_trywait()` can be used. The function returns -1 immediately if the semaphore cannot be decremented, without suspending the calling thread.

```
// attempt to decrement semaphore 'mysem'
err_val = sem_trywait(&mysen);
```

6.7.4.3 Destroying Semaphores

After all the threads that use a semaphore have terminated, the semaphore can be destroyed. This is carried out by function sem_destroy(). The following line of code destroys semaphore mysem.

```
err-val = sem_destroy(&mysem);   // destroy semaphore 'mysem'
```

6.8 Monitors

A *monitor* is a mechanism that implements mutual exclusion. It is a synchronization tool that operates on a higher level than a semaphore in the synchronization of processes. Monitors are abstract data types implemented as a class. Therefore, they use the encapsulation principle to integrate data and operations and to protect the private members; they are also normally implemented in object-oriented programming languages.

Only a single process can execute an operation of the monitor at any given time. The monitor object provides mutual exclusion, and its member function execution is treated as a critical section.

An arriving process must wait in the entry queue of the monitor before entering. After entering, a process can be suspended and later reactivated. Several queues are maintained by the monitor to hold waiting processes that have entered the monitor but have been suspended.

In addition to the entry queue, there are one or more condition queues. Each one corresponds to a *condition variable*, which is similar to a semaphore and is defined with two operations: wait and signal. These operations can be described as follows:

- A process that invokes the wait operation on condition variable x, releases mutual exclusion, places itself on the condition queue for x, and suspends itself.

- A process that invokes the signal operation on condition variable x, and reactivates one waiting process from the condition queue of x; the current process eventually releases mutual exclusion and exits the monitor. The reactivated process reevaluates the condition to continue execution.

A process that completes execution inside the monitor releases mutual exclusion and exits. A new process is then allowed to enter the monitor from the entry queue.

6.8.1 Synchronization with Monitors

In a manner similar to the use of semaphores, monitors are used to solve various synchronization problems. The main advantage of using monitors in solving synchronization problems is the higher-level construction.

Brinch Hansen is one of the researchers who initially proposed monitors as another synchronization tool. His approach for the semantics of monitors requires that a process that executes a `signal` operation must exit the monitor immediately. The `signal` statement must be the last one defined in the monitor function. Anthony Hoare, the other researcher who advocated monitors, proposed a slightly different semantics for monitors.

6.8.2 The Producer-Consumer Problem with a Monitor

The following pseudocode defines a monitor for the producer-consumer problem:

```
class Monitor_prodcon {
  private Condition full, empty;    // conditional variables
  private int num = 0;              // number of items in buffer

//
 public void insert (data: Item) {
    if num == N           // is buffer full?
    then
       full.wait();       // suspend producer
    endif;
      [ insert item in an empty slot of buffer ]
    increase num;
    if num == 1
    then
       empty.signal();    // reactivate consumer
 } // end insert
//
 public Item remove() {
    if num == 0           // is buffer empty?
    then
       empty.wait();      // suspend consumer
    [ full slot of buffer ]
    decrement num;
    if num == N -1
    then
       full.signal();     // reactivate producer
 } // end remove
} // end class Monitor_prodcon
```

The monitor, `Monitor_prodcon`, is defined as a class, and it includes as private attributes two condition variables, `full` and `empty`, and an integer variable, `num`, for the count of the number of data items in the buffer.

The description given of the behavior of a monitor corresponds to Hansen's approach; Hoare proposed a slightly different behavior for monitors.

Chapter 6 Synchronization Principles

The monitor class includes two public methods, `insert` and `remove`. The following are high-level definitions in pseudocode of the bodies of the producer and consumer processes:

```
while (true) {
  [ produce data_item ]
  Monitor_prodcon.insert(data_item);
} // end while
while (true) {
  data_item = Monitor_prodcon.remove();
  [ consume data_item ]
}  // end while
```

6.8.3 Monitor Synchronization with Java

The Java programming language does not directly support condition variables, so the wait and notify methods are used. The following Java code implements a monitor solution to the producer-consumer problem. The class `ProdCons` includes several inner classes: `Monitor`, `Producer`, and `Consumer`.

```
public class Procons
  static final int N = 0;
  static Producer prod = new Producer();
  static Consumer cons = new Consumer();
  static Monitor monitor = new Monitor();
  //
  // insert the three classes, Monitor, Producer, and Consumer
  //
  public static void main (String args[])
     // start the two threads
     prod.start();
     cons.start();
   // end main
   // end class Prodcons

static class Monitor
  private int data [] = new int[N]; // buffer with N slots
  private int num = 0;    // number of full slots in buffer
  private int i = 0;
  private int j  0;
//
 public synchronized void insert (int item)
    if (num == N)            // is buffer full?
       try
          wait();
```

6.8 Monitors

```
          catch ( InterruptedException e) ;

    data[j] = item;  // insert data item in buffer
    j = (j+1) % N;   // index for next slot to insert
    num++;
    if (num == 1)
      notify();      // reactivate consumer
  // end insert

//
 public synchronized int remove()
    int item;
    if (num == 0)    // is buffer empty?
      try
        wait();
        catch( InterruptedException e) ;

    item = data[i];  // get data item from buffer
    i = (i+1) % N              // index for next slot to remove
    num--;
    if (num == N-1)
       notify();     // reactivate producer
    return item;
  // end remove
    // end class Monitor

static class Producer extends Thread
  public void run()
    int item;
    while(true)
      item = generateItem();     // produce item
      monitor.insert(item);

   // end run
 // end class Producer

static class Consumer extends Thread
  public void run()
    int item;
    while(true)
       item = monitor.remove();
       useItem(item);    // consume item

   // end run
    // end class Consumer
```

6.8.4 Simulation Models Using Monitors

From the modeling point of view, the monitor is a resource; thus it is a passive object compared to processes, which are active objects. The simulation model of the producer-consumer problem with a monitor has seven classes: (1) *Buffer*, (2) *Condition*, (3) *Consprod*, (4) *Consumer*, (5) *PCmonitor*, (6) *Producer*, and (7) *Semaphore*. The Java implementation of the model is stored in the archive file `consprodm.jar`. The C++ implementation is stored in file `consprodm.cpp`.

The implementation of the producer and consumer processes in the model is relatively simple. All the synchronization work is carried out by the monitor object. The access to the shared buffer is handled directly through the monitor. It also handles the mutual exclusion and the ordering of the events: start to deposit a data item into the buffer and start to withdraw a data item from the buffer.

The producer process takes finite and random time to produce a character item, and then it invokes the *insert* operation of the monitor object, to deposit the data item into the shared buffer. To get a data item from the buffer, the consumer process invokes the *remove* operation and then takes a finite time to consume the character item.

This model also generates two output text files: the trace and the summary statistics. Listing 6.5 includes a partial listing of a simulation run of the simulation model that implements the monitor solution to the consumer-producer problem.

Listing 6.5 Partial trace of the consumer-producer model with a monitor.

```
Project: Consumer/Producer Problem-Monitors
Run at: Sat Sep 17 14:36:59 EDT 2006
Input Parameters:
Simulation period: 1750.0
Consumer mean consume interval: 17.65
Producer mean prod interval: 12.5
Mean interval in monitor: 6.75
Coefficient of variance: 0.13
Start Simulation
Time 0000.000 Producer begins producing item
Time 0000.000 Consumer accessing monitor at:
Time 0003.996 Producer produced item: K
Time 0003.996 Producer to access monitor
Time 0011.162 Producer completed access to monitor
Time 0011.162 Producer begins producing item
Time 0012.657 Producer produced item: e
Time 0012.657 Producer to access monitor
Time 0017.382 Character removed by consumer: K
Time 0023.124 Consumer accessing monitor at:
Time 0024.136 Producer completed access to monitor
```

6.8 Monitors

```
Time 0024.136 Producer begins producing item
Time 0028.198 Producer produced item: n
Time 0028.198 Producer to access monitor
Time 0030.729 Character removed by consumer: e
Time 0037.372 Consumer accessing monitor at:
Time 0037.724 Producer completed access to monitor
Time 0037.724 Producer begins producing item
Time 0043.068 Character removed by consumer: n
Time 0043.857 Consumer accessing monitor at:
Time 0047.797 Producer produced item: n
Time 0047.797 Producer to access monitor
Time 0055.731 Producer completed access to monitor
Time 0055.731 Producer begins producing item
Time 0061.329 Character removed by consumer: n
Time 0064.950 Producer produced item: e
Time 0064.950 Producer to access monitor
. . .
Time 1733.522 Producer to access monitor
Time 1737.088 Character removed by consumer: e
Time 1737.163 Consumer accessing monitor at:
Time 1742.952 Producer completed access to monitor
Time 1742.952 Producer begins producing item
Time 1749.450 Character removed by consumer: n
Time 1754.740 Producer produced item:
Time 1754.740 Producer to access monitor
Time 1763.255 Producer completed access to monitor
Time 1763.255 Producer terminating
Time 1763.617 Consumer terminating
```

The summary statistics are written to the second output file shown in Listing 6.6. It displays only one performance metric: the total wait period for the producer process and for the consumer process. Two other performance metrics can be calculated:

- Throughput, which is the number of times a consumer process accessed the shared buffer through the monitor and the number of times a producer accessed the shared buffer through the monitor.

- Average wait intervals for the consumer and the producer processes.

Listing 6.6 Summary statistics of the consumer-producer model with a monitor.

```
Project: Consumer/Producer Problem-Monitors
Run at: Sat Sep 17 14:36:59 EDT 2006
Input Parameters:
Simulation period: 1750.0
```

```
Consumer mean consume interval: 17.65
Producer mean prod interval: 12.5
Mean interval in monitor: 6.75
Coefficient of variance: 0.13
-------------------------------------------------------------
Results of simulation:
Producer total wait period: 0718.4358
Consumer total wait period: 0659.9947
```

6.9 Interprocess Communication

Interprocess communication (*IPC*) consists of mechanisms that enable processes to exchange data. This data is normally formatted into messages according to some predefined protocol. The transfer of messages among the communicating processes requires synchronization.

The operating system provides several IPC mechanisms and processes needed to invoke system calls. This section discusses asynchronous communication (indirect communication) via mailboxes, and synchronous communication (direct communication) via channels. Two simulation models are presented; the first represents asynchronous communication and the second, synchronous communication.

6.9.1 Asynchronous Communication

Two processes communicate indirectly via a *mailbox* that holds the message temporarily. There is no direct interaction between the sender process and the receiver process. The sender process sends a message to the receiver process through the mailbox.

Because the sender process does not have to wait until the receiver process gets the message from the mailbox, the sending and the receiving operations can occur at different times. Typically, the sending of a message is nonblocking and the receiving of a message is blocking. The sender does not need to wait, and it therefore does not block. The receiver is blocked until the requested message becomes available in the system mailbox.

A mailbox is a shared data structure that implements a queue and that can temporarily store messages. This data structure is an intermediate data storage that helps synchronize the sender and receiver processes. The mailbox storage will normally have capacity for several messages. The operation of placing a message in a mailbox by a sender process and the operation of taking the message from the mailbox by a receiver process can occur at different times.

Figure 6.10 shows a system mailbox in which the sender process sent the message and placed it in a slot of the mailbox; the receiver process will get the message from the mailbox.

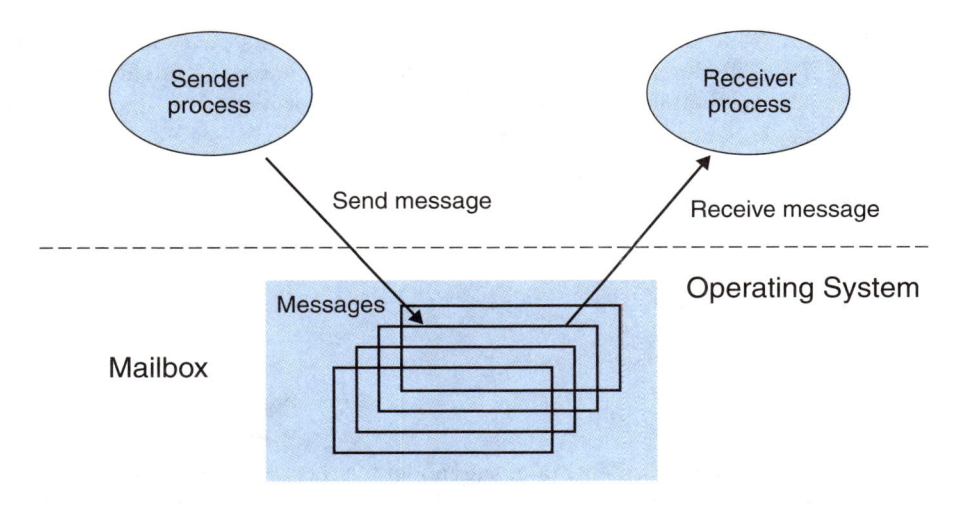

Figure 6.10 Two processes communicating via a mailbox.

The sender and/or receiver processes may have to wait if the mailbox is full or empty. If there is no free mailbox slot left, the sender process may have to wait until a message slot of the mailbox becomes available. Similarly, the receiver process may have to wait if the mailbox slots are empty, or if there is no message for it. A process continues with its independent activities after placing a message in the mailbox or retrieving a message from the mailbox.

Instead of a sender process or a receiver process having to wait, the sender process can poll the mailbox for availability of an empty message slot, or the receiver process can poll the mailbox for a requested message. Thus, the processes will not block (suspend) and can carry out some other activity until they can check the mailbox again.

In asynchronous communication, the processes involved do not directly interact and their activities are independent of each other. The receiver process will normally receive the message at some time after the sender has sent the message. The synchronization needed to access the mailbox is similar to the producer-consumer problem discussed previously.

6.9.2 Simulation Model for Asynchronous Communication

The Java implementation of the simulation model of the asynchronous communication consists of six classes: (1) *Acomm*, (2) *Mailbox*, (3) *Message*, (4) *Receiver*, (5) *Semaphore*, and (6) *Sender*. This model is stored in the archive file `acomm.jar`. The C++ implementation of the model also defines these classes and is stored in file `acomm.cpp`.

Class *Mailbox* is defined as an array of messages and an integer attribute that denotes the number of messages in the mailbox. An object of this class has the capacity to hold several messages, the number of which is defined in the symbolic constant

NUM_MESS. This class includes several methods that insert a message in the mailbox, check if the mailbox is full, return the number of messages in the mailbox, remove a message from the mailbox, and search a message for a specified receiver process.

Class *Message* is defined with the following attributes:

- Message sequence number (ID of the message)
- Time stamp
- Sender process
- Receiver process
- Data in the message

This model is an extension of the model for the producer-consumer problem. There are two counting semaphores and one binary semaphore to synchronize the use of the mailbox by the various processes.

The sender and receiver processes need the semaphores in order to check the number of available message slots in the mailbox and to have exclusive access to the mailbox when placing or retrieving a message. This model uses a constant of 1 time unit as the period that a process spends accessing the mailbox. This model supports several sender processes and receiver processes; this number is defined by the symbolic constant NUM_PROC.

This model also generates two output text files: the trace file and the summary statistics file. Listing 6.7 includes a partial output of the trace of a simulation run for the asynchronous communication model discussed previously. The trace shows all the different events involved in sending and receiving messages to and from the mailbox.

Listing 6.7 Trace of a simulation run for an asynchronous communication model.

```
Project: Asynchronous communication
Run at: Sat Sep 17 22:38:39 EDT 2006
Input Parameters:
Simulation period: 2560.0
Receiver mean consume interval: 43.0
Sender mean produce interval: 13.0
Number of rec/sender processes: 5
Max number of messages in mailbox: 12
Start Simulation
Time 0000.000 Receiver0 attempting comm
Time 0000.000 Receiver1 attempting comm
Time 0000.000 Receiver2 attempting comm
Time 0000.000 Receiver3 attempting comm
Time 0000.000 Receiver4 attempting comm
Time 0004.071 Sender1 attempting to access mailbox
```

```
Time 0004.072 Sender2 attempting to access mailbox
Time 0004.076 Sender0 attempting to access mailbox
Time 0004.080 Sender3 attempting to access mailbox
Time 0004.082 Sender4 attempting to access mailbox
Time 0005.821 Sender1 sent message # 1
Time 0007.170 Sender1 attempting to access mailbox
Time 0007.571 Sender2 sent message # 2
Time 0009.321 Sender0 sent message # 0
Time 0011.071 Sender3 sent message # 3
Time 0012.173 Sender3 attempting to access mailbox
Time 0012.821 Sender4 sent message # 4
Time 0014.971 No message for Receiver0
Time 0014.971 Receiver0 attempting comm
Time 0016.721 Sender1 sent message # 5
Time 0018.871 Receiver1 received message 5
Time 0018.871 Information Systems from sender: Sender1
Time 0020.909 Sender0 attempting to access mailbox
Time 0021.021 No message for Receiver2
Time 0021.021 Receiver2 attempting comm
Time 0023.171 No message for Receiver3
Time 0023.171 Receiver3 attempting comm
Time 0024.921 Sender3 sent message # 8
Time 0025.815 Sender1 attempting to access mailbox
Time 0026.024 Sender3 attempting to access mailbox
Time 0027.071 No message for Receiver4
Time 0027.071 Receiver4 attempting comm
Time 0029.221 No message for Receiver0
. . .
Time 1290.018 Sender4 terminating
Time 1292.396 Sender2 attempting to access mailbox
Time 1294.146 Sender2 sent message # 321
Time 1294.146 Sender2 terminating
Time 1294.508 Receiver0 terminating
Time 1295.216 Receiver2 terminating
Time 1302.390 Sender1 attempting to access mailbox
Time 1304.140 Sender1 sent message # 319
Time 1304.140 Sender1 terminating
Time 1320.503 Sender3 attempting to access mailbox
Time 1322.253 Sender3 sent message # 322
Time 1322.253 Sender3 terminating
```

Listing 6.8 shows the summary statistics of the asynchronous communication model. The only performance measure shown is the wait period for each of the processes that are involved in the asynchronous communication. These are the wait intervals that every process spends while attempting communication.

Listing 6.8 Summary statistics of the asynchronous communication model.

```
Project: Asynchronous communication
Run at: Sat Sep 17 22:38:39 EDT 2006
Input Parameters:
Simulation period: 2560.0
Receiver mean consume interval: 43.0
Sender mean produce interval: 13.0
Number of rec/sender processes: 5
Max number of messages in mailbox: 12
---------------------------------------------------------------
Results of simulation:
Sender0 total wait period: 0409.3330
Receiver0 total wait period: 0771.9168
Sender1 total wait period: 0405.6222
Receiver1 total wait period: 0918.9961
Sender2 total wait period: 0432.8186
Receiver2 total wait period: 0781.8411
Sender3 total wait period: 0476.7335
Receiver3 total wait period: 0797.1071
Sender4 total wait period: 0399.2811
Receiver4 total wait period: 0694.3857
Average sender wait: 0424.7577
Average receiver wait: 0792.8494
```

6.9.3 Synchronous Communication

Synchronous communication implies that the communication of a message between two processes involves a stronger synchronization than with asynchronous communication. The sender process or the receiver process can be blocked (suspended) until the communication occurs. Synchronous communication is also called direct communication because the sender process and the receiver process have a *joint activity* and both processes need to participate simultaneously during the *period of cooperation*. If a sender process attempts to send a message, it gets suspended if the receiver process is not ready to receive the message. In a similar manner, if a receiver process attempts to receive a message and the sender process does not cooperate at the same time, the receiver process gets suspended.

Instead of a mailbox, as required in indirect communication, a *channel*—a means of communication between the sender process and the receiver process—is established between two processes. Figure 6.11 shows the structure needed for direct communication between a sender process and a receiver process. The synchronization occurs when executing a *send* operation by the sender process simultaneously with a *receive* operation by the receiver process. The channel is used as a carrier of the message from the

Figure 6.11 Synchronous communication between two processes.

sender process to the receiver process. After the period of communication, the processes continue with their own independent activities.

In the simple case of synchronous communication, one sender process communicates with only one receiver process. This approach to communication is also known as a *rendezvous*. The communication may also be established so that a sender process can communicate with several receiver processes simultaneously.

6.9.4 Simulation Model for Synchronous Communication

A channel is the link that is established between a sender process and a receiver process. It is the software mechanism that enables the pair of processes to carry out a joint activity during a period of communication.

The Java implementation of the simulation model of the synchronous communication problem consists of five classes: (1) *Comchan*, (2) *Message*, (3) *Receiver*, (4) *Scomm*, and (5) *Sender*. The model is stored in the archive file `scomm.jar`. The C++ implementation of the model is stored in file `scomm.cpp`. The implementation of this simulation model is very different from the previous model (asynchronous communication) in that neither semaphores nor mailboxes are used.

Class *Comchan* defines a communication channel and it includes the main software mechanism used in the model to implement the joint cooperation of processes. It has an attribute of class *Waitq*, a library class of the PsimJ2 simulation package. An object of class *Comchan* represents a channel in the communication between a sender process and a receiver process.

The communication mechanism implemented in class *Waitq* involves one process (*the master*) as the active participant in the communication: It is the dominant process. The other process (*the slave*) behaves as a passive participant: It carries out the joint activity in a suspended state. During this period of communication, the sender process becomes subordinated (as a slave) to the receiver process. After the period of communication, the two processes continue their own independent activities.

If the sender process does not find the receiver process ready to communicate, the object of class *Waitq* suspends the sender process. If a receiver process does not find the sender process ready, the receiver process is suspended. For this, class *Waitq* defines two different queues to store suspended processes that are waiting: the master and the slave queues. One queue stores suspended master processes; the other queue stores suspended slave processes.

Chapter 6 Synchronization Principles

In the simulation model, the number of sender processes and the number of receiver processes is defined by constant NUM_PROC. The same number of channels is defined, one for each pair of processes. Every channel is represented by an object of class *Waitq*.

The trace of a simulation run of this model is shown in Listing 6.9 This is a partial listing with only the relevant events in the trace and the output computed. Listing 6.10 includes the summary statistics of the simulation run. The only performance measure shown is the total wait period for all the processes involved.

Listing 6.9 Trace of the model with synchronous communication.

```
Project: Synchronous communication with channels
Run at: Sat Sep 17 23:18:57 EDT 2006
Input Parameters:
Simulation period: 2560.0
Receiver mean consume interval: 43.0
Sender mean produce interval: 13.0
Number of rec/sender processes: 5
Start Simulation
Time 0000.000 Msg assembled: 0 Computer Science sender Sender0 rec Receiver0
Time 0000.000 Receiver0 attempting comm via Channel0
Time 0000.000 Msg assembled: 1 Information Systems sender Sender1 rec Receiver1
Time 0000.000 Receiver1 attempting comm via Channel1
Time 0000.000 Msg assembled: 2 Kennesaw State University sender Sender2 rec Receiver2
Time 0000.000 Receiver2 attempting comm via Channel2
Time 0000.000 Msg assembled: 3 1000 Chastain Road sender Sender3 rec Receiver3
Time 0000.000 Receiver3 attempting comm via Channel3
Time 0000.000 Msg assembled: 4 Kennesaw, GA sender Sender4 rec Receiver4
Time 0000.000 Receiver4 attempting comm via Channel4
Time 0004.071 Sender1 attempting to communicate via chan Channel1
Time 0004.072 Sender2 attempting to communicate via chan Channel2
Time 0004.076 Sender0 attempting to communicate via chan Channel0
Time 0004.080 Sender3 attempting to communicate via chan Channel3
Time 0004.082 Sender4 attempting to communicate via chan Channel4
Time 0006.821 Receiver1 received message 1 via channel Channel1
Time 0006.821 Information Systems from sender: Sender1
Time 0006.821 Sender1 sent message # 1
Time 0006.821 Msg assembled: 5 Kennesaw State University sender Sender1 rec Receiver1
Time 0006.822 Receiver2 received message 2 via channel Channel2
Time 0006.822 Kennesaw State University from sender: Sender2
Time 0006.822 Sender2 sent message # 2
Time 0006.822 Msg assembled: 6 1000 Chastain Road sender Sender2 rec Receiver2
Time 0006.826 Receiver0 received message 0 via channel Channel0
Time 0006.826 Computer Science from sender: Sender0
Time 0006.826 Sender0 sent message # 0
Time 0006.826 Msg assembled: 7 Information Systems sender Sender0 rec Receiver0
```

6.9 Interprocess Communication

```
Time 0006.830 Receiver3 received message 3 via channel Channel3
Time 0006.830 1000 Chastain Road from sender: Sender3
Time 0006.830 Sender3 sent message # 3
Time 0006.830 Msg assembled: 8 Kennesaw, GA sender Sender3 rec Receiver3
Time 0006.832 Receiver4 received message 4 via channel Channel4
Time 0006.832 Kennesaw, GA from sender: Sender4
Time 0006.832 Sender4 sent message # 4
Time 0006.832 Msg assembled: 9 USA sender Sender4 rec Receiver4
Time 0007.933 Sender3 attempting to communicate via chan Channel3
Time 0008.170 Sender1 attempting to communicate via chan Channel1
Time 0018.414 Sender0 attempting to communicate via chan Channel0
Time 0020.312 Receiver0 attempting comm via Channel0
Time 0020.312 Receiver1 attempting comm via Channel1
Time 0020.339 Receiver4 attempting comm via Channel4
Time 0020.340 Receiver2 attempting comm via Channel2
Time 0020.353 Receiver3 attempting comm via Channel3
Time 0023.062 Receiver0 received message 7 via channel Channel0
Time 0023.062 Information Systems from sender: Sender0
Time 0023.062 Sender0 sent message # 7
Time 0023.062 Msg assembled: 10 Kennesaw State University
              sender Sender0 rec Receiver0
Time 0023.062 Receiver1 received message 5 via channel Channel1
Time 0023.062 Kennesaw State University from sender: Sender1
. . .
Time 1258.544 USA from sender: Sender4
Time 1258.544 Sender4 sent message # 135
Time 1258.544 Msg assembled: 141 Computer Science sender Sender4 rec Receiver4
Time 1259.468 Sender3 attempting to communicate via chan Channel3
Time 1260.415 Sender1 attempting to communicate via chan Channel1
Time 1271.724 Sender0 attempting to communicate via chan Channel0
Time 1274.116 Sender4 attempting to communicate via chan Channel4
Time 1276.563 Receiver4 attempting comm via Channel4
Time 1279.313 Receiver4 received message 141 via channel Channel4
Time 1279.313 Computer Science from sender: Sender4
Time 1279.313 Sender4 sent message # 141
Time 1279.313 Msg assembled: 142 Information Systems sender Sender4 rec Receiver4
Time 1300.370 Receiver3 terminating
Time 1301.789 Receiver2 terminating
Time 1306.300 Sender4 attempting to communicate via chan Channel4
Time 1328.394 Receiver1 terminating
Time 1337.757 Receiver4 terminating
Time 1418.777 Receiver0 terminating
```

Chapter 6 Synchronization Principles

Listing 6.10 Summary statistics of a model with synchronous communication.

```
Project: Synchronous communication with channels
Run at: Sat Sep 17 23:18:57 EDT 2006
Input Parameters:
Simulation period: 2560.0
Receiver mean consume interval: 43.0
Sender mean produce interval: 13.0
Number of rec/sender processes: 5
-------------------------------------------------------------
Results of simulation:
Sender0 total wait period: 0843.0414
Receiver0 total wait period: 0151.7252
Sender1 total wait period: 0874.7892
Receiver1 total wait period: 0160.0617
Sender2 total wait period: 0915.6380
Receiver2 total wait period: 0149.7606
Sender3 total wait period: 0915.8063
Receiver3 total wait period: 0166.6394
Sender4 total wait period: 0951.4321
Receiver4 total wait period: 0128.3877
Average sender wait: 0900.1414
Average receiver wait: 0151.3149
```

6.10 Atomic Transactions

It will often be the case that multiple related data values need to be modified in a critical section. In real-world systems, those data values will often be in persistent storage (on a disk). Listing 6.11 shows a simple banking example. The modification of these values inside a critical section is called an *atomic transaction*.

Listing 6.11 Atomic transaction example.

```
Move $100.00 from Bank Account #1 to Bank Account #2
Lock accounts
   Decrement Account #1 balance
   Increment Account #2 balance
Unlock Accounts
```

Suppose that a system failure (e.g., a power outage) occurs in the middle of the critical section (Listing 6.12). Thus, when the system is restarted, there is a situation in which some but not all of the values have been modified. This violates the requirements for mutual exclusion of critical sections. At this point in time, the data that is modified by the critical section is in an indeterminate state, and it is unsafe to resume normal execution. What can we do about this problem?

Listing 6.12 System failure in an atomic transaction.

```
Move $100 from Bank Account #1 to Bank Account #2
Lock accounts
  Decrement Account #1 balance
System Failure
  Increment Account #2 balance
Unlock Accounts
```

We must include a *failure recovery*—a change in the transaction to ensure that the mutual exclusion requirements are met. There are two choices for this:

- Resume the interrupted transaction and run it to completion.
- Undo the incomplete parts of transactions already started.

On general-purpose systems, main memory contents are lost during the system failure, and we have no way to resume the interrupted transaction at precisely where it was at the time of the failure. Some embedded systems can do this, but it requires specialized hardware support.

Thus, general-purpose systems must *undo* the incomplete transaction to bring the system back to a safe state. There are two approaches to carry this out:

- Checkpoint-restart
- Transaction logging

With checkpoint-restart, the following procedure is followed:

- Periodically, record a checkpoint—the state of the system (with all completed transactions).
- After a system failure, restore the saved system status from the last checkpoint.

This procedure will restore the system to a safe state. Unfortunately, all transactions since the last checkpoint are lost. Thus, if these checkpoints are not performed frequently, there is a risk of losing many transactions.

With *transaction logging* (aka write-ahead logging), there are two steps to follow:

- Prior to each step of an Atomic Transaction, write the details of that step to a separate *Transaction Log* file.
- After a system failure, use the *Transaction Log* file to undo the steps of any incomplete transactions.

Listing 6.13 shows the transaction log entries for the previous banking example. To recover from a failure, the system will examine the transaction log and undo transactions that do not have an `End Transaction` marker. The information recorded for each step has sufficient detail to allow that step to be undone.

Listing 6.13 Transaction log example.

```
Begin Transaction
Decrement Account #1 by $100, giving balance xxx
Increment Account #2 by $100, giving balance yyy
End Transaction
```

Transaction logs are used by application programs and by the operating system. These two cases can be described as follows:

> A database engine will keep a transaction log of the modifications to the database. When you tell the database engine to do a `Commit`, what that is actually doing is writing an `End Transaction` record to the transaction log.

In Chapter 8 (File Management), we shall see how the operating system will use a transaction log to ensure the integrity of data structures on disk.

6.11 Summary

Synchronization is normally necessary when processes and threads execute concurrently. The main purpose of synchronization is the sharing of resources through the use of mutual exclusion. The other purpose is the coordination of the process interactions and thread.

This chapter presented the basic concepts of synchronization, and several case studies using simulation models have been discussed. Semaphores and monitors are the most commonly used synchronization tools used to solve problems requiring synchronization. Most operating systems provide semaphores. The producer-consumer problem (also known as the bounded-buffer problem), and the readers-writers problem are two classical case studies that describe and test synchronization mechanisms. These two problems are illustrated with simulation models.

Interprocess communication is a type of interaction among processes for message passing. The first general type of interprocess communication is asynchronous communication, in which processes do not directly interact because the message sending and receiving do not occur at the same time. Mailboxes are used as intermediate storage of messages. The mailboxes are maintained by the operating system. The basic synchronization technique is an extension of the one used to solve the producer-consumer problem. Thus, semaphores are used to synchronize access to a mailbox.

The second general type of interprocess communication is synchronous communication, in which processes directly interact during a period of cooperation. Channels are the communication media to link two (or more) processes in order to transfer messages from the sender process to the receiver process. When one process needs to communicate and the other process is not available, then the communication is not possible at that time instant and the process is suspended. When the other process becomes available to communicate, the first process is reactivated and the communication proceeds.

Key Terms

asynchronous communication	fair system	rendezvous
atomic transaction	interprocess communication	semaphore
binary semaphore	Java thread	shared resources
bounded-buffer problem	joint activity	signal
buffer slots	mailbox	slave
channel	master	starvation
condition variable	message	synchronized method
coordination	monitor	synchronous communication
counting semaphore	mutual exclusion	transaction logging
critical section	period of cooperation	checkpoint
entry section	producer-consumer problem	wait
event ordering	race condition	wait/notify mechanism
exit section	readers-writers problem	
failure recovery		

Exercises and Questions

1. The simulation model of the producer-consumer uses only one producer process and one consumer process. Is this correct for multiple producers and consumers? Explain. Modify the simulation model for multiple producers and consumers.

2. In the simulation model of the producer-consumer, would the `full` and `empty` semaphores be necessary if the buffer had a single slot? Explain. Implement the changes in the simulation model.

3. Expand the simulation model of the producer-consumer; include the counts of the number of insertions by the producer process and the number of removals by the consumer process. Carry out two or more simulation runs. Are the values of these counts the throughput for this model? Discuss and explain.

Chapter 6 Synchronization Principles

4. The simulation model presented for the readers-writers problem gives implicit priority to readers. Change the workload as necessary and run the model. What percentage of the writer processes starve (or do not complete execution)? Is this a good solution? Is it a fair synchronization solution?

5. Implement a simulation model that uses the second strategy for the readers-writers problem. For this, modify the model given for the first strategy and assign a higher priority to the writer processes. Writer processes should invoke the PsimJ2 `set_prio` method. Note that the highest priority is 0, so reader processes should be given a higher integer value for their lower priority.

6. Expand the simulation model of the producer-consumer problem that implements the monitor solution. The model should use multiple producer and consumer processes. Run the simulation model. Compare with the corresponding model that implements the semaphore solution.

7. The two simulation models given for the producer-consumer problem implement a semaphore solution and a monitor solution. Modify the simulation models so that they use the same workload and run both models again. Compare the performance measures.

8. Enhance the simulation models given for interprocess communication. Include additional performance measures. Discuss the relevance of the new performance measures. Run the simulation models and discuss the results.

9. Modify the simulation model of asynchronous communication. Increase the number of sender and receiver processes. What performance values do you observe? Where is the bottleneck of the system? What are the main limitations of this model? Discuss.

10. With synchronous communication, a receiver or sender process can check if the other process is waiting to communicate by polling the communication channel. A process can poll a channel and decide to carry out other activities when there is no communication possible. Modify the simulation model by including the `poll` method in class *Comchan* that defines communication channels. Use the `length` method in the PsimJ2 class *Waitq*. This method returns the number of slave processes that are waiting in the slave queue. The other method that can be used is `lengthm` that returns the number of master processes waiting in the master queue. After implementing the poll operation, carry out simulation runs. Discuss how the performance changes. What are the limitations of this new model?

11. In the simulation model of synchronous communication, assume that the sender process needs to send messages to several receiver processes. Enhance the simulation model for this. It would be more convenient to make the sender process be the master. A new queue should be defined in the sender process to place the receiver processes during the period of cooperation. Implement this new model and run the simulation.

Chapter 7
Deadlocks

7.1 Introduction

Processes that are executing concurrently in a multiprogramming environment may often reach a state of starvation or deadlock. Deadlock may occur when the operating system is attempting to allocate resources to a set of processes requesting these resources.

The basic principles of deadlock and the most common approaches used to deal with it—deadlock prevention, deadlock avoidance, and deadlock detection and recovery—are discussed in this chapter. The five dining philosophers—a classical problem used to explain synchronization and deadlock principles—illustrates why and how deadlock occurs as well as deadlock solutions. Several different simulation models of the dining philosophers problem are presented to demonstrate deadlock and solutions for preventing it.

7.2 Basic Principles of Deadlock

Deadlock is the state of indefinite waiting that processes may reach when competing for system resources or when attempting to communicate. When a process requests a resource to the operating system, it normally waits for the resource to become available. A process acquires a resource when the operating system allocates the resource to the process. After acquiring a resource, the process *holds* the resource.

The resources of concern are those that will normally not be shared, such as a printer unit, a magnetic tape unit, and a CD unit. These kinds of resources can only be acquired in a mutually exclusive manner.

During its normal execution, a process usually needs access to one or more resources or instances of a resource type. The following sequence of steps describes how a process acquires and uses resources:

1. Request one or more resource instances.

2. Acquire the resource instances if they are available. The operating system allocates an available resource when it is requested by a process. If the resource instances are not available, the process has to wait until the resource instances become available.

3. Use the resource instance for a finite time interval.

4. Release the resource instances. The operating system deallocates the resource instances and makes them available for other requesting processes.

Suppose there are two processes, $P1$ and $P2$, and two resource types, $R1$ and $R2$. The processes are attempting to complete the following sequence of steps in their executions:

1. Process $P1$ requests resource $R1$.

2. Process $P2$ requests resource $R2$.

3. Process $P1$ acquires resource $R1$.

4. Process $P2$ acquires resource $R2$.

5. Process $P1$ requests resource $R2$.

6. Process $P1$ is suspended because resource $R2$ is not available.

7. Process $P2$ requests resource $R1$.

8. Process $P2$ is suspended because resource $R1$ is not available.

9. The executions of both processes have been suspended.

The previous discussion is a simple example of deadlock because there are two processes each holding a resource but requesting a second resource that the other process holds. In this state, both processes are *blocked indefinitely*, waiting for each other to release a resource.

If the operating system does not avoid, prevent, or detect deadlock and recover, the deadlocked processes will be blocked forever and the resources that they hold will not be available for other processes.

7.2.1 Resource Allocation Graph

The *resource allocation graph* is a directed graph that is very useful in showing the state of a system. The two types of nodes that are included in the graph represent a set of processes, $P = \{P1, P2, P3, \cdots, Pn\}$, and a set of resource types, $R = \{R1, R2, R3, \cdots, Rm\}$. In the graph, a process is drawn as an oval or ellipse, and the resources are shown as rectangular boxes. The graph is an abstract description of the state of the system with respect to processes and resources.

There are two types of edges drawn as arrows. An edge from a process to a *resource type* indicates that the process is requesting one instance of the resource type. An edge from a resource type to a process indicates that one instance of the resource type has been allocated to the process. With these elements, the graph shows the processes that are either requesting resources and/or have acquired resources. The graph also shows the resources available and the ones that have been allocated.

Figure 7.1 shows a resource allocation graph with the two processes $P1$ and $P2$ in a deadlock state. The two resource types involved, $R1$ and $R2$, are shown with one instance each. The resource allocation graph is a standard type of diagram used to represent deadlock or the potential for deadlock. The graph shows that process $P1$ has acquired (holds) an instance of resource $R1$ and is requesting an instance of resource $R2$. Process $P2$ has acquired (holds) an instance of resource $R2$ and is requesting an instance of resource $R1$. Each process is waiting for the other to release the resource it needs, events that will never occur.

A more complex example would include a larger number of processes, resource types, and instances of each resource type. Figure 7.1 shows only one instance of each resource type.

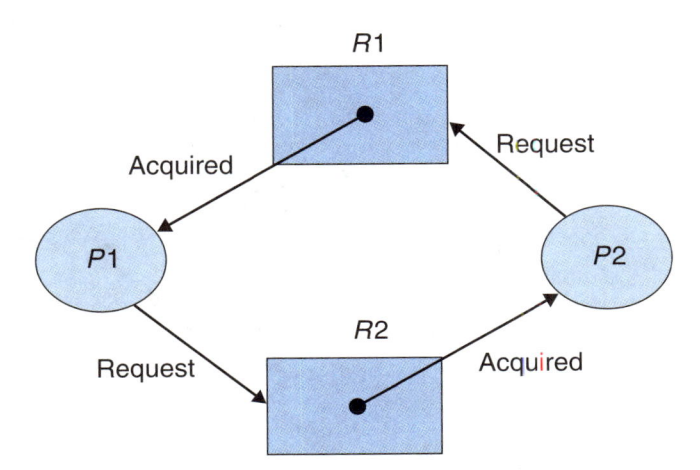

Figure 7.1 A resource allocation graph showing the deadlock of two processes.

7.2.2 Conditions for the Existence of Deadlock

Deadlock is possible if the following four conditions are present simultaneously:

1. *Mutual exclusion*: Only one process can access a resource at a time and the process has exclusive use of the resource.

2. *Hold and wait*: A process has acquired one or more resources (already holds these resources) and is requesting other resources.

3. *Circular wait*: A condition that is represented by a closed path (cycle) of resource allocations and requests. For example, process $P1$ holds resource $R1$ and is requesting resource $R2$; process $P2$ holds resource $R2$ and is requesting resource $R3$; process $P3$ holds resource $R3$ and is requesting resource $R1$ (held by $P1$). This situation can include more than three processes and resource types.

4. *No preemption*: A process cannot be interrupted and forced to release resources.

These conditions are necessary but not sufficient for deadlock to occur. This means that even if the four conditions are present, deadlock may not actually occur. The presence of the four conditions implies that there is potential for deadlock.

The examples that follow illustrate several system states represented by resource-allocation graphs. These are used to analyze the existence of the conditions for deadlock.

There are three processes ($P1$, $P2$, and $P3$) and three resource types ($R1$, $R2$, and $R3$). As shown in Figure 7.2, process $P1$ has acquired an instance of resource type $R1$; so $P1$ holds a unit of resource $R1$. Process $P2$ has acquired an instance of resource type $R2$. Process $P3$ has acquired an instance of resource type $R3$. Process $P1$ is requesting (and waiting for) an instance of resource type $R2$. Process $P2$ is requesting an instance of resource type $R3$.

In the state shown, the system is not in deadlock. Process $P3$ is not in a *hold and wait* condition, although $P1$ and $P2$ are. The processes are not in a *circular wait* condition.

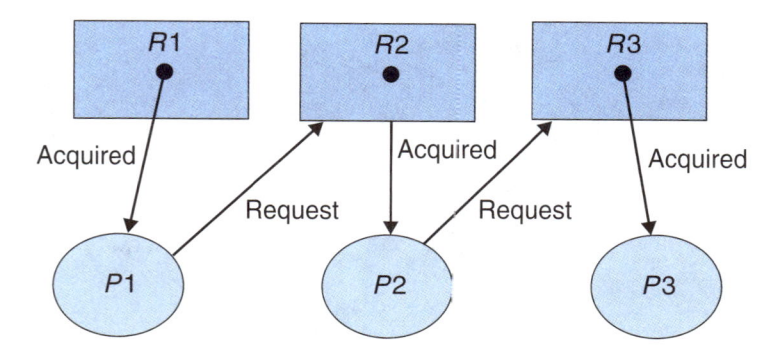

Figure 7.2 Resource allocation graph with three processes.

7.2 Basic Principles of Deadlock

Because there are not sufficient resources for the three processes to proceed concurrently in the system state described, we must find the order of how processes can execute. Process $P3$ is not requesting any resources; consequently, $P3$ can proceed immediately. The following sequence of events describes how processes $P1$, $P2$, and $P3$ can execute:

1. Process $P3$ starts executing using resource $R3$.
2. After a finite interval, process $P3$ releases resource $R3$.
3. Process $P2$ acquires resource $R3$.
4. Process $P2$ starts executing using resources $R2$ and $R3$.
5. After a finite interval, process $P2$ releases resources $R2$ and $R3$.
6. Process $P1$ acquires resource $R2$.
7. Process $P1$ starts executing using resources $R1$ and $R2$.
8. After a finite interval, process $P1$ releases resources $R1$ and $R2$.

Figure 7.3 shows an example of a system state that is slightly different than the one shown in the previous figure. The main differences are that process $P3$ is requesting resource $R1$ and there are two instances of resource $R1$. In this example, process $P3$ can start without waiting because there is an instance of resource $R1$ available that it can immediately acquire. There is no deadlock in the system and the sequence of events is very similar to the one discussed previously.

Figure 7.4 illustrates the presence of a cycle in a resource allocation graph with three processes. As in the previous example, process $P3$ requests an instance of resource type $R1$ and assumes one instance is immediately allocated to $P3$, since the system has two instances of resource $R1$. Process $P2$ is also requesting an instance of resource $R1$, and

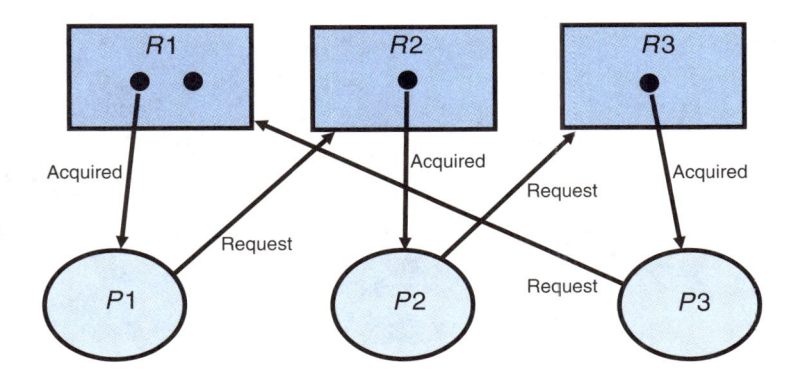

Figure 7.3 Another system state with three processes.

180 Chapter 7 Deadlocks

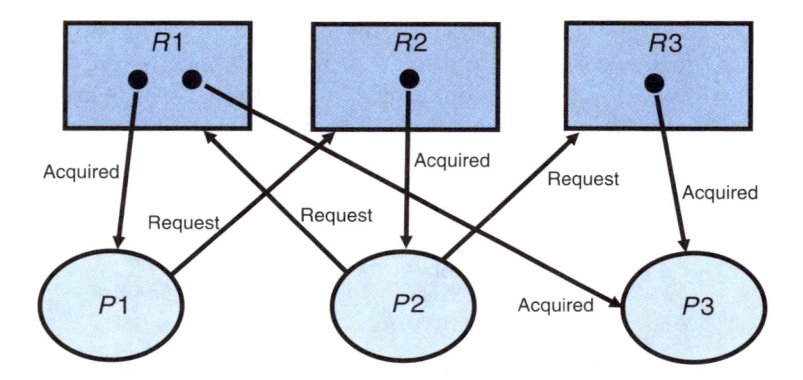

Figure 7.4 A cycle in a graph with three processes.

$P2$ must wait for the availability of resource $R1$. The following cycle can be identified in the graph: $P1 \rightarrow R2 \rightarrow P2 \rightarrow R1 \rightarrow P1$. There is no deadlock in this example because process $P3$ can proceed and eventually release resources $R1$ and $R3$. Process $P2$ can then acquire resource $R3$, for which it was waiting.

In the system state shown in Figure 7.5, there is deadlock because the three processes are blocked indefinitely, waiting for each other to release a resource. The four conditions for deadlock are true. Processes $P1$, $P2$, and $P3$ are in hold and wait because each is holding a resource and waiting for another resource. The main difference with

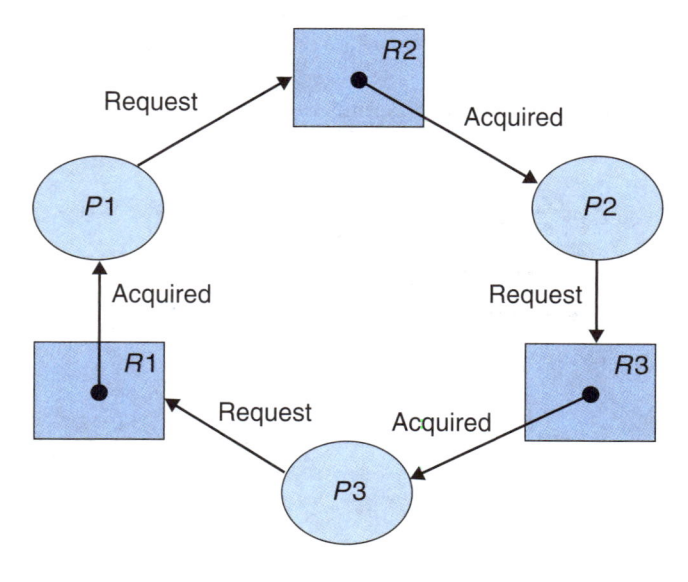

Figure 7.5 Resource allocation graph with a cycle.

the previous example is that there is only one instance of resource type $R1$, which means that process $P3$ must wait for resource $R1$.

In Figure 7.5, the circular wait condition is true for the three processes because there is a cycle in the graph following the arrows that represent resource allocations and resource requests, and there is a single instance of each resource type.

Deadlock can be considered worse than starvation: There is a collection of processes in indefinite waiting, and these processes are holding system resources.

7.3 The Dining Philosophers

The *dining philosophers* is an example of a classical synchronization problem and includes more detailed allocation and deallocation of resources for a set of five processes. Five philosophers spend their lives thinking and eating. When a philosopher is hungry, he or she sits at a round table that has five plates and five forks (or chopsticks), with a fork placed between each pair of plates. In the center of the table, there is a big bowl of spaghetti that represents an endless supply of food. Figure 7.6 shows the layout of the resources and the five philosophers at the table. The philosophers are represented by the position each takes at the table, labeled as $P0$, $P1$, $P2$, $P3$, and $P4$. The forks are represented by lines on both sides of every plate, $f0$, $f1$, $f2$, $f3$, and $f4$.

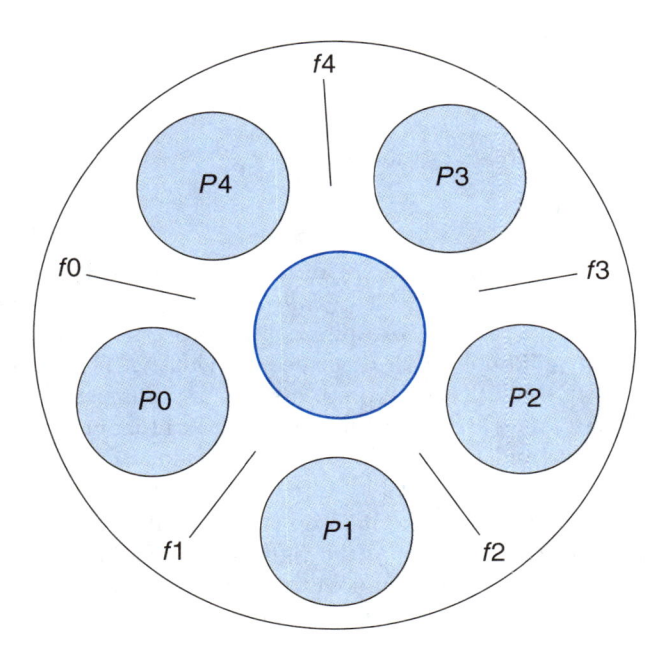

Figure 7.6 The five dining philosophers.

There are two basic activities carried out by every philosopher: thinking and eating. When a philosopher wants to eat, he (or she) attempts to pick up the two forks that are on either side of him (or her) and starts to eat. After eating, the philosopher puts down (releases) the two forks and returns to thinking. The resources that are relevant are the forks, which are necessary for eating and are scarce because there are only five units of that resource. The other resources are not relevant (plates, table, chairs, center bowl of food, etc.) since there is a sufficient number of these for the five philosophers.

The dining philosophers is an example of a problem in which deadlock can easily occur. When all philosophers are hungry, they will sit down at the same time. At this point in time, every philosopher will pick up the fork on the left side, then reach out for the fork on the right, which is not available. The four conditions for deadlock are now met and deadlock occurs.

The purpose of the problem described is to synchronize the activities of the philosophers so that each one can acquire and use two forks to start eating.

7.3.1 Modeling Deadlock

This section describes a simulation model that describes deadlock in the five philosophers problem. Each philosopher intends to carry out repeatedly the following sequence of steps:

1. Acquires his (or her) left fork.

2. Attempts to acquire the right fork.

3. Starts eating (if possible).

4. After eating, releases the forks.

5. Starts thinking.

The simulation model consists of three user-defined classes: *Philosopher*, *Philos1*, and *SimInputs*. The second class, *Philos1*, is the main class and defines the resources in the model and starts the five philosopher processes. The first class implements the behavior of a philosopher, as described previously. The third class, *SimInputs*, implements the GUI with the appropriate input parameter values for each simulation. The three classes are stored in the Java files: `Philosopher.java`, `Philos1.java`, and `SimInputs.java` and are stored in the archive file `philos1.jar`. The C++ implementation of this simulation model is stored in file `philos1.cpp`.

In the simulation model, a philosopher object attempts to acquire the left fork, with index *indexLeft*, then to acquire the right fork, with index *indexRight*. Each object of class *Philosopher* generates a random time interval for the duration of its eating activity, and another random time interval for the duration of its thinking activity. As mentioned before, a philosopher first eats, then thinks, and continues this cycle endlessly.

A resource type is declared as an object of the *PsimJ2* class *Res*. Each *Res* object is initialized with a number of resource items or units of that resource type. Each object of class *Res* has a queue for placing waiting processes. When a process requests a number of resource items from an object of the *Res* class and the number of resource items is not available, the process is automatically suspended and placed in the object's queue. When a process releases a number of resource items, the object of the *Res* class automatically reactivates the process waiting at the head of the queue.

The workload parameters for this model are the mean time to eat and the mean time to think. The other input parameters are the simulation period and the close activity time, which is the time that the philosophers will stop their normal activities and terminate. Figure 7.7 shows the GUI of the simulation model that represents deadlock in the dining philosophers problem.

Listing 7.1 shows a partial output of the trace of a simulation run of the model with the five philosophers problem with deadlock. Note that the simulation run results in deadlock. After starting, each one of the five philosopher objects acquires his or her left fork but cannot acquire the right fork. Every philosopher object holds his or her left fork and is waiting for the right neighbor to release his or her fork, an event that will never occur.

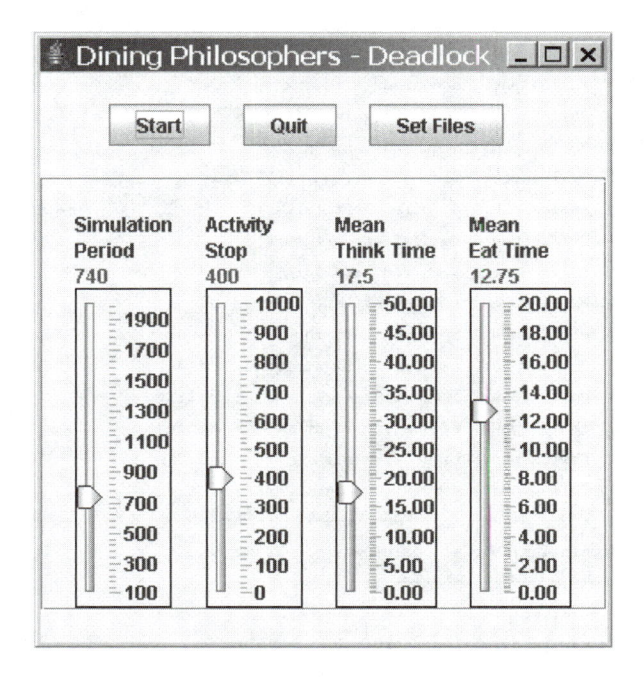

Figure 7.7 GUI of model with deadlock in the dining philosophers problem.

Chapter 7 Deadlocks

Listing 7.1 Trace output of the model with deadlock.

```
Project: Dining Philosophers - Deadlock
Run at: Sat Oct 01 17:15:39 EDT 2006 by jgarrido on Windows XP, localhost
-------------------------------------------------------
Input Parameters
Simulation Period: 740
Activity Stop: 400
Mean Think Time: 17.5

Mean Eat Time: 12.75
Project: Dining Philosophers - Deadlock
Run at: Sat Oct 01 17:15:40 EDT 2006
Start Simulation
Time 0000.000 Philosopher0 starts
Time 0000.000 Philosopher1 starts
Time 0000.000 Philosopher2 starts
Time 0000.000 Philosopher3 starts
Time 0000.000 Philosopher4 starts
Time 0000.000 Philosopher0 requesting left fork
Time 0000.000 Philosopher0 acquired left fork
Time 0000.000 Philosopher1 requesting left fork
Time 0000.000 Philosopher1 acquired left fork
Time 0000.000 Philosopher2 requesting left fork
Time 0000.000 Philosopher2 acquired left fork
Time 0000.000 Philosopher3 requesting left fork
Time 0000.000 Philosopher3 acquired left fork
Time 0000.000 Philosopher4 requesting left fork
Time 0000.000 Philosopher4 acquired left fork
Time 0000.000 Philosopher0 requesting right fork - waiting
Time 0000.000 Philosopher1 requesting right fork - waiting
Time 0000.000 Philosopher2 requesting right fork - waiting
Time 0000.000 Philosopher3 requesting right fork - waiting
Time 0000.000 Philosopher4 requesting right fork - waiting
-------------------------------------------------------
Results of simulation: Dining Philosophers - Deadlock
-------------------------------------------------------
Results of simulation:
Number of eating cycles Philosopher0 = 0
Total waiting time Philosopher0 = 0000.0000
Number of eating cycles Philosopher1 = 0
Total waiting time Philosopher1 = 0000.0000
Number of eating cycles Philosopher2 = 0
Total waiting time Philosopher2 = 0000.0000
Number of eating cycles Philosopher3 = 0
```

```
Total waiting time Philosopher3 = 0000.0000
Number of eating cycles Philosopher4 = 0
Total waiting time Philosopher4 = 0000.0000
Average time waiting:   0000.0000
```

7.3.2 Informal Solution to Deadlock

This section describes an informal solution to deadlock in the dining philosophers problem. Deadlock will not occur when the philosophers do not all sit at the table at the same time; therefore, if the five philosophers start thinking before eating, deadlock will not always occur. The reason for this is that the time interval to think is randomly generated so that the philosophers will not normally start to eat at the same time, and consequently deadlock will not always occur. This solution to deadlock shows that the ordering of events can make a big difference.

The simulation model consists of three user-defined classes: *Philosopher*, *Philos2*, and *SimInputs*. The second class, *Philos2*, is the main class, defining the resources in the model and starting the five philosopher processes. The first class, *Philosopher*, implements the behavior of a philosopher, as described previously. The third class, *SimInputs*, implements the GUI with the appropriate input parameter values for each simulation. The three classes are stored in the Java files: `Philosopher.java`, `Philos2.java`, and `SimInputs.java`, and are stored in the archive file `philos2.jar`. The C++ implementation of this simulation model is stored in file `philos2.cpp`.

In the simulation model, a philosopher object attempts to acquire the left fork, with index *indexLeft*, then attempts to acquire the right fork, with index *indexRight*. Each object of class *Philosopher* generates a random time interval for the duration of its eating activity, and another random time interval for the duration of its thinking activity. As mentioned before, this solution for deadlock specifies that a philosopher first thinks, then eats, and continues this cycle endlessly.

Every philosopher object will repeatedly follow a sequence of activities, until the simulation period ends. The sequence of activities for every philosopher object is now as follows:

1. Think for a time interval of `thinkPeriod` time units.

2. Attempt to acquire the left fork.

3. Attempt to acquire the right fork.

4. Eat for a time interval of `eatPeriod` time units.

Listing 7.2 shows a partial trace of a simulation run of the model with the informal solution to deadlock. The listing shows no deadlock for this particular run, but there is potential for deadlock.

Chapter 7 Deadlocks

Listing 7.2 Trace output of the model with solution to deadlock.

```
Project: Five Dining Philosophers
Run at: Sat Oct 01 19:01:53 EDT 2006 by jgarrido on Windows XP, localhost
-----------------------------------------------------
Input Parameters
Simulation Period: 740
Activity Stop: 400
Mean Think Time: 17.5
Mean Eat Time: 12.75

Project: Dining Philosophers - first solution
Run at: Sat Oct 01 19:01:53 EDT 2006
Start Simulation
Time 0000.000 Philosopher0 starts
Time 0000.000 Philosopher1 starts
Time 0000.000 Philosopher2 starts
Time 0000.000 Philosopher3 starts

Time 0000.000 Philosopher4 starts
Time 0000.000 Philosopher0 start think activity
Time 0000.000 Philosopher1 start think activity
Time 0000.000 Philosopher2 start think activity
Time 0000.000 Philosopher3 start think activity
Time 0000.000 Philosopher4 start think activity
Time 0005.263 Philosopher0 requesting left fork
Time 0005.263 Philosopher0 acquired left fork
Time 0005.263 Philosopher0 requesting right fork - waiting
Time 0005.263 Philosopher0 acquired right fork
Time 0005.263 Philosopher0 starts eating
Time 0008.710 Philosopher1 requesting left fork
Time 0009.097 Philosopher0 releasing forks
Time 0009.097 Philosopher0 start think activity
Time 0009.097 Philosopher1 acquired left fork
Time 0009.097 Philosopher1 requesting right fork - waiting
Time 0009.097 Philosopher1 acquired right fork
Time 0009.097 Philosopher1 starts eating
Time 0015.443 Philosopher1 releasing forks
Time 0015.443 Philosopher1 start think activity
Time 0019.589 Philosopher2 requesting left fork
Time 0019.589 Philosopher2 acquired left fork
Time 0019.589 Philosopher2 requesting right fork - waiting
Time 0019.589 Philosopher2 acquired right fork
Time 0019.589 Philosopher2 starts eating
. . .
```

```
Time 0380.304 Philosopher3 requesting right fork - waiting
Time 0380.304 Philosopher3 acquired right fork
Time 0380.304 Philosopher3 starts eating
Time 0385.697 Philosopher3 releasing forks
Time 0385.697 Philosopher3 start think activity
Time 0395.136 Philosopher3 requesting left fork
Time 0395.136 Philosopher3 acquired left fork
Time 0395.136 Philosopher3 requesting right fork - waiting
Time 0395.136 Philosopher3 acquired right fork
Time 0395.136 Philosopher3 starts eating
Time 0397.982 Philosopher4 requesting left fork
Time 0398.460 Philosopher3 releasing forks
Time 0398.460 Philosopher3 start think activity
Time 0398.460 Philosopher4 acquired left fork
Time 0398.460 Philosopher4 requesting right fork - waiting
Time 0401.655 Philosopher1 releasing forks
Time 0401.655 Philosopher1 terminating
Time 0401.655 Philosopher0 acquired right fork
Time 0401.655 Philosopher0 starts eating
Time 0401.655 Philosopher2 acquired left fork
Time 0401.655 Philosopher2 requesting right fork - waiting
Time 0401.655 Philosopher2 acquired right fork
Time 0401.655 Philosopher2 starts eating
Time 0404.378 Philosopher0 releasing forks
Time 0404.378 Philosopher0 terminating
Time 0404.378 Philosopher4 acquired right fork
Time 0404.378 Philosopher4 starts eating
Time 0408.844 Philosopher3 requesting left fork
Time 0411.255 Philosopher4 releasing forks
Time 0411.255 Philosopher4 terminating
Time 0419.987 Philosopher2 releasing forks
Time 0419.987 Philosopher2 terminating
Time 0419.987 Philosopher3 acquired left fork
Time 0419.987 Philosopher3 requesting right fork - waiting
Time 0419.987 Philosopher3 acquired right fork
Time 0419.987 Philosopher3 starts eating
Time 0427.553 Philosopher3 releasing forks
Time 0427.553 Philosopher3 terminating
```

Listing 7.3 includes the summary statistics for the simulation run mentioned. The performance measures displayed are the number of eating cycles and the average wait time of each philosopher object during the simulation period.

Listing 7.3 Summary statistics of the model with solution to deadlock.

```
Project: Five Dining Philosophers
Run at: Sat Oct 01 19:01:53 EDT 2006 by jgarrido on Windows XP, localhost
-----------------------------------------------------
Input Parameters
Simulation Period: 740
Activity Stop: 400
Mean Think Time: 17.5
Mean Eat Time: 12.75
Project: Dining Philosophers - first solution
Run at: Sat Oct 01 19:01:53 EDT 2006
-----------------------------------------------------
Results of simulation: Five Dining Philosophers
-----------------------------------------------------
Results of simulation:
Number of eating cycles Philosopher0 = 10
Total waiting time Philosopher0 = 0203.9259
Number of eating cycles Philosopher1 = 10
Total waiting time Philosopher1 = 0131.0330
Number of eating cycles Philosopher2 = 9
Total waiting time Philosopher2 = 0164.6285
Number of eating cycles Philosopher3 = 11
Total waiting time Philosopher3 = 0120.0247

Number of eating cycles Philosopher4 = 7
Total waiting time Philosopher4 = 0112.4418
Average time waiting:    0146.4108
```

7.4 Methods for Handling Deadlock

There are three general methods to handle deadlock:

- Prevention
- Avoidance
- Detection and recovery

The first two methods for dealing with deadlock guarantee that deadlock will not occur. The prevention methods are simpler and more straightforward to understand and learn. The main rationale used is to disallow at least one of the four conditions for deadlock. The deadlock avoidance methods use the current resource-allocation state of the system and the maximum resource claim of the processes. With this information, the operating system can decide to delay the allocation of resources to one or more processes.

The third method, detection and recovery, allows a system to reach a deadlock state. A detection algorithm periodically checks if the system has entered a deadlock state. Another algorithm is used to allow the system to recover from a deadlock state.

7.5 Deadlock Prevention

As mentioned before, there are four necessary conditions for deadlock to occur:

1. *Mutual exclusion*: Only one process can access a resource at a time and the process has exclusive use of the resource.

2. *Hold and wait*: A process has acquired one or more resources (already holds these resources) and is requesting other resources.

3. *Circular wait*: A condition that is represented by a cycle of resource allocations and requests. For example, process $P1$ holds resource $R1$ and is requesting resource $R2$; process $P2$ holds the resource $R2$ and is requesting resource $R3$; process $P3$ holds resource $R3$ and is requesting resource $R1$ (held by $P1$). This situation can include more than three processes and resource types.

4. *No preemption*: A process cannot be interrupted and forced to release resources.

Deadlock prevention methods ensure that at least one of the four conditions is never met (always false). To simplify the following discussion on deadlock prevention, assume that all resources must be accessed in a mutually exclusive manner, and that once a process has acquired a resource, it will not be forced to release the resource. This assumption implies that conditions 1 and 4 will be considered true.

The discussion of deadlock prevention will focus on the other two conditions: hold and wait, and circular wait. The two deadlock prevention techniques are described in the following section and each one is illustrated by means of a simulation model. Both models are variations of the dining philosophers problem.

7.5.1 Disallowing Hold and Wait

The strategy applied in these techniques for deadlock handling is to preclude a process from holding one or more resources and at the same time requesting other resources. There are two techniques to accomplish this:

- A process must acquire all the resources it needs before starting to use acquired resources.

- A process must release all resources it has acquired before requesting any new resources.

The first technique is more appropriate in batch systems, and the second in interactive systems. In both techniques, the performance of the operating system is decreased. The system throughput, resource utilization, and average wait time of processes are affected. Starvation is also possible because a low priority process may have to wait forever.

Applying deadlock prevention in the dining philosophers problem is carried out using the first technique. A philosopher process can acquire its left and right forks only if *both* forks are available. The checking for the availability of the two forks and the acquisition of both forks are carried out in a critical section. Only one philosopher process can be carrying out these activities at any time.

The solution to deadlock is implemented in Java in another simulation model of the dining philosophers problem. The two basic user-defined classes in the model are *Philoshw* and *Philosopher*. These classes are implemented in files `Philoshw.java` and `Philosophers.java`, and they are stored in the archive file `philoshw.jar`. The C++ version of the model is stored in file `philoshw.cpp`.

In this model, the execution for each philosopher object will keep repeating its sequence of activities, cycling until the simulation period ends. The following sequence of activities of a philosopher object is carried out repeatedly:

1. Check if both forks are available, then continue; otherwise wait.

2. Attempt to acquire the left fork.

3. Attempt to acquire the right fork.

4. Eat for a time interval of `eatPeriod` time units.

5. Think for a time interval of `thinkPeriod` time units.

The simulation model declares an array of resources called *fork* with five elements. The array represents five resource types with one resource instance each. This model uses a binary semaphore called *mutex* to implement the critical section in the philosopher processes.

The following portion of code includes a relevant part of class *Philosopher* implemented in Java with the critical section that checks for the availability of both forks.

```
// critical section
mutex.swait();   // attempt exclusive access for checking

// get number of resource instances available of each type
numLeftFork = Philoshw.fork[index].num_avail();
numRightFork = Philoshw.fork[indexRight].num_avail();
//
// are both forks (left and right) available?
if(numLeftFork > 0 && numRightFork > 0)
  {
  getLeftForks();
```

7.5 Deadlock Prevention

```
    getRightForks();
    //
    // release mutual exclusion so other philosophers can
    // attempt acquiring both forks
    mutex.signal();
    //
    startEating();
    releaseForks();
    done = true;       // done eating
 }
 else
  {
  mutex.signal(); // release mutual exclusion
  waitForForks(); // wait for forks
  // will have to repeat and try to acquire forks
}
```

After a philosopher process acquires both forks, it exits its critical section by releasing mutual exclusion and proceeds to eat. Other philosopher processes can concurrently attempt to acquire two other forks. After eating, a philosopher process releases both forks.

Listing 7.4 shows a partial trace of a simulation run of the dining philosophers problem that implements the deadlock solution by disallowing the hold and wait condition.

Listing 7.4 Partial trace of the philosophers' model that disallows hold and wait.

```
Project: Dining Philosophers - H&W
Run at: Sat Oct 01 23:07:24 EDT 2006
Input Parameters:
Simulation period: 250.75
Mean think period: 15.5
Mean eat period: 9.75
Start Simulation
Time 0000.000 Philosopher0 starts
Time 0000.000 Philosopher1 starts
Time 0000.000 Philosopher2 starts
Time 0000.000 Philosopher3 starts
Time 0000.000 Philosopher4 starts
Time 0000.000 Philosopher0 attempting exclusive access
Time 0000.000 Philosopher0 checking res availability
Time 0000.000 Philosopher0 requesting left fork
Time 0000.000 Philosopher0 acquired left fork
Time 0000.000 Philosopher0 requesting right fork
Time 0000.000 Philosopher0 acquired right fork
Time 0000.000 Philosopher0 starts eating
```

Chapter 7 Deadlocks

```
Time 0000.000 Philosopher1 attempting exclusive access
Time 0000.000 Philosopher1 checking res availability
Time 0000.000 Philosopher1 start waiting
Time 0000.000 Philosopher2 attempting exclusive access
Time 0000.000 Philosopher2 checking res availability
Time 0000.000 Philosopher2 requesting left fork
Time 0000.000 Philosopher2 acquired left fork
Time 0000.000 Philosopher2 requesting right fork
Time 0000.000 Philosopher2 acquired right fork
Time 0000.000 Philosopher2 starts eating
Time 0000.000 Philosopher3 attempting exclusive access
Time 0000.000 Philosopher3 checking res availability
Time 0000.000 Philosopher3 start waiting
Time 0000.000 Philosopher4 attempting exclusive access
Time 0000.000 Philosopher4 checking res availability
Time 0000.000 Philosopher4 start waiting
Time 0002.652 Philosopher0 releasing forks
Time 0002.652 Philosopher0 start think activity
Time 0002.652 Philosopher1 attempting exclusive access
Time 0002.652 Philosopher1 checking res availability
Time 0002.652 Philosopher1 start waiting
Time 0002.835 Philosopher2 releasing forks
Time 0002.835 Philosopher2 start think activity
Time 0002.835 Philosopher3 attempting exclusive access
Time 0002.835 Philosopher3 checking res availability
Time 0002.835 Philosopher3 requesting left fork
Time 0002.835 Philosopher3 acquired left fork
Time 0002.835 Philosopher3 requesting right fork
Time 0002.835 Philosopher3 acquired right fork
Time 0002.835 Philosopher3 starts eating
Time 0004.028 Philosopher3 releasing forks
. . .
Time 0169.546 Philosopher1 acquired left fork
Time 0169.546 Philosopher1 requesting right fork
Time 0169.546 Philosopher1 acquired right fork
Time 0169.546 Philosopher1 starts eating
Time 0183.782 Philosopher0 attempting exclusive access
Time 0183.782 Philosopher0 checking res availability
Time 0183.782 Philosopher0 start waiting
Time 0191.054 Philosopher1 releasing forks
Time 0191.054 Philosopher1 start think activity
Time 0191.054 Philosopher4 attempting exclusive access
Time 0191.054 Philosopher4 checking res availability
Time 0191.054 Philosopher4 requesting left fork
Time 0191.054 Philosopher4 acquired left fork
```

7.5 Deadlock Prevention

```
Time 0191.054 Philosopher4 requesting right fork
Time 0191.054 Philosopher4 acquired right fork
Time 0191.054 Philosopher4 starts eating
Time 0195.370 Philosopher3 terminating
Time 0204.254 Philosopher4 releasing forks
Time 0204.254 Philosopher4 start think activity
Time 0204.254 Philosopher2 attempting exclusive access
Time 0204.254 Philosopher2 checking res availability
Time 0204.254 Philosopher2 requesting left fork
Time 0204.254 Philosopher2 acquired left fork
Time 0204.254 Philosopher2 requesting right fork
Time 0204.254 Philosopher2 acquired right fork
Time 0204.254 Philosopher2 starts eating
Time 0225.240 Philosopher4 terminating
Time 0225.246 Philosopher1 terminating
Time 0235.224 Philosopher2 releasing forks
Time 0235.224 Philosopher2 start think activity
Time 0235.224 Philosopher0 attempting exclusive access
Time 0235.224 Philosopher0 checking res availability
Time 0235.224 Philosopher0 requesting left fork
Time 0235.224 Philosopher0 acquired left fork
Time 0235.224 Philosopher0 requesting right fork
Time 0235.224 Philosopher0 acquired right fork
Time 0235.224 Philosopher0 starts eating
Time 0247.012 Philosopher0 releasing forks
Time 0247.012 Philosopher0 start think activity
Time 0265.751 Philosopher0 terminating
Time 0284.459 Philosopher2 terminating
```

The main difference with the previous model is that this model allows at most two philosophers to simultaneously eat. Listing 7.5 shows the summary statistics of the simulation run for this model. The performance measures displayed are the number of eating cycles and the average wait time of each philosopher process.

Listing 7.5 Summary statistics of the simulation run for model that disallows hold and wait.

```
Project: Dining Philosophers - H&W
Run at: Sat Oct 01 23:07:24 EDT 2006
Input Parameters:
Simulation period: 250.75
Mean think period: 15.5
Mean eat period: 9.75
-----------------------------------------------------------
Results of simulation:
Number of eating cycles Philosopher0 = 6
```

```
Total waiting time Philosopher0 = 0113.5253
Number of eating cycles Philosopher1 = 4
Total waiting time Philosopher1 = 0066.7829
Number of eating cycles Philosopher2 = 6
Total waiting time Philosopher2 = 0108.2626
Number of eating cycles Philosopher3 = 6
Total waiting time Philosopher3 = 0041.0321
Number of eating cycles Philosopher4 = 6
Total waiting time Philosopher4 = 0101.1488
Average time waiting:   0086.1504
```

7.5.2 Disallowing Circular Wait

The circular wait condition exists in a collection of processes $P1$ to Pn, if process $P1$ is waiting for a resource held by $P2$, process $P2$ is waiting for a resource held by $P3$, and process Pn is waiting for a resource held by $P1$. The resource allocation graph clearly shows a cycle, as can be observed in Figure 7.8.

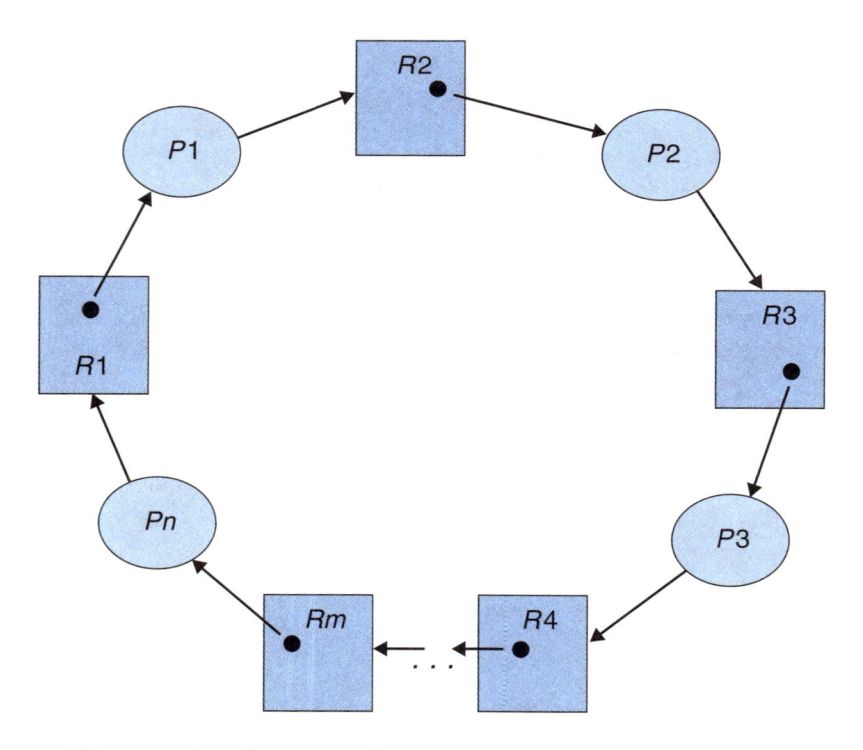

Figure 7.8 Resource allocation graph with a general cycle.

7.5 Deadlock Prevention

A technique for disallowing (preventing) the circular wait condition is to assign a *total ordering* to all the resource types in the system. Each resource type can be assigned a unique integer number, or an index number. A simple application of this ordering is to only allow a process to acquire a resource, R_k, if $R_k > R_j$ for some resource R_j that the process already holds.

If process Pi requests a resource, R_j, and the process already holds resource R_k such that $R_k > R_j$, the system would not allow the allocation of resources in this order. To follow the total order imposed by the system for resource allocation, process Pi must release resource R_k so that the process can acquire resource R_j and then acquire resource R_k.

In the dining philosophers problem, deadlock can be prevented if a total ordering is imposed on how the philosophers can acquire the forks. For example, the fork with index 0 (f_0) must be acquired before the fork with index 1 (f_1), and the fork with index 1 (f_1) must be acquired before acquiring the fork with index 2 (f_2).

The Java version of the simulation model that implements the solution to deadlock by preventing the circular wait condition is stored in file **philoscw.jar**. The C++ version of this model is stored in file **philoscw.cpp**. In this simulation model, a philosopher object first checks the index values of the two forks it needs, then it will attempt to acquire them in an increasing order of index value. The first four philosophers will acquire their left fork first, with index i (f_i), and then their right fork, with index $i+1$ (f_{i+1}). Philosopher 4 (the fifth philosopher) must now first acquire the right fork, with index 0 (f_0), then the left fork, with index 4 (f_4).

Each philosopher object will repeatedly execute its sequence of activities until the simulation period ends. The following sequence of activities will be carried out by a philosopher:

1. Check if the index value of the left fork is less than the index value of the right fork, then carry out Step 2 then Step 3; otherwise carry out Step 3, then Step 2.

2. Attempt to acquire the left fork.

3. Attempt to acquire the right fork.

4. Eat for a time interval of `eatPeriod` time units.

5. Think for a time interval of `thinkPeriod` time units.

Listing 7.6 includes a partial trace for a simulation run of the model that implements the deadlock prevention technique by disallowing circular wait.

Listing 7.6 Partial trace of the dining philosophers model that disallows circular wait.

```
Project: Dining Philosophers - CW
Run at: Sun Oct 02 12:49:17 EDT 2006
Input Parameters:
Simulation period: 250.75
Mean think period: 15.5
```

Chapter 7 Deadlocks

```
Mean eat period: 9.75
Start Simulation
Time 0000.000 Philosopher0 starts
Time 0000.000 Philosopher1 starts
Time 0000.000 Philosopher2 starts
Time 0000.000 Philosopher3 starts
Time 0000.000 Philosopher4 starts
Time 0000.000 Philosopher0 attempting to acquire forks
Time 0000.000 Philosopher0 requesting left fork
Time 0000.000 Philosopher0 acquired left fork
Time 0000.000 Philosopher0 requesting right fork
Time 0000.000 Philosopher0 acquired right fork
Time 0000.000 Philosopher0 starts eating
Time 0000.000 Philosopher1 attempting to acquire forks
Time 0000.000 Philosopher1 requesting left fork
Time 0000.000 Philosopher2 attempting to acquire forks
Time 0000.000 Philosopher2 requesting left fork
Time 0000.000 Philosopher2 acquired left fork
Time 0000.000 Philosopher2 requesting right fork
Time 0000.000 Philosopher2 acquired right fork
Time 0000.000 Philosopher2 starts eating
Time 0000.000 Philosopher3 attempting to acquire forks
Time 0000.000 Philosopher3 requesting left fork
Time 0000.000 Philosopher4 attempting to acquire forks
Time 0000.000 Philosopher4 requesting right fork
Time 0003.370 Philosopher0 releasing forks
Time 0003.370 Philosopher0 start think activity
Time 0003.370 Philosopher4 acquired right fork
Time 0003.370 Philosopher4 requesting left fork
Time 0003.370 Philosopher4 acquired left fork
Time 0003.370 Philosopher4 starts eating
Time 0003.370 Philosopher1 acquired left fork
Time 0003.370 Philosopher1 requesting right fork
Time 0008.727 Philosopher0 attempting to acquire forks
Time 0008.727 Philosopher0 requesting left fork
Time 0013.762 Philosopher4 releasing forks
Time 0013.762 Philosopher4 start think activity
Time 0013.762 Philosopher0 acquired left fork
Time 0013.762 Philosopher0 requesting right fork
Time 0018.334 Philosopher2 releasing forks
Time 0018.334 Philosopher2 start think activity
Time 0018.334 Philosopher1 acquired right fork
Time 0018.334 Philosopher1 starts eating
. . .
Time 0181.538 Philosopher0 releasing forks
```

```
Time 0181.538 Philosopher0 start think activity
Time 0181.653 Philosopher2 attempting to acquire forks
Time 0181.653 Philosopher2 requesting left fork
Time 0181.653 Philosopher2 acquired left fork
Time 0181.653 Philosopher2 requesting right fork
Time 0181.653 Philosopher2 acquired right fork
Time 0181.653 Philosopher2 starts eating
Time 0184.494 Philosopher1 attempting to acquire forks
Time 0184.494 Philosopher1 requesting left fork
Time 0184.494 Philosopher1 acquired left fork
Time 0184.494 Philosopher1 requesting right fork
Time 0185.422 Philosopher0 attempting to acquire forks
Time 0185.422 Philosopher0 requesting left fork
Time 0185.422 Philosopher0 acquired left fork
Time 0185.422 Philosopher0 requesting right fork
Time 0185.929 Philosopher2 releasing forks
Time 0185.929 Philosopher2 start think activity
Time 0185.929 Philosopher1 acquired right fork
Time 0185.929 Philosopher1 starts eating
Time 0186.311 Philosopher3 attempting to acquire forks
Time 0186.311 Philosopher3 requesting left fork
Time 0186.311 Philosopher3 acquired left fork
Time 0186.311 Philosopher3 requesting right fork
Time 0186.311 Philosopher3 acquired right fork
Time 0186.311 Philosopher3 starts eating
Time 0192.726 Philosopher2 terminating
Time 0199.556 Philosopher4 terminating
Time 0200.230 Philosopher1 releasing forks
Time 0200.230 Philosopher1 start think activity
Time 0200.230 Philosopher0 acquired right fork
Time 0200.230 Philosopher0 starts eating
Time 0208.225 Philosopher0 releasing forks
Time 0208.225 Philosopher0 start think activity
Time 0222.311 Philosopher3 releasing forks
Time 0222.311 Philosopher3 start think activity
Time 0222.966 Philosopher1 terminating
Time 0235.021 Philosopher3 terminating
Time 0265.457 Philosopher0 terminating
```

Listing 7.7 shows the summary statistics for the simulation of this model. The performance measures displayed are the number of eating cycles and the average wait time of each philosopher process. This method can be compared with the other two discussed previously, with respect to the performance measures to consider, and the overall advantages and disadvantages of each method. (See the questions at the end of the chapter for ideas on more detailed analysis.)

Listing 7.7 Summary statistics of the dining philosophers model that disallows circular wait.

```
Project: Dining Philosophers - CW
Run at: Sun Oct 02 12:49:17 EDT 2006
Input Parameters:
Simulation period: 250.75
Mean think period: 15.5
Mean eat period: 9.75
-------------------------------------------------------------
Results of simulation:
Number of eating cycles Philosopher0 = 11
Total waiting time Philosopher0 = 0101.8240
Number of eating cycles Philosopher1 = 6
Total waiting time Philosopher1 = 0033.1532
Number of eating cycles Philosopher2 = 9
Total waiting time Philosopher2 = 0062.5194
Number of eating cycles Philosopher3 = 11
Total waiting time Philosopher3 = 0027.0035
Number of eating cycles Philosopher4 = 6
Total waiting time Philosopher4 = 0040.9010
Average time waiting:   0053.0802
```

7.5.3 Model with Graphical Animation

This section briefly describes a simulation model of the dining philosophers problem with graphical animation. The model uses two techniques of deadlock prevention: disallow hold and wait, and disallow circular wait. The technique can be selected from the Options menu.

Three parameters are entered for each simulation run: the simulation period, the mean interval for eating, and the mean interval for thinking. The values initially shown are the default values that the simulation model uses for the run. Figure 7.9 shows the main screen with these default values of the input parameters. The initial state of the philosophers is also shown; all philosophers start thinking.

As the simulation run progresses, the clock advances the simulation time, and the state of the philosophers continuously changes. Figure 7.10 shows the philosophers' state at a different simulation time. Note that two philosophers are eating in this state and the simulation time is 40.73 time units.

At the end of the simulation run, the model displays the simulation results in the small pop-up window shown in Figure 7.11. Another option of the model is the generation of a trace file, if desired, and the naming of this file. The trace first appears on the screen, as shown in Figure 7.12, and will then be stored on the indicated file. The simulation model is implemented in Java, using the PsimJ2 simulation package, and consists of several classes stored in the archive file `philosanim.jar`.

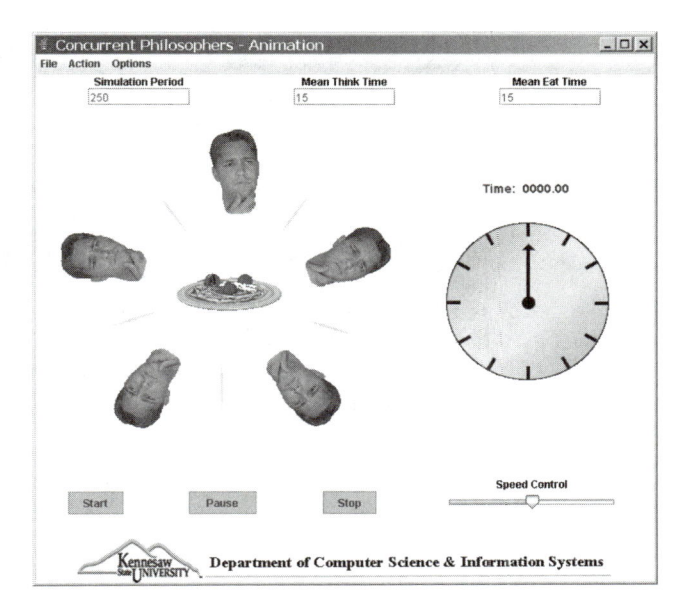

Figure 7.9 Initial state of the philosophers in the animation model.

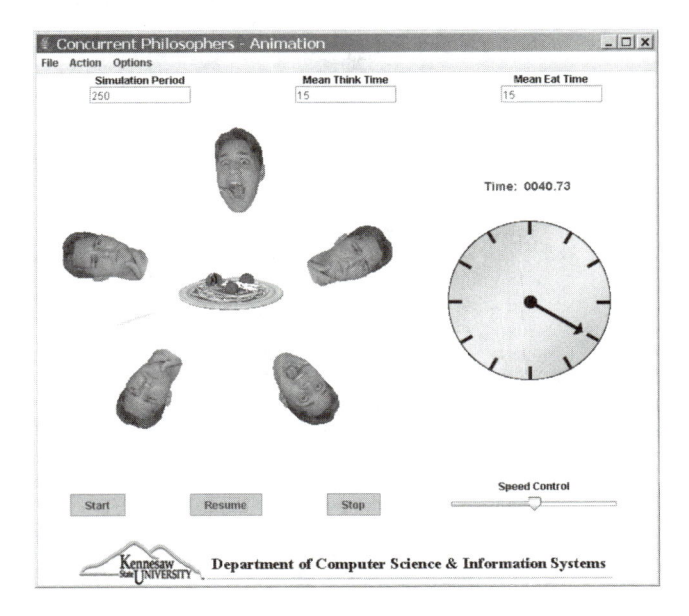

Figure 7.10 A different state of the philosophers in the animation model.

200　Chapter 7　Deadlocks

Performance Metrics Dis. Hold & Wait

Number of Eating Cycles for Philosopher 0 = 5
Total Waiting Time for Philosopher 0 = 116.46540242646225
Number of Eating Cycles for Philosopher 1 = 5
Total Waiting Time for Philosopher 1 = 110.09342846937471
Number of Eating Cycles for Philosopher 2 = 5
Total Waiting Time for Philosopher 2 = 90.6586627188641
Number of Eating Cycles for Philosopher 3 = 4
Total Waiting Time for Philosopher 3 = 30.06755144671201
Number of Eating Cycles for Philosopher 4 = 7
Total Waiting Time for Philosopher 4 = 80.80701525503692
Average Time Waiting = 85.61841206329

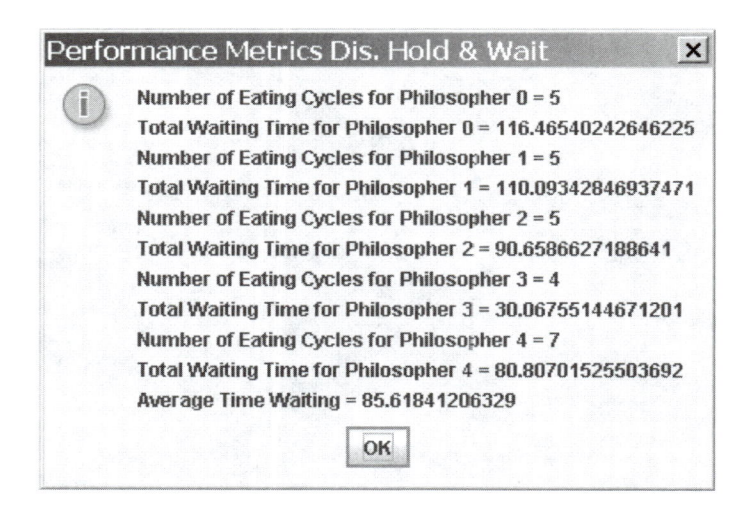

Figure 7.11　Results of the simulation run in the animation model.

Simulation Trace

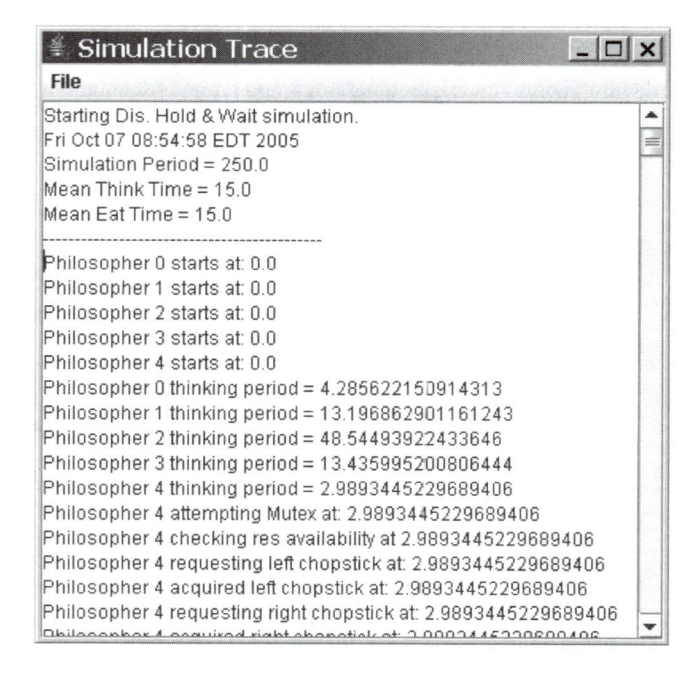

Starting Dis. Hold & Wait simulation.
Fri Oct 07 08:54:58 EDT 2005
Simulation Period = 250.0
Mean Think Time = 15.0
Mean Eat Time = 15.0

Philosopher 0 starts at: 0.0
Philosopher 1 starts at: 0.0
Philosopher 2 starts at: 0.0
Philosopher 3 starts at: 0.0
Philosopher 4 starts at: 0.0
Philosopher 0 thinking period = 4.285622150914313
Philosopher 1 thinking period = 13.196862901161243
Philosopher 2 thinking period = 48.544939224336465
Philosopher 3 thinking period = 13.435995200806444
Philosopher 4 thinking period = 2.9893445229689406
Philosopher 4 attempting Mutex at: 2.9893445229689406
Philosopher 4 checking res availability at 2.9893445229689406
Philosopher 4 requesting left chopstick at: 2.9893445229689406
Philosopher 4 acquired left chopstick at: 2.9893445229689406
Philosopher 4 requesting right chopstick at: 2.9893445229689406

Figure 7.12　Trace of the simulation run in the animation model.

7.6 Deadlock Avoidance

Avoidance techniques allow a system to change state by allocating resources only when it is certain that deadlock will not occur by subsequent resource allocations. The system analyzes the current resource allocation state to determine that it is a *safe state*. Each time there is a resource request, the system analyzes the current state by examining the allocation status of all resources and the current resource needs of the processes up to their *maximum claim*. The maximum resource claim of a process is the total number of resource instances that a process will ever request.

The goal of avoidance techniques is to determine if there is some *sequence* of resource requests, allocations, and deallocations that allow every process to eventually complete. If this sequence cannot be found, then the resource allocation state is said to be an unsafe state. The system is only required to allocate resources in some order to the requesting processes, not to simultaneously meet all maximum claims of the processes. This avoids deadlock, but if the system is in an unsafe state, then there is potential for deadlock to occur.

7.6.1 Banker's Algorithm

The *banker's algorithm* can be invoked by the operating system to check if the current resource-allocation state is a safe state. The resource-allocation state is defined by the total number of resources in the system, the number of allocated resources, and the maximum resource claim of the processes. The state is stored in the following data structures:

- A vector, **C**, with the total number of instances of every resource type in the system. The element, c_j, represents the number of resource instances of resource type j in the system.

- A matrix, A, with the number of resource instances of every resource type allocated to every process. The element, a_{ij} is the number of resource instances of resource type j that have been allocated to process i.

- A matrix, M, with the maximum claim of every resource type declared by every process. The element, m_{ij}, represents the maximum number of resource instances of resource type j, that will ever be requested by process i.

7.6.2 Applying the Banker's Algorithm

The following problem illustrates the application of the banker's algorithm to find out whether a system state is safe. For this, the algorithm looks for a safe sequence, which is some order of resource allocation that will maintain the system in a safe state. This sequence represents the order of how resources will be allocated to a set of processes. The order is denoted by $\langle P1, P2, P3, \ldots, Pn \rangle$.

Chapter 7 Deadlocks

A system has five processes: $P1$, $P2$, $P3$, $P4$, and $P5$. There are four resource types in the system: $R1$, $R2$, $R3$, and $R4$. The total numbers of resource units of each resource type are 5 units of $R1$, 6 units of $R2$, 8 units of $R3$, and 4 units of $R4$. This quantity of resources is written as (5, 6, 8, 4). Table 7.1 presents data for each process, the maximum claim, the resources allocated to the process, and the current resource needs of the process.

Table 7.1 Data for the Banker's Algorithm Problem

Process	Max Claim	Allocation	Need
$P1$	(3, 2, 2, 2)	(2, 1, 1, 0)	(1, 1, 1, 2)
$P2$	(2, 1, 1, 2)	(0, 1, 1, 0)	(2, 0, 0, 2)
$P3$	(1, 1, 3, 1)	(1, 1, 1, 0)	(0, 0, 2, 1)
$P4$	(3, 4, 2, 2)	(1, 1, 2, 1)	(2, 3, 0, 1)
$P5$	(2, 4, 1, 4)	(1, 2, 1, 1)	(1, 2, 0, 3)

The total number of allocated resources is (5, 6, 6, 2) and the total number of resources available in this initial state is (0, 0, 2, 2).

The algorithm carries out the following sequence of steps in finding a safe sequence:

1. Compare the resources available with the current needs of the processes. There are sufficient resources to satisfy the needs of process $P3$.

2. Process $P3$ acquires resources (0, 0, 2, 1). The resources available are now (0, 0, 0, 1).

3. After a finite time interval using the resources, process $P3$ releases all resources it holds, (1, 1, 3, 1). The available resources are now (1, 1, 3, 2).

4. There are sufficient resources to satisfy the needs of process $P1$. Process $P1$ acquires resources (1, 1, 1, 2) and the resources available are now (0, 0, 2, 0).

5. After a finite time interval using the resources, process $P1$ releases resources (3, 2, 2, 2). The available resources are now (3, 2, 4, 2).

6. Process $P2$ acquires resources (2, 0, 0, 2). The resources available are now (1, 2, 4, 0).

7. After a finite time interval using the resources, process $P2$ releases resources (2, 1, 1, 2). The resources available are now (3, 3, 5, 2).

8. Process $P4$ acquires resources (2, 3, 0, 1). The resources available are now (1, 0, 5, 1).

9. After a finite time interval using the resources, process *P*4 releases resources (3, 4, 2, 2). The resources available are now (4, 4, 7, 2).

10. Process *P*5 acquires resources (1, 2, 0, 2). The resources available are now (3, 2, 7, 0).

11. After a finite time interval using the resources, process *P*5 releases resources (2, 4, 1, 4). The resources available are now (5, 6, 8, 4) and these are equal to the total resources in the system.

The safe sequence of resource allocation found is $\langle P3, P1, P2, P4, P5 \rangle$; therefore, the state given is a safe state.

7.7 Deadlock Detection and Recovery

With the *deadlock detection* method, the operating system allocates resources to the requesting processes whenever sufficient resources are available. Since this may lead to deadlock, the operating system must periodically execute a deadlock detection algorithm.

7.7.1 Deadlock Detection

The operating system can check for deadlock every time a resource is allocated; this is early detection. Other algorithms are used to detect cycles in the resource allocation graph. The techniques are based on incremental changes to the system state. The algorithms attempt to find a process with its resource requests that can be allocated with the currently available resources. The resources are then allocated to and used by the process, and then they are released. This is repeated with the other processes. The processes that are in deadlock are identified, and a procedure is initiated to stop deadlock.

Deadlock detection involves maintaining information of the current resource allocation state and invoking an algorithm that uses the information of the resource allocation state to detect deadlock, if it has occurred.

The information about the resource allocation state is derived from data stored in the following data structures, for m resource types and n processes:

- A vector, *Resources*, of length m that stores the total resources of each type in the system.

- A vector, *Available*, of length m that stores the number of available resource instances of each resource type.

- An $n \times m$ matrix, *Allocation*, that stores the number of resource instances of each resource type that have been allocated to each process.

- An $n \times m$ matrix, *Request*, that stores the current resource request for each process.

Chapter 7 Deadlocks

The operating system monitors the allocation and deallocation of resources to and from processes and updates the resource allocation state.

A deadlock detection algorithm basically checks for cycles in the resource allocation graph. There are several algorithms developed for discovering cycles in the resource graph, but the simple algorithms can be applied only when there is one resource instance of every resource type.

An important issue is the frequency of invoking the deadlock detection algorithm. There are two approaches to consider:

- Deadlock can occur only when some process issues a request that cannot be immediately granted by the operating system. Thus, the deadlock detection algorithm can be invoked every time a process requests a resource that cannot be immediately granted (allocated). In this case, the operating system can directly identify the specific process that caused deadlock, in addition to the set of processes that are in deadlock. This approach involves considerable overhead.

- The detection algorithm is invoked periodically using a period not too long or too short. Since deadlock reduces the CPU utilization and the system throughput, the detection algorithm may be invoked when the CPU utilization drops below 40 percent.

7.7.2 Recovery

Once deadlock is detected, the operating system must attempt to recover. There are several approaches for deadlock recovery.

7.7.2.1 Aborting Processes

The simplest approach to deadlock recovery is to terminate one or more processes. An obvious process to kill is one in the circular wait cycle. A more complete strategy can be defined by the following:

- Terminate all processes that have been identified to be in deadlock.

- Preempt resources one by one and run the detection algorithm until deadlock ceases to exist. Roll back these processes to a state previous to their resource allocation.

- Terminate every process and run the detection algorithm to check if deadlock still exists, and continue until deadlock ceases to exist.

7.7.2.2 Rollback

With recovery via rollback, the system periodically stores the state of the system.

A checkpoint is a data structure that stores at least the state of a process, each resource state, and a time stamp. The checkpoints are stored on a file and are used to restart a process in a previous state before deadlock occurred.

The recovery procedure involves a rollback of every process in a deadlock state to a previous state that has been defined as a checkpoint and stored in a special file.

7.8 Summary

Deadlock occurs when the processes and/or threads in a group are blocked, waiting for each other. Each process needs two or more shared resource instances of a resource type. Each process or thread holds a resource and waits to acquire a resource instance that another process holds. There is indefinite waiting for all processes in the group. This state is called deadlock because each process is waiting for an event that will never occur.

The five dining philosophers illustrate a classical synchronization problem that is used to explain deadlock and some solutions to deadlock. The three general methods that operating systems use to handle deadlock are prevention, avoidance, and detection.

The main idea in deadlock prevention is to disallow one of the four conditions for deadlock. Most of the techniques disallow the hold and wait condition and the circular wait condition. Deadlock avoidance techniques depend on the maximum resource claim of the process so as not to let the system enter an unsafe state. The banker's algorithm is the most common technique for deadlock avoidance. Detection and recovery techniques are different because these allow the system to enter a deadlock state. A detection algorithm is executed frequently to detect deadlock. A recovery algorithm is then invoked to remove the processes involved in deadlock.

Several simulation models, which implement the dining philosophers problem, were presented in this chapter to show in detail how and why deadlock occurs, and three possible solutions to deadlock were discussed. Different values of performance measures were shown from the simulation runs.

Key Terms		
acquiring resources	deadlock avoidance	resource allocation graph
allocation order	deadlock detection	resource deallocation
available resources	deadlock prevention	resource instance
banker's algorithm	dining philosophers	resource item
blocked process	hold and wait	resource type
circular wait	holding resources	safe state
conditions for deadlock	maximum claim	
deadlock	releasing resources	

Exercises and Questions

1. Discuss in which practical cases the condition of nonpreemption would not hold. Give an example.

2. Explain and give examples of why deadlock may be considered worse than starvation. Is deadlock a form of starvation? Give examples.

3. Which of the techniques for deadlock prevention are easier to implement? Give your arguments.

4. Compare the first two simulation models presented in this chapter, in files `philos.jar` and `philos1.jar`. Carry out about three or more simulation runs. The philosopher processes in the second model have to think first, then eat. Since the philosopher processes take a random period to think, how effective is this solution to deadlock? Discuss your arguments.

5. Using the simulation model in `philoshhw.jar`, change the model to implement the disallowance of hold and wait in a different way. What advantages did you gain? Which one has better performance?

6. The *Res* resource class is used to create resource objects with resource items that processes can acquire in a mutually exclusive manner. Using this class, there is an implicit exclusive access to the resource items. In the simulation model that implements the solution to deadlock by disallowing the hold and wait condition, why is a critical section needed? Discuss all possibilities. Modify the model in file `philoshw.jar` to make a relevant change in the program and carry out a test simulation. Compare the performance measures.

7. Compare the two simulation models that implement solutions to deadlock prevention, in files `philoshw.jar` and `philoscw.jar`. Which one has better performance? What are the reasons for this? Discuss your arguments.

8. Using the same workload parameters, compare the models in files `philos1.jar`, `philoshw.jar`, and `philoscw.jar`. Where is the overhead in the solutions to deadlock? Give good arguments.

9. A system has four resources types with (5, 3, 5, 3) and five processes with a maximum resource claim: $P1$ with (2, 2, 1, 1), $P2$ with (1, 2, 1, 2), $P3$ with (1, 1, 2, 1), $P4$ with (3, 1, 2, 0), and $P5$ with (2, 1, 1, 0). The resource allocations are $P1$ with (1, 1, 0, 0), $P2$ with (0, 1, 1, 0), $P3$ with (1, 0, 1, 1), $P4$ with (2, 1, 2, 0), and $P5$ with (1, 0, 1, 0). Is this system in a safe state? Give good arguments.

10. Include additional performance measures and compare the two models that implement solutions to deadlock prevention, stored in files `philoshw.jar` and `philoscw.jar`. Use the same workload parameters. Which one has better performance? Discuss your arguments.

11. Extend the number of philosophers in the two models that implement solutions to deadlock prevention. The models would have more than five philosophers competing for forks. Is performance very different? Discuss.

Chapter 8

File Management

8.1 Introduction

In a computer system, the data should be organized in some convenient and efficient manner. In particular, users should be able to do two key tasks:

- Put data into files.

- Find and use files that have been previously created.

The file management subsystem of the operating system provides these capabilities. Actually, the operating system provides rudimentary capabilities to meet these needs. For example, The OS provides little support for how data is organized. Users will often rely on a database engine to provide a better organizational structure for data. Similarly, the typical OS provides only a very simple mechanism to find files. Internet search engines (such as Google) are far more sophisticated. While the features that the OS provides tend to be very simple, the more sophisticated features of database engines and Google are built on top of the OS features.

8.2 Files

A *file* is simply a sequence of bytes that have been stored in some device on the computer; Figure 8.1 illustrates this concept. Those bytes will contain whatever data we would like to store in the file—for example, a text file containing only the characters that we are interested in, a word processing document file that also contains data about how to format the text, and a database file that contains data organized in multiple tables. In general, the file management system does not have any knowledge about how the data

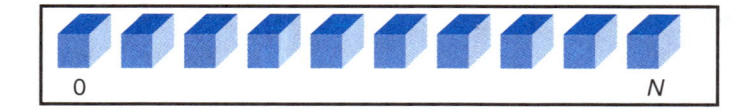

Figure 8.1 A file as a sequence of bytes.

in a file is organized. That is the responsibility of the application programs that create and use the file.

Note that other parts of the operating system (such as an audit log and the swap file) may create and use files. These other system components will be aware of the structure of the files they create and use.

A computer has volatile and nonvolatile memory. Volatile memory loses its contents if power goes away. The file management system will typically store files in nonvolatile memory. Examples of nonvolatile memory or permanent storage include the following:

- Disk drives
- Flash memory (memory stick)
- CDs and DVDs

After files have been stored on a storage device of the computer, users need to be able to find them at some later time. The basic mechanism that operating systems provide for this is the *filename*—the name chosen by the user to store a file. Files are then grouped together in a *folder* (also known as a *directory*). Later, a user who wants a file can ask if a file with a certain name exists in a particular folder.

8.2.1 File Attributes

In addition to a filename, a file will have a number of other attributes:

- *Size*: How much data is stored in the file?
- *Location*: Where is the file actually stored on the computer? Which device (disk) is it on? Where is it on that device? Is it even on this computer? Perhaps it is located on another computer somewhere else on the network.
- *Type*: What data is stored in this file? Is it a text file, video file, database, or something else? Usually the type is denoted in a *file extension* (the last part of a filename). On a modern system, this is used in conjunction with *file associations* to indicate what application should normally be executed with this file. Thus, MS Windows will have the Notepad application associated with files that have the `.txt` file extension. This allows users to double-click on the icon for a text file and the system will start up Notepad to work on that file. Note that one can change a file extension (thus changing which file association to use) without changing the

actual contents of a file. This can be used to the user's advantage or can cause unexpected results.

- *Permissions*: Who is allowed to use this file and what can they do with it? This topic will be discussed in detail in Chapter 11, which discusses security and protection.

- *Time stamps*: When was this file created? When was it last modified?

The attributes of a file are typically stored in the folder that contains the file. This data is stored in an area commonly called a *directory entry*.

8.2.2 Folders

An important attribute of the folder is the name given to it. Typically, a folder may contain files and other folders (commonly called subfolders or subdirectories). This results in a tree structure of folders and files. In Figure 8.2, folder *abc* contains folder *def* and file A1. Folder *def* contains files B1 and B2.

8.2.3 Pathnames

The *pathname* of a file specifies the sequence of *folders* users must traverse to travel down the tree to the file. Thus, the pathname for file B2 is *abc/def/B2*. This pathname actually describes the *absolute path* of the file, which is the sequence of folders users must travel from the root of the tree to the desired file. A *relative path* describes the sequence of folders users must traverse starting at some intermediate place on the absolute path.

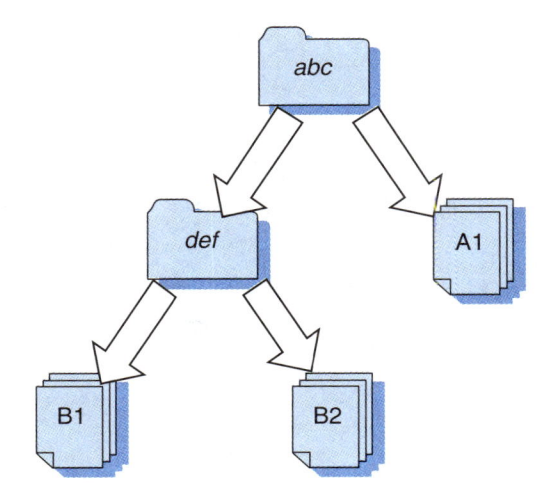

Figure 8.2 Tree structure of folders and files.

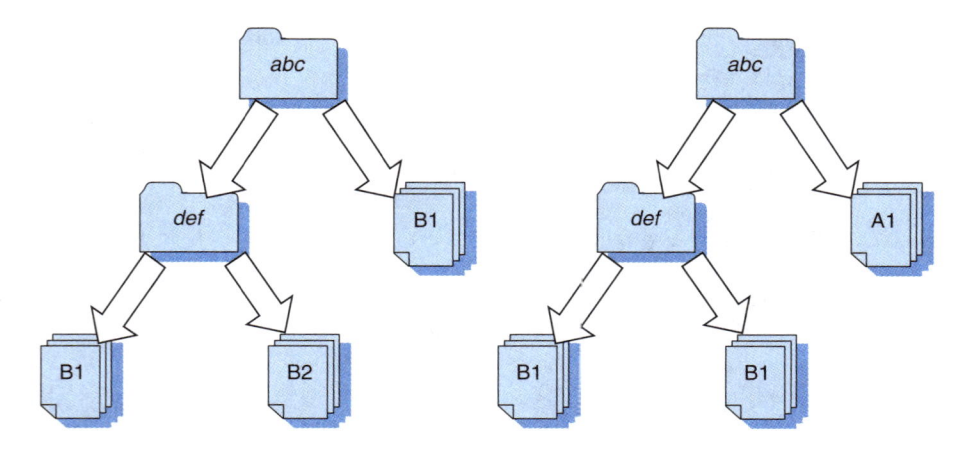

Figure 8.3 Legal and illegal tree structures.

The absolute path provides a unique identification for a file. Two different files can have the same filename as long as the resulting pathnames are unique. Thus two different folders can have a file named B1, but there cannot be two files named B1 in the same folder, as shown in Figure 8.3.

This pure tree structure is highly restrictive. Modern systems also support a mechanism that allows a file to appear to be in a different part of the tree structure than where it actually resides. This is called a *Shortcut* on Windows and a *Symbolic Link* on Unix/Linux. In Figure 8.4, file B2 appears to reside in folder *abc* (as well as folder *def*, where it truly resides).

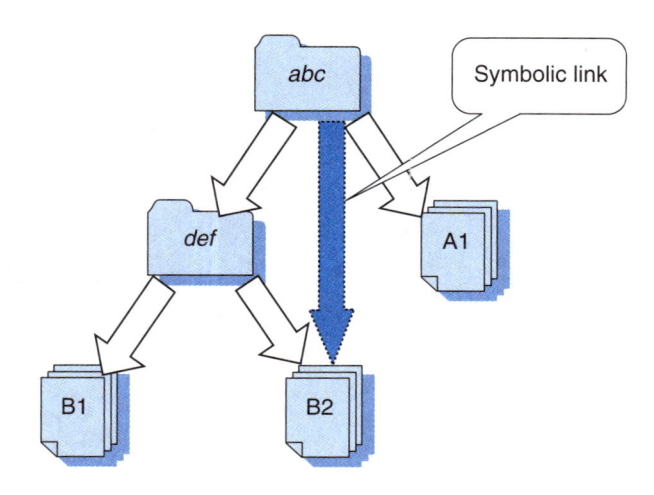

Figure 8.4 Example of a symbolic link.

8.3 Access Methods

An *access method* describes the manner and mechanisms by which a process accesses the data in a file. There are two common access methods:

- Sequential
- Random (or direct)

In the *sequential* access method, the file is read or written sequentially, starting at the beginning of the file and moving to the end. In the *random* access method, the application may choose to access any part of the file at any time. It is important to understand that the access method describes how the data is accessed and used. It has nothing to do with how the data has been stored in the file. A good analogy is a music CD. Users can choose to play the music tracks in order (sequentially) or they can choose shuffle play and the tracks will be played in a random order. The choice of how to access the tracks has no effect on how the tracks were recorded on the CD.

When a process needs to use a file, there are a number of operations it can perform:

- Open
- Close
- Read
- Write

8.3.1 Open

In order for a process to read data from a file or write data to a file, the OS needs to know where that file is located. That data is in the directory entry in the folder in which the file is located. Thus, the OS must traverse the absolute path of the file to locate this directory entry. Even if the pathname is very short, this will be a time-consuming process. If the pathname is long, this will be a very lengthy process. Carrying out this traversal every time an application wishes to read or write some data would add tremendous overhead to an already slow process. In effect, the OS would have to carry out several disk reads every time the application would want to do a disk read or write.

To avoid the pathname traversal overhead, the application program is required to execute an open system call for a file before it does any read or write requests. This allows the OS to carry out this directory traversal only once—at the time that the file is opened. The open request will cache the directory entry in main memory so that the OS can quickly access that data anytime it is needed in the future. The open request will return a *file handle*—a value that identifies the cached directory entry. That handle will then be used by the application in all future requests regarding that file. Figure 8.5 illustrates the file open operation.

212 Chapter 8 File Management

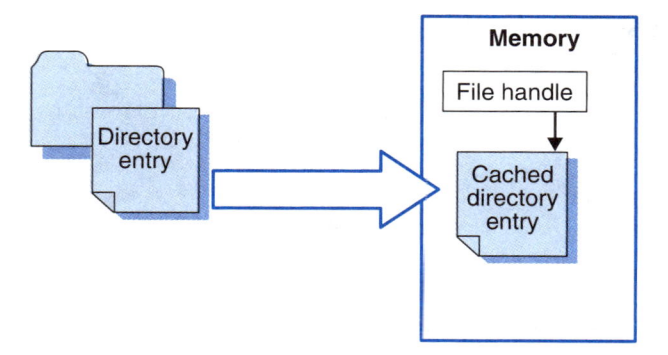

Figure 8.5 File open operation.

When an application carries out an open request, in addition to providing the pathname of the file, it will also indicate the following:

- Whether sequential or random access will be used.
- Whether the file will be read or written. If the file is to be written, it will also indicate whether it will start writing at the beginning of the file or it intends to append data to the end of the file.

8.3.2 Close

When an application is done using a file, it should close it. A *close system call* performs several functions:

- It will destroy the cached directory entry so that the file is no longer available for reads and writes.
- Under various schemes that are discussed in the next chapter, data may not be physically written to a file at the time that the application initially requests. If the application was writing to the file, the close operation will ensure that all data has actually been written to the file, as shown in Figure 8.6.

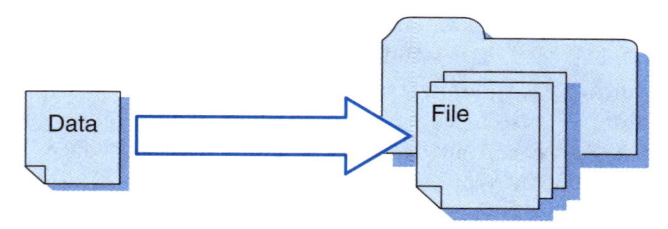

Figure 8.6 Close ensures data is written to the file specified.

- If the file is on removable media, the close operation will make the media available for removal. This will be discussed in more detail in Section 8.8.

8.3.3 Read

The purpose of the *read system call* is to read some data from the specified file into the memory space of the process that is requesting the data. For this, the file management system will need to know the following from the requesting process:

- Which file? The handle that was returned by the open call of the specified file is used to indicate this.

- Where is the data in the file? The typical application will not read an entire file at one time. It will read a portion of the file (a data block) and then later read another portion. Thus, the application needs to indicate to the OS which portion of the file to read.

- Where in the memory space of the process should this data be stored? The area in which the data will be stored is commonly called a *buffer*.

- How much data? How many bytes are to be read from the file? (What is the size of the data block being read?)

Thus, the read system call will be similar to the following line of pseudocode:

```
read(handle, file position, buffer, length);
```

The task carried out by this command is shown in Figure 8.7.

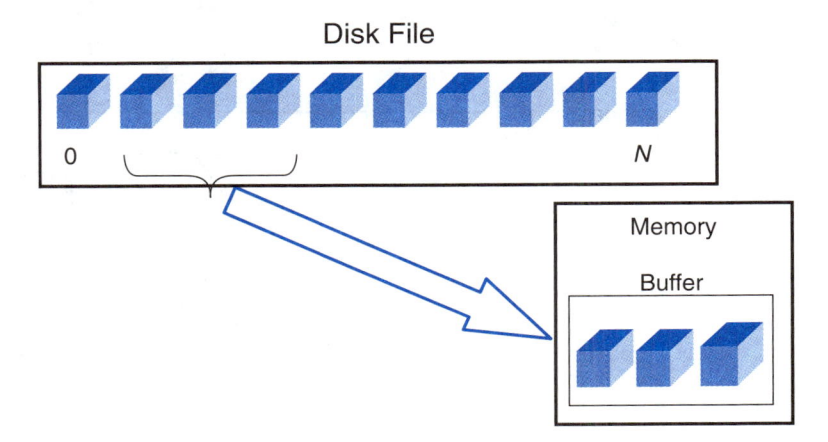

Figure 8.7 File read operation.

8.3.4 Write

A write operation is very similar to (but the opposite of) a read operation. The purpose of the write system call is to write some data to a file from the memory space of the process that owns the data. To carry this out, the file management system will need the following from the requesting process:

- Which file? The handle that was returned by the open call is used to indicate this.

- Where should the data be stored in the file? The typical application will not write an entire file at one time. It will write a portion of the file, a data block, and then later another portion. Thus, the application needs to indicate to the OS where in the file to put the data block.

- Where in the memory space of the process is the buffer that contains the data block that is to be written?

- How much data? How many bytes are to be written to the file? (What is the size of the data block?)

Thus, the write system call will be similar to the following line of pseudocode:

```
write(handle, file position, buffer, length);
```

The task carried out by this command is shown in Figure 8.8.

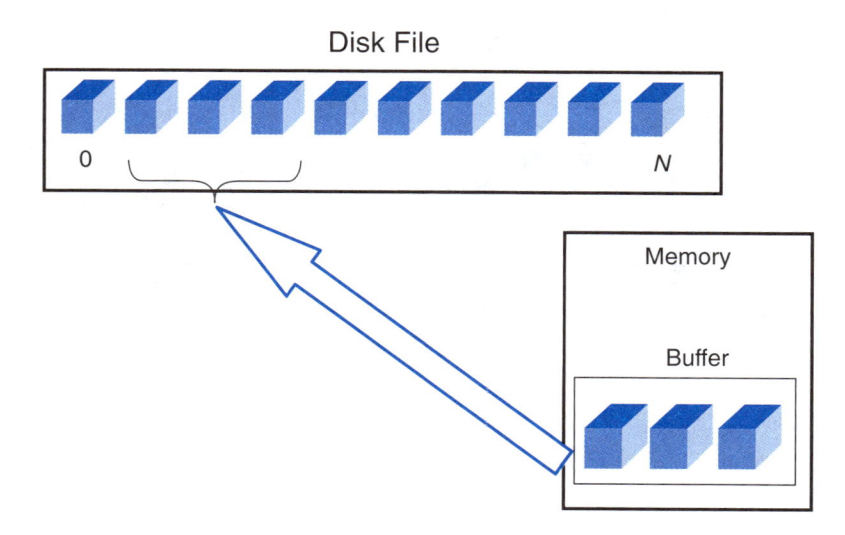

Figure 8.8 File write.

8.3.5 Sequential Access

If a process has opened a file for sequential access, the file management subsystem will keep track of the current file position for reading and writing. To carry this out, the system will maintain a *file position pointer* that will be the position of the next read or write. This value will be initialized during the open operation to one of two possible values:

- Set to 0 to start the reading or writing at the beginning of the file, the normal setting for this value.

- Set to the current size of the file, if the file is being opened to append data to the file.

After each read or write, the file position pointer will be incremented by the amount of data that was read or written. Since the file management subsystem is keeping track of the file position, the operating system typically will have another form of read and write system calls, in which the application does not specify a file position.

8.3.6 Streams, Pipes, and I/O Redirection

A *stream* is the flow of data bytes, one byte after another, into the process (for reading) and out of the process (for writing). This concept applies to sequential access and was originally invented for network I/O, but several modern programming environments (e.g., Java and the Windows .Net framework) have also incorporated it.

A *pipe* is a connection that is dynamically established between two processes. When a process reads data, the data will come from another process rather than from a file. Thus, a pipe has a process at one end that is writing to the pipe and another process reading data at the other end of the pipe. It is often the situation that one process will produce output that another process needs for input. Figure 8.9 illustrates the flow of data between two processes using a pipe.

Rather than having the first process write to a file and the second process read that file, we can save time by having each process communicate via a pipe. Using a pipe can improve system performance in two ways:

- By not using a file, the applications save time by not using disk I/O.

- A pipe has the characteristic that the receiving process can read whatever data has already been written. Thus we do not need to wait until the first process has

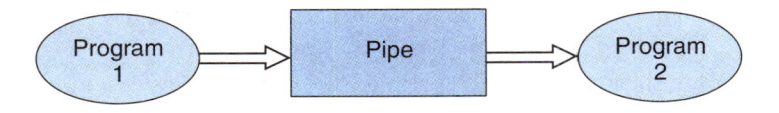

Figure 8.9 A pipe.

written all of the data before we start executing the second process. This creates a pipeline similar to an automobile assembly line to speed up overall performance.

A pipe will typically use a buffer in main memory as a temporary holding spot for the data that has been written by the first process. Notice that a pipe is actually an implementation of the producer-consumer problem discussed in Chapter 6.

When a process begins execution, the file management system will create three standard I/O files:

- *Standard input*, which will typically take input from the user keyboard.

- *Standard output*, which will typically write data to the user screen.

- *Standard error*, which is used for error messages from the process.

Each of these standard I/O files will be a pipe that is connected to a system module that communicates with an appropriate device. The command interpreter will also support *I/O redirection*. Using I/O redirection, the user can request the command interpreter to do the following:

- Take the data from a file or another process instead of from the standard input.

- Send data to a file or another process instead of to the standard output or standard error.

Table 8.1 shows several examples of I/O redirection. The pipes used in I/O redirection are unnamed, but it is also possible to have named pipes. Such pipes are a feature that support interprocess communication if the communicating processes are not being executed by the same parent process (command interpreter). This typically might happen if a server application and a client application are needing to communicate.

Table 8.1 I/O Redirection

Command	Action
`dir > tmp.txt`	Take the standard output from the `dir` application and write it to the file `tmp.txt`.
`more < tmp.txt`	The `more` application should use the file `tmp.txt` as its standard input.
`dir	more`	The standard output of the `dir` application will be used as the standard input for the `more` application.

8.3.7 Other I/O System Calls

In addition to the normal I/O system calls (open, close, read, write), several other I/O system calls are available. One of the most important is *flush*. If the data that is being written to a file represents an *atomic transaction*, then it is critical that the data actually be written to the file at a known time. If the system is using some kind of buffering scheme, this will not necessarily happen at a predictable time. A flush request tells the system to ignore whatever buffering scheme is being used and physically write out whatever data has been logically but not yet physically written.

8.4 Directory Functions

There are a number of operations or functions that can typically be specified with folders (directories):

- *Create file*: When a process opens a file that does not already exist, it must be created. In this situation, the open system call will use the create file function to allocate space for the file and create a directory entry for it.

- *Delete file*: Deletes space allocated to the file and its directory entry.

- *Rename file*: Changes the name recorded in the directory entry for a file.

- *File exist?*: Searches a folder to see if there is a directory entry whose name matches that of the desired file.

- *Directory list*: Returns a list of the directory entries in a folder.

- *Get and set attributes*: Returns various attributes from a directory entry or changes those attributes.

8.5 File Space Allocation

One of the major tasks for the file management subsystem is to allocate space for files. A simple mechanism for doing this is *contiguous allocation*. In this scheme, a contiguous section of the disk is allocated for a file. This scheme actually achieves optimal performance for the application that is reading/writing the file. Unfortunately, the contiguous allocation scheme has two major deficiencies:

- It is necessary to know how much space will be required for the file prior to creating the file. This usually is not possible.

- Because files are continually being created and deleted, after a system has run for some time, there may not be the necessary space in a contiguous chunk. The space will be typically available in smaller chunks scattered around the disk. One could move files around to create the necessary contiguous space, but that is an extremely time-consuming process that is best done when the system is not otherwise busy.

8.5.1 Cluster Allocation

To resolve these two problems, systems will commonly use *cluster allocation*—a scheme in which chunks of space are allocated to a file as a process that is writing the file needs them. A system that is using cluster allocation needs to remember where all of the clusters for a file are located. There are two approaches for carrying this out. The first uses *linked clusters*, a system in which clusters are linked together in a chain in such a manner that each cluster points to the next, as shown in Figure 8.10.

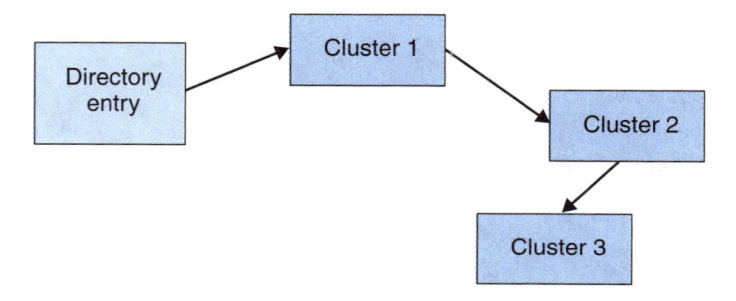

Figure 8.10 Linked clusters.

The second approach uses *indexed clusters*, a system in which the directory entry points to a file index block, which has an array of pointers to clusters. Figure 8.11 illustrates a file index block.

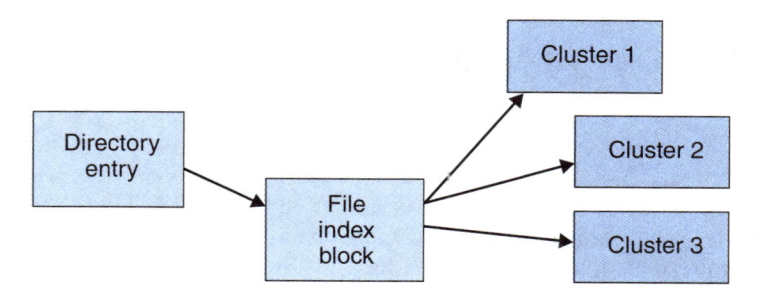

Figure 8.11 File index block.

8.5.2 Calculating Read/Write Addresses

When an application wishes to read or write data, the file management system must determine where the data actually is on disk. Figure 8.12 shows the address calculation with contiguous allocation. With this scheme, the calculation can simply be done with the following line of pseudocode:

```
Read/Write Address = DirectoryEntry.diskAddress +
                     File_Position_Pointer;
```

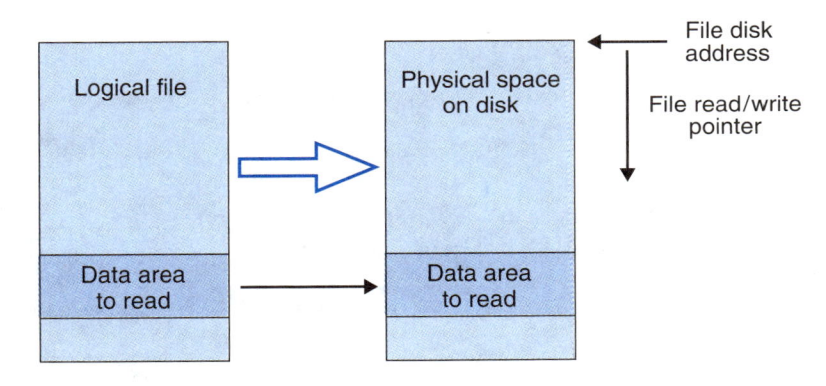

Figure 8.12 Read/write address calculation: contiguous allocation.

If cluster allocation is used, this calculation becomes more complicated. The system needs to scan through the various clusters, looking for the one that contains the desired data. The following portion of pseudocode shows how this can be implemented:

```
offset = File Position;
currentCluster = First Cluster;
while (currentCluster.size < offset)
{
    offset = offset - currentCluster.size;
    currentCluster = next cluster;
}
Read/write address = currentCluster.diskAddress + offset;
```

Figure 8.13 illustrates this scheme.

It is entirely possible that a single read/write request from the application program may cross the boundary between two clusters. This will certainly happen if the application read/write request is for more data than is in a single cluster. When this situation occurs, the file management system must take the single application I/O request and change it to multiple physical I/O requests, as shown in Figure 8.14.

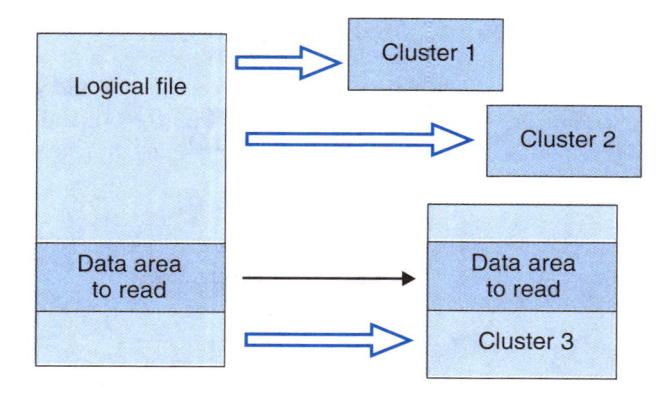

Figure 8.13 Read/write calculation: cluster allocation.

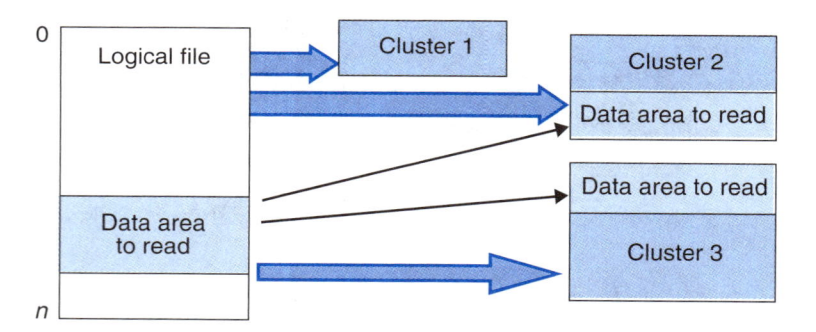

Figure 8.14 An I/O request across a cluster boundary.

8.5.3 Free Space Management

Just as the system needs to keep track of the clusters that have been allocated to each file, it must also practice free space management—the process of keeping track of the available (free) clusters. There are two commonly used schemes for accomplishing this. The first is the linked list, which is similar to how the clusters are managed for files, as shown in Figure 8.15.

The second scheme for managing free space is *bit mapping*—a scheme in which each bit in the bit map represents a cluster, as illustrated in Figure 8.16.

When a file is deleted, its clusters are moved back to the free list. For efficiency, the clusters are not erased. This fact has a dramatic impact on overall system security and the field of computer forensics.

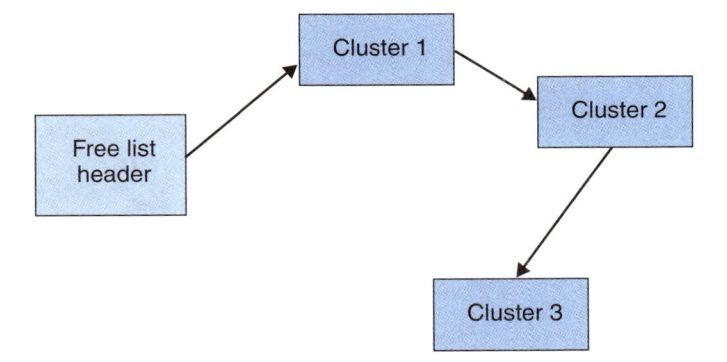

Figure 8.15 Linked list free space management.

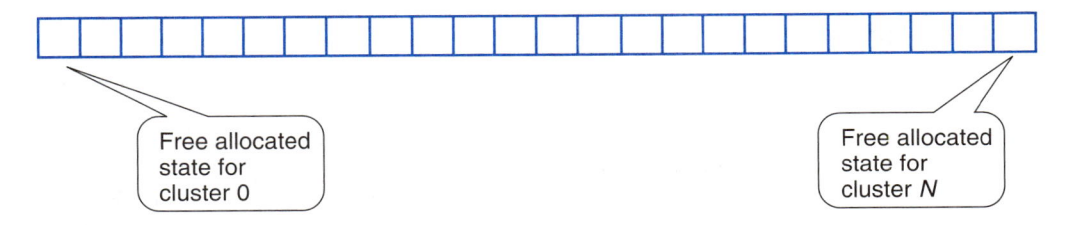

Figure 8.16 Bit mapped free space management.

8.5.4 Disk Fragmentation

All cluster allocation schemes suffer from two forms of disk fragmentation:

- *External fragmentation*: With this type of fragmentation, the space for a particular file may be broken into many clusters that are scattered all over the disk. The more clusters that there are, the poorer the performance will be. The file management system can try to reduce this effect by allocating larger clusters. Regardless of the size of the clusters, an actively used disk will, over time, tend to become very fragmented. Thus, periodically a defragmentation utility should be run. It is the job of this utility to take the scattered clusters of each file and rearrange them on the disk so that the clusters of a file are all physically adjacent, thus emulating contiguous allocation. This defragmentation also tends to put the free clusters into a contiguous area. Thus, for a while after defragmentation has been done, files will tend to be allocated contiguously.

- *Internal fragmentation*: If a small file is written on a system that is using large clusters, there can be a lot of disk space that is unused. This can result in a substantial amount of wasted disk space. Recently, the disk drive manufacturers have made substantial improvements in disk capacities. Thus, this issue is not currently a major concern.

8.5.5 Reliability of Disk Space Management

The process of allocating space for a file basically involves the following steps:

1. Locate a free cluster.

2. Update structure(s) to show that cluster is no longer available.

3. Add cluster to the allocation structure for the file.

Since multiple processes may need space allocated for files simultaneously, this procedure needs to be implemented as an atomic transaction. In addition, we want this procedure to be reliable in the face of power failures and other forms of system crashes.

To achieve that goal, it needs to be implemented as a multistage atomic transaction. As mentioned in Chapter 6 (which discusses synchronization), that generally requires the use of a transaction log (also known as journaling) to allow the system to easily restore itself to a consistent state upon restart after a system failure. As we shall see, some real-world systems implement this level of reliability and others do not.

8.6 Real-World Systems

A disk drive in a real-world system is typically organized in a specific manner. There is a *boot block*, which contains the code to do the initial boot of the system. There is typically a *partition control block*, which describes the partitions that follow. Then, there will be one or more partitions. One of these partitions is designated the active partition, and it will contain the operating system that is to be booted. This structure, shown in Figure 8.17, allows multiple operating systems to be installed on a single disk drive, each in a separate partition.

It is also possible to have each partition controlled by a different file system, which will thus use different strategies and provide different features. We now examine several real-world file systems:

- Microsoft FAT System

- Microsoft NTFS System

- Linux Ext2 and Ext3 Systems

- Other file systems

8.6 Real-World Systems 223

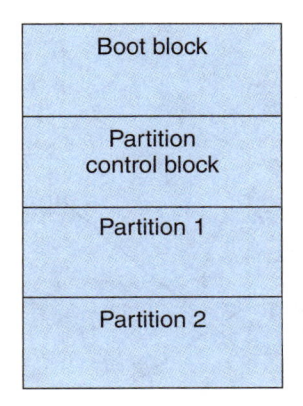

```
┌─────────────────────┐
│     Boot block      │   Contains code to do initial boot of system
│                     │   (located at fixed disk address)
├─────────────────────┤
│      Partition      │   Describes disk partitions
│   control block     │
├─────────────────────┤
│                     │
│     Partition 1     │
│                     │
├─────────────────────┤
│                     │
│     Partition 2     │
│                     │
└─────────────────────┘
```

Figure 8.17 Disk partitions.

8.6.1 Microsoft FAT System

The Microsoft Fat System was originally created for the MS-DOS operating system. It had a limitation of a 2GB maximum disk size. While this seemed gigantic when it was invented in the early 1980s, disk drive manufacturers surpassed this size in the mid-1990s. Thus, Microsoft created a new version, FAT-32, for Windows 98. Windows NT, 2000, XP, Vista, and 2003 Server also support FAT-32. Additionally, Linux includes support for FAT-32. Table 8.2 shows the characteristics of a FAT-32 system.

The FAT file system has a large table on disk called the file allocation table (FAT). The directory entry for a file points to an entry in the FAT. That entry points to the first cluster. If there is a second cluster, the first FAT entry points to a second FAT entry, which points to the second cluster, and so on. Thus, the FAT file system uses a linked clusters approach where the links go through the FAT entries rather than the actual clusters. This is illustrated in Figure 8.18.

Table 8.2 Microsoft FAT File System Characteristics

Cluster size	1K to 32K
Maximum partition size	2 terabytes
Maximum file size	4 gigabytes
Filenames	8 bit ASCII characters
File permissions supported?	No
Transaction log?	No

224 Chapter 8 File Management

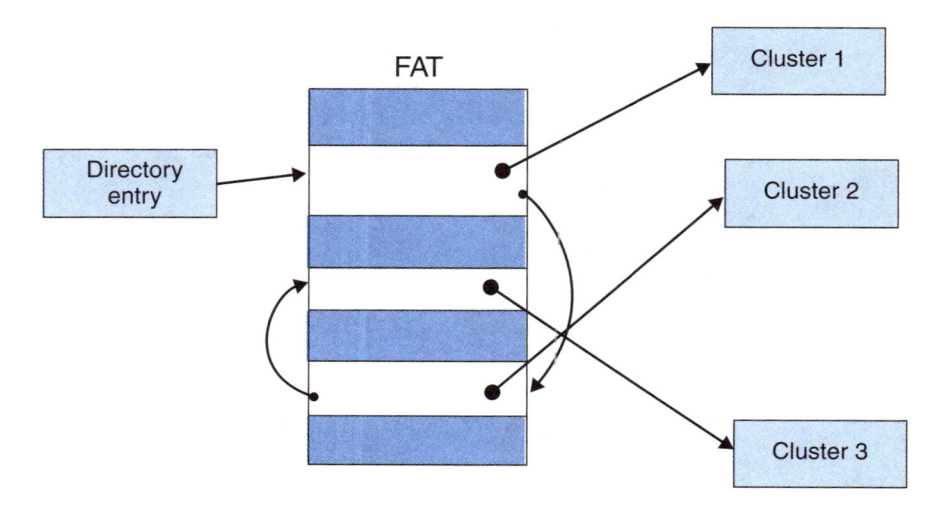

Figure 8.18 Microsoft FAT file system.

The FAT file system manages free space in a similar fashion. There is a free list of available clusters, which are linked together through FAT entries (see Figure 8.19). To allocate a cluster, the system moves a FAT entry from the free list to the end of the list of clusters for the file. This requires changing three pointers on disk. When a file is deleted, the entire FAT chain for the file can be moved to the free list. If the OS keeps track of where the end of the free list is, this can be done by changing one pointer. The FAT file system has no mechanisms to enforce permissions for accessing

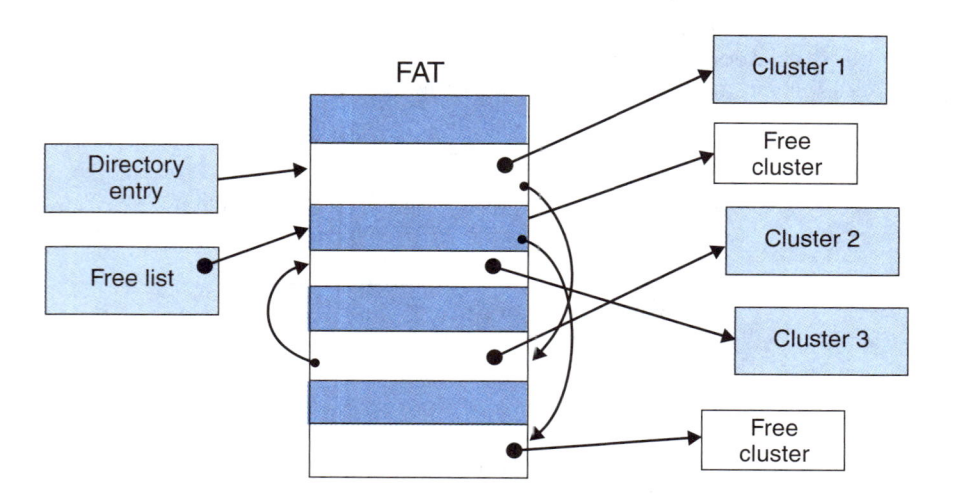

Figure 8.19 Free space handling in a FAT file system.

files. Consequently, anyone who has access to a computer that is using a FAT file system will be able to do whatever he or she wants to the files on that system.

The FAT file system does not maintain a transaction log to recover after a system failure. The Scandisk utility program must be run in any attempt to recover after a system failure. This has a number of problems:

- When the Scandisk utility starts, it has no idea where any possible problems might exist. Consequently, it must scan the entire disk and thus will take an extremely long time to execute.

- It will often run for a long time and find no problems. Because of this, users often elect not to run it.

- If there are indeed problems and users fail to run it for a long time, the problems can multiply.

- If there are multiple problems, a single execution of Scandisk may or may not find all of them. Thus, Scandisk should be run repeatedly until it reports that there are no problems.

- Sometimes the problems are so bad that Scandisk cannot properly correct them. In this case, it will save clusters that it cannot properly repair for the user to "do something with." Usually the user will not be able to do anything with these clusters and will thus lose data.

8.6.2 Microsoft NTFS System

The Microsoft New Technology File System (NTFS) was created as part of the Windows NT development effort to create a reliable system that could be used as a server by businesses. Windows NT, 2000, XP, 2003 Server, and Vista all support this system. The characteristics for NTFS are shown in Table 8.3.

Table 8.3 Microsoft NTFS File System Characteristics

Cluster size	512 to 64K
Maximum partition size	256 terabytes
Maximum file size	16 terabytes
Filenames	Unicode characters
File permissions supported?	Yes
Transaction log?	Yes

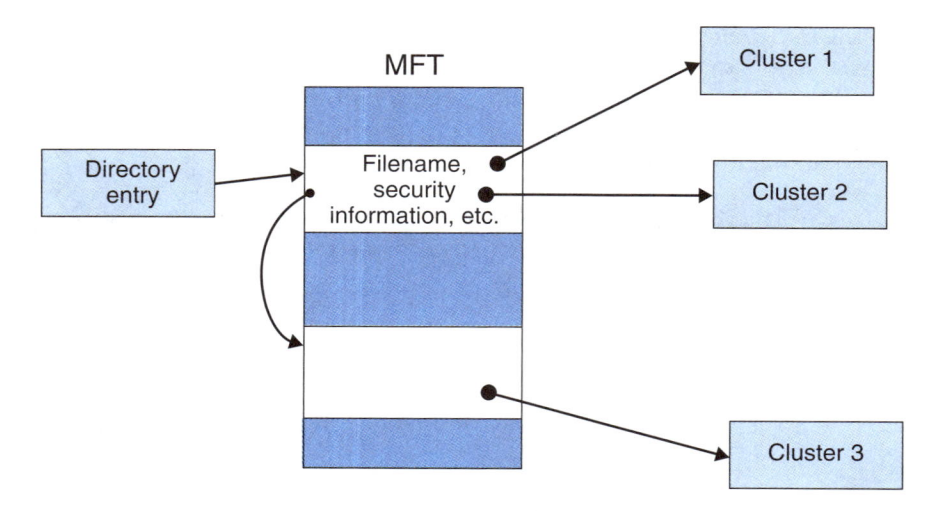

Figure 8.20 Microsoft NTFS MFT structure.

NTFS has a table on disk called the Master File Table (MFT). Each directory entry points to an entry in the MFT. The MFT entry will contain several data fields about the file, including security information and a list of pointers to allocated clusters. The MFT entries are a fixed size. Once the MFT is filled with pointers to clusters, another MFT entry will be allocated to hold additional cluster pointers. Thus, this system uses indexed clusters, with the MFT entry acting as the file index block. The NTFS MFT structure is shown in Figure 8.20.

NTFS uses a bit map to keep track of free clusters. It also provides a transaction logging (journaling) feature and a fairly general file permissions capability. In addition, when an NTFS file system is installed, you can optionally select that it should encrypt all data that is written to the disk.

8.6.3 Linux Ext2 and Ext3 Systems

The Linux Ext2 File System uses indexed clusters, similar to the Microsoft NTFS file system. Table 8.4 shows the characteristics for the Linux file system. Figure 8.21 shows the general structure of the file system.

Some important differences between the Ext2 and NTFS systems include the following:

- Ext2 does not support transaction logging (journaling). Ext3 is an extension of the Ext2 file system and does have a journaling capability.

- While Ext2 supports file permissions, it does not provide as much control over the permissions as NTFS. This topic will be discussed in more detail in Chapter 11.

Table 8.4 Linux Ext2 File System Characteristics

Cluster size	1 to 4K
Maximum partition size	4 terabytes
Maximum file size	4 terabytes
Filenames	8 bit ASCII characters
File permissions supported?	Yes
Transaction log?	Ext2 : No

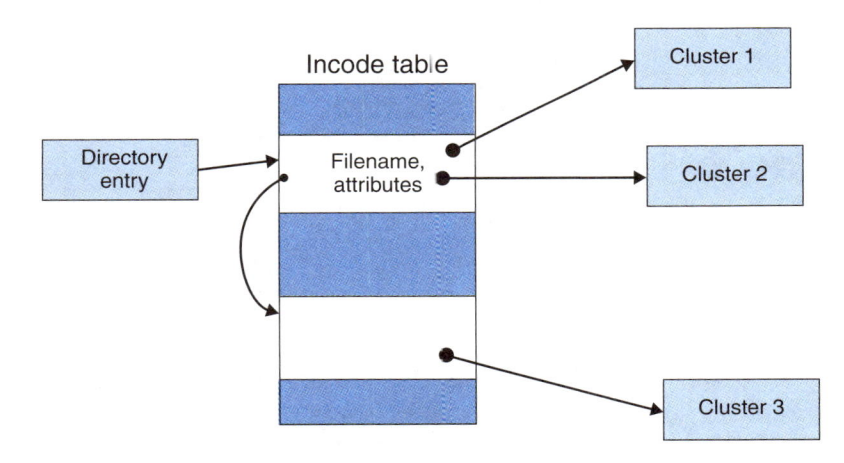

Figure 8.21 Linux Ext2 file system structure.

8.6.4 Mac OS X HFS+ Systems

HFS+ is the standard filesystem on Mac OS X and supports transaction logging (journaling), long filenames, symbolic links, and other features.

Table 8.5 MAC OS X HFS+ File System Characteristics

Cluster size	512 bytes or larger
Maximum partition size	2 terabytes
Maximum file size	
Filenames	Unicode characters
File permissions supported?	Yes
Transaction log?	Yes

8.6.5 Other File Systems

There are many other types of file systems. Examples include the following:

- *CD-ROMs*: The data on CD-ROMs is formatted with a file system scheme called ISO 9660, which allocates contiguous space for each file on the disk. Table 8.6 shows the characteristics of the ISO 9660 file system.

Table 8.6 ISO 9660 File System Characteristics

Cluster size	N/A
Maximum partition size	N/A
Maximum file size	700 MB
Filenames	8 bit ASCII characters
File permissions supported?	No
Transaction log?	No

- *Network File System (NFS)*: A Network File System (and other similar systems) allows a process on one computer to access a file that physically resides on another computer across the network. This file system does not implement any disk space allocation, but provides the mechanisms for the various file and directory access methods to communicate across the network.

8.7 Virtual File System

On any given computer, there will likely be multiple file systems. There will also be multiple device types and possibly multiple disk partitions, each with a different file system. The typical application does not care what device a file resides on, what type of device it is, or what file system is in use on that device. It simply wants to be able to use the file and the directory access methods discussed earlier. Thus, a modern operating system will include a *virtual file system* to provide this abstraction.

When an application carries out an I/O system call, the request will go to the virtual file system. It is the job of this system to determine which device the requested file resides on and to forward the request to the appropriate file system. Figure 8.22 shows the relationship of the application to the virtual file system and the underlying file systems.

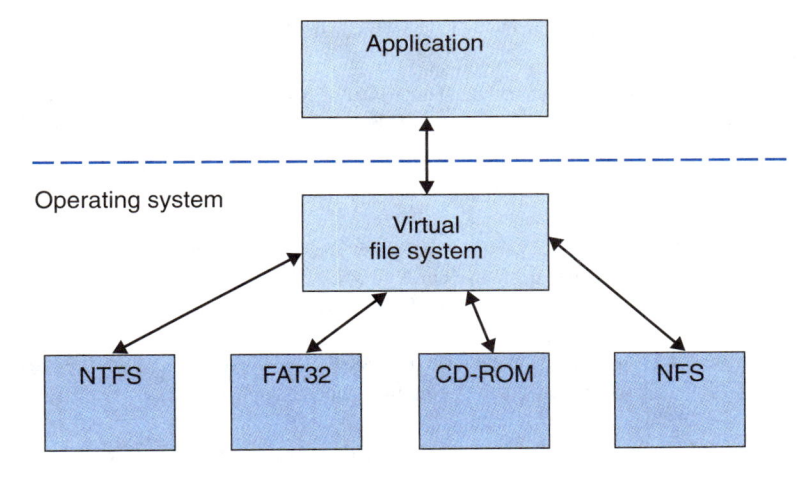

Figure 8.22 Virtual file system.

8.8 Removable Media

Files are commonly stored on removable media such as the following:

- CD
- USB memory stick
- Camera or Smartphone

When removable media is physically inserted/mounted on the computer, the file management subsystem needs to take two steps:

1. Determine the type of media that has been installed and start up the appropriate file system to manage it.
2. Inform the virtual file system of the presence of this new file system.

This procedure is commonly called *mounting* the file system. When the media is removed, the file management system needs to undo the two steps above through a process called *unmounting*. The terms *mount* and *unmount* originated years ago when tape reels were physically mounted on a drive to make the files on the tape available to the computer.

Suppose a process has opened a file that is on removable media. What happens when that media is removed? In a traditional system, the process will get an error the next time it attempts to do I/O to that file, which will typically cause the process to terminate abnormally.

On more modern systems, users can inform the file management system that they are planning to remove the media. The file management system will then send a message to the running processes to inform them that the media is about to be removed. Processes can take one of two possible actions:

- The process can cleanly stop itself or take some kind of recovery action that allows it to close files on that media. For example, Windows Explorer will close any window that is showing folders on that media.

- The process can ignore the message. In that case, the file management system will warn users that they should not remove the media.

In addition to mounting and unmounting physical media, it is also possible to mount/unmount a file system (or directory) that is on another computer across the network. On Windows, this is called *Map Network Drive*.

Users mounting a remote file system must specify a mount point—the position in the local directory structure where the remote file system is to appear. On Windows, users specify a drive letter for this; the dialog window shown in Figure 8.23 will appear. On Unix and Linux, the mount point can be any node in the directory tree structure. On Mac OS X, the mount point will be the shared devices folder that appears in the finder window.

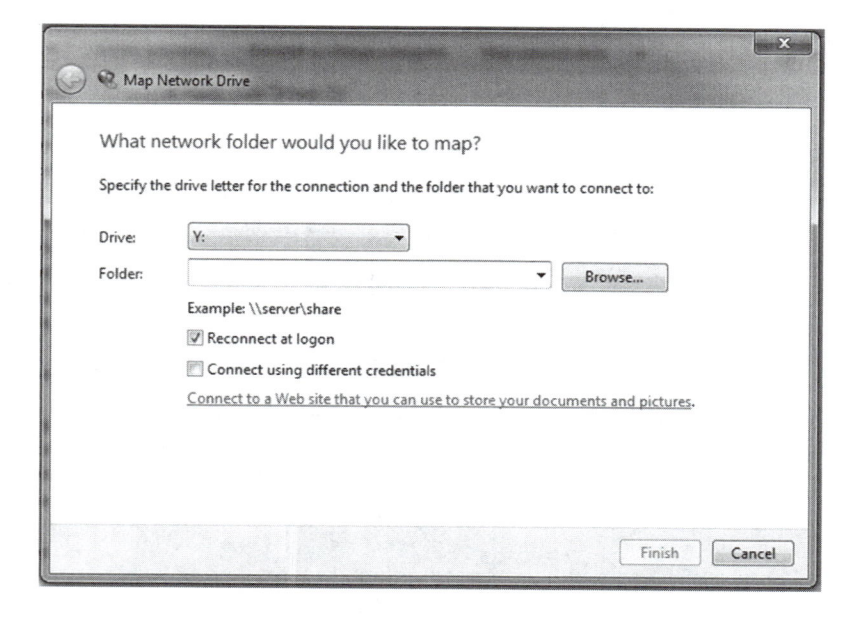

Figure 8.23 Microsoft Windows Map Network Drive.

8.9 Seeing the Future Now

The traditional directory tree structure for file systems was invented when disk space was very expensive; consequently, computers did not have a lot of it. At that time, a typical system might have several hundred files. Thus, it was not a large burden to find a particular file in the tree structure.

Today, computers often have much more disk space than the typical user actually needs, but there are often over 100,000 files stored on a system. This makes it extremely difficult to locate a particular file.

New operating systems are now becoming available that have Google-like capabilities to locate files locally on that computer. Both the Apple Mac OS X and Windows Vista have this feature. This capability scans a file when it is created to build a large index of its contents to be displayed when a search is performed.

8.10 Summary

Operating systems provide capabilities to store, locate, and retrieve data. The stored data is organized into files. The file management subsystem consists of the OS components that provide these facilities. In addition to providing the mechanisms for reading and writing data, the file management subsystem is responsible for organizing the files on physical media such as disks and CDs.

	Key Terms	
absolute path	file system	pathname
access method	filename	pipe
boot block	flush	random access
buffer	folder	read
close	HFS+	redirection
cluster allocation	I/O redirection	relative path
contiguous allocation	indexed clusters	sequential access
direction	internal	shortcut
directory entry	fragmentation	standard error
external fragmentation	linked clusters	standard input
FAT-32	Linux Ext2 and	standard output
file	Ext3 systems	stream
file association	NTFS	symbolic link
file extension	open	virtual file system
file handle	partition control write	write
file position pointer	block	

Exercises and Questions

1. In Java, the File class is used to represent the data in a directory entry. Write a program that uses the File class to print all the attributes of a file.

2. Write a program that uses each of the I/O system calls described in the section on access methods.

3. Write a program that searches a directory tree for a particular file.

4. Write pseudocode to map an application I/O request to physical I/O requests. Allow for the application request to cross cluster boundaries.

5. Write a report that explores the details of a real-world file system in much more detail than we have discussed here.

6. Write a program that simulates allocating and deallocating space for a file.

    a. Model the structures that are used in FAT-32.

    b. Model the structures that are used in NTFS.

    c. Model the structures that are used in Ext2.

Chapter 9

The I/O System

9.1 Introduction

The previous chapter explained how a file management system interfaces with application programs and allocates space for files. To be able to actually read and write data to and from those files, we need to use the input/output (I/O) system, which has two major objectives:

- Take an application I/O request and send it to the physical device, then take whatever response comes back from the device and send it to the application.

- Optimize the performance of the various I/O requests.

Additionally, the I/O system must provide mechanisms to *configure* the system— i.e., to inform the OS of exactly what *devices* are attached to the system and how to communicate with those devices.

9.2 I/O Hardware

Before we discuss how the operating system handles input and output, let's review how I/O hardware works. The general structure of a computer is shown in Figure 9.1. The most important information in this diagram is that each physical device has a *device interface* (also known as a device controller or peripheral controller). These device interfaces directly control the devices for the main CPU.

In order to control the devices, the device interfaces all have some level of intelligence (i.e., they are all actually small computers in their own right). The level of

234   Chapter 9   The I/O System

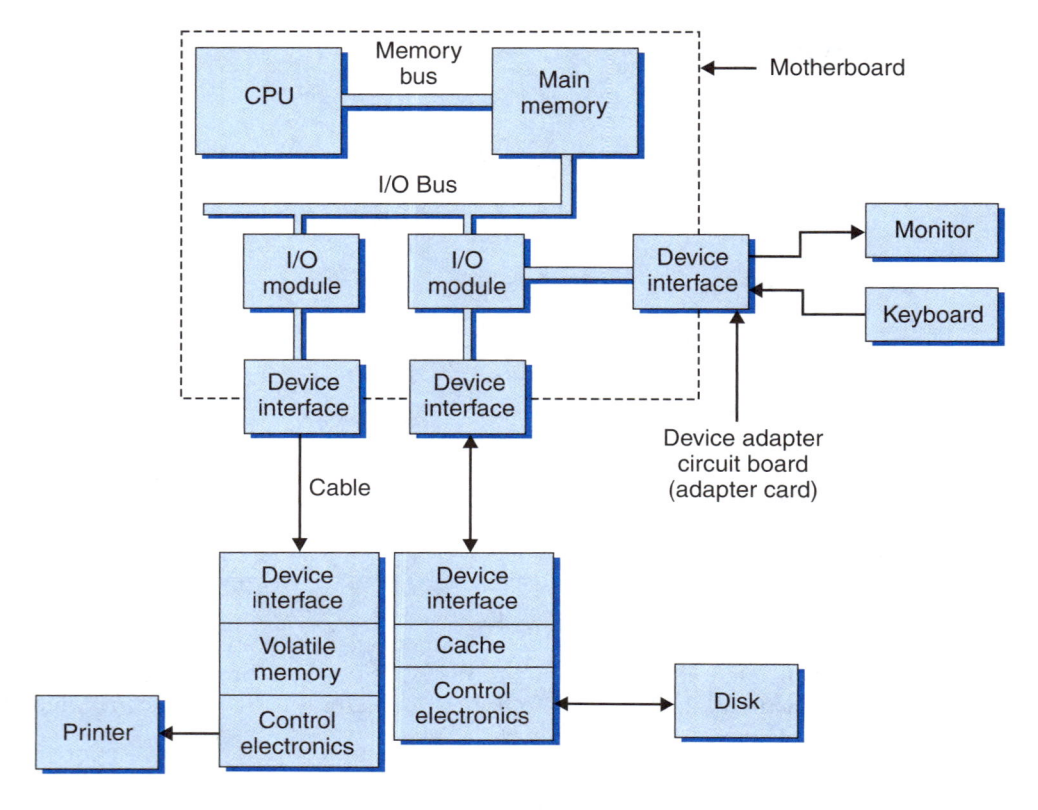

Figure 9.1 General structure of a computer.

intelligence in each device interface will vary tremendously, but they all have one very important attribute: These device interfaces are able to operate the devices at the same time that the main CPU is carrying out some other task.

The general procedure by which device interfaces operate is as follows:

1. The main CPU requests that the device interface carry out an operation.

2. The main CPU proceeds to carry out some other task while the device interface performs the requested operation.

3. When the operation is complete, the device interface generates an *interrupt* to the main CPU to inform it of the completion.

4. The operating system will respond to the I/O completion by informing the appropriate process.

Studying the general architecture of a computer system, several observations can be made:

1. The operating system is able to improve overall system performance if it can keep the various devices as busy as possible.

2. It is important for the operating system to handle device interrupts as quickly as possible.

    a. For interactive devices (keyboard, mouse, microphone), this can make the system more responsive.

    b. For communication devices (modem, Ethernet, etc.), this can affect the effective speed of the communications.

    c. For real-time systems, this can be the difference between the system operating correctly and the system malfunctioning.

In addition, since multiple devices are operating simultaneously, it is possible that several devices will want to send interrupts to the CPU at the same time, as shown in Figure 9.2. The operating system must be prepared to handle this situation.

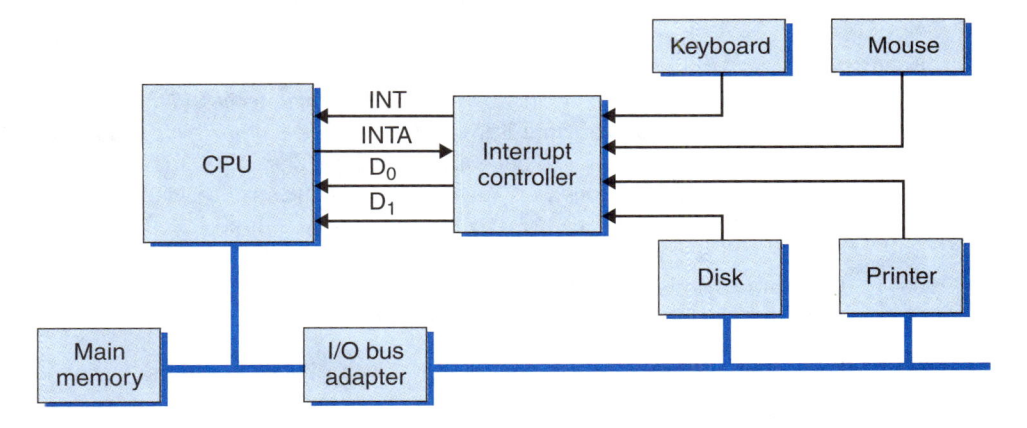

Figure 9.2 Hardware interrupt controller.

9.2.1 Direct Memory Access

As we discuss in more detail later in this chapter, each interrupt requires an amount of processing by an *interrupt service routine* in the operating system. Slow devices (such as a keyboard) will generate an interrupt to the main CPU after each byte is transferred. If a fast device such as a disk generated an interrupt for each byte, the operating system would spend most of its time handling these interrupts.

236　Chapter 9　The I/O System

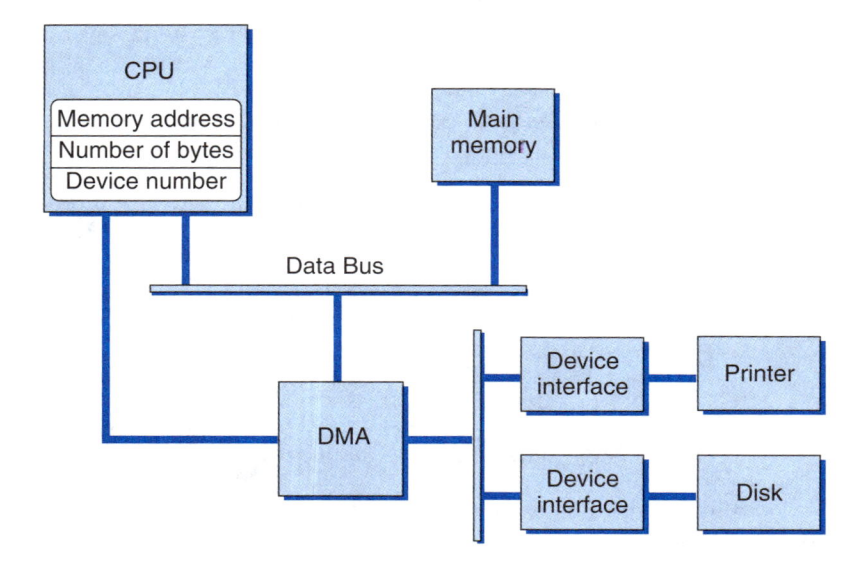

Figure 9.3　DMA hardware.

Thus, a typical computer will have *direct memory access* (*DMA*) hardware to reduce this overhead, as shown in Figure 9.3. With DMA hardware, an entire block of data is transferred between the device and memory. The DMA hardware generates one interrupt after the entire block is transferred, rather than after each byte.

The operating system uses the DMA hardware as follows:

1. The application performs a system call to read data from a file. The file system converts this into one or more physical read requests.

2. The device driver converts this request into a list of commands that indicate

    a. Memory address of the buffer
    b. Number of bytes to transfer
    c. Disk address

3. These commands are sent to the device interface hardware.

4. The device interface initiates and controls the disk operation. (The CPU is able to do other work while this disk operation is in process.)

5. The device interface uses the DMA hardware to transfer the data directly to/from the memory buffer (thus, the name direct memory access).

6. When the entire block of data has been transferred, the device interface sends an interrupt to the CPU to indicate the completion of the request.

9.2.2 Hard Disk Drives

The physical structure of a typical disk drive is shown in Figure 9.4. Each disk has one or more platters that are attached to a rotating spindle. Data is written to and read from the platters by read/write heads.

There is one head for each platter. The head is at the end of an arm that moves the head across the surface of the platter. With the arm stationary, the rotation of the platter creates a *track*—a circle under the head where data is recorded with the head in that position. All of the arms (and heads) will move in unison. Thus, each possible position of the arm forms a track on each platter.

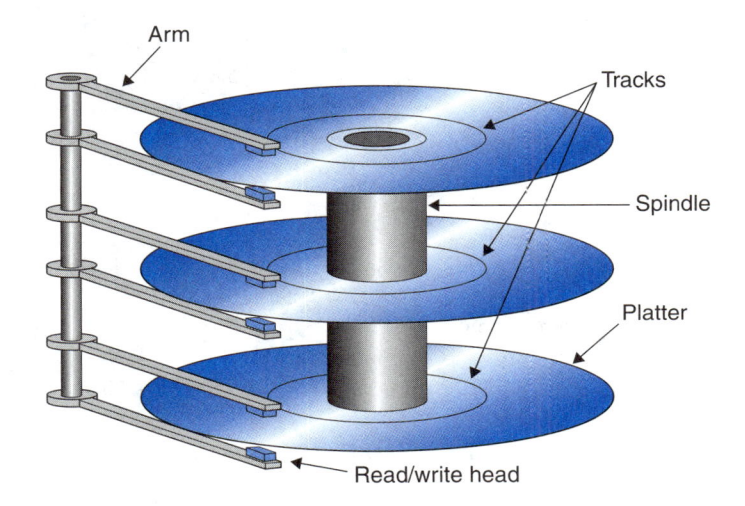

Figure 9.4 Disk drive mechanism.

To read or write data, the disk device must move the arm to the appropriate track. The time to carry this out is called *seek time*. The disk device must then wait for the desired data to rotate into position under the head. The time to carry this out is called *rotational latency*. The disk access time can be calculated as follows:

$$Disk\ access\ time = Seek\ time + Rotational\ latency$$

Each track is recorded in units called *sectors*—the smallest amount of data that can be physically read or written, as shown in Figure 9.5.

On a typical modern disk drive, seek time is about 8 milliseconds and rotational latency is about 4 milliseconds. Thus, the CPU can execute about 10 million to 30 million instructions in the time it takes to carry out one physical disk access. This is a dramatic difference and has a significant impact on system performance. We will be discussing this in the remainder of this chapter.

Some modern disk controllers have a large amount of cache memory and can carry out the following performance optimization. Once the head has been moved to the proper track and we are waiting for the desired sector to rotate into position, we can

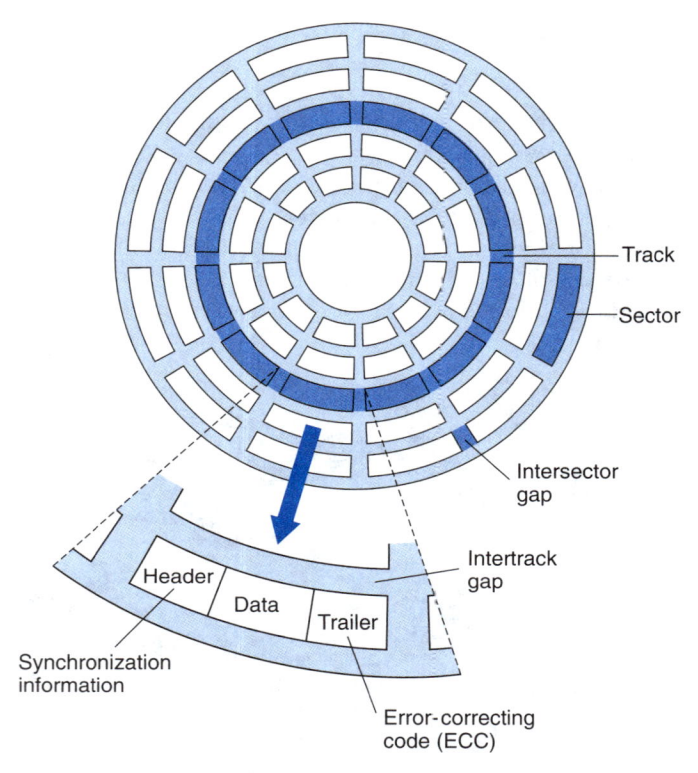

Figure 9.5 Disk sector format.

read other sectors into the cache memory as they appear under the head. Later, if there are requests from the CPU for those sectors, the disk controller can provide them immediately from the cache rather than having to access the disk drive again.

9.2.3 Solid State Disks

An emerging technology is Solid State Disks (SSD), which use some form of non-volatile electronic memory. This technology has much faster access time because there is no mechanical arm to move or rotational latency. However, currently its cost/bit is much higher than the mechanical form of disk drive. Consequently, it is typically limited to small portable devices such as:

- USB Memory Stick
- Camera
- Smartphone

9.3 Device I/O Structure

The overall device I/O structure of an operating system is depicted in Figure 9.6. There is a different *generic device driver* for each general type of media—for example, one for

9.3 Device I/O Structure

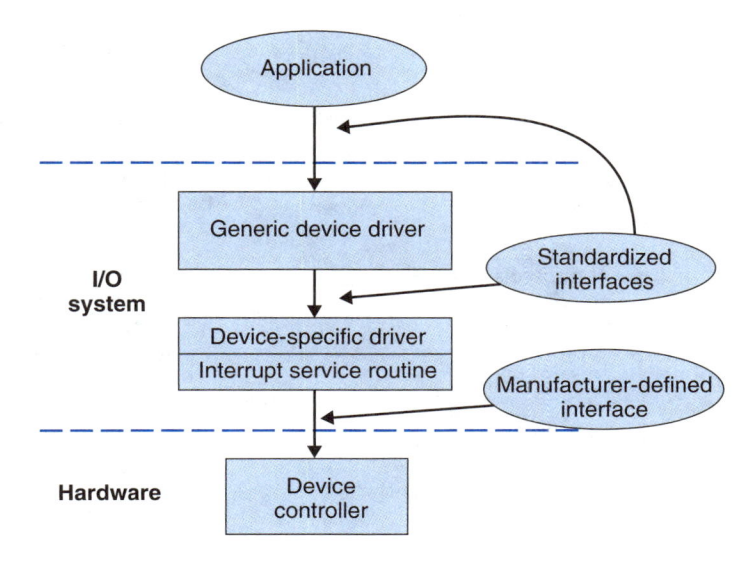

Figure 9.6 I/O system structure.

disks and another one for modems. The generic device driver is responsible for mapping the requests it receives into commands for its media type. Recall from the previous chapter that the file system will convert a logical I/O request from the application to one or more physical I/O requests that will be sent to the generic device driver.

Most devices have been designed with low-level, hardware-oriented interfaces that vary from manufacturer to manufacturer. Thus, the *device-specific driver* is responsible for translating generic commands from the device driver to manufacturer specific commands for the specific make and model of the device that is in use.

The diagram for the I/O system structure shows two standardized interfaces for generic device drivers and device-specific drivers, which allow people other than the OS provider to develop device drivers. Often, device manufacturers will develop the device-specific drivers for their hardware. For an open source system such as Linux, anybody can develop a new (and possibly better) device driver. Note that these standardized interfaces are unique to an operating system. The standards are different for different operating systems. Thus, a device driver for MS Windows will not work on Linux (and vice versa).

The occurrence and handling of an I/O request can be described as the following sequence of steps (also shown in Figure 9.7):

1. An I/O request is created by the application and is sent to the I/O system, which determines the appropriate generic device driver to handle it.

2. If this is a write request and the device does not use DMA, the generic device driver must obtain the data from the requesting process's memory. The generic device driver will then forward the request to the device-specific driver.

3. The device-specific driver will issue the specific sequence of commands that is required to have the device controller perform the desired action.

240 Chapter 9 The I/O System

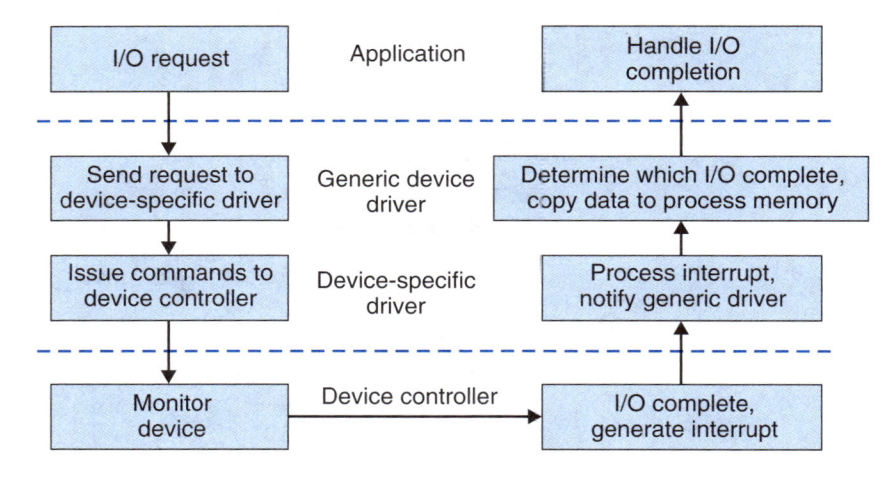

Figure 9.7 Stages of an I/O request.

4. The device controller monitors the status of the operation at the device.

5. When the operation has completed, the device controller generates an interrupt to the CPU.

6. The interrupt causes the CPU to suspend executing whatever thread is currently executing and jump to the interrupt service routine (ISR) in the device-specific driver.

7. The interrupt service routine will perform the device-specific commands that are required to determine the exact status of the device. It will then notify the generic device driver of the completion.

8. The generic device driver must determine which I/O request actually completed and which process/thread initiated the I/O request. If this is a read request and the device does not use DMA, then the generic device driver must copy the data into the requesting process's memory.

9. The requesting process is notified that the I/O request has completed. This typically means informing the CPU dispatcher that the process does not need to wait any longer.

These steps describe how a single I/O request is handled. However, in general, there may be many I/O requests for a device at the same time. These requests may come from multiple processes or from the same process. As with any *resource*, each device needs to have the following:

1. A queue of pending requests

2. A resource scheduler that determines the next request to execute

3. A mechanism to initiate the next request whenever a request completes

9.3 Device I/O Structure   241

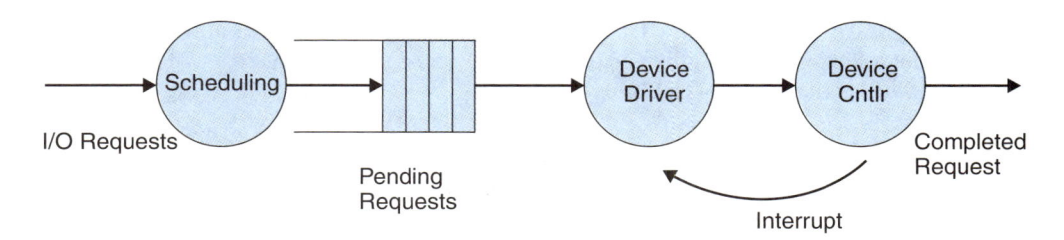

Figure 9.8 I/O request queuing.

The generic device driver handles the scheduling function, as shown in Figure 9.8. This is discussed in more detail in Section 9.4.3 on I/O scheduling.

9.3.1 Intelligent Buses

Newer systems will often support intelligent buses such as Universal Serial Bus (USB) or IEEE 1394 (FireWire). These buses have a high level of intelligence and are defined with software-oriented interfaces. As part of these software-oriented interfaces, all device-specific functionality is placed in the device controller. Thus, there is no need for device-specific drivers in the operating system. Because these buses often support multiple devices simultaneously, they will use communication protocols between the CPU and the device controllers (see Figure 9.9).

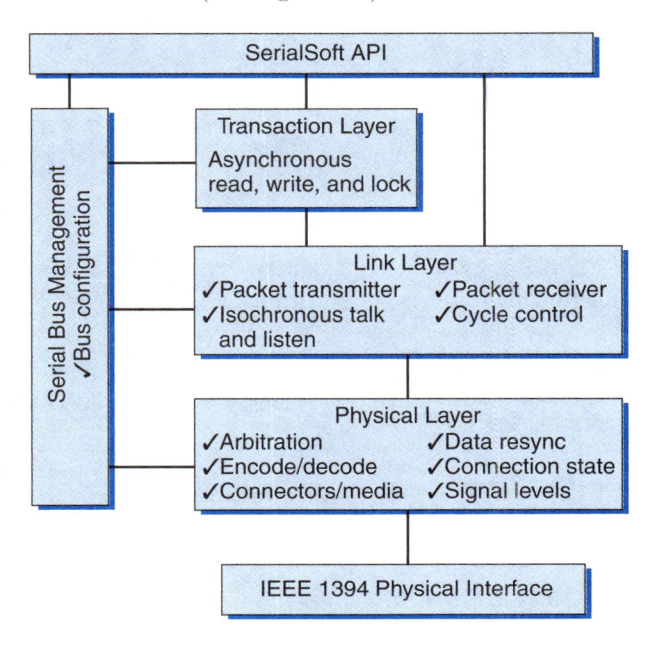

Figure 9.9 IEEE 1394 communication protocols.

242　Chapter 9　The I/O System

With this structure, the generic device driver will communicate with the device controller via a bus interface driver (see Figure 9.10). The stages of an I/O request now look like that shown in Figure 9.11.

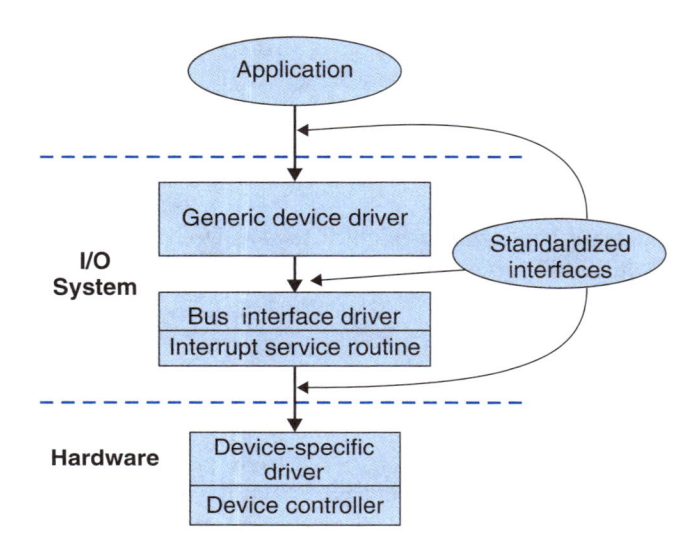

Figure 9.10　I/O system structure for intelligent buses.

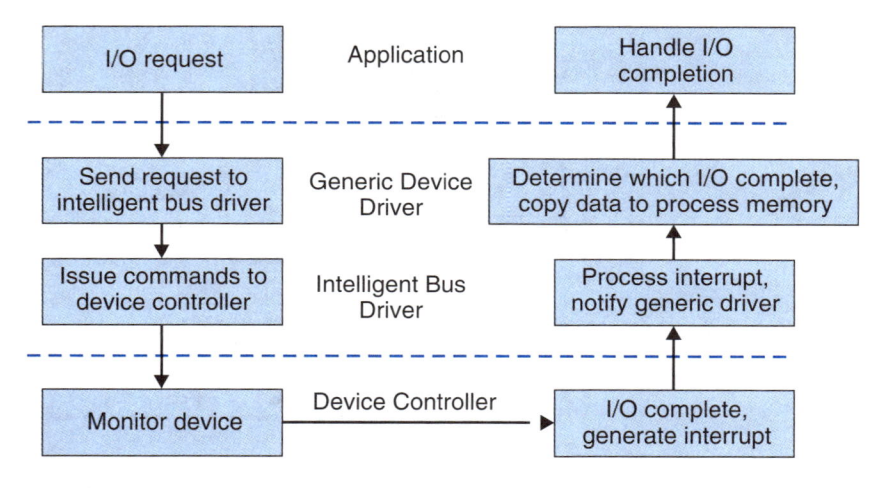

Figure 9.11　Stages of an intelligent bus I/O request.

9.3.2 Handling Multiple Devices Simultaneously

A system will typically have multiple devices operating simultaneously. Consequently, we will often have simultaneous (or near simultaneous) interrupts from these multiple devices. How is this handled?

At the hardware level, interrupts from different devices are given priority levels according to how fast the CPU needs to respond to the device interrupt. The OS needs to respond quickly to an interrupt for either of two reasons:

- To obtain information from the device controller before that information is lost
- To initiate the next operation before it is "too late"

Typically, the hardware works as shown in Figure 9.12. This mechanism handles the priority of the interrupt service routines. Because of this priority-based interrupt

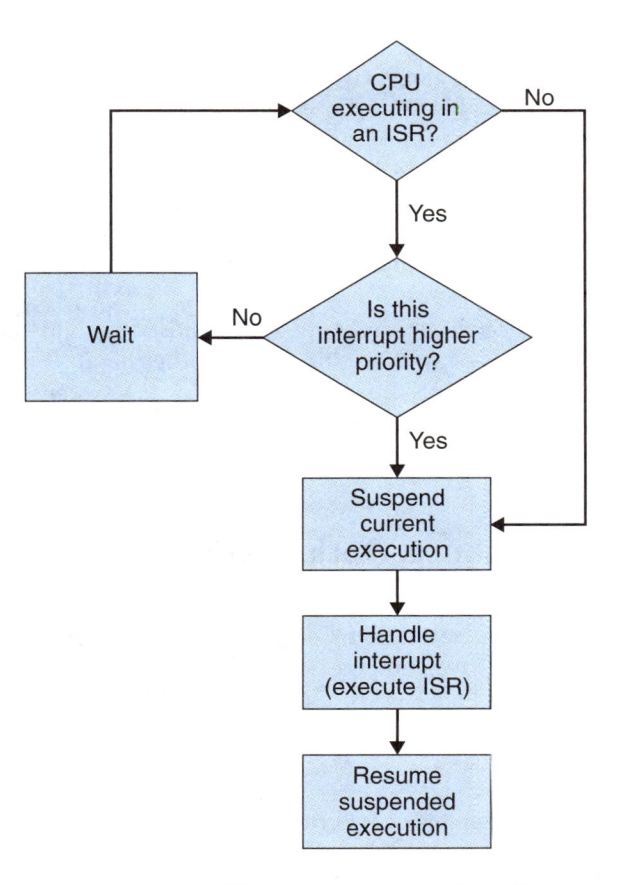

Figure 9.12 Hardware interrupt handling.

244 Chapter 9 The I/O System

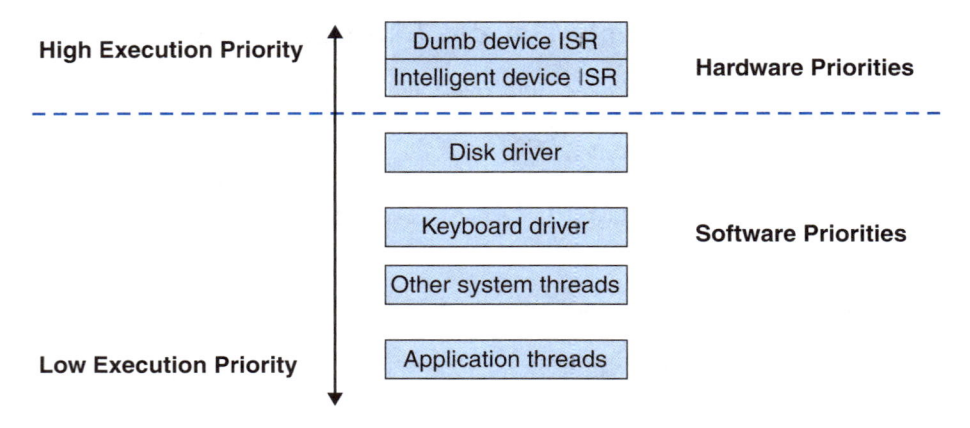

Figure 9.13 System execution priorities.

servicing, the interrupt service routines effectively have the highest execution priority in the entire system. Consequently, ISRs should be written to carry out only the minimal amount of work needed to achieve the two goals described above. They should then pass the request to the device driver(s).

In a typical system, device drivers execute as threads in the system process, with higher priority than other threads. Generally, the device driver thread(s) handling "important" devices such as disks will have higher priority than threads handling other devices (e.g., the keyboard). Figure 9.13 shows the typical overall system execution priorities.

Because device drivers execute as threads, they can lock system resources and perform other types of system calls. On the other hand, ISRs operate in a world that is half detailed hardware-oriented and half operating system. As such, the programming environment for ISRs tends to be constrained, and most normal system functions are unavailable.

9.4 I/O Performance Optimization

Why do we want to optimize I/O performance? Remember that on a typical modern computer, the CPU can execute 10 million instructions in the time it takes to carry out one disk I/O. Thus, *every* physical disk I/O has a dramatic impact on system performance. There are three ways of improving I/O performance, listed in order of decreasing effectiveness:

1. Reduce the number of I/O requests
2. Carry out buffering and/or caching
3. Schedule I/O requests

9.4.1 Reducing the Number of I/O Requests

The most efficient I/O request is one that is never requested.

The best way to improve I/O performance is to reduce the number of I/O requests that the application program makes. A simple example is illustrated by the following portion of SQL code:

```
SELECT Name from STUDENT_RECORDS
SELECT Address from STUDENT_RECORDS
```

Instead of this code, use the following:

```
SELECT Name, Address from STUDENT_RECORDS
```

Both of these examples obtain a list of student names and addresses. The first approach causes the database engine to read the STUDENT_RECORDS table from disk twice. The second approach requires that the table be read only once, thus saving a potentially significant amount of time.

We could create a similar example using basic file read and/or write system calls. Note that since these SQL statements are not directly file read or write system calls, it is easy to overlook them.

All real-world programs generate a significant amount of I/O requests. An application can obtain a considerable performance improvement by reducing the number of disk I/O requests. Programmers often spend a lot of time optimizing the code in a program without giving much thought to the disk I/O. Yet, it is usually easier to eliminate a single I/O request than it is to eliminate 10 million instructions. If this is an application that must support multiple simultaneous requests (e.g., a Web service), this will dramatically affect how well the application will scale up to support many users. That, in turn, will affect how much the organization must spend on computer hardware.

9.4.2 Buffering and Caching

The idea behind *buffering* is a simple one: If you cannot completely eliminate I/O, make the physical I/O requests as big as possible. This will reduce the number of physical I/O requests by the buffering factor used. For example, if we buffer three logical I/O requests per physical I/O request, the number of physical I/O requests will be one-third the number required without buffering. We carry this out by having the application's logical I/O requests copy data to/from a large memory buffer. The physical I/O requests then transfer the entire buffer. As an example, an application may wish to carry out a logical I/O request for each line of a text file. We can increase system performance by carrying out only one physical I/O request for a large group of lines.

Chapter 9 The I/O System

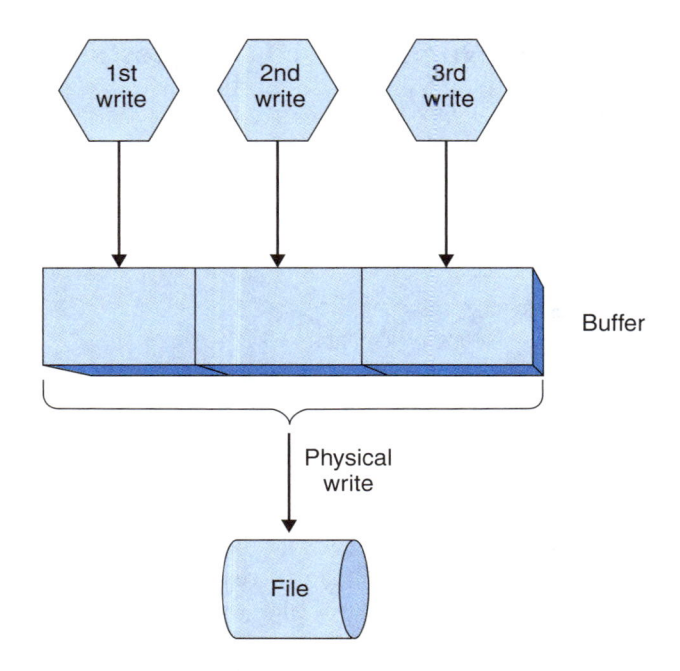

Figure 9.14 Buffered write.

The following general algorithm is used for buffered writes, which are shown in Figure 9.14:

```
Copy application data to buffer[Buffer_index]
Buffer_index = Buffer_index + logical_write_size
If Buffer_Index = Buffer_Size  // is Buffer now Full?
   Do physical write
   Buffer_index = 0
```

Figure 9.15 illustrates a buffered read, which would use this algorithm:

```
If Buffer_index == Buffer_Size  // Have we emptied the buffer?
  Do physical read
  Buffer_index = 0
Copy data from buffer[Buffer_index] to application
Buffer_index = Buffer_index + logical_read_size
```

Notice that with buffered writes, we are keeping data in volatile memory for a longer period before we physically write it to nonvolatile memory. Thus, we are incurring a greater risk that we will lose data if there is a system crash. Our overall application and system design should understand and handle this situation.

9.4 I/O Performance Optimization

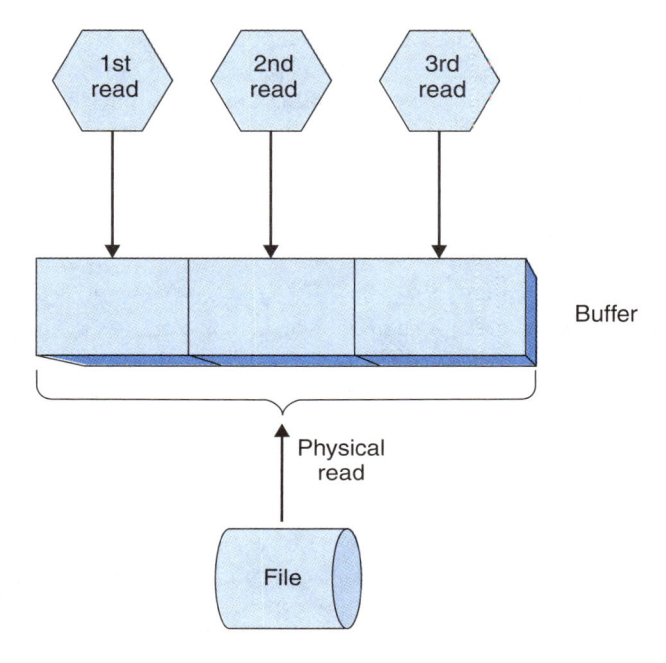

Figure 9.15 Buffered read.

If the data we are buffering is for an atomic transaction, we MUST transfer the data to nonvolatile memory when the atomic transaction completes. Otherwise, we will be violating the contract of the atomic transaction. For ordinary file I/O, the *flush* system call is used to carry this out. Flush effectively says to ignore the buffering and do a physical write immediately. If we are using a database engine, the *commit* command is used for this purpose.

Caching is a form of buffering in which data is kept around after it has been used in the hope that it will be used again. If we guess right and the data actually is used again, we can save considerable time because we have the data already in memory and do not have to access a physical device again. In the discussion of disk drives in Section 9.2.2, we saw how modern disk controllers will use caching. The operating system's memory management subsystem also uses caching.

Buffering and caching are examples of space–time tradeoffs. By using more memory space, we can potentially save time. For pure buffering, it is easy to make this calculation:

- Benefit (time saved) = (Buffer_Size / logical_read_size) × Disk access time
- Cost (memory space required) = buffer size

For caching, the cost (memory space required) can be easily calculated, but the benefit is not precisely quantifiable. The reason for this is that caching is attempting to predict the future behavior of the system. Since, in general, the future is not always precisely predictable, we cannot always implement the optimal behavior. The best we can do is hope to approximate the optimal behavior. What is possible is to estimate statistical probabilities of achieving a hit (i.e., desired data is in the cache). This probability will vary depending on how the cache is actually being used.

9.4.3   I/O Scheduling

For most devices, a FCFS (first-come first-served) scheduling algorithm is appropriate. For example, we want the segments of a music file to be played in sequential order. However, for some devices (disks especially), the order in which requests are processed is not inherently constrained by the device characteristics.

On a typical system, there will be pending disk I/O requests from many different processes. The correct functioning of these processes usually does not depend on the *order* in which the disk I/O operations actually occur. Thus, we will want the resource scheduler to attempt to optimize performance for devices such as disks. In the rare cases where the ordering of the disk I/O operations does matter, we would actually be carrying out interprocess communication and should use appropriate resource locks to avoid race conditions.

Because of the requirement for moving the arm (with the read/write head) and waiting for the disk to rotate into position, the hard disk's context switch time (i.e., the time to change from one request to another) is extremely high, especially compared with carrying out a CPU context switch. Thus, in disk scheduling, the duration of an actual read/write operation is much shorter than the duration of a context switch. A similar situation is observed in the case of a traveling service person who has to provide technical service to several customer sites distributed in some geographical area. The average time the service person takes to travel from one service site to another is generally much longer than the average service time at each site.

Additionally, for most devices, the time to execute a command is independent of the previous command. However, disk I/O has the attribute that the time it takes to carry out a complete I/O operation is dependent on what the previous operation was (i.e., Where did the previous operation move the arm?). This aspect of I/O processing is said to be state dependent and mainly affects the context switch time.

9.5   Hard Disk I/O Scheduling

There are four common hard disk I/O scheduling algorithms:

- First-come first-served (FCFS)
- Shortest seek time first (SSTF)
- Elevator (SCAN)
- Circular SCAN

9.5.1 First-Come First-Served Algorithm

First-come first-served (FCFS) scheduling services I/O requests in the order in which they arrive. It is, of course, the simplest scheduling algorithm and actually does no scheduling. It serves as a useful baseline to compare other scheduling algorithms. Consider the following example: There is a disk with 100 tracks and requests for tracks 44, 20, 95, 4, 50, 52, 47, 61, 87, and 25. The arm is currently at track 50. Figure 9.16 shows the arm movement for this example. We see in this figure that while the arm is moving from track 50 to track 44, it does not stop to service requests at intermediate locations (track 47). FCFS is actually a desirable scheduling algorithm for one type of "disk media." Consider flash memory devices (such as a USB memory stick). On these devices, there is no mechanical arm to move and the time to perform a request is not dependent on the previous request. In this situation, FCFS will provide performance as good as any other scheduling algorithm without the overhead. FCFS is also an appropriate scheduling scheme in situations in which it is known that only one application will be accessing the disk.

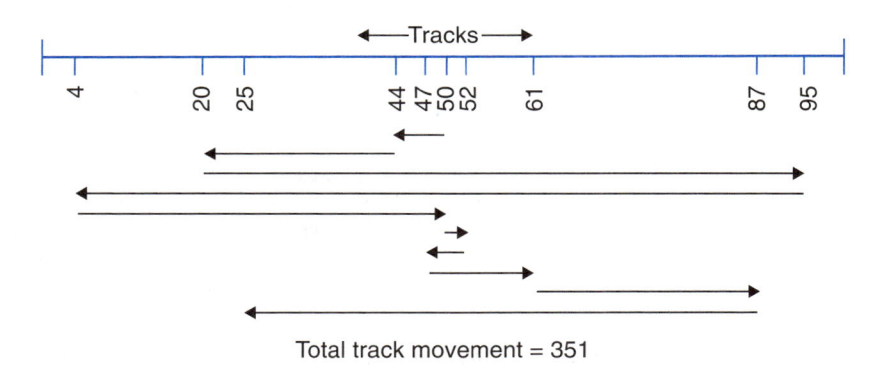

Figure 9.16 FCFS scheduling example.

9.5.2 Shortest Seek Time First Algorithm

The obvious optimization for disk I/O requests is to always handle the request that requires moving the arm the least amount—a process that is called shortest seek time first (SSTF). To illustrate this process, let's examine the same FCFS example but now use the SSTF algorithm, as shown in Figure 9.17. As is clear, there is a significant improvement. In this example, the disk arm moves less than half as many tracks. This algorithm provides "short-term optimality."

Now consider a situation in which there are many requests clustered together and one request is far away (at the other end of the disk). SSTF will spend its time processing the requests that are clustered together and ignore the far away request. If requests continue to arrive that are near the other requests, SSTF will continue to ignore the far

250 Chapter 9 The I/O System

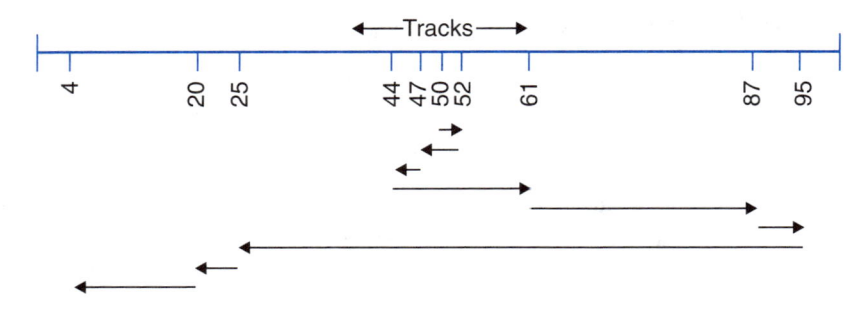

(SSTF scheduling diagram with tracks: 4, 20, 25, 44, 47, 50, 52, 61, 87, 95)

Total track movement = 152

Figure 9.17 SSTF scheduling example.

away request. Thus, it is possible for this scheduling algorithm to exhibit *starvation* of the far away requests.

9.5.3 Elevator (SCAN) Algorithm

In the elevator (SCAN) algorithm, once the arm starts moving in one direction, it keeps moving in that direction until the end is reached (the last track), then the disk arm will start moving in the other direction. A variation of this policy is the LOOK policy in which the disk arm moves in one direction as long as there are pending requests in that direction. Only after all requests have been exhausted ahead in the direction the arm has been moving, does it start moving in the other direction.

Figure 9.18 illustrates a SCAN scheduling algorithm that in this case clearly provides an improvement over SSTF. Because this algorithm continues to service I/O

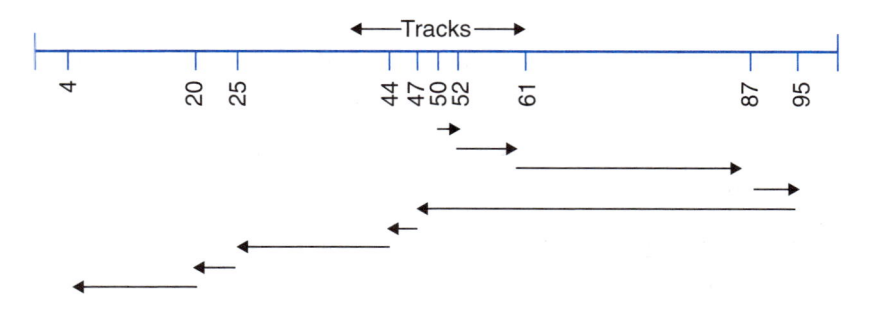

(SCAN scheduling diagram with tracks: 4, 20, 25, 44, 47, 50, 52, 61, 87, 95)

Total track movement = 136

Figure 9.18 SCAN scheduling example.

requests in one direction up to the last track before switching to the other direction, starvation of the I/O requests will not occur. We can see that SCAN requires the minimum amount of arm movement. That, along with the lack of starvation, makes this the most commonly used disk I/O scheduling algorithm.

9.5.4 Circular Scan Algorithm

The circular scan algorithm is similar to regular SCAN, except that the arm does not stop to handle requests while moving in the reverse direction. Instead, the arm moves all the way in the reverse direction and then starts processing requests in the forward direction. The example shown in Figure 9.19 illustrates that circular scan will not be as efficient as either SSTF or regular SCAN.

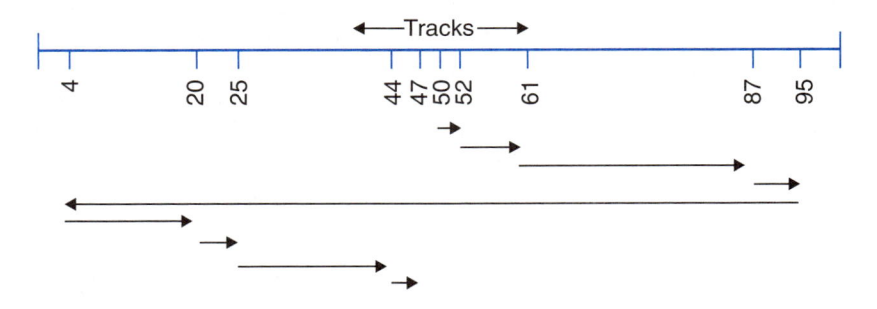

Total track movement = 236

Figure 9.19 Circular scan scheduling example.

9.5.5 Optimizing Rotational Latency

Since rotational latency can take as long as moving the disk arm, it would seem natural that we would also want to optimize this with two goals in mind:

1. Place requests for the same track together in the request queue.

2. Order those requests by rotational position of the desired sector relative to the current position of the disk.

Unfortunately, many modern disk controllers do not inform the operating system of the current rotational position. So, the OS cannot carry out the second part of this optimization. However, those disk controllers will typically accept many simultaneous requests and use their large cache memory to handle them, thus achieving the same effect.

9.5.6 Interaction of Disk Scheduling and Other System Functions

As we have just seen, the performance of the disk is greatly affected by how far the arm must move. Thus, it is easy to see that if files are close together on a disk, there will be less arm movement than if files are far apart. This leads to two observations we can make about disk space allocation that was discussed in the previous chapter:

- We would like the disk space allocation system to allocate clusters close together rather than scattered around the disk.

- We see why it is important to periodically defragment a disk.

There are a number of files and disk data structures that are frequently accessed. These include the swap file and disk space management structures (e.g., MFT). If these items are allocated on the center tracks, less arm movement will be required than if they are allocated at one end of the disk. In fact, we can generalize this observation to say that we can improve overall performance by allocating space from the center of the disk outward, rather than starting at one side of the disk and moving across.

We have focused on performance as the primary criteria for disk I/O scheduling. A system may also want to consider two other features:

- *Reliability*: We may want to give priority to disk I/Os related to updating the disk space management structures on a disk (e.g., MFT, inodes).

- *Overall system performance*: Certain system structures (e.g., swap file, Windows Registry) are accessed frequently and directly affect overall system performance. We may want to give priority to these over other I/O requests.

9.6 System Configuration

As previously mentioned, when a system powers on, it must be configured so that the operating system can answer the following questions:

- What devices are connected to the system?

- For each device, what are the addresses to be used to communicate with the device?

The traditional manner to configure a system is for a system administrator to manually provide this information to the operating system. Additionally, a device-specific driver typically needs to be installed to provide the communications with the device.

As more and more different types of devices became available and the typical owner of a computer became less and less experienced in managing computers, this approach became a support nightmare. The first step to alleviate this problem on PCs was the

Plug and Play feature introduced in Windows 95. This system attempted to automatically determine what devices were connected and how to communicate with them. However, because there had been few software-oriented standards for hardware devices, this feature often failed.

The next step was to have the device interfaces use *self-identification*—when a device is turned on, it automatically informs the operating system that it is present and provides information about itself and how to communicate with it. Self-Identification was introduced to PCs with the PCI Bus.

Note that this feature had been available in Apple MACs for almost a decade prior to the introduction of PCI Bus. Apple MACs used NuBus, which had been created by MIT in the late 1970s. While self-identification alleviated many problems, it still required the installation of a device-specific driver. With the introduction of USB (Universal Serial Bus) and FireWire (IEEE 1394), software-oriented standards were introduced. Figure 9.20 shows an example of the software protocols.

The introduction of these software-oriented protocols has the effect of moving the device-specific driver from the operating system into the device controller. With this approach, the operating system does not need to know any manufacturer-specific information. As long as there is an appropriate generic device driver, users can plug in a device of that type from any manufacturer and it will work properly.

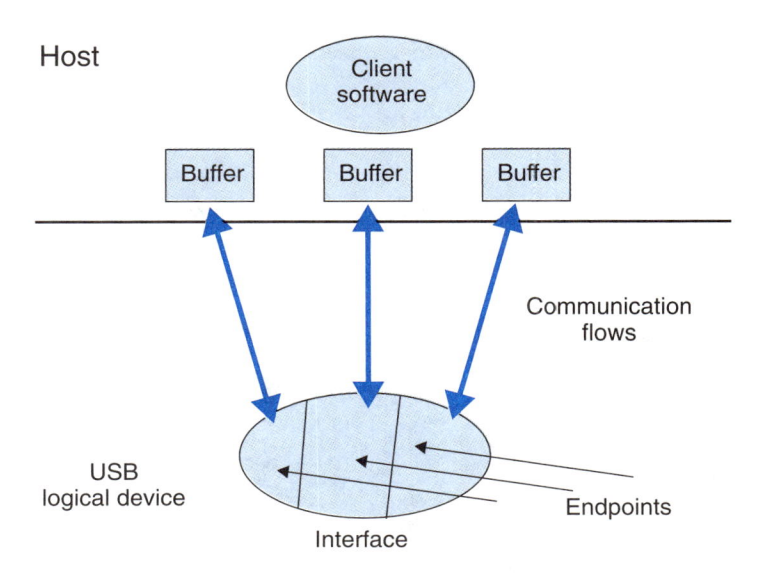

Figure 9.20 USB software-oriented design.

9.7 Hard Disk Scheduling Simulation Model

An interactive disk scheduling simulation model is available for exploring this aspect of an operating system. The simulation model can be run by selecting run simulations disk I/O. As shown in Figure 9.21, the user can set the following parameters:

1. Simulation period (how long to run the simulation)

2. Arrivals stop (when the simulation should stop creating new disk I/O requests)

3. Interarrival time (average time between disk I/O requests being created)

4. Disk tracks (number of tracks on the disk)

5. Seek time (average seek time for the disk)

6. Disk RPM (how fast the disk is spinning)

7. Disk transfer rate (how fast data is transferred by the disk)

8. Scheduler (which disk scheduling algorithm to use)

9. Distribution type (how the requests are distributed across the disk)

10. Standard deviation (applies if the distribution type is normal; see Appendix E)

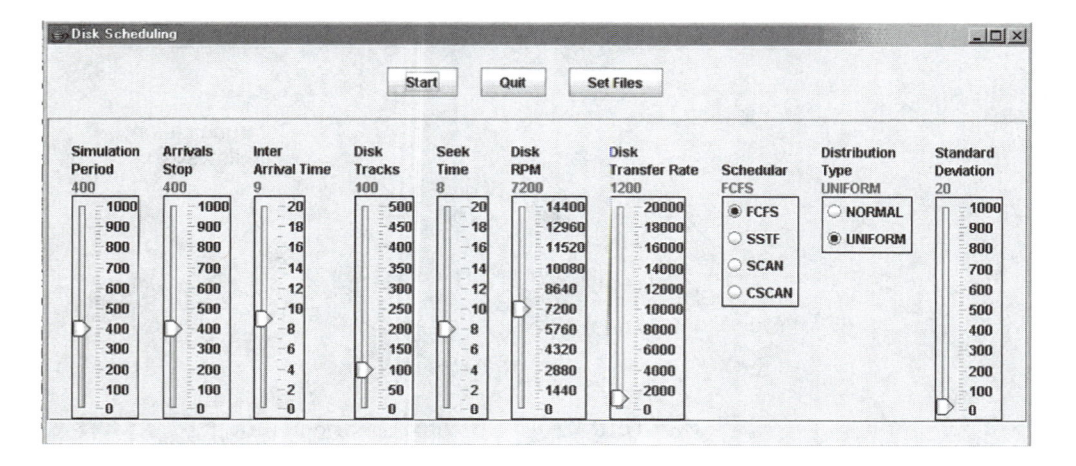

Figure 9.21 Disk scheduling parameters.

9.7 Hard Disk Scheduling Simulation Model

The simulation run will produce two plots:

- One showing the disk arm movement over time, as shown in Figure 9.22.
- The other showing the number of pending I/O requests over time, as shown in Figure 9.23.

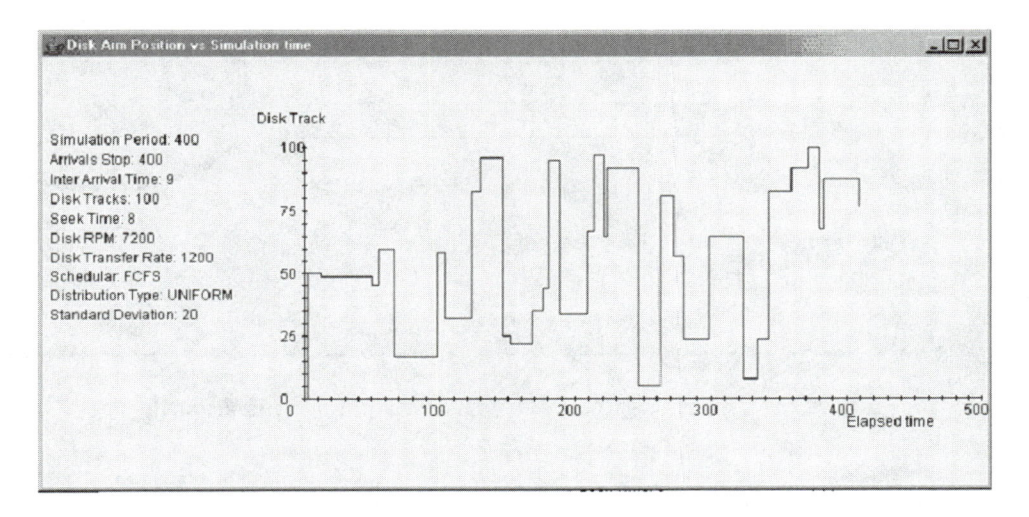

Figure 9.22 Disk arm movement.

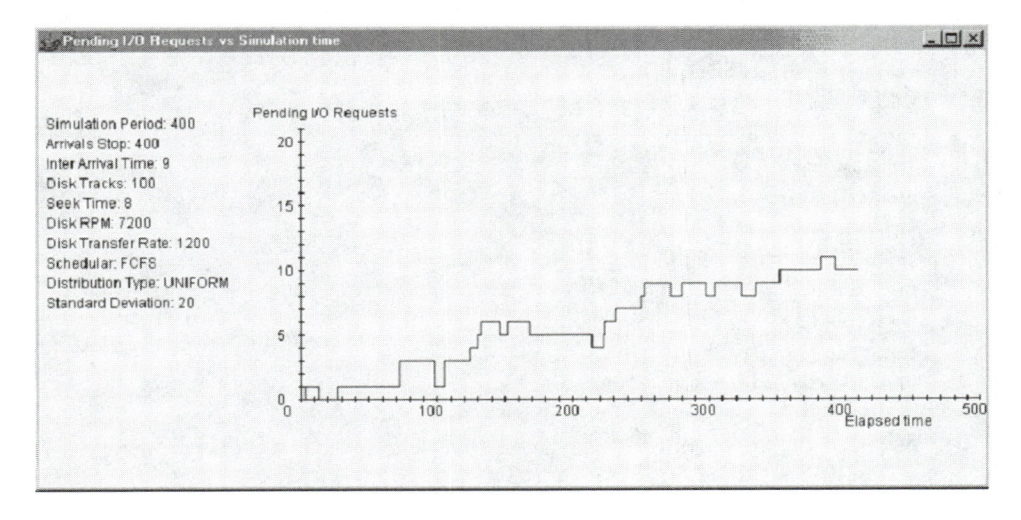

Figure 9.23 Number of pending I/O requests.

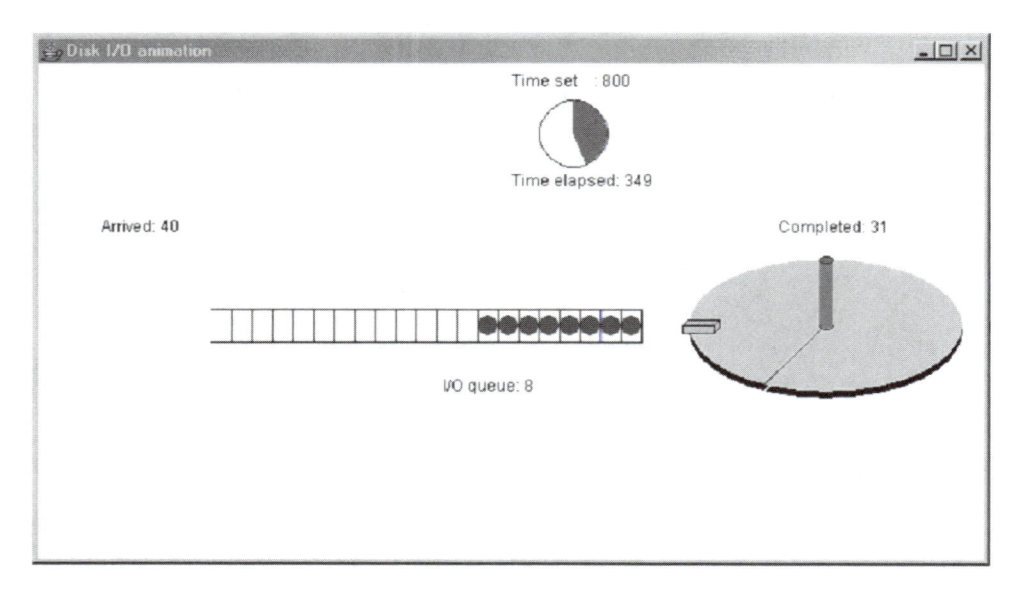

Figure 9.24 Disk scheduling animation.

In addition, there is an animation of the operation of the disk and its input queue (see Figure 9.24). Each simulation run will also produce a report such as the one shown in Listing 9.1.

Listing 9.1 Output listing of a disk scheduling animation.

```
Project: Disk Scheduling
Run at: Mon Mar 14 12:43:56 EST 2006 by RS on Windows XP, RichLaptop
------------------------------------------------------
Input Parameters
Simulation Period: 400
Arrivals Stop: 400
Inter Arrival Time: 9
Disk Tracks: 100
Seek Time: 8
Disk RPM: 7200
Disk Transfer Rate: 1200
Scheduler: FCFS
Distribution Type: UNIFORM
Standard Deviation: 20
------------------------------------------------------
Results of simulation:
Total number of I/O requests arrived: 46
Throughput:   34
Disk Request Mean Sojourn Time: 0059.040
```

```
Disk Utilization: 90%
Mean Disk Wait Time: 0048.423
Maximum Disk Wait Time: 0103.423
```

9.8 Summary

The I/O system of a computer enables users to store data to files and to retrieve that data at any time. The I/O system takes a read or write from an application and sends the appropriate I/O request to the corresponding physical device, and then handles the response from the device. The I/O system also maintains information about the available physical devices connected to the computer system.

Buffering and caching are techniques used to improve performance of the I/O system. The various hard disk scheduling techniques order the I/O requests to be serviced in such a manner as to minimize the seek time, which directly affects performance of the system. The simulation model described in this chapter helps to illustrate the behavior and the performance of the various disk scheduling techniques, given a queue of disk requests.

As the technology for solid state disks improves, we are likely to see more and more usage of this type of disk in future systems.

Key Terms		
access time	flush	seek time
buffering	generic device driver	self-identification
caching	intelligent bus	shortest seek time first
commit	interrupt	(SSTF)
device interface	interrupt service routine	space–time tradeoff
device-specific driver	rotational latency	starvation
direct memory access	SCAN	track
first-come first-served (FCFS)	sector	

Exercises and Questions

1. Two disk drives are available for a particular computer. Drive A has 5400 rpm, and drive B has 7200 rpm (and is more expensive). Which disk drive provides better performance? Explain your answer.

    a. Drive A

    b. Drive B

    c. Both have the same performance

    d. Not enough information to decide

2. Figure 9.13 indicates that the ISRs for "dumb devices" typically have the highest execution priority. Why is this?

3. Show that for any given set of requests, the SCAN disk scheduling algorithm moves the disk arm the least possible distance.

4. Show that SSTF will provide the same performance as SCAN only if its arm movement happens to be identical to that of SCAN.

5. Consider the disk scheduling examples in Figure 9.16 thru Figure 9.19. Suppose that just after the disk has processed the last request in the list, some additional requests arrive. Show that in this situation, circular SCAN will provide the same performance as regular SCAN.

6. Show why disk performance is improved if we allocate space from the center of the disk out, rather than starting at one side.

7. Which scheduling algorithm would be the best one to use for a music CD?

Chapter 10
Memory Management

10.1 Introduction

The major tasks of the memory manager are the allocation and deallocation of main memory. Because main memory is one of the most important resources in a computer system, the management of memory can significantly affect the performance of the computer system. Memory management is an important part of the functions of the operating system.

In simple operating systems without multiprogramming, memory management is extremely primitive; memory is allocated to only one program (or job) at a time. In early operating systems with multiprogramming, memory was divided into a number of *partitions*—blocks of contiguous memory that could be allocated to a process. The degree of multiprogramming determines the number of partitions in memory (i.e., the maximum number of processes that can reside in memory). When a process completes and terminates, memory is deallocated and the partition becomes available for allocation to another process.

One of the problems present in memory management with partitions is memory fragmentation—the existence of some amount of allocated memory that is not used by the process, or of relatively small memory blocks that cannot be allocated to a process. This problem reduces the memory utilization and can affect other system performance metrics.

The other approach to memory allocation uses smaller blocks of storage that are located in various places of physical memory in a noncontiguous manner. This approach dramatically minimizes the fragmentation problem.

Although at the present the cost of memory has significantly dropped, today's programs are larger and more complex and they demand more memory. The GUI requirements of programs, as well as the increasing complexity and size of the application problems, have in part triggered the trend of higher demand for memory.

The operating system with virtual memory management provides an abstraction of the memory space used by a program, independent of how this memory is actually

260   Chapter 10   Memory Management

implemented in the physical memory device. One advantage of virtual memory is that a program can reference more memory than what is available in main (physical) memory.

This chapter first discusses the basic concepts in contiguous memory allocation using partitions, then noncontiguous memory allocation using pages and segments. After this, virtual memory management is discussed. The chapter then reviews the most common static paging algorithms and presents two simulation models that compare three of these algorithms. The last part discusses a dynamic paging algorithm and presents a simulation model to illustrate its behavior and performance.

10.2   Process Address Space

A *logical address* is a reference to some location of a process.

The *process address space* is the set of logical addresses that a process references in its code. The operating system provides a mechanism that maps the logical addresses to physical addresses. When memory is allocated to the process, its set of logical addresses will be bound to physical addresses. Figure 10.1 illustrates a high-level view of the mapping of logical addresses to the physical addresses of two processes.

Three types of addresses are used in a program before and after memory is allocated:

1. *Symbolic addresses*: The addresses used in a source program. The variable names, symbolic constants, and instruction labels are the basic elements of the symbolic address space.

2. *Relative addresses*: A compiler converts symbolic addresses into relative addresses.

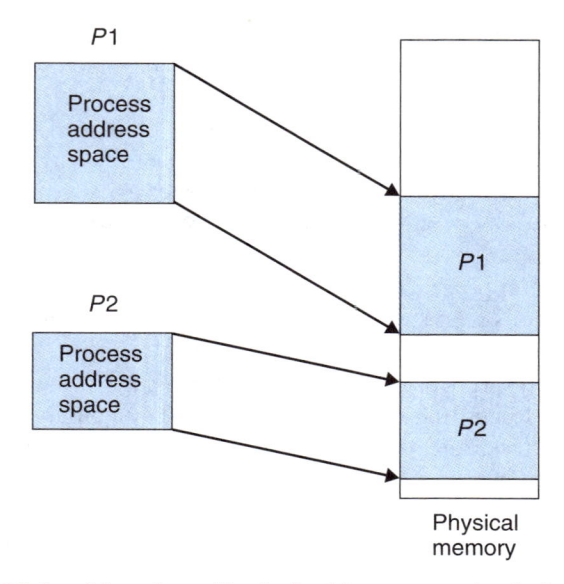

Figure 10.1   Mapping of logical addresses to physical addresses.

3. *Physical addresses*: The final address generated when a program is loaded and ready to execute in physical memory; the *loader* generates these addresses.

10.2.1 Binding

When using a compiled programming language such as C/C++, Ada, and Fortran, the compiler translates the source program with the symbolic addresses into an object program in machine language that includes relative or relocatable addresses.

The *linker* combines the object program with other necessary object modules into an absolute program, which also includes *logical addresses*. The absolute program defines the complete set of logical addresses that the program can reference: the process address space.

The memory manager allocates a block of memory locations to the absolute program and the loader moves the program into the allocated memory block.

At load time, the absolute program is loaded starting at a particular physical address in main memory. The relocatable addresses are mapped to physical addresses; each logical address is bound to a physical address in memory.

The absolute program becomes an executable program right after its logical addresses are translated (mapped) to the corresponding physical addresses. Figure 10.2

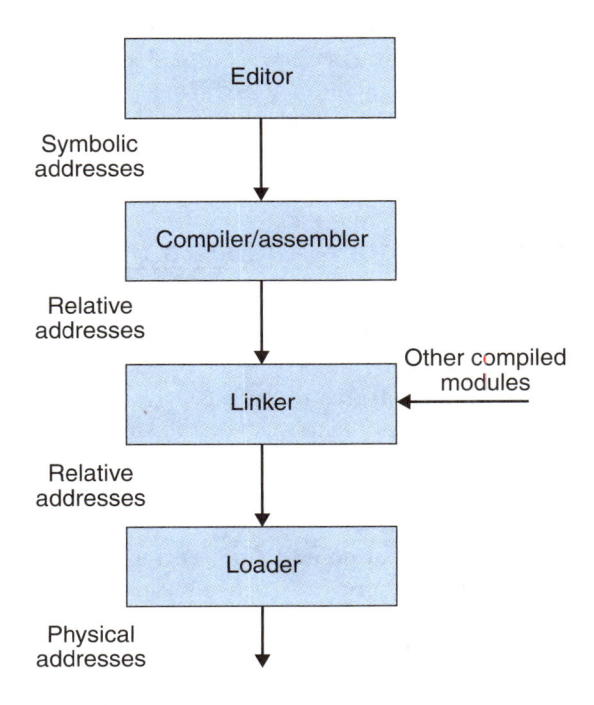

Figure 10.2 Types of addresses.

illustrates compilation, linkage, and loading of a program with the various types of addresses.

The general address translation procedure is called *address binding*. If the mapping (or conversion) of logical addresses to physical addresses is carried out before execution time, it is known as early or *static binding*. A more advanced binding technique delays the mapping from logical to physical addresses until the process starts to execute. This second type of binding is called late or *dynamic binding*.

10.2.2 Static and Dynamic Loading

With static loading, the absolute program (and data) is loaded into memory in order for execution to start. This is the type of loading mentioned in the previous section.

With dynamic loading, the modules of an external library needed by a program are not loaded with the program. The routines of the library are stored on a disk in relocatable form and are loaded into memory only when they are needed by the program. The main advantage of dynamic loading is the improved memory utilization.

10.2.3 Static and Dynamic Linking

When static linking is used, the linker combines all other modules needed by a program into a single absolute load module before execution of the program starts.

When dynamic linking is used, the building of the absolute form of a program is delayed until execution time. For every call to a routine of a library, a stub is executed to find the appropriate library in memory. This type of linking is commonly used with shared libraries such as Dynamic Linked Libraries (DLL). Only a single copy of a shared library is needed in memory.

10.3 Contiguous Memory Allocation

Operating systems with multiprogramming and simple memory management divide the system memory into *partitions*—blocks of contiguous memory, each one allocated to an active process. The degree of multiprogramming is determined by the number of partitions in memory. As mentioned before, when a process completes and terminates, its memory space is deallocated and that amount of memory becomes available. Known as *memory partitioning*, this type of memory management was used in the early multiprogramming operating systems.

In addition to the allocation and deallocation of partitions to and from processes, the memory manager also provides two additional basic functions. The first is the *protection* of the memory space in the partition allocated to a process from the memory references generated by a process in a different partition. The second function is the management of shared memory in a partition by two or more processes.

Partitioned memory allocation can be *fixed* or *dynamic*, depending on whether the

10.3 Contiguous Memory Allocation

partitions are fixed-sized or variable-sized blocks of memory. With fixed partitions, the number of partitions is fixed; with variable partitions, the number and size of partitions vary because these are dynamically created when memory is allocated to a process.

10.3.1 Fixed Partitions

In this memory management scheme, memory is divided into fixed-sized partitions that are not normally of the same size. One partition is allocated to each active process in the multiprogramming set. The number and the size of the partitions are fixed. There is one special partition, the system partition, in which the memory-resident portion of the operating system is always stored. The rest of the partitions are allocated to user processes.

The main limitation of fixed partitions is the fact that the entire partition is allocated to a process, even if the process does not use all the memory space of the partition. On the other extreme, a process larger than a partition cannot be allocated to that particular partition. The simple principle is that a partition must be large enough for a particular process in order for the system to allocate that partition to the process.

Figure 10.3 illustrates the fixed partitioning of memory. The system partition is configured from address 0 to address 100K. Partition 1 is configured from address

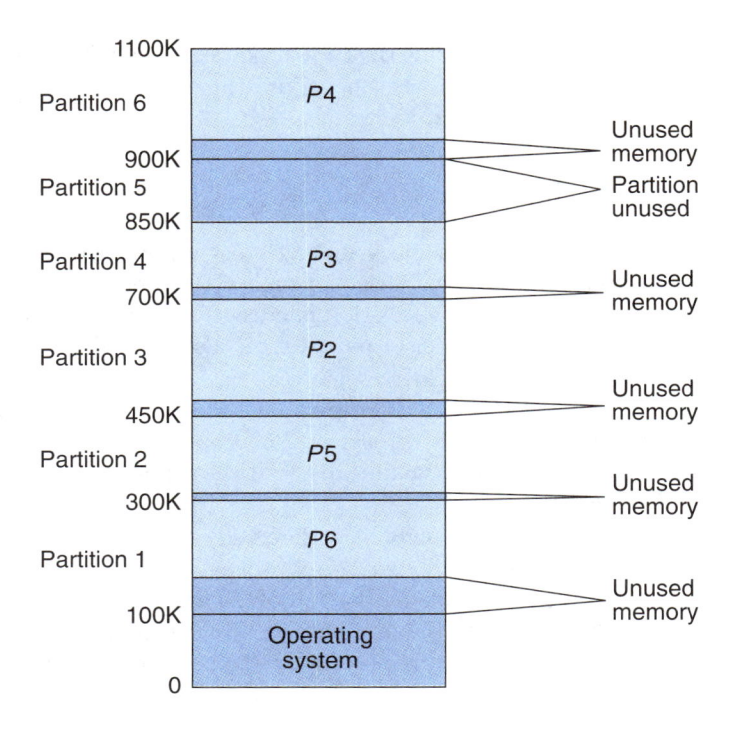

Figure 10.3 Fixed memory partitioning.

100K to address 300K, partition 2 from address 300K to address 450K, partition 3 from address 450K to address 700K, partition 4 from address 700K to address 850K, partition 5 from address 850K to address 900K, and partition 6 from address 900K to address 1100K.

The figure also shows five active processes that have been allocated partitions. Partition 3 has been allocated to process $P2$, partition 4 to $P3$, partition 6 to $P4$, partition 2 to $P5$, and partition 1 to $P6$. Partition 5 has not been allocated, so it is available. This partition has not been allocated because it is too small—only 50K memory units—compared to the memory requirements of the processes waiting for memory. The largest is partition 3 with a size of 350K.

An important problem in memory allocation with fixed partitions is *fragmentation*, the portion of memory allocated but not used. In Figure 10.3, the five processes that are in memory are each somewhat smaller than the allocated partition. The unused portion of memory inside a partition is called *internal fragmentation*.

The selection of a process from the input queue allocating a partition to it is an important issue in memory allocation. There are two general techniques for this:

- A technique using a queue for every partition. A process will be assigned the smallest partition large enough for the process. This technique minimizes the internal fragmentation.

- A technique using a single queue for the processes waiting for memory. The next process is selected from the queue and the system assigns the smallest available partition to the process.

10.3.2 Dynamic Partitions

Dynamic partitioning is a memory management scheme that uses variable size partitions; the system allocates a block of memory sufficiently large according to the requirements of a process. The partition is created dynamically, when there is sufficient memory available. The number of partitions is also variable.

The memory manager allocates memory to requesting processes until there is no more memory available or until there are no more processes waiting for memory. Assume that memory was allocated to processes $P6$, $P5$, $P2$, $P3$, and $P4$, in that order. The five partitions were created dynamically, and the amount of memory left is located at the top of memory.

Contiguous blocks of available (unallocated) memory are called *holes*. If a hole is sufficiently large, it can be allocated to a process of the same or smaller memory size. Assume that the memory hole at the top of Figure 10.4 (a) has a size of 200K bytes. At some later time instant, the system allocates memory to process $P7$ of size 125K. After allocating memory to this process, there is a smaller hole at the top of memory of size 75K, as shown in Figure 10.4 (b).

10.3 Contiguous Memory Allocation

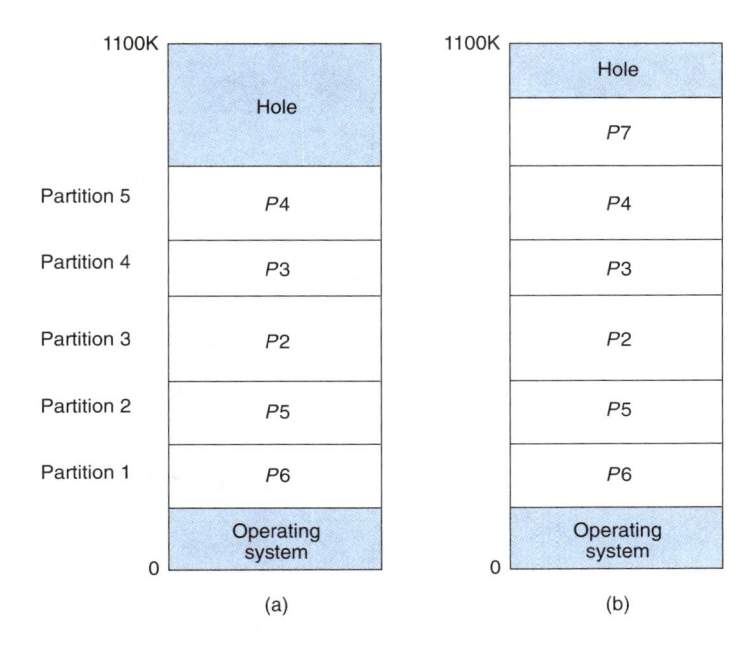

Figure 10.4 Allocating memory to a new process, $P7$, through a dynamic partition.

Assume that process $P5$ has a size of 200K. Figure 10.5 shows the memory state after the system deallocates the memory from process $P5$ and the process is removed from memory. The available memory left after this memory deallocation is of the same size as process $P5$, so a new hole is created of size 200K (the size of process $P5$). Consequently, there are now two holes in memory that are not contiguous (not adjacent to each other), the hole left by $P5$ of 200K and the hole at the top of memory of size 75K.

In dynamic partitioning, the holes represent the memory that is available, and if they are too small, they cannot be allocated. They represent *external fragmentation*. The total fragmentation in this case is 75K + 200K. The problem is that this total amount of memory is not contiguous memory; it is fragmented.

The operating system can use several techniques to allocate holes to processes requesting memory. The first technique is called *best-fit*: It selects the hole that is closest in size to the process. The second technique is called *first-fit*: It selects the first available hole that is large enough for the process. The third technique is called *next-fit*: It selects the next available hole that is large enough for the process, starting at the location of the last allocation.

The most appropriate allocation technique is not easy to determine. It depends on the arrival sequence of processes into the input queue and their corresponding sizes.

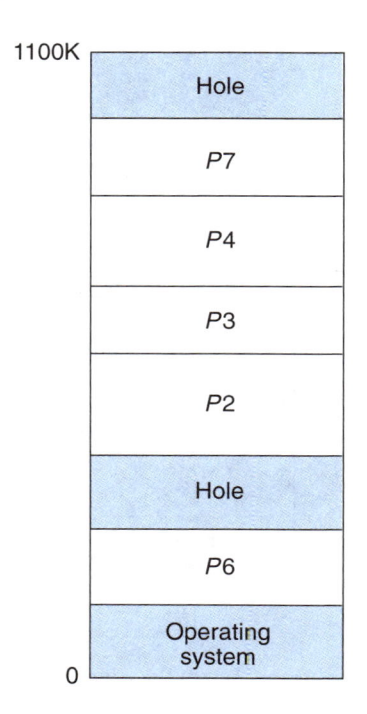

Figure 10.5 Removing process $P5$ from memory with dynamic partitioning.

At some particular time, the state of memory can become very fragmented, and will consist of a large number of relatively small holes. Since this memory cannot normally be allocated, the operating system uses a technique called *compaction* to solve or reduce external fragmentation. This technique consists of moving processes to different locations in memory in order to merge the small holes into larger holes. After compaction is carried out, the resulting holes can be allocated more easily. Figure 10.6 shows a big hole at the top of memory after compaction. Processes $P2$, $P3$, $P4$, and $P7$ have been moved to lower memory locations to create a larger hole (of size 275K) at the top of memory.

Dynamic partitioning requires the system to use *dynamic relocation*, a facility to relocate processes in memory, even after execution has begun. This is considered late binding. With hardware support, the relocation of the relative addresses can be performed each time the CPU makes a reference to memory, during the execution of a process.

Dynamic relocation is necessary to perform compaction since several processes are moved from their memory locations to other locations.

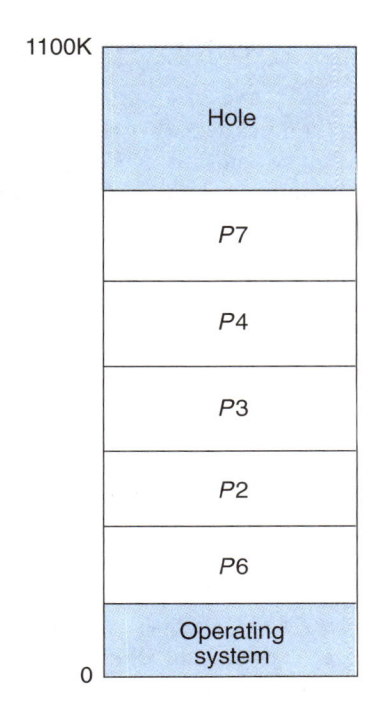

Figure 10.6 Memory after compaction in dynamic partitioning.

10.3.3 Swapping

Dynamic relocation is also important in *swapping*. When a process is blocked (suspended) while waiting for I/O service, the system assumes that the process will not become ready for a relatively long time interval. The system can swap out (or move) the blocked process to secondary storage (disk) and make that memory available to other processes. At some later time, the system swaps back the process from the secondary storage to main memory. The locations in memory into which the process is swapped back are not normally the same locations where the process was originally stored in main memory.

Performance is usually affected by swapping. The total overhead time includes the time it takes to move the entire process to a disk and to copy the process back to memory, as well as the time the process takes competing to regain main memory (memory allocation). In order for swapping to be effective, this total time must be less than the time the process is to spend blocked (waiting for I/O service).

Another important problem is the accumulated wait time of a process when there is not sufficient memory available for the process to be loaded and executed. These two quantities can be used as performance measures of the memory management subsystem.

10.4 Noncontiguous Memory Allocation

Fragmentation (internal and external) is the main problem in contiguous memory allocation. Modern operating systems use more advanced memory allocation schemes. This section discusses two common techniques for *noncontiguous memory allocation*: paging and segmentation.

10.4.1 Paging

With noncontiguous memory allocation, the process address space is divided into small fixed-sized blocks of logical memory called *pages*. The size of a process is consequently measured in the number of pages. In a similar manner, physical memory is divided into small fixed-sized blocks of (physical) memory called *frames*. If a 15-page process is waiting for memory, the system needs to find any 15 frames to allocate to this process.

The size of a page is a power of two—for example, a size of 1K = 1024 bytes. The size of a frame is the same as that of a page because the system allocates any available frame to a page of a process. The frames allocated to the pages of a process need not be contiguous; in general, the system can allocate any empty frame to a page of a particular process. With paging, there is no external fragmentation, but there is potential for a small amount of internal fragmentation that would occur on the last page of a process.

Figure 10.7 shows an example with paging in which the physical memory is divided into 32 frames, $f0$ to $f31$, and not all the frames have been allocated. The frames with the pages of a particular process are not all contiguous. Two examples of the frames that have been allocated are frame $f5$ allocated to page 0 of process $P3$ and frame $f20$ allocated to page 1 of process $P6$.

10.4.1.1 Logical Addresses

A logical address of a process consists of a page number and an offset. Any address referenced in a process is defined by the page that the address belongs to and the relative address within that page. When the system allocates a frame to this page, it translates this logical address into a physical address that consists of a frame number and the offset. For memory referencing, the system needs to know the correspondence of a page of a process to a frame in physical memory, and for this, it uses a *page table*. A page table is a data structure (array or linked list) used by the OS with data about the pages of a process. There is one table entry for every page.

Since the logical address of a process consists of the page number and the offset, the least significant bits of the address correspond to the offset, and the most significant bits to the page number. For example, Figure 10.8 shows a 20-bit address in a system

Frame	Contents
f31	
f30	P6 - page 3
f29	P5 - page 0
f28	P6 - page 4
f27	P5 - page 3
f26	
f25	P6 - page 2
f24	
f23	P6 - page 0
f22	
f21	P5 - page 1
f20	P6 - page 1
f19	
f18	P5 - page 2
f17	
f16	P3 - page 3
f15	P4 - page 2
f14	P4 - page 0
f13	
f12	P4 - page 1
f11	P2 - page 1
f10	P3 - page 1
f9	
f8	P3 - page 2
f7	P2 - page 0
f6	
f5	P3 - page 0
f4	
f3	
f2	Operating system
f1	Operating system
f0	

Figure 10.7 Example of paging.

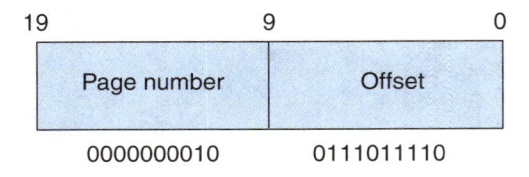

19	9	0
Page number	Offset	
0000000010	0111011110	

Figure 10.8 Logical address in paging.

that uses 1K pages. The lower 10 bits of the address are the offset. Because $2^{10} = 1024$, these lower 10 bits are sufficient to address any byte in a 1K-page. The higher 10 bits are used to reference the page number. The logical address in the example corresponds to page 2 and offset 478 (in decimal). The complete logical address in hexadecimal is 009DEh, which is calculated by adding the reference to the page number (00800h) and the offset (1DEh). The logical address of byte 0 in page 2 is actually 00800h because the offset is 0.

10.4.1.2 Address Translation

The operating system maintains a table or list of the currently empty (and available) frames. In addition to this table, for every process the system maintains a table with the frame allocation to each page of the process. Figure 10.9 illustrates the general concept of address translation.

Figure 10.10 shows a simplified structure of the page table for process $P3$ in the example discussed previously. With this page table and with hardware aid, the operating system can easily translate a logical address into a physical address at the execution time of a process. This is performed for every memory reference.

The translation is carried out by appending the frame number to the offset. Assume that page 2 in the previous example is allocated frame 4 and that the physical address is the one shown in Figure 10.11. The offset is the same as in the logical address and the frame number is 4, which in the high bits is 01000h. This hex value is added to the offset, which in the low 10-bit field is 1DEh. The complete physical address in hex is 011DEh.

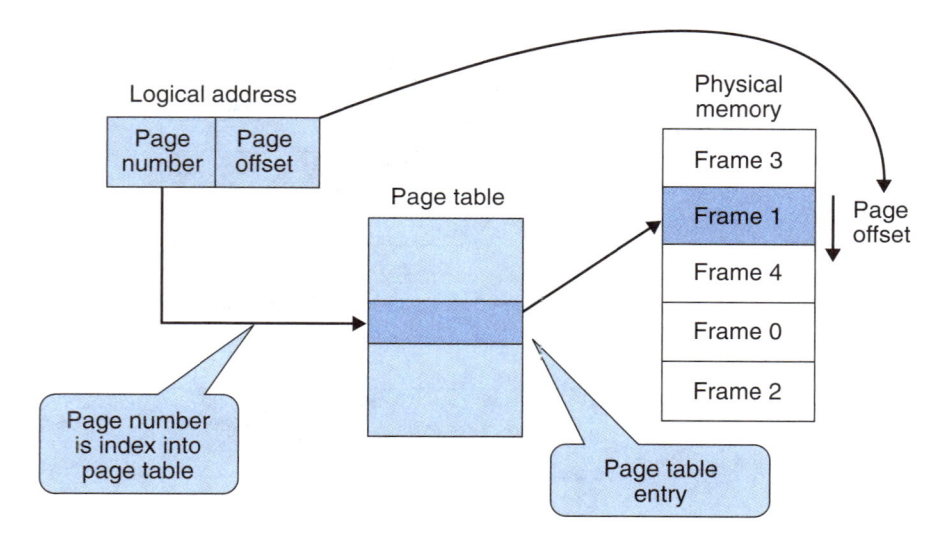

Figure 10.9 Address translation.

Page	Frame
0	f5
1	f10
2	f8
3	f16

Figure 10.10 Page table of process $P3$.

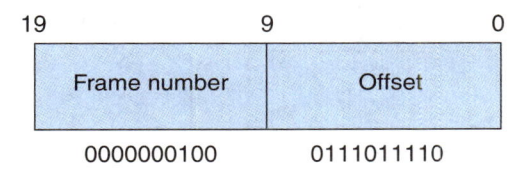

```
19                    9                    0
┌──────────────────┬──────────────────┐
│  Frame number    │     Offset       │
└──────────────────┴──────────────────┘
    0000000100         0111011110
```

Figure 10.11 Physical address.

10.4.2 Segmentation

Segments are variable-length modules of a program that correspond to logical units of the program; that is, segments represent the modular structure of how a program is organized. Each segment is actually a different logical address space of the program. Examples of segments are the program's main function, additional functions, data structures, and so on. Figure 10.12 (a) shows a program consisting of five segments, all of different sizes. Before a program can execute, all its segments need to be loaded noncontiguously into memory (these segments do not need to be contiguous in memory). For every segment, the operating system needs to find a contiguous block of available memory to allocate to the segment.

There are three main differences between segmentation and paging:

- Not all segments of a process are of the same size.

- The sizes of segments are relatively large compared to the size of a page.

- The number of segments of a process is relatively small.

The operating system maintains a *segment table* for every process and a list of free memory blocks. The segment table consists of an entry for every segment in a process. For each segment, the table stores the starting address of the segment and the length of the segment. When the system allocates memory to each segment of a process, a

272 Chapter 10 Memory Management

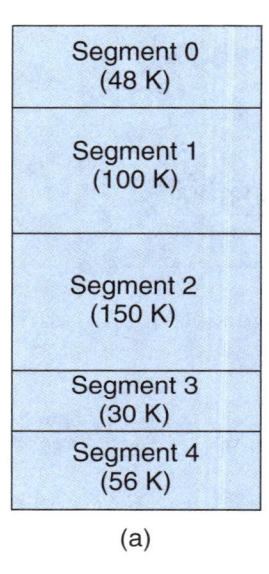

Start address	Segment size
10000	48K
20000	100K
80000	150K
50000	30K
60000	56K

(a) Segments: Segment 0 (48 K), Segment 1 (100 K), Segment 2 (150 K), Segment 3 (30 K), Segment 4 (56 K)

(b)

Figure 10.12 Example of segmentation.

segment table is set up for the process. Figure 10.12 (b) shows the segment table for the process in Figure 10.12 (a).

A logical address of a process consists of two parts: the segment number and an offset. For example, suppose a 20-bit address is used with 8 bits for the segment number and 12 bits for the segment offset. The maximum segment size is 4096 (2^{12}) and the maximum number of segments that can be referenced is 256 (2^8).

The translation of a logical address to a physical address with segmentation is carried out using the segment table. With the segment number in the left 8 bits of the logical address, the system looks up the segment number from the segment table. Using the length of the segment from the table, the system checks if the address is valid by comparing the segment length with the offset. The starting physical address of the segment is retrieved from the table and added to the offset.

10.5 Virtual Memory

The memory space of a process is normally divided into blocks that are either pages or segments. Virtual memory management takes advantage of the typical behavior of a process: Not all blocks of the process are needed simultaneously during the execution of a process. Therefore, not all the blocks of a process need separate main memory allocation. Thus, the physical address space of a process is smaller than its logical address space.

10.5.1 Basic Concepts

The *virtual address space* of a process is the entire set of all its addresses in the absolute program. After linkage, the absolute version of the program is stored on disk. The disk area that stores all the processes in absolute form is called the *virtual memory*. The *physical address space* of a process is much smaller than its virtual address because only a portion of the process will ever be loaded into main memory.

Assuming that virtual memory is implemented with paging, not all the pages of a process are stored in physical memory. A page reference is the page that has the address being referenced. The virtual memory manager swaps in a page of an executing process whenever the execution of a process references a page that is not in physical memory. Any unused page will normally be swapped out to a disk.

Figure 10.13 shows the logical address space of process $P3$ that consists of six pages, but only four of its pages are in memory. The figure also illustrates that there is a relation between the process and the virtual memory, in which the entire logical address space of the process is stored. The relation between physical memory and virtual memory is also shown.

The operating system should provide efficient means to translate virtual addresses to physical addresses. The size of the virtual address space is greater than the size of the physical address space. Thus, the operating system must also provide effective and efficient techniques to load the needed blocks of a program as it continues executing. Operating systems implement virtual memory management using *segments* or *pages*.

10.5.2 Process Locality

A process in execution only references a subset of its addresses during a specific interval of time. This behavior is called *reference locality*. A process executes in a series of phases and spends a finite amount of time in each phase, referencing a subset of its pages in each phase. This subset of pages is called a process locality.

Figure 10.14 illustrates the behavior of an executing process changing from one phase to another, each with a different locality. The figure shows four phases: In phase 1 the locality set is $\{1, 2, 3\}$, in phase 2 it is $\{2, 4, 5, 6, 7\}$, in phase 3 it is $\{1, 2, 8, 9, 10\}$, and in phase 4 it is $\{10, 11, 12, 13\}$.

The process starts execution in the first phase of execution referencing a subset of its pages (its virtual address space) and is spending a small amount of time in this phase. The process then moves to its next phase of execution and uses another subset of its pages for some other amount of time, and so on until the process terminates. Each subset of its pages is called a locality. The executing process changes from locality to locality.

Chapter 10 Memory Management

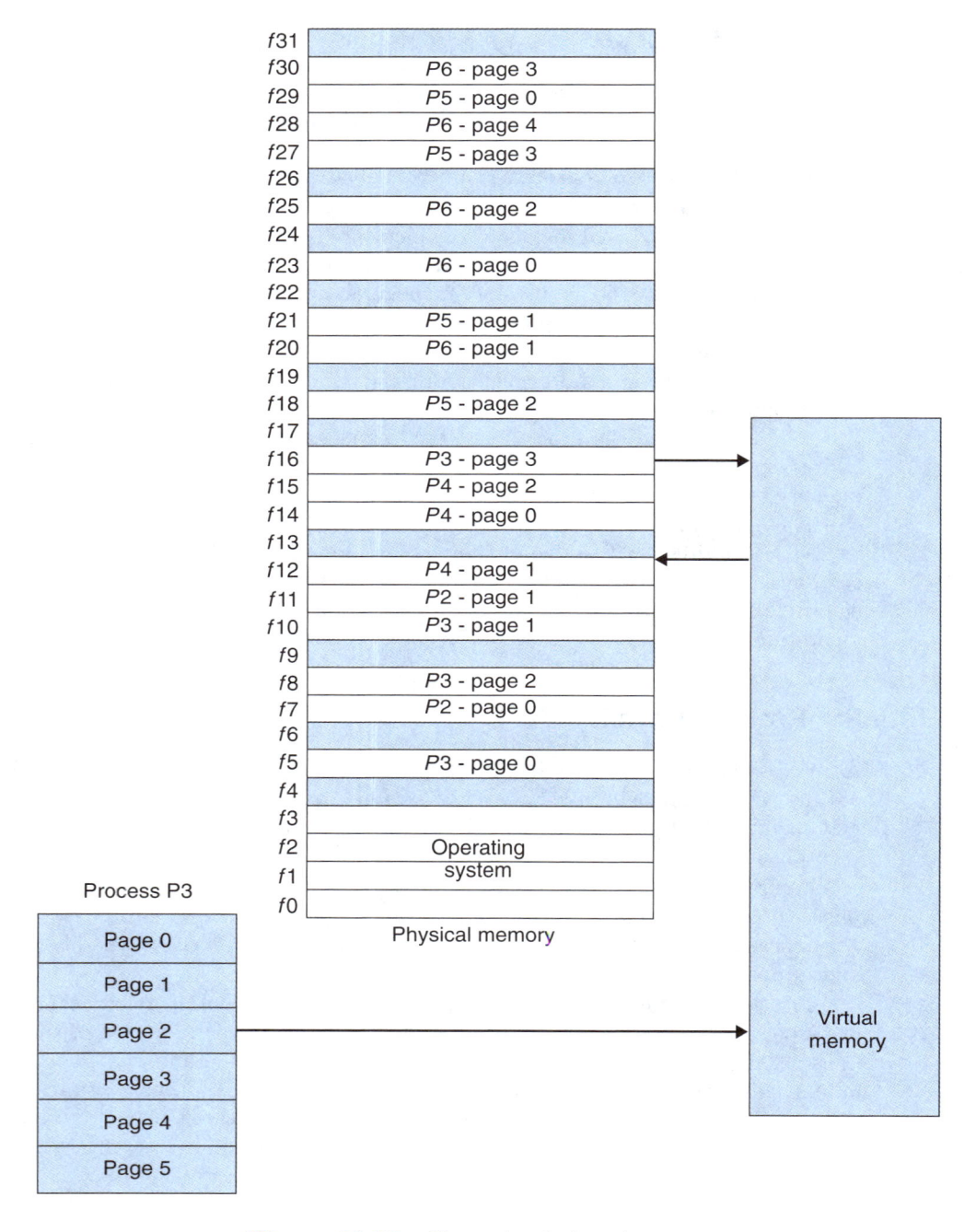

Figure 10.13 Example of virtual memory.

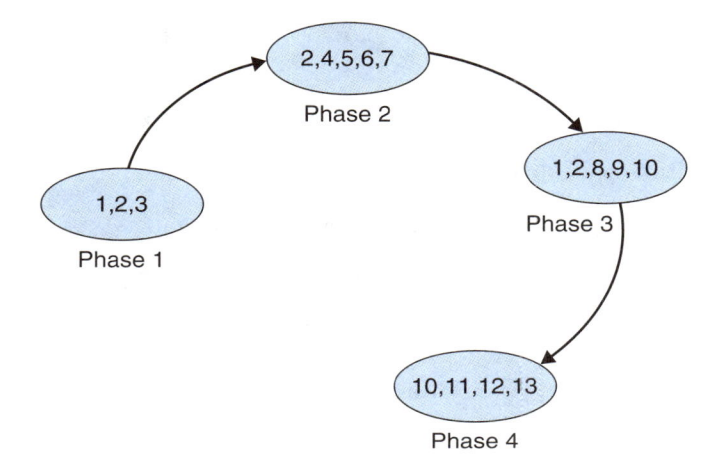

Figure 10.14 Example of localities of a process during execution.

10.5.3 Using Segments

Segments are user-defined logical modules in a program; they are variable-sized program units. Not all these segments are needed at once (this depends on the program's current locality), so the program executes with only a few segments loaded into memory.

At some particular time, the executing program will need another segment that is not in memory. At that time, the virtual memory subsystem transfers the needed segment from the appropriate secondary storage device to memory, replacing one of the segments already in memory. The replaced segment may be transferred back to the secondary storage device, if it has been modified since the last time it was loaded.

One difference between segmentation and paging is that with paging, there is no control from the user (or programmer) to divide the program into smaller units. The system has predefined the size of the pages, which are small fixed-sized units of storage. Physical memory is divided into *frames*, which store one page each. The following sections discuss virtual memory management with paging.

10.5.4 Memory Protection

Modern operating systems have memory protection that has two goals:

- Processes will not adversely affect other processes.

- Programming errors will be caught before large amounts of damage can be done.

The first goal is achieved by ensuring that a process can access memory only within its own address space. Thus, the operating system will block memory accesses for addresses that are beyond the bounds of the process's memory.

The second goal is achieved by portions of the process's memory being marked as follows:

- Read enabled: The memory can be read as data.
- Write enabled: Variables in this area can be changed.
- Execute enabled: The area contains instructions.

Depending on the hardware, the granularity of this memory protection could be individual pages or segments. The usage of these protections is shown in Table 10.1.

Table 10.1   Protection of Pages

R	W	E	Meaning usage
0	0	0	No access OS tables?
0	0	1	Execute-only instruction
0	1	0	Write-only feature not used
0	1	1	Write-execute feature not used
1	0	0	Read-only constants
1	0	1	Read-execute instructions, constants produced by some compilers
1	1	0	Read-write variables, stack, heap
1	1	1	Read-write-execute no protection produced by some compilers

10.5.5   Shared Memory

It is often useful for multiple processes to have access to shared code in memory, which is most often implemented for shared libraries. In this scenario, some of the code needed by a process will be in a dynamic linked library (DLL). When a process first attempts to use this library module, the OS will ensure that it is loaded into memory. If additional processes wish to use this library module, the OS will recognize that it is already loaded into memory and will arrange for the additional processes to have access to the module.

Dynamic linked libraries are used for common libraries that many applications use. They are also used for very large applications (e.g., Internet Explorer) that may have multiple instances running simultaneously.

Using shared libraries saves memory because only one copy of the library module needs to be loaded. Execution time is also saved for the additional processes that wish to use the library module.

It is also possible to use shared memory for interprocess communication. In this case, the shared memory would act as the buffer in a bounded buffer situation. However, this approach to interprocess communication is highly error-prone and very inflexible in its implementation. Most recent implementations of interprocess communication will use TCP/IP as the underlying structure.

10.5.6 Address Translation

The address translation used in virtual memory is similar to the one discussed for non-contiguous memory allocation with pages and segments. The translation procedure and the page table used in virtual memory are more complex.

During execution, for every virtual address referenced, the corresponding page is looked up in the page table of the process. First, the system needs to check if the referenced page corresponds to a valid reference. Second, it needs to find out whether the page is stored in physical memory. If it is, the system then finds out the frame that has been allocated to the page. The physical address is constructed using the frame address and the page offset. With this physical address, the main memory is accessed. Figure 10.15 illustrates the components necessary for address translation.

The page table uses the page number as the index to access the corresponding table entry. In addition to the frame number, an entry in the page table includes a bit that indicates if the page is currently stored in physical memory. If the page is not in physical

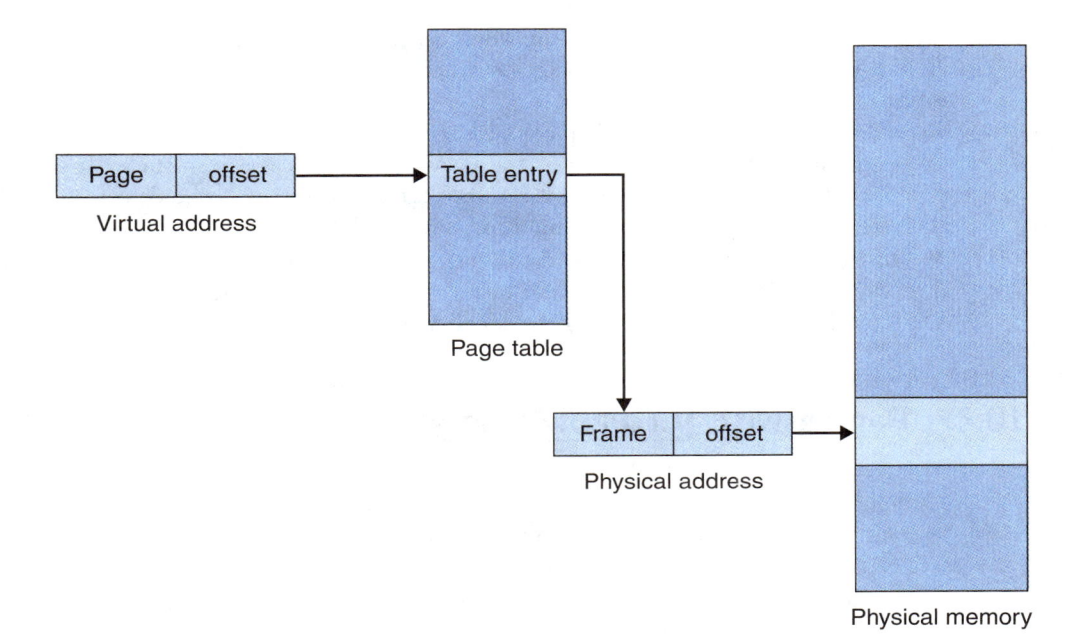

Figure 10.15 Address translation in virtual memory.

memory, the operating system interrupts the process and starts a routine that will fetch the page from virtual storage (disk). Another bit included in a table entry is one that indicates if the page has been modified since it was last loaded into physical memory. If the page has not been modified, then there is no need to swap the page back to virtual memory.

The page table of a process can be relatively large; the total number of entries in the table depends on the page size and the number of bits in an address. For example, in a system that uses 32-bit addresses, the total address space is 4 Gbytes. If the page size is 2K (2^{11}), the low 11 bits of the address correspond to the page offset. The high 21 bits of the address correspond to 2M, the maximum number of pages referenced by a process. The process's page table can have up to 2M (2^{21}) entries. Using these parameters, every process could require a huge space of memory for its page table.

Managing the page tables affects performance of the system. One solution for the huge storage space required by the page table is to store it in virtual memory and only load the part of the table with the entry of the page currently being referenced. A second technique that can be used is a two-level scheme in which a page directory is always kept in memory. Every entry in this page directory points to a page table. There exist other techniques for managing the page tables—for example, using an inverted page table.

10.5.7 Page Size Considerations

Small page sizes reduce the amount of internal fragmentation. In the best case, the internal fragmentation is zero. In the worst case, internal fragmentation is $K - 1$, where K is the size of a page. This is the case where a single byte is used in the last page of a process.

The disadvantage of small page size is the large number of pages required by a process, which increases the size of the page table. Another problem with small page size is that the total number of data units (bytes) to transfer to and from a disk with the virtual memory may be too small for efficient data transfer.

In the behavior of a process, if the page size is too small, there may be too many page faults, which are the events that occur when the referenced page is not in memory. This implies that the principle of the locality of a process would be less applicable.

10.6 Paging with Virtual Memory

As mentioned previously, the operating system translates a virtual address after a physical address after allocating a frame to a page when necessary. The system needs hardware support to carry out the translation from a virtual address to a physical address.

As a process proceeds in its execution, it references only a subset of its pages during any given time interval. These are the pages that the process needs to proceed in its current phase of execution; these pages are the current *locality* of the process.

10.6 Paging with Virtual Memory

Therefore, a process of size N pages is allocated a relatively small number of frames, M, with $M < N$. When the process references a page that is not in memory, a *page fault* occurs and the operating system interrupts the currently executing process and fetches the page from disk. At some later time, the process resumes execution.

In a system with virtual memory and paging, an executing process will eventually attempt to access a page that has not been loaded into memory. This event is known as a *page fault*, and the operating system then handles this event.

10.6.1 Paging Policies

Several important issues have to be resolved to completely implement virtual memory:

- When to swap in a page—the fetch policy.
- The selection of the page in memory to replace when there are no empty frames—the replacement policy.
- The selection of the frame in which to place the page that was fetched—the placement policy.
- The number of frames to allocate to a process.

10.6.1.1 Fetch Policy

For resolving the fetch policy, there are two approaches to consider:

- Demand paging, in which a page is not loaded until it is referenced by a process.
- Prepaging, in which a page is loaded before it is referenced by a process.

In demand paging, a process generates a page fault when it references a page that is not in memory. This can occur in either of the following conditions:

- The process is fetching an instruction.
- The process is fetching an operand of an instruction.

With prepaging, other pages are loaded into memory. It is not very useful if these additional pages loaded are not referenced soon by the process. Prepaging can be used initially when the process starts. These pages are loaded into memory from the secondary storage device (virtual memory).

10.6.1.2 Replacement Policy

The locality of a process consists of the subset of the pages that are used together at a particular time. As a process proceeds in its execution, its locality changes and one or more pages not in memory will be needed by the process in order to continue execution.

The following steps are carried out by the operating system when a page fault occurs:

1. The process that generated the page fault is suspended.

2. The operating system locates the referenced page in the secondary storage device, using the information in the page tables.

3. If there are no free frames, a page is selected to be replaced and this page is transferred back to the secondary storage device if necessary.

4. The referenced page is loaded into the selected frame, and the page and frame tables are updated.

5. The interrupted program is scheduled to resume execution.

If there are no free frames in memory, a page in memory is replaced to make available an empty frame for the new page. The replaced page may have to be transferred back into the secondary storage device, if it has been modified. There are several replacement policies that are discussed in the sections that follow.

The placement policy determines in which frame to store the fetched page. This is not a real issue in paged virtual memory management.

In a more detailed view, when a page fault occurs, the MMU (memory management unit) hardware will cause a page fault interrupt to the CPU. The operating system responds to the interrupt by taking the following steps to handle the page fault:

1. Verify that the page reference address is a valid (or potentially valid) address for the process that caused the page fault. If it is not, then the process will be terminated with a protection violation.

2. Locate a frame into which the desired page can be loaded. Clearly, a frame that is not currently being used is desired. If all frames are currently in use, choose a frame using one of the paging policies discussed next. This step is a resource allocation procedure and therefore must be performed under lock (since multiple processes may simultaneously need to have additional frames allocated).

3. Swap out the page that is currently occupying the frame that was selected in Step 2 above. This procedure can be optimized by noting that pages that have not changed do not need to be swapped out (a copy of the page already exists on the disk). Clearly, pages that do not have Write enabled cannot have changed, so they never need to be swapped out. Even a page that does have Write enabled may not have actually changed since it was loaded from a disk. In many systems, the MMU will mark a page entry whenever a write occurs to that page. The OS can examine this "modified" bit (also known as a "dirty" bit) to determine if it needs to swap out the page.

4. Load the desired page. The OS can locate a copy of the page on disk: either in the original program file (if it has never been loaded before) or in the swap file.

10.6.2 Frame Allocation

There are two general groups of paging algorithms: those that use *static allocation* and those that use *dynamic allocation*. In static allocation, the system allocates a fixed number of frames to a process. In dynamic allocation, the system dynamically changes the number of frames it allocates to a process during its execution.

The number of frames to allocate to a process is important for the performance of the system. In general, the more frames that are allocated to a process, the better the performance will be because there will be a reduced number of total page faults during the execution of a process. Too many frames allocated to a process would have the overall effect of reducing the degree of multiprogramming, which in turn reduces performance.

If the number of frames is too small, there will be too many page faults during execution of a process. An excessive number of page faults could lead to *thrashing*, a situation that can be worse than deadlock because one or more processes will be making no progress in their executions and it can completely bring the system down. This will be further discussed later in this chapter.

Two general schemes are used by the operating system to allocate frames to the various processes. The simplest one is called *equal allocation*, and it divides the available frames equally among the active processes. The second scheme is called *proportional allocation*, and in it, the number of frames is proportional to its size (in pages) and also depends on the priority of the process.

For page replacement, two schemes for frame allocation are defined: local and global allocation. With local allocation, a process can select frames only from its own set of frames. With global allocation, a process can select frames from the global set of frames.

10.6.3 Page Faults and Performance Issues

A page fault requires the operating system to handle the page fault, as discussed previously. The total time it takes to service a page fault includes several time components. The following are most relevant:

- The time interval to service the page fault interrupt.

- The time interval to store back (swap out) the replaced page to the secondary storage device.

- The time interval to load (swap in) the referenced page from the secondary storage device (disk unit).

- Delay in queuing for the secondary storage device.

- Delay in scheduling the process with the referenced page.

The most significant time component is the disk I/O time to swap out the replaced page and to swap in the referenced page. These I/O operations take several orders of magnitude more time than the access time to physical memory.

The execution of the process that caused a page fault includes delays caused by the page faults, and this accumulates to its total execution time. These additional delays are considered significant overhead. Assume that the normal execution time of process P_i without page faults is τ. The total execution interval, T_i, for process P_i depends on the number of page faults, n_f, and the interval for servicing each page fault, S_f. The total execution interval is defined by

$$T_i = \tau + n_f \times S_f.$$

The *page fault rate*, n_f/T_i, is the number of page faults per unit of execution time and should be kept as small as possible. The page fault rate depends on the following factors:

- The number of frames allocated to the process (P_i)

- The replacement algorithm

Because there are so many steps involved in carrying out page fault, performance is an important consideration and it is therefore necessary to minimize the number of page faults.

10.7 Paging Algorithms

Paging algorithms mainly implement the replacement policy. There are two groups of paging algorithms used in virtual memory management: (1) those based on static frame allocation and static paging algorithms and (2) those based on dynamic frame allocation and dynamic paging algorithms. The main difference between the two groups of algorithms is on how memory frames are allocated to the processes. To analyze these types of algorithms, first assume that each process references a sequence of pages during its execution; r_i is a reference to page i. This sequence is known as the page *reference stream*, R, and it is defined by

$$R = \langle r_1, r_2, r_3, \ldots r_k \rangle.$$

An example of a sequence of page references is $\langle 3, 6, 2, 1, 4, 7, 3, 5, 8, 9, 2, 8, 10, 7 \rangle$. The page reference stream represents the behavior of a process during execution. The page reference stream is used to test and evaluate the paging algorithms considered in the next sections. Most of the known paging algorithms use demand paging as the fetch policy.

10.7.1 Static Paging Algorithms

As mentioned previously, the static paging algorithms implement the replacement policy when the frame allocation to a process is fixed. This section discusses the three most common static paging algorithms: (1) first-in-first-out (FIFO) replacement, (2) optimal replacement, and (3) least recently used (LRU) replacement.

10.7.1.1 FIFO Algorithm

The FIFO algorithm is the simplest for replacement. When a page fault occurs and there are no empty frames for the process, the page selected to be replaced is the one that has been in memory the longest time—the oldest page. This selection of the page to replace is completely independent of the locality of the process. Thus, it does not follow very well the general behavior of processes. In practice, FIFO has the worst performance compared to the other algorithms. The only advantage of this algorithm is its simplicity and ease of implementation.

```
Page reference stream:
1 2 3 2 1 5 2 1 6 2 5 6 3 1 3 6 1 2 4 3

1 1 1 1 1 2 2 3 5 1 6 6 2 5 5 3 3 1 6 2
  2 2 2 2 3 3 5 1 6 2 2 5 3 3 1 1 6 2 4
    3 3 3 5 5 1 6 2 5 5 3 1 1 6 6 2 4 3
* * *       *     * * * *     *     * * *
```

FIFO
Total 14 page faults

Figure 10.16   FIFO page replacement.

Figure 10.16 illustrates the application of the FIFO algorithm to a page reference stream of 20 page references, which appears on the second line of the figure. This example assumes that three frames have been allocated to the process. Every column indicates the pages in memory after the page reference is processed.

The first page referenced is page 1. The system loads this page into one of the allocated frames and an asterisk or a star (*) placed at the bottom of the column indicates that a page fault occured. The next page that is referenced is page 2, which also generates a page fault. The next page referenced is page 3, which also causes a page fault. So the first three page references each caused a page fault and a star is placed at the bottom of the first three columns. At this point, pages 1, 2, and 3 have been loaded in the three frames allocated to the process.

The next page referenced is page 2 (see column 4), which does not cause a page fault because page 2 is already in physical memory. The next page referenced is page 1 (see column 5), which does not cause a page fault. The next page referenced is page 5 (column 6); it causes a page fault because page 5 is not in physical memory. Since there are no empty (available) frames for this process, a page replacement is necessary. The algorithm selects the oldest page in memory to be the one replaced, which is page 1. The page replaced is swapped out from memory, leaving an empty frame, and page 5 is swapped in and placed in this frame. Note that the most recently loaded page is placed at the bottom of the column; this is only for convenience. The current pages now in memory are pages 2, 3, and 5. A star is placed below the page numbers to indicate that there was a page fault for the current page reference.

The next page referenced is page 2 (see column 7) and since it is already in memory, no page fault is generated. The next page referenced is page 1, and it causes a page fault because page 1 is not currently in physical memory. There is also the need for a page replacement. Page 2 is the page that has been in memory for the longest time, so it is the page to be replaced. Page 2 is swapped out to disk and page 1 is swapped in and placed in the empty frame vacated by page 2. An asterisk is placed at the bottom of the column to indicate a page fault.

The procedure continues until all the page references have been processed. The total number of page faults is determined by counting the number of asterisks in the line below all columns. In the example with FIFO page replacement, the number of page faults is 13.

If the number of frames allocated to the process is increased using the same sequence of page references, the number of page faults will normally decrease.

10.7.1.2 Simulation Model with FIFO

The simulation model for the FIFO page replacement algorithm is relatively simple. The model consists of five Java classes: *Fifo*, *Fifopgrep*, *Genpgrefs*, *Rpage*, and *Simpinputs*. In the model, an object of class *Genpgrefs* generates the page reference stream of size 300 pages that is stored in array **prstream**. The size of the reference stream is defined by the symbolic constant **NUM_PAGES**.

The page references are generated randomly using a normal probability distribution and appropriate values for the mean and standard deviation. Using the normal distribution, the stream can reflect the fact that some of the pages referenced are more than other pages. Thus, this can simulate the locality of the process.

The number of frames allocated to the process is defined by the variable **M_FRAMES**. An array of pages, **list_page**, is maintained by the algorithm to store the different pages in the frames allocated to the process.

The algorithm calculates the number of page faults, which is stored in the variable **num_faults**. This quantity is computed in an object of class *Fifo* using the page references in the array **prstream** and the frames allocated to the process.

For every process, the pages already in memory are stored in the frame array, **list_page**. The array is always kept in order of loading each page. The last page of the array is the one to be replaced, the oldest page in memory for the process. The object of class *Fifo* carries out the following sequence of steps:

1. Get the next page from the page reference stream (**prstream**).

2. Determine if the referenced page is already in memory.

3. If the referenced page is not in memory, increment the number of page faults.

4. If there are no empty frames, remove the last page in the frame array, **list_page**.

5. Insert the current referenced page at the top position in the frame array.

10.7 Paging Algorithms

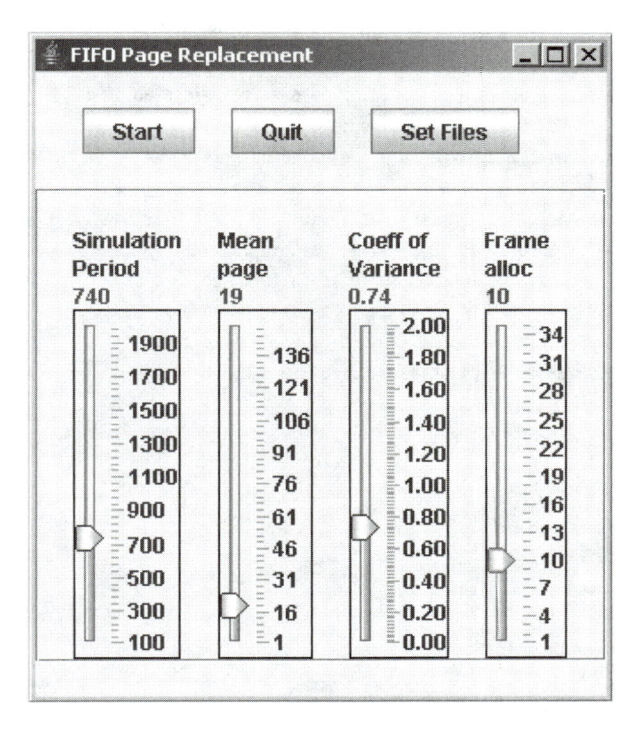

Figure 10.17 GUI for input parameters in FIFO model.

The model is implemented in Java with the PsimJ2 simulation package and is stored in the archive file `fifopgrep.jar`. The C++ version is stored in file `fifopgrep.cpp`.

Figure 10.17 shows the GUI for entering the input parameters in a simulation run for the model that implements FIFO page replacement. A user may set the values of the simulation period, the mean page for the generation of the page reference stream with normal distribution, the coefficient of variance, and the number of frames allocated to the process.

A partial trace output for a simulation run is shown in Listing 10.1. The first part shows the complete stream of page references that is randomly generated. The second part shows the actual trace. For each page reference, the trace includes the number of page faults so far, the number of pages in memory, and the list of current pages in memory.

Listing 10.1 Trace output of the model with FIFO page replacement.

```
Psim/Java project: FIFO Page Replacement
Simulation date: 10/18/2006 10:5
(Sequence of page references generated by the simulation model)
22 13 2 35 28 20 29 19 17 29 13 6 7 19 34 5 20 25 20 15 11 25 13
```

Chapter 10 Memory Management

```
19 13 33 31 10 13 19 8 31 20 26 7 10 25 3 2 19 1 19 20 5 10 9 15
34 13 18 27 20 31 16 22 6 28 3 33 8 10 1 18 33 6 2 18 11 19 1 30
28 16 19 19 5 17 4 25 19 3 11 10 12 22 20 6 26 20 6 16 5 30 26 11
5 29 30 27 3 16 34 28 14 27 31 12 19 10 4 23 20 21 19 8 23 30 18
28 16 18 14 17 34 1 7 23 4 33 14 30 26 20 20 22 5 18 23 14 28 28
31 12 18 12 29 14 10 20 31 9 11 21 27 4 6 30 15 26 25 29 10 35
26 1 14 29 15 34 18 4 26 32 27 21 23 23 21 34 6 20 25 27 8 34 31
15 31 9 11 30 8 3 16 12 20 18 12 21 22 33 5 16 21 21 14 18 14 30
21 25 6 17 10 23 17 10 28 14 30 19 19 16 13 19 14 20 23 8 9 32
22 4 9 15 7 24 2 28 25 5 21 31 19 12 10 29 17 11 6 30 2 22 18 5
16 14 25 17 26 20 9 3 16 8 3 31 13 18 25 7 8 19 21 24 15 23 11
11 3 12 6 13 23 35 13 21 17 20 23 34 21 32 13 3 28 20 34 5 9


FIFO page Replacement

Page referenced: 22
Number of pages in mem: 0
List Pages in mem: none
Page fault, accum pg faults: 1
Page referenced: 13
Number of pages in mem: 1
List Pages in mem: 22
Page fault, accum pg faults: 2
Page referenced: 2
Number of pages in mem: 2
List Pages in mem: 13 22
Page fault, accum pg faults: 3
Page referenced: 35
Number of pages in mem: 3
List Pages in mem: 2 13 22
Page fault, accum pg faults: 4
Page referenced: 28
Number of pages in mem: 4
List Pages in mem: 35 2 13 22
Page fault, accum pg faults: 5
Page referenced: 20
Number of pages in mem: 5
List Pages in mem: 28 35 2 13 22
Page fault, accum pg faults: 6
Page referenced: 29
Number of pages in mem: 6
List Pages in mem: 20 28 35 2 13 22
Page fault, accum pg faults: 7
Page referenced: 19
    . . .
```

10.7 Paging Algorithms

```
List Pages in mem: 32 21 34 20 17 35 13 6 12 3
Page referenced: 3
Number of pages in mem: 10
List Pages in mem: 32 21 34 20 17 35 13 6 12 3
Page referenced: 28
Number of pages in mem: 10
List Pages in mem: 32 21 34 20 17 35 13 6 12 3
Page fault, accum pg faults: 219
Page referenced: 20
Number of pages in mem: 10
List Pages in mem: 28 32 21 34 20 17 35 13 6 12
Page referenced: 34
Number of pages in mem: 10
List Pages in mem: 28 32 21 34 20 17 35 13 6 12
Page referenced: 5
Number of pages in mem: 10
List Pages in mem: 28 32 21 34 20 17 35 13 6 12
Page fault, accum pg faults: 220
Page referenced: 9
Number of pages in mem: 10
List Pages in mem: 5 28 32 21 34 20 17 35 13 6
Page fault, accum pg faults: 221
```

The summary statistics for the simulation run of the model with FIFO page replacement is shown in Listing 10.2. The results displayed in the summary statistics by the algorithm are the number of page faults and the proportion of page faults to page references.

Listing 10.2 Summary statistics of the model with FIFO page replacement.

```
Project: FIFO Page Replacement
Run at: Tue Oct 18 10:23:24 EDT 2006 by jgarrido on Windows XP, 130.218.248.234
-------------------------------------------------
Input Parameters
Simulation Period: 740
Mean page: 19
Coeff of Variance: 0.74
Frame alloc: 10 Project: FIFO Page Replacement
Run at: Tue Oct 18 10:23:24 EDT 2006
-------------------------------------------------
Results of simulation: FIFO Page Replacement
-------------------------------------------------
Total number of page faults: 221
Total number of page references: 300
Proportion of page faults to page refs:  0.737
```

In the FIFO algorithm, the number of page faults may increase even if the number of frames is increased. This behavior is known as *Belady's anomaly*. Because the FIFO algorithm is not a stack algorithm, it does not have the well-behaved characteristic of the optimal and LRU algorithms.

10.7.1.3 Optimal Algorithm

The optimal algorithm for page replacement requires knowledge of the entire page reference stream in advance. When a page fault occurs and there are no empty frames for the process, the algorithm looks ahead in the page reference stream to find out about future references to the pages currently in physical memory. The algorithm uses this "future" knowledge to choose the optimal page to be removed from memory. The approach used is to replace the page in memory that will not be used for the longest period. The optimal algorithm is not normally realizable in practice, but it serves as a reference for comparison with the other algorithms.

Figure 10.18 illustrates the application of the optimal algorithm to the page reference stream of 20 page references, which appears on the second line of the figure. This example assumes that three frames have been allocated to the process. Every column indicates the pages in memory after the page reference is processed. The page reference stream and the number of frames allocated to the process is the same as in the previous example.

The first page referenced is page 1. The system loads page 1 into one of the allocated frames and an asterisk or a star (*) placed at the bottom of the column indicates that a page fault occured. The next page referenced is page 2, which also generates a page fault. The next page referenced is page 3, which also causes a page fault. So each of the first three page references caused a page fault, which means that a star is placed at the bottom of the first three columns. At this point, pages 1, 2, and 3 have been loaded in the three frames allocated to the process.

The next page referenced is page 2, which does not cause a page fault because this page is already in physical memory. The next page referenced is page 1, which does

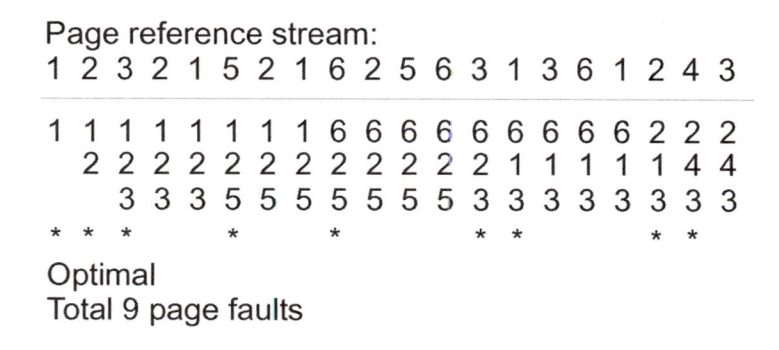

```
Page reference stream:
1 2 3 2 1 5 2 1 6 2 5 6 3 1 3 6 1 2 4 3

1 1 1 1 1 1 1 1 6 6 6 6 6 6 6 6 6 2 2 2
  2 2 2 2 2 2 2 2 2 2 2 2 1 1 1 1 1 4 4
    3 3 3 5 5 5 5 5 5 5 5 3 3 3 3 3 3 3
* * *     *     *         * *       * *
```

Optimal
Total 9 page faults

Figure 10.18   Optimal page replacement.

not cause a page fault. The next page referenced is page 5, which causes a page fault because this page is not currently in physical memory. A page replacement is necessary because there are no empty frames for this process. At this point in time, there are three pages currently in memory (page 1, page 2, and page 3) and the algorithm must decide which of these pages to replace. The algorithm looks ahead in the page reference stream and selects page 3 because this page will not be referenced as soon as the other pages in physical memory. Page 3 is swapped out from physical memory, and page 5 is swapped in and placed in the empty frame. An asterisk is placed below the column of the current page reference to indicate a page fault. As stated previously, the strategy used is to replace the page that will not be used for the longest period.

The next two page references (page 2 and page 1) cause no page faults because the pages are currently in physical memory. The next page referenced (page 6) is not in physical memory, so it causes a page fault. The algorithm looks ahead in the page reference stream and finds out that page 1 will not be referenced as soon as the other pages currently in memory, so page 1 is the selected page to be replaced. Page 1 is swapped out, and page 6 is swapped in. An asterisk is placed below the column of the current page reference to indicate a page fault.

The procedure continues until all the page references have been processed. The total number of page faults is determined by counting the number of asterisks in the line below all columns. In the example with optimal replacement, the number of page faults is 9, which is better than the number of page faults in the FIFO replacement example.

If the number of frames allocated to the process is increased using the same sequence of page references, the number of page faults will normally decrease.

10.7.1.4 Simulation Model with the Optimal Algorithm

The simulation model for the optimal page replacement algorithm consists of five Java classes: *Optimal*, *Optpgrep*, *Genpgrefs*, *Rpage*, and *Simpinputs*. In the model, an object of class *Genpgrefs* generates the page reference stream of size 300 pages that is stored in array `prstream`. The size of the reference stream is defined by the symbolic constant `NUM_PAGES`.

The pages referenced are generated randomly using a normal probability distribution and appropriate values for the mean and standard deviation. With this distribution, the stream reflects the fact that some of the pages are more frequently referenced than other pages. Thus, this can simulate the locality of the process.

The number of frames allocated to the process is defined by the variable `M_FRAMES`. An array of pages, `list_page`, is maintained by the algorithm to store the different pages in the frames allocated to the process.

The algorithm calculates the number of page faults, which is stored in the variable `num_faults`. These are computed in an object of class *Fifo* using the page references in the array `prstream` and the frames allocated to the process.

Array `list_page`, which holds the pages already in memory, is always kept in order of the next occurrence of each page in the page reference stream. The last page of the array is the one to be replaced, the page that will not be used in the near future. The algorithm carries out the following sequence of steps:

1. Copy the next page from the page reference stream (`prstream`).

2. Determine the next occurrence of this page in the page reference stream.

3. If the referenced page is not in memory, increment the number of page faults. If there are no empty frames, remove the last page in array `list_page`.

4. Insert the current referenced page at an appropriate position in the frame array, determined by the value of the next occurrence in the page stream.

The model is implemented in Java with the PsimJ2 simulation package and is stored in the archive file `optpgrep.jar`. The C++ version is stored in file `optpgrep.cpp`.

Figure 10.19 shows the GUI for entering the input parameters in a simulation run for the model that implements optimal page replacement. A user may set the values of the simulation period, the mean page for the generation of the page reference stream with normal distribution, the coefficient of variance, and the number of frames allocated to the process.

A partial trace output for a simulation run is shown in Listing 10.3. The first part shows the complete stream of page references that is randomly generated. The second part shows the actual trace. For each page reference, the trace includes the number of page faults so far, the number of pages in memory, and the list of current pages in memory.

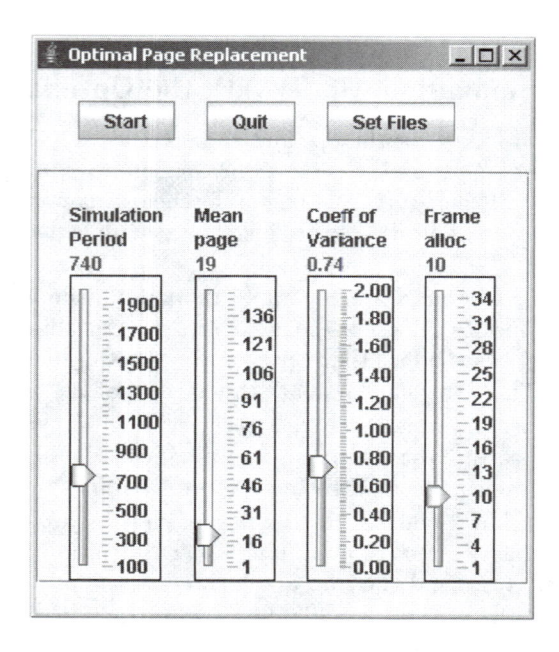

Figure 10.19 GUI for input parameters in the optimal model.

Listing 10.3 Trace output of the model with optimal page replacement.

```
Psim/Java project: Optimal Page Replacement

Simulation date: 10/18/2006 10:35
22 13 2 35 28 20 29 19 17 29 13 6 7 19 34 5 20 25 20 15
11 25 13 19 13 33 31 10 13 19 8 31 20 26 7 10 25 3 2 19
 1 19 20 5 10 9 15 34 13 18 27 20 31 16 22 6 28 3 33 8
10 1 18 33 6 2 18 11 19 1 30 28 16 19 19 5 17 4 25 19 3
11 10 12 22 20 6 26 20 6 16 5 30 26 11 5 29 30 27 3 16
34 28 14 27 31 12 19 10 4 23 20 21 19 8 23 30 18 28 16
18 14 17 34 1 7 23 4 33 14 30 26 20 20 22 5 18 23 14 28
 28 31 12 18 12 29 14 10 20 31 9 11 21 27 4 6 30 15 26
25 29 10 35 26 1 14 29 15 34 18 4 26 32 27 21 23 23 21
34 6 20 25 27 8 34 31 15 31 9 11 30 8 3 16 12 20 18 12
21 22 33 5 16 21 21 14 18 14 30 21 25 6 17 10 23 17 10
28 14 30 19 19 16 13 19 14 20 23 8 9 32 22 4 9 15 7 24
2 28 25 5 21 31 19 12 10 29 17 11 6 30 2 22 18 5 16 14
25 17 26 20 9 3 16 8 3 31 13 18 25 7 8 19 21 24 15 23
11 11 3 12 6 13 23 35 13 21 17 20 23 34 21 32 13 3 28
20 34 5 9


Optimal page Replacement

Page referenced: 22
Number of pages in mem: 0
List Pages in mem: none
Page fault, accum pg faults: 1
Page referenced: 13
Number of pages in mem: 1
List Pages in mem: 22
Page fault, accum pg faults: 2
Inserting page: 13 at index: 0
Page referenced: 2
Number of pages in mem: 2
List Pages in mem: 13 22
Page fault, accum pg faults: 3
Inserting page: 2 at index: 1
Page referenced: 35
Number of pages in mem: 3
List Pages in mem: 13 2 22
Page fault, accum pg faults: 4
Page referenced: 28
Number of pages in mem: 4
List Pages in mem: 13 2 22 35
Page fault, accum pg faults: 5
```

```
Inserting page: 28 at index: 3
Page referenced: 20
Number of pages in mem: 5
List Pages in mem: 13 2 22 28 35
Page fault, accum pg faults: 6
Inserting page: 20 at index: 1
Page referenced: 29
Number of pages in mem: 6
List Pages in mem: 13 20 2 22 28 35
Page fault, accum pg faults: 7
Inserting page: 29 at index: 0
Page referenced: 19
Number of pages in mem: 7
List Pages in mem: 29 13 20 2 22 28 35
Page fault, accum pg faults: 8
Inserting page: 19 at index: 2
Page referenced: 17
Number of pages in mem: 8
List Pages in mem: 29 13 19 20 2 22 28 35
Page fault, accum pg faults: 9
Inserting page: 17 at index: 7
 . . .
Page referenced: 21
Number of pages in mem: 10
List Pages in mem: 21 13 3 20 34 5 9 18 35 17
Page: 21 found at index: 0
Page referenced: 32
Number of pages in mem: 10
List Pages in mem: 13 3 20 34 5 9 18 35 17 21
Page fault, accum pg faults: 131
Frames full when referencing page 32
Page referenced: 13
Number of pages in mem: 10
List Pages in mem: 13 3 20 34 5 9 18 35 17 32
Page: 13 found at index: 0
Page referenced: 3
Number of pages in mem: 10
List Pages in mem: 3 20 34 5 9 18 35 17 32 13
Page: 3 found at index: 0
Page referenced: 28
Number of pages in mem: 10
List Pages in mem: 20 34 5 9 18 35 17 32 13 3
Page fault, accum pg faults: 132
Frames full when referencing page 28
Page referenced: 20
Number of pages in mem: 10
```

```
List Pages in mem: 20 34 5 9 18 35 17 32 13 28
Page: 20 found at index: 0
Page referenced: 34
Number of pages in mem: 10
List Pages in mem: 34 5 9 18 35 17 32 13 28 20
Page: 34 found at index: 0
Page referenced: 5
Number of pages in mem: 10
List Pages in mem: 5 9 18 35 17 32 13 28 20 34
Page: 5 found at index: 0
Page referenced: 9
Number of pages in mem: 10
List Pages in mem: 9 18 35 17 32 13 28 20 34 5
Page: 9 found at index: 0
```

The summary statistics for the simulation run of the model with optimal page replacement is shown in Listing 10.4. The results displayed in the summary statistics by the algorithm are the number of page faults and the proportion of page faults to page references.

Listing 10.4 Summary statistics of the model with optimal page replacement.

```
Project: Optimal Page Replacement
Run at: Tue Oct 18 10:35:51 EDT 2006 by jgarrido on Windows XP, 130.218.248.234
-------------------------------------------------
Input Parameters
Simulation Period: 740
Mean page: 19
Coeff of Variance: 0.74
Frame alloc: 10
Project: Optimal Page Replacement
Run at: Tue Oct 18 10:35:51 EDT 2006
-------------------------------------------------
Results of simulation: Optimal Page Replacement


-------------------------------------------------
Total number of page faults: 132
Total number of page references: 300
Proportion of page faults to page refs:  0.440
```

10.7.1.5 Least Recently Used

The least recently used (LRU) algorithm replaces the page that has not been used for the longest period. It assimilates past knowledge from the page reference stream, instead of future knowledge as used in the optimal algorithm. The assumption taken in the algorithm is that recent page references give a good estimation of page references in the near future. When a page fault occurs and there are no empty frames, the algorithm selects the least recently referenced page for replacement.

Figure 10.20 illustrates the application of the LRU algorithm to the page reference stream of 20 page references, which appears on the second line of the figure. This example assumes that three frames have been allocated to the process. Every column indicates the pages in memory after the page reference is processed. The page reference stream and the number of frames allocated to the process are the same as in the previous example.

```
Page reference stream:
1 2 3 2 1 5 2 1 6 2 5 6 3 1 3 6 1 2 4 3

1 1 1 1 3 2 1 5 2 1 6 2 5 6 6 1 3 6 1 2
    2 2 3 2 1 5 2 1 6 2 5 6 3 1 3 6 1 2 4
        3 2 1 5 2 1 6 2 5 6 3 1 3 6 1 2 4 3
* * *       *       *       *   * *           * * *
LRU
Total 11 page faults
```

Figure 10.20   LRU page replacement.

The first page referenced is page 1. The system loads page 1 into one of the allocated frames and an asterisk or a star (*) placed at the bottom of the column indicates that a page fault occured. The next page referenced is page 2, which also generates a page fault. The next page referenced is page 3, which also causes a page fault. So the first three page references caused a page fault each, and a star is placed at the bottom of the first three columns. At this point, pages 1, 2, and 3 have been loaded in the three frames allocated to the process.

The next page referenced is page 2, which does not cause a page fault because this page is already in physical memory. For convenience, page 2 is placed at the bottom of the column to indicate that it is the most recent referenced page. The next page referenced is page 1, which does not cause a page fault. Page 1 is placed at the bottom of the column. At this point, there are three pages currently in memory: page 1, page 2, and page 3.

The next page referenced is page 5 (column 6), which causes a page fault because this page is not currently in physical memory. A page replacement is necessary because there are no empty frames for this process and the algorithm has to select which of the pages currently in memory to replace. In this case, page 5 replaces page 3 (which was at the top of the list of pages in memory). Page 5 is indicated now at the bottom of the list.

Applying the LRU algorithm generates more page faults than the optimal algorithm, but with an appropriate number of frame allocations, the behavior can be acceptable in practice.

10.7.1.6 Simulation Model with LRU

The simulation model for the LRU page replacement algorithm consists of five Java classes: *Lru*, *Lrupgrep*, *Genpgrefs*, *Rpage*, and *Simpinputs*. In the model, an object of class *Genpgrefs* generates the page reference stream of size 300 pages that is stored in array `prstream`. The size of the reference stream is defined by the symbolic constant `NUM_PAGES`.

The page references are generated randomly using a normal probability distribution and appropriate values for the mean and standard deviation. With this distribution, the stream can reflect the fact that some of the pages referenced are more than other pages. This can thus simulate the locality of the process.

The number of frames allocated to the process is defined by the variable `M_FRAMES`. An array of pages, `list_page`, is maintained by the algorithm to store the different pages in the frames allocated to the process.

The algorithm calculates the number of page faults, which is stored in the variable `num_faults`. These are computed in an object of class *Fifo* using the page references in the array `prstream` and the frames allocated to the process.

Array `list_page`, which holds the pages already in memory, is always kept in order of the most recently referenced page to the least recently referenced page. The last page of the array is the one to be replaced, the page that was used least recently. The algorithm carries out the following sequence of steps:

1. Copy the next page from the page reference stream (`prstream`).

2. If the referenced page is in memory, remove this page from array `list_page`.

3. If the referenced page is not in memory, increment the number of page faults. If there are no empty frames, remove the last page in array `list_page`.

4. Insert the current referenced page at the top position in the frame array.

The model is implemented in Java with the PsimJ2 simulation package and is stored in the archive file `lrupgrep.jar`. The C++ version is stored in file `lrupgrep.cpp`.

Figure 10.21 shows the GUI for entering the input parameters in a simulation run for the model that implements the LRU page replacement. A user may set the values of the simulation period, the mean page for the generation of the page reference stream with normal distribution, the coefficient of variance, and the number of frames allocated to the process.

A partial trace output for a simulation run is shown in Listing 10.5. The first part shows the complete stream of page references that is randomly generated. The second

Chapter 10 Memory Management

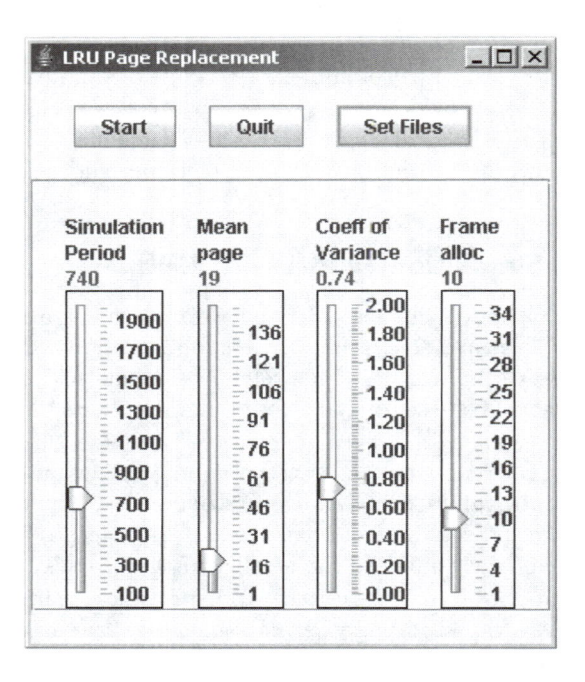

Figure 10.21 GUI for input parameters in LRU model.

part shows the actual trace. For each page reference, the trace includes the number of page faults so far, the number of pages in memory, and the list of current pages in memory.

Listing 10.5 Trace of the model with LRU page replacement.

```
Psim/Java project: LRU Page Replacement
Simulation date: 10/18/2006 10:31
22 13  2 35 28 20 29 19 17 29 13  6  7 19 34  5 20 25 20 15
 11 25 13 19 13 33 31 10 13 19  8 31 20 26  7 10 25  3  2
19  1 19 20  5 10  9 15 34 13 18 27 20 31 16 22  6 28  3 33
  8 10  1 18 33  6  2 18 11 19  1 30 28 16 19 19  5 17  4 25
19  3 11 10 12 22 20  6 26 20  6 16  5 30 26 11  5 29 30 27
  3 16 34 28 14 27 31 12 19 10  4 23 20 21 19  8 23 30 18
 28 16 18 14 17 34  1  7 23  4 33 14 30 26 20 20 22  5 18
23 14 28 28 31 12 18 12 29 14 10 20 31  9 11 21 27  4  6
 30 15 26 25 29 10 35 26  1 14 29 15 34 18  4 26 32 27
21 23 23 21 34  6 20 25 27  8 34 31 15 31  9 11 30  8  3 16
 12 20 18 12 21 22 33  5 16 21 21 14 18 14 30 21 25  6
17 10 23 17 10 28 14 30 19 19 16 13 19 14 20 23  8  9 32
 22  4  9 15  7 24  2 28 25  5 21 31 19 12 10 29 17 11  6 30
```

10.7 Paging Algorithms

```
 2 22 18  5 16 14 25 17 26 20  9  3 16  8  3 31 13 18 25  7
 8 19 21 24 15 23 11 11  3 12  6 13 23 35 13 21 17 20 23
34 21 32 13  3 28 20 34  5  9
```

LRU page Replacement

Page referenced: 22
Number of pages in mem: 0
List Pages in mem: none
Page fault, accum pg faults: 1
Page referenced: 13
Number of pages in mem: 1
List Pages in mem: 22
Page fault, accum pg faults: 2
Page referenced: 2
Number of pages in mem: 2
List Pages in mem: 13 22
Page fault, accum pg faults: 3
Page referenced: 35
Number of pages in mem: 3
List Pages in mem: 2 13 22
Page fault, accum pg faults: 4
Page referenced: 28
Number of pages in mem: 4
List Pages in mem: 35 2 13 22
Page fault, accum pg faults: 5
Page referenced: 20
Number of pages in mem: 5
List Pages in mem: 28 35 2 13 22
Page fault, accum pg faults: 6
Page referenced: 29
Number of pages in mem: 6
List Pages in mem: 20 28 35 2 13 22
Page fault, accum pg faults: 7
Page referenced: 19
Number of pages in mem: 7
List Pages in mem: 29 20 28 35 2 13 22
Page fault, accum pg faults: 8
Page referenced: 17
Number of pages in mem: 8
List Pages in mem: 19 29 20 28 35 2 13 22
Page fault, accum pg faults: 9
 . . .
Page referenced: 32
Number of pages in mem: 10

Chapter 10 Memory Management

```
List Pages in mem: 21 34 23 20 17 13 35 6 12 3
Page fault, accum pg faults: 209
Page referenced: 13
Number of pages in mem: 10
List Pages in mem: 32 21 34 23 20 17 13 35 6 12
Page: 13 found at index: 6
Page referenced: 3
Number of pages in mem: 10
List Pages in mem: 13 32 21 34 23 20 17 35 6 12
Page fault, accum pg faults: 210
Page referenced: 28
Number of pages in mem: 10
List Pages in mem: 3 13 32 21 34 23 20 17 35 6
Page fault, accum pg faults: 211
Page referenced: 20
Number of pages in mem: 10
List Pages in mem: 28 3 13 32 21 34 23 20 17 35
Page: 20 found at index: 7
Page referenced: 34
Number of pages in mem: 10
List Pages in mem: 20 28 3 13 32 21 34 23 17 35
Page: 34 found at index: 6
Page referenced: 5
Number of pages in mem: 10
List Pages in mem: 34 20 28 3 13 32 21 23 17 35
Page fault, accum pg faults: 212
Page referenced: 9
Number of pages in mem: 10
List Pages in mem: 5 34 20 28 3 13 32 21 23 17
Page fault, accum pg faults: 213
```

The summary statistics for the simulation run of the model with LRU page replacement is shown in Listing 10.6. The results displayed in the summary statistics by the algorithm are the number of page faults and the proportion of page faults to page references.

Listing 10.6 Summary statistics of the model with LRU page replacement.

```
Project: LRU Page Replacement
Run at: Tue Oct 18 10:31:06 EDT 2006 by jgarrido on Windows XP, 130.218.248.234
-------------------------------------------------
Input Parameters
Simulation Period: 740
Mean page: 19
```

```
Coeff of Variance: 0.74
Frame alloc: 10
Project: LRU Page Replacement
Run at: Tue Oct 18 10:31:06 EDT 2006
-------------------------------------------------------
Results of simulation: LRU Page Replacement
-------------------------------------------------------
Total number of page faults: 213
Total number of page references: 300
Proportion of page faults to page refs:  0.710
```

These last two algorithms are called *stack algorithms* because they have a well-behaved trend in the number of page faults for changes in the number of allocated frames. As the number of allocated frames increases, the number of page faults decreases.

10.7.2 Dynamic Paging Algorithms

As mentioned previously, the locality of a process changes as it continues execution. Figure 10.22 illustrates this behavior of a typical process in execution. In its next phase of execution, a process will reference a different set of pages and the number of pages referenced may also be different. The number of pages can decrease or increase with time. All this means that a process will require a number of frames allocated, which varies with time. The dynamic paging algorithms attempt to use this fact in allocating to a process an appropriate number of frames in a dynamic manner.

A dynamic paging algorithm takes the assumption that a process needs only enough frames for its current locality. If there are more frames allocated, there will not be

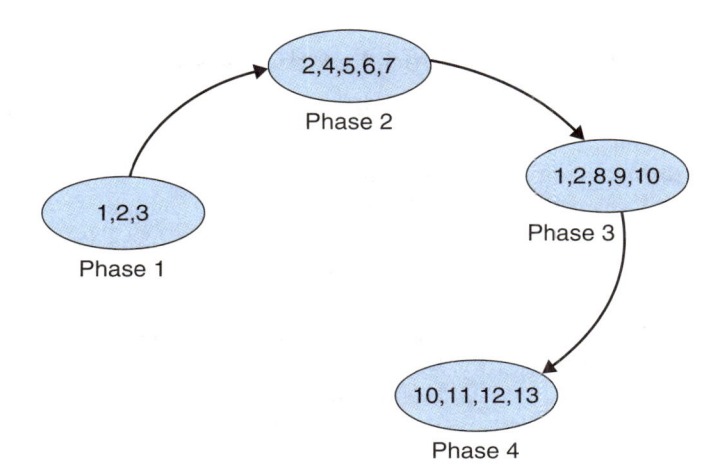

Figure 10.22 Example of localities of a process during execution.

improvement in its behavior; if there are fewer frames allocated, the number of page faults increases significantly.

10.7.2.1 The Working Set Algorithm

The working set algorithm estimates the number of frames needed by a process in its next execution phase based on its current memory requirements. Given the last *wsw* page references, the working set is the set of pages referenced in that window. The quantity *wsw* is called the *working set window*.

Figure 10.23 illustrates a working set window used in a process with the page reference stream of 20 page references that was used in previous examples. In the figure, the size of the working set window (*wsw*) is set to 8 and the working set (*ws*) is $\{1, 2, 3, 5\}$, at the point shown. At a different instance during execution of the process, the working set may be larger or smaller.

```
Page reference stream:
1 2 3 2 1 5 2 1 | 6 2 5 6 3 1 3 6 1 2 4 3

◄──────────────
wsw = 8
ws = {1,2,3,5}
```

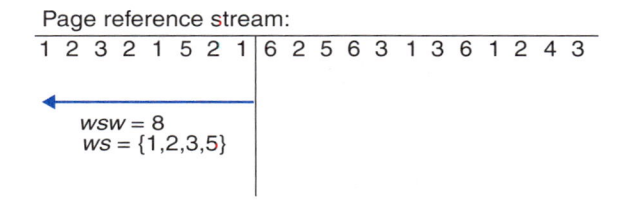

Figure 10.23 Working set window.

A good value of *wsw* results when the working set of a process equals its current locality. Based on the size of the working set, more frames can be allocated or deallocated to or from the process. The total number of pages that should be allocated to a process is the size of its working set.

10.7.2.2 Simulation Model of the Working Set Algorithm

The simulation model discussed here implements the working set algorithm using a selected value for the working set window. This model is a modified version of the model that implements the LRU algorithm. The two algorithms are similar in that both use the immediate past knowledge to predict memory requirements in the immediate future.

Figure 10.24 shows the GUI for entering the input parameters in a simulation run for the model that implements the working set algorithm. A user may set the values of the simulation period, the mean page for the generation of the page reference stream with normal distribution, the coefficient of variance, and the working set window assigned to the process. In the model, the size of the working set window is defined by the symbolic constant, `WS_WINDOW`. The page reference stream is also generated using a normal probability distribution. The number of different pages in the current working set window is stored in the attribute, `num_pagws`.

The first part of the main body of the simulation model is almost the same as the one for the LRU algorithm. The first important step determines if the referenced page

10.7 Paging Algorithms

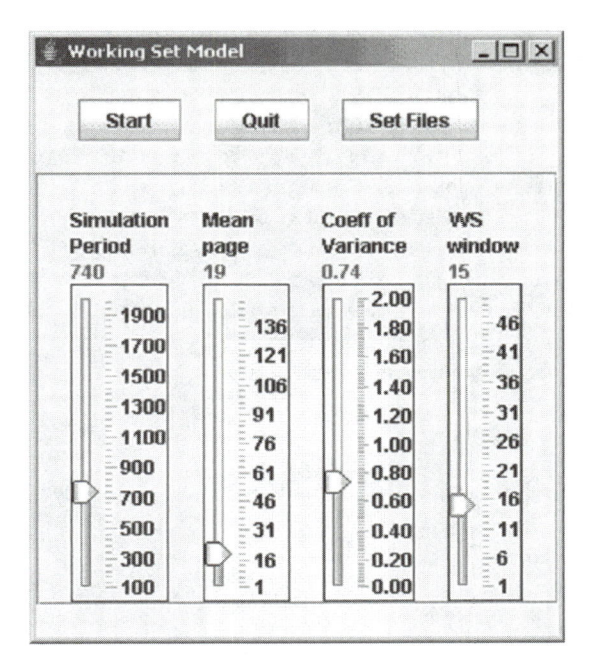

Figure 10.24 GUI of the working set model.

is already in memory. If the page is in memory, it is repositioned to the top of the stack, in array `list_page`. If the page is not in memory, a page fault occurs, the referenced page is swapped in and pushed to the top of the stack, and the page at the bottom of the stack is removed.

After this first part of the procedural implementation, the model computes the number of different pages, the working set, in the current working set window. This computation is carried out by the member function `pages_ws`, which counts the number of different pages in the last `WS_WINDOW` page references. This count is stored in attribute `num_pagws`. If this number is less than the number of allocated frames, then the number of frames is increased for this process. If the count is greater than the number of allocated frames, the number of frames is decreased by the difference between the count and the allocated frames.

Listing 10.7 shows a partial output of the trace of a simulation run of the simulation model of the working set algorithm. The trace shows how the number of frames allocated changes dynamically after every page reference.

Listing 10.7 Partial output of a simulation run for the working set model.

```
Psim/Java project: Working Set Model
Simulation date: 10/19/2006 14:41
22 13 2 35 28 20 29 19 17 29 13 6 7 19 34 5 20 25 20 15 11 25
 13 19 13 33 31 10 13 19 8 31 20 26 7 10 25 3 2 19 1 19 20 5
```

```
10  9 15 34 13 18 27 20 31 16 22  6 28  3 33  8 10  1 18 33  6  2 18
11 19  1 30 28 16 19 19  5 17  4 25 19  3 11 10 12 22 20  6 26 20
 6 16  5 30 26 11  5 29 30 27  3 16 34 28 14 27 31 12 19 10  4 23
20 21 19  8 23 30 18 28 16 18 14 17 34  1  7 23  4 33 14 30 26
20 20 22  5 18 23 14 28 28 31 12 18 12 29 14 10 20 31  9 11 21
27  4  6 30 15 26 25 29 10 35 26  1 14 29 15 34 18  4 26 32 27  2
 1 23 23 21 34  6 20 25 27  8 34 31 15 31  9 11 30  8  3 16 12 20
18 12 21 22 33  5 16 21 21 14 18 14 30 21 25  6 17 10 23 17 13
28 14 30 19 19 16 13 19 14 20 23  8  9 32 22  4  9 15  7 24  2 28
25  5 21 31 19 12 10 29 17 11  6 30  2 22 18  5 16 14 25 17 26
20  9  3 16  8  3 31 13 18 25  7  8 19 21 24 15 23 11 11  3 12  6 13
23 35 13 21 17 20 23 34 21 32 13  3 28 20 34  5  9

Working set algorithm

Page referenced: 22
Number of pages in mem: 0
List Pages in mem: none
Page fault, accum pg faults: 1

Number of frames allocated after ref page 22 is: 1
Page referenced: 13
Number of pages in mem: 1
List Pages in mem: 22
Page fault, accum pg faults: 2
Number of frames allocated after ref page 13 is: 2
Page referenced: 2
Number of pages in mem: 2

List Pages in mem: 13 22
Page fault, accum pg faults: 3
Number of frames allocated after ref page 2 is: 3
Page referenced: 35
Number of pages in mem: 3
List Pages in mem: 2 13 22
Page fault, accum pg faults: 4
Number of frames allocated after ref page 35 is: 4
Page referenced: 28
Number of pages in mem: 4
List Pages in mem: 35 2 13 22
Page fault, accum pg faults: 5
Number of frames allocated after ref page 28 is: 5
Page referenced: 20
Number of pages in mem: 5
List Pages in mem: 28 35 2 13 22
```

10.7 Paging Algorithms

```
Page fault, accum pg faults: 6
Number of frames allocated after ref page 20 is: 6
Page referenced: 29
Number of pages in mem: 6
List Pages in mem: 20 28 35 2 13 22
Page fault, accum pg faults: 7
Number of frames allocated after ref page 29 is: 7
Page referenced: 19
Number of pages in mem: 7
List Pages in mem: 29 20 28 35 2 13 22
Page fault, accum pg faults: 8
Number of frames allocated after ref page 19 is: 8
Page referenced: 17
Number of pages in mem: 8
List Pages in mem: 19 29 20 28 35 2 13 22
Page fault, accum pg faults: 9
Number of frames allocated after ref page 17 is: 9
. . .
Page referenced: 34
Number of pages in mem: 10
List Pages in mem: 20 28 3 13 32 21 34 23 17 35
Page: 34 found at index: 6
Number of frames allocated after ref page 34 is: 10
Page referenced: 5
Number of pages in mem: 10
List Pages in mem: 34 20 28 3 13 32 21 23 17 35
Page fault, accum pg faults: 196
Number of frames allocated after ref page 5 is: 11
Page referenced: 9
Number of pages in mem: 11
List Pages in mem: 5 34 20 28 3 13 32 21 23 17 35
Page fault, accum pg faults: 197
Number of frames allocated after ref page 9 is: 11
Decrease frame allocation by 1
```

Listing 10.8 shows the summary statistics for the simulation run. The listing includes the total number of page faults and the proportion of page faults to page references.

Listing 10.8 Summary statistics of the simulation run for the working set model.

```
Project: Working Set Model
Run at: Wed Oct 19 14:30:02 EDT 2006 by jgarrido on Windows XP, 130.218.248.234
------------------------------------------------------
Input Parameters
Simulation Period: 740
```

```
Mean page: 19
Coeff of Variance: 0.74
WS window: 15
Project: Working set algorithm
Run at: Wed Oct 19 14:30:02 EDT 2006
-----------------------------------------------------
Results of simulation: Working Set Model
-----------------------------------------------------
Total number of page faults: 197
Total number of page references: 300
Proportion of page faults to page refs:  0.657
```

The summary statistics output of the model discussed shows the number of page faults as the main result. This is considered an important performance measure in virtual memory management. The page fault rate determines the level of the more basic performance measures, such as throughput, CPU utilization, and response time.

The model is implemented in Java with the PsimJ2 simulation package and is stored in the archive file wspgrep.jar. The C++ version is stored in file wspgrep.cpp.

10.7.2.3 The Page Fault Frequency Algorithm

The page fault frequency algorithm is a dynamic paging algorithm that determines the page fault frequency of a process. If the page fault rate is too high, then the number of frames allocated is too small and it must be increased. If the page fault rate is too low, the algorithm must deallocate one or more frames.

This algorithm attempts to control the page fault rate by establishing the lower and upper bounds of page fault rates for a process. If the page fault rate of a process is less than the lower bound, a frame must be deallocated from this process. If the page fault rate is higher than the upper bound, then an additional frame must be allocated to the process. If there are no available frames, another process with a lower page fault rate will be suspended.

The operating system normally needs an estimate for the size of the working set window, or estimates of the bounds of the allowed page fault rate of a process in order to prevent thrashing.

10.8 Thrashing

Thrashing is a condition or state in the system into which all the time a process spends is dedicated for swapping pages; thus no computation is carried out by the process.

In principle, each active process should be allocated a sufficient number of frames for its current locality. If the number of frames allocated is too low, the execution of the process will generate an excessive number of page faults, and eventually the process will make no progress in its execution because it will spend practically all of its time paging—that is, swapping pages in and out. This condition is called *thrashing*.

The operating system should manage the allocation of frames in such a manner that, when it deallocates frames to one or more processes, it can increase the degree of multiprogramming, if necessary. When one or more processes need more frames, the system must suspend some other process to increase the number of frames available and to allocate these to the processes that need them.

One approach used to prevent thrashing is to determine or estimate, for every active process, the sizes of the localities of the process in order to decide on the appropriate number of frames to allocate to that process.

The performance of the system is affected by thrashing. The CPU utilization and throughput decrease at a very fast rate when thrashing occurs. The operating system increases the degree of multiprogramming in an attempt to improve the CPU utilization, and this might cause other processes to thrash, causing lower throughput and lower CPU utilization.

Thrashing of one process may cause other processes to thrash, if the operating system uses a global allocation strategy. This allocation strategy provides a global pool of frames for processes to select a replacement frame when needed. With local allocation, a process can select a replacement frame only from the set of frames already allocated to it.

10.8.1 Combining Paging with Segmentation

In Section 10.4.2, it was mentioned that with segmentation a program and data are divided into segments. Because these are logically independent address spaces of the program, there are several linear address spaces in a segmented program.

Segmentation has several advantages. First, it simplifies the handling of data structures for the implementation of segments. Second, it facilitates the sharing of procedures and data among several processes. The sharing of libraries is an important issue. Third, different kinds of protection can be applied to the various segments of a program.

With virtual memory management, segments of a program can be further divided into pages. Recall that a page is a unit of logical memory. In this scheme, only a few pages of a segment need to be allocated frames at any time, so an entire segment does not need to be loaded at one time. The first system to implement this scheme was Multics. In this system, an address consists of a segment number and the address within the segment, which is further divided into a page number and a 10-bit word within that page.

More recent implementations of combined segmentation and paging are aided by the hardware in a system.

10.9 Summary

Memory management deals with allocation and deallocation of memory to the various processes in the multiprogramming set. The manner in which this is carried out can significantly affect the performance of a system. Three address spaces are used to manage memory: (1) symbolic addresses, (2) relative addresses, and (3) physical addresses. These types of addresses are handled by the compiler, the linker, and the loader. Address binding is the mapping from a relative address to a physical address in memory. Late or dynamic binding delays the mapping to physical address to just before execution.

The operating system, aided by the hardware, must provide effective and efficient mechanisms to convert from symbolic to virtual addresses, then to physical addresses.

The two general approaches to memory allocation are contiguous and noncontiguous memory allocation. With contiguous memory allocation, physical memory is divided into partitions, contiguous blocks of memory for each process. Two types of memory partitions are static or fixed partitioning and dynamic or variable partitioning. Early operating systems with multiprogramming used these memory partitioning techniques.

With noncontiguous memory allocation, paging and segmentation are the two general approaches to allocate and manage memory. In virtual memory, the entire process does not have to be in memory to start and continue execution. With this characteristic of virtual memory, the operating system can use a higher degree of multiprogramming.

In virtual memory management, page faults occur when a process is referencing pages that are not in physical memory. Several algorithms exist to manage the fetch and replacement of pages (fetch and replacement policies). All the paging algorithms discussed in this chapter used demand paging. The static paging algorithms use a fixed frame allocation to the processes; the dynamic paging algorithms use a variable frame allocation based on the working set window.

During thrashing—a condition that occurs during execution of a process—the process spends most of its time swapping pages and thus makes no progress in its execution. The cause of thrashing is insufficient frame allocation; typically the number of frames allocated to a process is less than the size of its current locality.

Four simulation models in Java and C++ are included and discussed. The first three are implementations of the three static algorithms discussed: optimal, LRU, and FIFO. The fourth simulation model implements the working set algorithm. These models generate randomly the page reference streams and compute the total number of page faults for every algorithm as well as the proportion of page faults to page references.

	Key Terms	
address binding	internal fragmentation	proportional allocation
address translation	logical address	reference locality
Belady's anomaly	noncontiguous memory	relative address
contiguous allocation	allocation	relocatable program
dynamic allocation	page fault	replacement policy
dynamic relocation	page offset	segment table
equal allocation	page reference	segmentation
external fragmentation	page table	static allocation
fetch policy	paging	swapping
fragmentation	partitions	symbolic address
frame allocation	physical address	thrashing
frames	process address space	virtual memory
holes	process locality	working set window

Exercises and Questions

1. Is there external fragmentation in fixed partitioning? Discuss and give good arguments.

2. Refer to Figure 10.3; assume that the sizes of processes $P2$, $P3$, $P4$, $P5$, and $P6$ are 200K, 125K, 185K, 185K, and 175K, respectively. Calculate the total internal fragmentation and the percentage of memory actually used.

3. Refer to Figure 10.5; a new process, $P8$ of size 175K, is allocated memory. Calculate the total fragmentation.

4. A system uses a page size of 4 Kbytes, and a program of size 46 Kbytes is allocated memory. What is the fragmentation? Explain.

5. Refer to the system in Exercise 3. How many entries in the page table are defined for the process? (How large is the page table for this process?)

6. Refer to the system in Exercise 3. Explain the translation of a logical address to a physical address.

7. A system uses a page size of 8 Kbytes, and a process of size 42 is allocated memory. Calculate the fragmentation.

8. Refer to the system in Exercise 6. How many entries in the page table are defined for the process? (How large is the page table for this process?)

9. Refer to the system in Exercise 6. Explain the translation of a logical address to a physical address.

10. The number of page faults is the main performance measure in the simulation models presented. Why? Discuss. What other performance measures would be relevant?

11. Change the variance in the values for the page generation in the model presented. Implement the modified models for the static paging algorithms. Run the models with different variance values. Write the results in a table and in a chart using a spreadsheet program (such as Microsoft Excel). What do the variance values represent? Why would the variance values be useful in generating page reference streams?

12. Solve the previous question using the dynamic paging algorithm.

13. Modify the models with the static paging algorithms. Use an outer loop to change the number of allocated frames. Implement the simulation model and carry out several simulation runs. Write the values in a table and in a chart. Discuss your findings.

14. With dynamic allocation, develop a simulation model that implements the page fault rate threshold. Redesign the simulation model of the working set algorithm. Use two symbolic constants for each page fault rate found. Use the same page reference stream. Run the simulation model and compare its results to the model of the working set window. Discuss your observations.

15. During thrashing, the operating system attempts to increase the degree of multiprogramming. Explain why this action of the operating system is logical. Does it make sense? How can the operating system increase the number of allocated frames to thrashing processes?

Chapter 11
Security and Protection

11.1 Introduction

Computer security is based on the answers to two questions:

- Who do you trust?

- How much do you trust them?

The specific answers to these questions are the basis for a *security policy*. A typical policy will define *roles* and *access privileges* for company employees, contractors, vendors, customers, and others. All of the security mechanisms that we will discuss in this chapter are intended to enforce that security policy.

We often think of security as protecting a system from outsiders, but it must also protect it from insiders who are attempting (either accidentally or deliberately) to do things not allowed by the security policy.

Like the objects of an executing object-oriented program, resources are accessed by processes through operations defined by a capabilities list controlled by the appropriate operating system manager. *Protection* refers to the set of policies and mechanisms that define how resources and the operations defined on them are protected from processes. In order to avoid haphazard and indiscriminant use of the operations of a resource object, the memory manager maintains an access matrix that specifies which operations on each object are accessible to the various domains that can be assigned to processes.

External security refers to the way user programs access networks, servers, other hosts, and their resources and services. In contrast to protection, where a process hopes to gain straightforward access to an operation defined on a specific resource, security is about understanding how processes, by accident or by design, attempt to carry out some action to an operating system resource that could damage it or alter it in an unacceptable way.

Another important issue in security is *access*—the ability to access the resources of another computer across the Internet by using a protocol (SMTP, HTTP, FTP, TCP, UDP, etc.). Any Internet user has access to public domain resources (usually files and lightweight applications, most of which are on the Web) while more extended access is available across the Internet, on local area networks, and directly for those who have user accounts. Requests for user account access to networks and servers are controlled by login names and passwords and (for remote access) by IP addresses and port numbers. Users and processes are controlled in this way because untrusted users (which the system attempts to filter out by a firewall) are likely to cause deliberate damage by inserting *viruses*, *worms*, or *spyware* into the system. Such users may deliberately or accidentally exploit an application or operating system vulnerability (such as the potential of a text reader to overflow its buffer if too much data is sent or the capability of circumventing the login procedure with a trap door) that has not been patched.

11.2 Problems of Security

Security must defend a system and its computers against mistakes and malicious attacks by users and by automated or intelligent programs. A system vulnerability, such as the susceptibility of a buffer or a stack to data overflow into a protected memory space, may be exposed by a mistake (usually a programming error) or exploited on purpose. A malicious attack usually involves the deliberate installation of software on a computer, which can compromise either privacy or security. For instance, such an attack could install *spyware*, which could extract enough information from files to lead to *identity theft*, *credit card fraud*, or other financial loss. Such an attack could install a virus that alters the system (attributes or functions) in some way (usually the operating system or a popular application). Such an attack could install a worm that uses the system as a springboard to propagate itself to other machines and to launch attacks on other machines that it may not be able to access directly. The worm may reduce the performance of the system through a *denial of service attack*, a disruption that floods it with useless Internet packets.

There are thus several points of distinction between the problem of protection and the problem of security. Protection is hardware and software oriented. Security is primarily software oriented. Protection assumes that the user and the processes are legitimate for the system and have been assigned to the appropriate domain, while security does not. Protection focuses on protecting resources from unauthorized use, while security focuses on reducing, mitigating, or recovering from the damage caused by programming mistakes and the harmful side effects of malicious programming.

In the case of protection, the owner of a system creates processes that want to access system resources (both hardware and software) in valid ways. It is a question of assigning the process to the right domain. Thus, protection is a bookkeeping device administered by the operating system to make sure that the applications executed by authorized users do not attempt to access resources beyond the scope of the domains on which they are defined. In the case of security, users and automated programs that may or may not have authorization gain access to or somehow debilitate system resources and data (deliberately or by accident). Having gained access, or even by attempting to gain access, such programs are able to damage or change the system or reduce its capability of responding to legitimate requests.

11.3 Security and Protection Components

The security of a system depends on the following components:

- Physical security
- User authentication
- Protection
- Secure communications
- People

As we shall discuss throughout the rest of this chapter, it is often desirable to use several of these security components so that if one component is breached, the others will still protect the system.

11.3.1 Physical Security

A computer must be protected against being lost or stolen; otherwise, it is highly vulnerable. Additionally, when a computer or disk drive is discarded, the disk drive should be erased to ensure that others do not have access to important information. As discussed in Chapter 8, the contents of deleted files remain on the disk. Consequently, this erasure procedure should physically write to the disk, not just delete files.

If a portable computer contains highly sensitive information (e.g., credit card numbers), then it is advisable that those files and/or the entire disk be encrypted. This will reduce the possibility of this information being maliciously accessed if the computer is lost or stolen.

It is common for modern computers to have a wireless communications capability such as WiFi or Bluetooth. These wireless capabilities add useful features to the computer, but they also open up holes in the physical security of the system. Thus, it is important that other security mechanisms such as user authentication and encryption be used with all wireless communications.

11.3.2 User Authentication

User authentication is the action of the system verifying (to the best of its knowledge) that users are who they say they are and that those users are permitted access to the system. User authentication can be in the form of *Something You Know*. This usually consists of a login name, a password, and a (network) domain name. The security of such basic login schemes can be enhanced by requiring periodic password updates, requiring a minimum password length and/or requiring that a minimum number of different types of characters (e.g., alpha, numeric) be used in a password so as to render it harder to guess. Usually, after the nth failed login attempt, further attempts by that user are disabled.

User authentication can also be achieved via *Something You Have*. Examples of this are a special ID card that is swiped or otherwise read by the computer. This technique is often used on manufacturing lines or by servers at a restaurant. This authentication technique is vulnerable to the card being lost or stolen. If it is a simple magnetic stripe card, then it can also be forged.

Newer systems will combine Something You Have with Something You Know. An example of this is using a *SmartCard*—a card that the user plugs into a port on the computer—for login purposes. The user will then be asked for a pin code (Something You Know), which will then be encrypted by the SmartCard. The encrypted value is sent to the network host, which will then verify it.

There are several forms of biometrics that are now starting to be used for user authentication:

- *Fingerprint*: Laptop computers are available that verify the user's fingerprint for logon.

- *Voice print*: User's voice is checked and verified.

- *Retina scan*: While very accurate, this is cumbersome to do and is currently restricted to very limited applications.

- *Facial imaging*: Currently, this technique is not accurate enough to uniquely identify an individual.

11.3.3 Protection

A resource is an object controlled by the operating system. It may be a software object such as a file or an application, or it may be a hardware object such as main memory, the CPU, or a peripheral device. An operation is a function defined on that resource. In the case of a file, for instance, operations that a process may execute on a file are create, open, copy, read, write, execute, close, and so forth.

A *domain* specifies the resources that a particular process may access. Protection on the system consists of giving resource access to domains that should have it and denying it to domains that should not have it. Consider the following example:

- A company has a Human Resources database and an Order database (the Resources).

- The HR department should have read and write access to the HR database.

- The Payroll department should have read access to the HR database.

11.3 Security and Protection Components

- The Order Entry and Manufacturing departments should have read and write access to the Order database.

- All others typically would have no access to these databases.

A domain can be modeled as a set of ordered pairs (R, O), which specify access rights. The first component refers to the ith resource denoted by the subscript i and the second component refers to a set of k operations defined on resource i. The domain is denoted as $(R_i, \{O_1, O_2, \ldots\})$.

For example, let F be the generic symbol for a file. Then the access right-ordered pair for a file and its operations is $(F, \{create, open, read, write, execute, close\})$ operations defined on that resource.

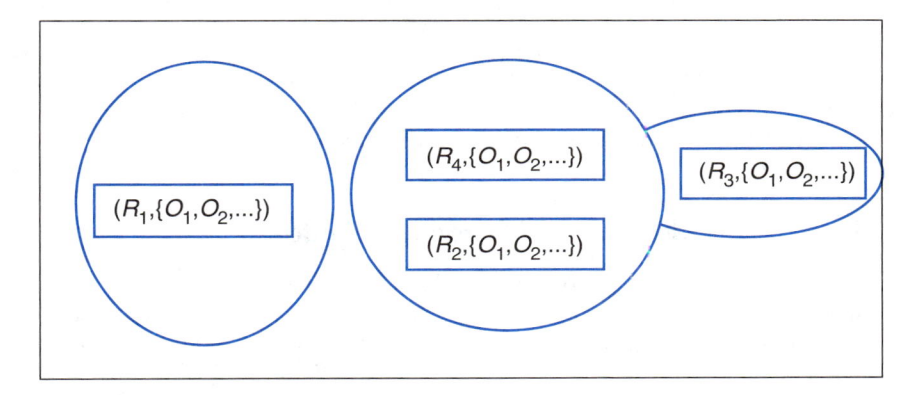

Figure 11.1 Three disjoint sets of access rights.

In Figure 11.1, the domains are denoted by ovals. The left and right domains consist of a single ordered pair, while the center domain consists of two ordered pairs. If one (or more) ordered pairs appear in the intersection of two domains, then the access right pair(s) are shared by the domains. The problem with the representation in Figure 11.1 is that it is not amenable to easy implementation.

11.3.3.1 Domains on Unix/Linux

The owner of a Unix file specifies three domains when creating a file—owner, group, and world—and three operations—read, write, and execute. The access rights to the file for each domain are specified by a group of three consecutive binary digits and separated from other domains by a hyphen (−) and are specified by the following code: $b_1 b_2 b_3 - b_4 b_5 b_6 - b_7 b_8 b_9$.

The first binary digit in each group of three specifies the read access; the second specifies the write access; the third specifies the execute access. If the binary digit is 1, access is permitted; otherwise it is denied. Only the owner of the file or a system administrator with access to the directory containing the file can change the access rights to the file.

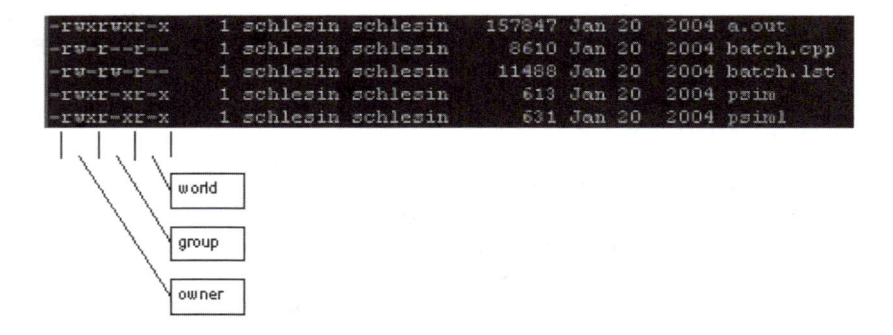

Figure 11.2 Example of permission settings on Linux.

In Figure 11.2, the owner has read and write permissions, but not execute permission, for the file `batch.cpp`. Since this file is a text file, it makes no sense to have execute permission. The group has read and execute permissions for psiml. The group does not have write permission, so no members of the group (except the owner) can change the file.

11.3.3.2 Domains on Microsoft Windows

MS Windows uses a more general domain model than Unix. On Windows, you can specify a set of individual users and a set of groups. Each of those users and groups can have different access rights for a resource. In Figure 11.3, the group named Users can

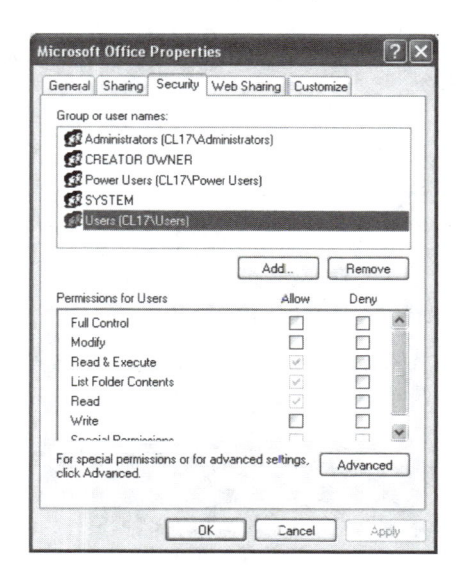

Figure 11.3 Example of permission settings on Windows.

list the contents of the folder Microsoft Office and read and execute it. Other groups may have a different set of permissions.

11.3.3.3 The Access Matrix

The domains in a system are typically modeled via an *access matrix* denoted by A. The rows of A consist of domains, the columns of A consist of objects, and the allowed operations are inserted into the cells of A. Table 11.1 shows an example of resource protection. Table 11.2 shows the access matrix for the company example.

Sometimes a domain itself can be listed as a resource (see Table 11.3). As a complex program evolves, it may want to switch domains to complete further tasks. A good example of this is when an installer program asks to run as the system administrator.

More flexibility/change can be introduced into the access matrix by introducing the operations of copy, owner, and control to the cells.

The copy right allows a process or the operating system to copy an operation for a resource defined on one domain to another domain for that same resource (same column). The owner right allows a process defined on one domain to add (or remove) an operation to (from) another domain for a particular resource by changing any cell

Table 11.1   An Access Matrix for Resource Protection

Domains/Resources	R_1	R_2	R_3	R_4
D_1	Stack alloc			
D_2		o, r, w, c	p	
D_3				ss, st, sth

Table 11.2   Access Matrix for a Company Example

Domains/Resources	HR Database	Order Database
Human resources	read, write	
Payroll	read	
Order entry		read, write
Manufacturing		read, write
Others		

Table 11.3 An Extended Access Matrix for Processes That Are Able to Switch Domains

Domains/Resources	R_1	R_2	R_3	R_4	D_1	D_2	D_3
D_1	ss, st					sw	
D_2		o, r, w, c	p		sw		sw
D_3				o, sth, cn, c	sw		

Table 11.4 An Access Matrix Where Domain Has Owner Rights and Copy(*) Rights

Domains/Resources	R_1	R_2	R_3	R_4
D_1	Stack alloc			
D_2		o, r*, w*, c	p*	
D_3		r, w		ss, st, sth

in the same (resource) column. Table 11.4 shows an access matrix in which certain domains have owner and/or copy rights.

Now the process defined on D_2 will remove read and write access for the file R_2 for D_3 and exercise the copy right to add print access to the file R_3 to D_3. Table 11.5 shows the access matrix after this change.

Table 11.5 Modified Access Matrix with Domain Access Rights

Domains/Resources	R_1	R_2	R_3	R_4
D_1	Stack alloc			
D_2		o, r*, w*, c	p*	
D_3			p	ss, st, sth

11.3.3.4 Memory Protection

Memory protection is a special case of protection in which the operating system will set up the appropriate access tables, but the enforcement is handled by the hardware. Memory protection is used to help ensure that a program bug does not have a dangerous effect. Typically, permission bits for read, write, and execute will be associated with each entry in the page table. The operating system will set these bits based on information that the compiler places in the program file for the program being executed. Table 11.6 shows the meaning and usage of the various combinations of permission bits.

Table 11.6 Memory Protection

Read	Write	Execute	Meaning	Usage
0	0	1	Execute-only	Instructions
0	1	0	Write-only	Not used
0	1	1	Write-execute	Not used
1	0	0	Read-only	Constants
1	0	1	Read-execute	Instructions, constants
1	1	0	Read-write	Data
1	1	1	Read-write-exec	No protection

Although the concept of having separate read, write, and execute permissions was developed about 40 years ago, not all CPUs support this concept. Some have no memory protection support and others only support read and write permissions. In fact, the CPUs used in PCs did not support a separate execute permission until 2006. The lack of execute permission provides an opening for hackers to penetrate a system.

Without a separate execute permission, any data area of a program is effectively executable. Thus, if a hacker can trick a program into executing something in its data, the program can be led to execute instructions provided by the hacker (in what the program believes is data). This is the basis for the Buffer Overflow and Stack Overflow security attacks.

Note that since the OS sets the permission bits based on the information provided by the compiler, it is necessary for the application developer to take advantage of this security feature in order for it to be fully enabled.

11.3.3.5 Capabilities and Higher Level Protection

Analyzing the rows across the access matrix provides a list of objects and the operations that a process defined on the domain can access on these objects. A list of all objects accessible to a domain (together with the operations allowed on these objects) is called a *capability list*. The address of an object is referred to as its *capability*. Possession of the capability implies access to all operations defined on the object.

The capability list of a domain is not accessible to the process executing on that domain. The capability list is itself a protected object maintained by the operating system. Capabilities are distinguished from other kinds of objects by a tag or by an extended address, part of which is accessible to the program process and the other part, containing the capability list, is accessible to the operating system only.

Normally protection is implemented at the hardware/software interface by the operating system kernel. Some protection can be implemented in hardware to reduce the overhead of having the kernel inspect and validate every attempt to access a resource. However, protection can also be implemented at the compiler level or even at the (programming) language (source code) level. Such a scheme can increase the flexibility of a protection policy. One way to extend flexibility is to allow applications programmers to define functions that perform operations on resources suitable to that particular application.

Control of the access to a shared resource can be made by extending the data type syntax of a programming language. For instance, the access to a file created by a program can also be controlled by that program with this type of facility (e.g., by opening a file for reading or writing for processes defined on specified domains). Each application can define its own access control matrix for the resources that it requires, rather than allowing the kernel to control the overall access matrix for all applications.

The advantage of such a system is that protection needs are declared at the beginning of a program instead of programmed as a sequence of calls on the operating system. Such an arrangement appears to be independent of the operating system. But in fact, the protection enforcement mechanism is usually left up to the kernel of the operating system.

A disadvantage of program- (or compiler-) based protection is that a priori assumptions are made by the applications programmer (compiler) about the objects of the system and the operations that can be performed on them. Compiler-based protection ignores the problem of enforcement. By leaving enforcement up to some other entity, it is not completely solving the protection problem. Ultimately, platform-independent access control is more of a goal than an accomplished fact. The application program must collaborate with hardware or the operating system kernel to correctly interpret, and then enforce and implement, the protection schemes it defines.

If the compiler or interpreter happens to provide software for enforcing protection, then it is easier to change it than to change hardware or kernel code. The tradeoff for the enhanced flexibility of higher-level software implementations of protection is the reduced efficiency relative to lower-level software and hardware implementations.

Recent versions of the Java programming language implement language-based protection. The Java Virtual Machine (JVM) loads a class in response to a program's request to create instances (objects) of that class. Java implements protection at the class level rather than at the process level. Pairs of classes can be labeled as mutually distrusting. Individual classes are labeled as trusted or untrusted. The JVM assigns a protection domain to untrusted classes and mediates protection between mutually distrusting classes.

Depending on the protection domain assigned to the class by the JVM, the method requiring a resource (object) may assert the privilege of being able to access a particular operation (method) of that resource. Every thread in the JVM maintains a stack of calls to methods in the process of execution. For each class, the stack frame is annotated with the resource access privileges allowed for each class. When an object of that class requests access to a protected resource, the stack frame annotation is checked before permission is granted; the technical term for this procedure is *stack inspection*. If access to a resource is denied to an object based on the protection domain of the method's class, then Java throws an exception.

The reason this scheme works is that, unlike programs in other programming languages, Java programs cannot directly access memory. In particular, untrusted programs are not able to manipulate their own stacks and thus change the resource access privileges assigned by the JVM.

11.3.4 Secure Communications

A system must ensure that its communications with other systems are secure. In today's world, any communications over the Internet are vulnerable to eavesdropping (see Figure 11.4). Similarly, any communications over a Wi-Fi wireless link can be intercepted. Thus, encryption should be used for any data transmitted where the physical security of the communication lines cannot be guaranteed.

Encryption is the process of scrambling data so that only an authorized receiver can unscramble it. There are two basic operations:

- Ciphertext = Encrypt(plaintext, key1)
- Plaintext = Decrypt(ciphertext, key2)

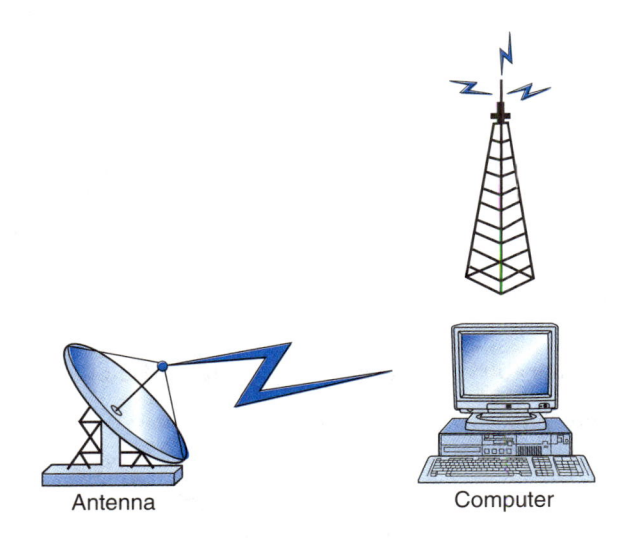

Figure 11.4 Eavesdropping.

A *symmetric encryption system* is one in which $key1 = key2$. The sender and receiver use the same key to encrypt and decrypt the data. This type of system requires that the key be kept secret. Consequently, it also requires a separate secure communications channel for the sender and receiver to communicate the key. Examples of this type of system are Data Encryption Standard (DES) and the Advanced Encryption Standard (AES).

DES was developed in the 1970s and became the standard for most encryption, especially in the financial industry. It uses a 56 bit key, which was effectively unbreakable in the 1970s; however, advances in computer technology have made it vulnerable. Thus it is now being replaced by AES, which gives the user the option of the size of key to use (128, 192, or 256 bits). This flexibility should make this system safe for the foreseeable future.

In an *asymmetric encryption system*, $key1 \neq key2$. Thus, one key is used to encrypt the data, and another is used to decrypt it. With this type of system, one of the keys (called the Public Key) is published (to the world). The other (the Private Key) is kept secret. For example, anybody can encrypt a message with Bill's public key and be confident that only Bill can decrypt it (since only he knows his private key). On the other hand, if Bill encrypts a message with his private key, anybody can decrypt it using Bill's public key. Thus, Bill can *sign* a message and anyone can verify that signature. This is called a *digital signature*, an important feature of the modern online world. When a new software component or update to an existing component is downloaded, digital signatures allow you to verify that a software component that is to be downloaded over the Internet was indeed created by whomever claims to have created it.

In modern systems, both symmetric and asymmetric systems are commonly used. Asymmetric systems provide flexibility. Symmetric systems are much faster than asymmetric systems, so a common arrangement is to use an asymmetric system to set up an encrypted communication link and a symmetric system to exchange large amounts of data.

11.3.5 Digital Certificates

A digital certificate is a mechanism that allows users to verify the authenticity of a document. When the concept was first invented. it was thought that this would be used to vouch for the authenticity of emails, legal documents, etc. While digital certificates are used for these purposes, their most common function has become verifying the authenticity of executable files downloaded from the Web.

A digital certificate system should have the following characteristics:

- It is *verifiable*. Anybody that receives the document should be able to perform a calculation to verify the accuracy of the certificate.

- It is *not forgeable*. Only the person, company, or computer system that purports to have created the certificate can actually create it.

As discussed earlier, you can create a digital certificate by encrypting a file with your private key. In practice, this leads to a very slow authentication process. To improve performance, the file to be authenticated is *hashed* to produce a relatively short *message digest*. You can then use your private key to encrypt just the hash value.

Depending on the particular hash function that is used, this message digest will be anywhere from 128 to 256 bits. A hash function $h = H(M)$ is designed to meet the following criteria:

- It can be applied to any size of message M.

- It produces a fixed-length output h.

- It is easy to compute $h = H(M)$ for any message M.

- It is a one-way function. For a given hash value, it is not feasible to find the original message M.

- It has collision resistance. For a given message M_1, it is not feasible to find another message M_2 that has the same hash value.

A number of hash functions are in use, including MD5, SHA-1, and SHA-256. Weaknesses have been discovered in MD5 and SHA-1, thus it is currently recommended that SHA-256 be used.

Let us suppose that you receive a certificate that purports to come from Company XYZ. How do you know that this is not a forgery? There are two approaches to creating certificates:

- *Self-certification*: In this approach, a company announces its public key ahead of time. To verify a document, you obtain that company's public key and then use it to verify the certificate. This is relatively straightforward but leads to the question of whether you can really trust that company's public key. Perhaps it was published by a forger.

- *Trusted party*: In this approach, a trusted third party signs the certificate. Since you trust the third party, you can trust the authenticity of the document. This approach leads to a question of who are the trusted third parties and how do you know if you can trust them?

In practice, the term *digital certificate* usually refers to a file that conforms to the X.509 international standard. An X.509 file will include demographic information (name, address of the creator of the certificate). The X.509 standard utilizes a trusted third-party mechanism—a set of companies/organizations that are globally trusted. A digital certificate (called a *root certificate*) identifying each of these companies is included with the operating system. On MS Windows, you can view these certificates by selecting Control Panel → Internet Options → Content → Certificates (see Figure 11.5).

If a company wishes to publish a digital certificate, it must provide that certificate to one of these *trusted root authorities*, who will then sign it with their private key. Thus a digital certificate will include an identification of the trusted signer of that certificate. You can then look at that signer's digital certificate to obtain the public key to verify the certificate that you are looking at.

Chapter 11 Security and Protection

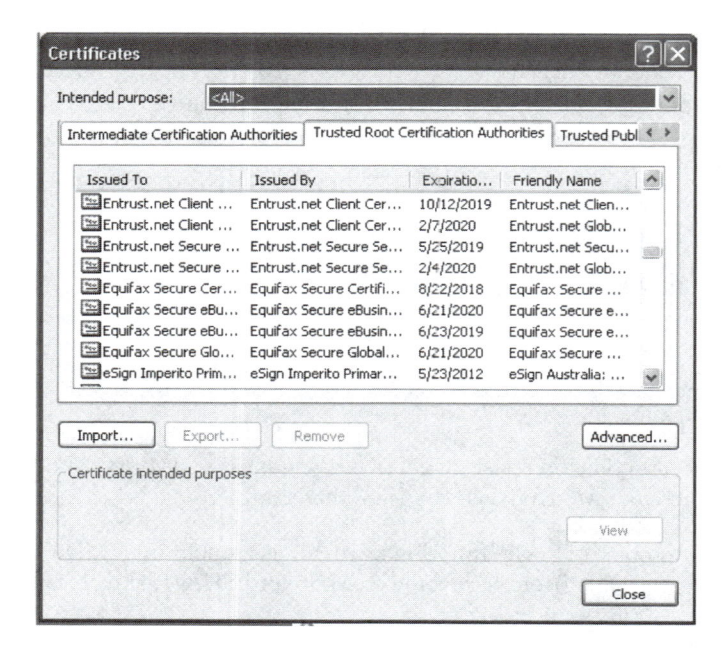

Figure 11.5 Root certificates.

Let's consider an example. Managers at Company XYZ have created a digital certificate that they wish to publish. To guarantee the authenticity of the certificate, they submit it to Company ABC, which is a designated root certificate authority. ABC verifies that XYZ is a valid company and then places their name in the certificate and signs the certificate with ABC's private key.

If you were to receive this signed certificate, you could verify its authenticity with the following steps:

1. Obtain the signer's name from the certificate.

2. Look up the signer's root certificate and obtain his or her public key.

3. Use that public key to decrypt the hash in the original certificate.

4. Verify the accuracy of the hash.

After completing these steps, you would know that this certificate was created by Company XYZ.

A digital certificate can be attached to a file that is intended for download over the Internet. In that case, what is being hashed is the entire file. Once this certificate has been properly signed by a root authority, any user can download it and be assured that it was created by the company that purports to have created it.

11.3.6 People

The people who use a system must be properly trained in basic security concepts and the protection of information. No matter how secure the system is technically, if the users do not practice good security procedures, the system will be vulnerable.

11.4 System Vulnerabilities

Software vulnerabilities are inherent in the operating system and most application programs. In some cases, they were deliberately designed by the programmer in order to facilitate his or her use of the program. In other cases, they are fundamental software defects that were not anticipated at design time.

11.4.1 Social Engineering

Social engineering is an attempt made by an attacker who pretends to be a trusted individual or institution in order to convince someone to divulge confidential information such as passwords or account numbers. There are two common examples:

- *Phishing* is the act of sending out an email that appears to be from a trusted institution, such as the receiver's bank. The user is asked to click on a web link to enter the desired confidential information. The link, of course, takes the user to an attacker's website rather than the trusted institution.

- *Pretexting* involves an attacker who makes a phone call to someone in an organization and poses as someone else and asks for confidential information.

11.4.2 Trojan Horse Programs

A *Trojan horse* is a program that masquerades as something beneficial but actually causes damage or invades privacy. It can also be a beneficial program that is accidentally or deliberately misused by a programmer. A prime example of a Trojan horse program is a terminal login emulator that hijacks/overrides an ATM or other password access controlled system.

In the first attempt to access a secure system, the user unwittingly communicates with the Trojan horse terminal emulator that intervenes between the user and the legitimate login software. The Trojan horse program logs the keystrokes that the user makes and then returns a message to the user that the password has been entered incorrectly and to try to login again. Having acquired the user's authentication data, the Trojan horse then permits the user to access the true terminal login software the next time. The user is none the wiser. The transaction is successfully completed and the user imagines that he or she must have keyed in the wrong PIN number on the first attempt. The Trojan horse then communicates the vital login information across the Internet to its control program.

11.4.3 Spyware

Spyware includes relatively innocuous *software cookies* that monitor the user's browser habits and report them back to an application when the computer is online. Browsers can be set so that a pop-up dialog box requests the browser's permission to deposit a cookie on the disk drive in exchange for access to the services provided by the website. A common form of spyware will hijack the user's web browser so that web searches are diverted to an unexpected website. Other spyware can search the hard drive for personal information, including social security numbers, credit card numbers, driver's license numbers, and other data that could be used to profile individuals, steal identities, or perpetrate credit card or other financial fraud (such as providing account numbers for bogus e-commerce and e-banking transactions).

11.4.4 Trap Doors

A *trap door* is a program fragment that issues a sequence of commands (sometimes just a special password) that the program writers have inserted to circumvent the security system that they designed to control access to their programs. Since these trap doors are not registered as normal logins, programmers who design software with trap doors have used them to carry out illegal activities undetected. Such activities include changing data in a database or tampering with accounting procedures and diverting funds from a group of accounts to a private account.

A trap door written into the login procedure is relatively easy to detect. Trap doors may be written into compilers by applications programmers. The compiler automatically adds a trap door to the executable file of any commercial software it compiles. Thus, the trap door code could not be discovered by examining the source code of the programs. The source code of such a customized compiler (which might be hard to acquire and hard to find once acquired) would have to be examined to locate the trap door.

11.4.5 Database Access Vulnerabilities

The dialog query entry text box for SQL and other database program user interfaces is supposed to be used for valid queries. However, if the program does insufficient checking of user input and simply inserts the user's text into an SQL query string, it is possible for the user to get the program to perform SQL functions that it was not intended to do. This is called an SQL injection attack.

11.4.6 Buffer and Stack Overflow

In many applications where the user must enter data into an input field, the user sends more data than the program anticipates. The data can eventually *overflow* the memory space allocated to the program and enter into a secure area in memory, such as the stack or kernel memory space (see Figure 11.6). The malicious hacker will tamper with pointers to execute code included as part of the data so that, instead of returning to the

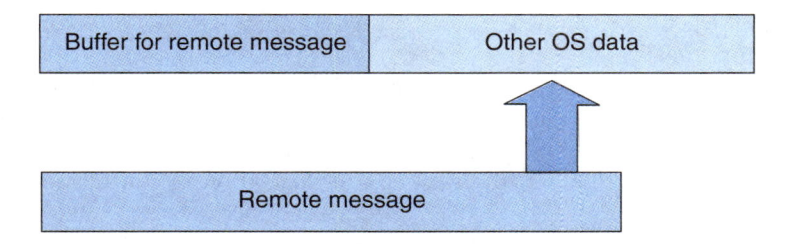

Figure 11.6 Buffer overflow illustration.

application, control is transferred to malicious code that is then executed in a secure area. Processes executing in secure areas of memory are associated with domains having broad access to a variety of resources.

Password files (stored in the root of the file system) can be located by programs running in kernel memory, and core dump files of crashed programs (intended to be used for debugging) can be sifted for useful information about the system and its programs. When vulnerability appears in a network access program, it is particularly pernicious because the attacker can use it to obtain information about the system and to execute malicious programs on the system.

Notice that both database vulnerabilities and buffer/stack overflows occur because the programmer made assumptions about the length or format of input data. One must always completely validate user input before accepting it.

11.5 Invasive and Malicious Software

Invasive and malicious software includes *viruses* and *worms* and any other programs that have the property of being self-replicating and/or self-propagating (they can spread themselves from one computer to another).

In addition to the ability to replicate themselves (often in hard-to-find places such as the boot sector of another file), viruses typically have harmful side effects. Some viruses can do something relatively innocuous such as changing wallpaper, posting flamboyant messages on the desktop, or otherwise changing the appearance of the graphical interface to the operating system. Other viruses can destabilize the operating system by deleting files, disabling applications, and causing other problems.

Viruses can be inadvertently transferred when files from a disk inserted into an external drive are copied to the internal hard disk. Viruses can also be transferred to the (internal) hard disk when email attachments are opened or downloaded. Viruses are fragments of operating system script code found in parts of files, sometimes hidden in the boot sector. Opening such a file can cause the virus script to execute. The first thing the virus code usually does is make a copy of itself to one or more files in the local file system. The adverse side effects caused when the virus changes the attributes of an object (e.g., by changing the registry in Windows) often appear after rebooting the machine.

Worms are complete programs or sets of collaborating programs that have the ability to transfer themselves from one machine to another and to communicate with each other or to receive commands from a master program on a remote machine. They can transfer themselves to any computer logged on to the Internet that they are able to access.

In addition to the ability to migrate from one machine to another, worms often have additional capabilities. An important one is that most worms have to report back to a master process the exact machine and the conduit they used (IP address, port number, and domain) to install themselves successfully. Using this information, the master process can send command signals across the Internet to launch a distributed denial of service attack on one or more servers.

11.6 Defending the System and the User

The system can be defended against viruses in two ways. The best method of protection against viruses is to practice safe computing. This entails common sense practices such as setting the web browser to detect/reject cookies and not opening or downloading email attachments from untrusted or unknown correspondents.

But no matter how careful you might be, using the Internet and/or inserting disks into external drives and copying files from them to the hard disk drive or executing applications on them, viruses will end up infesting your computer. The best way to eliminate these viruses is by installing antivirus software that will scan all files for viruses and remove or quarantine those that it discovers. Antivirus software should be updated often since it is only good against viruses that the programmers deemed were prevalent at the time it was written.

It is more difficult to defend the system against worms. A worm often gains access to a system by exploiting known vulnerabilities of system applications, such as the buffer overflow vulnerability of some network applications. Any system that a human user can access can be accessed automatically by a worm. Worms are also harder to delete. Since most worms on a system will be executing, the worm file cannot be simply deleted, as is the case with a virus. However, worms in the process of execution can be deleted with the aid of the process manager and the file manager.

For servers and other computers with broadband access that are always on and have a fixed IP address, the best way to defend against worms and unauthorized users is to control Internet access on a machine by installing a *firewall*—a program that filters out harmful data by using high-level application gateways and low-level router gateways. Low-level filters specify protocols that allow specific IP addresses to use specific port numbers to access a specific service and deny connection to that address, port, and service to all others. Filters can be circumvented by standard techniques such as IP address spoofing. When hackers discover IP addresses, port numbers, services, and domains to which a firewall grants connections and system access and the association between the port numbers and the services, they can spoof one of these IP addresses. The acceptable IP addresses and port numbers can be inserted into the headers of the packets that the program uses to initiate or terminate communication with the machine (e.g., SYN, ACK, RST, and FIN packets). With the aid of this information, the intruder can tunnel into the network using the protocols acceptable to the firewall.

Apart from preventive measures, the best overall strategy is to conduct periodic checkups of the system/network server/network host when it is running and connected to the Internet for any length of time. The periodic checkup may include any of the following: conducting virus scans with antivirus software, file checksum verifications, process and thread inspections (especially network daemons to locate any unidentified processes that have been running for a long time), using specialized software to search for spyware and viruses, checking access protection data for system files and other resources such as device drivers, requiring users to change passwords that are easy to guess or are out of date, and deleting unexpected pointers in the directory search path.

To defend against identity theft and financial fraud, it is good practice to avoid entering information that could be used to identify an individual into (insecure) web page dialog boxes.

11.7 Intrusion Detection Management

There are two basic patterns for intrusion detection: *signature-based detection* and *anomaly detection*. Like antivirus software, *signature detection* looks for known patterns of behavior established by previous attacks. For instance, multiple logons to an account indicate that an intruder may be trying to guess the password to an account. An application that scans port numbers by sending premature FIN packets indicates that an attacker is looking for open ports, while a connection followed by the transmission of an inordinate amount of data can indicate that the attacker is looking to exploit a buffer overflow to obtain a variety of sensitive system information that may include passwords and IP addresses that could provide access to system accounts.

Anomaly detection is a process that looks for unusual patterns in computer behavior. For instance, a worm program exploiting a port or network application daemon might be detected by the transfer of unusually large amounts of data that would not normally be transferred when the daemon is in that particular state.

In addition to scanning for attack patterns or anomalous behavior on the current state of the machine, intruders who may no longer be active or are temporarily quiescent can be detected by processing the log and audit files. With the aid of these files, past attack patterns can be detected and anomalous events can be analyzed. Information from log and audit files can be cross referenced with the information obtained from the scan of the most recent state of the machine to provide further evidence of the presence of an intruder.

In either case, if an intrusion into the system is suspected, appropriate action can be taken. A system administrator can be warned. Anomalous processes can be deleted from the system. A virtual resource, called a honey pot, can be set up to lure the intruder into the system and extract information about the intruder program while it attempts to exploit the resource.

11.8 Security and Privacy

As we have said, *security* involves preventing the unauthorized access to information. This is different from *privacy*, which involves preventing the unauthorized disclosure of information. What is the difference? Employees who may be authorized to access certain information violate a company's privacy policy if they disclose that information to someone who is not authorized to see it.

Current commercial operating systems do nothing to enforce privacy restrictions. Once authorized users obtain information, the system allows them to do whatever they like with that information. That is because the operating system considers information to be just a set of bits, with no understanding of what those bits represent. Thus, in today's world, enforcing a privacy policy is something that is a training and administrative issue with no technical support.

11.9 Secure Systems Versus Systems Security

Most operating systems and applications in common use at the time this book was written were designed with the goal of maximum connectivity and ease of use. Software plugins are developed by industry or open source programmers to cover up additional vulnerabilities as they are discovered or exposed. When vulnerabilities for an application or an operating system are discovered, the information about the availability of patches and the patches themselves are posted on websites or emailed to users and systems managers.

As new viruses are discovered, antivirus software is updated to recognize their signatures so that the new releases can be removed or at least quarantined. As specific websites with unacceptable content and addresses that send junk email proliferate, application-level filters for browsers and email applications can be updated and adjusted as needed. Security requires overhead, but overhead becomes faster and cheaper as system hardware and software evolves.

What if worrying about systems security was not an afterthought and operating systems designers created an operating system with the forethought to build security in from the foundation up? How can this be done without compromising connectivity and ease of use? An attempt to design a secure system that is easy to use and can handle insecurity from the foundation up has already been attempted with the Java programming language and the Java Virtual Machine (JVM). The basic strategy is to protect the management of main memory from the programmer. Main memory is viewed as the essential source of program and operating system vulnerability.

The Java programming language does not allow its objects to directly access main memory. Moreover, various processes are classified and labeled as trustworthy or not and then allowed appropriate access by the JVM by indelibly marking the stack frame where the object is loaded and which the Java programs executing the object are unable to access.

The three main vulnerabilities related to viruses and worms of an operating system (for a single host machine, a server, or a network of machines) are memory for process storage, disk drives for file storage, and the TCP/IP network protocol and the login procedure for Internet communication. Any attempt to design a future operating system with security built into the architecture must try to extend what the designers of the Java programming language did to the broader scope of the entire operating system, the network, and the resources that they manage.

11.10 Summary

This chapter defines security and protection, and explores the organization of resource protection. Domains are defined for processes. Each process is eligible to execute zero or more operations on each hardware/software resource. Protection can be expressed in terms of the access matrix, which can be extended to allow processes defined on one domain to switch to another, or to copy, add, or delete operations from one matrix cell to another. The access matrix can be implemented globally by storing and then searching ordered triples in a table. It can also be implemented by looking at the list of capabilities available to each domain on each resource.

The problem of security was discussed and contrasted to that of protection. The discussion of security begins with the observation that most systems and applications have vulnerabilities that can be accidentally or deliberately triggered to impair the system. A host of security threats, such as worms, viruses, and spyware, are discussed, as are software countermeasures for each of these threats, such as firewalls, antivirus software, and spyware. Despite the availability of these software countermeasures, the problem is that intruders still manage to access system resources and log on to system accounts. When they do, subtler means must be used to identify their presence. The two main techniques for detecting intruders are to look for pattern signatures and anomalies that can be found by looking at the present state of the system or at information about past system activity available in log and audit files.

Key Terms

access matrix	domain	root certificate
access privilege	external security	security policy
address spoof	firewall	signature detection
anomaly detection	gateway	smartcard
antivirus software	identity theft	software cookie
asymmetric encryption	intrusion detection	spyware
authentication	message digest	stack inspection
capability	packet filter	symmetric encryption
credit card fraud	phishing	system vulnerability
cryptography	pretexting	trap door
denial of service attack	protection	tunnel
	rights	virus
digital signature	role	worm

Exercises and Questions

1. List the access rights and sketch the domain implementations for the Unix file access specification given in Section 11.3.3. (*Hint*: There are a multitude of possible domains. Choose two reasonable file policies that you, as the owner of the file, might want to implement as domains for processes wanting to access the files in your directory. In each case, list the ordered pairs and sketch the relationship between the three domains in a Venn diagram, such as the one shown in Figure 11.1).

2. Sketch a domain implementation in which $i < j \Rightarrow D_i \subseteq D_j; i, j = 1, ..., 5$. Can you explain why this is called a ring implementation? If your program had a process that you wanted to have at least as many access rights as any other process could have, which domain would you select for it?

3. Write a program in pseudocode to implement an access matrix so an operating systems manager can control access to processes associated with domains that request resources from objects. Explain how you would attempt to write a similar program to implement domains of access right pairs. Why is the first task easier?

4. Write a program to implement an access matrix with a global table. When an operation M on D is executed on a resource R in domain D, the program searches the table for the ordered triple (M,D,O). Each time a process, defined on domain D, tries to execute an operation on resource O, the global table is checked for a match. If the ordered triple is located, the operation is permitted; otherwise an exception is thrown.

5. For Table 11.2, explain what kind of process could have access to domains 1, 2, and 3. What kind of resources could R_1, R_2, R_3, and R_4 be?

6. With regard to Table 11.3, define a process that would need to carry out the various operations and domain switches. Describe a scenario in which the switch operation could be used to complete a useful workload and execution cycle for the application.

7. Define a third access matrix modifier called *control* that is applicable to domain objects only. When the word *control* appears in the cell of an access matrix, the process defined on that domain has the ability to change other cells in the same row. Add the word *control* to cell a_{27} in Table 11.3. Show the matrix that results when the process with domain D_2 uses its control to remove the operations that a process defined on D_3 can access on R_4 and to add the operations that a process defined on D_3 can access on R_2.

8. Download a Java compiler/interpreter and use it to load and run an untrusted applet from a web page. Modify the applet to invoke a method to access a resource that should be protected from an untrusted class, hence not be accepted by the JVM. Check if the applet is able to access the resource or whether Java throws the exception as promised and discontinues the execution of the applet.

9. A computer has a one or ten gigahertz processor on a computer connected to a server on an Internet connection that transfers information at a rate of 10 or 100 megabits per second. Suppose that a program running on this computer is dedicated to cracking passwords. Compute how long it will take a program to guess the following passwords by trial and error:

    a. A 6-character password in which each character is a letter in the English alphabet.

    b. A 6-character password in which each character is a letter or a digit.

    c. A 10-character password in which each character is selected from among 36 different Unicode characters.

10. In the Windows operating system, object attributes (properties determined by data) of software objects are stored in a registry. Write an innocuous virus code fragment and insert it into a text file. Attach the text file to an email message and send it to yourself. When you open/download the attachment, the virus fragment should copy itself to a file in a specified directory location and exhibit a harmless side effect, such as changing the wallpaper of the desktop to your school colors by changing the registry. When you reboot the machine, the appearance of the desktop graphical interface should change.

11. Use the file search engine on your operating system file manager to locate the virus in Exercise 10 by matching it to key script commands in the code fragment that uniquely identify it. Now write your own file search program to first locate and then either quarantine or delete the innocuous virus that you created.

12. Write a white paper on how to redesign the file system manager and the directory that would make the file system secure from processes and threads in a manner analogous to the way Sun Microsystems designed the Java language (as mediated by the JVM compiler/interpreter) to make main memory secure from processes and threads.

Chapter 12

Networking and Distributed Systems

12.1 Introduction

The networking of computer systems together has profoundly changed the way that we use computers. It has opened up new uses for the machines in assisting humans in obtaining information, and new ways for us to interact. The development of the Internet, the Web (and browsers and web pages), email, and distributed computing applications has changed and enriched our lives. This area has an engineering foundation in understanding the electronics and signal-processing issues that make fast communication between computers possible. This area also includes management issues: Organizations are now dependent on their computers and the ability to move information from machine to machine for fast communications.

Computers have been linked together for the transfer of data since early in the digital age. The ability to move data and information between systems over phone landlines and dedicated circuits has been common since the 1960s. Moving email between systems is also an old idea, implemented by linking systems together with a dedicated circuit, and allowing systems to pass email messages between each other.

The Internet is a key concept in the evolution of computing that takes these ideas to the next level, allowing a greater degree of integration of software and data residing on different systems that are geographically distant than was previously possible. The development of the Internet also created new, powerful applications in the World Wide Web, in the various forms of e-commerce. The Internet grew out of academic research, and research sponsored by the U.S. Department of Defense. The Internet is a system of high bandwidth links connecting routers, hubs, and gateways, providing very fast connectivity between computing machines located anywhere on the planet with Internet access.

The creation of the World Wide Web and Hypertext Markup Language resulted in a "killer application" that made the Internet useful for everyone, not just computing professionals and scientists. The hypertext concept was popularized by Apple Computers as a way for computer users to find, organize, and access their data. When extended across the Internet, the Web allows users to find, link to, and access data stored on web pages that can reside anywhere in the world.

- RESOLUTION: The Federal Networking Council (FNC) agrees that the following language reflects our definition of the term 'Internet'. 'Internet' refers to the global information system that—

  (i) is logically linked together by a globally unique address space based on the Internet Protocol (IP) or its subsequent extensions/follow-ons;

  (ii) is able to support communications using the Transmission Control Protocol/Internet Protocol (TCP/IP) suite or its subsequent extensions/follow-ons, and/or other IP-compatible protocols; and

  (iii) provides, uses, or makes accessible, either publicly or privately, high-level services layered on the communications and related infrastructure described herein.
  –Unanimous resolution, Federal Networking Council, October 24, 1995.

The Internet is a network that links networks of computers, or a meta-network. It is a dynamically changing interconnection of thousands of individual networks with millions of computers and users, working through a standardized set of protocols for data transmission and control of the communications process.

The architecture of the Internet is design to interconnect networks through a common protocol TCP/IP. The TCP/IP protocol is designed to connect any networks together, regardless of the specific hardware and internal protocols running internal to those networks. By adding the TCP/IP protocols and creating a physical connection with the Internet, any node on any connected network can communicate seamlessly with any other node on the interconnected networks. TCP/IP is an open standard, allowing any company to produce hardware and software that is compatible with the Internet, and to allow the Internet to grow and develop on an unprecedented scale.

The architecture of the Internet is a complex weaving of many networks interconnected at multiple levels. The Internet backbone consists of multiple very high bandwidth communication links, which handle the long distance transfer of information, and are operated by large telecommunications companies. Many cross-connections between backbone sections and bandwidth providers create multiple redundant paths through the Internet. Many branches and subbranches connect either directly or indirectly to the Internet backbone.

Data moves through the Internet in packets, which can be routed from segment to segment automatically by network routing computers that rely on the Internet's addressing protocol. Each network and each machine on the Internet has a unique address, so that any computer in the world that is connected to the Internet can be identified unambiguously. Starting from the source, each communication packet is routed up in the hierarchy of interconnected networks, and is then routed back down through the networks to its destination. Routing within both the source and destination networks is provided by the local network, while Internet service providers and backbone operators provide the routing at the higher levels.

The mechanism that provides the service to route packets between source and destination is in the two protocols that are the key innovation in building the Internet: Transmission Control Protocol (TCP), and Internet Protocol (IP), called TCP/IP.

12.2 Ethernet

In order for computers to be able to exchange information through a network, both machines must be configured to support the following requirements:

- *Medium*: Computers are networked through a physical medium, whether a network cable, Internet provider, wireless/radio network, etc.

- *Protocol*: A protocol is a plan or set of standards for arranging bits in messages, so that both source and destination have the same expectations for formatting data. The protocol includes a frame or a packet definition, which specifies how bits and bytes will be organized and grouped together for transmission.

- *Control protocol*: This is the strategy that will be used to allow multiple machines to share the transmission medium in a logical way. The control protocol may be concerned about fairness, so that all machines have a chance to use the shared media, and concerned about the quality of service, verifying that packets have been received and received correctly.

One of the most common networking standards in use is Ethernet. Ethernet is a relatively old standard, as its origins stretch back to the Second World War, in the design of a network of radio stations that share access to a common set of radio frequencies. With Ethernet, there is a common shared media, which can be cable, twisted-pair, wireless radio frequency, and other media. The basic control strategy that governs the use of that shared media can be described with an acronym: CSMA/CD.

CSMA/CD stands for:

- *Carrier sense*: A machine that needs to send data will first listen to the media to see whether it is idle or in use (listen before talk).

- *Multiple access*: Multiple devices can share the use of the medium by following these rules for access.

- *Collision detection*: (Listen while talk.) Even when machines listen to the media for it to be idle before transmitting, there is a possibility that more than one machine can transmit on top of each other, called a collision. This occurs when multiple machines are waiting for the media to become idle when an ongoing transmission completes. More than one machine may detect that the medium is idle at the same time, and may begin to transmit. Multiple machines transmitting at the same time result in garbled signals—no message gets through correctly. It is critical that collisions be detected when they occur so that frames containing data can be retransmitted. Collisions are detected by having the transmitting machines monitor the media while transmitting and comparing the signals actually on the media to what it is sending. If the signals don't match, a collision has occurred. When a collision is detected, all transmitting machines will immediately cease transmission, and will send a jamming signal to ensure that all machines detected either the collision or the jamming signal. Then, the transmitting machines wait a random amount of time (in order to space out the retransmissions) and then listen for the media to go idle in order to retransmit.

One of the interesting features of the Ethernet protocol is that its behavior is non-deterministic. That is, its performance will vary depending on the quantity of traffic. The more traffic on the network, the greater the chance of accidental collisions as stations jump on an idle media at the same moment. These collisions waste bandwidth both during the collision itself and through the required jamming signals and subsequent retransmissions. So, as an Ethernet system approaches heavy use and collisions consume more and more bandwidth, its efficiency and useful bandwidth begins to decline.

There are alternative media access control (MAC) protocols that do not suffer the performance degradation under heavy load that is characteristic of the Ethernet. An example alternative involves token passing. A token is a special logical right to use the shared media. The station that holds the token may broadcast without fear of collision or interruption, as no other station holds the token. Token-passing strategies require that machines hold onto the token for a limited duration, in order to allow other machines a chance to transmit on the shared medium. The token is then passed along to the next machine in line.

The improved performance of token passing comes at the cost of a more complex protocol and control logic. Token-passing protocols must allow for stations to join or leave the network and the sequence of token passing. A machine could be shut down (or crash) while holding the token, requiring a protocol algorithm for detecting this occurence and generating a new token. Various other situations must be accounted for in logic, all of which have been successfully implemented.

Ethernet became widely adopted as a standard networking interface during the 1980s, when the manufacturing cost differential between simple Ethernet and more sophisticated protocols was relatively large. Ethernet's competitive cost advantage due to its initial lower cost to manufacture network controllers won out over more complicated protocols that perform more efficiently. Ethernet won in the marketplace based on the manufacturing economics of the time, and has since become a universal standard in spite of the performance limitations of its original MAC strategy.

Current Ethernet technologies are no longer limited by the media contention issues of its original design. Ethernet has evolved significantly over time as technology has improved. The original Ethernet media was a thick cable (about the diameter of a nickel). This evolved to a more convenient and less expensive thin cable (similar to a cable TV cable), and then to networking using twisted pairs of wires, similar to telephone wires. Of course, wireless Ethernet is now widely used, with the media being radio frequencies rather than physical cables or wires. As the media has evolved and changed, so has the control protocol for managing the media. But the frame structure part of the Ethernet protocol has remained constant throughout, facilitating software compatibility, back-

| Start | Dest | Source | T | Data | Frame |

Figure 12.1 Ethernet frame structure.

ward compatibility, and interfacing with other protocols. The frame structure can be thought of as the Ethernet's interface to other protocols, applications, and operating systems. The underlying mechanics can evolve without affecting compatibility as long as this interface has remained constant.

Figure 12.1 illustrates the basic structure of an Ethernet frame.

The frame is divided into fields, each a set string of bits with a different meaning. The first field (START) is a preamble that the network cards use to synchronize to the detectors on the network cards for the rest of the transmission. The DEST and SOURCE fields are the address of the destination and source machines. The T field is for the type of Ethernet frame. The DATA field can be of variable length, holding from 46 to 1500 bytes of data. The final field is a frame check sequence that is used to check for transmission errors.

The SOURCE and DESTINATION fields are each 6 bytes long, allowing 248 different addresses, which vastly exceeds the number of humans on the planet. This very large number of different possible addresses seems excessive, especially considering that the number of network nodes (machines) on a single Ethernet network is performance limited (more recent Ethernet variations have greater capacities and speeds than the original design). The reason for the large number of possible addresses is to allow the assignment of blocks of addresses to different network interface board manufacturers, in order to guarantee that no Ethernet board would be sold that duplicates another address on an existing board. And also to guarantee that as technology advances, old boards can be just thrown away and replaced with new without worrying about recovering or "trading in" the old Ethernet addresses for reassignment and reuse.

12.3   Internetworking and TCP/IP

The Internet was created to link multiple networks together (internetworking) in order to exchange data and information between systems located on different networks. Networking protocols (like Ethernet) could not be extended to and expanded to support millions of machines located literally around the globe. The decision was made to create a new communication protocol that will handle internetworking tasks, which is a layer of software on top of the existing networking protocols already in widespread use. The new Internetworking protocols support and interact with existing networking protocols without requiring change or modification. These Internetwork protocols are described as TCP and IP, though there are actually a number of specialized variations on these models in use for specific purposes. TCP stands for transmission control pro-

Chapter 12 Networking and Distributed Systems

tocol whereas IP stands for internetwork protocol. These protocols were designed to work with existing networking protocols (like Ethernet) and not to replace them. The concept of encapsulation is used for this interaction. Basically, the data from the application that is to be communicated from source to destination is first inserted into TCP packets. These are passed down to the IP software layer that adds its control information. Then these packets are passed down to the MAC layer for assembly into MAC frames for transmission on the local network (Figure 12.2), so that multiple levels of communication protocol information encapsulates the data. The MAC layer frame is transmitted on the source network to the local Internet gateway. The Internet gateway strips off the MAC layer frame information, leaving the TCP and IP control information and the data in packet form. TCP and IP are used to send and route the packets over the Internet to the destination network.

At the destination network, the TCP/IP packets are assembled into frames for the destination network and transmitted to the destination machine. The destination machine strips off the MAC layer control information, the IP layer header information, and the TCP header information and assembles the data from the packets and delivers them to the destination application.

Figure 12.3 illustrates how data is encapsulated with control information at each level of protocol. The data is first encapsulated with the TCP control information in

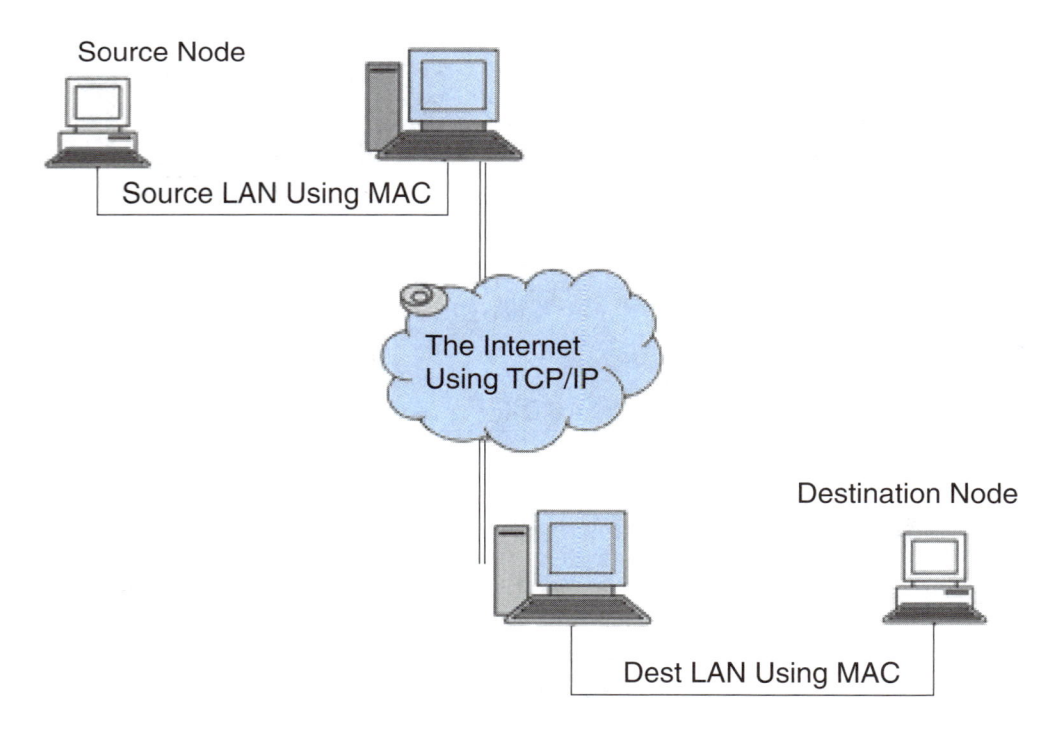

Figure 12.2 Internetworking across LANs and the Internet.

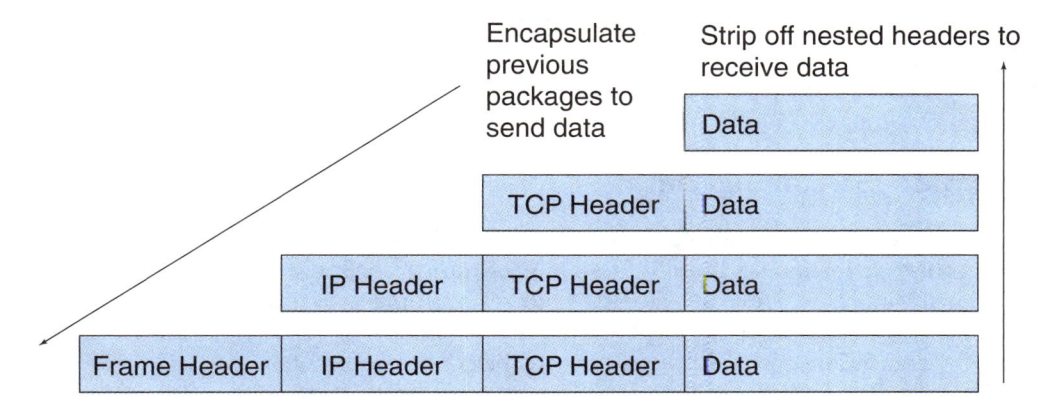

Figure 12.3   Encapsulation of protocol headers and data.

a header. That combined control/data packet is then presented to the next protocol layer (IP) as data, and receives another header around it. Finally, the packet with both IP and TCP control information is presented to the lowest networking-level protocol (e.g., Ethernet), and is further encapsulated with another layer of control information. This process of encapsulation can go on for multiple levels. In fact, some applications encapsulate control information along with the data itself.

At each level of transmission and reception, the protocol headers are either added when transmitting, or stripped off when receiving.

12.3.1 Connection Oriented Versus Connectionless

The IP protocol is a connectionless protocol, which means that packets are routed from the source to destination through multiple routers connecting different segments of the Internet. Each router decides how to pass the packet along by looking at the destination address information in the packet and consulting its internal tables on connections. As traffic on the Internet fluctuates, it is possible that routers will route some packets one way, and some another. Consequently, using a connectionless scheme, it is possible that some packets will arrive out of order, thus requiring the ability to properly order and recombine packets to recreate the data at the destination. IP includes positioning data in its packets so that the message can be reconstructed in the proper order.

TCP is a connection-oriented protocol, which means that a temporary connection of links is created from source to destination across the Internet. This requires that each router between communicating machines be involved in creating a temporary virtual connection. Special overhead control messages are sent to create the virtual connection, and to take it down when finished. Through paying the cost of the overhead messages and time to establish the virtual connection up-front, the routing of packets is simplified, with no decision making needed at each router. Each router simply passes the packets along to the next device programmed in the sequence. Setting up a virtual connection can take network traffic and load into account, but once established, the virtual connection is generally not changed. Connection-oriented virtual connections can provide a higher level of service, guaranteeing that packets will arrive and that they will arrive in order.

12.3.2 Streaming Data

Streams of data are used to broadcast or transmit audio and video across the Internet. Streams are literally a stream of data from source to destination that captures an audio or audio + video broadcast. Multiple protocols have been implemented to stream data over the Internet; some are essentially connectionless, whereas others are connection-oriented, plus there are blended aspects of both. Each protocol may implement a different level of service and reliability, some guaranteeing the arrival of all packets in a stream, whereas others allow the loss of some data.

Lossless streams often involve buffering the data—requiring a wait while a video is downloaded, for instance. The buffering delay allows for time for the protocol to analyze the arriving stream of data, and retransmit any lost or corrupted packets in the stream. Streams that allow data loss can show up as lower quality, for instance, as choppy video that stalls briefly at times. Often it is acceptable to lose some data in a video stream, as in web conferencing or distance learning, where the instructor's or participant's web camera image may appear choppy and not fluid. But the transmission of information vital to successful communication may not allow data loss. For instance, losing part of an audio communication or broadcast may compromise the effectiveness of communication if some words are missed, or part of a musical broadcast is lost.

12.4 World Wide Web

The World Wide Web is a way of using the Internet to request and retrieve information, and to interact with remote computer systems. The Web could be considered to be an application on the Internet. The Web consists of four concepts:

- *Markup language*: This is the language that specifies codes that allow the developer to format the appearance of web pages. The web browser must understand and be able to interpret these codes, which are standardized as HTML (hypertext mark-up language). For instance, to designate that text is to appear in bold, a web page might contain the following line:

    The word <strong> BOLD</strong> is in bold text.

    The <strong> and </strong> are used to begin and end the section of text that is to be displayed in bold typeface.

- *Uniform resource locator* (*URL*): This is a label for the address and location of a page or resource somewhere on the Internet. This label is translated to an actual IP address by servers on the Internet. An example URL is

    http://www.nsf.gov/

    which is the URL for the U.S. Government's National Science Foundation.

- *Hypertext or hyperlinks*: These are embedded links in a web page that can be used to link pages together. The pages can be on different computer systems anywhere on the Internet. Hyperlinks can also be used within a document to allow the users to quickly jump or navigate from place to place within the document. An example of a hyperlink that can be embedded in a web page to link to the Linux operating system organization's home page:

  <A href=" http://www.linux.org/"> Linux </A>

  Observe that this hyperlink has a URL embedded within it between the double-quotes ("). Note also the use of the markup-language < and > to begin and end the HTML commands. The name "Linux" is a label that appears on the web page, that when clicked on or selected, directs the user's browser to go to the URL for the Linux organization.

- *Client-server model of computing*: This is the idea that an application can be composed of parts that may exist at different machines connected by the Internet, that work together. In regard to the Web, there are at least two machines that work together:

  - The user's PC is the client.
  - A server with web pages or web applications.

  There are a number of other machines that work behind the scenes to make the Internet work, and to handle functions like translating the URLs into IP addresses.

12.5 DNS and DHCP

Because Internet addresses are numbers, intelligible names are assigned in place of Internet addresses, for our convenience in everyday use. This requires the use of a translation process to convert a user-friendly web address into an actual numeric address. The Domain Name System (DNS) does this translation. As an example, the U.S. President's website at www.whitehouse.gov is translated to an IP address of **92.123.72.136**. The address of the U.S. National Science Foundation (www.nsf.gov) is **128.150.4.107**. There are web-based tools that can be used to perform an address look up for finding the IP address of a domain name or website.

The DNS actually consists of a set of many name-translating servers, organized as a distributed database in a hierarchy based on the domain and subdomains that they serve. Domain names consist of one or more labels, separated by dots (periods). The hierarchy of domains starts from the right. The top-level domain of www.whitehouse.gov is "gov". Web users are familiar with many different top-level domains like .com, .net, and .edu.

A host name is a set of domain-name labels to translate to an actual IP address. The domain name www.whitehouse.gov is also a host name because it translates to **92.123.72.136** but "gov", while a valid domain name, it is not a complete host name. The multiple levels of domain-name translating servers are each responsible for translating different labels in a domain name. So to make a complete translation, multiple DNS servers may be involved, each doing a part of the translation, with multiple messages communicated between servers.

The process of translating an Internet address into an actual numeric address consists of a number of steps, as the translation process goes from high-level domains to lower-level domains:

1. Each computer needs an address of a server. To translate the highest-level domain of an address (i.e., .com, .net, .gov) the system accesses a root server.

2. A system that needs to use the DNS is configured with the known addresses of the root servers. This is often stored in a file of root hints, which are updated periodically by an administrator from a reliable source.

3. Messages are sent to query one of the root servers to find the server that is responsible for the desired top-level domain (TLD).

4. Then, messages are sent to the obtained TLD DNS server requesting the address of a DNS server that can provide the translation for the second-level domain. That server is then queried for the translation, and then also queried for the address of the next-level DNS server that can provide the translation of the next-level domain name.

5. Step 4 is repeated until the entire domain name has been translated into an actual IP address, which is then returned to the computer generating the request.

12.5.1 DNS Caching

Because the Internet is very heavily used, DNS allows for caching of records to improve performance and reduce the DNS traffic on the system. Caching is the idea of holding local and temporary copies of needed data in order to minimize the number of DNS accesses (and time required) that must go through the translation process to the original sources. When a requested DNS entry can be found in the local and temporary storage (the cache), the cache provides the needed address without the need for additional time and communications bandwidth to go to the original source.

Caching is used in many places throughout computing in order to speed up access. It is also described as reducing latency, which is the time required to complete a process, and reducing overall bandwidth (traffic on the network), which can also reduce the delay time. For instance, computer systems use caching to speed up disk processing. A portion of the disk data can be temporarily stored in memory on the disk controller, resulting in a hard disk that performs faster. Caching is also used for improving Internet performance, which happens at a number of levels. For instance, Internet domain-name translations can be cached on a local system, managed by the operating system or web browser. Web pages themselves can also be cached on a local system, or on servers on the Internet.

DNS caches temporarily hold a domain name to IP-address translation for a fixed period of time, which can be configured as a time_to_live (TTL). When the TTL expires, the data stored in the cache is declared invalid, and must be refreshed from the DNS servers. The TTL is set by the administrator of the DNS server that provides the translation, and the period of time may vary from just seconds to days or even weeks.

An interesting consequence of caching addresses is that a change in a DNS domain name to a different IP address does not take effect immediately for all machines, but instead takes time to propagate throughout the Internet, as cached values TTL expire and the data is refreshed with the new address. Obviously then, when changing IP addresses for a domain name, it is helpful to provide a temporary workaround so that the old IP addresses will continue to work, while waiting for TTLs to expire and force an update of the new address.

12.5.2 DHCP

DHCP stands for Dynamic Host Configuration Protocol. It is a networking protocol used for setting up and configuring computers to use the Internet. In order for a computer to use the Internet, it needs to be configured with an initial Internet address, and the address servers it needs to use. One specific server machine needs to be able to find (for Internet access) the address of a DNS server, for translating to numeric Internet addresses.

Network administrators can set up a DHCP server. Computers access the DHCP server for configuration information needed. By using DHCP, administrators can maintain a single repository for configuration information that all machines query. This is much easier to maintain than individually configuring all machines on a network.

DHCP is based on a client/server architecture; client machines broadcast a request for configuration information, and the DHCP server responds with the needed data from its internal database. It has a pool of IP addresses it can allocate to clients. It also has the default gateway address, domain name, subnet masks, and so on. DHCP can allocate IP addresses using dynamic, automatic, or static allocation schemes:

- *Dynamic allocation*: A range of IP addresses is allocated to the DHCP server that it can use to assign. Client machines request and release IP addresses from this pool. In this scheme, there is no attempt made to ensure that a client machine gets the same address. IP addresses can be allocated to clients for a controlled and limited time period.

- *Automatic allocation*: IP addresses are assigned to clients from the pool allocated to that DHCP server. The DHCP server maintains a table of MAC-layer addresses and IP addresses that have been assigned to that MAC-layer address. Each time a client starts up and requests an IP address, the server does a table look up to provide one of the same addresses previously allocated if available.

- *Static allocation*: This method is more restrictive than automatic allocation. IP addresses are permanently assigned to clients from the pool allocated to that DHCP server. The DHCP server maintains a table of MAC-layer addresses and IP addresses. Each time a client starts up and requests an IP address, the server does a table look up to provide the same address previously allocated. The DHCP server can be set up to deny IP-address assignments from machines (based on their MAC-addresses) that have not been previously configured in its database.

12.6 Parallel Computing

Regardless how much faster each generation of computer chip design increases computing power, there is always a need and desire for more computing power. We seem to have an insatiable need to do more computing in less time. Increasing computing power enables the solution in a timely fashion of problems that would previously be impractical to solve. Increasing computing power makes it possible to enhance programs with additional features and capabilities that enhance the human–computer interaction—like voice-recognition interfaces, 3-D graphics, virtual-reality interfaces, and intelligent interfaces.

Each generation of computer chip design improves performance by miniaturizing the transistors on the chip. Small transistors mean that more can be packed in the same space and smaller transistors require less energy to operate. Transistors that need less energy to run (often revealed in the voltages necessary to run the devices—5V, 3.3V, 2.2V, 1.1V, 0.7V) generate less heat as wasted energy, allowing a denser packing of transistors without temperatures reaching the failure point. Smaller transistors that operate on less power switch faster, and shorter connections between transistors allow for chips to operate at higher clock speeds.

But regardless of how the physicists and engineers improve our computing devices with each generation (early chips ran at 4000 cycles per second and less, current chips run at 3,000,000+ cycles per second), there is a need for more computing power. An alternative approach to achieving higher power is through parallel processing, where multiple processors are combined to complete a workload in less time.

Parallel computing systems also offer the possibility of a higher degree of fault tolerance. If a single processor in a system of multiple redundant processors fails, the entire system can continue to function, but at reduced power. Redundancy can be applied to many aspects of a computing system, allowing systems with multiple processors, buses, disk drives, memories, caches, network interfaces, and so on. Figure 12.4 illustrates the basic foundation concept behind parallel computing. In this example, there are four processors available for concurrent execution of this process. The process also happens to be divisible into 10 discrete pieces, at most four of which can be executed in different processors concurrently. The process has some set-up work at the beginning that can only be executed on a single processor. Similarly, there is some work at the conclusion of the process where results are collated and consolidated that must be executed on a single processor.

In Figure 12.4, an abstract process to be computed is composed of 10 blocks of processing, each requiring the same time to complete. When executed on a single processor (executed in serial), 10 time units are required to complete the work. But when taking advantage of the four processors available, then running the same process on the parallel-processing multiprocessor machine, the work is completed in only four time units.

> **An example parallel process of 10 time units:**
> S – Serial or nonparallel parts of the process
> A – All A parts can be executed concurrently
> B – All B parts can be executed concurrently
>
> All A parts must be completed prior to executing any of the B parts
>
> **Executed on a single processor:**
>
> | S | A | A | A | A | B | B | B | B | S |
>
> Ten units of time to complete
>
> **Executed in parallel on four processors:**
>
> $$Speedup = \frac{Serial\ Time}{Parallel\ Time} = \frac{10}{4} = 2.5$$
>
> $$Efficiency = \frac{Speedup}{Processors} = \frac{2.5}{4} = 62.5\%$$
>
> Four units of time to complete

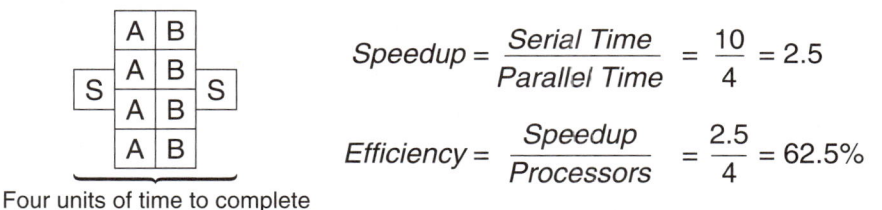

Figure 12.4 Understanding parallel speedup of computing.

It is useful to measure the performance improvement of a parallel machine. One measure used is called SPEEDUP, which is the ratio of the serial time divided by the parallel time.

$$Speedup = \frac{Serial\ Time}{Parallel\ Time} = \frac{10}{4} = 2.5$$

$$Efficiency = \frac{Speedup}{Processors} = \frac{2.5}{4} = 62.5\%$$

Another performance measure is EFFICIENCY, which gives an idea of how much of the available computing power is applied to the problem, as opposed to sitting idle. Efficiency is the ratio of the speedup obtained on a particular system, over the number of processors or processing elements on the system.

These concepts about parallel processing were first observed by Gene Amdahl, and when formulated a different way, are known as Amdahl's law. Amdahl's formulation focuses on the fraction or percentage of the workload that can be done in parallel, and the percentage that must be completed in serial. These two fractions add up to 100%. The parallel percentage is executed on the parallel processors and will take proportionately less time to complete. The ratio of the serial workload divided by the parallel workload (composed of the parallel and serial fractions) defines speedup.

12.6.1 Simple Model of Parallel Speedup

In the following formulation, the parallel fraction of the work is represented as α, and the serial percentage is then $1 - \alpha$.

$$Speedup = \frac{Serial\ Time}{Parallel\ Time} = \frac{1}{(1-\alpha) + \frac{\alpha}{n}}$$

where

$$\alpha = \text{fraction of work that can be done in parallel}$$
$$1 - \alpha = \text{fraction of work that must be done in serial}$$
$$n = \text{number of processors}$$

This simple analytical model, also known as Amdahl's law, is not the final word on parallel processing speedup. It is a simple model with a number of implied assumptions. These assumptions mean that it is a correct and complete model only for a simplistic system. Specifically, the following assumptions are implied but specifically acknowledged in the model, each of which have historically represented opportunities for investigators to expand our knowledge of parallel processing beyond this baseline model:

- The workload consists of a single process to be executed. The extension to the simple model is to consider running multiple programs (processes) simultaneously, where each process may use a different subset of the available processes.

- The process runs at just one constant degree of parallelism (the process always uses exactly n parallel processors for the portion of the program that can run in parallel, with no serial component). The extension is to recognize that many processes will be able to use a varying number of processors, sometimes leaving processors idle, and sometimes needing more processors than are available.

- The process and the work that is to be completed is constant, and will not be scaled up or increased in size in order to take advantage of a larger number of available processors. The extension recognizes that with a bigger machine (more processors), a larger workload may be attempted.

- Parallelism exists at a single level (Amdahl's model is at the processor level). Recent work has identified parallelism at more than five distinct levels, and that the incorporation of multiple simultaneous levels of parallelism yields greater speedups.

12.6.2 Limitations of Parallel Speedup

It is instructive to consider how much performance improvement is possible and practical through parallel computing. Consider the denominator of the simple analytical model:

$$Speedup = \frac{1}{(1-\alpha) + \frac{\alpha}{n}}$$

The denominator has two parts that are summed together, only one of which changes as the number of processors (n) changes, the other being a constant based on the serial fraction of the workload. Consider the break point where these two halves of the denominator are equal:

$$(1-\alpha) = \frac{\alpha}{n}$$

At this point, increasing the number of processors assigned to the task can drive the right half of the equation (α/n) close to zero, thus halving the denominator of the equation. Thus, beyond this break point, the speedup can be at most nearly doubled, regardless of the number of available processors, even if there is an infinite number of processors available (and this would also require that the task can utilize an infinite number of processors—a very unlikely condition for a real-world process). At this extreme, the time required to complete the task can at best be halved.

Beyond this break point where the two halves of the denominator are equal, throwing additional processors at a task will produce only limited speedup and time savings. Beyond this break point, the speedup is limited more by $1-\alpha$, the fraction of work that must be done in serial, rather than the number of processors available.

For $\alpha = 90\%$, the break point is at

$$(1-\alpha) = \frac{\alpha}{n}$$
$$(1-0.90) = \frac{0.90}{n}$$
$$n = 9$$

Inserting these values for α and n yields a speed at the balance point of 5. Scaling the number of processors to drive α/n toward zero can decrease the denominator approaching 0.10, yielding a speedup approaching 10.

For $\alpha = 99\%$, the break point is at

$$(1-\alpha) = \frac{\alpha}{n}$$
$$(1-0.99) = \frac{0.99}{n}$$
$$n = 99$$

For $\alpha = 99.9\%$, the break point is at

$$(1-\alpha) = \frac{\alpha}{n}$$
$$(1-0.999) = \frac{0.999}{n}$$
$$n = 999$$

So when the relationship between the two parts of the denominator are $(1-\alpha) < \frac{\alpha}{n}$ it may then be reasonable to increase the number of processors assigned to the task, in order to increase speedup and reduce the time required to complete the task. Conversely, when $(1-\alpha) > \frac{\alpha}{n}$ it is not likely to be efficient to allocate additional computing power to the task that will return only marginal increases in speedup and reductions in time to workload completion.

This inherent limitation in realizable speedup was observed early on, and was considered to be discouraging to further exploration of parallel processing. But through examining types of problems and algorithms that exhibit very large parallel fractions (and very small serial fractions of work), it was realized that there are situations where the break point as defined by $1 - \alpha$ can be very small, thus allowing the efficient use of a very large number of processors. Many scientific and engineering problems and simulation model systems exhibit these characteristics. In these problems, the degree of accuracy of the simulation and reliability of the problem solution is increased with very large data sets or very large numbers of points to be simulated. This class of problems can efficiently use a large number of processors.

But by far the most common application of computing for general purposes does not require and may not easily utilize the power of parallel processing at extreme levels. Consequently, most computers and PCs are sold with a single or a small number of processors. Finally, there are the rare situations where a large number of processors are available, more than can be efficiently utilized, but which will otherwise sit idle. For those cases, it is sensible to utilize the computing resources even if they make only modest contributions to speedup. When the number of available processors is beyond the number utilized efficiently at the break point, researchers even consider expanding the work to be completed (scaling the work) in order to make efficient use of the available processors. Of course this only makes sense when there is real value to be returned by scaling the work to utilize a larger number of processors.

Diminishing Returns of Parallel Speedup

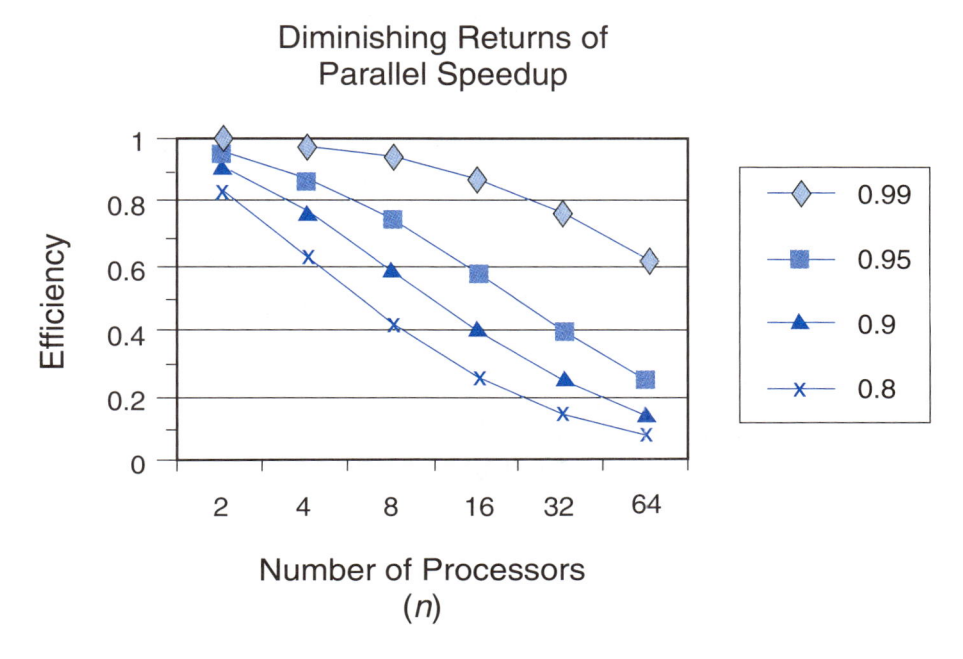

Figure 12.5 Diminishing returns of parallel speedup.

Figure 12.5 illustrates the problem with diminishing returns from parallel processing. The figure charts the efficiency (the parallel speedup divided by the number of processors used) that results with four applications that have different parallel fractions of work. As increasing numbers of processors are allocated to the task, the overall efficiency declines dramatically. Parallel fractions from 99% to 80% are illustrated. Applications with parallel fractions below 80% will result in even worse efficiency, whereas those with parallel fractions above 99% will perform better. There are scientific and engineering number-crunching applications with very high parallel fractions above 99%, for which parallel processing is very effective.

12.6.3 Multiple Levels of Parallelism

The most common approach to realizing greater speedups from parallel processing is to use the hardware resources to accommodate multiple levels of parallelism in the software by building machines with multiple hardware levels of parallelism. A fraction of the hardware resources is committed to each level, instead of all hardware being dedicated at a single level. By using this strategy, the parallel speedup realized at each level is toward the more efficient end of the speedup curve (to the right in Figure 12.5), and suffers less from the problem of diminishing returns as the number of processing

350 Chapter 12 Networking and Distributed Systems

Hardware Parallel Element	Software Parallelism
Pipeline stages	Intra-instruction
Superscalar: multiple pipelines	Inter-instruction
Multi-core: multiple processor cores in a chip	Thread/process
Multiple processor on a board or blade	Thread/process
Multiple processors/boards/blades in a cluster	Thread/process
Multiple clusters in a system	Thread/process
Multiple tiers, distributed and grid computing	Process/application

Table 12.1 Levels of Parallelism

elements increase. As an example, the modern personal computer often has multiple levels of parallel hardware, sometimes as many as three:

- Multiple processors
- Each processor may have multiple processing cores
- Each core will have multiple pipelines.

Note that in Table 12.1 multiple levels of hardware that implement different levels of parallelism at the thread/process level are common, illustrating that "nested" levels or parallelism are possible (i.e., parallel processes may contain parallel threads that each contain grains or blocks of code that can be executed in parallel).

12.7 Cluster and Grid Computing

The study of parallel processing also focuses on the architecture of different types of parallel machines. Designs often consist of hundreds or thousands of off-the-shelf processors integrated into a single system. The buses and interconnects that allow the processors to work together are a critical component of a parallel machine, as limitations in communication capability severely limit the speedup that can be realized.

Programming languages and operating systems for parallel machines are another related area of study and research. High-level languages that are designed specifically for parallel processing or extensions to existing languages to support parallel processing are needed to support parallel processing, as well as operating systems that are extended or enhanced to coordinate the functioning of many processors.

Parallel programming utilizes programming constructs that are not present in normal (nonparallel) programming. Languages specific to parallel processing have been created, but the most fruitful approach has been to add parallel extensions to an existing programming language. Similarities exist between parallel programming language features and features required for multithreaded programming. The following example constructs illustrate some of the important programming concepts needed for parallel programming:

- *Par*: Defines a block of code as executable in parallel, often includes the number of parallel code pieces or threads to create.

- *Public/private*: Used to specify what variables can be shared between parallel sections, and what variables are unique to each thread.

- *Distribute*: A mechanism to distribute data sequentially to parallel code pieces, generally by distributing elements or rows/columns of an array.

- *Synchronize*: Used to JOIN the parallel threads of execution, by forcing waits until all parallel threads or code blocks complete to this point.

- *Critical*: Defines a block of code to be a "critical section" that allows execution by only one thread/processor at a time.

Clustered computing architectures build high-performance multiprocessor machines by grouping processors together in clusters, and then combining the clusters together. Clustering processors together works efficiently for a wide range of applications, because each cluster contains localized cache or memory storage with a local communication pathway. This architecture compartmentalizes communication traffic and sharing of data within clusters, which allows multiple clusters to be grouped together while avoiding forcing the communication interconnections to become a bottleneck to performance.

Figure 12.6 shows a conceptual diagram of a clustered multiprocessor computer architecture. Four clusters of processors are shown, each with an internal bus and an internal cache memory for high-speed communication and processing within the clusters. The clusters are then interconnected with a second interconnect that not only allows the clusters to communicate with other clusters, but also provides access to memory and I/O devices. Other cluster configurations are possible with different variations of

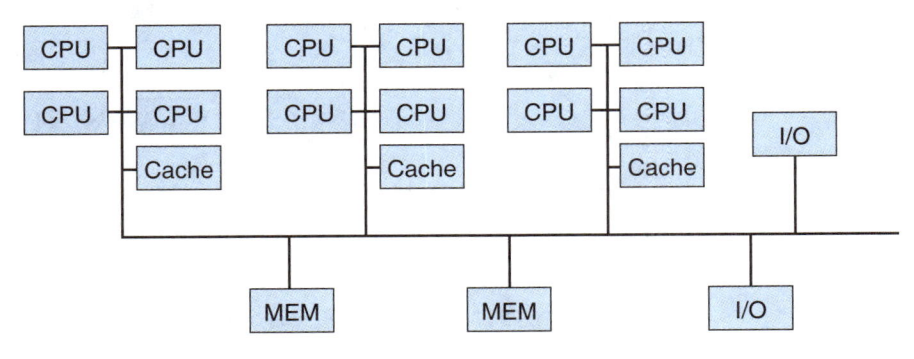

Figure 12.6 Clustered computer architecture.

processors, buses, cache, memory and disk storage within the cluster (intracluster), and different interconnection topologies to connect the clusters together (shown here is a single bus intercluster interconnect).

One commercially available clustered architecture is a blade cluster. Each blade contains two or more processors, each processor chip has its own cache, and there is both cache and memory on each blade. The blades are then interconnected with a high-speed network. The physical construction is that each blade is a separate board (like a motherboard), with the processors and components mounted. Multiple blades can be assembled in a chassis backplane, where each blade connects to the backplane for power, intracluster networking, and access outside the cluster to the Internet and other resources.

Figure 12.7 shows a blade-cluster architecture with three blades. Each blade contains two processors, cache, memory, disk storage, and two network interface units. One network interface unit connects to the intercluster network that integrates the clusters into one high-performance machine. One or more blades can be connected to the outside world for communication; generally one blade is designated as the "master" or controller blade through which the clustered machine communicates with the rest of the world.

Note that the diagram shows two levels of clustering: (1) the cluster of two processors that make up a blade, and (2) the clustering that integrates the blades into a larger machine.

It is also interesting to consider the levels of parallel processing that may exist in a clustered multiprocessor: Each CPU may contain multiple pipelines. A pipeline performs a low level of parallel processing to speed up the processing of instructions (level 1), and each modern processor contains multiple pipelines (level 2). Modern CPU

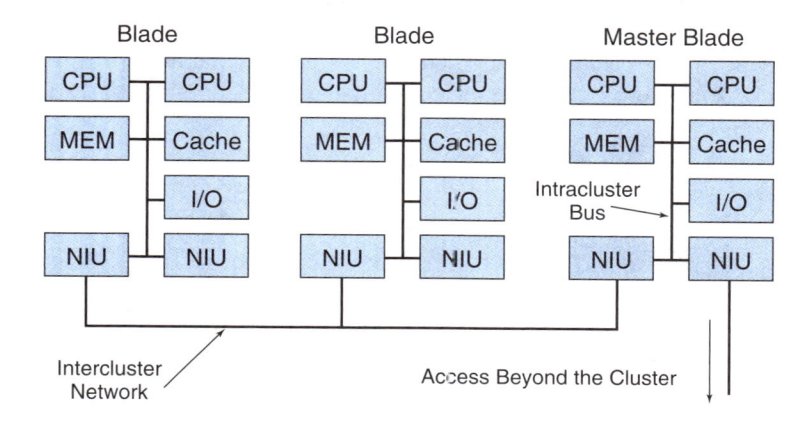

Figure 12.7 A blade cluster architecture.

chips are being constructed with multiple "cores"—that is, multiple separate processors are integrated together in a single chip, sharing some components (level 3). The blade cluster illustrated previously combines two processor chips together on a single blade (level 4) and then combines multiple blades together for the clustered computer (level 5). Multiple clustered multiprocessors can also be integrated to create an even larger parallel processing machine with another level of interconnection (level 6). One such implementation design concept is called grid computing.

Grid computing is a modern form of distributed computing that coordinates the activities of many parallel processors distributed geographically over a wide area. It is called grid computing because the idea is to create a computing grid similar to the electrical power grid: one simply plugs in and taps the power needed. In grid computing, one simply accesses the grid with an application and the grid uses available computing power to work the application.

Grid computing involves coordinating and sharing computing resources (often clusters of processors as well as supercomputers), applications, data, and storage. Grid computing is an evolving area of research where the software technology to seamlessly integrate many machines together to create the grid is continuing to evolve.

Many researchers and scientific and technology organizations will have an occasional need for high levels of computing power. But the cost of assembling a very large supercomputer at the needed level of power may be prohibitive. Grid computing offers a solution, where through sharing resources by contributing to the grid, organizations can then lay claim to occasionally use the larger resources of the shared grid, thus avoiding the high cost of creating supercomputing levels of computing power needed for only occasional use and specialized problems.

Note that Figure 12.8 illustrates two critical principles of building high-performance computing systems:

1. *Replication at many levels*: Multiple CPUs on a blade, multiple blades in a cluster, and multiple clusters in a grid.

2. *Interconnection hierarchy*: Multiple interconnects are needed to allow communication between the different levels in an architecture. At each level in hierarchical computer architecture, most of the traffic at that level of device or grouping is local, and stays within that device or grouping. Only a small fraction of the communication reaches outside that level.

On a grid system, only a small fraction of the overall communication occurs on the grid interconnect itself (which is most likely the Internet). This allows for the interconnect hierarchy to have different bandwidth capabilities and response times (latency) at each level, in order to match the bandwidth required. The overall workload must be balanced across the processors, but just as importantly, the bandwidth requirements

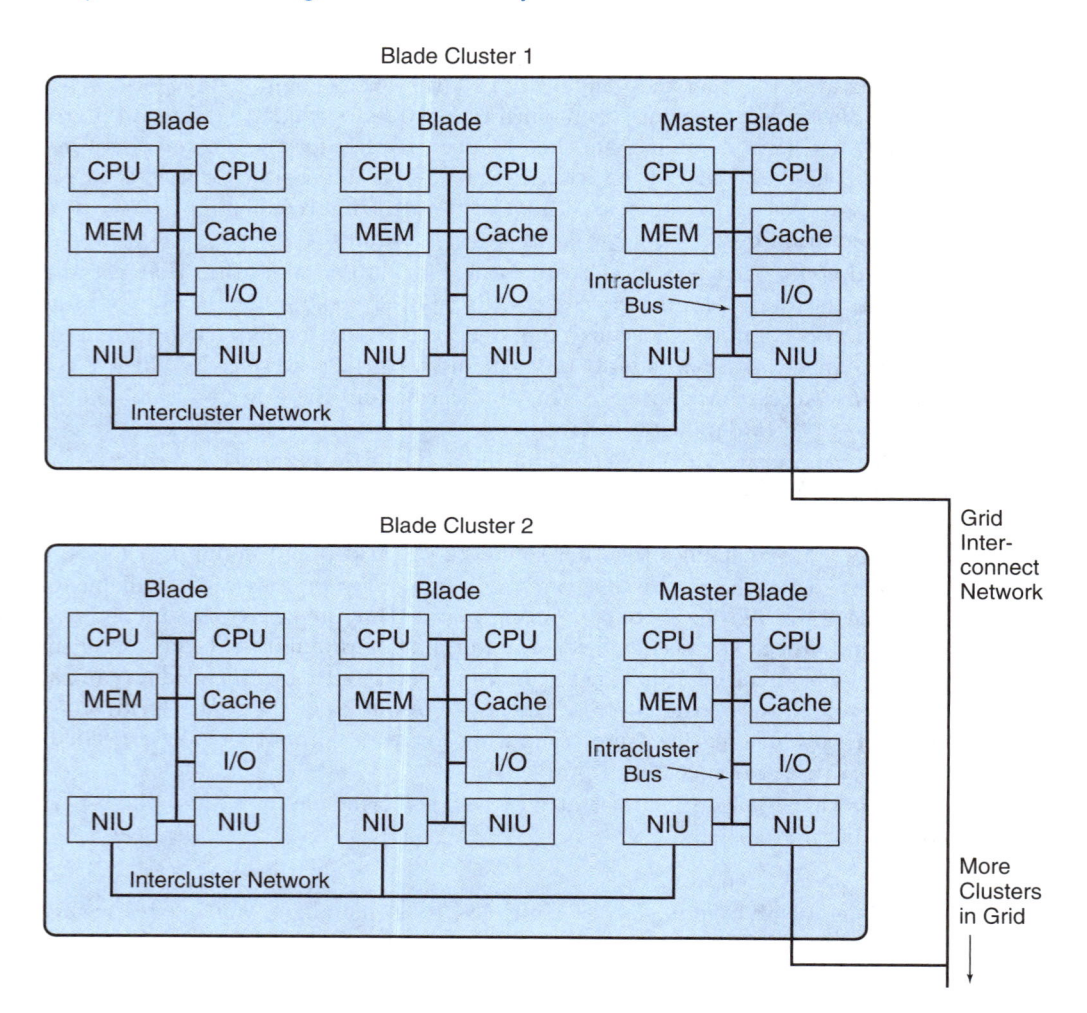

Figure 12.8 A grid architecture.

must also be balanced across the interconnect hierarchy. Any one interconnect could become a bottleneck that limits overall performance.

Amdahl's simple model of parallel processing speedup has been extended to allow for the performance effect of the interconnection network latency and contention. Each system will have an average latency for its interconnect while running the parallel workload. The average latency will change depending on how much of the processing requires communication, and the fraction of the communication that occurs at each level of the interconnect. So this average depends not only on the system architecture, but also on the characteristics of the workload.

$$Speedup = \frac{1}{(1-\alpha) + \alpha L + \frac{\alpha}{n}}$$

where

α = fraction of work that can be executed in parallel
n = number of processors or processing elements
L = average latency over the entire network

The average latency can be measured in terms of the time to process an instruction. So an average latency of 1 represents that each instruction requires an extra delay equal to the processing time of an extra instruction just for the communication. An unlikely average interconnect latency of zero means that the interconnection network performs perfectly, or that there is no communication involved. The communication delays force the processor to sit idle while waiting for communication.

Some example speedup values for two architectures (with 10 processors and with 1000 processors) are shown in Table 12.2.

From the table it is clear that the interconnection network and communication delays can dominate the performance of parallel systems. This implies that for best performance, the allocation of the workload across the grid nodes must be done with knowledge of how the application will communicate with other processors in other nodes. Allocation with this knowledge will allow the performance bottlenecks that will smother the parallel speedup and are to be avoided.

α	n	L	Speedup	
90%	10	0.00	$\frac{1}{0.19}$	5.263
90%	10	0.01	$\frac{1}{0.199}$	5.025
90%	10	0.50	$\frac{1}{0.64}$	1.563
99%	1000	0.00	$\frac{1}{0.01099}$	90.992
99%	1000	0.01	$\frac{1}{0.02089}$	47.870
99%	1000	0.50	$\frac{1}{0.50599}$	1.976

Table 12.2 Effect of Interconnect Performance on Parallel Speedup

12.8 Distributed Application Technologies

Distributed computing is related to parallel computing, and the two are really different aspects of the same ideas. As technology has evolved, computers have become highly parallel devices with multiple levels of parallel hardware to support concurrent processing at different levels: pipelined processors, multicore processors, multiprocessor CPUs, and distributed computers across a network or the Internet. Distributed processing can be thought of as parallel computing, where the multiple parallel processors are distributed across a network—potentially distributed geographically around the nation and the globe. There are three closely related aspects to consider: the distributed and parallel hardware system, the parallel-distributed software (operating systems and programming language), and the application or algorithm to run on the system to accomplish some useful task.

Figure 12.9 illustrates the continuum of parallel computer systems. Figure 12.9(a) illustrates a distributed computing system, basically a network of unspecified nodes interconnected, shown as a graph with nodes (vertices) and edges (connecting links). Figure 12.9(b) shows the same architecture with a bit more detail, with the nodes

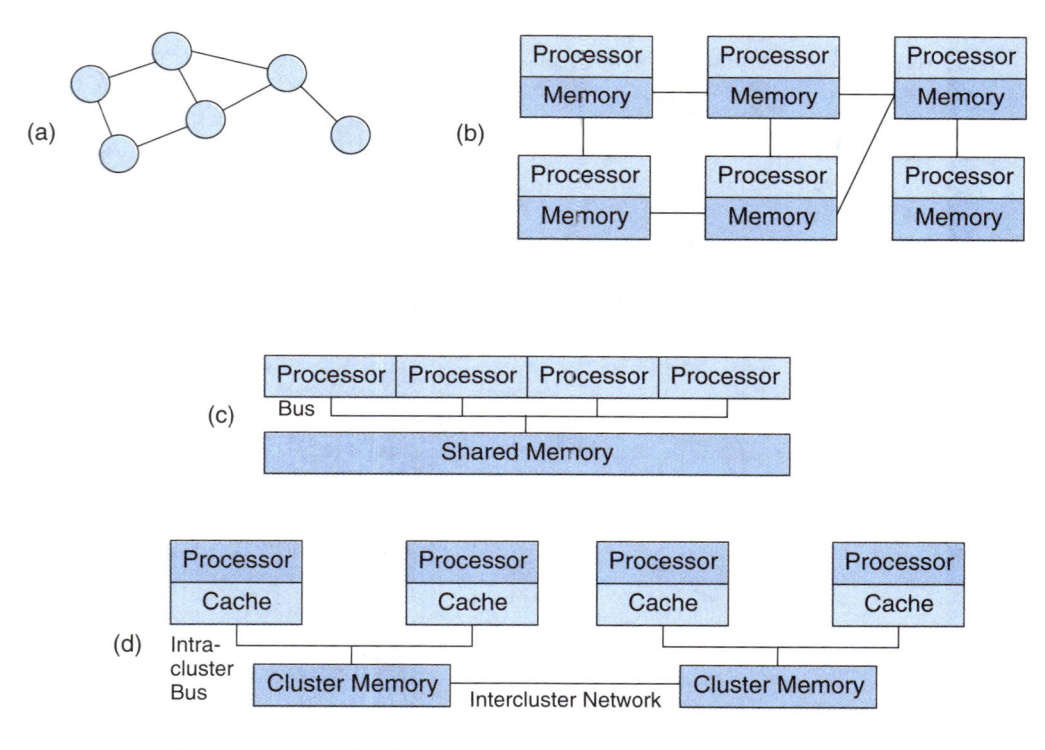

Figure 12.9 Continuum of parallel and distributed systems.

shown as individual processors with their own memories. This kind of architecture is a loosely coupled architecture, because each computer is discrete and capable of separate processing without dependency on the other machines in the network. In order to do useful work as a parallel machine, the computers must be able to communicate over the network.

The time required to communicate between machines is a critical aspect of parallel and distributed computing. A process or algorithm that will run on multiple computers that requires a large amount of communication between machines must run on a system with little communication delay in order to be effective. A process that has very little communication between machines can run effectively on a system with slow or low-bandwidth communication links.

Figure 12.9(c) illustrates a tightly coupled computer architecture. In this machine, the processors all share the same memory through a shared bus. The processors can't help but interact and interfere with each other through the shared memory. The advantage of this architecture is that the time for machines to communicate is minimal: the sender stores data in memory, and the receiver simply reads the data from memory. But multiple processors sharing the same bus system introduces contention and slow downs while one processor must wait for another to finish its access to memory.

Figure 12.9(d) shows a modern solution to the contention problem of shared-memory multiprocessors by introducing cache to reduce the frequency of CPU accesses to memory, as many requests for data will be satisfied by the cache. The other aspect of this architecture is the clustering of processors, which tends to "compartmentalize" communications and also helps to reduce contention with multiple shared buses in place of a single bus. This architecture illustrates a two-level architecture, with the first level being two processors sharing access to memory within a cluster, and the second level being the interconnection between the clusters. In this two-level architecture, there are actually three different data-access speeds: (1) processor to cache access time is the fastest, (2) processor to local memory access time is fast, and (3) processor to remote memory (in the other cluster) access time has the slowest response time.

12.8.1 Distributed Software Architectures

The architecture of distributed software systems focuses on how/where processing is located on the nodes of the system, and how they interact. These software architectures share similarities in concept with the physical architectures described above, but are specific to the software design, and do not specify the hardware of physical architecture. The software design architecture is independent of the physical design, though it has been shown that performance can be optimized if the hardware architecture supports and maps the software communication architecture well.

- *Client-server*: The application software on the client workstation interacts with the user to obtain inputs and data, and is responsible for communicating that information to the server. The client also presents information to the user. The data resides on the server, and most of the processing occurs on the server. Depending on the software system in use, the client may do some preprocessing of commands/requests before transmitting them to the server. Client-server is also a 2-tier architecture.

- *3-tier architecture*: A middle tier is introduced between the client and the server. The middle tier handles data input, formatting, and presentation functions, allowing the third tier (the data server) to handle just the work of storing and manipulating the data. An example might be a large database system as the third tier, and the middle tier handles all interaction with clients that could come from a a variety of technologies. The middle tier may format information for the client into web pages, allowing users to interact through a web browser.

- *N-tier architectures*: Use multiple middle tiers between the client and the data server. These are often enterprise systems.

- *Peer-to-peer*: Here all machines are at the same level in terms of responsibility and workload. All peers can be both clients and servers for other peers. Peer-to-peer can be complex for a sophisticated system, due to the amount of coordination and communication needed between peers.

The method for coordinating work and for communication of data between machines (nodes) is message passing. Machines in the system may communicate directly with each other through message passing using the underlying Internet and networking protocols. Nodes may also pass messages through other nodes in the distributed system, or even pass messages to a centralized "switchboard-type" node. In practice, peer-to-peer direct message passing is the most common mode of communication between nodes on the Internet.

12.8.2 Software Interface: ODBC

Open database connectivity (ODBC) is a standardized software interface to allow a distributed system access to a wide variety of database management systems (DBMS). It is nonproprietary, so is independent of the programming language or scripting language used for the access logic, but also independent of any particular DBMS and operating system.

ODBC functions as a middleware software tier or interface between the application and the DBMS. The application uses the ODBC syntax and commands to create queries that will be translated and passed through to the DBMS. ODBC provides a software Application Programming Interface (API) for interacting with relational database systems, and also for nonrelational DBMS. Drivers for particular DBMS systems are installed into the ODBC software tier to allow access to a specific DBMS. Drivers exist for all major DBMS as well as non-DBMS and other file systems. DBMS drives include Oracle, DB2, Microsoft SQL Server, Sybase, MySQL, Microsoft Access, and many others. ODBC has been developed for many operating systems, including Microsoft Windows, Unix, Linux, OS/2, OS/400, IBM i5/OS, and Mac OS X. Microsoft released the first ODBC implementation as a set of DLLs for Microsoft Windows, and ODBC is now integrated into the Windows OS standard package and installation.

Key Terms		
clustered multiprocessor	DNS	media access control (MAC)
connection-oriented/	encapsulation	middleware
connectionless	ethernet	ODBC
CSMA/CD	frame	parallel speedup
DHCP	grid computing	protocol
diminishing returns	HTML	TCP/IP
distributed system	Internet	

Exercises and Questions

1. Describe how CSMA/CD works to control media access.

2. Describe how the Internet works with existing networking protocols. Consider an alternative approach to the TCP/IP strategy (one that was actually considered)—creating a new networking protocol from scratch that can simultaneously be both a networking protocol and an Internet working protocol. Describe some advantages and disadvantages of this alternative approach.

3. What does the Internet do?

4. Research on the Internet to learn about alternative networking protocols to the Ethernet. Choose one and describe its functioning using no more than a single page.

5. Explain the concept of encapsulation in regard to networking protocols.

6. Research the World Wide Web and find two URLs of websites that you find interesting.

7. Research on the Internet to find two additional HTML codes.

8. Research on the Internet to find out what XML is. Describe and explain what XML is and how it differs from HTML.

9. How is parallel processing speedup achieved in general?

10. Calculate the speedup and efficiency that will be achieved, using Amdahl's simple model, for a system with 10 processors and a parallel fraction of 90%.

11. Calculate the speedup and efficiency that will be achieved using Amdahl's simple model, for a system with 100 processors and a parallel fraction of 90%.

12. Use the enhanced speedup model to recompute your answers for questions 10 and 11 using an average latency of 0.25 (0.25 means that every four instructions require communication time equivalent to a single instruction time).

13. Describe the architecture of a grid computing system.

14. Calculate the theoretical performance for a grid system with 256 processors, running an application with a parallel fraction of 99.9%, and a system interconnect average latency of 0.03.

15. Explain how a clustered multiprocessor architecture helps to limit the effect of communication slowdowns due to contention.

16. List some database systems with known ODBC drivers.

17. Discuss in no more than a paragraph, the advantages of using a middleware technology like ODBC for building distributed applications.

Chapter 13
Virtual Machines

13.1 Introduction

A virtual machine provides the ability to run a guest operating system and its applications on top of a different host operating system. This feature can be very useful.

- It allows a user to run applications that were written for a different operating system.
    - For example, one can run Windows applications on an Apple Mac or a Linux system while still being able to run applications that are native to that system.
    - Windows 7 includes a virtual machine that runs Windows XP (for business applications that have not been migrated off of Windows XP).
- Similarly, a server is able to run applications that were written for different operating systems. This can save money as the company may be able to buy and maintain fewer servers.
- In an environment, such as a call center, where many desktop users will work with the same system configuration, one can have a central server run a virtual machine for each user, with the desktop acting solely as a human interface device. This has the potential of saving hardware costs, as well as ongoing maintenance and support costs.
- It allows easy configuration of systems for application regression testing. One simply saves a system configuration and then uses it to test a new version of an application. Figure 13.1 illustrates this idea. This ability to save and run multiple system configurations greatly simplifies the task of testing an application across many different types of hardware and software configurations.

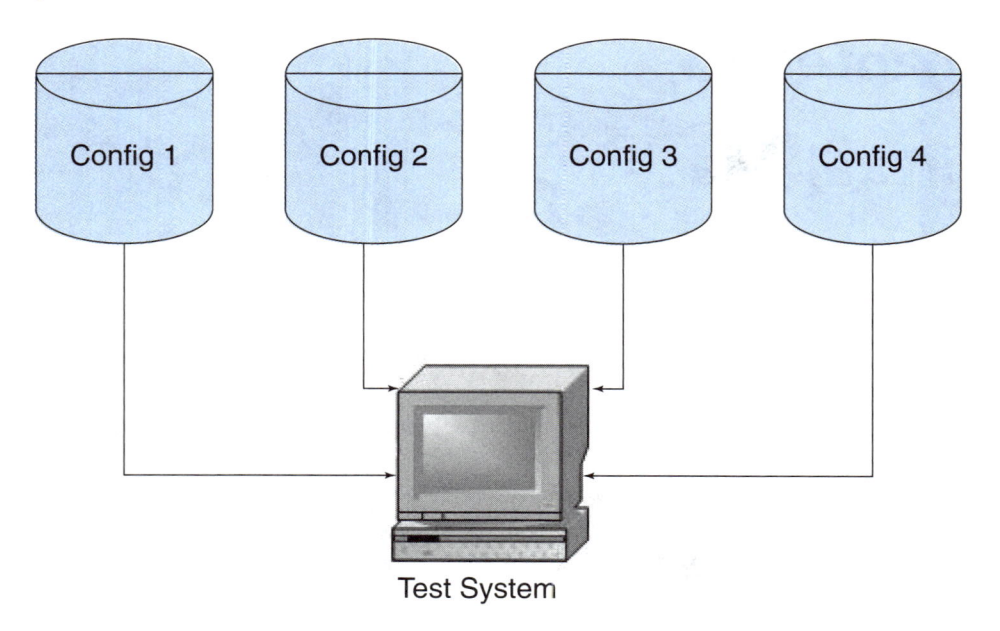

Figure 13.1 Multiple virtual machine configurations.

13.2 Overall Virtual Machine Structure

Figure 13.2 shows the structure of a system running a virtual machine.

The key component of this structure is the virtual machine monitor (VMM). This module acts as an interface between each Guest OS and the host OS. The VMM must ensure that the following conditions are met:

- *Fidelity*: Programs running in the virtual machine must execute the same as they would on the real computer hardware, aside from some minor timing effects.

- *Performance*: The performance of the virtual machine must be similar to the performance of a real computer. There have been attempts to create virtual machines to allow programs written for one CPU to be able to run on another type of CPU. Unfortunately, the overhead to interpret and execute the non-native instructions is so high that the performance of such systems has often not been acceptable. Thus, virtual machines that meet this requirement will typically be designed for the same generic type of CPU as the underlying actual hardware.

- *Safety*: Programs running on the virtual machine must not be able to interfere with the operation of the host OS or other programs running on the computer.

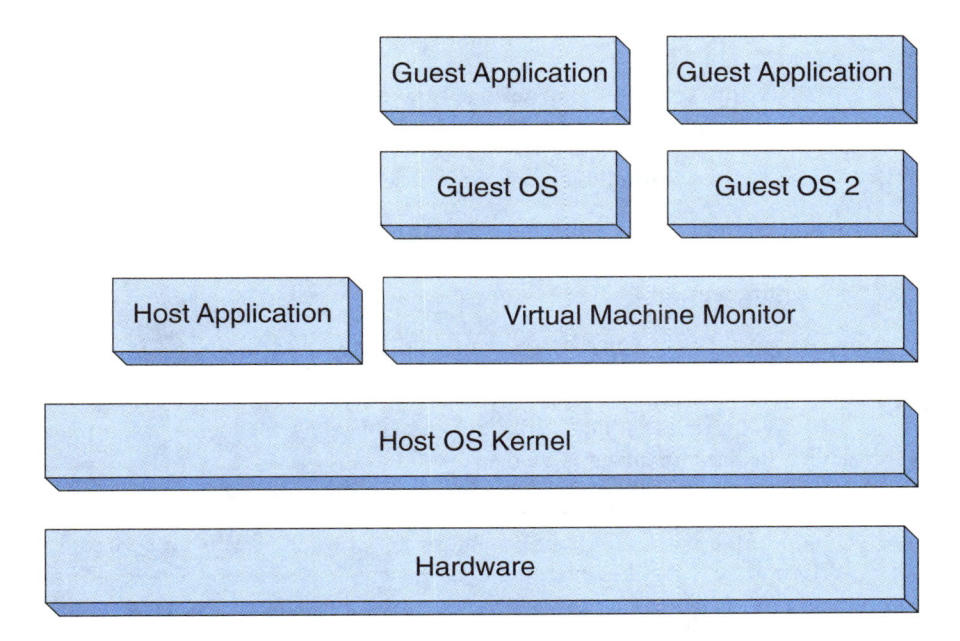

Figure 13.2 Virtual machine structure.

13.3 Hardware Interface

13.3.1 Instruction Execution

A computer has three types of instructions:

- *Ordinary instructions*: These perform some operation on the data of the program or change the flow of execution in the program. Examples include multiply, test, jump, etc.

- *Privileged instructions*: These which manipulate the state of the computer. Examples include instructions to set the current memory mapping and instructions to do input/output. As discussed in earlier chapters, privileged instructions may only be executed when the computer is operating in "OS mode." When a privileged instruction is executed in User Mode, typically a trap occurs and the executing program is terminated by the OS.

- *Sensitive instructions*: Their functionality depends on whether the computer is in user mode or OS mode. Sensitive instructions will typically either:
    - Report the state of the computer (such as whether the computer is in OS mode or user mode).

- Provide reduced functionality if they are executed in user mode.

Typically, sensitive instructions may be executed by any program running on the computer.

Thus, a critical implementation requirement is that if a computer has only user and OS modes:

- A guest OS will need to execute in user mode in order to guarantee the safety requirement.
- A guest OS will need to execute as if it is in OS mode to guarantee the fidelity requirement.

Resolving this conflict while achieving the Performance requirement is the core difficulty in implementing a VMM.

- Privileged instructions must be controlled in a more granular fashion than on a computer without virtual machine functionality. Without virtual machine functionality, the following logic controls the execution of privileged instructions:
  - If the computer is in user mode, privileged instructions are not allowed.
  - If the computer is in OS mode, any privileged instruction is allowed.

  On a computer with a virtual machine, the following logic is required:
  - If the guest OS is executing an application, privileged instructions are not allowed.
  - If the guest OS executes a privileged instruction, that instruction must be interpreted to determine whether it is to be allowed or possibly a mapping performed to actually execute a similar but different privileged instruction.
  - Native host OS applications may not execute privileged instructions.
  - The host OS may execute privileged instructions, as before.
- Similarly, in order for a virtual machine to operate properly, any sensitive instructions that it executes must report the state of the virtual machine, not the state of the underlying host computer.

Two mechanisms have been commonly used by VMMs to ensure the proper expected execution of a guest OS:

- *Trap and emulate*: In this model, all privileged and sensitive instructions are trapped and emulated with the proper mapping. Additionally, the actual page table is configured so that all guest OS accesses to critical memory areas (such as memory-mapped devices and what the guest OS believes is the page table) are also trapped.

- *Binary translation*: On computers where trap and emulate cannot be used with all privileged and sensitive instructions, binary translation will interpret and translate a segment of guest OS code before it is executed. This is similar to the just-in-time translation that is used on some optimizing Java compilers.

  This approach is necessary if there are any sensitive instructions that act differently depending on whether they are executed in user mode or OS mode. The computer chips used in PCs have this problem and, thus, force the use of binary translation by their VMMs.

13.3.2 Software Trap Handling

A software trap occurs on any of the following conditions:

- A system call is executed. Note that an OS may do system calls itself (for example, to write to a file)

- A page fault occurs

- A privileged instruction is executed in nonprivileged mode

- A memory protection violation occurs

The following steps (shown in Figure 13.3) are required to handle a software trap from a guest application:

1. The trap goes to the host OS kernel.

2. The host OS kernel determines that the trap came from a virtual machine and passes the trap to the VMM.

3. The VMM determines that the trap came from a Guest application and passes the trap to the guest OS.

The following steps (shown in Figure 13.4) are required to handle a software trap from a guest OS:

1. The trap goes to the host OS kernel.

2. The host OS kernel determines that the trap came from a virtual machine and passes the trap to the VMM.

3. The VMM determines that the trap came from a guest OS. The trap is passed to the guest OS if it is a system call. Otherwise, the VMM handles it itself.

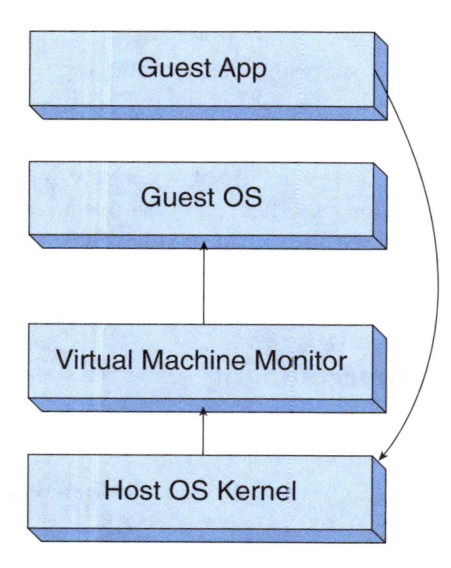

Figure 13.3 Guest application trap handling.

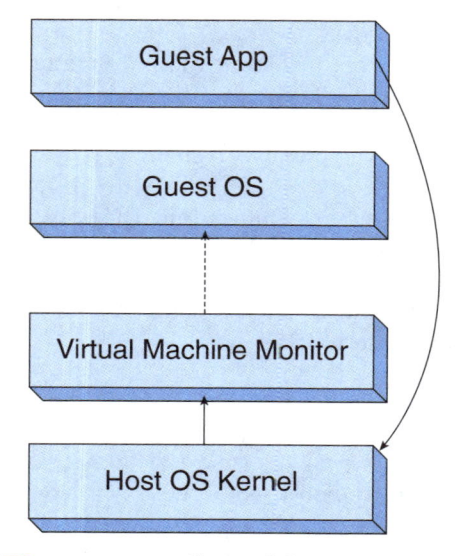

Figure 13.4 Guest OS trap handling.

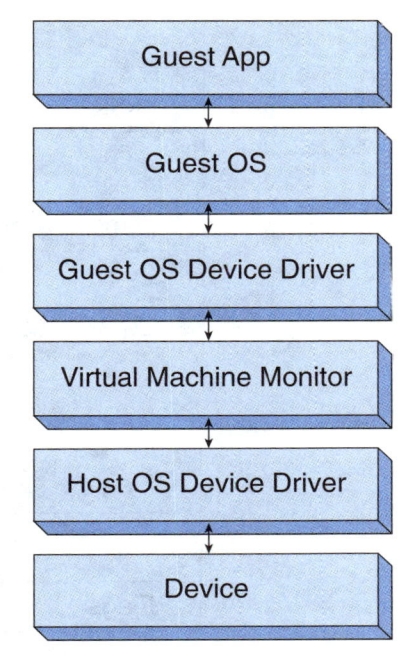

Figure 13.5 Virtual machine I/O.

13.3.3 Device Input/Output

The structure to support I/O for a virtual machine looks like Figure 13.5. The I/O requests from a guest OS device driver are intercepted, interpreted, validated, and remapped by a device emulation component of the VMM. This mapping is fairly straightforward for devices that use DMA. This is because there is typically a single privileged instruction executed to actually initiate the I/O. For non-DMA devices, multiple privileged instructions are often required, which makes the validation and interpretation more difficult.

13.3.4 Memory Management

The MMU hardware maintains the TLB, which is a high-speed cache of page table entries. Whenever a TLB Miss occurs, the MMU hardware looks up the entry in the page table. This is particularly complicated for a Virtual Machine. Figure 13.6 shows that page table lookups are a two-stage process:

1. The guest logical address must be mapped to a guest physical address.

2. The guest physical address must be mapped to a host physical address.

368 Chapter 13 Virtual Machines

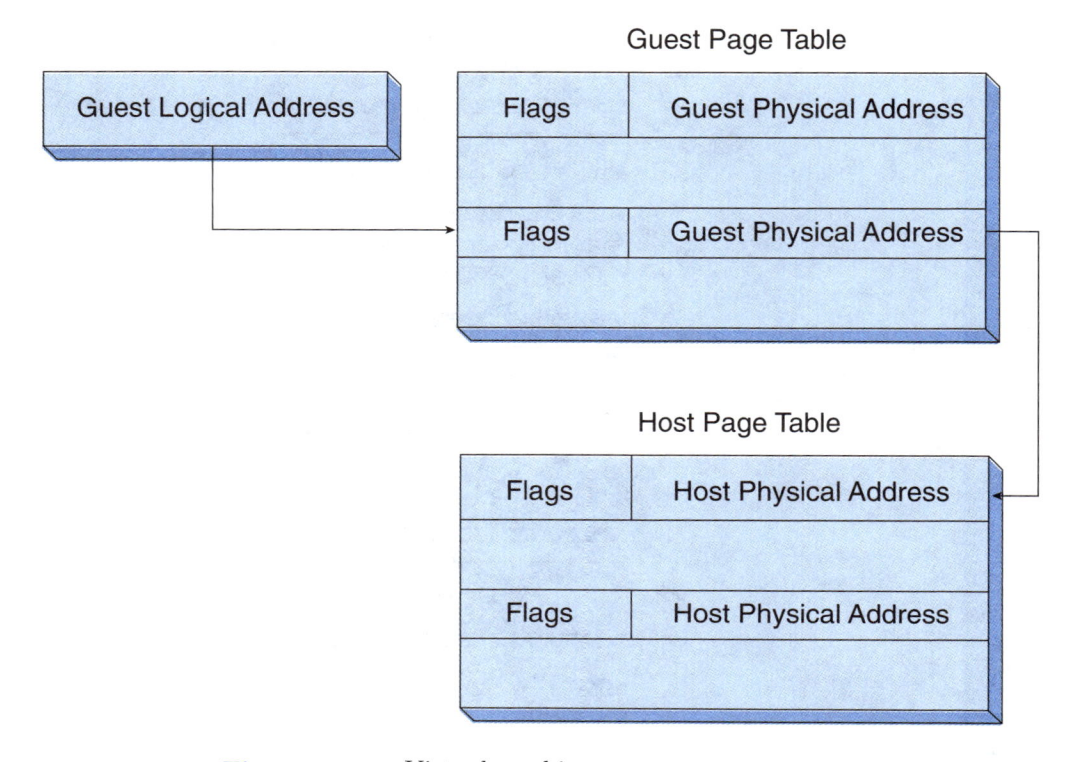

Figure 13.6 Virtual machine memory management.

On a typical CPU, the MMU can only do the second level of this mapping. Thus, the VMM must configure the system so that a trap occurs on all TLB misses. The VMM must then do the first level of mapping. This process adds a significant amount of overhead to the execution of the virtual machine.

13.4 Hardware Enhancements

Modern CPUs that support virtual machines may include the following enhanced features:

13.4.1 Additional Execution Modes

This allows the system to easily distinguish whether a particular operation is being performed by:

- A guest application
- A guest OS

- The VMM
- A host application
- The host OS

In particular, the handling of software traps is much simplified because a software trap will go directly to the component that should handle it. See Figures 13.7 and 13.8.

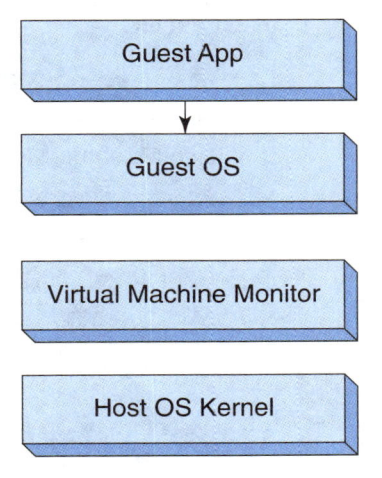

Figure 13.7 Guest application trap handling.

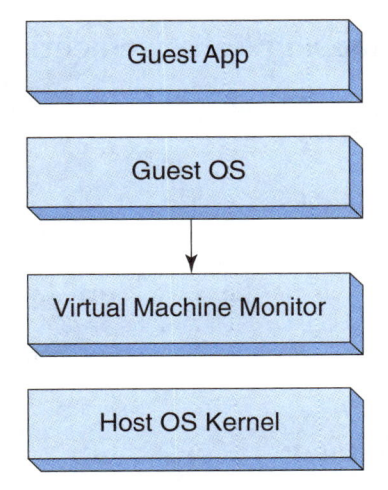

Figure 13.8 Guest OS trap handling.

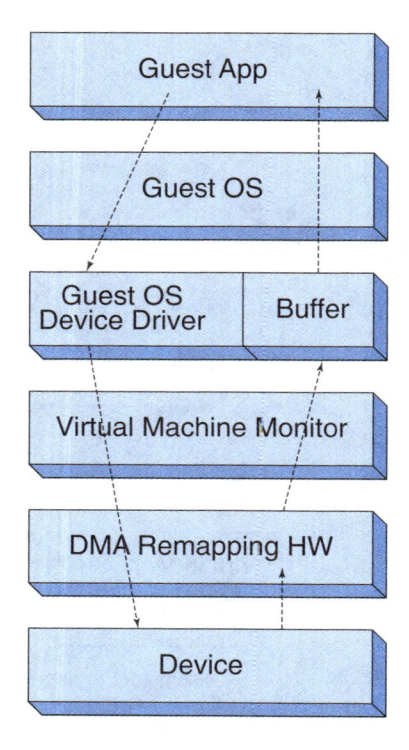

Figure 13.9 Virtual machine mapping of I/O.

13.4.2 Memory Mapping Enhancements

Some newer CPUs provide support for the MMU hardware to perform all levels of the page table lookup process described earlier. This is a significant reduction of system overhead.

Another enhancement is to have the DMA hardware also perform mapping for virtual machine addresses. This is illustrated in Figure 13.9. With this functionality, the mapping of virtual machine I/O requests is performed by a hardware component. The key to enabling this functionality is that I/O requests are memory mapped and performed by DMA hardware. Thus, it is a relatively straightforward enhancement to the DMA hardware to perform the necessary memory mapping for its requests.

13.5 Mapping Devices to Host OS Structures

Normally, an OS assumes that it is in complete control of the hardware. A guest OS is not in control of the underlying hardware. Thus, to provide the necessary functionality, certain virtual machine devices will typically be mapped to structures provided by the host OS, rather than directly to a physical device.

- The guest system's disk will typically be mapped to a file on the host OS. It is this feature that allows multiple system configurations to be created, saved, and used later for regression testing.

- The screen of the guest system will be mapped onto a window of the host OS. If this feature was not available, then one could not simultaneously use applications from more than one operating system. Thus, the desired usability of the system really depends on this feature.

- The guest system's mouse and keyboard will be mapped to the application mouse and keyboard provided by the host OS. This is necessary to properly support having a guest OS's screen appear in a window of the host OS.

- The guest system's network interface will typically be mapped to a network port provided by the host OS. This feature allows the guest OS to effectively share the network interface hardware of the computer. Without this feature, each guest OS would need its own network interface hardware.

    It is also possible to isolate the virtual machine from the Internet by either disabling its network or giving it a network connection only to the host.

- The guest system's printer will be mapped to a printer interface provided by the host OS. This feature is similar to sharing the network interface. Without it, each guest OS would require its own printer.

Mapping of devices can be handled by appropriate interception and interpretation of the privileged instructions that the guest OS device drivers execute to manipulate these devices, as well as trapping accesses to memory-mapped areas for these devices.

A much more efficient approach is to install special device drivers in the guest OS. These device drivers know they are part of a virtual machine and make the appropriate system calls to the host OS, rather than attempting to execute privileged instructions or access memory-mapped fields for a device. Figure 13.10 illustrates this. This replacement of portions of the guest OS is known as para-virtualization.

13.6 Unmapped Devices

Some devices (such as a USB-connected microscope) cannot be mapped. In order for the virtual machine to access these devices, it must obtain exclusive control of these devices. If the virtual machine did not have exclusive control of such a device, there would be many possible conflicts with the host OS or other applications on the host system. For example, without exclusive control of a microscope, two different systems could simultaneously tell it to change the zoom level. This is clearly a race condition.

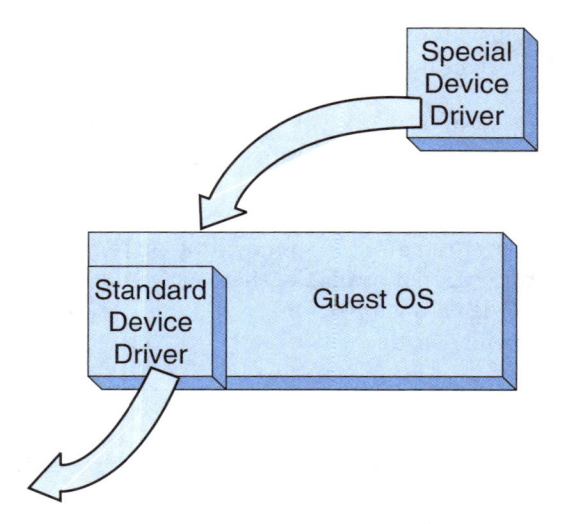

Figure 13.10 Driver replacement.

13.7 Virtual Machine Integration

Integration is a set of features that (while not necessary) make the overall system more useful. Examples include:

- Making the file system of the host OS accessible to the guest OS. This allows multiple operating systems (and their applications) to access the same data files. This applies not only to the files on the host system's main disk but also files on connectible devices such as a USB memory stick or digital camera.

  By *not* configuring this feature for a particular virtual machine, that virtual machine will tend to be isolated from the host system. This can prevent malware from migrating from a guest system to the host system and, thus, provides an extra level of security. This can be extremely useful for working in environments where one *knows* that malware will be present. Computer security research is a good example of where this would be desirable.

  Implementation of this feature simply requires the VMM to make host system files available to a network file system.

- Sharing the clipboard between the guest and host systems. This allows a user to copy/cut and paste data between applications on the guest and host systems (or between two different guest systems).

  Implementation requires replacing a guest OS's clipboard-handling module with one that uses the host OS system calls for the clipboard.

- Having a window in the guest OS appear as a window in the host OS. This avoids the extra effort for the user to switch first from a host window to the guest OS window and then to a window of a guest application.

  Implementation requires replacing the guest OS window handler with one that uses host OS system calls.

- Allowing a user to launch a guest application directly from the host OS. Once again, this avoids the extra effort for the user to switch first from a host window to the guest OS window and then to launch a guest application.

  This can be implemented with a host OS shell script.

13.8 Summary

As discussed in the introduction, virtual machines have many advantages. Implementation of a VMM requires a very detailed understanding of the underlying computer hardware. Many conventional CPUs were not designed for virtual machine implementation, thus impacting the complexity and performance of such systems. As newer CPUs become available with designs that provide more support for virtual machines, this complexity will be reduced and performance improved.

Today, virtual machine support is typically an extra add-on that is purchased separately from the OS. In the future, computers may come with a hypervisor (an OS kernel with just the functionality required to support virtual machines). On this type of system, all user-level operating systems would operate on a virtual machine, which would potentially provide an additional level of security. CPUs would need to have all of the hardware enhancements described earlier to make this type of system practical. It would be highly desirable for these hypervisors to have a standard interface for virtual machines, much as the PC Bios provided a standard interface for first generation PCs.

Key Terms		
binary translation	ordinary instruction	software trap
driver replacement	OS mode	TLB miss
fidelity	page fault	trap-and-emulate
guest OS	page table	unmapped devices
host OS	para-virtualization	user mode
hypervisor	performance	virtual machine monitor
mapped devices	privileged instruction	(VMM)
memory protection violation	safety	
MMU	sensitive instruction	

Exercises and Questions

1. Install a virtual machine on a computer. Student versions of virtual machine software are generally available under academic licenses from the developers.

2. Research the details of the virtualization features in CPUs from Intel and AMD.

3. Research the virtualization features provided by IBM mainframe computers.

4. Use the modeling framework to create a model of the two-level memory mapping required for a virtual machine.

Appendix A
Introduction to Using Linux

A.1 Introduction

Linux is a multiuser, multitasking operating system that is a variant of Unix and performs many of the same functions. To acquire Linux is to purchase a Linux distribution, an organized bundle that includes the kernel (core of the operating system) and a large set of utility programs with an installation utility. Some of the most widely used Linux distributions are Red Hat, Caldera, SuSe, Debian, and Slackware.

A user interacts with Linux using one of several available interfaces that are grouped into two categories:

- A text-based command line interface
- A graphical user interface (GUI)

Linux has several graphical user interfaces available, such as GNU Network Object Model Environment (GNOME) and the K Desktop Environment (KDE). In addition to the graphical interfaces, the command line is commonly used. The Command Line Interpreter, called the *shell*, accepts commands in text form and executes them one after the other.

When you connect to a Linux system via a network or start Linux in a standalone computer, a login screen will appear (Figure A.1). This console window will display a line at which you should type your user ID. After you press the Enter key, another line will appear on which you should type your password.

After you have logged in, a command prompt will appear as a $ symbol. This prompt indicates that the shell is ready to accept a command. In Figure A.1, the line with the prompt contains:

```
[Home directory/current directory] $
```

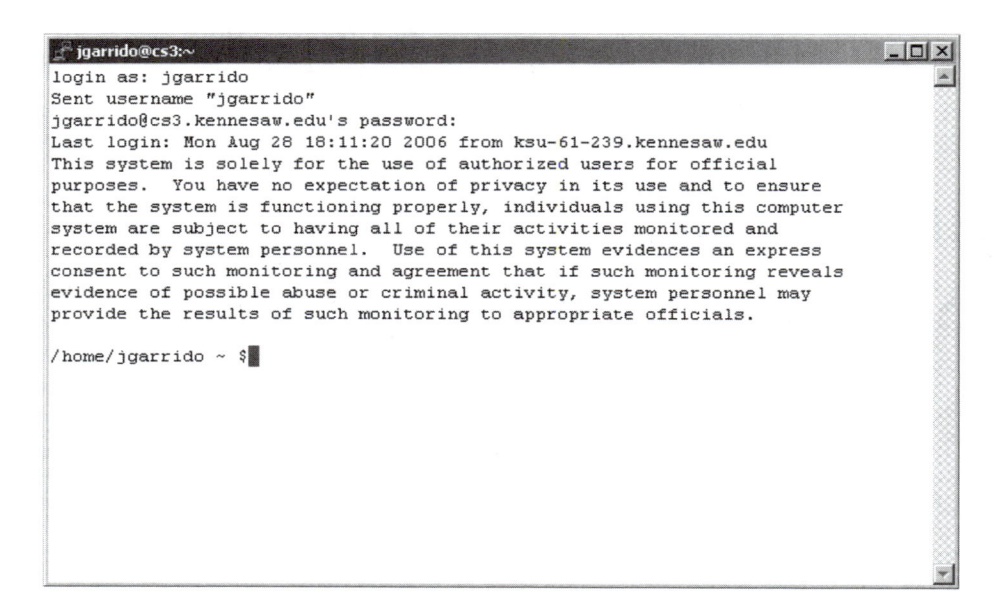

```
jgarrido@cs3:~
login as: jgarrido
Sent username "jgarrido"
jgarrido@cs3.kennesaw.edu's password:
Last login: Mon Aug 28 18:11:20 2006 from ksu-61-239.kennesaw.edu
This system is solely for the use of authorized users for official
purposes.  You have no expectation of privacy in its use and to ensure
that the system is functioning properly, individuals using this computer
system are subject to having all of their activities monitored and
recorded by system personnel.  Use of this system evidences an express
consent to such monitoring and agreement that if such monitoring reveals
evidence of possible abuse or criminal activity, system personnel may
provide the results of such monitoring to appropriate officials.

/home/jgarrido ~ $
```

Figure A.1 Login screen.

A.2 Command-Line Interface

This section explains the basic use of the command-line interface and the most common commands used in Linux. Each command has a name, followed by a set of parameters. In general, commands are entered using the keyboard (standard input) and the system response appears on the screen (standard output). The shell accepts and executes the commands as they are entered by the user.

The shell is the command interpreter. Linux has many different shells available, among them are the following:

- Bourne
- Korn
- C shell
- Bash (default on Linux)
- tcsh

While these shells vary in some of the more complex features that they provide, they all have the same basic usage. This section presents a quick introduction to using the most basic Linux commands.

A.3 Files and Directories

In Linux, there are three types of files: (1) ordinary files, (2) directories, and (3) device files. An ordinary file is simply a named, organized collection of data. A file can contain data or a program (in binary or in source form). A directory file allows a convenient way to organize files and subdirectories. The top directory is the system root, denoted by a forward slash (/). All other directories and files are located under the system root.

When you are working with a *Linux shell*, you navigate the system's directory structure to perform the desired operations. The shell has the concept of the *Current Directory*, which is the directory that you are currently working in. When you login, the shell will initially position you at your *Home Directory*, which is the unique directory provided for each user of the system. For example: /home/jgarrido is a home directory.

In addition to your home directory, the system usually has other directories with various system files that you may use. Some common system directories are shown in Table A.1.

Table A.1 System Directories

/bin	Contains binary or executable files.
/usr	Contains user libraries and applications.
/etc	Typically contains configuration information.
/tmp	Directory for temporary files.
/dev	Contains device drivers for the hardware components.

A.3.1 Specifying Paths

A directory or file is specified by typing the *path* to the desired directory or file. A path consists of the names of directories in the directory tree structure, with a "/" between directory names. (Note that Windows uses "\" to separate directory names). If the path begins with a directory (or file) name, then the path begins at the *current directory*. If the path begins with a "/", then the path begins at the root of the entire directory structure on this system.

An absolute path includes the complete and hierarchical structure. To access a file with the indicated absolute path, Linux starts at the top and searches downward through every directory specified. For example, /home/jgarrido/psim3/batch.cpp is an absolute path of file batch.cpp. A relative path specifies the location of a file in relation to the current working directory.

Appendix A   Introduction to Using Linux

Unlike MS Windows, Linux pathnames are case-sensitive. Thus, `MyFile`, `myfile`, and `MYFILE` all specify different files.

There are two special directory names (a single period, and 2 consecutive periods):

- A reference to the current directory is specified as "." in the command line.

- A reference to the parent directory one level up in the tree is specified with ".." in the command line.

Thus, the command `ls ..` will display the parent directory.

A.3.2   Wildcards

When using the Bash shell, it is possible to select several filenames that have some sequence of characters in common. Some commands allow you to specify more than one file or directory. The special characters that are used are wildcard characters. There are three wildcards:

- If you specify a "?" in a directory or filename, it will match any character in that position. Thus `h?` will match `he` or `hf`, but not `her`.

- Similarly, if you specify "*" in a directory or filename, it will match any sequence of characters in that position. Thus `h*` will match `he`, `hf`, or `her`.

- A pair of square brackets "[]" enclosing a list of characters allows the shell to match individual characters of the list.

The following examples show the convenience of using wildcards with the `ls` command:

```
ls *.dat
ls re*asd
ls *.?
ls bat[edfg].cpp
ls [a-j]*.dat
```

A.4   Basic Commands

A.4.1   The `passwd` Command

The `passwd` command is used to change your password. It will prompt you to enter your current password and then ask you to enter your new password twice. For example,

```
passwd
Changing password for user jgarrido.
```

```
Changing password for jgarrido
(current) UNIX password:
New UNIX password:
Retype new UNIX password:
passwd: all authentication tokens updated successfully.
```

A.4.2 The `man` Command

To request help, if you cannot remember what the parameters to a command are, or the specific use of a command, you can type the `man` command. If you type `man commandname`, it will display the manual page for that command, including the parameters for that command. It accepts wildcards, so if you cannot remember exactly how the command is spelled, you can use a wildcard to have it try to match the name of the desired command. For example, the following command typed at the the shell prompt will display the manual command page shown in Figure A.2:

```
man passwd
```

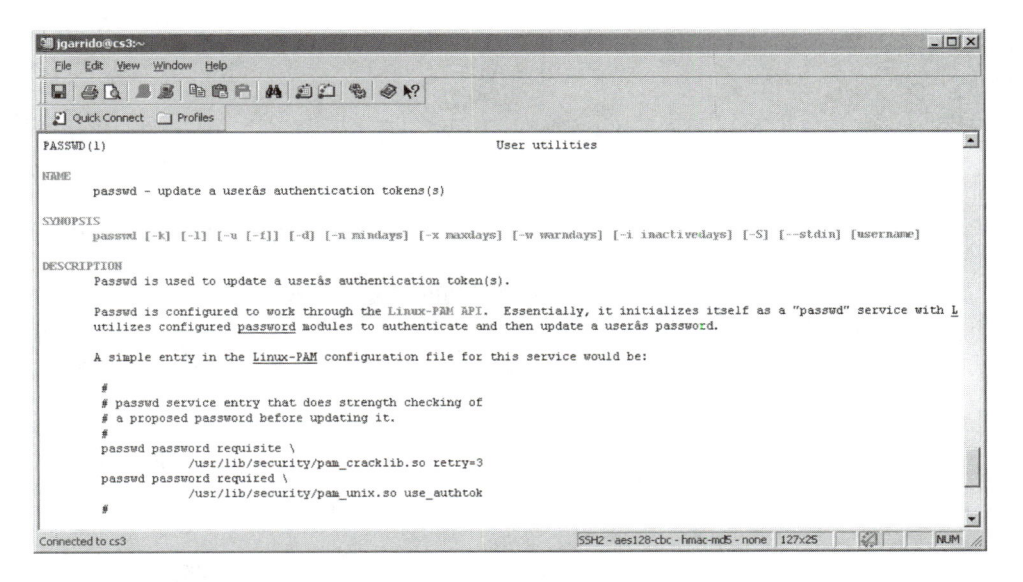

Figure A.2 Manual page for the `passwd` command.

A.4.3 The `ls` Command

The `ls` (list directory) command is used to provide a directory listing. It has the following format:

```
ls [options] directory-name
```

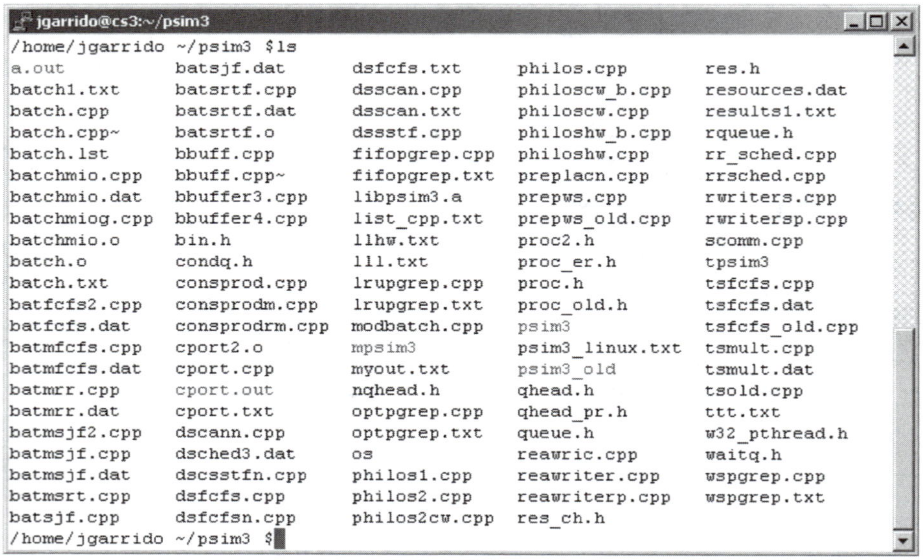

380　Appendix A　Introduction to Using Linux

```
jgarrido@cs3:~/psim3                                                    _ □ ×
/home/jgarrido  ~/psim3 $ls
a.out          batsjf.dat     dsfcfs.txt      philos.cpp       res.h
batch1.txt     batsrtf.cpp    dsscan.cpp      philoscw_b.cpp   resources.dat
batch.cpp      batsrtf.dat    dsscan.txt      philoscw.cpp     results1.txt
batch.cpp~     batsrtf.o      dssstf.cpp      philoshw_b.cpp   rqueue.h
batch.lst      bbuff.cpp      fifopgrep.cpp   philoshw.cpp     rr_sched.cpp
batchmio.cpp   bbuff.cpp~     fifopgrep.txt   preplacn.cpp     rrsched.cpp
batchmio.dat   bbuffer3.cpp   libpsim3.a      prepws.cpp       rwriters.cpp
batchmiog.cpp  bbuffer4.cpp   list_cpp.txt    prepws_old.cpp   rwritersp.cpp
batchmio.o     bin.h          llhw.txt        proc2.h          scomm.cpp
batch.o        condq.h        lll.txt         proc_er.h        tpsim3
batch.txt      consprod.cpp   lrupgrep.cpp    proc.h           tsfcfs.cpp
batfcfs2.cpp   consprodm.cpp  lrupgrep.txt    proc_old.h       tsfcfs.dat
batfcfs.dat    consprodrm.cpp modbatch.cpp    psim3            tsfcfs_old.cpp
batmfcfs.cpp   cport2.o       mpsim3          psim3_linux.txt  tsmult.cpp
batmfcfs.dat   cport.cpp      myout.txt       psim3_old        tsmult.dat
batmrr.cpp     cport.out      nqhead.h        qhead.h          tsold.cpp
batmrr.dat     cport.txt      optpgrep.cpp    qhead_pr.h       ttt.txt
batmsjf2.cpp   dscann.cpp     optpgrep.txt    queue.h          w32_pthread.h
batmsjf.cpp    dsched3.dat    os              reawric.cpp      waitq.h
batmsjf.dat    dscsstfn.cpp   philos1.cpp     reawriter.cpp    wspgrep.cpp
batmsrt.cpp    dsfcfs.cpp     philos2.cpp     reawriterp.cpp   wspgrep.txt
batsjf.cpp     dsfcfsn.cpp    philos2cw.cpp   res_ch.h
/home/jgarrido  ~/psim3 $
```

Figure A.3　The ls command.

This command will provide a listing of the specified directory. If the directory name is omitted, it will provide a listing of the current directory. Figure A.3 shows the result of using the ls command without including a directory name.

The ls command provides several options. The most important ones are **long** listing (-l), list all files (including the system files) (-a), and list files by order of date and time starting with the most recent (-t). To use the **long** listing option, type the ls command with a hyphen and a letter l, -l. For example:

```
ls -l
```

The command will list all the files and folders in the current directory with the **long** listing option. With the long option, detailed information about the files and subdirectories (subfolders) is shown. Figure A.4 shows the ls command with the long option. The additional information displayed includes the file type, the permissions mode, the owner of the file, the size, the date and time of last update, and other data about the file.

Typing the ls command and the name of a directory displays all the files and subdirectories in the specified directory. By typing ls os in the command line, the ls command is used with the os directory. Figure A.5 shows that the specified directory contains eight files.

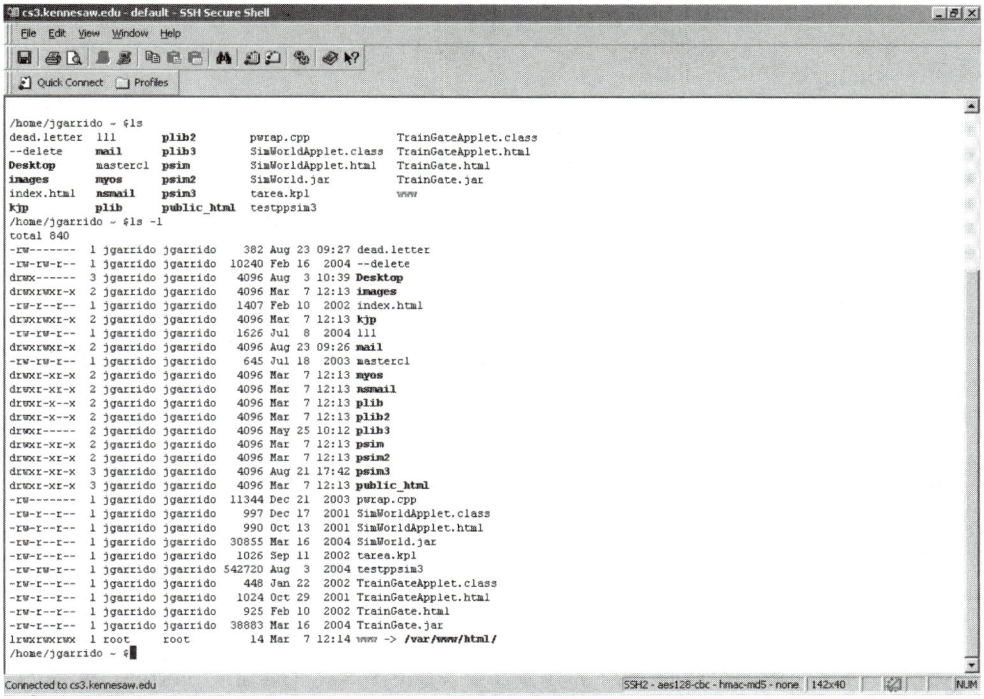

A.4 Basic Commands   381

Figure A.4 The `ls` command with the `long` option.

Figure A.5 The `ls` command on the `os` directory.

A.4.4 The `cp` Command

The `cp` command will copy one or more files from one directory to another. The original files are not changed. The command has the following format:

```
cp [options] source destination
```

This command will copy a source file on some directory to a destination directory. You can use wildcards to specify more than one file or directory to be copied. For example,

```
cp psim2/rrsched.cpp psim3
cp data/*.dat mydir/data
```

The first line copies the file `rrsched.cpp` from the `psim2` subdirectory to directory `psim3`. The second line copies all the files with a `.dat` extension to subdirectory `mydir/data`.

The most common options of the `cp` command are the following: interactive option `-i`, which prompts the user when a file will be overwritten; recursive option `-r`, which can copy directories and their files; and verbose `-v`, which displays the name of each file copied.

A.4.5 The mv Command

The `mv` command can be used to change the name of a file (or directory). This can also be done with the `cp` command. The `mv` command has the following format:

```
mv [options] source target
```

Some of the options for this command (interactive and verbose options) are similar to the ones for command `cp`. The following example illustrates the use of the `mv` command.

```
mv rrsched.cpp timesh.cpp
mv my.dat mydir/data
```

The first line of the example changes the name of file `rrsched.cpp` to `timesh.cpp`. The second line moves file `my.dat` to directory `mydir/data`.

A.4.6 The rm Command

The `rm` command will remove (delete) a file from the directory where it is currently located. The command has the following format:

```
rm [options] filename
```

This command will remove (delete) the specified file from the current directory. The following example shows the use of the `rm` command:

```
rm rrsched.cpp
rm mydat/*.dat
```

The first line in the example deletes file `rrsched.cpp` from the current working directory. The second line removes all the files whose names end with `.dat`. The most common options of the `rm` command are the following: interactive option `-i`, which prompts the user when a file will be removed; recursive option `-r`, which will remove entire directories (all their files); and verbose `-v`, which displays the name of each file before removing it.

A.4.7 The `cd` Command

The `cd` command (change directory) changes the current directory to the one specified. The command has the following format:

```
cd directory-path
```

This command will change the current directory to the specified directory. Thus, the command line `cd ..` will move to the parent directory. When specifying a directory, be careful to include (or not include) the beginning "/" depending on whether you are intending to use an absolute or relative path. If a directory name is not given, the `cd` command changes to the user's home directory. For example,

```
cd
cd psim3/data
cd /usr/misc
```

The first line of the example changes to the user's home directory. The second line changes to directory `psim3/data`, which is a subdirectory under the current directory. The third line changes to directory `/usr/misc`, for which an absolute path is given.

A.4.8 The `mkdir` Command

The `mkdir` command (make directory) creates a new directory with the specified name. The newly created directory is empty (it has no files). The command has the following format:

```
mkdir directory-name
```

This command will create a new directory with the specified name. One usually uses this with a relative path to create a subdirectory, but it is possible to specify an absolute path. For example,

```
mkdir data/models
```

The `mkdir` command in the example creates a new subdirectory called `models` located on the subdirectory `data`.

A.4.9 The `rmdir` Command

The `rmdir` (remove directory) command removes a directory with the specified name. The command has the following format:

```
rmdir directory-name
```

This command will remove (delete) the specified subdirectory from the current directory. The following example removes directory `psim3/data` from the current working directory:

```
rmdir psim3/data
```

A.4.10 I/O Redirection and Pipe Operators

In Linux, three default files are available for most commands: (1) standard input, (2) standard output, and (3) standard error. Using direction and piping, the shell user can change these defaults. With *I/O redirection*, the shell can do the following:

- Take input from another file, called *input redirection*.
- Send output to another file, called *output redirection*.

Input redirection is carried out by using the less-than symbol ($<$). The command will take the file specified after the ($<$) symbol as the input. For example, the executable file `a.out` will execute with data from the file `myfile.dat`:

```
a.out < myfile.dat
```

Output redirection is carried out by using the greater-than symbol ($>$). The command will take the file specified after the ($>$) as the output. For example, the executable file `a.out` will execute and send the results to the file `myresult.dat`:

```
a.out > myresult.dat
```

With pipes, the standard output of a command can be connected to the standard input of another command. Several commands can be connected with pipes, which use the pipe character (|) between commands. For example, a pipe can be used with the `ls` command and the `more` command:

```
ls -l | more
```

The pipe between these two commands is useful because there will be too much data to be displayed by the `ls` command. The output of this command is sent as input

Table A.2 I/O Redirection

Command	Action
`ls > tmp.txt`	Take the standard output from the `ls` command and write it to the file `tmp.txt`.
`xyz < tmp.txt`	The xyz application will use the file `tmp.txt` as its standard input.
`ls	xyz`	The standard output of the `ls` command will be used as the standard input for the xyz application.

to the `more` command, and the data is displayed by the `more` command screen by screen. Table A.2 shows several simple examples of I/O redirection and piping.

The `tee` command sends the output of a command to a file, and the pipe sends the output to another command. For example,

```
./a.out | tee myout.txt | more
```

The first command executes the file `a.out` and sends the output to file `myout.txt` and is also displayed on the screen by the `more` command.

A.5 Shell Variables

In Linux, there are two types of variables that are used with the shell:

- System variables, which are created and maintained by Linux itself. This type of variable is defined in CAPITAL LETTERS.
- User-defined variables, which are created and maintained by the user. The name of this type of variable is defined in lowercase letters.

The following are examples of system variables:

```
HOME=/home/vivek
PATH=/usr/bin:/sbin:/bin:/usr/sbin
SHELL=/bin/bash
USERNAME=vivek
```

To print the contents of a system variable, you must use the character $ followed by the variable name. For example, you can print the value of the variables with the `echo` command, as follows:

```
echo        $USERNAME
echo        $HOME
echo        $SHELL
```

The following example defines a user variable called `vech` having value *Bus*, and a variable called **n** having value 10.

```
vech=Bus
no=10      # this is ok
10=no      # Error,Value must be on right side of = sign.
```

To print the content of variable `vech`, you must use the character ($) followed by the variable name. For example,

```
echo $vech # will print 'Bus'
echo $n    # will print value of 'n'
echo vech  # prints 'vech' instead of its value 'Bus'
echo n     # prints 'n' instead of its value '10'
```

Associated with each user login are a set of environment variables. The `set` command is used to change the value of an environment variable. The set command has the following format:

```
set variable=value
```

Used with no parameters, the command will display the values of all environment variables (see Figures A.6 and A.7).

An important environment variable is `PATH`. This variable has a list of directories in which the system will look for the program file whenever you request that an application be executed.

A.5.1 The pwd Command

The `pwd` command will print (display) the absolute name of the current working directory. The command will display the full pathname of the current directory. A dot (.) references the current working directory and is used in other commands that manipulate files and directories (`ls`, `cp`, `mv`, `mkdir`, and `rmdir`, among others).

A.5 Shell Variables

```
/home/jgarrido ~/psim3 $set
BASH=/bin/bash
BASH_ARGC=()
BASH_ARGV=()
BASH_ENV=/home/jgarrido/.bashrc
BASH_LINENO=()
BASH_SOURCE=()
BASH_VERSINFO=([0]="3" [1]="00" [2]="15" [3]="1" [4]="release" [5]="x86_64-redhat-linux-gnu")
BASH_VERSION='3.00.15(1)-release'
COLORS=/etc/DIR_COLORS.xterm
COLUMNS=80
DIRSTACK=()
EUID=1374
GROUPS=()
G_BROKEN_FILENAMES=1
HISTFILE=/home/jgarrido/.bash_history
HISTFILESIZE=1000
HISTSIZE=1000
HOME=/home/jgarrido
HOSTNAME=cs3.kennesaw.edu
HOSTTYPE=x86_64
IFS=$' \t\n'
INPUTRC=/etc/inputrc
JAVA_HOME=/usr/java/jdk1.3.0_02
KDEDIR=/usr
LANG=en_US.UTF-8
LESSOPEN='|/usr/bin/lesspipe.sh %s'
LINES=6
LOGNAME=jgarrido
LS_COLORS='no=00:fi=00:di=00;34:ln=00;36:pi=40;33:so=00;35:bd=40;33;01:cd=40;33;01:or=01;05;37;41:mi=01;05;37;41:ex=00;32:*.cmd=00;32:*.exe=00;32:*.com=00;32:*.btm=00;32:*.bat=00;32:*.sh=00;32:*.csh=00;32:*.tar=00;31:*.tgz=00;31:*.arj=00;31
```

Figure A.6 A listing of environment variables.

```
35:*.xbm=00;35:*.xpm=00;35:*.png=00;35:*.tif=00;35:'
MACHTYPE=x86_64-redhat-linux-gnu
MAIL=/var/spool/mail/jgarrido
MAILCHECK=60
OLDPWD=/home/jgarrido
OPTERR=1
OPTIND=1
OSTYPE=linux-gnu
PATH=/usr/java/jdk1.3.0_02/bin:/usr/kerberos/bin:/usr/local/bin:/bin:/usr/bin:/usr/X11R6/bin:/home/jgarrido/bin:/usr/psim
PIPESTATUS=([0]="0")
PPID=22160
PROMPT_COMMAND='echo -ne "\033]0;${USER}@${HOSTNAME%%.*}:${PWD/#$HOME/~}\007"'
PS1='/home/jgarrido \w $'
PS2='> '
PS4='+ '
PWD=/home/jgarrido/psim3
SHELL=/bin/bash
SHELLOPTS=braceexpand:emacs:hashall:histexpand:history:interactive-comments:monitor
SHLVL=1
SSH_ASKPASS=/usr/libexec/openssh/gnome-ssh-askpass
SSH_CLIENT='::ffff:130.218.248.234 4367 22'
SSH_CONNECTION='::ffff:130.218.248.234 4367 ::ffff:130.218.248.40 22'
SSH_TTY=/dev/pts/4
SUPPORTED=zh_CN.UTF-8:zh_CN:zh:fr_FR.UTF-8:fr_FR:fr:de_DE.UTF-8:de_DE:de:ja_JP.UTF-8:ja_JP:ja:es_ES.UTF-8:es_ES:es:en_US.UTF-8:en_US:en
TERM=xterm
UID=1374
USER=jgarrido
USERNAME=
_=os
/home/jgarrido ~/psim3 $
```

Figure A.7 Another listing of environment variables.

388   Appendix A   Introduction to Using Linux

A.5.2 The `more` Command

The `more` command will display the contents of a file one page at a time. In using this command, Linux assumes that the specified file is a text file (or a file that can be viewed on the screen). This command can also be used with a pipe to display the output of another command:

```
more mydata.dat
ls | more
```

The first line of this example lists the contents of file `mydata.dat` one page at a time. The second line displays a listing of the current directory one page at a time.

A.5.3 The `exit` Command

The `exit` command can be used to log out of Linux. When you are done using Linux, type the `exit` command. This will cause the shell to terminate and you will be logged off the system. This command is normally used in a script file (a command file) to exit with an optional integer error code.

A.6 Text Editing

There are several text editors available for Linux. The three most popular are (1) `vi`, (2) `pico`, and (3) `emacs`. Figure A.8 shows the screen that appears when using pico. To edit a file with `pico`, simply type the following command:

```
pico filename
```

In the command line, `filename` is the name of the file to be edited. The top part of the screen in Figure A.8 shows part of the file being edited. The last two lines of

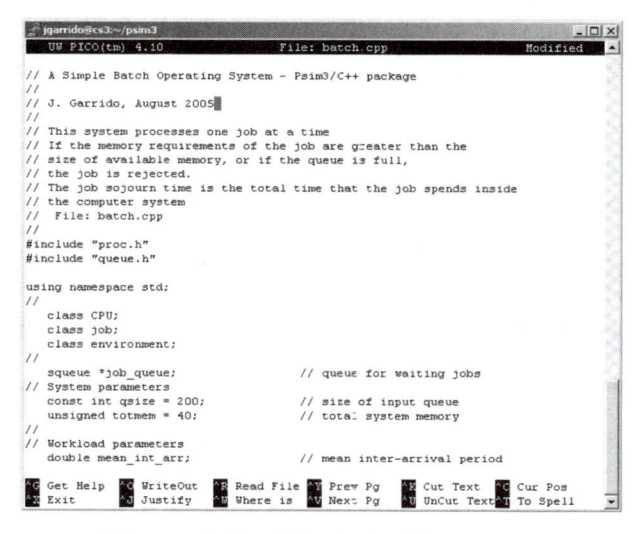

Figure A.8   Pico text editor screen.

the screen show the editing commands that you can use. The (ˆ) character refers to the *Ctrl* key. Thus, *Ctrl-G* is the editing command that will open the help pages and *Ctrl-X* will exit the editor. Refer to the Help screen (by using *Ctrl-G*) for a complete discussion of the available editing commands.

A.7 File Access Permissions

A user may deny or allow access to files and directories; these are normally called permission modes. The following types of permission modes are allowed for files and directories:

- Read (`r`)
- Write (`w`)
- Execute (`x`)

In Linux, there are three types of users for file access:

- Owner of the file or directory (user)
- Group (users in the same group as the owner)
- Others (all other users)

A user can change the file permissions on one or more files and directories by using the `chmod` command. The following example changes the permission mode to give read access permission to all users for file `batch.cpp`, and changes the permission mode to remove write permission to other users:

```
chmod a+r batch.cpp
chmod o-w batch.cpp
```

When writing a shell script, it is necessary to change permission and enable execute permission of the script file to the user or owner of the file. The following example gives execute permission to the user for the (script) file `myscript`.

```
chmod u+x myscript
```

A.8 The cat Command

The `cat` command is used to display the contents of a text file. If the file is too big, only the last part would be shown on the screen; in this case, the `more` command would be more appropriate. For example, to display on the screen the contents of file `mytasks.txt`, the following command line is needed:

```
cat mytasks.txt
```

Another important purpose of the `cat` command is to join two or more files one after the other. In the following example, three files—`alpha`, `beta`, and `gamma`—are chained together. The redirection operator is required to create the output file

```
cat alpha beta gamma > myfile
```

The `cat` command can also be used to append data to a file using the append ($\gg$) operator. The following example illustrates the use of the append operator to append data to the end of an existing file. The example shows that data from file `res.h` is appended to the end of file `batch.txt`:

```
cat res.h >> batch.txt
more batch.txt
```

A.9 Commands for Process Control

A shell command can be internal (built-in) or external. Internal commands are part of the Linux system. The external commands are the utilities in Linux, application programs, or script files. Linux creates a new process for every external command that is started and assigns a process ID number (PID) to every process created.

The `ps` command lists the active processes of the user. With the `l` option, this command displays a long listing of the data about the processes:

```
/home/jgarrido ~ $ps
PID TTY          TIME CMD
4618 pts/3    00:00:00 bash
4644 pts/3    00:00:00 ps
/home/jgarrido ~ $


/home/jgarrido ~ $ps -l
F S   UID   PID  PPID  C PRI  NI ADDR SZ WCHAN  TTY      TIME CMD
0 S  1374  5279  5277  0  75   0 - 13493 wait   pts/3 00:00:00 bash
0 R  1374  5318  5279  0  76   0 -  1093 -      pts/3 00:00:00 ps
/home/jgarrido ~ $ps -lj
F S   UID   PID  PPID  PGID   SID  C PRI  NI ADDR SZ WCHAN  TTY      TIME CMD
```

```
0 S  1374  5279  5277  5279  5279  0  76  0 - 13493 wait pts/3    00:00:00 bash
0 R  1374  5319  5279  5319  5279  0  76  0 -  1093 -    pts/3    00:00:00 ps
/home/jgarrido ~ $
```

The `ps` command with the `l` option displays the attribute values of the processes. The most important of these are the `PID` and the process state.

When users need to force the termination of a process, they can use the `kill` command, which sends a signal to terminate the specified process. Users can terminate only processes that they own. The general syntax for this command is

```
kill [options] pid
```

For example, in the following example, the first line will terminate process 15097 and the second line will terminate process 15083 by sending it a signal with number 9:

```
kill 15097
kill -9 15083
```

A.10 Foreground and Background Processes

When a process is started in a Linux shell, the user waits until the process terminates and Linux displays the shell prompt. Processes that execute in this manner run in the *foreground*. For long-running processes, Linux allows the user to start a process so it will execute in the *background*. Processes that run in the background have a lower priority than processes in the foreground.

For processes to start execution in the background, the user needs to type the name of the command, followed by the ampersand (&) symbol. To start a process called `myjob` as a background process, type `myjob &`. The following example shows the start of the script file `psim3` in the background:

```
./psim3 batch.cpp &
[1] 5325
```

The Linux shell returns two numbers when a background process is started by the user, the job number (in brackets) for the process, and its PID. In the second command line of the previous example, `1` is the job number and `5325` is its PID.

A background job (a process running in the background) can be brought to run in the foreground with the `fg` command. The job number has to be specified as an argument to the command:

```
pico tarea.kpl &
[1] 15165
fg %1
pico tarea.kpl
```

In this example, the Pico editor is started as a background job with job number 1. The next command makes the shell bring the background job to the foreground. The Pico screen will be shown with the file `tarea.kpl` and editing can proceed normally.

Another use of the `fg` command is to resume a suspended process. A process running in the foreground can be suspended by the <Ctrl-Z> key combination. It can later be resumed by using the `fg` command and the job number of the process. A suspended process can be resumed to run in the background using the `bg` command and the job number.

A.11 Script Files

A shell script is basically a text file with shell commands. The shell executes the script by reading and executing the commands line by line. The syntax of script files is relatively simple, similar to that of invoking and chaining together utilities at the command line.

A shell script is a *quick and dirty* method of prototyping a complex application. Achieving a limited subset of the functionality to work in a shell script is often a useful first stage in project development. Shell scripting provides the user with the ability to decompose complex projects into simpler subtasks and to chain together components and utilities.

A shell script file must be readable and executable to the user of the script. The `chmod` command must be used to change these permissions modes of the script file.

A.11.1 Comments in Scripts

Comment lines are lines that begin with a # symbol. Comments may also follow the end of a command or the whitespace at the beginning of a line. For example,

```
# This line is a comment.
    echo "A comment will follow."  # Comment here.
    #       ^ Note whitespace before #
       # A tab precedes this comment.
```

A.11.2 Positional Parameters

The shell uses positional parameters to store the values of command-line arguments, and they are used as read-only variables in the script. A $ symbol precedes the parameter number. The parameters in the script are numbered 0-9. In addition to positional parameters, a script file normally uses system and user variables. The following two command lines are included in a script file:

```
rm $1  # remove file $1
echo $1 $2
```

A.11.3 Command Substitution

Command substitution evaluates a command and makes available the output of the command for assignment to a variable. The format of this is `` `command` ``, a notation that uses backquotes or backticks. An alternative notation is $(command). For example,

```
echo Current date is:  `date`
echo Today is:  $(date)
mydate=`date`
```

A.11.4 The test Command

The test command is used to test or evaluate the conditions formulated in loops and branches. You can use the command to do the following:

- Compare numbers.
- Compare strings.
- Check files.

The test command has two syntaxes:

- Uses the keyword *test* before the expression to be evaluated.
- Uses brackets to enclose the expression to be evaluated.

The test command also supports several operators:

- Testing files and integers.
- Testing and comparing strings.
- Logically connecting two or more expressions to form complex expressions.

Table A.3 shows several operators used in the test command that evaluate expressions with numbers. Table A.4 shows several operators used in the test command that

Table A.3 Test Command Operators for Expressions with Numbers

Operator	Action
n1 -eq n2	Evaluates to True if n1 and n2 are equal
n1 -le n2	Evaluates to True if n1 is less than or equal to n2
n1 ge n2	Evaluates to True if n1 is greater than or equal to n2
n1 gt n2	Evaluates to True if n1 is greater than n2
n1 ne n2	Evaluates to True if n1 and n2 are not equal

Table A.4 Test Command Operators for Expressions with Strings

Operator	Action
str1	Evaluates to True if str1 is not an empty string
str1 = str2	Evaluates to True if str1 and str2 are equal
str1 != str2	Evaluates to True if str1 and str2 are not equal
n str1	Evaluates to True if the length of str1 is greater than zero
z str1	Evaluates to True if the length of str1 is zero

Table A.5 Test Command Operators for Expressions with Files

Operator	Action
f file	Evaluates to True if file is an ordinary file
d file	Evaluates to True if file is a directory
e file	Evaluates to True if file exists
s file	Evaluates to True if file is nonempty
r file	Evaluates to True if file is readable
w file	Evaluates to True if file is writable
x file	Evaluates to True if file is executable

evaluate expressions with strings. Table A.5 shows several operators used in the `test` command that evaluate expressions with files.

A.11.5 The `if` and the `test` Commands

The basic form of the `if` command is used for two-way branching in the flow of control of the execution of the script. The expression in the `if` statement can be evaluated with the `test` command, which returns True or False after evaluating the expression. The following example illustrates the use of the `if` and `test` commands.

```
if test $# -ne 1   # number of arguments is not 1
    then
    echo Error in number of arguments
    exit 1
fi
```

```
#
if [ -f $1 ]
    then
        echo File is:   $1
    else
        echo File $1 is not an ordinary file
        exit 1
fi
```

The following script file, called `psim3`, uses most of the commands discussed previously.

```
# Script for compilation of a C++ model and linking with the
# Psim3 and Pthread libraries
clear
echo '----------------------------------------------------------------'
echo '----- Psim 3.0 C++ package for object oriented simulation -----'
echo '-------   (C) J. M. Garrido, 1997, 1999, 2004, 2006   ---------'
echo 'Date: ' `date`
rm a.out    # delete previous executable
# the following line invokes the GNU C++ compiler/linker
g++ $1 -lpthread /home/jgarrido/psim3/libpsim3.a
-I/home/jgarrido/psim3
#   Check if everything was ok
if [ -x a.out ]   # file exists and is executable?
  then
     echo "a.out created."
  else
     echo *** Compilation or linkage problems found ***"
     exit 1
fi                      # change to endif for tcsh
echo '                          '
exit 0
```

A.11.6 The set Command

When used with arguments, the `set` command allows you to reset positional parameters. After resetting the parameters, the old parameters are lost. The positional parameters can be saved in a variable. Command substitution can be used with the `set` command. The following script file includes several examples using the `set` command.

```
# Script name: posparam
# Example script using set command
echo "Total number of arguments: " $#
echo "All arguments: " $*
echo "1st is: " $1
```

```
echo "2nd is: " $2
prevargs=$*      # save arguments
set V W X Y Z    # resetting positional parameters
echo "New parameters are: " $*
echo "Number of new parameters: " $#
set `date`       # Reset parameters with command
                 # could also be typed as $(date)
echo $*          # display new parameters
echo "Today is: " $2 $3 $6
echo Previous parameters are: " $prevargs
set $prevargs
echo $3 $1 $2 $4
exit 0
```

The following command lines execute the script file and show the output produced by the script:

```
/home/jgarrido ~ $./posparam a b c d
Total number of arguments:  4
All arguments:   a b c d
1st is:  a
2nd is:  b
New parameters are:  V W X Y Z
Number of new parameters:  5
Fri Sep 15 13:39:06 EDT 2006
Today is:  Sep 15 2006
Old parameters are:  a b c d
c a b d
/home/jgarrido ~ $
```

A.11.7 Mutibranch with the `if` Command

The `if` command can be used for multiway branching, which is considered an extension of the basic structure of the `if` command. The general syntax for this is as follows:

```
if expr1
    then
          commands
    elif expr2
          commands
    elif expr3
          commands
     . . .
    else
          commands
fi
```

The following example illustrates the use of the multibranch `if` command in a shell script.

```
if [ -f $1 ]
   then
        echo File $1 is an ordinary file
        exit 0
   elif [ -d $1 ]
        nfiles = $(ls $1 | wc w)
        echo The number of files in $1 is:   $nfiles
        exit 0
   else
        echo Argument $1 is not file or directory
        exit 1
fi
```

A.11.8 Repetition with the `for` Command

The `for` command is used for repetitive execution of a block of commands in a shell script. The repetitions of a block of commands are normally known as loops. The number of times the block of commands is repeated depends on the number of words in the argument list. These words are assigned to the specified variable one by one and the commands in the command block are executed for every assignment. The general syntax of this command is as follows:

```
for variable [in argument list]
do
       command block
done
```

The following example shows a short script file with a `for` loop:

```
# File: loopex1. Example of for-loop
for system in  Linux Windows Solaris OS2 MacOSX
do
    echo $system
done
```

The execution of the script file is shown in the following listing:

```
./loopex1
Linux
Windows
Solaris
OS2
MacOSX
```

A.11.9 Repetition with the `while` Command

The `while` loop allows repeated execution of a block of commands based on a condition of an expression. The general syntax of the `while` command is as follows:

```
while expression
do
        command-block
done
```

The expression in the `while` command is evaluated, and if it is true, the command block is executed and the expression is again evaluated. The sequence is repeated until the expression evaluates to false. The following example of a script file shows a `while` loop:

```
# while example
#secret code
secretcode=Jose
echo n "Enter guess: "
read yguess
while [ $secretcode != $yguess ]
do
        echo "Wrong guess"
        echo n "Enter guess again: "
        read yguess
done
echo Good guess
exit 0
```

The loop command is often used with the `break` and `continue` commands, which are used to interrupt the sequential execution of the loop body. The `break` command transfers control to the command following `done`, terminating the loop prematurely. The `continue` command transfers control to `done`, which results in the evaluation of the condition again.

A.12 Searching Data in Files

Linux provides several utilities that search for lines with specific data in text lines. These utilities are `grep`, `egrep`, and `fgrep`. For example, the following command line uses the `grep` command and will search for the lines in file `pwrap.cpp` that contain the string `include`:

```
/home/jgarrido ~ $grep -n include pwrap.cpp
42:#include "pthread.h"
```

A.12 Searching Data in Files

```
43:#include <iostream.h>
165://#include <unistd.h> //included to test sleep(), usleep(),
         wait()
210:    /*this is included to adjust
/home/jgarrido ~ $
```

As the following example shows, the `grep` command also allows the search of a string in multiple files, using a wildcard:

```
/home/jgarrido ~ $grep -n include *.cpp
dscann.cpp:10:// A disk service includes the rotational delay,
         seek delay, and
dscann.cpp:18:#include "proc.h"
dscann.cpp:19:#include "queue.h"    // additional library classes
dscsstfn.cpp:10:// A disk service includes the rotational delay,
         seek delay, and
dscsstfn.cpp:19:#include "proc.h"
dscsstfn.cpp:20:#include "queue.h"    // additional library classes
```

The `grep` command can also list names of files. The following uses the `grep` command with the l option to display the names of the files where string `include` is found:

```
home/jgarrido ~ $grep -l include *.cpp
dscann.cpp
dscsstfn.cpp
dsfcfs.cpp
dsfcfsn.cpp
dsscan.cpp
dssstf.cpp
pwrap.cpp
/home/jgarrido ~ $
```

Regular expressions can be used with the `grep` command. For example, the following command line uses the `grep` command to display lines in file `dsscan.cpp` that start with letters d through f:

```
/home/jgarrido ~ $grep '^[d-f]' dsscan.cpp
double rev_time = 4;        // revolution time (msec.)
double transfer_rate = 3;   // in Mb/sec (Kb/msec)
double seek_tpc = 15.6;     // seek time per cylinder (msec.)
double simperiod;           // simulation period
```

Appendix A   Introduction to Using Linux

The following command lines provide more examples using the `grep` command with regular expressions:

```
grep '[a-f]{6}' pwrap.cpp
grep '<cl'myfile.dat
grep 'et\>Š myfile.dat
egrep n "lass|object" pwrap.cpp
egrep v "class|object" pwrap.cpp
egrep "^O" pwrap.cpp
egrep "^O|^C" pwrap.cpp
```

The `egrep` command does not directly accept a string as input; it accepts files. When there is no file specified, the `egrep` command takes input from standard input. The following script file takes two input strings as parameters and checks if one string is a substring of the other. The script file converts the first string into a file with the `echo` command. The file created by executing the `echo` command is piped into the `egrep` command:

```
# An example script file that locates a substring using egrep
# Script file: testegrep
#
if [ $# != 2 ]
then
     echo "Two parameters are required"
     exit 1
fi
#
# egrep does not directly accept a string as input
if echo $1 |  egrep $2 > myfile
then
     echo " $2 is in $1"
else
     echo "Not found"
fi
exit 0
```

The command line shows the execution of the `testegrep` script file and the output produced:

```
/home/jgarrido ~ $./testegrep September emb
 emb is in September
/home/jgarrido ~ $
```

A.13 Evaluating Expressions

The `expr` command evaluates an expression and sends the result to standard output. The expressions can be used to manipulate numbers and strings. The following operators used with the `expr` command manipulate strings.

With `arg1:arg2`, the `expr` command searches for the pattern `arg2` (a regular expression) in `arg1`. The result is the number of characters that match. The following examples show the use of the (:) operator.

```
# number of lowercase letters at the beginning of var1
expr $var1 : '[a-z]*'
#Match the lowercase letters at the beginning of var1
expr $var1 : '\([a-z]*\)'
#Truncate var1 if it contains five or more chars
Expr $var1 : '\(ã..\)' \| $var1
#Rename file to its first five letters
Mv $mf `expr $mf : '\(ã..\)' \| $mf`
```

With the `index string character-list` format, the `expr` command searches the `string` for the first possible character in the `character list`. The following example illustrates the use of the `index` operator of the `expr` command.

```
/home/jgarrido ~ $expr index "jose" def
4
```

With the `length string` format, the `expr` command gets the length of the `string` variable. The following example illustrates the use of the `length` operator of the `expr` command.

```
/home/jgarrido ~ $expr length "kennesaw"
8
```

With the `substr string start length` format, the `expr` command searches for the portion of the `string` variable starting at the specified location. The following example illustrates the use of the `subr` operator of the `expr` command:

```
/home/jgarrido ~ $expr substr "kennesaw" 5 3
esa
```

Writing more powerful shell scripts is possible with additional external commands (shell utilities), such as `sed` and `awk`.

A.14 Connecting to a Remote Linux Server

Your PC or workstation can operate as a terminal that allows access to a remote Linux server. For this, a terminal emulator program is needed. Such programs support up to two modes of operation: text command and graphics modes. As discussed previously, two types of interfaces exist to access a Linux system:

- Command-line interface, which is character-oriented (text-based).

- Graphical user interface (GUI), which is graphics-oriented and is intended to access a Linux system using a desktop environment such as KDE and GNOME.

A.14.1 The Putty Program

The Putty program, a free Telnet/SSH Client, is an example of a simple setup for terminal emulation. This program does not include an SSH file transfer facility. After downloading the program, simply start its execution (by double clicking on it).

When started, it opens a window requesting the IP address of the server and the protocol (SSH). Figure A.9 shows the program's dialog box when started. After the

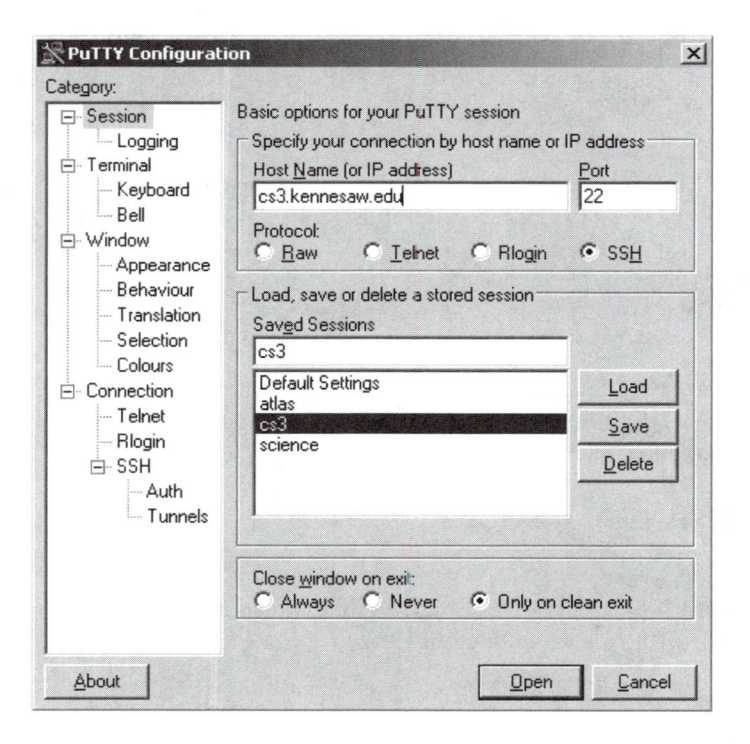

Figure A.9 The Putty program dialog box.

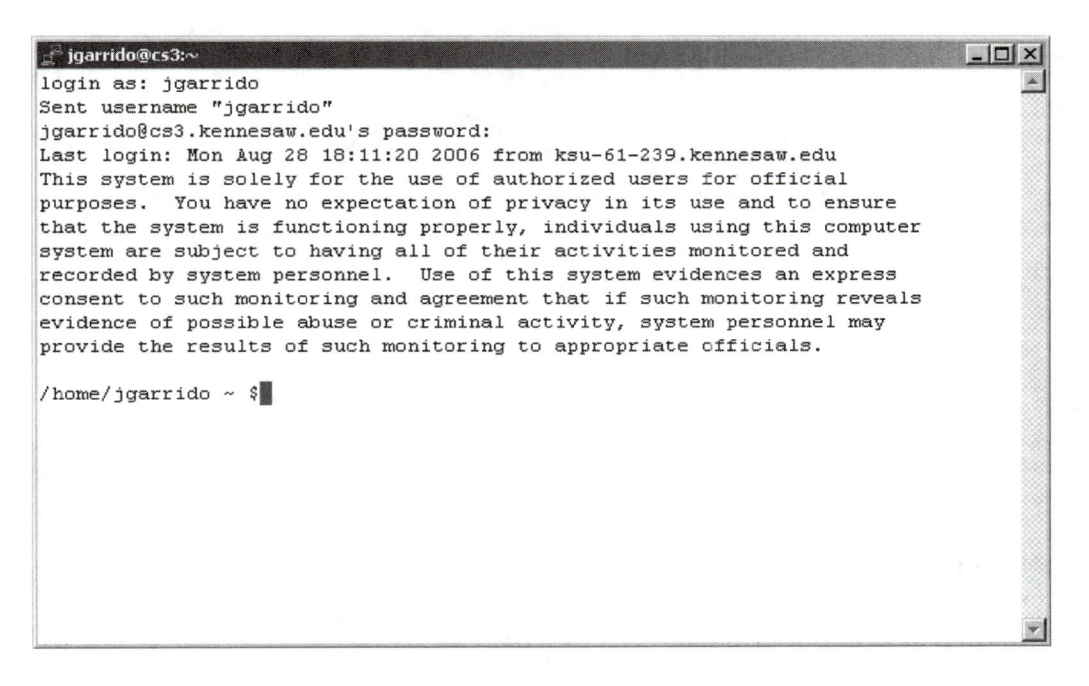

```
jgarrido@cs3:~
login as: jgarrido
Sent username "jgarrido"
jgarrido@cs3.kennesaw.edu's password:
Last login: Mon Aug 28 18:11:20 2006 from ksu-61-239.kennesaw.edu
This system is solely for the use of authorized users for official
purposes.  You have no expectation of privacy in its use and to ensure
that the system is functioning properly, individuals using this computer
system are subject to having all of their activities monitored and
recorded by system personnel.  Use of this system evidences an express
consent to such monitoring and agreement that if such monitoring reveals
evidence of possible abuse or criminal activity, system personnel may
provide the results of such monitoring to appropriate officials.

/home/jgarrido ~ $
```

Figure A.10 Window with the Linux login screen.

connection is established, the user can login to Linux in the normal way, as shown in Figure A.10.

A.14.2 SSH Client

There are many other SSH programs for Windows on the Web. An example of these programs is SSH Client for Windows, which is available free to students and faculty of some colleges and universities. This program can be downloaded by carrying out the following steps:

1. Search the web page www.kennesaw.edu.
2. Select/click on *Computing Resources*.
3. Select *IT Service Desk*, then *Software Downloads*.
4. Click on SSH.exe to download the install program.
5. After downloading, execute the Install program.

Two modes of operation are provided by the SSH Client for Windows utility:

- Secure File Transfer Client
- Secure Shell Client

404   Appendix A   Introduction to Using Linux

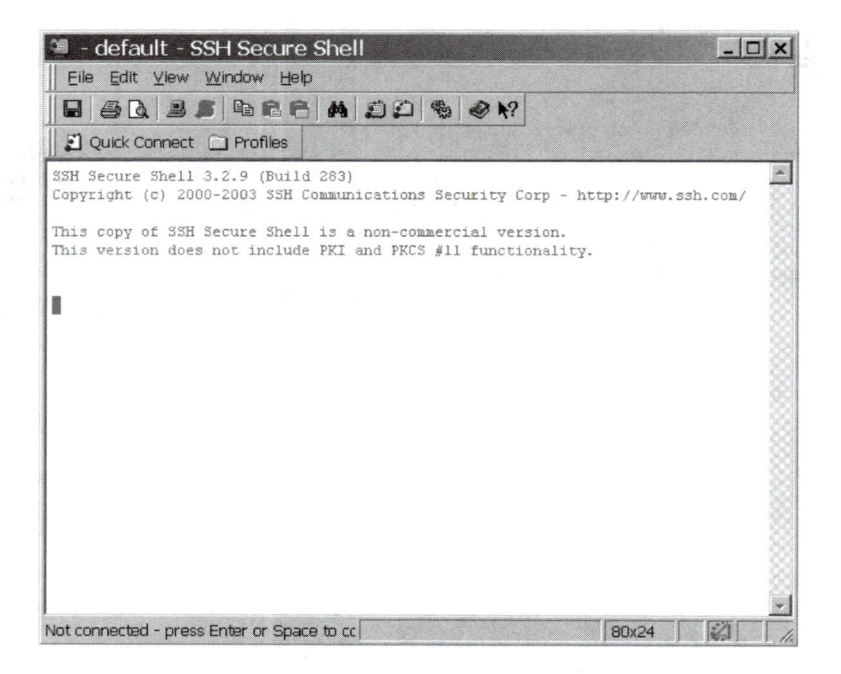

Figure A.11   Window of SSH Shell Client when started.

Carry out the following steps to connect to a Linux server with the Secure Shell Client:

1. Make sure you are connected to the Internet.

2. Start the Secure Shell Client to connect to a remote Unix server. Figure A.11 shows the window of SSH Shell Client when started.

3. Type `cs3.kennesaw.edu`.

4. Log on to Linux on the CS3 server.

5. Start using the appropriate Linux shell.

After you click on the window or press the Enter key, the dialog box shown in Figure A.12 appears. Type the name of the server and your user account name, and then click on the Connect button.

When connection to the server is established, SSH Shell Client presents another dialog box requesting a password, as shown in Figure A.13. Type your password in this dialog box.

After login, the Linux prompt will appear on the next line to indicate that Linux is waiting for a command. Figure A.14 shows the window with the Linux prompt after login using the SSH Secure Shell program. The prompt is shown by the $ symbol and it indicates that the Linux shell is waiting for a command.

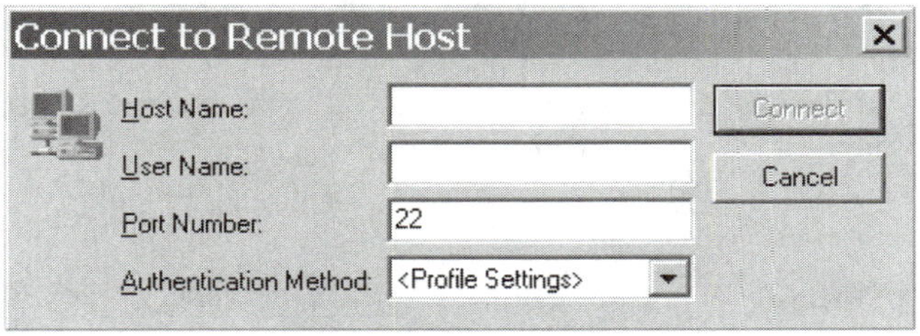

A.14 Connecting to a Remote Linux Server

Figure A.12 Dialog box shown when connection is to be established by SSH Shell Client.

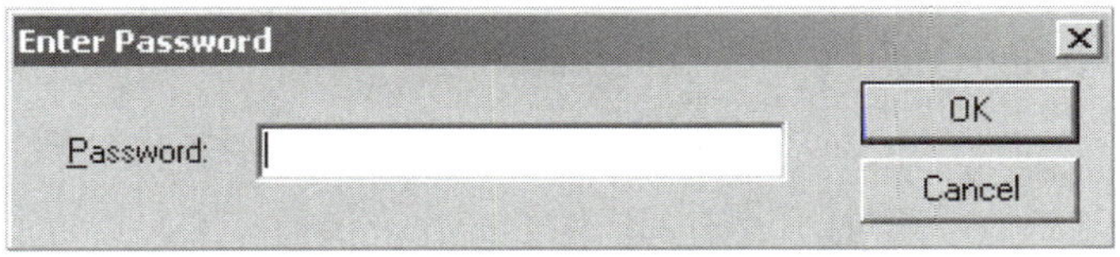

Figure A.13 Password dialog box.

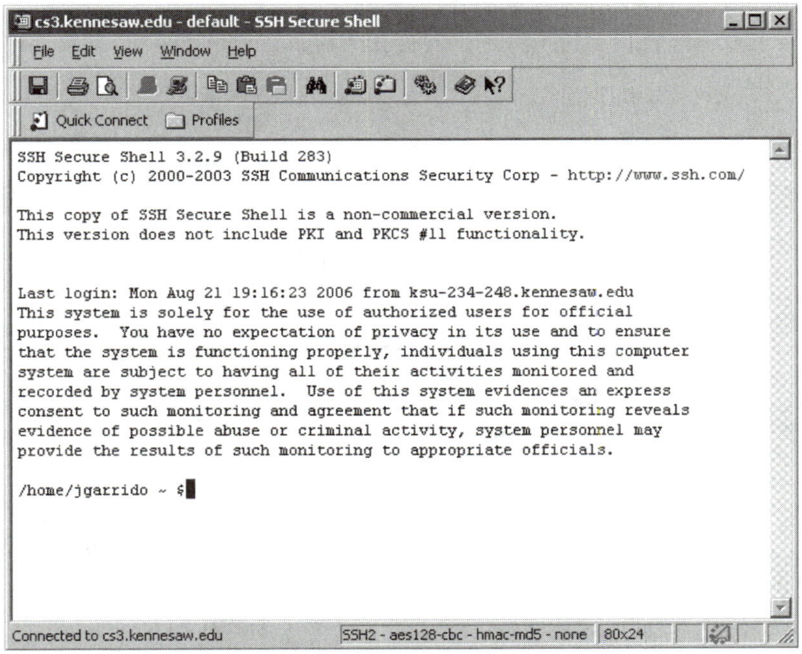

Figure A.14 Window with SSH Shell Client after login.

A.14.3 X-Window and Graphical Desktops

The X-Window system supports graphical user interface (GUI) on Linux. There are two popular graphical desktop environments used for this:

- The K Desktop Environment (KDE)
- GNU Network Object Model Environment (GNOME)

To access a remote Linux server with a GUI interface, you need an X-window package that runs on MS Windows (or on a Mac). An example of a good X-window package is Xming. You need the main release and the font package. Carry out the following steps to install and configure SSH and Xming:

1. Download the Xming program from

    http://sourceforge.net/projects/xming

2. Install the Xming X-window package.
3. Start SSH Shell Client.
4. Select File.
5. Select Profiles and Edit profiles.
6. Select Tunneling.
7. Mark *Tunnel X11 Connections*.
8. Click Ok.

To start a graphical desktop (based on X-window) on Linux, carry out one or more of the following tasks:

1. On the SSH Shell Client (or Putty), start an X terminal by typing `xterm`
2. On the new terminal screen, type `konqueror`. This is the advanced file manager in Red Hat Enterprise Linux.
3. If you want to start the KDE system, type `startkde`.

You can also type `xclock` on the initial terminal or in an Xterm, and Linux will respond by displaying a clock, as shown in Figure A.15.

Figure A.15 Clock shown using Xming.

A.14.4 Using the K Desktop Environment

The K Desktop Environment (KDE) is a graphical desktop that includes a window manager, a file manager, and utilities for most other Linux tasks. The interface is similar to the one found on Mac OS and MS Windows. Figure A.16 shows the KDE

Figure A.16 The KDE desktop.

Figure A.17 The kicker panel.

desktop, and at the bottom of the screen the KDE kicker panel, which is also shown in Figure A.17, appears. A user can access most of the KDE functions from this panel, which is also called a *kicker* because any application can be started from the menu that appears by clicking the first icon on the left (a red hat). This icon enables the KDE Application Starter.

One of the necessary steps when in the KDE desktop is to edit a file using the KEdit editor program. To start the KEdit editor, type KEdit on an Xterm terminal window. Figure A.18 shows the KEdit screen.

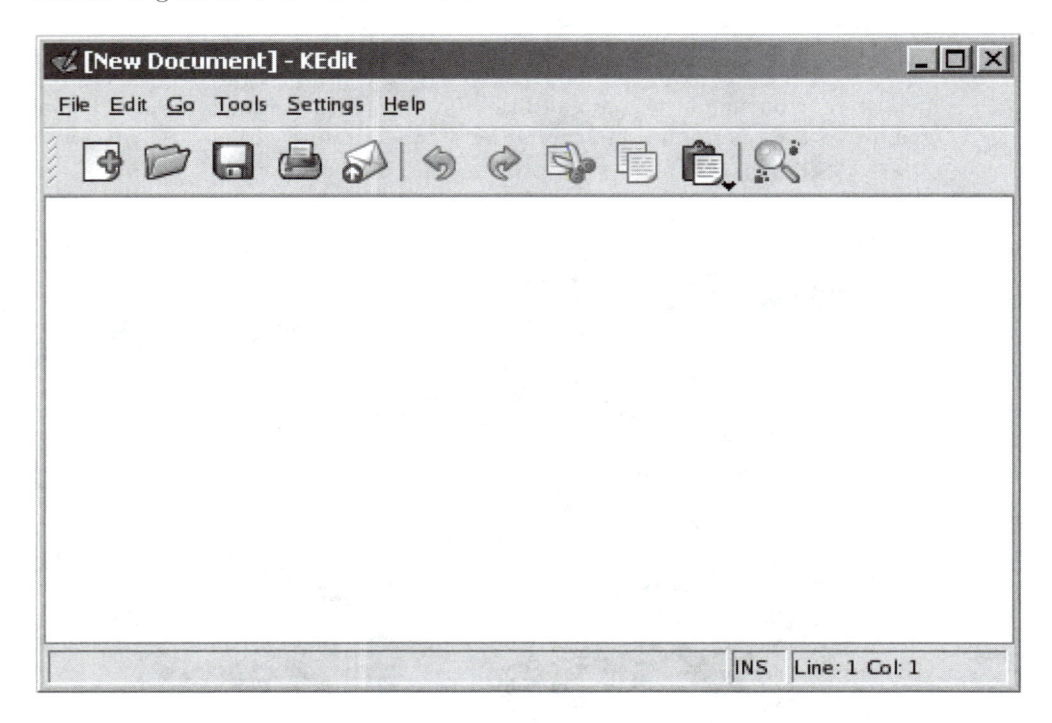

Figure A.18 The KEdit screen.

Appendix B
Java and POSIX Threads

B.1 Introduction

This appendix presents an overview of the important concepts of threads. The first part presents an overview of the most relevant Java threads, and the second half presents an overview of POSIX threads, known as *Pthreads* and used with the C++ and C programming languages. Only the basic concepts of threads are discussed; more advanced concepts appear in several specialized books listed in the bibliography.

B.2 Threads

As mentioned in Section 2.3, operating systems support computational units called *threads*. Called a *lightweight process*, a thread is a dynamic component of a process. Several threads are usually created within a single process. These threads share part of the program code and resources of the process.

Most modern operating systems support a feature called *multithreading*—multiple threads of execution within a single process. The operating system manages processes and threads in a multiprogramming environment, and from the computational point of view, the execution of threads is handled much more efficiently than the execution of processes. The modern view of threads represents them as the active elements of computation within a process. All threads that belong to a process share the state and resources of the process. Figure B.1 illustrates the concept of multiple threads in a process.

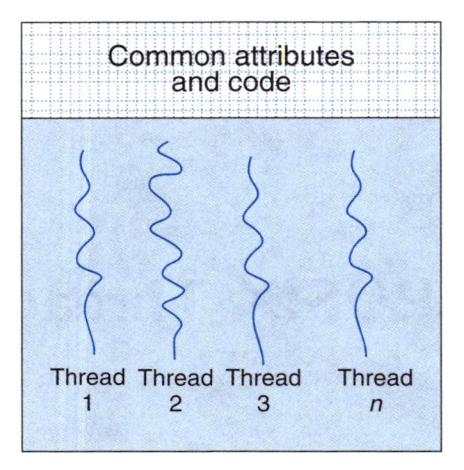

Figure B.1 Threads in a process.

B.3 Object-Oriented Concepts and Threads in Java

Java is a pure object-oriented programming language with several important characteristics:

- Method *main* is included in one of the classes of the application being developed. This class would normally be included in the controlling class, or the *main* class. This is not applicable to applets.

- No global variables or objects are allowed.

- Members of a class are public, private, or protected. These keywords are called the *access modifiers*.

- Members of a base class can be redefined, or overridden in a derived class (subclass), when using inheritance.

- The class definitions should include one or more constructors.

- The only way to manipulate objects after they are created is via their references. In Java, the reference types are classes, interfaces, and arrays. Unreferenced objects are automatically destroyed by the garbage collector mechanism in Java.

B.3.1 Inheritance

B.3.1.1 Base and Derived Classes

Object-oriented programming enhances reuse by the application of inheritance. All the members of a *base class* are inherited by a *subclass*, which is also called a *derived class*. In Java, all the members of a base class can be redefined (i.e., reimplemented) in the subclass. In this way, when a subclass redefines one or more inherited methods, it is considered a specialization of the base class. Usually, a subclass includes its own members in addition to the inherited members. In this second case, the subclass is considered an extension of the base class. In general, a subclass can be a specialization and/or an extension of the base class.

In Java, the definition of a subclass needs to indicate that it inherits the features of a base class by using the *extends* keyword followed by the name of the base class. For example, in the definition of the `Car` class, it inherits the `Motor_vehicle` class. The first class is the derived class and the second is the base class. The Java code for this relationship is as follows:

```
class Car extends Motor_vehicle
{
   // complete class implementation
   ...
}
```

Classes `Truck` and `Motorcycle` also inherit class `Motor_vehicle`. Class `Truck` has a similar header as class `Car`. The following code shows this:

```
class Truck extends Motor_vehicle
{
   // complete class implementation
   ...
}

class Motorcycle extends Motor_vehicle
{
   // complete class implementation
   ...

}
```

When a subclass redefines (overrides) one or more methods defined in the base class, then there will be two versions for these methods. One is the base class version; the other is the subclass version (the redefined version). If the subclass needs to invoke a method of the base class, it needs to explicitly indicate base class ownership with the `super` keyword. For example, the following invokes the `stop` method of the base class:

```
super.stop();      // invoke stop() of the base class
```

B.3.1.2 Constructors of the Subclasses

All members of a base class are inherited by a subclass, except the constructor of the base class. The constructor of the subclass will normally need to invoke the constructor of the base class. This is necessary for the proper initialization of base class attributes that are used in the subclass.

To invoke the constructor of the base class, the keyword `super` is used for the name of this constructor. For example, assume that in the constructor for class `Car` a parameter is needed for the initial number of miles. The following Java code implements (partially) the constructor for class `Car` that invokes the base class constructor with an integer parameter that represents the number of miles. If there is no explicit call to the constructor of the base class, then the default constructor is called implicitly.

```
public void Car (int i_miles) {
   // invoke the base class constructor with number miles
   super (i_miles);
   // additional instructions
   ...
}
```

B.3.2 Abstract Classes

Methods in a class that are only declared and have no implementation are called *abstract methods*. To declare an abstract method, the keyword `abstract` is written before the method modifiers. The following statement declares an abstract method called `stop`:

```
abstract public void stop();
```

A class that has one or more abstract methods is called an *abstract class*. It is normally used as a base class, and the methods are implemented in a subclass. It is used to emphasize that the base class is a more general class than the subclasses and to promote uniformity in the methods implemented in all subclasses. The name of the methods, the numbers and type of parameter, and the return type for the methods cannot be changed by the subclasses.

Abstract classes cannot be instantiated—that is, objects cannot be created of abstract classes. The following Java code implements (partially) the definition of an abstract class called `Vehicle`.

```
public abstract class Vehicle
{
   // definition
   ...
}
```

B.3.3 Polymorphism

An important aspect of inheritance is that a reference to an object of a class can be declared and assigned to a reference of an object of a subclass. For example, consider the base class `Motor_vehicle` described above: Three subclasses were defined: `Car`, `Truck`, and `Motorcycle`.

An object reference of class `Motor_vehicle` can be declared, even if the class is an abstract class. Objects of the subclasses can be created in the usual manner; this is shown below in the following code:

```
Motor_vehicle my_vehicle; // object reference declaration
...
Car my_car = new Car ();  // reference to a newly created object
Truck my_truck = new Truck();
Motorcycle my_cycle = new Motorcycle ();
```

Now the object reference of the base class can be assigned to reference an object of any of the subclasses. On the left-hand side of the assignment statement, only object references of the same class or of a more general class (a base class) can be used.

```
// my_vehicle references the same object as does my_truck
my_vehicle = my_truck;
```

Polymorphism is a technique that allows a call to a method of an object, from a reference of base class. This is considered a *polymorphic call* because the version of the method invoked depends on the object that is being referred to at that time. The following Java code shows a polymorphic call to method `drive`.

```
my_vehicle.drive();      // a polymorphic call to Drive()
```

In this case, the version of the method `drive` to execute is the one that is implemented for object of class `Truck`. In general, the decision of which implementation of a method to use is carried out at run time and depends on the object being referenced. The rule for polymorphism is that the class of the object, not the class of the reference, is what determines which method to invoke.

B.3.4 Classes and Interfaces

An *interface* is an extreme case of an abstract class. It only declares methods and constants (final and static attributes). Like abstract classes, implementation of all methods declared in an interface is deferred to subclasses. An interface cannot be instantiated; the interface is public and its members are public. No constructors are allowed. To define an interface, the keyword `interface` is used before its name. The following code defines an interface called `Animal` with two method declarations.

```
interface Animal {
   int get_count();
   void display (String cc);
}
```

Instead of inheriting a base class, a class *implements* an interface. The following code implements the `Animal` interface:

```
public class Cat implements Animal {
  int get_count() {
     ...
  }
  //
  void display (String x)
  {
     ...
  }
  // other members of class Cat
  ...
}  // end of class Cat
```

Java does not support multiple inheritance—that is, a subclass inheriting from two or more different base classes. Instead, a class can implement more than one interface.

B.3.5 Exceptions

An *exception* is an abnormal condition in a program that can be caught at run time; the problem that caused the exception can be corrected and the program will continue. Java includes mechanisms for dealing with exceptions, so these can be detected and handled.

There are several types of exceptions in Java; the `try` and `catch` statements are provided to detect and handle exceptions in a consistent way.

Dealing with exceptions involves three main steps:

1. Identify the block of statements in the code that might raise an exception.

2. Determine the type of exception(s) that might occur.

3. Decide what instructions to execute when the exception is caught; this is the exception handling part.

When a sequence of instructions that might raise an exception is identified, it should be enclosed in a `try` block (of statements). The `catch` block immediately follows the `try` block; it encloses instructions to be executed if the exception type specified occurs. The instructions in the `catch` block correspond to the code for handling the exception type specified as the parameter for the `catch` statement.

In the following code, invoking method `display` of object `my_obj` might throw an exception; the message in the `catch` block is printed on the console if the exception `ex` is thrown.

```
try {
   my_obj.display(); // this method might throw an exception
}
catch ( NumberFormatException ex) {
```

```
        System.out.println( "Number format exception caught ");
}
```

B.3.6 Java Threads

A program can have multiple execution paths (sequential flows of control) called *threads*. Java provides various ways to create and manipulate threads as objects. A thread is called a lightweight process because it executes concurrently with other threads within a single program.

As mentioned in Chapter 1, the *active* objects in the conceptual model are implemented as threads in Java. These objects execute concurrently to compete for exclusive access to resources and/or to interact among themselves in some synchronized fashion.

B.3.6.1 Using Threads

There are five general steps to use threads in Java:

1. Define one or more classes with thread behavior. These are the user-defined thread classes that:

    - inherit class `Thread`, or
    - implement the `Runnable` interface.

2. Redefine the special thread method `run` for each thread class.

3. Create one or more thread objects from each of these classes.

4. Start the thread objects with the special thread method, `start`.

5. Manipulate the thread objects with the thread methods available from the `Thread` class (or from the `Runnable` interface).

The simplest way to define a class with thread behavior is to use the `Thread` class (from the Java library) as the base class. In addition to the inherited attributes and methods, the subclass will normally include its own methods with additional behavior. Method `run` has to be overridden (redefined). This method defines and controls the behavior of a user-defined thread class, and it is implicitly invoked by method `start`. For a given program, several classes with thread behavior would normally be defined.

In addition to the object threads created from the user-defined thread classes, the Java Virtual Machine (JVM) creates and starts several system threads implicitly. One of these is the main thread that starts when the main method begins execution. Another system thread is the garbage collector thread. If the application includes graphics, the JVM starts one or more graphics threads.

B.3.6.2 Inheriting the Thread Class

A user-defined class will normally extend the Java `Thread` library class. The following code defines class `Mythread`:

```
public class Mythread extends Thread
{
  private String thread_name;
  // constructor
  Mythread ( String tname ) {
     thread_name = new String ( tname );
  }
  // override method run()
  public void run () {
    setName ( thread_name );
    System.out.println ( " New thread: " + thread_name );
  }
  //
  // define additional features
} // end of class Mythread
```

Class `Mythread` inherits the `Thread` class and overrides method `run`. It defines a constructor to initialize the name of the object. From method `main` of the program, for example, a thread of class `Mythread` can be created and started. Using this method for defining threads, every instance of class `Mythread` is a thread object. The following code creates a thread object and starts it, in addition to this object; it also implicitly creates the main thread:

```
public static void main (String [] args) {
   Mythread mythr_obj = new Mythread ("my new thread");
   mythr_obj.start(); // start execution of the thread object
   ...
   System.out.println("Main thread");
}
```

Method `start` is one of the methods of class `Thread`. After the thread object is created, it needs to start execution. Invoking the `start` method begins execution of the thread object. As mentioned above, this method implicitly invokes method `run`, which defines the actual behavior of the thread object.

The first activity carried out by the thread object above and defined in method `run` is to set the name of the thread object. Method `setName` of class `Thread` is invoked to set the name of the thread object. This is one of several methods defined in the `Thread` class.

One of the most common applications of threads is GUI implementations, and one of the major concerns in user-interface implementations is to keep the user interface alive and responding to user-generated events. To accomplish this, a thread is defined for the basic GUI, and different threads are defined for the major tasks of the application.

B.3.6.3 Other Basic Thread Methods

There are several methods defined in the `Thread` class. The previous section explained the use of three of them: `run`, `start`, and `setName`. Since more than one thread may execute a method, it can be very convenient or useful to have a reference to the thread that is currently executing a portion of code.

The static method `currentThread` returns a reference to the currently executing thread at the particular point in time. A thread reference needs to have been declared before invoking `currentThread` to get the value of the reference to the current thread. The following portion of code declares a thread reference, then gets the reference to the current thread by invoking the static method `currentThread`:

```
Thread mythread;    // a thread reference declaration

...
// get reference to the currently running thread
mythread = Thread.currentThread();
```

After a reference to the current thread is known, several nonstatic `Thread` methods can be invoked. One of these is the method to get the name of the current thread. The method `getName` returns a string with the name of the thread. Assume that the method to set the name of the thread has been previously called. The following statements simply get the name of the thread and assigns it to a string object:

```
String mythread_name;   // a string object ref declaration
...
mythread_name = mythread.getName(); // get name of current thread
```

A thread begins execution when its `start` method is invoked; at this point in time, the thread becomes alive. It will remain alive until its `run` method returns, or when it is terminated. To check if a thread is alive, the boolean method `isAlive` can be used. The following code checks if a thread is alive, then prints a message on the screen:

```
// mythread is a reference to a thread object
...
if ( mythread.isAlive() ) {
   System.out.println("Thread: " + mythread.getName() +

      " is alive");
   ...
}
else {
   system.out.println ("Thread is not alive");
   ...
}
```

B.3.6.4 A Thread Suspending Itself

A thread can be suspended for a given period, then reactivated. Method `sleep` can be used by a thread to suspend itself; the method is a static method that requires an argument of type `long`. The following line of code calls method `sleep` with an argument of value 10000 to suspend a thread for 10 seconds:

```
Thread.sleep ( 10000 );
```

While the thread is suspended, it can be interrupted by another thread; Java requires placing this call within a `try` block so it can check for an exception. The code is as follows:

```
try {
    Thread.sleep ( 10000 );
}
catch (InterruptedException e)  {
    // ignore exception
}
```

B.3.6.5 Implementing the Runnable Interface

As mentioned before, in Java a class can only inherit a single base class—that is, multiple inheritance is not supported. However, a class can implement multiple interfaces. Therefore, when it becomes impractical for a class to inherit the `Thread` class, it can implement the `Runnable` interface.

Similar to the manner used above to define a class for thread objects, implementing the `Runnable` interface requires the class to completely define method `run`. There is a minor difference in defining a thread class by implementing the `Runnable` interface, compared to the technique used above. An instance of the class is passed as an argument to the `Thread` constructor.

There are six general steps used to declare and define a thread object:

1. Define a thread class by implementing the `Runnable` interface.

2. Declare and create an object of the class implementing the `Runnable` interface.

3. Declare and create a thread object by invoking the thread constructor using the instance of the class in the previous step, as an argument.

4. Start the thread object by invoking its start method.

5. Manipulate the thread object by invoking the various thread methods.

6. Indicate to the garbage collector to destroy the thread object.

The following Java code defines a class that implements the `Runnable` interface and includes a definition of the `run` method:

```java
public class Otherthread implements Runnable {
  // declaration of attributes
  ...
  // definition of private and public methods
  ...
  // definition of the run() method
  public void run () {
     System.out.println ("Thread: " + getName () );
     ...
  }
}        // end of class
```

This class can now be instantiated, and `Thread` objects can be created and manipulated. This is accomplished by the following code of method `main`:

```java
public static void main ( String [] args ) {
   private Otherthread classobj;
   ...
   // create object of this class
   classobj = new Otherthread ();
   // now create thread object
   Thread mythread = new Thread ( classobj );
   mythread.start ();   // start execution of thread


   ...
}     // end main()
```

B.3.6.6 Interrupting a Thread Object

There are several ways for one thread to stop another thread. The most straightforward way is to have one thread interrupt a second thread. The first thread can do this by invoking the `interrupt` method of the second thread. In the following example, the main thread interrupts the thread that it has created and started previously. The main method described above now includes a call to the interrupt method of the second thread:

```java
...
// time after starting thread object mythread, interrupt it
mythread.interrupt ();
...
```

The interrupted thread will have a special interrupt flag set to indicate that it has been interrupted. If the thread being interrupted is sleeping, an exception is thrown (as shown above). The block of instructions to execute when this event occurs (interrupt) is placed in a `catch` block.

```
try {
    Thread.sleep ( 10000 );
}
catch ( InterruptedException e )  {
    // just a message to screen
    System.out.println ("Thread interrupted ....");
}
```

When a thread is interrupted, its interrupted flag is set. This is reflected in its interrupted status, which will indicate whether the thread was interrupted. The call to method `sleep` above clears the interrupted flag when it throws the exception. Usually, when a thread is executing a method and it is interrupted, it should be able to raise an exception of type `InterruptedException`.

To check the interrupted status of a thread, the `isInterrupted` method is called. This method returns `true` if the thread has been interrupted and `false` if the thread has not been interrupted. This method does not change the interrupted status of the thread. For example, the following code checks for the interrupted flag and executes appropriate instructions in a thread:

```
...
if ( isInterrupted () ) {
    ...         // appropriate instructions
    System.out.println ( "Thread was interrupted, ..." );
}
else {
    ...         // other instructions
    System.out.println ( "Thread was not interrupted, ..." );
}
...
```

To check and clear the interrupted flag in a thread, the `interrupted` method is invoked; it is a static method of class `Thread`. The following code invokes this method and displays the interrupted status of the thread:

```
System.out.println ( "Status for thread: " +
    Thread.interrupted () );
```

B.3.6.7 Thread Priorities in Java

Scheduling is the selection of which thread to execute next. Threads are normally scheduled with their default priorities. The application threads (including the main thread) have a default priority of 5. The system threads, such as the thread of the garbage collector and AWT windows thread, have a higher priority (in the range of 6 to 10).

To change the priority of threads, Java provides several constants and methods used for priority assignments. Any priority changes must be done with care, and JVM may not actually use the new priorities in the expected manner.

B.3 Object-Oriented Concepts and Threads in Java

To get the current priority of a thread, the `getPriority` method is invoked. To set the priority of a thread to a different value, the `setPriority` method is invoked. The priority is an integer value. A thread can be rescheduled to execute any time after a pause by relinquishing the processor to another thread. The `yield` static method indicates the scheduler to execute the next pending thread. The code that follows gets the priority of a thread. If it is 5 or less, it is set to the maximum priority possible; otherwise the current thread yields the processor to another scheduled thread.

```
int my_prior;
...
my_prior = mythread.getPriority();
if ( my_prior <= 5 )
    mythread.setPriority ( Thread.MAX_PRIORITY);
else
    Thread.yield();     // yield execution of this thread
...
```

B.3.6.8 Simple Thread Synchronization

A thread can obtain a *lock* on an object by invoking a synchronized instance method of that object. In this case, only one thread can invoke a synchronized method; all other threads are excluded from invoking the method and have to wait. The threads that are waiting are suspended (or blocked) until one is enabled to invoke the method.

A synchronized instance method is a nonstatic method that includes the `synchronized` modifier in the method header. This type of method ensures that only one thread can be executing the method at a time. The code that follows defines a class that includes a synchronized method as one of its members. The main method instantiates this class and two threads that invoke the synchronized method of the object created.

```
public class My_exclusive extends Object {

   // several member definitions
   //
   // method can only be invoked by one thread at a time
   public synchronized void exclusive_method (){
       ...
   }
} // end of class definition




public static void main ( String [] args ) {
   My_exclusive my_obj = new My_exclusive ();
   //
   // creating two threads and passing object
```

```
// as argument to constructor

Thread_class my_thread1 = new Thread_class (my_obj);
Thread_class my_thread2 = new Thread_class (my_obj);
...
// the two threads will invoke method
// exclusive_method of the object
my_thread1.start();
my_thread2.start();
```

In some applications, there is no need to synchronize a complete method; a *synchronized block* is used instead. This can be more efficient as it reduces the time that the object lock is held. The other advantage is that it allows the thread to get a lock on a different object if necessary. The following code defines a synchronized block on object `my_obj`:

```
synchronized ( my_obj ) {
  // block of statements
  ...
}
```

Although using a synchronized block can be more efficient than synchronized methods, you should be very careful when using them. Their use can easily lead to an unstructured solution that is difficult to understand. Additionally, their use can more easily lead to deadlock situations. Good object-oriented design would put the locking code in methods in the object being locked.

B.3.6.9 Wait/Notify Mechanism in Threads

A convenient way for threads to accomplish some level of communication is to synchronize through the wait/notify mechanism. Basically, a thread will *suspend* itself waiting for a condition until it is notified that there has been a change. This condition will typically be a check on the value of a variable. A second thread changes the condition and notifies the first thread. At this instant, the first thread can continue, if possible.

In the simplest case, a thread first acquires a lock on a member object, then it invokes the `wait` method on that object. The thread releases the lock on the object and is suspended until notified or interrupted.

The second thread attempts to get the lock on the object. If this is not possible, the thread waits until it can get exclusive access to the lock on the same object. As soon as the thread gets access to the lock for the object, the thread invokes the `notify` method. The following code accomplished the suspension of the first thread:

```
synchronized ( my_object ) {
  try {
    my_object.wait();
  }
```

```
catch ( InterruptedException x ) {
  System.out.println ( "Thread interrupted on wait " );
}
```

Good object-oriented design will have the wait and notify calls in the same class. Otherwise, it is extremely difficult to understand the functioning of a multithreaded application.

B.4 POSIX Threads

POSIX threads, also known as *Pthreads*, are not really object-oriented; they were developed to be used with the C programming language. For C++, we can define a wrapper class as defining the basic thread class, then instantiate or inherit the class from a subclass. The Psim3 simulation package, which is used to implement the simulation models discussed in this book, was developed with Pthreads.

Pthreads follow the IEEE Portable Operating System Interface (POSIX) standards. Part of this standard covers threads and includes the application programming interface (API) that supports threads.

Every thread has the following parameters associated with it:

- A thread ID, which uniquely identifies the thread. The thread ID is returned when the thread is created.

- An attribute object, which is used to configure the thread. Normally the default values are used for the attribute object.

- A *start function*, which is called when the thread is created.

- An argument of the start function call. If more than one argument is required in the function call, then the argument should point to a data structure.

B.4.1 Creating POSIX Threads

The prototype of the function to create a thread within a process is as follows:

```
int pthread_create (pthread_t *thread_id,
                    pthread_attr_t *attr,
                    void *(*start_function)(void *),
                    void *arg);
```

A process, or application, may create several threads by invoking the `pthread_create` function.

The following portion of code is an example of creating a thread that calls the `func1` function when it is created:

```
Pthread_t tid;
int error_code;
//
// create a new thread
//
error_code = pthread_create (&tid, NULL, func1, arg1);

. . .
void * func1 (void *arg) {
  //
  // code for func1
  //
}
```

In the Psim3 simulation package, member function `pstart()` of class `process` includes the Pthread function `pthread_create` to create a thread. Thus, a new thread is created when the `pstart()` function is called on a process object—an instance of a user-defined class that inherits class `process`.

B.4.2 Basic Synchronization of Pthreads

B.4.2.1 Waiting for Termination

When a thread has to wait for another thread to complete, the first thread has to invoke `pthread_join(..)`. A call to this function suspends the first thread until the second thread exits or returns. The first thread invokes `pthread_join(..)` and needs the thread ID of the second thread as one of the arguments in the function call. The following line of code invokes the function using the thread ID, `Tid2`, of the second thread.

```
error_code = pthread_join(Tid2, NULL);
```

Threads that can be *joined* are also called *nondetached threads*; threads that cannot be joined are called *detached threads*. By default, threads that are created are joinable. Threads that are to be detached can be created by first changing the attribute in the attribute object of the thread. The following line of code changes this:

```
pthread_attr_setdetachstate(&attr, PTHREAD_CREATE_DETACHED);
```

An existing thread can be detached by invoking the following function:

```
int pthread_detach( pthread_t tid);
```

B.4.2.2 Termination of a Thread

A thread normally terminates when it returns from its *start function*, which is the code body of the thread. Another way a thread terminates is by calling the `pthread_exit()` function. The prototype of this function is

```
int pthread_exit( void *thes);
```

Parameter `thes` is the thread's exit status. A detached thread should not exit with this parameter different than NULL.

A thread may be terminated by another thread. If a first thread needs to terminate a second thread with a thread ID, `tid2`, then the following line of code in the first thread will terminate the second thread:

```
pthread_cancel(thid2);   // cancel thread thid2
```

B.4.3 Mutual Exclusion

In Chapter 6, the main concepts and principles of synchronization were discussed. Mutual exclusion is an important approach used for a set of processes, (and/or threads) to share resources in a mutually exclusive manner.

With POSIX, mutual exclusion is used with *mutex variables*, also called *mutexes*. These are normally declared as global static variables of type `pthread_mutex_t`. The usage of these variables is similar to binary semaphores used for mutual exclusion, discussed in Chapter 6.

In order to initialize a mutex variable, its attribute object needs to be initialized. The following lines of code declare and initialize a mutex attribute object with its default values:

```
pthread_mutex_t mymtx;          // mutex variable declaration
pthread_mutexattr_t mymtx_attr; // attributes object of a mutex
. . .
err_val = pthread_mutexattr_init (&mymtx_attr); // initialize attr
```

The default attributes object will allow sharing of the mutex variable by threads within the same process. If needed, the `PROCESS_SHARED` attribute will have to be set to share the mutex variable by all threads in multiple processes. The following line of code sets this attribute:

```
err_val = pthread_mutexattr_setpshared (&mymtx_attr,
             THREAD_PROCESS_SHARED);
```

Once the attributes object of a mutex variable is initialized, the variable can then be used as a simple mutually exclusive lock in the critical sections of the threads that share a resource.

Recall that before the critical section of a process, the *entry section* executes, and after the critical section, the *exit section* executes. Once the attributes object of a mutex variable is initialized, the variable can then be used as a simple mutually exclusive lock in the critical sections of the threads that share a resource.

Function `pthread_mutex_lock()` is used to implement the *entry section*, and function `pthread_mutex_unlock()` is used to implement the *exit section*.

The critical section in the *start* function of a thread accesses a shared resource in a mutually exclusive manner. The mutex variable `mymtx` has been declared and initialized. The attributes object `mymtx_attr` of the mutex variable has also been initialized. The threads that accessed a shared resource have been created. The following lines of code implement the entry section, the critical section, and the exit section in a thread:

```
pthread_mutex_lock(mymtx);      // entry section with mutex 'mymtx'
    // critical section
pthread_mutex_unlock(mymtx);    // exit section
```

B.4.4 Semaphores

Semaphores are used to synchronize threads within a process and are similar to mutex variables. Semaphores are variables of type `sem_t` and have to be initialized to an appropriate value.

B.4.4.1 Initializing Semaphores

Function `sem_init()` is used to initialize the semaphore to an integer value. The following lines of code declare and initialize a semaphore to the value 4:

```
sem_t mysem;               // semaphore variable
. . .
sem_init (&mysem, 0, 4);   // initialize semaphore to 4
```

In the call to function `sem_init()`, the first argument is a reference to the semaphore variable, the second argument with value zero indicates that the semaphore is shared among threads within a process, and the third argument is the value to which the semaphore variable is initialized. Thus, the semaphore `mysem` is defined as a counting semaphore.

B.4.4.2 Decrementing and Incrementing Semaphores

Decrementing the value of a semaphore is carried out by function `sem_wait()`. If the semaphore cannot be decremented because its current value is zero, the thread invoking this function is suspended. Incrementing a semaphore is carried out by function `sem_post()`. This function also reactivates any waiting threads that have been suspended. The following lines of code invoke both functions with semaphore `mysem`, which was intialized previously:

```
sem_wait(&mysem);      // decrement semaphore 'mysem'
   . . .
sem_post(&mysem);      // increment semaphore 'mysem'
```

With these functions to increment and decrement semaphores and with the use of mutex variables, synchronization problems such as the bounded-buffer problem and the readers-writers problem can easily be solved using threads.

To check if a semaphore can be decremented without the thread that invokes the function being suspended, function `sem_trywait()` can be used. The function returns -1 immediately if the semaphore cannot be decremented, without suspending the calling thread.

```
// attempt to decrement semaphore 'mysem'
err_val = sem_trywait(&mysem);
```

B.4.4.3 Destroying Semaphores

After all the threads that use a semaphore have terminated, the semaphore can be destroyed. This is carried out by function `sem_destroy()`. The following line of code destroys semaphore `mysem`:

```
err-val = sem_destroy(&mysem);   // destroy semaphore 'mysem'
```

B.4.5 Condition Variables

Condition variables can be used to make a thread wait for an event to happen. A condition variable is an object that consists of three components: the condition variable, an associative mutex variable, and a condition. One thread invokes a wait on a condition variable to check the condition. Another thread will change the state of the condition and signal the condition variable.

Declaration and initialization of a condition variable and its attributes object is shown in the following lines of code:

```
pthread_cond_t condv;          // declare cond variable 'condv'
pthread_condattr_t cond_attr;  // declare attributes object
   . . .
pthread_condattr_init(&cond_attr);    // initialize attr object
   . . .
// initializes the cond variable
pthread_cond_init(condv, &cond_attr);
```

When a thread invokes the wait function on a condition variable, the function will carry out the following sequence of steps:

1. Lock the mutex variable to allow only one thread at a time to examine and alter parameters that affect the condition.

2. Evaluate the condition.

3. If the condition is not true, suspend the thread.

4. If the condition is true, carry out the specified task.

5. Unlock the mutex variable.

These steps are coded in C in the following lines of code:

```
pthread_mutex_lock(&mmtx);     // lock mutex variable
while (! condt)
   pthread_cond_wait(&condv, &mmtx); // cond var wait
task();                        // carry out some task
pthread_mutex_unlock(&mmtx);
```

The mutex variable is automatically released when the thread starts to wait on the condition.

When another thread changes the state of the condition and invokes the function to signal the condition variable, the function will carry out the following sequence of steps:

1. Lock the mutex variable.

2. Change the state of the condition (set to true).

3. Reactivate one or more threads that are waiting.

4. Unlock the mutex variable.

The following lines of code implement the sequence of steps, listed previously, in a second thread:

```
pthread_mutex_lock(&mmtx);
   . . .
   condt = true;               // alter state of condition
pthread_mutex_unlock(&mmtx);
pthread_cond_signal(&condv);   // signal condition var
```

More advanced concepts with threads, such as signaling, is outside the scope of this short overview of threads. For a more detailed discussion, see Lewis and Berg (1998) and Norton and Dipasquale (1997) in the bibliography.

B.4.6 Scheduling and Priorities of POSIX Threads

The default scheduling approach used in POSIX threads is the *process scheduling scope*, a process in which each thread competes for system resources with all other similar threads within the process. These threads are unbound, which means that a thread does not directly bind to a kernel entity.

A thread can temporarily change its scheduling by releasing or yielding the CPU to another thread. The function call `sched_yield()` in a thread will allow another thread to run.

POSIX defined three real-time scheduling policies for threads: (1) FIFO (with priorities), (2) round robin, and (3) another policy that may be specified by a particular implementation. When a thread is created, it has a given scheduling policy and a priority. These two can be changed dynamically after the thread starts execution.

The scheduling policies contain at least 32 priority values. To get the minimum and maximum priority values, POSIX provides two functions that are specified by the following function prototypes:

```
int sched_get_priority_min (int sched_policy);

int sched_get_priority_max (int sched_policy);
```

The integer parameter `sched_policy` has three possible values: (1) SCHED_FIFO, (2) SCHED_RR, and (3) SCHED_OTHER.

The scheduling parameter of a thread is a data structure having several components, with scheduling priority being one of them. The scheduling policy and scheduling parameter can be changed with the function call in the following code:

```
struct sched_param s_param;   // scheduling parameter
. . .
s_param.sched_priority = priority_val;
err_val = pthread_setschedparam (th_id, sched_policy, &s_param);
```

Appendix C
The Java Modeling Framework

C.1 Introduction

The simulation models implemented in Java that are used throughout this textbook are based on a modeling framework—an extension to the PsimJ library, which consists of the classes for developing simulation models with Java.

The framework allows students of operating systems to develop their own models of OS components without having to integrate components into a real operating system. Students should be able to use this framework if they have completed a Java programming course. Examples of the types of OS components that can be developed include the following:

- Job scheduler
- CPU scheduler
- Producer-consumer or reader-writer
- Disk space management
- Disk request scheduler
- Page replacement algorithm
- File protection system

C.2 Basic Structure of a Model

A simulation model normally has the following components:

- *Input parameters* that provide any needed parameters for the model execution.

- One or more *processes* that perform the operations of the model. A `Process` is an active element that is actually a separately running thread.

- *Output* that consists of a trace file of events that happen during the execution of the model and a summary file with any desired statistical or summary information.

- An optional *graphical display* that can show plots of values that vary over time and (if desired) an animation of the model's execution.

C.2.1 Simulation Model

To develop your own model, you should define a subclass of class `Model`, which is defined in the framework. This subclass will need to have the program's *main* method, which should invoke method `main` of class `Model`, passing it a string with the name of this model and the command-line arguments.

This user-defined class, the main class, needs to instantiate the framework's class `SimInputs` for reading the input parameters for this model, using a statement similar to the following:

```
private static SimInputs simIn = new SimInputs();
```

In the above statement, `SimInputs` is a subclass of the `Input` class (discussed in Section C.2.2). The constructor of this class should invoke the constructor of class `Model` using `super(simIn)`.

The subclass of the `Model` class will need to implement the methods shown in Table C.1.

C.2.2 Input Parameters

The class `SimInputs` (a subclass of the `Input` class) defines all input parameters. Each parameter can be one of the following:

- An `IntegerParameter` that has a name, minimum value, maximum value, and default value.

- A `DoubleParameter` that has a name, minimum value, maximum value, and default value.

- A `SelectionParameter` that has a name, set of possible options, and default value.

Table C.1 Methods in Class `Model`

`void main(String[] args, String name)`	The model's main class is passed the command-line arguments and the model's name.
`Model(Input simIn)`	The constructor for the `Model` class should be passed the set of `Input` parameters.
`void begin()`	This method is called by the UI when the user pushes the start button. It should create any processes (`RequestProcessors`) that are always present in the system and then use the start method to begin executing those processes.
`void reportStatistics()`	This method is called at the end of the simulation run. It can be used to print any desired information.
`void Main_body()`	The model is itself a process, and you may use the `Main_body` method to perform any activity that needs to occur after the simulation starts.

Table C.2 Input Parameters

`IntegerParameter (String name, int minimum, int, maximum, int default)`	The constructor for an `IntegerParameter` specifies a name, minimum, maximum, and default values.
`DoubleParameter (String name, int minimum, int, maximum, int default)`	The constructor for a `DoubleParameter` specifies a name, minimum, maximum, and default values.
`SelectionParameter (String name, String[] options, String default)`	The constructor for a `SelectionParameter` specifies a name, a set of choices for the user, and default values.

The modeling framework will automatically use the set of parameters to construct a GUI for the user to set the desired values. Note that the input parameters should not be declared to be private (see Table C.2).

C.2.3 Class Input

The `Input` class has a number of utility methods for working with the input parameters (see Table C.3).

Table C.3 Input Methods

`double getParameterValue (String name)`	Returns the value of the input parameter with the specified name.
`String[] getFormattedInputParameters`	Returns an array of strings, each representing a printable display of an input parameter.

C.2.4 Class UI

The *UI* class uses the `InputParameters` in `SimInputs` to create a GUI frame to allow the user to specify the particular parameter values to be used for this execution. When the user presses the `Start` button, the begin method in the `Model` class will be called.

C.2.5 Processes

A typical model will have many processes, each performing some specific task. A process is used to model any active component. Examples include a CPU, a job executing in the system, and a web server. You can create your own processes by creating a subclass of `psimjava.Process`. A process will normally invoke the methods listed in Table C.4.

C.2.6 The `RequestProcessor`

A common type of process is a `RequestProcessor`, which repeatedly takes in `Requests` and performs some service based on the attributes of the request. Examples include a CPU and a web server. A `RequestProcessor` has a `Schedular` that determines the order in which the requests will be serviced. A request is itself a process, allowing it to perform actions as desired. `RequestProcessor` is an abstract class that the user must subclass to provide the desired specific functionality (i.e., what the `RequestProcessor` actually does).

In a typical model, requests arrive in the system and are scheduled for a `RequestProcessor`. When the scheduler determines it is appropriate to handle the request, the `RequestProcessor` performs the desired action. At this point, the request either terminates or is scheduled for another `RequestProcessor`. The methods available to a `RequestProcessor` are listed in Table C.5.

C.2.7 Request

A `Request` object is a subclass of the `Process` class, with the additional attributes and associated methods listed in Table C.6. Typically, a model will extend `Request` to define attributes and behaviors that are unique to that model.

Table C.4 Process Methods

`Process(String name)`	When you construct a `Process`, you must provide a name for it.
`void start()`	This method must be called to start the `Process` actually executing. Depending on the model, this method may be called by the process's constructor or by another component of the system.
`void Main_body()`	This method is called by the modeling framework to have the `Process` perform its function. In this method, the `Process` will interact with other system components and use the other `Process` methods to perform its function.
`void delay(double time)`	A `Process` may use this method to delay its execution for the specified amount of time. This is used in the simulation models to simulate the time it takes to do some activity.
`void deactivate (Process process)`	This method causes the specified `Process` to be suspended until it is reactivated.
`boolean idle()`	Returns true if the `Process` has been suspended.
`void reactivate (Process process)`	This method reactivates the specified `Process`.
`void terminate()`	This method is called by the `Process` to stop execution.

C.2.8 Schedular

A `Schedular` is used by a `RequestProcessor` to determine the order in which requests should be serviced. Actual schedulers are subclasses of the abstract `Schedular` class and may override its methods as necessary (Table C.7).

A commonly used subclass is `FCFSschedular`, which implements a simple first-come-first-served scheduling algorithm. It can be used with either a bounded or an unbounded queue. It will also examine the request's access type to determine whether shared access is allowed.

Another available schedular is `PriorityScheduler`, which will find the highest priority available request (Table C.8).

Table C.5 The Methods Available to a `RequestProcessor`

`RequestProcessor(String name, SimInputs sIn, Schedular sched)`	When you construct a `RequestProcessor`, you must provide a name, the input parameters, and a schedular.
`RequestProcessor(String name, SimInputs sIn)`	This is an alternate form of the constructor for a `RequestProcessor`. If this form is used, then the `setSchedular` method must be called to specify the schedular prior to attempting to actually handle any requests.
`void setSchedular (Schedular sched)`	Specifies the schedular to be used by this `RequestProcessor`.
`void serviceRequest (Request currentRequest)`	This method is called to actually service a `Request`.
`void schedule (Request newRequest)`	This method is called by other model components to have a request scheduled for this `RequestProcessor`. The default implementation simply passes the `Request` along to the `Schedular`. This method can be overridden to perform some unique activity when a `Request` occurs. It is possible for this method to throw a `RejectedRequestException`.
`void requestComplete (Request rqst)`	This method is called to indicate that the processing of a `Request` is completed.
`void reportStatistics()`	This method is called at the end of execution to provide a report of any desired statistics.
`void drawGraphic (Graphic g, int x, int y)`	This method may be called from the animation module to draw a graphic image of the `RequestProcessor`. The image will be drawn at the specified coordinates on the specified graphics canvas.

Table C.6 Request Class

`void setRequestPriority(int priority)`	Sets the priority of this `Request`. Zero is the highest priority.
`int getRequestPriority()`	Returns the priority of this `Request`.
`void setRequestType(int priority)`	Sets the type of the request to either `EXCLUSIVE_ACCESS` or `SHARED_ACCESS`. This indicates whether the `RequestProcessor` can share access for this particular `Request` with other requests. The default is `EXCLUSIVE_ACCESS`.
`int getRequestType()`	Returns the access type of this `Request`.
`void setStartWaitTime (double time)`	Called to save the time at which this `Request` starts waiting.
`int getStartWaitTime()`	Called to obtain the previously saved `StartWaitTime`.

Table C.7 Schedular Class

`Schedular(String name)`	The constructor specifies a name for this `Schedular`. It uses a queue of unbounded size.
`Schedular(String name, int qsize)`	This constructor creates a `Schedular` that works with a queue of the specified size.
`void schedule(Request newRequest)`	This method is called to place a request into the schedular's queue. This method can throw a `RejectedRequestException`.
`Request getNextRequest()`	This method returns the next `Request` to be serviced.
`void RequestComplete (Request rqst)`	This method should be called by the `RequestProcessor` to indicate that it has completed processing of the specified `Request`.
`int getNumberWaitingRequests()`	This method returns a count of the number of waiting Requests.

Table C.8 PrioritySchedular Class

`PrioritySchedular(String name, int numberPriorities, int qsize)`	This constructor creates a `PrioritySchedular` with the specified number of priorities and queue size for each priority level. Within a priority level, requests are handled on a first-come-first-served basis.
`PrioritySchedular(String name, Schedular... schedulars)`	This constructor creates a `PrioritySchedular` in which the schedular to use for each priority level is specified as arguments to the constructor or in an array.

The second form of the `PrioritySchedular` constructor allows the user to create a priority schedular, in which a different scheduling algorithm is used for each priority level. An example where this might be used is a disk request schedular that uses FCFS for high-priority requests and a performance-based algorithm (e.g., SSTF) for lower-priority requests.

Many applications will create their own schedulars. In the typical manner in which this is carried out, the schedule method places requests on the queue and `getNextRequest` searches the queue for the next `Request` to process. This will thus override `getNextRequest` to implement the desired scheduling algorithm. Typically, the schedule method is overridden only to perform some test to determine if this is a valid `Request`. Be sure that all methods in a `Schedular` class are *synchronized* to avoid possible race conditions.

C.2.9 The `IncomingRequestGenerator` Class

Many models require initial (incoming) requests to initiate processing in the system. The `IncomingRequestGenerator` class will create such requests based on a Poisson distribution. This class provides the timing of when new requests are created. The user must create a subclass that creates the actual requests (Table C.9).

Table C.9 IncomingRequestGenerator Class

`IncomingRequestGenerator (String name, SimInputs sIn)`	When you construct an `IncomingRequestGenerator`, you must provide a name and the simulation inputs.
`abstract void generateRequest(int requestNumber)`	The concrete subclass must implement this method to actually create (and schedule) an incoming request.

C.2.10 `ResourceManager`

A `ResourceManager` manages a resource—an inactive entity—such as Memory (Table C.10).

C.2.11 The `Output` Class

The `Output` class is used to create printed trace and summary reports. All of its methods are static (Table C.11).

C.2.12 Simulation Display

You can create an on-screen display of your model's activity by creating a subclass of the `Display` class. The frames of the on-screen display will typically be plots of some variables over time and possibly an animation of the model's activity. The `Display` class will automatically cause the frames of the on-screen display to be periodically updated. This is shown in Table C.12.

C.2.13 The `Plotter` Class

The `Plotter` class is an abstract subclass of `JFrame` that creates a plot of some variable over time. It is the responsibility of a concrete subclass to provide the value of the variable being plotted (Table C.13).

Table C.10 `ResourceManager` Class

`ResourceManager(String name, SimInputs sIn, int numberResources)`	When you construct a `ResourceManager`, you must provide a name, the simulation inputs, and the quantity of this type of resource in the system.
`void acquire(int qty)`	This method is called to allocate the specified quantity of this resource. If the requested quantity is unavailable, the requesting `Process` is suspended until more resources become available.
`void release(int qty)`	This method is called to release the specified quantity of the resource.
`void reportStatistics()`	This method should be called at the end of execution to provide a report of any desired statistics.

Appendix C The Java Modeling Framework

Table C.11 Output Methods

Output.setOptions (String[] args)	Called by the modelling framework to provide the command-line arguments to the Output class.
Output.newInstance()	Called from the UI to open the trace and report files.
Output.trace(double time, String msg)	Prints a line in the Trace file that has the specified simulation time and message.
Output.trace(String msg)	Prints a line in the Trace file that has the specified message.
Output.report(String msg)	Prints the specified message in both the Trace and Summary files.
Output.close()	Closes the Trace and Summary files.

Table C.12 The Display Class

Display(Input in)	The constructor for the on-screen display needs to have the input parameters passed to it.
add(JFrame frame)	Adds a frame for the on-screen display.

Table C.13 The Plotter Class

Plotter(String title, String yAxisLabel, String[] legend, int x, int y, Input in)	The constructor for a Plotter requires a title for the frame, a label for the y axis, a legend for the plot, the x and y positions for the frame, and the model input parameters.
abstract int getScale()	The concrete subclass must supply the maximum expected value for the y axis.
abstract int getPlotY()	The concrete subclass must supply the current value of the variable being plotted.
void paint(Graphics g)	Periodically called by the Display class to update the plot.

Table C.14 The `QPlotter` Class

`QPlotter(String title, String yAxisLabel, String[] legend, int x, int y, Input in, RequestProcessor process)`	The constructor for a `Plotter` requires a title for the frame, a label for the y axis, a legend for the plot, the x and y positions for the frame, the model input parameters, and the `RequestProcessor`.

C.2.14 The `QPlotter` Subclass

`QPlotter` is a concrete subclass of class `Plotter`, which plots the number of waiting requests for a `RequestProcessor` (Table C.14).

C.2.15 Animation

If animation is desired, it should be done in a class that extends `JFrame`, with that frame being added to the `Display` object's list of frames. This will cause the animation's paint method to be periodically called to redisplay the state of the model, thus providing for an animated image. Animation can use the following features:

- `QGraphic` and `SchedularGraphic` can be used to draw queues.
- A `drawGraphic` method that can be used to draw a `RequestProcessor`.

Users, of course, are free to develop their own drawing and animation features.

C.2.16 The `QGraphic` Abstract Class

`QGraphic` is an abstract class that will display a queue for an animation (see Tables C.15 and C.16).

Table C.15 `QGraphic` Constants

`LEFT`	Draws a horizontal queue with the head on the left.
`RIGHT`	Draws a horizontal queue with the head on the right.
`TOP`	Draws a vertical queue with the head at the top.
`BOTTOM`	Draws a vertical queue with the head at the bottom.

Table C.16 QGraphic Methods

`QGraphic(int x, int y, Dimension orientation)`	Create a queue image at the specified coordinates with the specified orientation.
`abstract int getQlength()`	Returns the current length of the queue.
`void paint(Graphics g)`	Must be called from the animation's paint method to repaint the queue.

Table C.17 SchedularGraphic Class

`SchedularGraphic (int x, int y, Dimension orientation, RequestProcessor process)`	Draws a queue at the specified coordinates with the specified orientation for the schedular queue of the specified `RequestProcessor`.

C.2.17 The `SchedularGraphic` Concrete Subclass

`SchedularGraphic` is a concrete subclass of `QGraphic` that will display a schedular queue. The constructor of the class is specified in Table C.17.

C.2.18 Random Number Generator Classes

There are several random number generators in the simulation package PsimJ, as shown in the subsections that follow:

C.2.18.1 The `Randint` Class

An object of class `Randint` generates random numbers from a uniform distribution between 0.0 and 1.0, as shown in Table C.18.

C.2.18.2 The `Erand` Class

An object of class `Erand` produces random numbers from an exponential probability distribution, as shown in Table C.19.

C.2.18.3 The `Normal` Class

An object of class `Normal` generates random numbers from a normal probability distribution, as shown in Table C.20.

Table C.18 `Randint` Methods

`Randint(long seed)`	Creates a random number generator, using the specified seed value.
`Randint()`	Creates a random number generator, using the processor timer for the seed. This implies that there will be a different random stream of numbers for every simulation run.
`void seed(long useed)`	Used to specify a value for a random number generator's seed.
`float fdraw()`	Produces a new random number between 0.0 and 1.0.

Table C.19 `Erand` Methods

`Erand(double emean, long seed)`	Creates an exponential random number generator with the specified mean, using the specified seed value.
`Erand(double emean)`	Creates an exponential random number generator with the specified mean, using the processor timer for the seed. This implies that there will be a different random stream of numbers for every simulation run.
`double fdraw()`	Generates a new random number using the specified exponential distribution.

C.2.18.4 The `Poisson` Class

An object of class `Poisson` produces random numbers from a Poisson distribution, as shown in Table C.21.

C.2.18.5 The `Urand` Class

An object of class `Urand` produces random numbers from a uniform distribution, as shown in Table C.22.

Table C.20 Normal Methods

`Normal(long mean, long stdev, int seed)`	Creates a normal distribution random number generator with the specified mean and standard deviation, using the specified seed value.
`Normal(long mean, long stdev)`	Creates a normal distribution random number generator with the specified mean and standard deviation, using the processor timer for the seed. This implies that there will be a different random stream of numbers for every simulation run.
`Normal(double rmean, double rstd, int seed)`	Creates a normal distribution random number generator with the specified mean and standard deviation, using the specified seed value.
`Normal(double rmean, double rstd)`	Creates a normal distribution random number generator with the specified mean and standard deviation, using the processor timer for the seed. This implies that there will be a different random stream of numbers for every simulation run.
`double fdraw()`	Produces a new random number using the specified normal distribution.

Table C.21 Poisson Methods

`Poisson(double prate, double pperiod, int seed)`	Creates a Poisson distribution random number generator with the arrival rate and period of arrivals, using the specified seed value.
`Poisson(double prate, double pperiod)`	Creates a Poisson distribution random number generator with the arrival rate and period of arrivals, using the processor timer for the seed. This implies that there will be a different random stream of numbers for every simulation run.
`float fdraw()`	Produces a new random number using the specified Poisson distribution.

Table C.22 Urand Methods

`Urand(long low, long high, long useed)`	Creates a uniform distribution random number generator with the specified low and high values, using the specified seed value.
`Urand(long low, long high)`	Creates a uniform distribution random number generator with the specified low and high values, using the processor timer for the seed. This implies that there will be a different random stream of numbers for every simulation run.
`Urand(double flow, double fhigh, long seed)`	Creates a uniform distribution random number generator with the specified low and high values, using the specified seed value.
`Urand(double flow, double fhigh)`	Creates a uniform distribution random number generator with the specified low and high values, using the processor timer for the seed. This implies that there will be a different random stream of numbers for every simulation run.
`double fdraw()`	Produces a new random number using the specified uniform distribution.

C.2.19 The `Statistic` Class

An object of the `Statistic` class is used to maintain information about a statistic of the simulation. It provides a convenient way to accumulate and report information about a model. The methods of the class are listed in Table C.23. The methods that can be used for formatting information for printing are passed one of the fields to specify the format to be used, as shown in Table C.24.

Table C.23 Statistic Class

`Statistic(String name)`	Assigns a name to statistics.
`void accumulate(double value)`	Accumulates the specified value for this statistic.
`int getNumberValues()`	Returns a count of the number of accumulated values.
`double getTotal()`	Returns the total of all accumulated values.
`double getMean()`	Returns the mean of all accumulated values.
`double getMaximum()`	Returns the maximum of all accumulated values.
`String formatTotal(NumberFormat fmt)`	Returns a total of all accumulated values formatted according to the specified format.
`String formatMean(NumberFormat fmt)`	Returns the mean of all accumulated values formatted according to the specified format.
`String formatMaximum(NumberFormat fmt)`	Returns the maximum of all accumulated values formatted according to the specified format.
`String formatRatio(double value, NumberFormat fmt)`	Returns the ratio of the total of all accumulated values divided by the specified value. The result is formatted according to the specified format.

Table C.24 Statistic Formats

`TIME`	Format for printing Time.
`INTEGER`	Format for printing an Integer.
`PERCENT`	Format for printing a percentage.

C.3 Java Coding Recommendations

When writing a Java program that uses this modeling framework, the following guidelines are recommended:

- Use the sample code on the CD as a starting point.

- Any outside objects that are needed by a class should be passed to that class (typically in the constructor).

- The methods that already exist in the framework should provide any needed functionality for communication between processes. If new methods are needed for an interaction between two processes, be absolutely sure that they are *synchronized* to avoid race conditions.

- If your model appears to do nothing or to stop operating, check that you are invoking the `start` method for each `Process` in your model. Also check that deactivated processes are being properly reactivated.

- Never use `public` instance variables. These violate encapsulation and are an invitation to make a mess of your program.

- While it is common to use `public static final` to define constants, you should NEVER use public static variables. They will make a mess of your program, and their use in a multithreaded application such as this modeling framework can also create race conditions.

C.4 The Simulation Package on CD-ROM

C.4.1 Files on the CD-ROM

The following groups of files are found on the CD-ROM provided with this book:

- The Java files with the source programs for each of the simulation models. For each model, a `jar` file is included. These are stored in the `pjava` directory.

- The PsimJ library that consists of the Java-compiled classes located in the `psimjava` subdirectory under the `pjava` directory.

C.4.2 Compiling with Java and the PsimJ Library

The Java source programs that implement simulation models that use the PsimJ package should link with the simulation package.

Your compiler options should be set to include the external library by indicating the directory where the library is located. The PsimJ library was compiled to be stored in a directory called `psimjava`.

For example, we have installed each of the simulation models on a subdirectory under the directory `pjava`. The simulation library is stored in the subdirectory `psimjava` under the directory `pjava`.

To compile a Java source program that implements a simulation model, the command is

```
javac -classpath c:\pjava *.java
```

This command will compile all the Java source files in the current subdirectory and search for the PsimJ classes in the `psimjava` subdirectory under the `pjava` directory.

The following command is used to execute the Java program, for which the name of the main class is `Acomm`:

```
java -classpath c:\pjava;. Acomm
```

When using the jGRASP development environment, the PsimJ library should be stored in a subdirectory called `psimjava` under the `classes` subdirectory under jGRASP's `extensions` directory.

In JBuilder, use Options, Configure, Library to add `psimjava` to the list of libraries that the compiler knows about. Then use Project, Properties, Required Libraries to add `psimjava` to the set of libraries to be used in this project.

C.4.3 Example Program

An example program in source code written using this modeling framework is included next. Listings C.1 through C.12 are the simulation models of disk I/O referred to in Chapter 9 and serve as a guide for developing other models.

Listing C.1 Source code of class `SimInputs` of the simulation model for Disk I/O.

```
package disksimulator;
import psimjava.*;
/**
 * <p>Title: Disk Scheduling Simulation</p>
 *
 * <p>Description: Define Input Parameters for this simulation</p>
 *
 * <p>Copyright: Copyright (c) 2004-2007</p>
 *
 * <p>Kennesaw State University </p>
 *
 * @author Rich Schlesinger
 * @version 1.0
 */
/*
```

C.4 The Simulation Package on CD-ROM

```
 * Defining the Parameters requires defining an
 * IntegerParameter, DobuleParameter, or SelectionParameter
 * (as appropriate) for each Parameter
 *    An IntegerParameter requires a Name, minimum value, maximum value,
 *        and default value
 *    A DoubleParameter requires a Name, minimum value, maximum value,
 *        and default value
 *    A SelectionParameter requires a Name, array of possible values,
 *        and default value
 */

public class SimInputs extends Input{
    static {DISPLAY_SUPPORTED=true;}
    //---------------------------------------------------------------------

    public IntegerParameter simperiod =
        new IntegerParameter("Simulation Period", 0, 1000, 400);
    //---------------------------------------------------------------------
    //
    //---------------------------------------------------------------------
    //The following 2 parameters MUST be present if the Arrivals class is used
    public IntegerParameter close_arrival =
        new IntegerParameter("Arrivals Stop", 0, 1000, 400);

    public IntegerParameter mean_int_arr =
        new IntegerParameter("Inter Arrival Time", 0, 20, 9);
    //---------------------------------------------------------------------
    //
    //---------------------------------------------------------------------
    // Model-Specific Parameters
    //
    public IntegerParameter disktracks =
        new IntegerParameter("Disk Tracks", 0, 2000, 1000);

    public IntegerParameter diskMeanSeek =
        new IntegerParameter("Seek Time", 0, 20, 8);

    public IntegerParameter rpm =
        new IntegerParameter("Disk RPM", 0, 14400, 7200);

    public IntegerParameter transRate =
        new IntegerParameter("Disk Transfer Rate", 0, 20000, 1000);

    private static final String[] algs = {"FCFS", "SSTF", "SCAN", "CSCAN"};
    public SelectionParameter algorithm =
```

```
            new SelectionParameter("Schedular", algs, "FCFS");

    private static final String[] distributionTypes = {"NORMAL","UNIFORM"};
    public SelectionParameter distType =
        new SelectionParameter("Distribution Type",distributionTypes,"UNIFORM");

    public IntegerParameter stdDev =
        new IntegerParameter("Standard Deviation", 0, 100, 20);

////////////////////////////////////////////////////////////////////////////
}
```

Listing C.2 Source code of class `DiskSim` of the simulation model for Disk I/O.

```
package disksimulator;

/**
 * <p>Title: Disk Scheduling Simulation</p>
 *
 * <p>Description: Implements Disk I/O Simulation </p>
 *
 * <p>Copyright: Copyright (c) 2004-2007</p>
 *
 * <p>Kennesaw State University </p>
 *
 * @author Rich Schlesinger
 * @version 1.0
 */
import psimjava.*;

public class DiskSim extends Model {
    // Processes to start up
    private Disk disk; // I/O device server
    private GenDiskRequests arrive;
    private static SimInputs simIn = new SimInputs();
    ////////////////////////////////////////////////////////////////////////
    public DiskSim() {
        super(simIn);
    }
    ////////////////////////////////////////////////////////////////////////
    // create and start main thread
    public static void main(String[] args) {
        Model.main(args,"Disk Scheduling");
    }
```

```
//////////////////////////////////////////////////////////////////
// Called to begin the simulation
public void begin() {
    modelBegin(simIn);
    disk = new Disk("Disk", simIn);
    arrive = new GenDiskRequests("Arrivals ", simIn, disk);
    start();
    if (Model.isDisplayRequested()) {
        new SimDisplay(simIn, arrive, disk);
    }
}
//////////////////////////////////////////////////////////////////
// Main body of the simulation
public void Main_body() {
    // I/O device object
    disk.start();
    // create the Arrivals process, which will itself create
    // the arriving jobs. All jobs are of the same type
    arrive.start();
    startSimulation();
} // end Main_body
//
// display output on summary file
//////////////////////////////////////////////////////////////////
// Print out final statistics
public void reportStatistics() {
    arrive.reportStatistics();
    DiskRequest.reportStatistics();
    disk.reportStatistics();
}
} // end class DiskSim
```

Listing C.3 Source code of class `GenDiskRequests` of the simulation model for disk I/O.

```
package disksimulator;
/**
 * <p>Title: Disk Scheduling Simulation</p>
 *
 * <p>Description: Generates Incoming Disk I/O Requests </p>
 *
 * <p>Copyright: Copyright (c) 2004-2007</p>
 *
 * <p>Kennesaw State University </p>
 *
```

```java
 * @author Rich Schlesinger
 * @version 1.0
 */
import psimjava.*;

public class GenDiskRequests extends IncomingRequestGenerator {
    // Input Parameters

    // References
    private Disk disk;
    private RandomGenerator nDisksergen; // random disk track
    private Urand diskRequestSizegen; // random DiskRequest size

    // Computed Values
    private int numBytes; // DiskRequest transfer size
    private int desiredTrack;
    private int arrived;

    ////////////////////////////////////////////////////////////////////////
    public GenDiskRequests(String s, SimInputs sIn, Disk disk) {
        super(s, sIn);
        this.disk = disk;
        // create objects for generation of random variables

        if (sIn.distType.getValue().equals("NORMAL")) {
            nDisksergen = new Normal(disk.getNumberTracks() / 2,
                                    sIn.stdDev.getValue());
        }
        else {
            nDisksergen = new Urand(0, disk.getNumberTracks());
        }
        diskRequestSizegen = new Urand(1, disk.getBytesPerTrack());
    }

    ////////////////////////////////////////////////////////////////////////
    // Create a Disk I/O Request
    protected void generateRequest(int requestNum) {
        arrived = requestNum;
        // Generate desired track and number bytes
        desiredTrack = (int) nDisksergen.draw();
        // Make sure track number is in proper range
        desiredTrack = Math.max(Math.min(desiredTrack, disk.getNumberTracks()), 0);

        // Generate size of I/O request
        numBytes = (int) diskRequestSizegen.draw();
```

C.4 The Simulation Package on CD-ROM 453

```
        // Create and schedule this Disk request
        DiskRequest diskRequest = new DiskRequest(requestNum,
                                                  desiredTrack,
                                                  numBytes,
                                                  get_clock());
        try {
            disk.schedule(diskRequest);
        }
        catch (RejectedRequestException e) {
            // No requests ever rejected in this model
        }
    }
    //////////////////////////////////////////////////////////////////////
    public void reportStatistics() {
        Output.report("Total number of I/O requests arrived: " +
                      arrived);
    }

}
```

Listing C.4 Source code of class `DiskRequest` of the simulation model for disk I/O.

```
package disksimulator;
import psimjava.*;
/**
 * <p>Title: Disk Scheduling Simulation</p>
 *
 * <p>Description: Implements Disk Request </p>
 *
 * <p>Copyright: Copyright (c) 2004-2007</p>
 *
 * <p>Kennesaw State University </p>
 *
 * @author Rich Schlesinger
 * @version 1.0
 */
public class DiskRequest extends Request {
    private int track; // Track to seek to
    private int numBytes; // Number bytes to transfer

    private double arrivalTime; // arrival time of request
    private double startTime; // time disk starts processing request
```

```
private static Statistic waitTime = new Statistic("Wait Time");
// request sojourn time
private static Statistic sojournTime = new Statistic("Sojourn Time");


////////////////////////////////////////////////////////////////////
public DiskRequest(long requestNum, int track, int numBytes,
                   double arrivalTime) {
    super("Request " + requestNum);
    this.arrivalTime = arrivalTime;
    this.track = track; // Track number to move to
    this.numBytes = numBytes; // Number bytes to transfer
    Output.trace(arrivalTime, getName() +
                        " arrives for track " + track +
                        ", bytes =" + numBytes);
}


////////////////////////////////////////////////////////////////////
// Get track number
public int getTrack() {
    return track;
}


////////////////////////////////////////////////////////////////////
// Get number bytes
public int getNumberBytes() {
    return numBytes;
}


////////////////////////////////////////////////////////////////////
// Called upon completion of this request
public void requestComplete(double completionTime) {
    Output.trace(completionTime, "Completed " + getName());
    // request sojourn time
    sojournTime.accumulate(completionTime - arrivalTime);
    waitTime.accumulate(startTime - arrivalTime); // request wait time
}


////////////////////////////////////////////////////////////////////
public static int getCompleted() {
    return sojournTime.getNumberOfValues();
}


////////////////////////////////////////////////////////////////////
// Called at end of simulation to report accumulated statistics
public static void reportStatistics() {
```

```
            int completedRequests = sojournTime.getNumberOfValues();
            Output.report("Throughput:   " + completedRequests);

            if (completedRequests > 0) {
                Output.report("Disk Request " +
                  sojournTime.formatMean(Statistic.TIME));
            }
        }
    }
}
```

Listing C.5 Source code of class `Disk` of the simulation model for disk I/O.

```
package disksimulator;
import psimjava.*;
/**
 * <p>Title: Disk Scheduling Simulation</p>
 *
 * <p>Description: Implements Disk Request Processor</p>
 *
 * <p>Copyright: Copyright (c) 2004-2007</p>
 *
 * <p>Kennesaw State University </p>
 *
 * @author Rich Schlesinger
 * @version 1.0
 */
import psimjava.*;
import java.text.DecimalFormat;

//
public class Disk extends RequestProcessor {
    // Simulation Parameters
    private int numberTracks; // number tracks on this disk
    private int RPM; // mean time to rotate into position
    private double transferRate; // Disk transfer rate

    // References
    private DiskRequest currentDiskRequest; // DiskRequest currently being serviced
    private Urand rotationGenerator;

    // Calculated values
    private double singleTrackSeekTime; // Time to seek a single track
    private static final int bytesPerTrack = 10000;
```

```java
// Current values
private int currentTrack; // Current track position
// formatting string;
private static final DecimalFormat fmt = new DecimalFormat("0.###");
////////////////////////////////////////////////////////////////////////
// Create disk and its associated attributes
public Disk(String s, SimInputs sIn) {
    super(s,sIn);
    setSchedular(getSchedular(sIn.algorithm.getValue()));

    numberTracks = sIn.disktracks.getValue();
    // Arm starts in middle of disk
    currentTrack = numberTracks / 2;
    singleTrackSeekTime = 8.0 / numberTracks;
    RPM = sIn.rpm.getValue();
    rotationGenerator = new Urand(0.0, 1000.0 / (RPM / 60));
    transferRate = sIn.transRate.getValue();
}

////////////////////////////////////////////////////////////////////////
// Creates the Schedular for this simulation
private Schedular getSchedular(String alg) {
    Schedular sched=null;
    if (alg.equals("FCFS")) {
        sched = new FCFSschedular();
    }
    else if (alg.equals("SSTF")) {
        sched = new SSTFschedular(this);
    }
    else if (alg.equals("SCAN")) {
        sched = new SCANschedular(this);
    }
    else if (alg.equals("CSCAN")) {
        sched = new CSCANschedular(this);
    }
    return sched;
}
////////////////////////////////////////////////////////////////////////
public int getNumberTracks() {
    return numberTracks;
}
```

```
////////////////////////////////////////////////////////////////////////
public int getBytesPerTrack() {
    return bytesPerTrack;
}


////////////////////////////////////////////////////////////////////////
public int getCurrentTrack() {
    return currentTrack;
}


////////////////////////////////////////////////////////////////////////
// Process a disk I/O request
protected void serviceRequest(Request request) {
    currentDiskRequest = (DiskRequest)request;
    Output.trace(get_clock(), get_name() + " starting to service " +
                 currentDiskRequest.get_name());
    double seekTime = singleTrackSeekTime *
        Math.abs(currentTrack - currentDiskRequest.getTrack());
    double transferTime = currentDiskRequest.getNumberBytes() /
        transferRate;
    Output.trace(get_clock(),
                 "Moving to track " + currentDiskRequest.getTrack());
    double rotationalLatency = rotationGenerator.fdraw();
    Output.trace(get_clock(), "Seek Time=" + seekTime +
                 " latency=" + fmt.format(rotationalLatency) +
                 " transfer time=" + transferTime);
    currentDiskRequest.setWaitStartTime(get_clock());
    delay(seekTime);
    currentTrack = currentDiskRequest.getTrack();
    // Delay for rotational latency
    delay(rotationalLatency);
    // delay for data transfer
    delay(transferTime);
    currentDiskRequest.requestComplete(get_clock());
    requestComplete(currentDiskRequest);
}
}
```

Listing C.6 Source code of class CSCANschedular of the simulation model for disk I/O.

```
package disksimulator;
import psimjava.*;
/**
 * <p>Title: Disk Scheduling Simulation</p>
```

```
 * <p>Description: Implements Circular SCAN scheduling algorithm</p>
 * <p>Copyright: Copyright (c) 2004-2007</p>
 * <p>Kennesaw State University </p>
 * @author Rich Schlesinger
 * @version 1.0
 */
public class CSCANschedular extends SCANschedular {
    private Disk disk;
    public CSCANschedular(Disk disk) {
        super("CSCAN");
        this.disk = disk;
    }
    /**
     * Return next request to be processed
     * Scan for nearest request in Forward direction
     *     If none found, re-scan starting at track 0
     * @return DiskRequest to be processed (or null if none pending)
     */
    public synchronized Request getNextRequest() {
        // Immediate return if no pending requests
        if (requests.size() == 0) {
            return null;
        }
        currentTrack = disk.getCurrentTrack();
        // Scan for nearest request ahead of us
        DiskRequest nextRequest = scan(FORWARD);
        if (nextRequest == null) {
            //No request found ahead of us
            //Restart at track 0
            currentTrack = 0;
            nextRequest = scan(FORWARD);
        }
        return nextRequest;
    }
}
```

Listing C.7 Source code of class **SCANschedular** of the simulation model for disk I/O.

```
package disksimulator;
import psimjava.*;

/**
 * <p>Title: Disk Scheduling Simulation</p>
 *
 * <p>Description: Implements SCAN scheduling algorithm</p>
```

```
 *
 * <p>Copyright: Copyright (c) 2004-2007</p>
 *
 * <p>Kennesaw State University </p>
 *
 * @author Rich Schlesinger
 * @version 1.0
 */
public class SCANschedular extends Schedular {
    protected static final int FORWARD  = +1;
    protected static final int BACKWARD = -1;
    private int direction = FORWARD;

    protected int currentTrack;
    private Disk disk;

    public SCANschedular(Disk disk) {
        super("SCAN");
        this.disk = disk;
    }
    ////////////////////////////////////////////////////////////////////
    public SCANschedular(String name) {
        super(name);
    }
    ////////////////////////////////////////////////////////////////////
    /**
     * Return next request to be processed
     * Scan queue looking for nearest request in current direction
     *    If none found, reverse direction and repeat scan
     * @return DiskRequest to be processed (or null if none pending)
     */
    public synchronized Request getNextRequest() {
        // Immediate return if no pending requests
        if (requests.size() == 0) {
            return null;
        }
        currentTrack = disk.getCurrentTrack();
        // Scan for request in the current direction
        DiskRequest nextRequest = scan(direction);
        if (nextRequest == null) {
            //No request in current direction
            //Reverse direction and look for request
            direction = -direction;
            nextRequest = scan(direction);
        }
```

```java
            updateSchedularInfo(nextRequest);
            return nextRequest;
        }
        //////////////////////////////////////////////////////////////////////
        // Scans request queue in one direction or the other
        protected DiskRequest scan(int direction) {
            //looking for nearest request that is > current position
            int requestDistance;

            DiskRequest closestRequest = null;
            int closestDistance = Integer.MAX_VALUE / 2;

            for (Request d1 : requests) {
                DiskRequest d = (DiskRequest)d1;
                requestDistance = direction * (d.getTrack() - currentTrack);
                //If requestDistance is negative, then it is in the opposite direction
                if ( (requestDistance >= 0) & (requestDistance < closestDistance)) {
                    closestDistance = requestDistance;
                    closestRequest = d;
                }
            }
            requests.remove(closestRequest);
            return closestRequest;
        }
    }
```

Listing C.8 Source code of class `SSTFschedular` of the simulation model for disk I/O.

```java
package disksimulator;
import psimjava.*;
/**
 * <p>Title: Disk Scheduling Simulation</p>
 * <p>Description: Implements SSTF scheduling algorithm</p>
 * <p>Copyright: Copyright (c) 2004-2007</p>
 * <p>Kennesaw State University </p>
 * @author Rich Schlesinger
 * @version 1.0
 */
public class SSTFschedular extends Schedular {
    private Disk disk;
    public SSTFschedular(Disk disk) {
        super("SSTF");
        this.disk = disk;
    }
```

```
////////////////////////////////////////////////////////////////////////////
/**
 * Return next request to be processed
 * Searches queue for request nearest to current position
 * @return DiskRequest to be processed (or null if none pending)
 */
public synchronized Request getNextRequest() {
    // If no pending requests, return null
    if (requests.size() == 0) {
        return null;
    }
    int requestDistance;
    int currentTrack = disk.getCurrentTrack();
    Request closestRequest = null;
    int closestDistance = Integer.MAX_VALUE / 2;

    // Scan list looking for request with minimum distance
    // from current position
    for (Request d : requests) {
        requestDistance = Math.abs(((DiskRequest)d).getTrack() - currentTrack);
        if (requestDistance < closestDistance) {
            // Found a closer request
            closestDistance = requestDistance;
            closestRequest = d;
        }
    }
    // Remove desired request from list
    requests.remove(closestRequest);
    updateSchedularInfo(closestRequest);
    return closestRequest;
}
}
```

Listing C.9 Source code of class `SimDisplay` of the simulation model for disk I/O.

```
package disksimulator;
import psimjava.*;

/**
 * <p>Title: Disk Scheduling Simulation</p>
 *
 * <p>Description: Creates overall Graphic display</p>
 *
 * <p>Copyright: Copyright (c) 2004-2007</p>
```

```
 *
 * <p>Kennesaw State University </p>
 *
 * @author Rich Schlesinger
 * @version 1.0
 */
public class SimDisplay extends Display {
    private static final int frameWidth = 700;
    private static final int frameHeight = 400;

    public SimDisplay(SimInputs simIn, GenDiskRequests arrive, Disk disk) {
        super(simIn);

        String[] legend = simIn.getFormattedInputParameters();

        // Create activity animation
        add(85, 25, new Animation(simIn,arrive, disk));

        // Plot the Pending request queue
        add(500, 450, new QPlotter("Pending I/O Requests vs Simulation time",
                                   "Pending I/O Requests",
                                   legend,
                                   frameWidth,
                                   frameHeight,
                                   simIn,
                                   disk));

        // Plot the disk arm movement
        add(10, 450, new ArmPlotter(legend,
                                    frameWidth,
                                    frameHeight,
                                    simIn,
                                    disk));

    }
}
```

Listing C.10 Source code of class `Animation` of the simulation model for disk I/O.

```
package disksimulator;
import psimjava.*;
import javax.swing.JFrame;
import java.awt.Color;
import java.awt.Graphics;
```

```java
/**
 * <p>Title: Disk Scheduling Simulation</p>
 *
 * <p>Description: Class to display an animation of the disk operation</p>
 *
 * <p>Copyright: Copyright (c) 2004-2007</p>
 *
 * <p>Kennesaw State University: </p>
 *
 * @author Rich Schlesinger
 * @version 1.0
 */
////////////////////////////////////////////////////////////////////////
public class Animation extends JFrame {
    private static final int FrameWidth = 700;
    private static final int FrameHeight = 400;

    private SchedularGraphic qDraw;
    private ClockGraphic clockDraw; // elapsed-time clock
    private DiskGraphic diskDraw; // Disk graphic

    private static final int DISK_WIDTH = 200;
    private static final int DISK_HEIGHT = 100;
    private int DISK_x = FrameWidth - DISK_WIDTH - 20;
    private int DISK_y = (FrameHeight - DISK_HEIGHT) / 2 + 20;

    private GenDiskRequests arrive;
    private Disk disk;

    public Animation(SimInputs theInputs, GenDiskRequests arrive, Disk disk) {
        super("Disk I/O Animation");
        this.arrive = arrive;
        this.disk = disk;

        setSize(FrameWidth, FrameHeight);

        //Create the graphics to be shown on the Animation

        // Simulation clock
        clockDraw = new ClockGraphic(420, 50, theInputs.simperiod.getValue());

        // The disk
        diskDraw = new DiskGraphic(DISK_x, DISK_y, DISK_WIDTH, DISK_HEIGHT,
                                   disk);
```

Appendix C The Java Modeling Framework

```
            // The disk Schedular Queue
            qDraw = new SchedularGraphic(DISK_x - 50,
                                        DISK_y + DISK_HEIGHT / 2 -
                                        QGraphic.QH / 2,
                                        SchedularGraphic.RIGHT,
                                        disk);

        setBackground(Color.white);

    }

    //---------------------------------------------------------------------
    public void paint(Graphics g) {
        //MUST call the JFrame's paint method
        super.paint(g);

        // Display the various status info
        String mssgArrived = "Arrived: " + arrive.getArrived();
        String mssgCompleted = "Completed: " + DiskRequest.getCompleted();
        String mssgIOq = "I/O queue: " + disk.getNumberWaitingRequests();

        // setBackground(Color.lightGray);
        g.drawString(mssgArrived, 50, 150);
        g.drawString(mssgCompleted, 545, 150);
        g.drawString(mssgIOq, 300, DISK_y + DISK_HEIGHT);

        // Repaint each of the animation objects
        clockDraw.paint(g);
        diskDraw.paint(g);
        qDraw.paint(g);

    }
}
```

Listing C.11 Source code of class `ArmPlotter` of the simulation model for disk I/O.

```
package disksimulator;
import psimjava.*;
/**
 * <p>Title: Disk Scheduling Simulation</p>
 *
 * <p>Description: Class to dplot the arm position</p>
 *
```

```
 * <p>Copyright: Copyright (c) 2004-2007</p>
 *
 * <p>Kennesaw State University: </p>
 *
 * @author Rich Schlesinger
 * @version 1.0
 */
////////////////////////////////////////////////////////////////////////
class ArmPlotter extends Plotter {
    Disk disk;

    // Create the Arm plot graphic by subclassing the Plotter class
    public ArmPlotter(String[] legend,
                      int x,
                      int y,
                      SimInputs simIn,
                      Disk disk) {
        super("Disk Arm Position vs Simulation time",
              "Disk Track",
              legend, x, y, simIn);
        this.disk = disk;

    }
    ////////////////////////////////////////////////////////////////////////
    // Return the current track number to be used as the
    // Y coordinate for the plot
    public int getPlotY() {
        return disk.getCurrentTrack();
    }
    ////////////////////////////////////////////////////////////////////////
    // Return the number of tracks for the scale on the Y axis
    public int getScale() {
        return disk.getNumberTracks();
    }
}
```

Listing C.12 Source code of class `DiskGraphic` of the simulation model for disk I/O.

```
package disksimulator;

import java.awt.*;

/**
 * <p>Title: Disk Scheduling Simulation</p>
```

```java
 *
 * <p>Description:Display a graphic of a disk (with arm) </p>
 *
 * <p>Copyright: Copyright (c) 2004-2007</p>
 *
 * <p>Kennesaw State University </p>
 *
 * @author Rich Schlesinger
 * @version 1.0
 */
public class DiskGraphic {
    // Position, size info for the disk
    private int x;
    private int y;
    private int width;
    private int height;
    private int thickness = 5;

    // Position, size info for the disk spindle
    private int spindle_x;
    private int spindle_y;
    private int spindle_width;
    private int spindle_height;
    private int spindleOval_height;

    // Info from the simulated disk
    private Disk disk;
    private int numberTracks;

    // Arm drawing parameters
    private int xArm;
    private int yArm;
    private int heightArm;
    private int widthArm;
    private int backArmWidth,backArmHeight;
    private Polygon arm = new Polygon();

    private int arcAngle = 180;

    private static final Color spindleColor = Color.MAGENTA;
    /**
     * Object to represent rotating disk (with moving arm)
     * @param x int      - x position of disk image
     * @param y int      - y position of disk image
     * @param width int  - width of disk image
```

C.4 The Simulation Package on CD-ROM

```
 * @param height int - height of disk image
 * @param disk Disk  - the disk that this animation represents
 */
public DiskGraphic(int x, int y, int width, int height, Disk disk) {
    this.x = x;
    this.y = y;
    this.width = width;
    this.height = height;
    this.disk = disk;

    spindle_width = width / 20;
    spindle_height = height / 2;
    spindle_x = x + width / 2 - spindle_width / 2;
    spindle_y = y;

    spindleOval_height = (int) ( (float) height / width * spindle_width);

    numberTracks = disk.getNumberTracks();
    xArm = x - 5;
    yArm = y + height / 2;
    heightArm = height / 15;
    backArmWidth = heightArm-2;
    backArmHeight = backArmWidth;
}

////////////////////////////////////////////////////////////////////////
public void paint(Graphics g) {
    arcAngle = (arcAngle + 4) % 360;

    //Side & bottom of platter
    g.setColor(Color.BLACK);
    g.fillOval(x, y + thickness, width, height);

    // Line on surface to give illusion of movement
    g.setColor(Color.WHITE);
    g.fillArc(x, y + thickness, width, height, arcAngle, 1);

    // Top surface of platter
    g.setColor(Color.LIGHT_GRAY);
    g.fillOval(x, y, width, height);

    // Line on surface to give illusion of movement
    g.setColor(Color.RED);
    g.fillArc(x, y, width, height, arcAngle, 1);
```

```java
        // Bottom curve of spindle
        g.setColor(spindleColor);
        g.fillOval(spindle_x,
                    spindle_y + spindle_height - spindleOval_height / 2,
                    spindle_width, spindleOval_height);
        g.setColor(Color.BLACK);
        g.drawOval(spindle_x,
                    spindle_y + spindle_height - spindleOval_height / 2,
                    spindle_width, spindleOval_height);
        // Spindle body
        g.setColor(spindleColor);
        g.fillRect(spindle_x, spindle_y, spindle_width, spindle_height);
        // Top oval of spindle
        g.setColor(spindleColor);
        g.fillOval(spindle_x,
                    spindle_y - spindleOval_height / 2,
                    spindle_width, spindleOval_height);
        g.setColor(Color.BLACK);
        g.drawOval(spindle_x,
                    spindle_y - spindleOval_height / 2,
                    spindle_width, spindleOval_height);
        // arc on spindle top to give illusion of movement
        g.setColor(Color.RED);
        g.fillArc(spindle_x,
                    spindle_y - spindleOval_height / 2,
                    spindle_width, spindleOval_height,
                    arcAngle, 45);

        //Disk Arm
        drawArm(g);
    }
    private void drawArm(Graphics g) {
        // Create a polygon to represent the current arm shape
        widthArm = (width / 2) * disk.getCurrentTrack() / numberTracks;
        arm.reset();
        arm.addPoint(xArm,yArm);
        arm.addPoint(xArm,yArm+heightArm);
        arm.addPoint(xArm+widthArm,yArm+heightArm);
        arm.addPoint(xArm+widthArm+backArmWidth,yArm+heightArm-backArmHeight);
        arm.addPoint(xArm+widthArm+backArmWidth,yArm-backArmHeight);
        arm.addPoint(xArm+backArmWidth,yArm-backArmHeight);

        g.setColor(Color.CYAN);
        g.fillPolygon(arm);
```

```
        arm.addPoint(xArm,yArm);
        arm.addPoint(xArm+widthArm,yArm);
        arm.addPoint(xArm+widthArm+backArmWidth,yArm-backArmHeight);
        arm.addPoint(xArm+widthArm,yArm);
        arm.addPoint(xArm+widthArm,yArm+heightArm);
        g.setColor(Color.BLACK);

        // Draw the arm
        g.drawPolyline(arm.xpoints,arm.ypoints,arm.npoints);
    }
}
```

Appendix D
Psim3

D.1 The Psim3 Library

The Psim3 simulation library is a set of C++ classes that implements the mechanisms necessary to carry out simulation runs using the object-oriented approach. The original meaning of Psim was "process simulation." For constructing simulation models, these library classes provide the following facilities:

- The definition of active objects, which are instantiations of subclasses of class *process*.

- The starting of a simulation run that will execute for a predetermined period, called the simulation period.

- The generation of random numbers, each from specified probability distribution.

Every user program that implements a simulation model with the Psim3 library needs to include the header file, `proc.h` as follows:

```
#include "proc.h"
```

This gives the simulation model access to all the class specifications in the basic Psim3 library. The most important class in the library is class `process`. An active object in a simulation model is an object of a user-defined subclass of class `process`. Note that in Psim3, an active object is also referred to as a `process`.

D.1.1 The Time Dimension

Time is treated as a dense number; the type chosen for these values are of type `double` in C++. In all implementations using Psim3, variables that refer to time need to be of type `double`. For example, to assign a variable `current_time`, the time of the system clock, the following syntax is used:

```
double current_time;
...
current_time = get_clock();   // get the time of system clock
```

D.1.2 Defining Active Objects

A simulation model in Psim3 must define one or more subclasses of the Psim3 class `process`. The active objects are then created as instances of these subclasses. To define an active object in a simulation model implemented in C++, the program must define a class with an appropriate name and inherit the `process` class from the Psim3 library. For example:

```
class server: public process {
   // private features
   ...
public:
   server( char *serv_name);     // constructor
   Main_body(void);
   // other public features
};
```

The code definition in a simulation model defines a subclass, called *server*, that inherits the `process` class from the Psim3 library. The public qualifier used to inherit the library class allows access to all the features of the `process` class. As any other class, class `server` includes definitions of its private features (data members and member functions) and its public features. All instances of the defined class `server` will behave as active objects.

Two of the public features defined above are important and must be included in every class that represents an active object in the simulation model:

- The constructor (`server`), which is an operation that is executed when an object of the class is created. The only parameter required is a character string for the name of the active object.

- The function, `Main_body`, which is present in every subclass of class `process` in the simulation model. This function defines all the activities that are to be carried out by the active objects of this subclass. The name of this function (`Main_body`) is pre-defined for all subclasses of class `process`.

D.1.3 Running a Simulation

To define a simulation, a C++ program that implements a simulation model needs to declare and create an object of class *simulation* in its main function. The instantiation of this class requires a title for the simulation model. This is another Psim3 library class that a model needs to access. The following is an example of an instantiation of the simulation class:

```
simulation srun("Simple Batch System");
```

The C++ statement declares and creates an object called *srun*. The object created includes the title of the model, or the object can be used as a title for the simulation run (i.e., every simulation run can have a different title).

To start a simulation run and to let it execute for a specified period, the member function, `start_sim`, must be invoked from the object of class simulation created above, as in the following example:

```
double simperiod = 450.75;
...
srun.start_sim(simperiod);
```

The first line declares a variable, `simperiod`, of type `double`. This variable represents the simulation period for the simulation run. Recall that all variables and objects that refer to the time dimension must be declared with this type. The `simperiod` variable is used in the second C++ statement above as a parameter when invoking the `start_sim` member function that belongs to `srun` (which is an object of the simulation class). In this case, the simulation runs for 450.75 time units.

Instead of an object of class *simulation*, a pointer of class `simulation` can be declared and initialized by creating an object of class `simulation`. For example:

```
simulation *srun;
...
srun = new simulation("Simple Batch System");
...
srun->start_sim(simperiod);
```

After the simulation run completes, the C++ program normally computes the summary statistics as final results and displays these results.

D.1.4 Features in Class process

When a user defines a subclass of class `process` in a simulation model, the subclass will have access to all the features inherited from the Psim3 `process` class. These features are specified in the `proc.h` header file. Some of these features are inherited from upper-level base classes. An active object is an instantiation of a user-defined subclass of the Psim3 class `process`.

Only the public features are discussed here. The features that follow are briefly discussed with examples. The user should refer to the `proc.h` header file.

D.1.4.1 Name of an Active Object

The name of an active object is assigned when this object is created using the constructor. The only parameter required in the constructor is the name. The t_name data member is a pointer to a character string with the name of the active object. For example, consider class server, a subclass of the Psim3 class process. The following code displays the name of an active object of class server:

```
server * mach1;
...
mach1 = new server("machine_A"); // create new server
...
cout << "Name of process: " <<  mach1->t_name << endl;
```

In the code, mach1 is the reference to an object of type server. A new object is created and assigned to this reference. In the last line, the name of the object (referenced by mach1) is displayed on the screen. To display the name of an active object, use t_name as follows:

```
cout << "Name of this active object: " << t_name << "\n";
```

D.1.4.2 The Simulation Clock

As stated above, the time dimension uses type double in C++. The simulation clock has the current time of the simulation. To access the simulation clock, the get_clock Psim3 library function must be used, as in the following example:

```
double arrival_time;
...
arrival_time = get_clock();
```

The arrival_time variable is declared of type double, and it gets the value returned by the function get_clock.

D.1.4.3 Priority of an Active Object

The priority of an active object is an integer value and represents its relative importance in relation to other processes. The highest priority value is 0. Psim3 supports priority values up to 3. To access the priority of an active process, the member function get_prio must be invoked. For example, to access the priority of another active object, invoke the function in the following manner:

```
server * mach1;
...
int s_prio;
s_prio = mach1->get_prio();
```

The first line declares a pointer to an active object of class server. The next line declares an integer variable to store the priority of the object. The third line invokes the `get_prio` member function in the object referenced by `mach1` and assigns it to the integer variable `s_prio`.

To set the priority of an active object, the object must invoke the `set_prio` member function with an integer parameter. For example, suppose an active object needs to set its priority to 1. The following C++ statement sets the active object's priority to 1:

```
set_prio(1);
```

Now suppose that an active object needs to increase the value of its priority by 1. The following statements accomplish this:

```
int my_priority;
...
my_priority = get_prio();     // get current priority
my_priority++;                // increment current priority
set_prio(my_priority);        // set new priority
```

D.1.4.4 States of an Active Object

There are three predefined states for an active object: IDLE, RUNNING, and TERMINATED. The state of an active object cannot be directly set since the simulation executive directly controls the scheduling of active objects. However, the state of an active object can be accessed by the `rdstate` member function. When invoked, this function returns any of the previously mentioned values. The function is normally called (or invoked) to check the state of an active object (process). For example, the following statement checks if active object `mach1` is in the RUNNING state:

```
server * mach1;
if ( mach1->rdstate() == RUNNING) {
   // carry out some activities if true
   ...
}
```

Note that in Psim3, an active object is also referred to as a process. To facilitate the implementation of processes, another member function, `idle`, is also provided in the Psim3 library. This function tests if the process is idle and returns true or false. The following is the easiest way to check if a process is idle:

```
if (! mach1->idle()) {
   // activities if process is not idle
   ...
}
```

Another similar member function provided in the Psim3 library is the function *pending*. This function returns true if the process is not terminated; otherwise it returns false.

D.1.5 Scheduling a Process

The dynamic behavior of a system is dependent on the scheduling of processes during an observation period or the simulation period. To schedule a process means to place it in an event list with a time stamp so that the simulation executive will execute its appropriate phase when the system clock reaches that time.

The `delay` member function is used for this type of scheduling in Psim3. For example, suppose a process is to be scheduled 5.65 time units from the current clock time. The following line of code implements this scheduling:

```
delay(5.65);
```

The delay member function will normally place the process in the event list to be executed at 5.65 time units from the current simulation time. The simulation executive will resume execution of this process after 5.65 time units from the current clock time.

The delay operation is applied to simulate an activity that has a certain time duration, or to simulate a wait activity. This function is also used to reactivate a process that has been suspended. For example, assume that a process referenced by `mach1` has been suspended; another process can reactivate it using a delay with a value of 0.0, as in the following example:

```
server *mach1;
...
mach1->delay(0.0);   // reactivate barber
```

Process `mach1` of type `server` will now be reactivated, which means scheduling the process now. This process will change its state from IDLE to RUNNING.

D.1.6 Suspending a Process

When a process has to suspend itself or another process, it invokes the `suspend` member function. This function takes the process away from the event list (if it has been scheduled) and changes its state from RUNNING to IDLE. In many practical cases, a suspended process is placed in a queue. For example, the following C++ code suspends the process `mach1` (defined above):

```
mach1->suspend(); // suspend barber
```

In Psim3 there are two other member functions of class `process` that can also suspend a process: `deactivate` and `sleep`. Refer to the header file `proc.h`.

D.1.7 Interrupting a Process

A process can interrupt another process that is carrying out some activity. The interrupting process uses an interrupt level (an integer). The interrupted process senses the interrupt and examines the *interrupted* data member, which has the value of the interrupt level. The function member `p_interrupt` interrupts the process and returns the remaining time left for the current interrupted activity. The following C++ code shows how to interrupt process `barber` with interrupt level 2.

```
int int_lev = 2;   // interrupt level
double rem_time;
rem_time = mach1->p_interrupt(int_lev);
```

As before, the type for the remaining time variable, `rem_time`, is `double`. This value may be useful to control the interval that the interrupted process will continue to execute when it is allowed to resume its activities.

The interrupted process will decide what instructions to execute when it receives the interrupt; the decision is based on the value of the interrupt level by invoking the `int_level` member function. The C++ code that follows implements the interrupt activities for the interrupted process:

```
int int_lev;                   // interrupt level
...
delay(act_period);
int_lev = int_level();         // get the interrupt level
if (interrupted == 2) {        // process interrupted with level 2
    int_time = get_clock();    // carry out some task
    ...
}
else {
    ...                        // otherwise, carry out another task
}
```

The value of 0 for the `interrupted` data member means that there was no interruption during the activities of the process, which has a normal duration period, `act_period`.

D.1.8 Terminating a Process

A process can terminate itself or terminate another process. The function member `terminate` is invoked to terminate a process normally. In the following line of code, a process terminates itself:

```
terminate();
```

D.2 The Queue Library

D.2.1 General Description

The queue library provides two queue classes and is designed to be used with the basic Psim3 library. A simulation model that requires simple queues or priority queues must access these queue classes. The queue library provides two classes:

- The `squeue` class for simple queues
- The `pqueue` class for priority queues

All simulation models that use queues must include the `queue.h` header file at the top of the program. This gives the program implementing the simulation model access to the queue classes, as in this example:

```
#include "queue.h"
```

D.2.2 Features of Class `squeue`

The most relevant features of the class `squeue` for simple queues are the following:

- The constructor for creating a simple queue requires the name of the queue and the queue size. This last parameter is optional; if not included, the assigned default size is 1000. For example, the following C++ statements declare and create a simple queue, `serv_queue` with an assigned name "Server Queue" and a size of 15 jobs:

    ```
    squeue *serv_queue;      // declare simple queue
    ...
    // now create simple queue
    serv_queue = new squeue("Server Queue", 15);
    ```

- To get the current size of a simple queue, the `length` function is provided. This function returns an integer value that corresponds to the current length of the queue. For example, to get the current length of `serv_queue` (defined above), a process uses the following statements:

    ```
    int serv_length;                         // length of server queue
    serv_length = serv_queue->length(); // get queue length
    ```

- To check for the general states of the queue, empty or full, the `full` and `empty` functions are provided. These functions return a Boolean value (true or false). For example, to check if `serv_queue` (defined above) is full, a process uses the following C++ statements:

```
if( serv_queue->full()) {
   // if queue is full execute instructions here
   ...
}
else
   // queue is not full
   ...
```

In a similar manner, the empty function checks if a queue is empty.

- The function `into` is used to insert a process into a simple queue. The only parameter required by this function is the process to insert; this process becomes the new process at the tail of the queue. The size of the queue is increased by one. For example to insert process `serv_obj` into the simple queue, `serv_queue`, another process uses the following C++ statements:

   ```
   server *serv_obj; // reference to a server process
   ...
   // enqueue server process
   serv_queue->into(serv_obj);
   ```

- The function `out` removes the process from the head of a simple queue. This function requires no parameters. The size of the queue is reduced by one, as a result of this operation. For example, to remove a `server` process from `serv_queue` and assign a reference `serv_obj` to it, a process uses the following statement:

   ```
   serv_obj = (server*) serv_queue->out();
   ```

   The casting for pointer to `server` is necessary to specify the type of the process dequeued.

For special scheduling that may be needed in some simulation models, the following functions, which do not follow the conventional rules for queue processing, are provided:

- The function `last` removes the last process inserted to the queue (i.e., the process at the tail of the queue). This is an abnormal operation; the usual operation is to remove the process at the head of the queue. This function requires no parameters. For example, to remove a `server` process from the tail of `serv_queue` (the last process inserted) and assign a reference `serv_obj` to it, a process uses the following statement:

   ```
   serv_obj = (server*) serv_queue->last();
   ```

- The function `back` inserts a process to the head of a queue and requires a reference to the process as the only parameter. This is another abnormal operation. For example, to insert process `serv_obj` to the head of a simple queue, `serv_queue`, a process uses the following C++ statement:

```
// put back server process into queue
serv_queue->back(serv_obj);
```

- The function `remov` removes a specified process from the queue. This function requires the reference to the process as the only parameter. For example, to remove the process referenced by `serv_obj` from queue `serv_queue`, a process uses the following statement:

```
serv_queue->remov(serv_obj); // remove process
```

D.2.3 Features of Class `pqueue`

The most relevant features of class `pqueue` used for priority queues are the following:

- The constructor for creating a priority queue requires the name of the queue, the number of different priorities, and the queue size for all priorities. The last two parameters are optional; if not included, the number of priorities is assigned the value 10 and the assigned default queue size is 1000 for every priority. For example, the following C++ statements declare and create a priority queue, `serv_queue`, with an assigned name "Server Queue," using 10 different priorities and a size of 15 server processes for every priority:

```
pqueue *serv_queue     // declare priority queue
...
// create priority queue
serv_queue = new pqueue("Server Queue", 10, 15);
```

- To get the current size (total number of processes) of a priority queue, the function `length` is provided. This function returns an integer value that corresponds to the current length of the queue. For example, to get the current length of `serv_queue` defined above, a process uses the following statements:

```
serv_queue->length();    // get queue length
```

- To get the number of processes of a specified priority in a queue, the function `plength` is provided. The only parameter required is the priority. The function returns an integer that corresponds to the number of processes found with the specified priority. For example, to get the current number of processes in `serv_queue`, with priority `1_prio`, a process uses the following statements:

```
int num_proc_prio;    // number of processes with priority
```

```
int l_prio;          // priority
. . .
// get queue length
num_proc_prio = serv_queue->plength(l_prio);
```

- To test if the number of processes of a specified priority is zero, the function **pempty** is provided. As before, this function needs only one parameter, the **priority**. The function returns a Boolean value (true or false). For example, to test if the number of processes with priority l_prio in serv_queue is zero, a process uses the following statements:

```
if (serv_queue->pempty(l_prio)) {
   // execute if no processes with priority l_prio
}
```

- To test if the number of processes of a specified priority has reached its limit (upper bound), the function **pfull** is provided. As before, this function needs only one parameter, the **priority**. The function returns a Boolean value (true or false). For example, to test if the number of processes with priority l_prio in queue serv_queue has reached its limit, a process uses the following statements:

```
if (serv_queue->pfull(l_prio)) {
   // execute if queue with priority l_prio is full
}
```

- To test if the complete priority queue is empty, the function **empty** is provided. This function requires no parameters and returns a Boolean value. For example, to check if serv_queue is empty (for all priorities), a process uses the following statements:

```
if (serv_queue->empty()) {
   // execute if the queue is empty
   . . .
}
```

- The function **into** is used to insert a process into a priority queue. The only parameter required by this function is the process to insert; its priority is implicit. This process becomes the new process at the tail of the priority group, with its implicit priority. The size of the corresponding priority group is increased by one. For example, to insert process serv_obj into the priority queue, serv_queue, a process uses the following C++ statements:

```
// reference to a server process
server *serv_obj;
```

```
...
// enqueue server process
serv_queue->into(serv_obj);
```

- The function **out** removes the highest priority process from the priority queue. If there are several processes with the same high priority, the process at the head of the queue is removed. This function requires no parameters. For example, to remove the highest priority process from **serv_queue** and assign it a reference **serv_obj**, a process uses the following statement:

```
serv_obj = (server*) serv_queue->out();
```

The casting for pointer to class **server** is necessary to specify the type of process dequeued.

- The function **pout** removes the next process with a specified priority from the queue. The process removed is the one at the head of its priority group. The only required priority for this function is the priority of the process. For example, to remove the next **server** process with priority **m_prio** from **serv_queue** and assign it to reference **serv_obj**, a process uses the following statement:

```
serv_obj = (server*) serv_queue->pout(m_prio);
```

As in simple queues, for special scheduling that may be needed in some simulation models, the following functions, which do not follow the conventional rules for queue processing, are provided:

- The function **plast** removes the last process inserted into the queue with a specified priority (i.e., the process at the tail of the priority group in the queue). This is another abnormal operation. This function requires the priority as the only parameter. For example, to remove the last **server** process that was inserted into **serv_queue** with priority **l_prio** and assign it to reference **serv_obj**, a process uses the following statement:

```
serv_obj = (server*) serv_queue->plast(l_prio);
```

- The function **llast** removes the last process inserted to the queue with the lowest priority in the queue (i.e., the process at the tail of the lowest priority group in the queue). This is another abnormal operation. This function requires no parameters. For example, to remove the last **server** process with the lowest priority that was inserted into **serv_queue** and assigned to reference **serv_obj**, a process uses the following statement:

```
serv_obj = (server*) serv_queue->llast();
```

- The function `pllast` removes the last process inserted to the queue with the lowest priority lower than the specified priority (i.e., the process at the tail of the lowest priority group with a priority lower than the specified priority). This is another abnormal operation. This function requires the specified priority as the only parameter. For example, to remove the last `server` process with the lowest priority lower than `ll_prio` that was inserted into the `serv_queue` and assign it to reference `serv_obj`, a process uses the following statement:

  ```
  serv_obj = (server*) serv_queue->pllast(ll_prio);
  ```

- The function `pback` inserts a process to the head of its priority group in a queue and requires a reference to the process as the only parameter. This function uses the implicit priority of the process. This is another abnormal operation. For example, to insert process `serv_obj` into the head of `serv_queue`, a process uses the following C++ statement:

  ```
  // put back server into serv_queue
  serv_queue->pback(serv_obj);
  ```

- The function `remov` removes a specified process from the priority queue. This function requires the reference to the process as the only parameter. For example, to remove the process referenced by `serv_obj` from `serv_queue`, a process uses the following statement:

  ```
  serv_queue->remov(serv_obj); // remove process serv_obj
  ```

D.3 The Resource Library

D.3.1 General Description

The resource library includes classes for the synchronization of processes that use resources. This library provides two classes:

- The `res` class for mutually exclusive resource synchronization.
- The `bin` class for producer-consumer resource synchronization.

All simulation models that use the first resource class must include the `res.h` header file at the top of the program. This gives the program implementing the simulation model access to the first resource class, as in the following example:

```
#include "res.h"
```

All simulation models that use the second resource class must include the `bin.h` header file at the top of the program. This gives the program implementing the simulation model access to the second resource class, as in the following example:

```
#include "bin.h"
```

D.3.2 Relevant Features of the `res` Class

The most relevant features of the resource class `res` are the following:

- The constructor for creating a resource pool of this class requires the name of the resource pool and the pool size. This last parameter defines the initial number of available resource items in the resource pool. For example, the following C++ statements declare and create a resource pool, `serv_res`, with an assigned name "Server Resource" and a size of 15 resource items:

    ```
    res *serv_res;          // declare resource pool
    ...
    // create resource pool
    serv_res = new res("Server Resource", 15);
    ```

- To get the number of available resource items in a resource pool, the function `num_avail` is provided. This function requires no parameters and returns an integer value that corresponds to the number of available resource items found in the resource pool. For example, to get the current number of available resource items in the resource pool `serv_res`, which was defined above, a process uses the following C++ statements:

    ```
    int num_res;
    ...
    num_res = serv_res->num_avail();
    ```

- For resource allocation to a process, the `acquire` function is provided. This function allows a process to acquire a specified number of resource items from a resource pool only when there are sufficient resources available. The number of requested resources is specified as the only parameter. When the number of resources is not sufficient, the process is suspended. For example, if the process needs to acquire five resource items from the `serv_res` resource pool (defined above), the process uses the following statements:

    ```
    serv_res->acquire(5))
    ```

    If the process is suspended because of insufficient resources, it will be restarted by another process that releases resource items.

- When a process needs to release resources, it invokes the `release` function, which de-allocates a specified number of resource items that the process holds. This function requires a parameter that corresponds to the number of resource items to release. The function has no return value. For example if a process is to release three resources from the `serv_res` resource pool (defined above), it uses the following statement:

    ```
    serv_res->release(3);
    ```

D.3.3 Features in Class `bin`

The most relevant features of the resource class `bin` are the following:

- The constructor for creating a `bin` resource container requires the name of the resource container and the initial container size. This last parameter defines the initial number of available resources in the resource container. For example, the following C++ statements declare and create a `bin` resource container, `serv_cont`, with an assigned name "Server Bin" and a size of 15 resource items:

   ```
   bin *serv_cont; // declare resource container
   ...
   // create a resource container (bin pool)
   serv_cont = new bin("Server Bin", 15);
   ```

- To get the number of available resource items in a `bin` resource container, the function `num_avail` is provided. This function requires no parameters and returns an integer value that corresponds to the number of available resource items found in the `bin` resource container. For example, to get the current number of available resource items in the resource container `serv_cont`, which was defined above, a process uses the following C++ statements:

   ```
   int num_cont;
   ...
   num_cont = serv_cont->num_avail();
   ```

- For a process to take a number of resources from a `bin` resource container, it must use the function `take`. If the number of resources in the `bin` container is sufficient, function `take` returns and the process can proceed; otherwise the process is suspended. If the operation succeeds, the number of resources in the `bin` container is decreased by the number of resource items taken by the process. For example, if a process needs to take five resource items from the `serv_cont` container (defined above), the following statements can be used:

   ```
   serv_cont->take(5);   // take 5 items from serv_cont
     // execute when there are sufficient resources
     ...
   ```

- When a process needs to place (or give) resource items to a `bin` container, it invokes the `give` function, which places a specified number of container items into the container. This function requires a parameter that corresponds to the number of resource items to place in the `bin` container. The function has no return value. For example, if a process is to place three resource items in the `serv_cont` container (defined above), it uses the following statement:

   ```
   serv_cont->give(3);   // place 3 items into serv_cont
   ```

D.4 The waitq Class

Class `waitq` manipulates the cooperation of processes. Objects of this class are used as a synchronization mechanism for the process cooperation. This synchronization allows one process to dominate and is treated as the master process; the other processes are treated as passive slaves.

All simulation models that need to use the `waitq` class must include the header file `waitq.h`, as in the following statement:

```
#include "waitq.h"
```

The relevant operations are as follows:

- The constructor for creating a synchronization object for cooperation requires a name and an optional number of priorities. This last parameter is needed for the hidden priority queues, one for the master processes and one for the slave processes. The default value for this parameter is 10. For example, to create a synchronization object with name "Cooperating Server," and with 10 priorities (the default number), a simulation model uses the following statements:

    ```
    waitq *coopt_serv;    // declaring a ref of class waitq
    ...
    coopt_serv = new waitq("Cooperating Server");
    ```

- To get the length of the *slave queue* (i.e., the number of `slave` processes waiting on the synchronization object), the function `length` is provided. This function returns an integer value with the number of `slave` processes waiting. For example, to get the number of slave processes waiting in the `coopt_serv` object defined above, a process uses the following statements:

    ```
    int num_slaves;
    ...
    num_slaves = coopt_serv->length();
    ```

- To get the length of the *master queue* (i.e., the number of `master` processes waiting on the synchronization object), the function `lengthm` is provided. This function returns an integer value with the number of master processes waiting. For example, to get the number of master processes waiting in the `coopt_serv` object defined above, a process uses the following statements:

    ```
    int num_master;
    ...
    num_master = coopt_serv->lengthm();
    ```

- A `slave` process that needs to cooperate with a `master` process must invoke the `wait` function. This function returns no value and does not require a parameter. If there is not a `master` process available, the `slave` process invoking this function is suspended. For example, a `slave` process attempting cooperation with a `master` process using the synchronization object `coopt_serv` (defined above) uses the following statements:

  ```
  coopt_serv->wait();    // wait for master process
  ...
  ```

- A master process that needs to cooperate with slave processes must invoke the `coopt` function. This function returns a reference (or a pointer) to the `slave` process retrieved from the `slave` queue. The function requires no parameters. If there is no slave process available in the slave queue, the master process invoking this function is suspended and placed in the master queue. For example, a master process that needs to cooperate with a slave process using the `coopt_serv` synchronization object uses the following statements:

  ```
  coopt_serv->coopt()
    // execute, a slave process was found
        ...
  ```

D.5 The condq Class

Class condq handles the waiting of processes for a specified condition (also called *conditional waiting*). Objects of this class are used as a synchronization mechanism for the processes to evaluate the specified condition and wait if the condition is not true. This synchronization allows processes to wait in a conditional queue by priority.

All simulation models that need to use class condq must include the header file condq.h, as in the following statement:

```
#include "condq.h"
```

The relevant operations are as follows:

- The constructor for creating a synchronization object for conditional waiting requires a name and an optional number of priorities. This last parameter is needed for the hidden priority queue of processes. For example, to create a synchronization object with name "CondServ" and with six priorities, a simulation model uses the following statements:

  ```
  condq *cond_serv;
  ...
  cond_serv = new condq("CondServ", 6);
  ```

- The member function `waituntil` evaluates the specified condition and suspends the process if the condition is not true. The suspended process is placed in priority queue of the `condq` object. The function has only one parameter, a Boolean value of the condition. The function returns a Boolean value, which is false if the condition evaluates to false; otherwise the function returns true. The condition specified in the parameter is a Boolean function with no parameter. For example, a process that uses a condition `cond_a` and synchronizes with a `condq` object, `cond_serv` (created above), uses the following statements:

    ```
    bool test_val;

    bool cond_a;
    . . .
    test_val = false;

    while (! Test_val)
       cond_serv->waituntil(cond_a);
    // execute if cond_a is true
    ```

- The member function `signal` reactivates the processes at the head of the priority queue in the `condq` object. The reactivated processes will evaluate their condition and may be suspended again. This function requires no parameter and returns no value. For example, a process that signals the `condq` object `cond_serv` (created above) uses the following statement:

    ```
    cond_serv->signal();
    ```

- The member function `setall` sets the internal flag for the evaluation mode in the `condq` object. If this flag is set to true, the `signal` function allows all waiting processes to test their condition. This function requires one parameter, the Boolean value for setting the flag. The function returns no parameter. For example, a process that needs to set the flag so that all processes will be allowed to test their condition on the `cond_serv` object (defined above) uses the following statement:

    ```
    cond_serv->setall(true);
    ```

- The function member `length` returns the number of processes in the conditional queue of a `condq` object. This function returns an integer value that corresponds to the conditional queue length. The function requires no parameter. For example, a process that needs to get the number of processes in the conditional queue in the `cond_serv` object (defined above) uses the following statements:

    ```
    int cond_num;
    cond_num = cond_serv->length();
    ```

D.6 Random Numbers

A random variable is *discrete* if its cumulative distribution function only changes value at certain points $x_1, x_2, \ldots$ and remains constant between these points. The function $F(X)$ has values $p_1, p_2, \ldots$ at these points, and $p_1 + p_2 + \ldots = 1$. A random variable is *continuous* if its cumulative distribution function is continuous everywhere.

The following distribution functions are provided in Psim3:

- Uniform
- Binomial
- Geometric
- Poisson
- Exponential
- Normal

Psim3 provides several C++ classes for random number generators that use different probability distributions. The following classes are the most common ones that provide the random number generators:

- `randint`, for uniformly distributed random numbers between 0.0 and 1.0.
- `erand`, for the generation of random numbers from an exponential distribution.
- `poisson`, for the generation of random numbers from a Poisson distribution.
- `normal`, for the generation of random numbers from a normal distribution.
- `urand`, for the generation of random numbers within a specified range and using a uniform probability distribution.

For summary documentation of all classes, consult the header file `proc.h` in the CD-ROM provided and in the Psim web pages.

D.6.1 Class `randint`

Class `randint` provides the most basic type of random number generation. The class uses a primitive uniform distribution. The description below gives some details on the member functions in class `randint`.

- `randint(unsigned int seed=0)`. This is the constructor for the random number generator object of class `randint`. The parameter `seed` is used to set the random number stream. This constructor is used to create a random number generator object. For example, the following C++ code declares and creates a random number generator object with 3 as the value of the seed.

```
// declare reference to random generator
randint *ran_gen1;
...
ran_gen1 = new randint(3);  // create rand gen
...
```

If the seed argument is not specified when invoking the constructor, the random generator object uses the processor timer for the seed. This implies that there will be a different random stream of numbers for every simulation run.

- `void seed(unsigned int useed)`. This function sets the seed for the random number stream. The parameter `useed` is the value for the seed. This member function is used when the random generator object has already been created and there is a need to set a value for the seed. For example, the following C++ code sets the seed to 7 for generator object `ran_gen1` defined above:

```
ran_gen1->seed(7);   // set seed to 7
...
```

- `double fdraw()`. This member function generates a random number between 0.0 to 1.0, using a generator object already created. For example, the following C++ code generates a random number from the generator object `ran_gen1` defined above and stores the number in variable `ran_value`:

```
double ran_value;
...
ran_value = ran_gen1->fdraw();  // generate a random number
...
```

- `long draw()`. This member function generates a random number between 0 to RAND_MAX, using a generator object already created. For example, the following C++ code generates a random number from the generator object `ran_gen2` and stores the number in variable `ran2_value`:

```
long ran2_value;
...
ran2_value = ran_gen2->draw();  // generate a random number
...
```

Every time the simulation model needs a random number, it calls the `draw` or the `fdraw` function that returns a "random" number.

D.6.2 Class `erand`

Class `erand` provides random number generation using an exponential distribution. The description below gives some details of the member functions in class `erand`.

- `erand(double emean, unsigned int eseed=0)`. This is the constructor for initializing the exponential random number generator. The parameters are `emean`, the mean value of the distribution and `essed`, the seed value for selecting a random stream. The overloaded constructor `erand(long emean, unsigned int eseed=0)`. These constructors are used to create a random number generator object. The arguments to be supplied are the mean value of the samples, and the seed (optional argument). For example, the following C++ code declares and creates a random number generator object `ran_gen` with a mean of 34.5 and 3 as the value of the seed.

```
// declare reference to random generator
erand *ran_gen;
...
ran_gen = new erand(34.5, 3); // create rand gen
...
```

- `double fdraw()`. This member function generates a random number using the exponential distribution with the mean value given in the constructor. For example, the following C++ code generates a random number of type `double` using random generator `ran_gen` (created above) and stores the random number in variable `ran_value`.

```
double ran_value;
...
ran_value = ran_gen->fdraw();
...
```

If the seed argument is not specified when invoking the constructor, the random generator object uses the processor timer for the seed. This implies that there will be a different random stream of numbers for every simulation run.

D.6.3 Class `normal`

Class `normal` provides random number generation using a normal distribution between two given values. The description below presents details of the member functions in class `normal`.

- `normal(long mean, long stdev, unsigned int seed=0)`. This is the constructor for the random number generator object using the normal distribution. The parameters are `mean`, the mean value of the distribution, `stdev`, the value of the standard deviation, and `seed`, the value to set the random stream. The overloaded constructor is

```
public Normal(double rmean, double rstd, unsigned int seed=0)
```

The constructor is used to create and initialize a random number generator object using a normal distribution with the given value of the mean, the standard deviation, and the value of the seed (optional argument). For example, the following C++ code declares and creates a random number generator object `norm_gen` with a mean of 22.5 and standard deviation of 1.3:

```
normal *norm_gen;   // declare reference to random generator
...
norm_gen = new normal(22.5, 1.3); // create rand gen
...
```

- `double fdraw()`. This member function generates a random number using the normal distribution with the mean value and the standard deviation given in the constructor. For example, the following C++ code generates a random number of type `double` using random generator `norm_gen` (created above) and stores the random number in variable `ran_value`.

```
double ran_value;
...
ran_value = norm_gen->fdraw(); // generate a random number
...
```

If the seed argument is not specified when invoking the constructor, the random generator object uses the processor timer for the seed. This implies that there will be a different random stream of numbers for every simulation run.

D.6.4 Class `poisson`

Class `poisson` provides random number generation using a Poisson distribution. The description below presents details of the member functions in this class.

- The constructor used to initialize a random number generator using a Poisson distribution is

```
poisson(double prate, double pperiod, unsigned int seed=0)
```

The parameters of the constructor are `prate`, the rate of arrival (arrivals per unit time), `pperiod`, the period considered for arrivals, and `seed`, the seed for selecting an appropriate random stream. The constructor is used to create and initialize a random number generator object with the given value of the arrival rate, the period for arrivals, and the value of the seed (optional argument). For example, the following C++ code declares and creates a random number generator object `poisson_gen` with mean 18.45 (arrivals per time unit) and arrivals period of 10.5 time units:

```
normal *poisson_gen; // declare reference to random generator
...
// create rand genenerator
poisson_gen = new poisson(18.45, 10.5);
...
```

- `int fdraw()`. This member function generates a random number using the Poisson distribution with the values of the arrival rate, the period for the arrivals, and the seed, given in the constructor. For example, the following C++ code generates a random number of type `int` using random generator `poisson_gen` (created above) and stores the random number in variable `ran_value`:

```
int ran_value;
...
ran_value = poisson_gen->fdraw();
...
```

If the seed argument is not specified when invoking the constructor, the random generator object uses the processor timer for the seed. This implies that there will be a different random stream of numbers for every simulation run.

D.6.5 Class urand

Class `urand` provides random number generation using a uniform distribution between the values given. The description below presents details of the member functions in class `urand`.

- `urand(long low, long high, unsigned int useed=0)`. This is the constructor for the random number generator with uniform distribution. The parameters are `low`, the low bound for the range of values, `high`, the upper bound for the range of values, and `useed`, the seed to set the random stream.

    The following constructor for random number generator with uniform distribution and values of type `double` is used:

    `urand(double flow, double fhigh, unsigned int useed=0)`

    The parameters are `flow`, the low bound for the range of values, `fhigh`, the upper bound for the range of values, and `useed`. The constructor is used to create and initialize a random number generator object with the given value of the low bound and high bound as well as the value of the seed (optional argument). For example, the following C++ code declares and creates a random number generator object `unif_gen` with a low bound of 6.35 and a high bound of 35.55.

```
normal *unif_gen; // declare reference to random generator
...
unif_gen = new urand(6.35, 35.55); // create rand generator
...
```

- `double fdraw()`. This member function generates a random number using the uniform distribution with the low and high limits given in the constructor. For example, the following C++ code generates a random number of type `double` using random generator `unif_gen` (created above) and stores the random number in variable `ran_value`.

```
double ran_value;
...
ran_value = unif_gen->fdraw();
...
```

If the seed argument is not specified when invoking the constructor, the random generator object uses the processor timer for the seed. This implies that there will be a different random stream of numbers for every simulation run.

D.7 The Simulation Package on CD-ROM

D.7.1 Files on the CD-ROM

The following groups of files are found on the CD-ROM provided with this book:

- The binary libraries of the Psim3 package, located in the `psim3` directory, are as follows:
  - `psim3.lib`, the Psim3 library compiled with Visual C++ 6.0.
  - `libpsim3.a`, the Psim3 library built with the GNU C++ (MinGW) compiler for Windows.
  - `libpsim3_solaris.a`, the Psim3 library for Sun Solaris, compiled with the GNU C++ compiler.
  - `libpsim3_linux.a`, the Psim3 library built with the GNU C++ compiler on Red Hat Linux 7.3.
  - The header files of the Psim3 library and the Pthreads library.
- The C++ files for the simulation models described in this book, located in the `psim3/models` directory.

D.7.2 Brief Instructions for Compiling and Linking

For compiling and linking the source files of the simulation models, note that the two external libraries necessary are the Psim3 and the Pthreads libraries. With the development environment and compiler used, the compilation should be carried out with the necessary source files, including the header files `proc.h` and `pthread.h`.

For the linking step, the appropriate version of the Psim3 and Pthreads library needs to be included in the project file or the make file. For example, the following DOS command is used for compiling and linking a source C++ program (e.g., batch.cpp) on Windows with the GNU C++ (MinGW) compiler:

```
g++ batch.cpp libpsim3.a libpthreadGC.a
```

We have copied this single command into a batch file called `psim3.bat`. Assuming that the current directory is `psim3\models` and the program in file `batfcfs.cpp` is to be compiled and linked, then the command line at the DOS prompt is

```
c:\psim3\models> psim3 batfcfs.cpp
```

Additional instructions and information are included in the file `readme.txt`.

Appendix E
Overview of Probability Theory

E.1 Introduction

This appendix includes the basic concepts and principles of probability theory used for describing the behavior of *stochastic models*—models that represent systems with uncertain behavior that includes random variables. The discussion includes the basic principles of probability theory and random variables. Only the relevant concepts of random number usage that are necessary for the construction of simulation models are explained.

Probability concepts are necessary to help understand the construction of simulation models with the appropriate random number generators using the appropriate probability distributions.

E.2 Basic Concepts

A *set* is a collection of distinct elements (duplicate elements are not allowed). This collection is usually enclosed within braces. For example, set S is defined as $\{a, b, c, d, e\}$. An element that belongs to a set is said to be a member of the set. If an element e is a member of set S, the membership of element e is denoted as $e \in S$. If element z is not a member of set S, it is denoted as $z \notin S$.

The following are basic definitions in set theory:

- An empty set is also a valid set; it is called a null set that contains no elements and is denoted as $\emptyset$.

- The union of two sets A and B is another set with all the elements contained in either of these two sets. The union of sets A and B is denoted as $A \cup B$.

- The intersection of two sets A and B is another set with only the elements contained in both sets. This intersection is denoted as $A \cap B$.

- The subset S of a set A is a set with the elements that are also contained in set A. In other words, S contains some or all the elements in A and is denoted as $S \subset A$.

- The universe is a set that contains all possible elements and is denoted as Ω.

- The complement of a set A is another set with all the elements that are not contained in set A; it is denoted as $\neg A$.

- Two sets A and B are mutually exclusive if they contain no common elements; they are denoted as $A \cap B = \emptyset$.

Probability is the likelihood or chance that a particular event will occur. Each possible type of occurrence is referred to as an *event*. An *experiment* is an activity that has exactly one outcome. A *sample space* of an experiment is the collection of all possible outcomes of that experiment. The sample space is the collection of all possible events and is usually called the *universe*. A particular outcome is called a *sample point*.

Certain outcomes or collection of outcomes in a sample space are called *events*. An event occurs if the outcome of an experiment is one of the sample points in the set that defines the event.

In studying the behavior of systems, the models are used to represent the behavior of systems over multiple experiments. Each experiment defines several possible outcomes. Therefore, the relative frequency of an outcome is what is important in probability theory. This is the number of occurrences of a particular outcome in a large number of repetitions of the experiment.

E.3 Probability of an Event

The probability of an event is measured by the relative frequency of an outcome and is defined by a function P that assigns a real number to an event. For example, the probability of event A is denoted $P(A)$.

The joint probability of two events A and B is the probability of the two events occurring simultaneously:

$$P(A \cap B) = P(A) \times P(B).$$

The probability of occurrence of either event A or event B or both A and B is

$$P(A \cup B) = P(A) + P(B)P(A \cap B).$$

The probability function must satisfy the following rules (axioms):

1. For every event A, $0 \leq P(A) \leq 1$.
2. The probability of any event or set of events in the universe is
$$P(\Omega) = 1.$$
3. If A and B are mutually exclusive events,
$$P(A \cap B) = 0$$
and
$$P(A \cup B) = P(A) + P(B).$$

In addition to the previous rules, the following definitions are fundamental:

1. The conditional probability of event B given that event A has occurred, denoted by $P(B|A)$, is defined by
$$P(B|A) = P(A \cap B)/P(A).$$

2. Two events A and B are independent if their occurrence is unrelated and the relation is defined as
$$P(B|A) = P(B)$$
or
$$P(A|B) = P(A).$$

If events A and B are independent, then
$$P(A \cap B) = P(A) \times P(B).$$

E.4 Random Numbers

To study the long-term behavior of a system, a series of independent repetitions of an experiment is carried out, reflecting many different aspects (random variables) of the system. Each repetition generates an event corresponding to a random variable defined for the experiment.

In statistics, the term *stochastic process* refers to a series of repetitions of an experiment or a sequence of events observed through time. More formally, a stochastic process is a set of random variables as functions of time. Note that some random variables are continuous-time—that is, they are defined for any value of time (for $t \geq 0$). Other random variables are discrete-time, defined only at specific points in time.

A Poisson process is an example of a stochastic process. The sequence of Bernoulli trials is another example of a stochastic process, called a *Bernoulli process*.

The simulation models studied in this book are the models for the simulation of stochastic processes. For these models, it is necessary to generate the values for the various random variables that represent the different *events*. To accomplish this, almost all the programs for the simulation models include calls to routines that generate random numbers based on appropriate distributions.

The basic generation of random (or more precisely, pseudorandom) numbers is carried out with a uniform distribution. The generation of pseudorandom numbers with the other distributions uses transformation methods starting with the uniform distribution as a base. The Psim simulation package does precisely this. It provides not only routines for the generation of pseudorandom numbers with a uniform distribution but also routines for the most common distributions. Each time a routine that generates pseudorandom numbers is called, it generates a number. A sequence of these numbers will be generated by successive calls to the appropriate routine that generates pseudorandom numbers.

The main characteristic of a pseudorandom stream of numbers is that the stream or sequence of numbers will be the same each time the program, which calls the routine to generate these numbers, is executed. When there is a need to generate a different sequence of such numbers, the value of the seed has to be changed. By default, the PsimJ and Psim3 packages use the system clock time as the seed for the generation of random numbers. But when there is a need to reproduce the same sequence of numbers, a seed is necessary (usually an odd value).

For example, to generate a sequence of random numbers with the Poisson distribution, the simulation model first needs to call the initial setup routine named *poisson*. The parameters needed for the call are the value of the arrival rate and the interval considered. Every time the simulation model needs a random number, it includes a call to the *draw* routine that returns a random number.

The expected value (also known as the average or mean) of a random variable is the weighted sum of all its values. The weight of a value is the probability of that value of the random variable.

In cases where the random variable X is discrete and has values $x_1, x_2, \ldots$ with probabilities $p_1, p_2, \ldots$, the expected value of X is defined as

$$E[X] = \sum_{i=1}^{\infty} p_i x_i.$$

In cases where the random variable X is continuous, the expected value of X is defined by the integral

$$E[X] = \int_0^{\infty} x f(x) dx.$$

The variance of the random variable X is defined as

$$\text{Var}[X] = E[(X - E[X])^2] = E[X^2] - (E[X])^2.$$

The variance of the random variable X is a measure of the spread of X around its mean. The standard deviation of X is defined as the square root of its variance and is denoted by σ.

Two random variables, X and Y, which are not uncorrelated, have their covariance defined by
$$\text{Cov}[X,Y] = E[XY] - E[X]E[Y].$$

If random variables X and Y are uncorrelated, then their covariance is zero.

E.5 Probability Distribution Functions

A random variable is a function that assigns a real number to a sample point or outcome in the sample space. This function assigns a real number to an event. The probability that a random variable X does not exceed a real value x is defined as function $F(x) = P(X \leq x)$—what is called the *cumulative distribution function* for random variable X. $F(x)$ has the following properties:

- $F(-\infty) = 0$

- $F(\infty) = 1$

- If $x \leq y$ then $F(x) \leq F(y)$.

A random variable is *discrete* if its cumulative distribution function changes value only at certain points $x_1, x_2, \ldots$ and remains constant between these points. The function $F(X)$ has values $p_1, p_2, \ldots$ at these points, and $p_1 + p_2 + \ldots = 1$. A random variable is *continuous* if its cumulative distribution function is continuous everywhere.

The *probability density function* $f(x)$ is defined as the derivative of the cumulative distribution function $F'(x)$. It follows that $F(x)$ can also be derived from the integral of $f(x)$. Then the probability that the random variable X has a value in the interval (a, b) is calculated by

$$P(a < X < b) = F(b) - F(a) = \int_a^b f(x).$$

The cumulative distribution functions are normally useful for calculating probabilities, and probability density functions are normally useful for calculating expected values (average values of the random variables).

There are two types of probability distribution: *theoretical* and *empirical*. The probability distribution for a random variable is theoretical if the collection of values of outcomes and probability can be obtained from a mathematical expression that represents some phenomenon of interest.

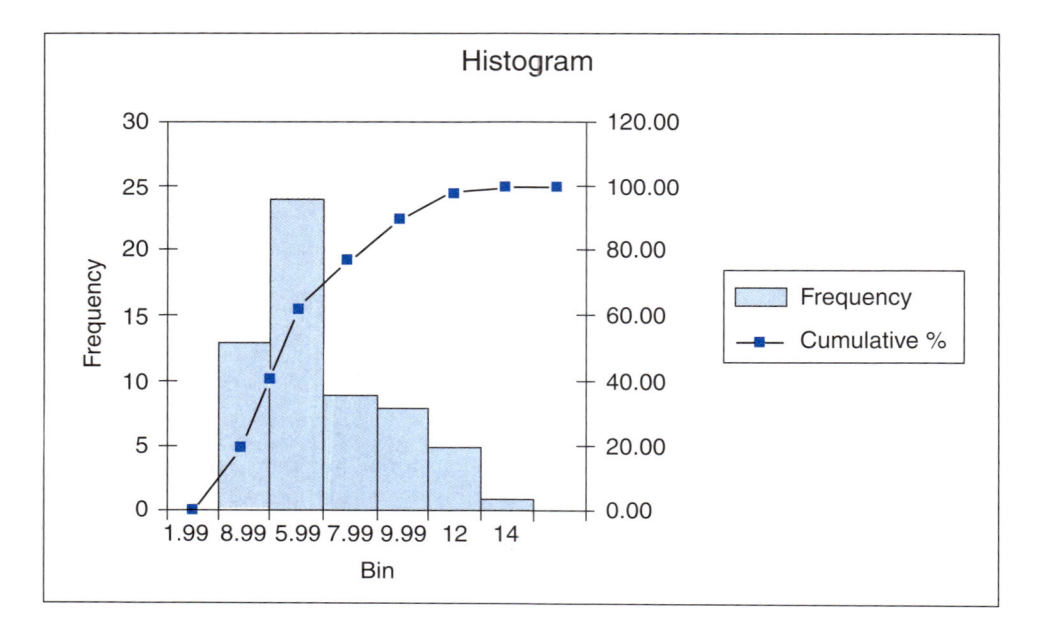

Figure E.1 Example of a histogram.

The empirical probability distributions are defined using a series of probability/value pairs representing a histogram of data values that can be returned. The empirical distributions are used instead of theoretical distributions when the data have unusual characteristics or when none of the theoretical distributions provide a good fit. A *histogram* is used to describe numerical data that have been grouped into frequency, relative frequency, or percentage distributions. The histogram consists of vertical bar charts in which the rectangular bars are constructed at the boundaries of each group or class. Figure E.1 shows an example of a typical histogram constructed with Microsoft Excel.

The following theoretical distribution functions are some of the most widely used for simulation performance modeling of systems:

- Binomial
- Geometric
- Poisson
- Uniform
- Exponential
- Normal

The first three distribution functions are discrete, and the last two are continuous; the uniform distribution can be continuous or discrete. In some practical problems,

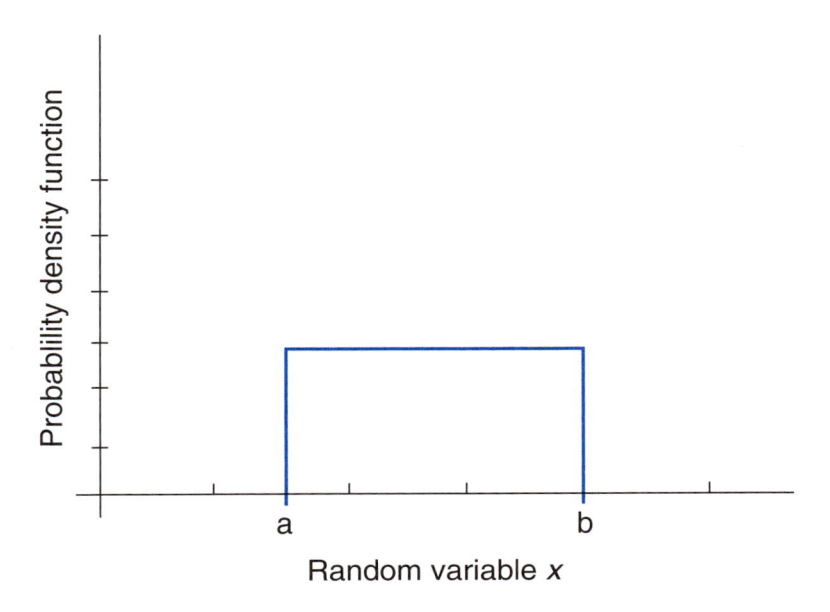

Figure E.2 A uniform distribution.

such as rolling a fair die, the discrete random variable of interest is said to follow a *uniform probability distribution*. The relevant characteristic of the uniform distribution is that all outcomes of the random variable are equally likely to occur. For example, the probability that any face of the fair die turns up is the same, 1/6, since there are six faces (six possible outcomes). Figure E.2 shows a graph with a uniform distribution, constructed with MathWorks MATLAB®.

E.5.1 The Geometric Distribution

Consider an experiment with two possible outcomes: success and failure (for example, flipping a coin with outcomes head as success and tail as failure). The experiment assigns to failure the probability p (therefore $q = 1 - p$ is the probability of success). The experiment is repeated a number of times under identical conditions. This series of experiments is called a sequence of Bernoulli trials. The random variable K is the number of trials made until the occurrence of the first success. The probability that the random variable K has a value equal to or less than k is determined by

$$P(K \leq k) = F(k) = \sum_{n=0}^{k}(1-p)p^n = 1 - p^{k+1}.$$

The expected value of the random variable K is defined as

$$E[K] = p/(1-p).$$

The variance of the random variable K is defined as

$$\text{Var}[K] = p/(1-p)^2.$$

The geometric distribution is the only discrete distribution with the *memory-less* property. If after k trials a success has not occurred, the probability that at least l additional trials are required is independent of k.

E.5.2 The Binomial Distribution

Consider a similar experiment as the one considered with the geometric distribution, in which there are two possible outcomes, success and failure. A random variable S is the number of successes in the first n trials. Given that the probability of a success is p, the probability that a given set of s trials result in successes (and a set of $n-s$ result in failures is q) is given by

$$P[s \text{ successes in } n \text{ trials}] = (1-p)^s p^{n-s}.$$

The probability that s successes occur from all possible combinations of n trials and s successes is

$$P[s] = \binom{n}{k}(1-p)^s p^{n-s}.$$

The cumulative distribution function for the binomial distribution is

$$F(s) = \sum_{m=0}^{s} \binom{n}{k}(1-p)^s p^{n-s}.$$

The expected value of the random variable S is defined as

$$E[S] = n(1-p).$$

The variance of the random variable S is defined as

$$\text{Var}[S] = np(1-p).$$

E.5.3 The Exponential Distribution

The exponential distribution is a continuous distribution that describes a type of experiment with successes that occur at some rate λ. A random variable T is the period until the next success. Since the distribution is continuous, a success can occur at any

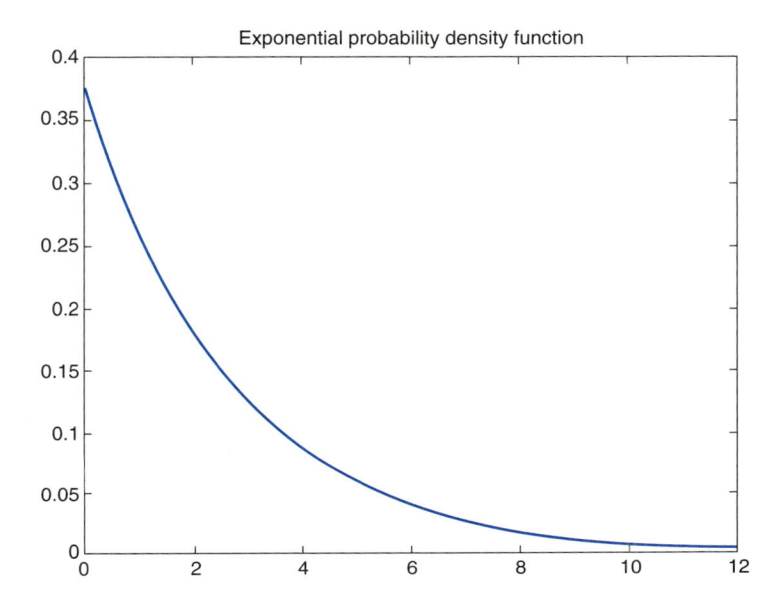

Figure E.3 A negative exponential distribution.

instant of time between 0 and ∞. The probability that the next success will occur at the instant equal to or less than t is given by

$$P[T \leq t] = F(t) = 1 - e^{-\lambda t}.$$

The expected value of the random variable T is defined as

$$E[T] = \frac{1}{\lambda}.$$

The variance of the random variable T is defined as

$$\mathrm{Var}[T] = \frac{1}{\lambda^2}.$$

The exponential distribution has the memory-less property. If the sequence of trials with the experiment has been in progress for some time τ, the probability that it will continue for some additional period y is independent of τ. Figure E.3 shows a graph of an exponential distribution.

E.5.4 The Poisson Distribution

Consider the same kind of experiment as for the exponential distribution, with successes that occur at some rate λ. The Poisson distribution is commonly used to represent the number of arrivals over a given interval. For a fixed period of time T, the probability of k successes is given by the expression

$$P[k \text{ successes in period } T] = \frac{(\lambda T)^k}{k!} e^{-\lambda T}.$$

The cumulative distribution is defined as

$$F[k] = \sum_{n=0}^{k} \frac{(\lambda T)^k}{k!} e^{-\lambda T}.$$

The expected value and the variance of the random variable K are both equal to λ.

The sequence of trials of the experiment that represents independent instances of occurrences of successes and that is distributed exponentially with mean λ is called a *Poisson process* or *Poisson stream*. A success in this type of experiment can represent the arrival of a job, the completion of service, or the response by a user.

E.5.5 The Uniform Distribution

The uniform distribution is one of the most fundamental distributions to use, and in simulation it is the basic distribution to generate random numbers. It is used when only the bounds of a random variable are known. Given a as the lower limit of the random variable X and b as the upper limit, the probability density function is given by

$$f(x) = \frac{1}{b-a}.$$

Look again at the graph with a uniform distribution shown in Figure E.2. The mean of the random variable X is $(a+b)/2$. The variance of the random variable X is given by $(b-a)^2/12$. If the random variable is discrete, it has only a finite number of values, each with the same probability.

E.5.6 The Normal Distribution

The normal distribution has a probability density function given by

$$f(x) = \frac{1}{\sigma\sqrt{2\pi}} e^{-(x-\mu)^2/2\sigma^2}.$$

The random variable X has mean μ and variance σ^2. When $\mu = 0$ and $\sigma = 1$, the function is called the unit normal distribution or standard normal distribution. The sum of several independent random variables is approximately a normal distribution. Figure E.4 shows a graph with a normal distribution.

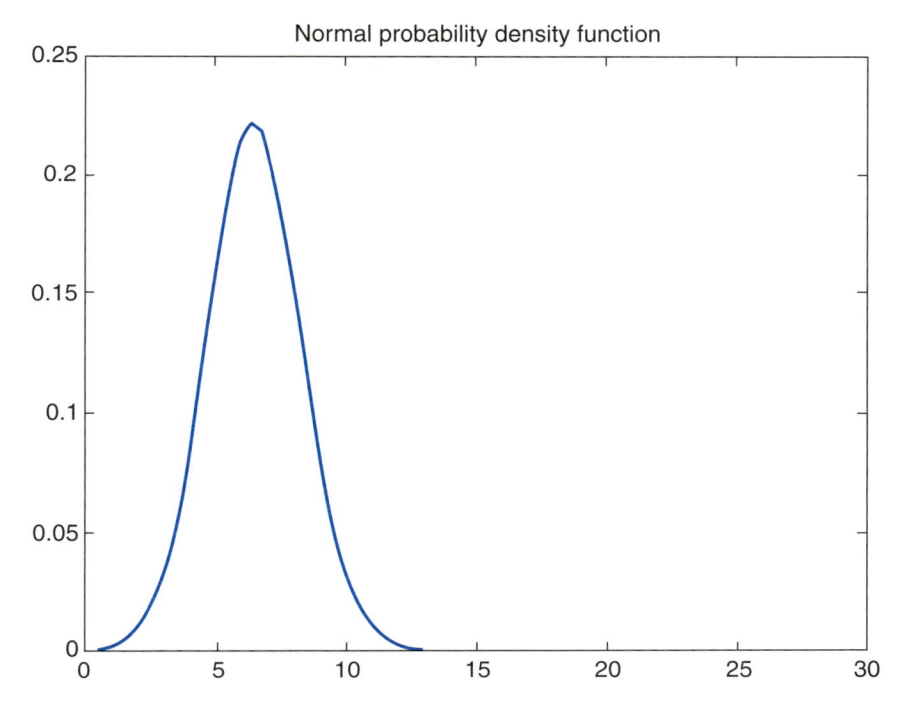

Figure E.4 A normal distribution.

E.6 Statistics

The simulation models are used to help evaluate the performance measures of a system. Normally, the basic data output from a simulation run is called the *trace*. This contains the values of the random variables, the times of occurrence of these values (events), and all other data about the state of the system being modeled.

Since the traces from simulation runs constitute a massive amount of data, summary statistics are much more useful to present the results of the different simulation runs. These summary statistics must reflect the characteristics of the stochastic process being modeled.

The most common statistics used to represent the results of simulation runs are as follows:

- The mean (or average), which gives the fundamental characteristic of the data.

- The standard deviation, the most common index of dispersion to summarize variability of the data.

- A frequency plot, or histogram, the simplest way to represent distribution of the data.

The histogram captures the number of times that different values of a random variable have occurred in the simulation run. It collects the frequency for all relevant values of the random variable and plots these values. If these frequency values are divided by the total number of observations, an empirical probability density function is obtained.

The main advantage of using the mean and the standard deviations is that these can be computed by accumulating values of the random variable while the simulation run is carried out. A histogram needs much more storage, especially if there is a large number of random variables.

E.7 Analyzing Sample Data

Reliable estimates of the performance measures of interest can be obtained by carrying out certain statistical analysis of the collected data. There are two common analysis methods used:

- Point estimation, which is a single value of the sample data of interest.

- Interval estimation, which is a pair of values, $[l, u]$, of the sample data; also called the confidence interval.

With interval estimation, the desired parameter to be estimated lies between the two values, l and u, that define the interval with a given probability. Both point and interval estimations are needed for meaningful data interpretation. It is useful to have the confidence interval be short and to have the desired quantity found in the interval with a high probability.

For example, the sample mean, $\bar{x}$, is an approximation (estimate) of the population mean, μ. If there is a finite number, n, of samples, then there are n estimates of the mean. Since it is not feasible to obtain the exact value of the population mean, one approach to follow is to find the probability that the population mean is within a certain interval $[l, u]$. This probability is expressed as

$$P[l \leq mu \leq u] = 1 - q.$$

The interval $[l, u]$ is called the confidence interval, and the value $1 - q$ is called the confidence coefficient. The method consists of finding the bounds for the interval and the probability that the population mean (μ) is within that interval.

Simulation results depend on two types of input. The first is the system parameter, also called the configuration parameter. An example of a system parameter is the number of servers. The second type of input is the workload parameter that is a random sample from the various probability distributions. Examples of workload parameters are interarrival and service periods.

It is important to differentiate between the effects of variations of the random samples and of the configuration parameters. Otherwise, the interpretation of the results will not be correct.

To obtain improved accuracy of the estimates of performance measures, variance reduction methods are used.

E.8 State-Dependent Models

Markov models represent systems that exhibit *dependencies* in their state changes (transitions). In these systems, the next state depends on the sequence of previous states. An example of such systems is a disk device, in which the next cylinder/sector to access depends on previous addresses of read/write operations.

In a continuous state space system, such as a free-falling object, the altitude (or height) of the object can take any *real* value and there is an infinite number of states. An example of a discrete state space system is the simple car-wash system; the state of the system depends on the number of customers (vehicles) waiting in the queue. These systems have a *countable* number of states that are clearly defined.

E.8.1 State Dependence

A system can be defined with a discrete state space, $\{s_1, s_2, \ldots s_k\}$, and with the following sequence of states that represent the execution up to the present:

$$Q = <s_1, s_9, s_2, s_4, s_4, s_1>.$$

The sequence Q defines the states in the order that the system has passed through. The dependency of the next state, S, on the previous sequence of states is expressed as the probability

$$P[S = s_k | Q].$$

This expresses the probability that the next state is s_k, given that the previous sequence of states is Q. In other words, to find the probability of the next state, all previous states and their ordering—the system's entire past history of state changes— need to be known.

Stochastic systems, in which the next state in a system depends only on the current state, are called Markov processes.

Some stochastic systems have the memory-less property because there is no dependency of the state changes in the model of the system. An example of this type of property is found in a Poisson process.

E.8.2 Stochastic Matrices

For systems with dependencies in their state changes, the amount of time spent in any state is memory-less, and if time is measured as a continuous variable, then the amount of time (period) spent in a state has an exponential distribution.

Assume that the parameters of the system are independent of time and depend only on the state of the system. The representation of a Markov chain is then simple. The most common representations are stochastic matrices and stochastic state-transition diagrams.

In stochastic matrices, the rows represent the current state and the columns represent the next states. The value of the matrix at row i and column j is the probability that the next state is j given that the current state is i. Since all these values are probabilities, the sum of all the values in every row is equal to 1.

In the state-transition diagram, circles represent states and the arrows joining the states represent the transitions. The probability of a transition is written as the label of the corresponding arrow (directed arc).

An example of a Markov chain is a model of a process in an operating system. There are six states in this process:

- Ready: The process is waiting for service from the CPU.
- Running: The process is receiving service from the CPU.
- Wait: The process is waiting for service from an I/O device.
- Suspended: The process is waiting for some event to occur.
- I/O: The process is receiving service from an I/O device.
- Terminated: The process has completed execution.

The stochastic matrix for this model of a process may be similar to the table shown below.

States	Ready	Running	Wait	Suspended	I/O	Terminated
Ready	0.0	1	0.0	0.0	0.0	0.0
Running	0.25	0	0.4	0.2	0.0	0.15
Wait	0	0	0	0	1	0
Suspended	1	0	0	0	0	0
I/O	0.8	0	0	0	0	0.2
Terminated	0	0	0	0	0	0

Appendix F
Using the C++ Models

F.1 Using Linux

At Kennesaw State University, the Department of Computer Science and Information Systems mainly uses the CS3 server that runs under Linux (Red Hat Linux Enterprise Server 4). On CS3, the Psim3 library, the header files, and the simulation models are stored in the folder /home/jgarrido/psim3. The GNU C++ compiler was used to create the Psim3 library. In addition to the Psim3 library, the Pthreads library is also needed to create the executable simulation models. To connect to the CS3 server, use Secure Shell Client and use cs3.kennesaw.edu as the name of the server (host). When you are connected to CS3, type your user name, then your password to log in.

On the Linux operating system, the *bash* shell is the default shell. After you log in, the shell types a dollar sign ($) as the system prompt. This indicates that the shell is waiting for a command. It is recommended that you create a working directory for your files under your root directory. You can use the mkdir command to make a new directory under the current directory, then change to the new directory with the cd command. For example,

```
mkdir myos
cd myos
```

Copy the psim3 script file and the files that implement the desired simulation model, such as batch.cpp, and batsjf.cpp. In Linux, the dot (.) indicates the currently working directory. The following example shows how to copy the relevant files from the /home/jgarrido/psim3 directory (on CS3) to your working directory:

```
cp /home/jgarrido/psim3/batch.cpp .
cp /home/jgarrido/psim3/batsjf.cpp .
cp /home/jgarrido/psim3/psim3 .
```

When using a similar system with Linux, carry out the following changes to the specified files supplied on the CD. The script file to compile and link a C++ program with the Psim3 and Pthreads libraries is `psim3_linux`. This file should be renamed to `psim3`. The library `libpsim3_linux` should be renamed to `libpsim3.a`. To edit a text file (C++ source file), use any editor, such as `pico` or `emacs`. To start the `pico` editor, type the following command:

```
pico batch.cpp
```

To compile, link, and create the executable file (`a.out`) with the `batch.cpp` file, type the following command:

```
./psim3 batch.cpp
```

The dot and the forward slash (./) must be included before any commands (executable or script file) that are stored in your working directory. The `psim3` file is a script that includes the actual commands that clear the screen, type a few text lines, and invoke the GNU compiler with the options to link the compiled program with the Psim3 and Pthreads libraries. This command produces an executable file called `a.out`, which is the default name of the executable file after compiling and linking.

All necessary files and libraries are included in the CD and in the Psim web pages. When using a similar system, such as Sun Solaris, carry out the following changes to the specified files supplied on the CD. The script file to compile and link a C++ program with the Psim3 and Pthreads libraries is `psim3_solaris`. This file should be renamed to `psim3`. The library `libpsim3_solaris` should be renamed to `libpsim3.a`. The following command will run the executable program produced above:

```
./a.out
```

To redirect the output to a file `simul.txt`, use

```
./a.out > simul.txt
```

To read the `simul.txt` file, which is your program's output, use this command:

```
more simul.txt
```

To transfer the output file to your PC, use a file transfer utility program, such as SSH Secure File Transfer Client.

You can rename a file to any appropriate name. To rename the executable file `a.out` to `batch.exe`, type the command:

```
mv a.out batch
```

F.2 Using Unix (Sun Solaris)

Another server that is used at KSU is *Atlas*, which runs under Sun Solaris 9.1. To access this server, connect to `atlas.kennesaw.edu`, and then log in. The Psim3 library, header files, and C++ programs are stored on folder `/home/jgarrido/psim3`. The rest of the task in using this installation of Unix (Sun Solaris/SunOS) is almost the same as for the Linux system on the CS3 server. The GNU C++ compiler was used to create the Psim3 library. In addition to the Psim3 library, the Pthreads library is also needed to create the executable simulation models. All necessary files and libraries are included in the CD and in the Psim web pages.

F.3 Using Microsoft Windows

When using MS Windows, open a DOS window and check that the PATH is appropriate. Create a new directory (for example, `os_models`), and copy from the CD the models (implemented in C++), the header files, and the Psim3 library (`libpsim3.a`). The Pthreads library files (`libpthreadGC.a` and `pthreadGC.dll`) are assumed to be included with the C++ compiler but are also included on the CD. The GNU C++ compiler was used to create the Psim3 library. In addition to the Psim3 library, the Pthreads library is also needed to create the executable simulation models.

To compile, link, and create an executable file on the DOS prompt, use the `psim3.bat` batch file. For example, to compile and link the file `batmio.cpp`, type the following command:

```
C:\models> psim3 batmio.cpp
```

To execute the program and run the corresponding simulation model, type the name of the default executable file:

```
C:\models> a.exe
```

To redirect the output to a file `simul.txt`, type the command line

```
C:\models>a.exe > simul.txt
```

All necessary files and libraries are included in the CD and are also available from the Psim web pages.

Note: To use the Microsoft Visual C++ (version 6.0 and later), the files `psim3_vcpp.lib`, `pthreadVC.lib`, and `pthreadVCE.dll` are needed to link to the C++ program. All these files have to be specified when building the project in Visual C++. Check the Visual C++ documentation to see how to create and build projects.

Appendix G
The Computer System: An Overview

The computer is a machine that follows instructions written by humans. It has no inherent intelligence of its own (at present), but follows "captured" human intelligence that has been rendered into a form the machine can follow. The machine itself is primarily electronic, with the movement and storage of electricity and electric charges representing data and information. As the data (electrical values) flow through the computer system they can be changed and manipulated according to mechanical rules that the computer must follow. Those rules are created and designed by human intelligence. This chapter examines the construction of a computer system by dissecting the machine to its fundamental components, and examining the construction of those components and how they work together.

G.1 Computer System Components

Examining a computer system from a high-level point of view reveals that a computer has six basic components or categories of components:

- *CPU*: The Central Processing Unit. In common usage, this term is often used to describe the box or enclosure within which the computer components reside. But to a computer scientist, the central processing unit is the processor chip that can interpret and execute the instructions in a computer program (software).

- *Main Memory* (*Also called primary storage*): This is working storage for programs and information, which is used while the compute is turned on and running. Main

515

memory is generally not permanent or fixed storage, its contents are wiped clean when the machine is powered-down.

- *Storage (Also called secondary storage)*: This term covers a variety of types of devices to store and retrieve data, information, and software programs. Devices range in speed, amount of storage, and cost. These can include hard drives, floppy drives, ram drives, CDs, memory sticks, SD-cards, etc.

- *Input/Output Devices*: This is a category of devices used to provide input to the machine, or display output for the user, or to communicate with other computers. Devices in this category include: monitor, keyboard, mouse, network card, modem, camera, printers, scanners, etc.

- *Bus*: An electrical highway that is used to connect the components. The bus is multiple wires, so that many bits can be communicated between devices at the same time. It is typical for a computer system to have two or more buses.

- *Operating System*: This is the software program that makes the computing hardware usable. The operating system includes low-level software for controlling the hardware devices, as well as software for managing programs and the resources in the computer system. The operating system includes software that provides a user interface into the system—typically a Graphical User Interface (GUI), though other types of interfaces are possible. The operating system also generally provides a programming interface: a way for programmers to utilize portions of the operating system routines in developing software. Most of the operating system is software, which resides in secondary storage and is loaded into the computer's memory when the computer boots up. Usually, a small portion of system code is stored in hardware in a chip, and may be called a Basic Input-Output System (BIOS), which contains instructions for loading and starting the operating system.

Figure G.1 illustrates a high-level diagram of a simple computing system. It shows the operating system and storage separately, though the operating system is software that resides on a storage device, (usually a hard disk drive), that is also used to store software applications and data. The other storage device (labeled "Storage") represents optional hard disk drives, but also optical drives, floppy drives, memory sticks, SD-cards, and other storage device technologies.

G.2 The Central Processing Unit (CPU)

The central processing unit (CPU) is the part of the computer system that contains the logic used to execute or process instructions, which then cause the computer do work. The CPU is a single chip that is the master of all the other devices in the system and any secondary processors.

G.2 The Central Processing Unit (CPU)

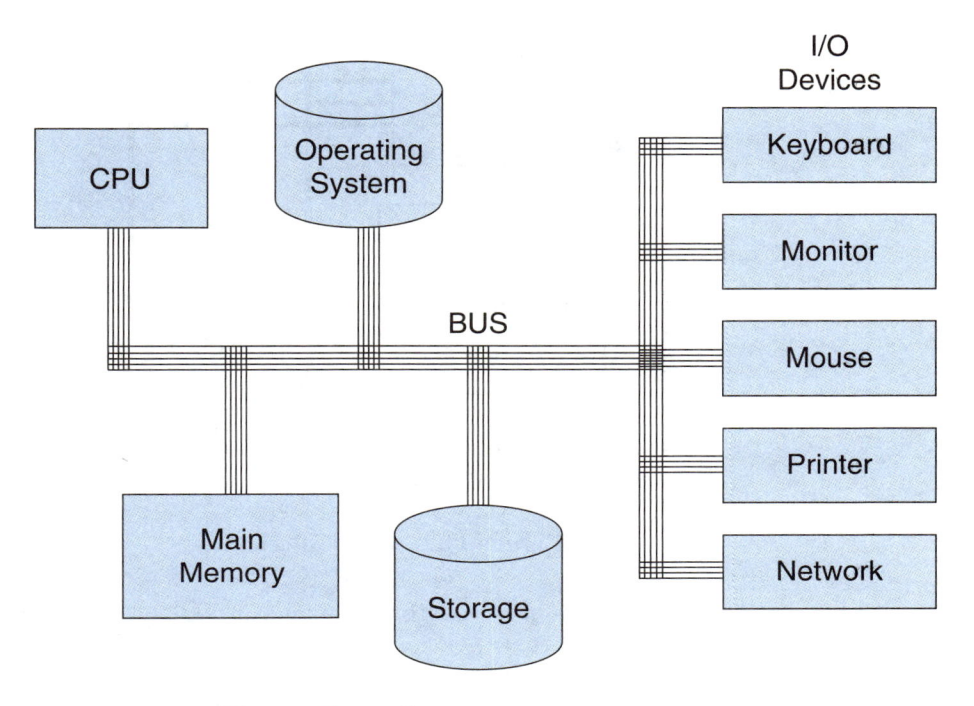

Figure G.1 Computer system components.

The CPU chip itself is quite small, the size of a fingernail or smaller. Because it is enveloped in a plastic or ceramic package, the CPU chip, when handled, appears larger, perhaps an inch by an inch in size, give-or-take. The ceramic enclosure around the CPU chip protects the fragile CPU, connects input and output wires to pins on the chip for easy connection to the rest of the computer system, and is involved in transferring waste heat away from the chip. Depending on how fast the CPU operates, many chips can generate sufficient heat to cause internal failures unless the excess heat is dealt with in some way with fans and radiator fins.

Inside the CPU everything is stored as numbers, represented inside the computer with binary digits. The meaning or interpretation of these numbers depends on what information is being stored: video recordings, sound files, graphic images, words and text, and of course mathematical or accounting numbers. All these types of information are stored as data using binary numbers inside the computer.

The binary number system has only two digits: zero and one. This two-digit system turns out to be convenient to build and manufacture using modern digital electronics technologies. A binary representation of the number eighteen for instance, looks like this in binary:

10010

Appendix G The Computer System: An Overview

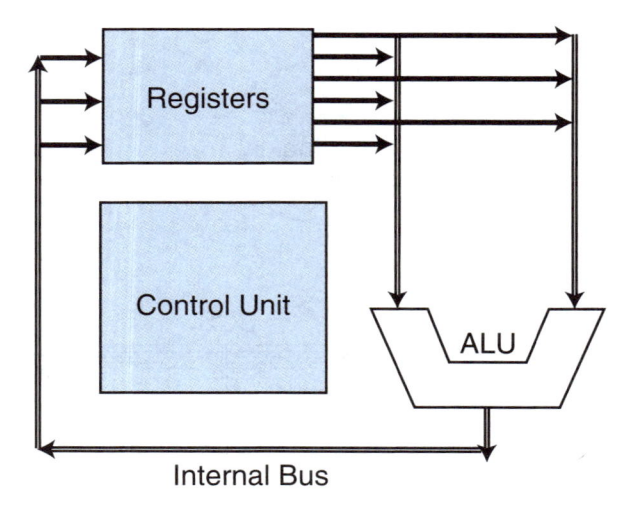

Figure G.2 CPU internals.

All information that we manipulate with computers, including names, pictures. and music, must be translated at some point by the computer and computer software, into simple binary representations. This translation can occur at a number of different times using a small number of ways to represent data and information in binary digits (0,1) called bits. The CPU operates on values represented as binary digits, and in fact, has no "knowledge" about the meaning of the binary numbers, or what they represent in our world. It simple-mindedly manipulates the data represented by binary numbers as it is told to do so by its programs, which are also translated or converted into binary representations themselves before the computer can work with them. The computer itself has no intelligence of its own, and all of its abilities are simply the result of capturing the intelligence and logic of its makers (both hardware designers and software programmers).

A simple central processing unit contains three basic components. Modern advanced processors blur these distinct components and include additional performance-enhancing features, but the three primary components of a simple CPU are:

1. *Registers*: a set of temporary storage locations for numbers while the CPU is working with them. If the intention is to add two numbers together, usually, each number would first be loaded from memory into a register, prior to the adding process. Then, the result of the addition might be stored temporarily in a register, prior to being stored back to the computer's main memory. The CPU can act upon the data stored in its internal registers much more quickly than if it was to work directly with data stored in memory.

2. *Arithmetic Logic Unit (ALU)*: this is the logic that can do operations with binary numbers. In addition to basic math functions like addition, subtraction, multiplication, and division, the ALU can also manipulate numbers in other ways and

compare numbers together for equality and inequalities (greater than, less than).

3. *Control Unit*: This component is the logic that is written into the hardware chip that determines the sequence of events needed to process instructions. Things like: how to decode an instruction; and how to move data from one register to the ALU; where to put results from the ALU; and which instruction should be processed next, etc., are all functions that are encoded in the CPU chip as part of the control logic or control unit of the processor.

Note in Figure G.2, that data flows through the CPU in a cycle, from registers to the ALU, where values are processed, and then the result flows back to be stored in a register.

G.3 Computer Instructions

The computer is a machine that processes instructions. Each single instruction does only a very small task, but the computer can process instructions at such a high rate of speed (millions or billions of instructions per second) that the computer can perform a tremendous quantity of computing work in a short period of time. At the lowest level, computer instructions are represented as numbers stored using the binary number system. The computer's central processing unit (CPU) must examine each instruction that is to be processed, in order to determine what function must be performed (i.e., math operation or other), and what data will be manipulated. This is called decoding the instruction.

The following is a representative assembly-language instruction that adds the contents of two registers together. This operation is abbreviated with ADR, which means to ADd Registers.

ADR R1 R2

Assembly language is a low-level programming language that is closely associated with the machine language that the computer "understands." The assembly language code can be directly translated (by an assembler program) into machine code, which the computer can then process:

010000 0001 0010

The computer is designed to process machine code instructions that are hard for humans to work with. The difficulty of machine code programming led to the creation of assembly language. Assembly language is much easier to work with than machine code, but even assembly is too close to the complexity of the computer hardware, and it is also difficult and tedious to work with. Consequently, even higher-level programming languages have been developed and are in use. This is an example of shifting work from the human programmer to the machine, as higher-level languages require more computer time to convert to machine-readable form, but the tradeoff is worth it.

```
   6         4      4     =14 bits
┌────────┬───────┬───────┐
│   Op   │  R1   │  R2   │
└────────┴───────┴───────┘

   R1 ← R1  Op  R2
```

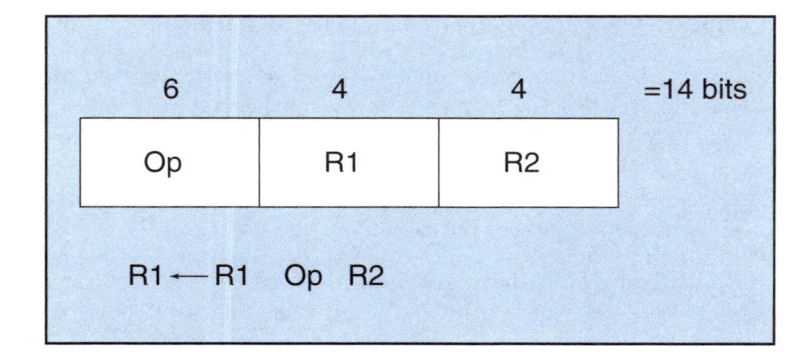

Figure G.3 Simple instruction format.

Machine code and assembly language are organized in an instruction format, with fields that indicate the operation to be performed (Operation Code, shortened to Op-Code or Op), and operands that the instruction will operate on (R1 and R2 are registers).

In Figure G.3, there are fields for the operation code (Op) and two operands (registers R1 and R2). The operation code specifies what operation is to be done, and the operands hold the data that is to be manipulated or modified.

G.4 Fetch/Decode/Execute/Interrupt Cycle

The computer is a digital and electronic machine that processes instructions. Both the instructions themselves and the logic that is needed to process those instructions should be considered to be "captured" human intelligence and logic, which has been incorporated into a machine. The logic that is needed to process computer instructions can be quite complex. As an introduction, the following explains the cycle that the CPU repeats millions or billions of times per second in executing instructions.

1. *Instruction Fetch*: The next instruction to be processed by the CPU must be fetched from the memory into the CPU, where it is stored in a register expressly designed to hold instructions. Fetching an instruction will generally require a single cycle. On some systems with very large instruction formats, a number of processor/bus cycles may be required to fetch an instruction, depending on the width of the instruction and the width of the bus, measured in bits. The logic to do an instruction fetch is part of the control unit of the CPU.

2. *Instruction Decode*: Determines what the instruction is supposed to do, in particular, what operation or manipulation will be performed on the data, and what operands (data) are required before the instruction can execute. Usually, operands will be required to be loaded into registers in the CPU.

3. *Operand Fetch*: Operands that are not already stored in CPU registers may be loaded from memory into registers. If multiple operands are required for the instruction, some computer systems may require multiple fetches from memory to registers. The number of operands that are allowed, and whether or not they must already be in registers inside the CPU, or can be in memory, are key design points in building processor chips. The control unit has the logic needed to fetch operands from memory and store them in registers.

4. *Instruction Execution*: After all operands are ready, and what operation is to be performed has been determined, in this phase of the instruction execution cycle, the CPU control unit instructs the arithmetic logic unit (ALU) to execute the operation on the operands.

5. *Check for Interrupts*: The last phase in the cycle has the CPU pausing to check before executing the next instruction, for signals requesting the CPU's attention. Other devices, events, or inputs may require processing by the CPU, forcing the CPU to interrupt the current program it is executing, to do other things. When a CPU "services" an interrupt, it first saves its place in its current processing, then switches to running other programs and instructions to service the interrupt. Then, after the needed processing is complete, the CPU returns to the "saved place" in its processing and picks up where it left off.

Figure G.4 illustrates this instruction execution cycle, and also illustrates another important idea. Some stages in the cycle are handled internally within the CPU chip itself, while other stages require communication with memory or other devices in the computer. When communication between the CPU and other devices is required, a bus is used to communicate signals and data in bits. That bus is shared by all devices in the computer system, and has the potential to be a bottleneck: the bus can handle only one request at a time, and only one device in the computer can use the bus at a time.

G.5 Simple Computer Instructions

As an example, consider the simple computing function of adding two numbers together. The numbers to be added (operands) are stored in the computer's memory. The result that is computed must also be stored back into memory. For the CPU to do the addition, the operands must first be copied from memory into registers.

```
LOAD R1 Num1
LOAD R2 Num2
ADR R1 R2
STOR R1 Result
```

The initial state of the computer system prior to executing any of these instructions is as follows:

Appendix G The Computer System: An Overview

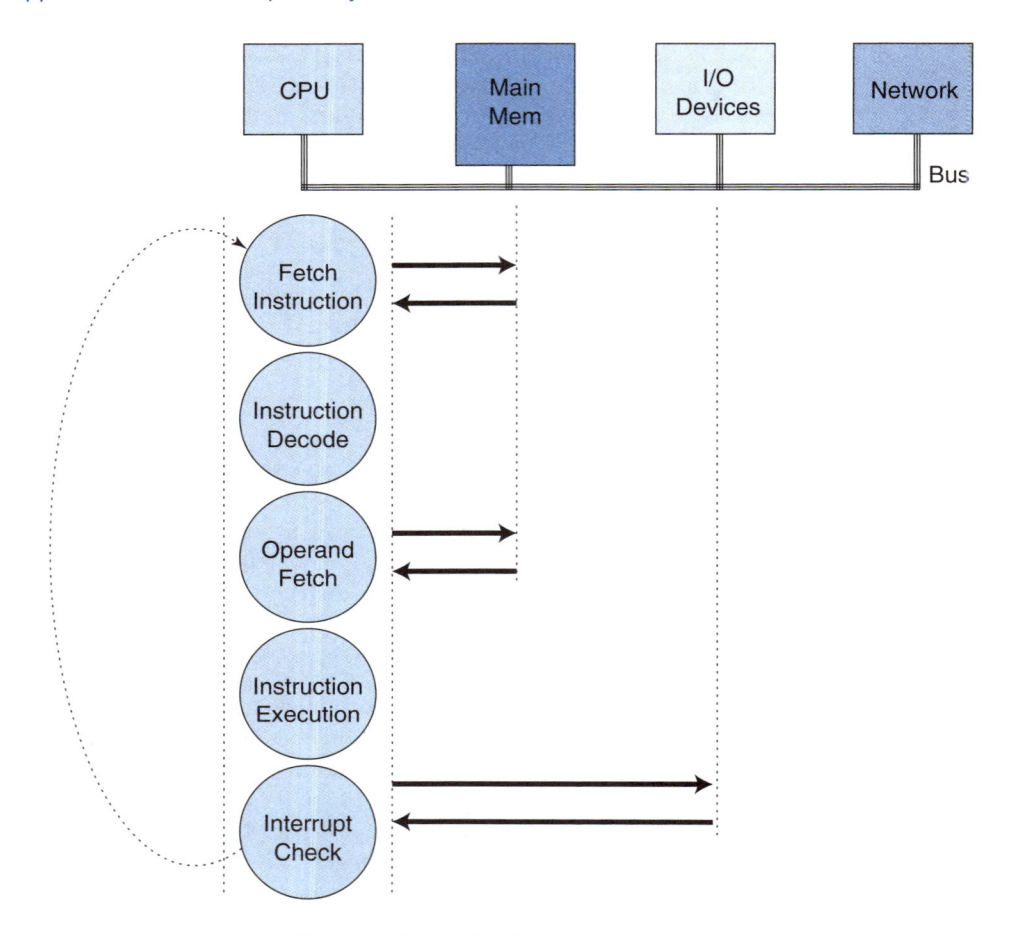

Figure G.4 CPU instruction cycle.

Register 1 empty
Register 2 empty
Number 1 = 4
Number 2 = 5
Result empty

The current "state" of the computer system can be conveniently displayed in Figure G.5, which shows both the contents of the CPU's registers, and the contents of memory:

Note that the sum overwrites the original contents of register R1. Registers are used for temporary storage.

G.5 Simple Computer Instructions

CPU	
Register	Contents
R1	
R2	

Memory	
Location	Contents
Num1	4
Num2	5
Result	

(a) Initial State of the CPU and Memory

CPU	
Register	Contents
R1	4
R2	

Memory	
Location	Contents
Num1	4
Num2	5
Result	

(b) After executing the first instruction:
LOAD R1 Num1

CPU	
Register	Contents
R1	4
R2	5

Memory	
Location	Contents
Num1	4
Num2	5
Result	

(c) After executing the second instruction:
LOAD R2 Num1

CPU	
Register	Contents
R1	9
R2	5

Memory	
Location	Contents
Num1	4
Num2	5
Result	

(d) After executing the third instruction:
ADR R1 R2

CPU	
Register	Contents
R1	9
R2	5

Memory	
Location	Contents
Num1	4
Num2	5
Result	9

(e) After executing the fourth instruction:
STOR R1 Result

Figure G.5 Instruction execution.

This example illustrated in Figure G.5 shows that a number of instructions are required to accomplish a modest amount of work. Some operations may even require substantially more instructions than this simple addition example. The power of the computer is that it can process millions and billions of instructions per second, each doing only a small portion of a task, but because so many instructions can be completed in a small amount of time, the computer can be extremely powerful.

The previous example also illustrates low-level programming functions in an assembly language programming. Programming at this level is painstaking and tedious, so we have developed higher-level languages that make the process easier and less trying for human programmers. In high-level languages, a single instruction can be written that accomplishes the work of the four assembly instructions in the example:

LOAD R1 Num1
LOAD R2 Num2
ADR R1 R2
STOR R1 Result

can be accomplished in a high-level language with a single instruction or programming statement:

Result = Num1 + Num2

G.6 Computer Architecture Layers

A computer system can be viewed as being composed of a set of layers of functionality. This conceptual point-of-view of examining complex systems in layers is used in many areas of computing. This decomposition-by-layer technique is used in building and analyzing networking protocols, building and configuring operating systems, building and integrating multi-tiered computer systems and grid computer systems, to the development of application programs. It is just one way to apply the divide-and-conquer approach to problem solving that allows us to look at a small portion of a large and complex system, and then understand and design each portion individually.

In computer architecture, each layer is constructed on top of the layer before it, and each layer then becomes a foundation for the layers that are created on top of it (Figure G.6). The complexity and details of the foundational layers that are below any given layer are abstracted for the layers built above it. In this way, the complexity and details can be "black-boxed" and hidden, in order to focus on the current layer and its mechanics. Each layer uses the constructions of the previous layers as building-blocks to support the new layer's construction.

This approach is similar to that used in software design, and the point is the same: managing the complexity of the system and design. The following layers create a computing system.

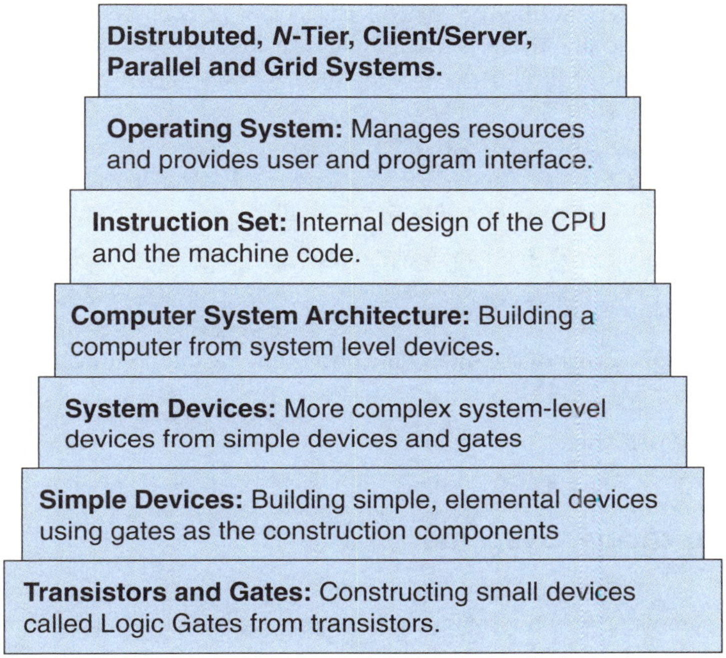

G.6 Computer Architecture Layers

Distrubuted, *N*-Tier, Client/Server, Parallel and Grid Systems.

Operating System: Manages resources and provides user and program interface.

Instruction Set: Internal design of the CPU and the machine code.

Computer System Architecture: Building a computer from system level devices.

System Devices: More complex system-level devices from simple devices and gates

Simple Devices: Building simple, elemental devices using gates as the construction components

Transistors and Gates: Constructing small devices called Logic Gates from transistors.

Figure G.6 Computer system design layers.

1. *Transistors and Gates*: constructing small devices called logic gates from transistors.

2. *Simple Devices*: building simple, elemental devices using gates as the construction components.

3. *System Devices*: building more complex devices (like registers, comparators, and memory) from simple devices.

4. *Computer System Architecture and Components*: building a computer from system-level devices.

5. *Instruction Set*: specifying the CPU internal architecture and capabilities with the instruction set. The instruction set specifies the programmer's interface to the hardware, both machine code and assembly language.

6. *Operating Systems*: provides basic functionality to the device, a user interface to the computer system, and a programmer's interface to the system.

7. *Distributed, N-Tier, Client/Server, and Parallel Systems*: interconnecting many computing systems together to work cooperatively.

The understanding of each of the layers of a computer system and the interdependencies of the layers is the foundation for understanding and comparing different computer system designs. Note that there are architectural designs at multiple levels in a computer:

- Architecture of the CPU
- Architecture of the computer system
- Architecture of the operating system
- Architecture of the computing applications
- Architecture of the interconnections linking one computing system to many others.

Each of these different layers represents a different focus of study, with separate courses and research tracks in each area.

G.7 Operating Systems

The operating system provides very important functions that convert a set of computing hardware into a usable system:

- Manage the resources of the computer system
- Provide a user interface
- Provide a programming interface
- Provide a networking interface

G.7.1 Manage the Resources of the Computer System

Disk space, input/output devices, and CPU processing time are resources that need to be managed efficiently and effectively. The operating system provides a mechanism for organizing the data storage for efficient access. Secondary storage is organized in order to make efficient use of the available space but also to maximize performance by minimizing the physical movement of components inside the disk drive. Disk drives contain read/write heads that float above the surface of the disk and must be moved back and forth over the disk surface. Since physically moving this component is very slow compared to the speed of the other parts of a computer system, it is critical to overall performance to organize the storage to minimize this drag on performance. An efficient mechanism for labeling files on the disk, indexing files, and locating files is provided by the operating system.

The computer consists of a number of input and output devices, from disk drives to monitors to printers and network interfaces. Each of these devices requires access and

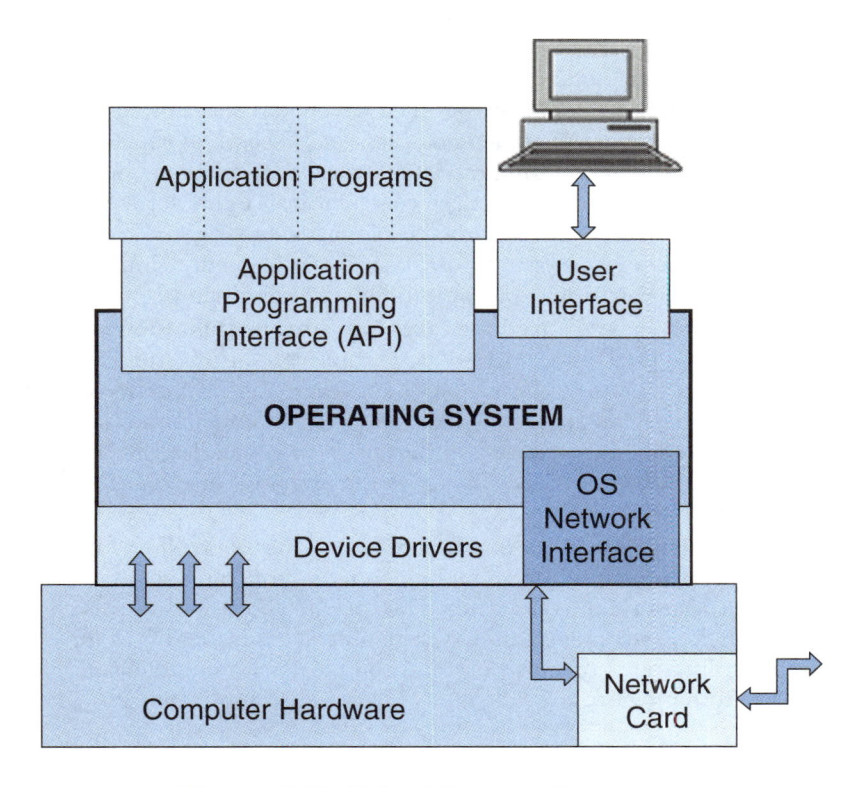

Figure G.7 Role of the operating system.

control through a defined process. The operating system contains device-driver software specific to each hardware device. The operating system also controls which process or user program is granted access to specific devices and manages that overall process to avoid conflicts and interference.

Managing the CPU processing is particularly interesting when the computer can run multiple processes at the same time, and can support multiple users on the system at the same time. A strategy that allocates CPU time in small pieces to each running process is called time-slicing and allows the user to multi-task. The strategies and algorithms devised to accomplish this very important function are particularly intriguing, as they must perform their function fairly and without wasting processing time.

G.7.2 Provide a User Interface

Users must have a way to interact with the computer and the software applications. This is accomplished through a software component that is part of the operating system.

The simplest form of user interface is a command-line interface, which allows the user to type (or speak) commands to the system. The user must know the language and syntax for providing commands, which can be arcane and complex at times. A more user-friendly interface that demands less of the user is the *Graphical User Interface* (*GUI*), which provides a kind of virtual world with pictures and graphics that the user can manipulate and interact with to control the system. More recent investigations have extended this concept through the development of a virtual environment and interface designed to allow humans to interact with the machines similarly to the way that we interact with other people and objects in our daily living.

The object behind this design trend is to make this Human–Computer Interaction (HCI) simpler and more natural and intuitive, shifting more of the communication effort from the human to the machine. The command-line interface requires that humans study and learn a language that the computer can understand (more work for us), while a virtual interface is software and hardware that handles the translation effort for us. In all cases, the user interface insulates the human users from the internal complexities of the computer.

The strategic decisions of where to place the work/effort and complexity between the main components of a system: human users, software, and hardware, is a pervasively interesting question in computing. The specific allocations of this effort fluctuates with technological developments and ever greater demands and uses for computing systems. The general trend is to shift work and complexity from humans into software, and from software to hardware.

G.7.3 Provide a Programming Interface

The operating system contains the software code needed to interact with the hardware systems in the computer. Applications software should use this system software to access resources in a controlled fashion, so the operating system must provide a way for applications to hook into these services. Often called the API (application programming interface), the OS manufacturer provides a defined interface as a set of modules or functions that can be called from within program software.

G.7.4 Process Execution Mode

Process privileges and execution mode are important ideas for protecting the operating system and other user processes. This section explains how a process obtains services and resources from the operating system by running in privileged mode, as implemented in Unix and Linux and similar operating systems.

When a process needs an OS service or resource, it actually changes from its current non-privileged user mode to a privileged kernel or OS mode. This change occurs when the process executes a software interrupt (or trap) instruction, which acts similarly to a hardware interrupt. Then the process itself executes the operating system code and routines needed to provide the desired service. Conceptually, rather than have a process generate a formal request to an "operating system entity" and wait for that entity to provide the service, the process itself becomes the operating system (temporarily) in order to run the OS code to provide its own services.

A process executing in privileged mode executes OS software and routines that are a part of the OS core or kernel. Those routines execute in a privileged memory space occupied by the OS, with access to data structures and information that the OS is managing. When the process has completed its required service, it switches back to nonprivileged mode to continue processing.

This change in mode is called a mode switch, which is different from a context switch, to be discussed later.

There are a number of advantages to this mode-switch approach. Security and permissions can be explicitly applied when a process needs to transition from nonprivileged to privileged mode. A process attempting an inappropriate action can be denied at this point, resulting in a protection violation interrupt. Also, this mechanism avoids a potential performance bottleneck, which would otherwise occur if a single OS entity were satisfying requests. With privileged-mode transitions, it becomes possible for multiple processes running at the same time, to be executing system code to handle their requirements, avoiding stop and wait times that would otherwise occur.

G.7.5 Provide a Networking Interface

Computers are networked together through local area networks (LANs) and the Internet, to allow users to exchange information and access programs and resources on other machines. The software to manage the network interface unit (NIU) and to control access to the Internet and to provide a World Wide Web browser as a user interface, has been incorporated into and integrated with the operating system. The programming interface (API) also includes a way for software to access networked resources and the Internet through operating system provided functions.

G.8 Language Translation

Programming a computer in its basic machine code of zeros and ones is inherently hard for humans, as machine code instructions are closely related to the internal design and construction of the processor itself. We prefer to use more human-friendly languages and high-level programming languages that are human-centric interfaces to communicate with our computing machines. At some point a translation must occur, to convert our instructions into a form that the computer can understand—primitive bits that can be either zero or one.

Fundamental to this concept is the shifting of work from the human to the computer with human-friendly interfaces that require more work on the machine's part, and less work for the human programmer.

```
  2    6    4    4    = 16 bits
┌──┬──────┬────┬────┐
│00│  Op  │ R1 │ R2 │
└──┴──────┴────┴────┘
     R1 ← R1 Op R2
```

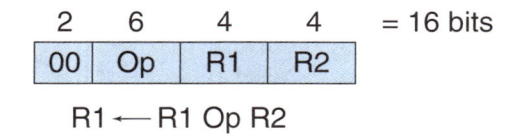

Figure G.8 Machine instruction format.

A machine code instruction is composed of a set of fields (like a record in a database), where each field has a specific use, and specific binary number codes in those fields represent different operations and events. For instance, Figure G.8 illustrates a machine instruction format for a simple computer system.

The numbers above the format are the number of bits allowed in each field. This instruction format has four fields, and the total number of bits in the instruction is 16.

The leftmost field (two bits in size) indicates the specific instruction format. The 00 in this field indicates that this is the layout for instructions of type 00. Since two bits are allowed for this field, there are four basic instruction types for this computer ($2^2 = 4$), type 00, type 01, type 10, and type 11.

Counting from the left, the second field is used to indicate the operation code, or opcode. This is the specific operation that the computer is to perform, like add, subtract, etc. Since there are six bits allowed for this field, there are ($2^6 = 64$) different operations (instructions) possible in instruction format type 00.

The third field from the left is 4 bits in size, allowing 16 combinations. This field represents the operand that the instruction will work with. Operands like registers and memory locations hold data values to be processed. For this type of instruction, the operands are all numbers stored in registers in the CPU, because the only operands allowed by the format are of type register. Any of the 16 registers could be listed in an instruction as either of the two operands. Other formats will allow operands that are stored in memory, which are referenced with an address. The fourth field is also a register operand.

The representation directly beneath the figure is a logical representation of what this instruction type does: It takes two operands stored in registers (R1 and R2) and combines them/modifies them in some way as specified by the operation code, with the result then being stored back into the same register and replacing the first operand (R1).

Each field is stored as a binary (unsigned) value, so if the desired operation is to add the two operands together, the Opcode must be represented or coded as the correct binary number. For instance, the 6-bit OpCode for adding two registers together might be 010000.

Specifying, in binary, the operand registers is simple:

Register 1 = 0001 (binary value of 1 in 4 bits)
Register 2 = 0010
Register 3 = 0011
Register 4 = 0100
Etc.

So an entire 16-bit instruction to add the contents of two registers can be represented as bits for each of the four fields:

00 010000 0001 0100

From this set of bits, it is clear that this is an instruction of type 00 (which allows two registers as its operands), the operation is an add operation, and the two values to be added are stored in registers 1 and 4.

Machine code instruction formats are actually closely tied to the internal design of the CPU itself. A specific CPU is designed to "understand" a specific machine code language, with definitions for instruction formats, opcodes, and the number of registers that are specific to this CPU. The hardware circuits that are able to "understand" a machine code instruction are part of the CPU called the decoder. The decoder literally decodes the 0s and 1s in a machine code instruction into the correct hardware-level actions needed to execute the instruction.

G.8.1 Assembly Language

Working in binary is particularly difficult for humans, as it is tiresome, and we are very prone to errors at this level. An easier language, called assembly language, was developed to make the programming process less tiresome. Assembly language itself did not add additional new capabilities or features to the machine, or change its machine code. It simply substituted a more human-friendly set of symbols or acronyms to replace the raw bits. For instance,

ADR R1 R2

is an assembly-language representation of the same machine-code instruction previously considered. ADR means to add two registers together, while R1 and R2 specify the registers to be added. It is understood that for this particular instruction format (00), the result of the operation always replaces the first operand by storing the result in the location of the first operand. Other, more complex, formats might have a separate field for specifying where the result is to be stored. A program to translate assembly language into its proper machine code is called an assembler.

Later, assembly languages began to evolve by offering improved features through a system of "macros." Macros allow blocks or sections of often repeated assembly code to be abstracted, and represented with an abbreviation. The programmer could write "macro1:" in place of the block of code containing many instructions. When translating the assembly language to machine code, the assembler will literally substitute the predefined block of instructions for each instance of the macro label, and then translate each instruction in that block.

G.8.2 High-Level Languages

Assembly language generates 1:1 machine code instructions when translated: one machine code instruction for each assembly instruction. As computing evolved, the need for more powerful and higher-level programming languages that are easier to work with became apparent. In high-level programming languages, a single instruction might be used in place of a handfull or many machine-language instructions that are often used together in the same repetitive pattern. For instance, the instruction

Sum = Number1 + Number2

might represent the four machine-language instructions to load the operands (Number1, Number2) from the computer's memory into two registers (two machine instructions), add them together (one machine instruction), and then store the result back to memory at the location called Sum (one machine instruction).

Languages like C, C++, Cobol, Fortran, and Pascal are all compiled languages, where the program that is run that does the translation of the high-level program instruction to machine code, is called a compiler. The compiler will run through the set of instructions written in the high-level language and will create a new machine-code program. The high-level program instructions cannot be run by the computer directly, but the new machine-code program that results from the translation by the compiler, CAN be executed by the computer (Figure G.9). This translation (compiling) need be done only once for a finished program and the machine-code program that results may be executed as many times as desired. However, if the high-level language program is modified, the program must then be recompiled to create a new executable machine-code program.

An alternative translation mechanism for high-level languages is called an interpreter. An interpreter does not produce a machine code program to be run. Instead, the interpreter translates one high-level language instruction at a time, and immediately passes that translated instruction to the processor to be executed (Figure G.10). Interpreted computer languages are traditionally slower than compiled language programs because each instruction must be translated while the program is being run, and instructions that are repeated may have to be retranslated each time. Interpreted languages include BASIC and VisualBASIC.

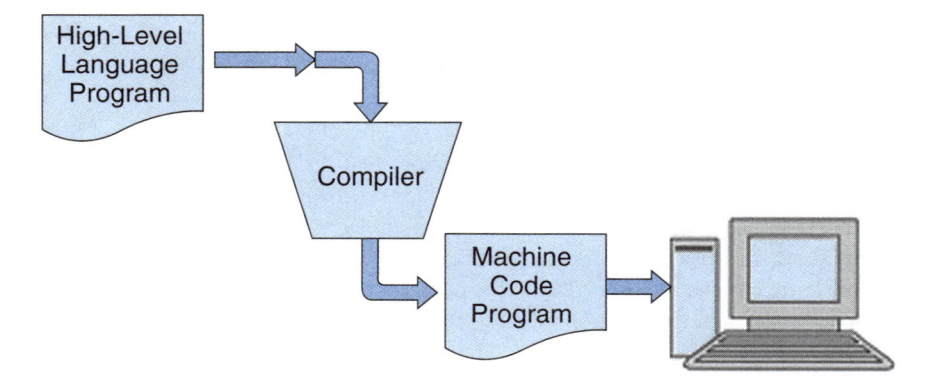

Figure G.9 Compiling a program.

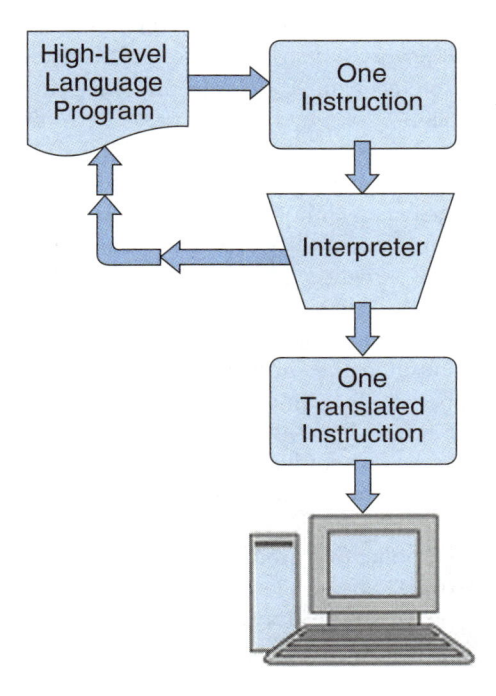

Figure G.10 Interpreting a program.

A modern take on interpretation has evolved for the Java language and Internet, where an interpreter/run-time environment is installed on each computer that will run Java. The interpreter/run-time environment is specific to the processor and machine code that it will run on. Then, any Java program can be run on any machine anywhere, independent of the machine code and processor type. This run-anywhere flexibility is very powerful and useful, and has contributed to Java's acceptance as a modern programming language.

G.8.3 Byte Code and the Virtual Machine

An intermediate language translation concept has evolved that shares aspects of both a compiler and an interpreter. The goal is to improve performance over that of an interpreter, while creating a way to make programs more portable.

Each computer processor has its own machine code, which is unique to that processor family. Yet we use many different types of processors in different computers, from mainframes to servers to PCs to personal digital assistants (PDAs) and embedded machines. To make a program written in some language portable to different CPU architectures, either an interpreter or a compiler must be developed specifically for that machine. Furthermore, the program must then be compiled using the compiler for that target CPU so the program can be run by that machine.

The software engineer must either compile his program for each CPU architecture that users might choose, or, send the source code to every user for them to compile on their machines. Neither is a satisfactory solution.

A better solution, which has been applied to a number of languages, is to develop an intermediate step between compilers and interpreters that has the advantages of decent performance and easy portability. For the Java language, the Java program must be translated into what is called byte code, and the byte code can be downloaded and distributed over the Internet. The byte code is a partially compiled program that runs on an abstract or "virtual" machine. The user must use a software program on their machine (the virtual machine software) to run the Java code.

Using this concept, Java programs can be run on any machine that has a "Java Virtual Machine." An application written in Java is then easily portable to any machine architecture without conflicts, because the application is compiled to run on the virtual machine, not the target machine's CPU architecture. Figure G.11 illustrates this process.

The universal application and adoption of the Internet and its associated technologies and protocols, has accelerated the need for portable applications that can be downloaded from a site on the Internet, and run on any machine that has a Java virtual machine.

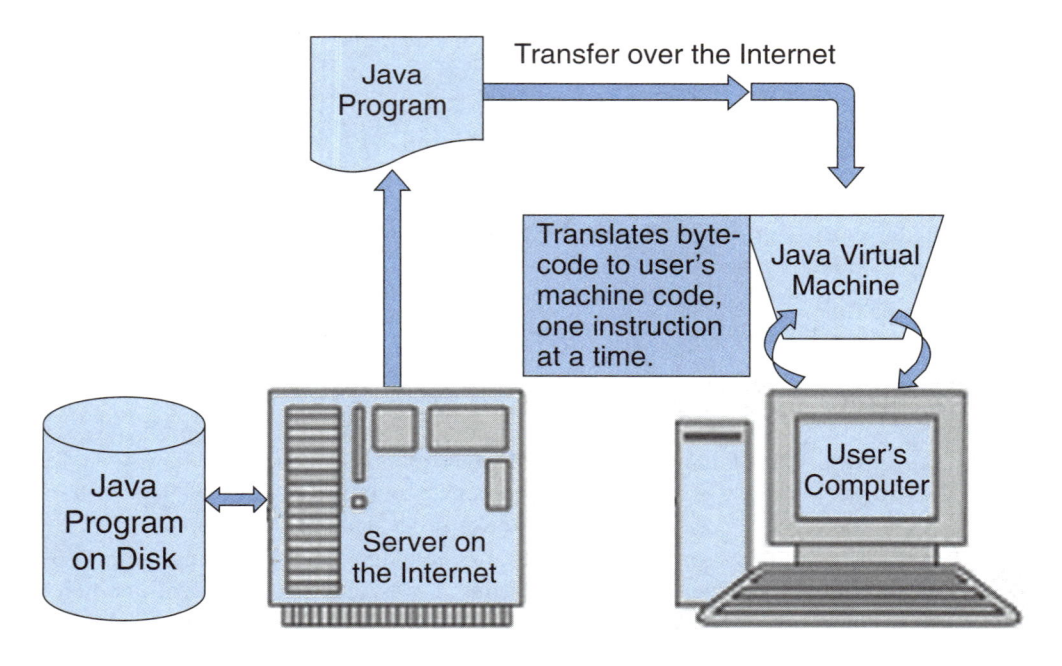

Figure G.11 Java virtual machine.

G.9   CPU Internal Structure

The internal design of the central processing unit (CPU) makes for a fascinating study for a couple of reasons:

1. The internal design of the CPU reflects the design of the machine language, to the point where the computer's low-level machine language is almost a specification for the design of the CPU itself! That is, when a designer decides what functions and operations the machine will perform at the low level, that design will require specific hardware capabilities. Making the desired low-level functions possible will require specific hardware and internal pathways. So the design of the machine language also specifies the hardware devices and pathways that will be required internally inside the CPU.

2. The second fascinating investigation is exploring enhancements to the basic computer architecture that have evolved over the years, which maximize the power and speed of the CPU.

The CPU is traditionally described as having three primary components: A set of registers for storing values, an arithmetic logic unit (ALU) that can manipulate values (math and bit manipulations), and a control unit, that controls the sequence of events inside the CPU, and orchestrates the Fetch/Decode/Execute cycle.

What needs to be added to this short list is an "interface" to the outside world: special registers for communicating data and addresses to the system bus, and internal buses for moving values around inside the CPU itself.

The control unit won't be shown in the diagram as a separate piece or component, as in actuality, it is arrayed on the CPU chip where it is needed, and where space is available. Figure G.12 shows a simple arrangement of CPU components.

Figure G.12 shows that internal buses connect the set of registers to the ALU. Note that there is a cycle, where values flow from the registers to the ALU, are processed in the ALU, and then flow back to registers.

The A Latch is needed because of the flow of voltage levels through the system—recall that all these components are constructed from gates and transistors that take inputs and create outputs. The A Latch is a separate register that is needed to hold a register value constant while it is *also* an input to the ALU for processing. This is needed when the result of the ALU processing is intended to go back into, and replace, the contents of one of the source registers. Without the A Latch, the voltages would race through the ALU, through the registers, and then back again to the ALU, so the ALU would then see the resulting value appearing as its input, causing further changes. To understand this fully, imagine if a register value contained the number "2", which was to be incremented by one. Without the A Latch to hold the "2" constant, the 2 would be incremented by the ALU to 3, flow into the register and be stored as a 3, but also flow back to the ALU as a 3, to be incremented (again) to a 4, and back to the registers, etc. So in the case when a single register is both a source of the data value, and the destination for the manipulated value, the A Latch is necessary. In the case

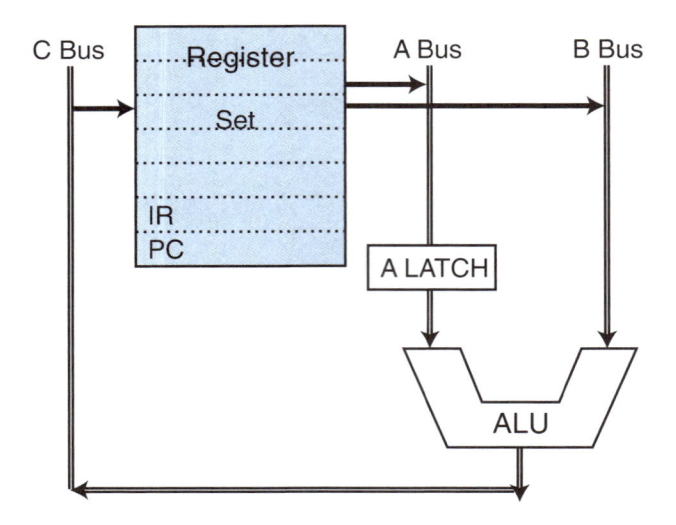

Figure G.12 Internal CPU architecture of a simple computer.

where the result from the ALU operation is to be stored in a different register from the source, the A Latch is not necessary.

The job of the control unit is to set the correct registers to produce their outputs on one or the other of the buses going to the ALU, set the ALU to do the desired operation, and sets the correct register to receive a new value from the ALU. The control unit decodes the current instruction (based on the bits of the instruction itself) to determine the correct settings for all these devices and buses, and controls the sequence of operations.

G.9.1 Adding the System Bus Interface

The CPU construction so far does not have a way to communicate with the outside world (the system bus, memory, I/O devices, etc.). The CPU connects to the system bus, which contains bus lines for exchanging data, and bus lines for specifying an address. The address lines are used both for specifying the addresses of instructions and the addresses of data. Similarly, the data lines are used both for moving instructions from memory to the CPU, and for moving data between the memory and the CPU. A special register is needed for storing an address that connects directly to the bus address lines, and a special register is needed for storing data values that is connected directly to the bus data lines. Figure G.13 illustrates these additions.

The MDR register is a memory data register, used for exchanging data and instructions between the CPU and memory (and possibly other devices). The MAR is a memory address register, used for specifying an address in memory to either read from or write to (and for communicating with other devices as well). Consider what is to

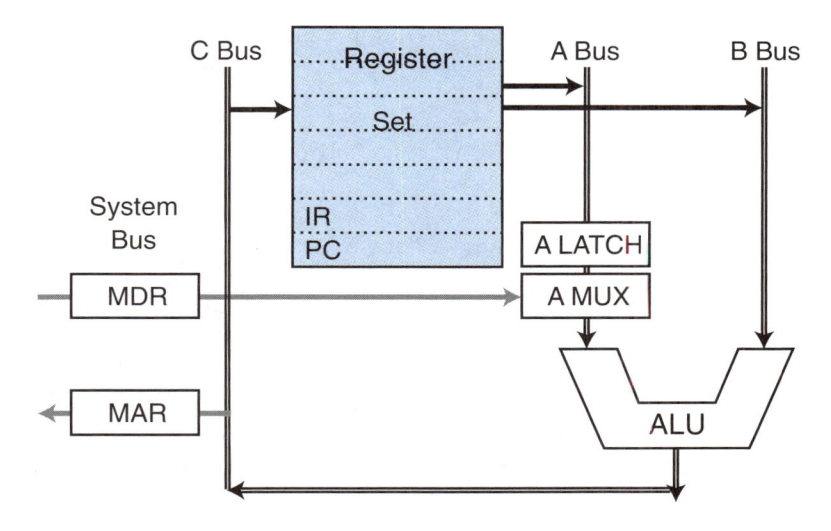

Figure G.13 CPU architecture with external bus interface.

happen in the case where the contents of a register are to be added with a value stored in memory, with the result to be stored back into a different register in the CPU:

1. The first step is to move the address of the data value that is to be loaded from memory, out to the bus. This address can be derived from a field in the instruction itself (details on how this is done are reserved for later study). The address flows from a special register called the instruction register, which contains the current instruction to be processed. The address flows through the ALU (without being changed) to the MAR, where it appears on the system bus.

2. The memory is "watching" the bus, and observes when a new address is posted to the address lines for it to work with. The memory internally processes the address and finds the values stored at the address.

3. The memory places the data values on the bus for the CPU to see.

4. The CPU latches on to the data on the bus, which is stored in the MDR within the CPU.

5. The MDR also connects through the A MUX to inputs to the ALU, so the ALU can then add the memory value from the MDR together with another value stored in a register. The A MUX is a multiplexer, which allows either the value from the MDR to flow into the ALU, or, it allows a value from a register to flow into the ALU. The A MUX then functions like a switch, allowing two possible inputs to that side of the ALU. The control unit circuitry determines what the proper switch setting should be for the A MUX, and controls the A MUX with a signal line.

6. The ALU then adds the value from memory on the A MUX input together with a value from a register on the other input side of the ALU, to produce the desired result.

7. The result from the ALU then flows back along the bus to be stored in a different register in the register set.

What about the case where a data value from a register passes through the ALU, to be stored out to memory? The CPU internal diagram must be modified to add a multiplexer to the MDR, so that a value coming from the ALU can be stored into the MDR. The MDR must work both ways, both to store a value going from the CPU to memory, and to store a value going from memory to the CPU.

Figure G.14 illustrates the new connection from the ALU to the MDR. The MDR now has two possible sources of data, either from the bus (not shown), or from the output of the ALU. The MDR needs the ability to choose which source to take a value from. It will be integrated with a multiplexer to allow that choice, which will be controlled by the control unit logic and circuits. The rest of the simple CPU internal wiring is logically determined by the required movement of data between the parts of the CPU and the system bus. The design of the processor instruction set (the set of instructions that the CPU must implement, which programmers use to control the machine) determines what the CPU must do. Thus, the design of the set of instructions that are to be implemented generally precedes the design of the CPU internal architecture itself.

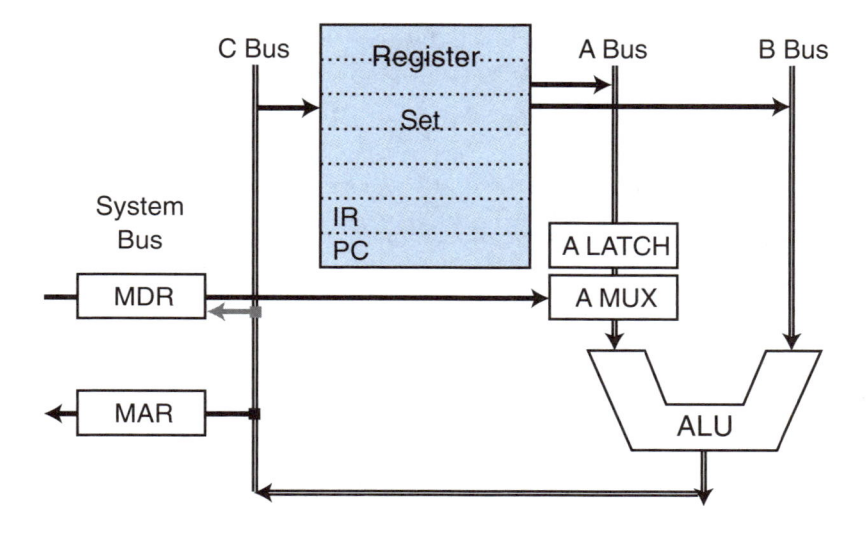

Figure G.14 CPU architecture with bi-directional MDR.

G.9.2 Supporting the Instruction Fetch

A special case for accessing the system bus exists when the CPU needs to fetch a new instruction. The program counter (PC) is a special register that is used to hold the address of the next instruction in the program. To fetch the next instruction, two things need to happen concurrently:

- The address of the next instruction (in the PC) must be placed in the MAR, so that memory will provide the next instruction to the CPU.
- The contents of the PC must be incremented, so that the PC will have the address of the next instruction to be executed (after the one being fetched concurrently).

The existing pathways can be used to increment the PC: Send the PC out on the A Bus through the A Latch to the ALU, where it is incremented, then out to the C Bus and back to the PC in the register set. The PC must be placed into the MAR, and this must occur prior to being incremented. So this means that the PC must also get to the MAR without going through the ALU. This requires an additional pathway in the CPU internal architecture, as shown in Figure G.15.

G.9.3 Detailed Program Execution

A more sophisticated version of executing the program than what was presented earlier includes more details. Specifically, the program itself is also stored in the computer's memory, and each instruction must be fetched from memory into the CPU before it can

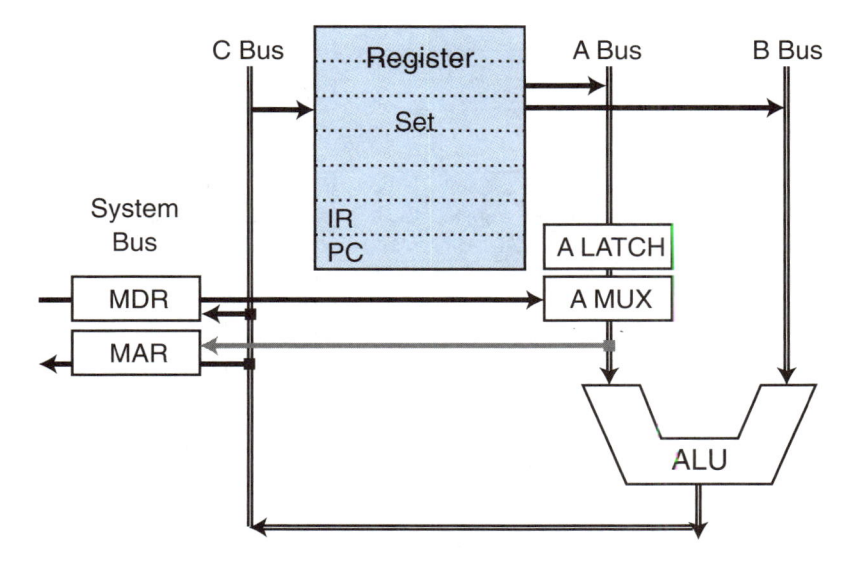

Figure G.15 CPU with instruction fetch support.

be executed. The CPU has a special register that is used to store the current instruction being executed called the instruction register, abbreviated IR.

The computer's memory consists of a set of storage locations each with a unique address—like a postal address. These addresses are numbers, and each memory storage location is numbered sequentially. Names like NUM1 and NUM2 are associated with specific addresses. In Figure G.16, NUM1 is an alias for the location 00.

CPU	
Reg	Contents
IR	
PC	04
R1	
R2	

Memory	
Location	Contents
00: Num1	4
01: Num2	5
02: Result	
03:	
04:	LOAD R1 NUM1
05:	LOAD R2 NUM2
06:	ADR R1 R2
07:	STOR R1 Result

(a) Initial State

CPU	
Reg	Contents
IR	LOAD R1 NUM1
PC	05
R1	
R2	

Memory	
Location	Contents
00: Num1	4
01: Num2	5
02: Result	
03:	
04:	LOAD R1 NUM1
05:	LOAD R2 NUM2
06:	ADR R1 R2
07:	STOR R1 Result

(b) First Instruction Fetched

CPU	
Reg	Contents
IR	LOAD R1 NUM1
PC	05
R1	4
R2	

Memory	
Location	Contents
00: Num1	4
01: Num2	5
02: Result	
03:	
04:	LOAD R1 NUM1
05:	LOAD R2 NUM2
06:	ADR R1 R2
07:	STOR R1 Result

(c) First Instruction Executed

Figure G.16 Detailed instruction execution.

G.9 CPU Internal Structure

CPU		Memory	
Reg	Contents	Location	Contents
IR	LOAD R2 NUM2	00: Num1	4
PC	06	01: Num2	5
		02: Result	
R1	4	03:	
R2		04:	LOAD R1 NUM1
		05:	LOAD R2 NUM2
		06:	ADR R1 R2
		07:	STOR R1 Result

(d) Second Instruction Fetched

CPU		Memory	
Reg	Contents	Location	Contents
IR	LOAD R2 NUM2	00: Num1	4
PC	06	01: Num2	5
		02: Result	
R1	4	03:	
R2	5	04:	LOAD R1 NUM1
		05:	LOAD R2 NUM2
		06:	ADR R1 R2
		07:	STOR R1 Result

(e) Second Instruction Executed

Figure G.16 Detailed instruction execution (continued).

The CPU has another special register that is used to store the address of the next instruction to be executed called the program counter, abbreviated PC.

Each time an instruction or data value is needed from memory, the CPU must first send the address over the system's bus.

1. The initial state of the computer prior to executing the program is shown in (Figure G.16(a)). The program counter is set to the address of the first instruction of the program.

2. The first step is to load the first instruction of the program from memory into the CPU's instruction register (IR). At the same time that this is occurring, the program counter (PC) is updated for the next instruction (Figure G.16(b)).

3. Next, the first instruction is executed, which loads the number stored at location 00 (Num1) into Register 1 (Figure G.16(c)).

4. After executing the first instruction, the CPU must fetch the second instruction (which is stored at location 05 in memory (Figure G.16(d)).

5. The second instruction is now executed by the computer (Figure G.16(e)).

6. The program execution continues to completion. The next step is to load the next instruction that is to be executed. It is recommended that the student walk through the remainder of the program as an exercise.

G.10 CPU Performance Enhancement: Pipeline

The CPU construction illustrated to this point is consistent with the design of early electronic computers from the 1950s into the 1970s. In the modern computer CPU, a number of interesting, clever, and sophisticated performance-enhancing features have been added to this simple construction, in order to achieve much higher performance from the CPU, as measured in the number of instructions processed in a unit of time. One such performance enhancement feature is the pipeline, and another is the use of cache (covered later in this chapter).

The key to the pipeline is the observation that all instructions go through a similar set of stages while being processed (Figure G.17).

The instruction execution cycle consists of five stages, the first four of which can create a pipeline inside the CPU:

1. Fetch the next instruction
2. Decode the instruction
3. Fetch any operands needed from memory
4. Execute the instruction

Each of these stages requires some hardware in the control unit, or the ALU itself. When an instruction is being fetched, the other hardware used for the other stages is idle. Similarly, when the ALU is executing the desired operation, the other hardware components are waiting while that occurs. The key concept behind pipelined instruction execution is to run instructions though all stages of the pipeline simultaneously, so that all of the hardware stages are working rather than idle (Figure G.18).

This produces a speedup of processing due to the parallel execution of multiple instructions at the same time (though each instruction is in a different stage of execution).

Figure G.19 shows a pipeline executing instructions over time. In the first cycle, the first instruction is fetched, and another instruction enters the pipeline in each successive cycle. The first instruction does not complete until after it has passed through all four pipeline stages, after cycle 4. This time delay between when the first instruction enters the pipeline, and when the first instruction is complete is called the pipeline load time.

After the first instruction is completed, all remaining instructions complete in the next successive cycles, without this delay. The pipeline load time applies to the first instruction only.

Once the pipeline has been loaded, the instructions are completed about four times faster. The speedup in processing is roughly equal to the number of stages in the pipeline, in this case four.

G.10 CPU Performance Enhancement: Pipeline

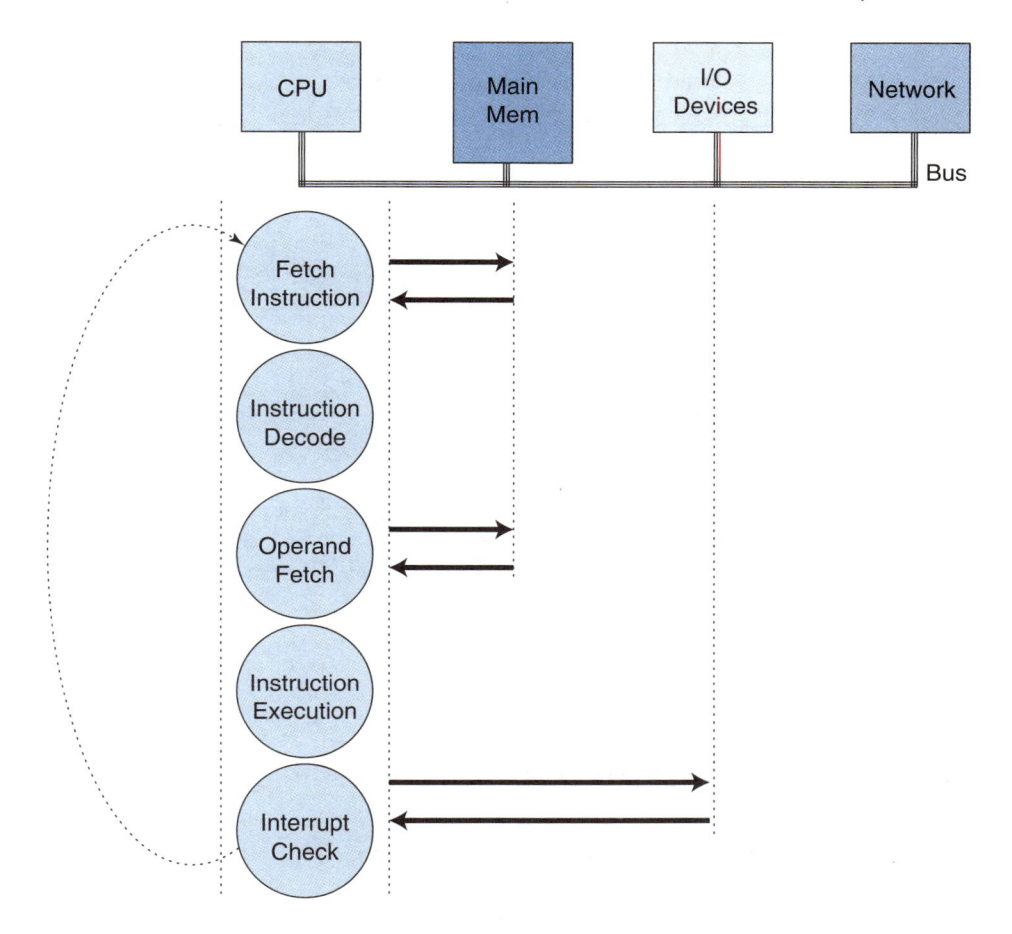

Figure G.17 CPU instruction execution cycle.

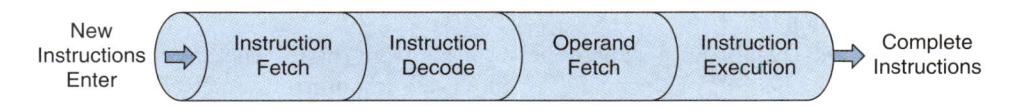

Figure G.18 Four-stage pipeline.

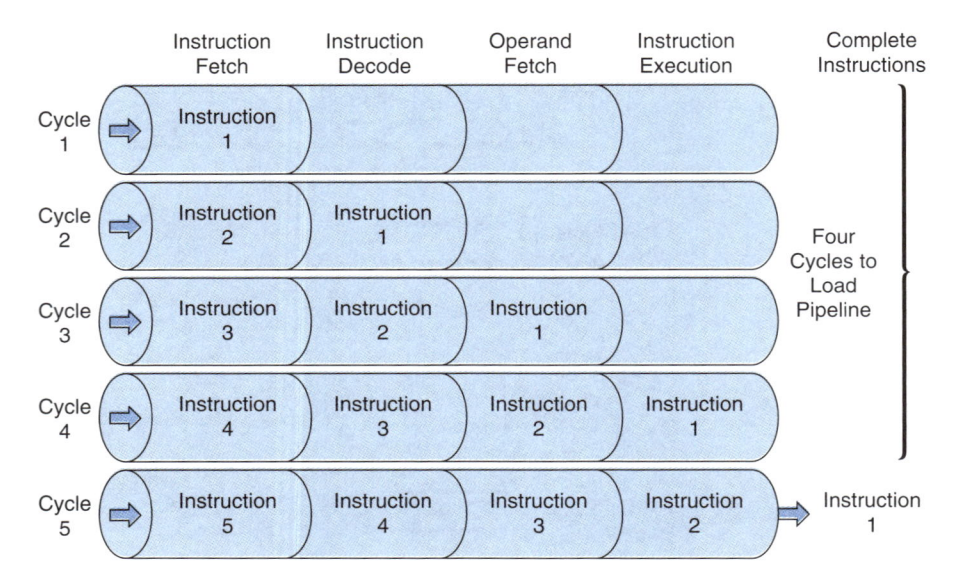

Figure G.19 Instructions flowing through a pipeline.

G.11 System Performance Enhancement: Cache

Cache is an important technology that is used to improve many aspects of computing systems. The basic idea is to use a small amount of high-speed and local memory as temporary storage, in order to buffer the interaction with a slower device. The most needed data is kept in the fast cache, and the machine only has to look in the slower memory or on the slower device when it needs something that is not in the cache. Cache can improve the performance of a computing system tremendously, as the frequency of a machine finding what it needs in cache can be extremely high (99% or more for some applications).

Cache can be applied across computing from the Internet and the World Wide Web, to inside the CPU chip itself. All modern computer systems utilize cache in multiple places in the system.

G.11.1 The Need for Cache

Historically, memory performance has not kept pace with processor performance, creating a disparity between two critical components of a computer system. Or, put another way, the cost of making memory perform at a certain level is much higher than the cost of making a processor that runs at that same speed. This disparity in performance potentially creates a performance bottleneck that limits the overall speed of a computer system to the speed of the memory system. In addition, the Von Neumann computer system architecture exacerbates this disparity by requiring multiple memory accesses for each instruction. In addition to fetching the instruction from memory, many instructions also require one or more operands that also come from memory along with the instruction.

The use of pipelines as a technique that increases the number of instructions that can be completed in a given time period, further multiplies this problem. Increasing the number of instructions and operands that can be processed further increases the memory/bus bandwidth required to keep up with the demands of the processor. (Here, bandwidth is used in its common computing meaning, being the communication requirement in terms of bits per second, rather than its more traditional communications usage as a range of radio frequencies.)

Clearly, computer system performance has, in fact, continued to increase as the performance of processors also continues to increase, since computers continue to get more powerful and faster with each generation. This implies that there must, in fact, be a practical solution to this performance disparity, one that mitigates the performance bottleneck effects. That solution is caching.

Caching is a technique that reduces the data transfer demands of the processor that go over the bus to the memory. By holding the instructions and data values currently being used in a small, relatively expensive but very high-speed memory called a cache, the CPU will often find the data that it needs in the cache. The cache is fast enough to keep up with the demands of high-speed processors, so accessing data and instructions in the cache does not slow down the processor. It is only when the processor requests access to memory that is NOT currently in the temporary high-speed cache, that a request for data or instructions must go out on the bus to the system memory. The idea is that most of the time, the processor can get what it needs from the high-speed cache, and only occasionally it will have to slow down to load a new block of data or instructions from memory into the cache. Following that loading of a block of data or

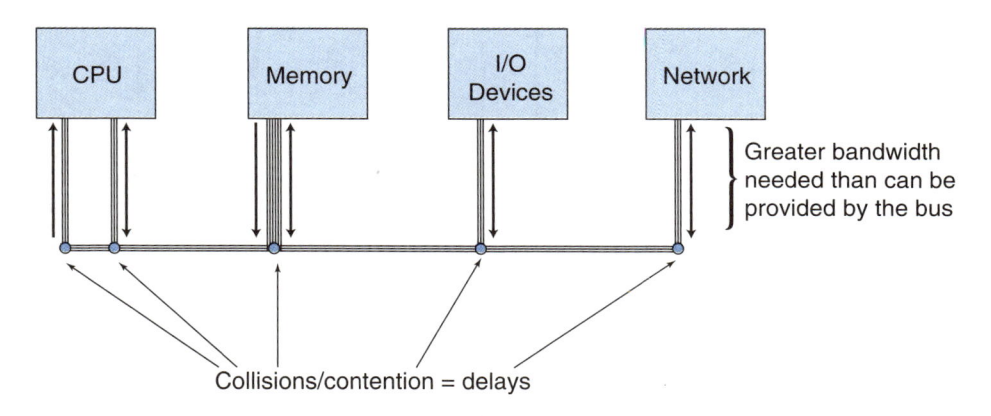

Figure G.20 Von Neumann bottleneck.

instructions into the cache, the processor can then proceed again at high speed.

Caching is a mechanism that has turned out to be highly effective. It has been applied to a number of different problems in computing where a disparity in speed of access exists:

- Caching blocks of memory to solve the disparity between the performance of the CPU and memory. This cache is located on the processor side of the bus, so that memory requests that are satisfied by the cache do not need to use the bus, freeing that resource for other uses.

- Caching hard drive data to mitigate the performance disparity between the hard-drive and main memory.

- Caching blocks of memory that are in use by multiple processors in a multi-processor or multi-computer parallel system, to mitigate the time-to-access (called latency) between memory that is local to one processor, and is non-local to other processors and is accessed by distant processors at a higher latency than the access time from the local processor.

- Caching blocks of data in a multiple processor system in order to reduce the bandwidth requirements on the interconnection network between the processors. Reducing the bandwidth requirements of the processors on the bus/memory system allows more processors to access a shared bus or interconnection network before the bandwidth demands overload the interconnection network bandwidth capability.

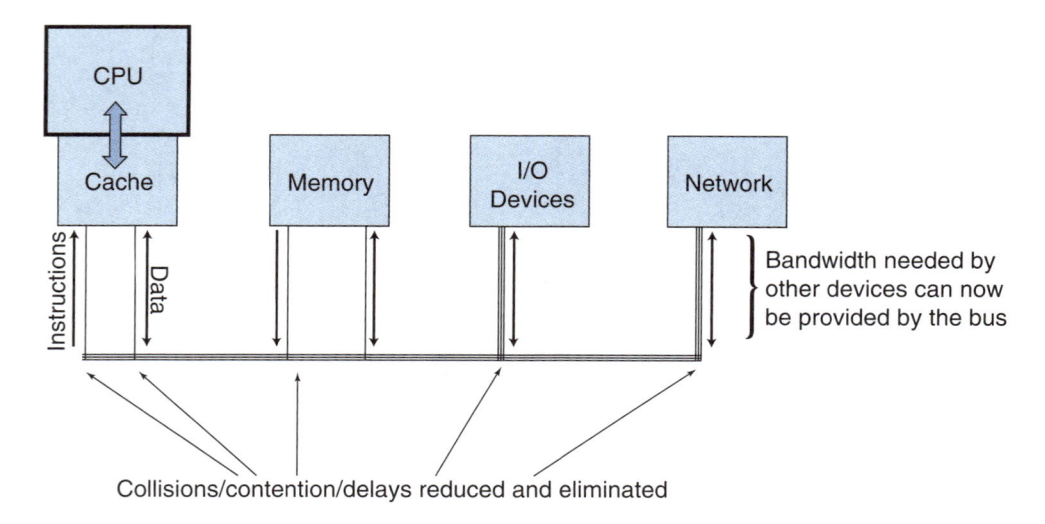

Figure G.21 System with cache reduces contention.

- Caching blocks of data in a communication system like the Internet, to mitigate the effects of communication latency for data (or web pages) that are held remote from the requesting processor, and to reduce the overall bandwidth demands on a system with hundreds, thousands, or millions of computers.

- Caching information about running programs in a multiple-user system, where the operating system must share the CPU between many users and between many running programs. Caching is used to reduce the amount of time required to switch from one running program (called a process) to another process. The switching is called a "context switch," and this special-purpose cache for this purpose might be called a register set or register file.

It turns out that caching in practice is highly successful, and its universal and wide application to many different problems where there is a performance disparity, or a need to reduce interconnect bandwidth, leads to the description of cache as the "universal computing band-aid."

It is worth considering the principles behind caching and considering why it works so well. The foundation observations behind caching are the locality principles. These have to do with the patterns of access in memory locations over time by the processor.

- *Temporal Locality*: The most recently accessed memory locations are more likely to be accessed again in the immediate future, than are less recently accessed memory locations.

- *Spatial Locality*: Blocks of memory that are near to the most recently accessed memory block, are more likely to be accessed in the future than are blocks that are farther away.

What characteristics of programs, when they are being executed, yield these observations?

- Programs contain loops that repeat the same instructions in the same areas of code (both locality principles). These loops may repeat anywhere from a handful of times to millions of times.

- Programs are sequential: the next instruction is the most likely to be needed instruction (spatial).

- Data processing is often sequential: data may be organized in fields and records, and may be accessed in the order that they are stored in the system.

Memory is cached in blocks—anywhere from 0.5 to 2K bytes per block are common. The two locality principles imply that it makes sense to store the memory blocks that are most likely to be accessed memory in the future in expensive high-speed memory. This will yield a high probability that many accesses will be satisfied by the cache, yielding, on average, a faster memory response time.

These two principles say that the most recently accessed memory block is very likely to be accessed again, so it pays off to store it in the high-speed cache. Less likely to be accessed blocks will be stored in slower memory, and perhaps even on secondary storage (disk) in a virtual memory system. Some percentage of memory accesses will be satisfied very quickly (low latency) in the cache, while the remainder will require access to the slower memory. The average rate of access will be between the low latency cache and the high latency memory. The greater the percentage that can be handled by the cache, the lower the average memory access latency.

G.11.2 Cache Performance

The computer system has memory storage components that respond at different speeds, building inherent performance disparities. A memory latency hierarchy exists in computer systems:

- CPU cache
- Memory
- Hard disk
- Networked storage
- CD or tape storage

Cache improves the average performance of a system:

- The accesses or requests that are satisfied by the cache are termed "hits" in the cache. This fraction of memory accesses occur at the speed of the fast cache.
- The accesses or requests that are not satisfied by the cache (have to go out to memory or other storage) are termed "cache misses." This percentage of requests for memory/memory-access occurs at the slower latency of the system memory.

All requests for memory are satisfied by either the cache or the system memory. This leads to a simple way to model the performance improvements that result from the use of cache.

$$\text{Prob(hit)} + \text{Prob(miss)} = 1$$

Average system request access performance then is:

$$\text{Prob(hit)}*\text{Time(cache)} + (1\text{-Prob(hit)})*\text{Time(miss)}$$

An example:

$$\text{Cache access time} = 5 \text{ nanoseconds}$$
$$\text{Memory access time} = 50 \text{ nanoseconds}$$
$$\text{Cache hit rate} = 90\%(0.9)$$

$$\begin{aligned}
\text{Average Latency} &= \text{Prob(hit)} * \text{Time(cache)} + (1 - \text{Prob(hit)}) * \text{Time(miss)} \\
&= 0.9(5) + 0.1(50) \\
&= 4.5 + 5 = 9.5\text{ns}
\end{aligned}$$

G.11 System Performance Enhancement: Cache

Observe that the average system latency with cache at 9.5ns is much better than the performance of the memory alone (50ns). An obvious question is to wonder if high cache hit rates are reasonable in the real world? Experience has demonstrated that the answer to this question is yes! In fact, in many cases, cache hit rates in the high 90s are common. The following calculations illustrate the average latencies that result from varying cache hit rates:

Hit Rate			
50%	$0.50(5) + 0.50(50)$	$= 2.50 + 25$	$= 27.50$ns
90%	$0.90(5) + 0.10(50)$	$= 4.50 + 5$	$= 9.50$ns
95%	$0.95(5) + 0.05(50)$	$= 4.75 + 2.5$	$= 7.25$ns
99%	$0.99(5) + 0.01(50)$	$= 4.95 + 0.5$	$= 5.45$ns

The effectiveness of caching also depends on the performance disparity between the cache and the memory. When there are large differences, there are large payoffs to using caching:

Cache access time = 5ns, Memory access time = 50 ns
Cache hit rate = 95% (0.95)
Ave Mem Latency $0.95(5) + 0.05(50) = 4.75 + 2.5 = 7.25$ns
Large disparity: 50ns down to 7.25ns == 85.5% improvement!
Cache access time = 5ns, Memory access time = 10ns
Cache hit rate = 95% (0.95)
Ave Mem Latency $0.95(5) + 0.05(10) = 4.75 + 0.5 = 5.25$ns
Smaller disparity: 10ns down to 5.25ns == 47.5% improvement.

Other issues with caching must wait for future exploration:

- What about cache writes?

- How to manage the blocks in cache (block replacement)?

- How to find the desired memory block in the cache?

Caveats:

- The calculations shown above are somewhat simplified:

    - Memory speed is time to read a single value

    - What about blocks of memory? — these take longer load times

    - Cache Writes? — write to cache

    - Finding a cache block, or freeing a spot for the new block

- The "miss penalty" could be much worse than our simplified analysis.

G.11.3 Fully Associative Cache

This section will end with an example of a fully associative cache. Fully associative cache allows blocks to be stored at any location inside the cache. This freedom to store blocks is very flexible and contributes to good performance, but the tradeoff is that the computer will have to check all blocks in the cache to find the particular memory block desired. Part of the address of the memory block will be used as a tag in the cache, in order to identify the desired cache block.

Example: A computer system has

128MB (million bytes) of Memory (2^{27} bytes),
1MB of cache memory (2^{20} bytes),
1KB cache and memory block size (2^{10} bytes),

From these specifics, information about the cache and memory can be deduced:

- The number of blocks in the cache = $2^{20} / 2^{10} = 2^{10}$ = one thousand or 1K blocks.

- The fraction of memory that can be held in cache = 1MB/128MB = 0.78%.

Since a block can be stored anywhere in the cache, a method of identifying the specific cache block is needed. In fully associative cache the memory address is divided into two fields, a tag to identify the block, and an offset (or internal block address) to specify the location of the memory desired within the cache block itself. All of the cache block tags must be compared with the tag bits from the address.

The necessity of comparing all tags for all cache blocks is reasonably expensive hardware, and the cost grows as the size of the cache grows. This cost constrains the fully-associative method to be restricted to small caches. Other variations on cache design have been developed that trade-off optimum performance for reduced cost.

Figure G.22 illustrates the process of accessing a cache block from a 27-bit address. Since the cache block is 1KB (2^{10}) in size, 10 bits in the address are required to locate

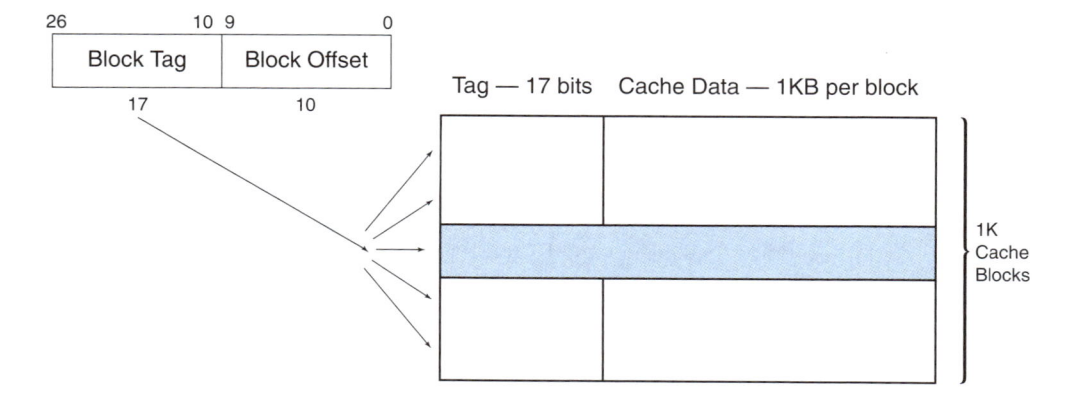

Figure G.22 Fully associative cache.

the byte within the block (the block offset). The remaining bits of the address are used as the tag bits that uniquely identify each block, and are used for the comparison.

The cache of Figure G.22 requires a parallel comparison of Tags of all 1024 blocks that are in the cache, against the Tag bits from the address. Requiring this many parallel comparisons in turn, requires a substantial hardware cost, making this design a large and expensive fully-associative cache.

Key Terms

arithmetic logic unit	assembly language	average latency
bus	cache	cache block
compiler	computer system components	control unit
CPU	fully-associative cache	high-level language
input/output	instruction execution cycle	instruction format
interpreter	machine code	memory
opcode	operand	OS mode
pipeline	register	software interrupt
user mode	virtual machine	

Exercises and Questions

Computer Architecture

1. Explain the architecture layer concept, and why it is useful to view computer systems using this conceptual model.

2. List and describe the basic components of a computer system.

3. Describe the role of the CPU in a computer system.

4. Explain the cycle that the CPU goes through in executing instructions.

5. Explain what the ADR instruction of Section G.3 does.

6. If you were to add a subtract instruction to the simple programming instructions of Section G.3, explain in detail, what your instruction would do.

7. Draw a diagram like those shown in Section G.3, showing a simple computer system with three registers containing the numbers 3, 5, and 7, and three memory locations containing the number 2, 4, and 8.

8. Design a program of simple computer instructions (as in Section G.3) that will add two numbers together that are stored in memory locations named NUM2 and

NUM3, and put the result of the addition into memory at the location labeled NUM1.

CPU Function

1. Explain the sequence and flow through the internal CPU that is required to store a data value from a register to a memory location.

2. Explain the sequence and flow through the internal CPU that is required to move a data value from a register into the CPU.

3. Explain the sequence and flow through the internal CPU that is required to add two operands (values stored in registers) together, and store the result back into the register of one of the operands.

4. Explain the sequence and flow through the internal CPU that is required to add two operands (values stored in registers) together, and store the result to a memory location.

5. What is the speedup that could be obtained from a 5-stage pipeline, disregarding the pipeline load time?

6. Consider the simple pipeline of Figure G.18. Which stages in the pipeline access memory, and which stages are completed entirely within the CPU itself?

7. The bus and memory can typically allow the CPU to access one value at a time in memory. If two pipeline stages both need to access memory at the same time, one stage or the other will have to wait (stall). Suggest a possible fix for this problem (called a "structural hazard").

8. Complete the program walkthrough of Section G.9.

Language Translation

1. Explain the difference between a high-level language and assembly language.

2. Why is translation necessary?

3. What does a machine-code instruction format do?

4. Using the instruction format explained in section G.8, write a machine code instruction that will add the contents of register 4 with register 5, with the result replacing the contents of register 5.

5. If the opcode for multiply is 000100, write a machine code instruction that will multiply register 2 and register 4, with the result replacing the contents of register 4.

6. What is the difference between an interpreter and a compiler?

7. Why are interpreted languages slower than compiled languages?

8. What are the advantages of the byte code/virtual machine concept?

Cache

1. What is the purpose of caching in a computer system?

2. Explain why caching works

3. Calculate the average latency for a system with:
   - Cache access time = 2 nanoseconds
   - Memory access time = 50 nanosecond
   - Cache hit rate = 98% (0.98)

4. Consider a computer system with a hard drive of 100GB in size with an average access time of 20ms (milliseconds). You are considering purchasing software to cache the disk using the computer's main memory. By using 200 megabytes of your machine's main memory, you expect to see hit rates to the memory used as disk cache of 95%. The latency for a cache hit (hit in the memory used to cache the disk) is 500ns (nanoseconds). A millisecond is 10^{-3}, and a nanosecond is 10^{-9}. Calculate the average latency time for disk access with the disk cache software. What percentage of improvement was achieved?

5. Where can a block be stored in a fully-associative cache?

6. What is the primary disadvantage (that increases cost) of the fully-associative cache organization?

Bibliography

Almeida, V. A. F., D. A. Menasce, and D. W. Dowdy. *Capacity Planning and Performance Modeling: From Mainframes to Client-Server Systems*. Englewood Cliffs, NJ: Prentice Hall, 1994.

Ash, Carol. *The Probability Tutoring Book*. Piscataway, NJ: IEEE Press, 1993.

Banks, J., and J. S. Carson. *Discrete-Event System Simulation*. Englewood Cliffs, NJ: Prentice Hall, 1984.

Blanchette, Jasmin, and Mark Summerfield. *C++ Gui Programming with Qt3*. Englewood Cliffs, NJ: Prentice Hall, 2004.

Deitel, H. M., P. J. Deitel, and D. R. Choffnes. *Operating Systems*, 3rd ed. Upper Saddle River, NJ: Pearson Prentice Hall, 2004.

Douglas, Bruce P. *Real-Time UML Second Edition Developing Efficient Objects for Embedded Systems*. Reading, MA: Addison Wesley Longman, 2000.

Dowdy, Larry, and Craig Lowery. *P. S. to Operating Systems*. Englewood Cliffs, NJ: Prentice Hall, 1993.

Fishwick, Paul A. *Simulation Model Design and Execution Building Digital Worlds*. Englewood Cliffs, NJ: Prentice Hall, 1995.

Flynn, I. M., and A. M. McHoes. *Understanding Operating Systems*. Pacific Grove, CA: Brooks/Cole, 1991.

Goodman, Roe. *Introduction to Stochastic Models*. Reading, MA: Addison-Wesley, 1988.

Jain, Raj. *The Art of Computer Systems Performance Analysis*. New York: Wiley, 1991.

King, Peter J. B. *Computer and Communication Systems Performance Modelling*. Hemel Hempstead, England: Prentice Hall International, 1990.

Kleijnen, Jack P. C. *Simulation: A Statistical Perspective*. New York: Wiley, 1992.

Lewis, Bil, and Daniel J. Berg. *Multithreaded Programming with PTHREADS*. Mountain View, CA: Sun Microsystems Press (Prentice Hall), 1998.

Medhi, J. *Stochastic Processes*, 2nd ed. New York: Wiley, 1994.

Bibliography

Mitrani, I. *Simulation Techniques for Discrete Event Systems.* Cambridge, England: Cambridge University Press, 1982 (reprinted 1986).

Molloy, M. K. *Fundamentals of Performance Modeling.* New York: MacMillan, 1989.

Nelson, Barry L. *Stochastic Modeling, Analysis and Simulation.* New York: McGraw-Hill, 1995.

Norton, Scott J., and Mark D. Dipasquale. *The Multithreaded Programming Guide: Threadtime.* Upper Saddle River, NJ: Prentice Hall, 1997.

Nutt, Gary. *Operating Systems: A Modern Perspective*, 3rd Ed. Boston, MA: Addison Wesley Longman, 2004.

Schwetman, Herb. "Using CSIM to Model Complex Systems. " *Proceedings of the 1988 Winter Simulation Conference.* San Diego, December 1988, pp. 246–253.

Selic, B., G. Gullekson, and P. T. Ward. *Real-Time Object-Oriented Modeling* New York: Wiley, 1994.

Silberschatz, A., P. B. Galvin, and G. Gagne. *Operating Systems Concepts*, 6th ed. New York: Wiley, 2002.

Stallings, William. *Operating Systems Internals and Design Principles*, 4th ed. Upper Saddle River, NJ: Prentice Hall, 2001.

Tanner, Mike. *Practical Queuing Analysis.* New York: McGraw-Hill, 1995.

Tannenbaum, Andrew S. *Modern Operating Systems*, 2nd ed. Upper Saddle River, NJ: Prentice Hall, 2001.

Index

abstract method, 412
abstraction, 1
access matrix, 315
access method, 211
    sequential, 211
address, 260
    binding, 262
    physical, 261
    relative, 260
    relocatable, 261
    space, 260
    symbolic, 260
    translation, 268, 277
aging, 151
allocation state, 201
Amdahl's law, 346
Android, 9
anomaly detection, 327
application programming interface (API), 528
application software, 2
arithmetic logic unit (ALU), 518, 538
arrivals, 506
assembly language, 519, 520, 524, 531
asymmetric encryption, 320
atomic transaction, 170
average, 500

batch, 45
batch systems, 7
best fit, 265
binary digits, 518
biometrics, 312
blocked indefinitely, 176
boot block, 222

bottleneck, 58, 127
break point/balance point, 347, 348
buffer, 136
buffered writes, 246
buffering factor, 245
bus, 516, 536

caching, 247, 342, 544, 548, 550
capability, 318
capacity, 58
circular scan, 251
circular wait, 178, 189
class, 132, 141, 410
    base, 411
    derived, 411
    interface, 413
    main, 141
    members, 410
    monitor, 156
    Res, 183
    semaphore, 141
    semaphores, 132
    thread, 138
    waitq, 167
client-Server, 357
cluster, 350, 352
cluster allocation, 218
communication, 162
    channel, 166
    indirect, 162
    mailbox, 162, 164
    message, 163
compaction, 266
compiler, 261, 532
computer system, 517

Index

concurrency, 172
condition queues, 156
condition variables, 158
confidence interval, 508
configure I/O, 233
connectionless, 339
connection-oriented, 339
contention, 354
context switch, 9, 64, 74, 83, 103
context switching, 6
contiguous allocation, 262
control unit, 519
cookies, 324
CPU, 39, 61, 515, 516, 535
CPU burst, 32, 63, 66, 69, 78
CPU scheduler, 79
CPU service, 78–80, 82–87, 98–100, 102, 103, 108, 110, 116
CPU utilization, 37, 40, 41, 56, 58, 59
critical section, 131, 134
cumulative distribution, 501

data buffer, 216
data, files, 207
data, storing, 207
database engine, 207
deadline, 117
deadlock avoidance, 201
deadlock detection, 203
deadlock prevention, 189
defend system, 310
demand paging, 279
denial of service, 310
denying access, 312
device address, 252
device controller, 240
device driver, 238, 239
device interfaces, 233
device interrupt, 235
devices, 233
DHCP, 341, 343
digital certificates, 320
digital signature, 320
dining philosophers, 181
directory entry, 211
handle, 211
disk, 237
disk context switch, 248
disk fragmentation, 221
external, 221
internal, 221
disk scheduling model, 254
disk, platters, 237
disk, track, 237
distributed computing, 356
distribution functions, 489, 502
DNS, 341, 342
domain, 312, 313
domain model, 314
dynamic binding, 262
dynamic paging, 282, 299
dynamic partitions, 264
dynamic priority, 115
dynamic relocation, 266

efficiency, 345
encapsulation, 156
encryption, 319
entry section, 134
estimates, 508
ethernet, 335
event, 498
event ordering 135
events, 39, 43–46, 49, 53, 183, 499
random, 45
exception, 414
exchange data, 162
execution ordering, 135, 179
exit section, 134
experiment, 498
external fragmentation, 265
external security, 309

failure, 504
failure recovery, 171
fair system, 151
fairness, 41, 80, 82, 83, 92, 108, 116, 127, 145

FAT system, 223
fault frequency, 304
FCFS, 82, 249
file, 207
    access permissions, 209
    buffer, 213
    close, 212
    create, 217
    delete, 217
    extension, 208
    filename, 208
    location, 208
    operations, 211
    pointer, 215
    read, 213
    rename, 217
    size, 208
    space allocation, 217
    type, 208
    write, 214
firewall, 326
flash memory, 208
flush, 217, 247
folder, 209
fragmentation, 264, 268, 278
    external, 265
    internal, 264
frame, 268, 275
frame number, 270
frames, 268, 275
frequency, 498

Gantt chart, 83, 85
graph cycle, 179, 194
graphical animation, 142
graphical user interface (GUI), 516, 528
grid, 350

high-level language/programming, 519, 524, 531
histogram, 502, 508
hold and wait, 178, 189
holes, 264
home directory, 377
Human–Computer Interface (HCI), 528

hypertext markup language (HTML), 340

I/O, 61
    burst, 32, 63, 66, 67, 69, 78
    device, 233, 516
    device, mapping, 371
    performance, 244
    queue, 63
    redirection, 216, 384
    request, 239
    request queue, 240
    requests, 248
    scheduling, 248, 251
    service, 78, 81
indefinite waiting, 176
independent activity, 167
inheritance, 410
input queue, 38, 39, 44, 49
instruction, ordinary, 363
instruction, privileged, 363
instruction, sensitive, 363
intelligent bus, 241
interactive, 99
interactive systems, 7
interconnection, 353
interfaces, 239
internal fragmentation, 264
internet, 333
internetworking, 337
interpretation, 115, 532
interprocess communication, 129
interrupt, 234
interrupt service, 235, 243
interrupted, 98
intrusion detection, 327
IP addresses, 327, 334, 337
iPhone OS, 9

Java, threads, 22, 415
job, 8
joint activity, 166

kernel, 5

latency, 354
levels of parallelism, 349

lightweight process, 19
linker, 261
Linux, 375
Linux Ext2, 226
LJF, 82
loader, 261
locality, 273, 279
logical address, 260, 261, 268
loosely-coupled, 357

machine code, 520, 529
main, 432
maximum claim, 201
mean, 500
measurements, 40
memory, 259
    main, 515
    nonvolatile, 208
    partitions, 259
memory capacity, 43
memory demand, 43
memory partitioning, 259, 262
memory protection, 262, 317
memory-less, 504, 505
message, 166
message transfer, 162
method overriding, 411
model, 38
model animation, 256
models, 37–39, 42, 44–46, 56, 59
    continuous, 44
    deterministic, 43
    discrete-event, 44
    graphical, 38
    mathematical, 38
    performance, 40
    physical, 38
    simulation, 42, 43, 45
    state, 44
    stochastic, 43, 45
monitors, 129, 132, 156
multiclass, 80, 82, 92, 101, 108, 116
multiple inheritance, 414

multiprogramming, 16, 31, 61, 64, 65, 67–71, 73, 74, 259, 262
    degree of, 31, 62, 65, 70
multithreading, 19, 20
mutual exclusion, 130, 160, 178, 189

next-fit, 265
no preemption, 178
noncontiguous allocation, 268
nonpreemption, 189
nonpreemptive scheduling, 81
Normal distribution, 142
NTFS, 225
N-tier, 358
NuBus, 253

object, active, 46, 65
object, passive, 46
objects, concurrent, 22, 415
ODBC, 358
open request, 212
operating system, 2, 516
    categories, 7
    examples, 9
    functions, 6
    goals, 2
    guest, 361, 364, 365, 368
    host, 361, 364, 365, 368
    interfaces, 3
    services, 2
operation code, 520
overflow, 324
overhead, 34
overlapped CPU and I/O, 64, 74
overlapping CPU and I/O, 33

page, 273
page fault, 279
page fault frequency, 304
page faults, 278, 281, 282, 284
page replacement, 280
page table, 268, 270
pages, 268

paging, 268
parallel computing, 344
partition, 262
    fixed, 263
    variable, 264
partition control, 222
pathname, 209
PCB, 18
PCI bus, 253
peer-to-peer, 358
performance, 41, 56, 114, 165, 233, 252, 260, 267, 304, 507
performance analysis, 38
performance measures, 145
performance metric, 40
performance metrics, 39–41, 43, 44, 59, 89
periodic process, 117
phishing, 323
pipe, 215
pipeline, 542
plug and play, 253
polymorphism, 413
POSIX threads, 28
preemptive, 80–82, 103, 108
preemptive scheduling, 81, 98
priority, 79–82, 92, 94, 101, 108, 110, 117, 124, 146, 151
priority queue, 94, 110, 148
privacy, 328
probability, 498
    conditional, 499
    continuous, 489, 501, 504
    density, 501
    discrete, 489, 501
    measure, 498
process, 8, 15, 64
    active, 305
    behavior, 32
    blocked, 176
    cooperation, 166
    coordination, 129
    creation, 16
    descriptor, 18
    interact, 163
    locality, 278
    management, 16
    nonterminating, 138
    reactivated, 137
    speed, 130
    states, 16
    suspended, 163
    wait, 138, 145, 163
    waiting, 176
process control block, 18
program, 1
    execute, 1
    link, 1
    load, 1
    translation, 1
programs, 1
protection, 309
protocols, 253, 335
pseudorandom, 500
Psim, Bin, 141
Psim3, 145, 471, 472
PsimJ, 431
PsimJ2, 141
Pthreads, 28, 152, 423

queue, 37–39, 43, 46, 47, 49, 58, 59, 61–65, 74
    I/O, 63
    input, 62, 69, 71
    ready, 62, 63, 66, 78, 94, 110
    size, 43

race condition, 130
random variable, 501
random variables, 501
readers-writers, 146
ready queue, 62, 63
ready state, 17
real-time, 117
reference locality, 273
reference stream, 282
register, 518, 538
reliability, 252
removable media, 229
rendezvous, 167

Index

resource, 77, 160, 240
resource allocation, 16, 177
resource type, 176
resources, 130, 175, 259
    acquiring, 175, 182, 195
    active, 16
    allocation, 176
    allocation graph, 177
    allocation state, 177, 188
    available, 175
    passive, 16
    requesting, 175
    shared, 130
    using, 176
rotational latency, 237
RR, 82
run state, 17
running, 16

safe state, 201
sample point, 498
sample space, 498
SCAN, 250
scheduler, 33
scheduling mechanism, 77
scheduling policies, 80
scheduling policy, 77
secondary storage, 516
secure communication, 319
seed, 500
seek time, 237
segment, 273
segment table, 271
segmentation, 271
segments, 271
self-certification, 321
semaphores, 129, 132
    binary, 133, 148, 190
    counting, 133
    objects, 132
    P, 133
    signal, 133
    V, 133
    wait, 133
service demand, 32, 63

set, 497
    complement, 498
    empty, 497
    intersection, 498
    membership, 497
    union, 498
shared buffer, 136
shared memory, 357
short-term scheduling, 78
simulation models, 43
simulation run, 44
single-class system, 80, 87
SJF, 82
software, cookies, 324
software components, 1
software trap, 365
solid state disk, 238
source program, 1
space management, 220
space–time tradeoffs, 247
speedup, 345
sporadic process, 117
spyware, 310, 324
SRT, 82
SSTF, 249
standard I/O, 216
starvation, 80, 92, 108, 146, 151, 181, 250
state dependency, 248
state diagram, 17
state transition, 510
static binding, 262
static paging, 282
station, 62
stochastic matrices, 510
storage device, 207
stream, 215
streaming, 340
subclass, 410, 411
    constructor, 411
success, 504
successive, 500
summary statistics, 89
suspended, 18
swapping, 267

symmetric encryption, 320
synchronization, 129
synchronized, 139
system behavior, 37
    dynamic, 44
system commands, 8
system defense, 326
system objects, 38
system parameters, 40, 42, 43, 49
system queues, 31
system resources, 2
system software, 2

TCP/IP, 334, 337
thrashing, 304, 305
thread, 19, 26, 28, 244, 419, 421
    descriptor, 20
    notify, 422
    objects, 139
    reference, 24, 417
thread methods, 24
throughput, 40, 41, 43, 56, 59
time quantum, 98
time-sharing, 82, 98
time slice, 78, 81, 82, 98–101, 103
total ordering, 195
trace, 43, 44, 49, 53
traces, 507
transition, 509
trap door, 324

Trojan horse, 323
trusted party, 321

UML, 46
universe, 498
Unix, 10
USB, 253
USB memory stick, 229
user authentication, 311
utilization, 32

virtual address space, 273
virtual file system, 228
virtual machine, 361, 533
    integration, 372
    monitor, 362
virtual memory, 272
virus, 325
viruses, 310
vulnerability, 325

wait state, 17
wait time, 40
Windows, 11
working set, 300
workload, 39, 41, 80
    parameters, 40, 41
World Wide Web, 333
worms, 310, 325